英汉双

编著 蔺红英 张杰

外文出版社

英汉及汉文同义词词典

编者的话

"Thesaurus"一般译作"同义词辞典",但是它的含义与汉语的"同义词辞典"有所不同。因为在英语国家,与文字打交道的人通常要备一本 Thesaurus,以供随时查阅,这是因为,Thesaurus 的作用不像中文同义词辞典那样通过提供二三个意思相近、用法亦相同的词语来提高你在遣词造句时的措辞准确度,而是将与某一词条意思相关的大量单词和词组尽数罗列,以便为使用者在各种语境场合下提供丰富而又最恰当的参考用词。

Thesaurus 在英文辞书中是一大种类,各大著名辞书出版商均有自己的 Thesaurus,其中最著名的版本是 Roget's Thesaurus,但 Thesaurus 未被"中国本土化",我们的读者使用起来终究不甚实用。

有鉴于此,我们特编撰了这本适合中国读者的 Thesaurus,以添补国内这一空白。首先我们为每个入选的英文词条加上中文释义,这就为许多英文初学者使用本辞典提供了方便之门;同时,我们所选用的词条都是中国读者常用的、较容易掌握的单词和词组,而将不常用的、不易掌握的单词和词组放入"同义词"之列,以大量不常用的"支持"少数常用的,这样,读者在学习英文时,有本书在手,就相当于单词量遽增数倍。经常使用,无疑会扩大词汇量,提高英文阅读能力和写作能力,实属英文学习的得力助手。

1999 年 8 月
编者谨识

Q	q	445
R	r	449
S	s	484
T	t	557
U	u	590
V	v	602
W	w	609
Y	y	629
Z	z	630

目 录

A	a	1
B	b	40
C	c	76
D	d	134
E	e	184
F	f	217
G	g	254
H	h	272
I	i	294
J	j	319
K	k	324
L	l	328
M	m	348
N	n	377
O	o	387
P	p	400

A

abandon v.
- 抛弃 desert, leave, forsake, jilt, leave in the lurch, maroon, strand, leave behind, scrap.
- 放弃 renounce, resign, give up, forgo, relinquish, surrender, yield, waive, drop, call it a day, call it quits, throw in the towel, vacate, evacuate, withdraw from, quit.

abandoned adj.
- 被弃的 deserted, unoccupied, derelict, neglected, forsaken, forlorn, desolate.
- 堕落的 dissolute, uninhibited, wanton, wicked, licentious.

abandonment n.
- 抛弃 desertion, neglect.
- 放弃 renunciation, resignation, relinquishment, surrender, sacrifice, waiver, discontinuation.

abashed adj.
- 惭愧的 ashamed, humble, embarrassed.
- 迷惑的 confused, bewildered.

abate v.
- 减少 decrease, reduce.
- 减弱 moderate, subside.

abbey n.
- 修道院,寺院 monastery, priory, friary, convent, nunnery, cloister.

abbreviate v.
- 缩;略 shorten, cut, abridge, summarize, digest, condense, compress, reduce, lessen, shrink, contract.

abbreviation n.
- 缩写,略语 shortening, abridgement, summarization, summary, synopsis, resume, precis, abstract, digest, compression, reduction, contraction.

abdomen n.
- 腹部 belly, guts, stomach, tummy, paunch, midriff.

abide v.
- 容忍 bear, stand, endure, tolerate, put up with, stomach, accept.
- 停留 remain, last, endure, continue, persist.

abide by
- 履行 fulfil, discharge, carry out, stand by, hold to, keep to.
- 遵守 obey, observe, follow, comply with, adhere to, conform to, submit to, go along with, agree to.

ability n.
- 能力 capability, capacity, faculty, facility, potentiality, power.
- 才能 skill, dexterity, deftness, adeptness, competence, proficiency, qualification, aptitude, talent, gift, endowment, knack, flair, touch, expertise, know how, genius, forte, strength.

abject adj.

☞ 下贱的 contemptible.
☞ 不幸的 miserable.

ablaze adj.
☞ 着火的 blazing, flaming, burning, on fire, ignited, lighted, alight.
☞ 激动的 impassioned, passionate, fervent, ardent.

able adj.
☞ 能干的 capable, fit, fitted, dexterous, adroit, deft, adept, competent, proficient, qualified, practised, experienced, skilled, accomplished, clever, expert, masterly, skilful, ingenious, talented, gifted, strong.

abnormal adj.
☞ 不正常的 odd, strange, singular, peculiar, curious, queer, weird, eccentric, paranormal, unnatural, uncanny, extraordinary, exceptional, unusual, uncommon.

abolish v.
☞ 取消 do away with, annul, nullify, invalidate, quash, repeal, rescind, revoke, cancel, obliterate, blot out, suppress, destroy, eliminate, eradicate, get rid of, stamp out, end, put an end to, terminate.

abolition n.
☞ 废止 annulment, nullification, invalidation, quashing, repeal, abrogation, cancellation, obliteration, suppression, eradication, extinction, end, ending, termination.

abortion n.
☞ 流产,失败 miscarriage, termination, frustration, failure, misadventure.

abortive adj.
☞ 失败的,夭折的 failed, unsuccessful, fruitless, unproductive, barren, sterile, vain, idle, futile, useless, ineffective, unavailing.

about prep.
☞ 关于 regarding, concerning, relating to, referring to, connected with, concerned with, as regards, with regard to, with reference to.
☞ 接近 close to, near, nearby, beside, adjacent to.
☞ 在……四周 round, around, surrounding, encircling, encompassing, throughout, all over.
adv.
☞ 大约 around, approximately, roughly, in the region of, more or less, almost, nearly, approaching, nearly.
☞ 四处 to and fro, hear and there, from place to place.

about to
☞ 将要 on the point of, on the verge of, all but, ready to, intending to, preparing to.

above prep.
☞ 在……之上 over, higher than, on top of, superior to, in excess of, exceeding, surpassing, beyond, before, prior to.
adv.
☞ 在上(方) overhead, aloft, on high, earlier.
adj.
☞ 上述的 above-mentioned,

above-stated, foregoing, preceding, previous, earlier, prior.

abroad *adv*.
- 在(到)国外 overseas, in foreign parts, out of the country, far and wide, widely, extensively.
- 广布地,四播地 at large, around, about, circulating, current.

abrupt *adj*.
- 陡的 sheer, precipitous, steep, sharp.
- 唐突的 bruesque, curt, terse, short, brisk, snappy, gruff, rude, uncivil, impolite, blunt, direct.
- 突然的 sudden, unexpected, unforeseen, surprising, quick, rapid, swift, hasty, hurried, precipitate.

absence *n*.
- 缺席 non-attendance, nonappearance, truancy, non existence, absentation.
- 缺乏 lack, need, want, deficiency, dearth, scarcity, unavailability, omission, vacancy.

absent *adj*.
- 缺的 missing, not present, away, out, unavailable, gone, lacking, truant, wanting.
- 溜号的 inattentive, daydreaming, dreamy, faraway, elsewhere, absentminded, vacant, vague, distracted, preoccupied, unaware, oblivious, unheeding.

absent-minded *adj*.
- 心不在焉的 forgetful, scatterbrained, absent, abstracted, withdrawn, faraway, distracted, preoccupied, absorbed, engrossed, pensive, musing, dreaming, dreamy, inattentive, unaware, oblivious, unconscious, heedless, unheeding.

absolute *adj*.
- 完全的 utter, total, complete, entire, full, thorough, exhaustive, supreme, consummate, definitive, conclusive, final, categorical, definite, unequivocal.
- 绝对的 omnipotent, totalitarian, autocratic, tyrannical, despotic, dictatorial, sovereign, unlimited, unrestricted.

absolutely *adv*.
- 完全地 utterly, totally, dead, completely, entirely, fully, wholly, thoroughly, exhaustively, perfectly, supremely, conclusively, finally, categorically, definitely, positively, unequivocally.

absorb *v*.
- 吸收 take in, ingest, drink in, imbibe, suck up, soak up, consume, devour, engulf, digest.
- 热衷 engross, involve, fascinate, enthral, monopolize, preoccupy.

absorbing *adj*.
- 吸引人的 interesting, amusing, entertaining, diverting, engrossing, preoccupying, intriguing,

fascinating, captivating, enthralling, spellbinding.

abstract *adj*.
- 抽象的 non-concrete, conceptual, intellectual, hypothetical, theoretical, unpractical, unrealistic, general, generalized, indefinite, metaphysical, philosophical.

n.
- 大纲 synopsis, outline, summary, recapitulation, resume, precis, epitome, digest, abridgement, compression.

v.
- 概括 summarize, outline, precis, digest, condense, compress, abridge, abbreviate, shorten.
- 转移 extract, remove, withdraw, isolate, detach, dissociate, separate.

abstraction *n*.
- 概念 idea, notion, concept, thought, conception, theory, hypothesis, theorem, formula, generalization, generality.
- 心不在焉 inattention, dreaminess, absent-mindedness, distraction, pensiveness, preoccupation, absorption.
- 提炼 extraction, withdrawal, isolation, separation.

absurd *adj*.
- 荒谬的 ridiculous, ludicrous, preposterous, fantastic, incongruous, illogical, paradoxical, implausible, untenable, unreasonable, irrational, nonsensical, meaningless, senseless.

abundant *adj*.
- 丰富的 plentiful, in plenty, full, filled, well-supplied, ample, generous, bountiful, rich, copious, profuse, lavish, exuberant, teeming, overflowing.

abuse *v*.
- 滥用 misuse, misapply, exploit, take advantage of, oppress, ill-treat, maltreat, hurt, injure, molest, damage, spoil, harm.
- 辱骂 insult, swear at, defame, libel, slander, smear, disparage, malign, revile, scold, upbraid.

n.
- 滥用 misuse, misapplication, exploitation, imposition, oppression, wrong, ill-treatment, maltreatment, hurt, injury, molestation, damage, spoiling, harm.
- 辱骂 insults, swearing, cursing, offence, defamation, libel, slander, disparagement, reproach, scolding, upbraiding, tirade.

academic *adj*.
- 学术的 scholarly, erudite, learned, well-read, studious, bookish, scholastic, pedagogical.
- 理论上的 theoretical, hypothetical, conjectural, speculative, notional, abstract, impractical.

n.
- 学者 professor, don, master, fellow, lecturer, tutor, student, scholar, man of letters, pedant.

accelerate *v*.

- 加速 quicken, speed, speed up, pick up speed, step up, expedite, hurry, hasten, precipitate, stimulate, facilitate, advance, further, promote, forward.

accent n.
- 口音 pronunciation, enunciation, articulation, brogue, twang, tone, pitch, intonation, inflection, accentuation.

accept v.
- 认可 acknowledge, recognize, admit, allow, approve, agree to, consent to, take on, adopt.
- 忍受 tolerate, put up with, stand, bear, abide, face up to, yield to.
- 接受 take, receive, obtain, acquire, gain, secure.

acceptable adj.
- 令人满意的 satisfactory, tolerable, moderate, passable, adequate, all right, ok, so-so, unexceptionable, admissible, suitable, conventional, correct, desirable, pleasant, gratifying, welcome.

access n.
- 进入(接近)许可、方法 admission, admittance, entry, entering, entrance, gateway, door, key, approach, passage, road, path, course.

accessible adj.
- 可接近的 reachable, get-at-able, attainable, achievable, possible, obtainable, available, on hand, ready, handy, convenient, near, nearby.

accident n.
- 偶然 chance, hazard, fortuity, luck, fortune, fate, serendipity, contingency, fluke.
- 厄运 misfortune, mischance, misadventure, mishap, casualty, blow, calamity, disaster.
- 事故 collision, crash, pile-up.

accidental adj.
- 意外的 unintentional, unintended, inadvertent, unplanned, uncalculated, unexpected, unforeseen, unlooked-for.

acclaim v.
- 称赞 praise, commend, extol, exalt, honour, hail, salute, welcome, applaud, clap.

n.
- 喝彩 acclamation, praise, commendation, homage, tribute, eulogy, exaltation, honour, welcome, approbation, approval, applause, ovation, clapping.

accommodate v.
- 供住宿 lodge, board, put up, house, shelter.
- 帮助 oblige, help, assist, aid, serve, provide, supply, comply, conform.
- 适应 adapt, accustom, acclimatize, adjust, modify, fit, harmonize, reconcile, settle, compose.

accommodating adj.
- 肯通融的、亲切的 obliging, indulgent, helpful, co-operative, willing, kind, considerate, unselfish, sympathetic, friendly, hospitable.

accompany v.
- 陪伴 escort, attend, convoy, chaperon, usher, conduct, follow.
- 与……同时发生 coexist, coincide, belong to, go with, complement, supplement.

accomplish v.
- 实现 achieve, attain, do, perform, carry out, execute, fulfil, discharge, finish, complete, conclude, consummate, realize, effect, bring about, engineer, produce, abtain.

accomplished adj.
- 娴熟的,多才多艺的 skilled, professional, practised, proficient, gifted, talented, skilful, adroit, adept, expert, masterly, consummate, polished, cultivated.

accomplishment n.
- 技能 skill, art, aptitude, faculty, ability, capability, proficiency, gift, talent, forte.
- 成就 exploit, feat, deed, stroke, triumph.
- 完成 achievement, attainment, doing, performance, carrying out, execution, fulfilment, discharge, finishing, completion, conclusion, consummation, perfection, realization, fruition, production.

accord v.
- 与……符合 agree, concur, harmonize, match, conform, correspond, suit.
- 给与(某人) give, tender, grant, allow, bestow, endow, confer.

n.
- 协调 accordance, agreement, assent, unanimity, concert, unity, correspondence, conformity, harmony.

according to
- 依据 in accordance with, in keeping with, in conformity with, in line with, consistent with, commensurate with, in proportion to, in relation to, after, in the light of, in the manner of, after the manner of.

accordingly adv.
- 因此 in accordance, in accord with, correspondingly, so, as a result, consequently, in consequence, therefore, thus, hence.

account n.
- 帐目,计算 ledger, book, books, register, inventory, statement, invoice, bill, tab, charge, reckoning, computation, tally, score, balance.
- 记述 narrative, story, tale, chronicle, history, memoir, record, statement, report, communique, write-up, version, portrayal, sketch, description, presentation, explanation.

account for
- 解释 explain, elucidate, illuminate, clear up, rationalize, justify, vindicate, answer for.

accountable adj.
- 为……负有责任 answerable, responsible, liable, amenable, obliged, bound.

accumulate v.
- 积累 gather, assemble, collect, amass, aggregate,

cumulate, accrue, grow, increase, multiply, build up, pile up, hoard, stockpile.

accurate *adj*.
☞ 准确的 correct, right, unerring, precise, exact, well-directed, spot-on, faultless, perfect, sound, authentic, factual, nice, true, truthful, veracious, just, proper, close, faithful, well-judged, careful, rigorous, scrupulous, meticulous, strict, minute.

accusation *n*.
☞ 控告 charge, allegation, impeachment, recrimination, complaint, incrimination.

accuse *v*.
☞ 控告 charge, indict, impugn, denounce, arraign, impeach, cite, allege, attribute, impute, blame, censure, recriminate, incriminate, criminate, inform against.

accustomed *adj*.
☞ 习惯于…… used, in the habit of, given to, confirmed, seasoned, hardened, inured, disciplined, trained, adapted, acclimatized, acquainted, familiar, wonted, habitual.

ache *v*.
☞ 痛 hurt, be sore, pain, suffer, agonize, throb, pound, twinge, smart, sting.
☞ 渴望 yearn, long, pine, hanker, desire, crave, hunger, thirst, itch.
n.
☞ 疼痛 pain, hurt, soreness, suffering, anguish, agony, throb, throbbing, pounding, pang, twinge, smarting, stinging.

achieve *v*.
☞ 取得 accomplish, attain, reach, get, obtain, acquire, procure, gain, earn, win, succeed, manage, do, perform, carry out.

achievement *n*.
☞ 成就 act, deed, exploit, feat, effort.
☞ 实现 accomplishment, attainment, acquirement, performance.

acid *adj*.
☞ 酸的 sour, bitter, tart, vinegary, sharp, pungent, acerbic, caustic, corrosive, stinging.

acknowledge *v*.
☞ 致意，招呼 greet, address, notice, recognize.
☞ 承认 admit, confess, own up to, declare, recognize, accept, grant, allow, concede.
☞ 收悉 answer, reply to, respond to, confirm.

acknowledged *adj*.
☞ 获认同的 recognized, accepted, approved, accredited, declared, professed, attested, avowed, confirmed.

acknowledgement *n*.
☞ 承认 admission, confession, declaration, profession, recognition, acceptance.
☞ 收悉 answer, reply, response, reaction, affirmation.
☞ 致谢 gratitude, thanks, appreciation, tribute.

acquaint *v*.

☞ 使……熟悉 accustom, familiarize, tell, notify, advise, inform, brief, enlighten.

acquaintance n.
☞ 了解,熟悉 awareness, knowledge, understanding, experience, familiarity, intimacy, relationship, association, fellowship, companionship.
☞ 熟人 friend, companion, colleague, associate, contact.

acquire v.
☞ 获得 buy, purchase, procure, appropriate, obtain, get, receive, collect, pick up, gather, net, gain, secure, earn, win, achieve, attain, realize.

acquisition n.
☞ 获得 purchase, buy, procurement, appropriation, gain, securing, achievement, attainment, accession, takeover, property, possession.

acrid adj.
☞ 尖刻的 pungent, sharp, stinging, acid, burning, caustic, acerbic, biting, cutting, incisive, trenchant, sarcastic, sardonic, bitter.

act n.
☞ 行为 deed, action, undertaking, enterprise, operation, manoeuvre, move, step, doing, execution, accomplishment, achievement, exploit, feat, stroke.
☞ 法令 law, statute, ordinance, edict, decree, resolution, measure, bill.

v.
☞ 行动 behave, conduct, exert, make, work, function, operate, do, execute, carry out.
☞ 假扮 pretend, feign, put on, assume, simulate, mimic, imitate, impersonate, portray, represent, mime, play, perform, snact.

act on
☞ 作用 affect, influence, alter, modify, change, transform.

action n.
☞ 行动 act, move, deed, exploit, feat, activity, liveliness, spirit, energy, vigour, power, force, exercise, exertion, work, functioning, operation, mechanism, movement, motion.
☞ 诉讼 litigation, lawsuit, suit, case, prosecution.
☞ 战斗 warfare, battle, conflict, combat, fight, fray, engagement, skirmish, clash.

activate v.
☞ 激活 start, initiate, trigger, set off, fire, switch on, set in motion, mobilize, propel, move, stir, rouse, arouse, stimulate, motivate, prompt, animate, energize, impel.

active adj.
☞ 积极的 busy, occupied, on the go, industrious, diligent, hard working, forceful, spirited, vital, forward, enterprising, enthusiastic, devoted, engaged, involved, committed, militant, activist.
☞ 活跃的 agile, nimble, sprightly, light-footed, quick, alert, animated, lively, energetic, vigorous.

☞ 活动中的 in operation, functioning, working, running.

activity n.
☞ 活跃 liveliness, life, activeness, action, motion, movement, commotion, bustle, hustle, industry, labour, exertion, exercise.

☞ 活动 occupation, job, work, act, deed, project, scheme, task, venture, enterprise, endeavour, undertaking, pursuit, hobby, pastime, interest.

actor n.
☞ 演员 actress, play-actor, comedian, tragedian, ham, player, performer, artist, impersonator, mime.

actual adj.
☞ 真正的 real, existent, substantial, tangible, material, physical, concrete, positive, definite, absolute, certain, unquestionable, indisputable, confirmed, verified, factual, truthful, true, genuine, legitimate, bona fide, authentic, realistic.

actually adv.
☞ 实际上 in fact, as a matter of fact, as it happens, in truth, in reality, really, truly, indeed, absolutely.

adapt v.
☞ 使适应(配),改编 alter, change, qualify, modify, adjust, convert, remodel, customize, fit, tailor, fashion, shape, harmonize, match, suit, conform, comply, prepare, familiarize, acclimatize.

adaptation n.
☞ 适应(配),改编 alteration, change, shift, transformation, modification, adjustment, accommodation, conversion, remodelling, reworking, reshaping, refitting, revision, variation, version.

add v.
☞ 附加,添加 append, annex, affix, attach, tack on, join, combine, supplement, augment.

add up
☞ 相加 add, sum up, tot up, total, tally, count (up), reckon, compute.

☞ 总计达 amount, come to, constitute, include.

addicted adj.
☞ 上瘾的 dependent, hooked, obsessed, absorbed, devoted, dedicated, fond, inclined, disposed, accustomed.

addiction n.
☞ 上瘾 dependence, craving, habit, obsession.

addition n.
☞ 加法;增加 adding, annexation, accession, extension, enlargement, increasing, increase, gain.

☞ 附加 adjunct, supplement, additive, addendum, appendix, appendage, accessory, attachment, extra, increment.

in addition
☞ 此外 additionally, too, also, as well, besides, moreover, further, furthermore, over and above.

additional adj.

☞ 附加的 added, extra, supplementary, spare, more, further, increased, other, new, fresh.

address n.
☞ 住址 residence, dwelling, abode, house, home, lodging, direction, inscription, whereabouts, location, situation, place.
☞ 致辞 speech, talk, lecture, sermon, discourse, dissertation.
v.
☞ 说话,演讲 lecture, speak to, talk to, greet, salute, hail, invoke, accost, approach, buttonhole.

adept adj.
☞ 老练,善长 skilled, accomplished, expert, masterly, experienced, versed, practised, polished, proficient, able, adroit, deft, nimble.

adequate adj.
☞ 足够的 enough, sufficient, commensurate, requisite, suitable, fit, able, competent, capable, serviceable, fit, able, competent, capable, acceptable, satisfactory.

adhere v.
☞ 粘着,附着 stick, glue, paste, cement, fix, fasten, attach, join, link, combine, coalesce, cohere, hold, cling, cleave to.
☞ 追随,遵守 observe, follow, abide by, comply with, fulfil, obey, keep, heed, respect, stand by.

adhesive adj.
☞ 有粘性的 sticky, tacky, self-adhesive, gummed, gummy, gluey, adherent, adhering, sticking, clinging, holding, attaching, cohesive.
n.
☞ 粘着剂 glue, gum, paste, cement.

adjust v.
☞ 调节 modify, change, adapt, alter, convert, dispose, shape, remodel, fit, accommodate, suit, measure, rectify, regulate, balance, temper, tune, fine-tune, fix, set, arrange, compose, settle, square.
☞ 使……适应 accustom, habituate, acclimatize, reconcile, harmonize, conform.

adjustment n.
☞ 调节 modification, change, adaptation, alteration, conversion, remodelling, shaping, fitting, accommodation, restification, regulation, tuning, fixing, setting, arranging, arrangement, ordering, settlement.

administer v.
☞ 给予 give, provide, supply, distribute, dole out, dispense, measure out, mete out, execute, impose apply.
☞ 管理 govern, rule, lead, head, preside over, officiate, manage, run, organize, direct, conduct, control, regulate, superintend, supervise, oversee.

administration n.
☞ 管理 administering, governing, ruling, leadership, management, execution, running, organization, direction,

control, superintendence, supervision, overseeing.
☞ 行政机构 governing, body, regime, government, ministry, leadership, directorship, management, executive, term of office.

administrative *adj.*
☞ 管理上的;行政上的 governmental, legislative, authoritative, directorial, managerial, management, executive, organizational, regulatory, supervisory.

admirable *adj.*
☞ 可钦佩的 praiseworthy, commendable, laudable, creditable, deserving, worthy, respected, fine, excellent, superior, wonderful, exquisite, choice, rare, valuable.

admiration *n.*
☞ 钦佩 esteem, regard, respect, reverence, veneration, worship, idolism, adoration, affection, approval, praise, appreciation, pleasure, delight, wonder, astonishment, amazement, surprise.

admire *v.*
☞ 钦佩 esteem, respect, revere, venerate, worship, idolize, adore, approve, praise, laud, applaud, appreciate, value.

admissible *adj.*
☞ 容许的;有权进入的 acceptable, tolerable, tolerated, passable, allowable, permissible, allowed, permitted, lawful, legitimate, justifiable.

admission *n.*
☞ 准入 confession, granting, acknowledgement, recognition, acceptance, allowance, concession, disclosure, divulgence, revelation, expose.

admit *v.*
☞ 承认 confess, own (up), grant, acknowledge, recognize, accept, allow, concede, agree, affirm, declare, profess, disclose, divulge, reveal.
☞ 准入 let in, allow to enter, give access, accept, receive, take in, introduce, initiate.

adolescence *n.*
☞ 青春期 teens, puberty, youth, minority, boyhood, girlhood, development, immaturity, youthfulness, boyishness, girlishness.

adolescent *adj.*
☞ 青春期的 teenage, young, youthful, juvenile, puerile, boyish, girlish, immature, growing, developing.
n.
☞ 青春期少男少女 teenager, youth, juvenile, minor.

adopt *v.*
☞ 接受,采用 take on, accept, assume, take up, appropriate, embrace, follow, choose, select, take in, foster, support, maintain, back, endorse, ratify, approve.

adore *v.*
☞ 崇拜 love, cherish, dote on, admire, esteem, honour, revere, venerate, worship, idolize, exalt, glorify.

adorn *v.*

☞装饰 decorate, deck, bedeck, ornament, crown, trim, garnish, gild, enhance, embellish, doll up, enrich, grace.

adult *adj.*
☞成人的 grown-up, of age, full-grown, fully grown, developed, mature, ripe.

advance *v.*
☞推进 proceed, go forward, move on, go ahead, progress, prosper, flourish, thrive, improve.
☞促进 accelerate, speed, hasten, send forward.
☞提升 further, promote, upgrade, foster, support, assist, benefit, facilitate, increase, grow.
☞提出 present, submit, suggest, allege, cite, bring forward, offer, provide, supply, furnish.
☞预付 lend, loan, pay beforehand, pay, give.
n.
☞前进,进步 progress, forward movement, onward movement, headway, step, advancement, furtherance, breakthrough, development, growth, increase, improvement, amelioration.
☞预付款 deposit, payment, prepayment.

in advance
☞提前 beforehand, previously, early, earlier, sooner, ahead, in front, in the lead, in the forefront.

advanced *adj.*
☞先进的 leading, foremost, ahead, forward, precocious, progressive, forward-looking, advantgarde, ultra-modern, sophisticated, complex, higher.

advantage *n.*
☞利益 asset, blessing, benefit, good, welfare, interest, service, help, aid, assistance, use, avail, convenience, usefulness, utility, profit, gain, start.
☞优势 lead, edge, upper hand, superiority, precedence, preeminence, sway.

advantageous *adj.*
☞有利的 beneficial, favourable, opportune, convenient, helpful, useful, worthwhile, valuable, profitable, gainful, remunerative, rewarding.

adventure *n.*
☞冒险 exploit, venture, undertaking, enterprise, risk, hazard, chance, speculation, experience, incident, occurrence.

adventurous *adj.*
☞冒险的 daring, intrepid, bold, audacious, headstrong, impetuous, reckless, rash, risky, venturesome, enterprising.

adverse *adj.*
☞相反的,敌对的 hostile, antagonistic, opposing, opposite, counter, contrary, conflicting, counter-productive, negative, disadvatageous, unfavourable, inauspicious, unfortunate, unlucky, inopportune.

adversity *n.*
☞厄运 misfortune, ill fortune,

bad luck, ill luck, reverse, hardship, hard times, misery, wretchedness, affliction, suffering, distress, sorrow, woe.

advertise v.
☞ 宣传 publicize, promote, push, plug, praise, trumpet, blazon, herald, announce, declare, proclaim, broadcast, publish, display, make known, inform, notify.

advertisement n.
☞ 广告 advert, ad, commercial, publicity, promotion, plug, display, blurb, announcement, notice, poster, bill, placard, leaflet, handbill, circular, handout, propaganda.

advice n.
☞ 忠告 warning, caution, dos and don'ts, injunction, instruction, counsel, help, guidance, direction, suggestion, recommendation, opinion, view.
☞ 建议 notification, notice, memorandum, communication, information, intelligence.

advise v.
☞ 忠告 counsel, guide, warn, forewarn, caution, instruct, teach, tutor, suggest, recommend, commend, urge.
☞ 建议 notify, inform, tell, acquaint, make known, report.

adviser n.
☞ 顾问 counsellor, consultant, authority, guide, teacher, tutor, instructor, coach, helper, aide, right-hand, instructor, coach, helper, aide, right-hand man, mentor, confidant(e), counsel, lawyer.

advocate v.
☞ 倡议 defend, champion, campaign for, press for, argue for, plead for, justify, urge, encourage, advise, recommend, propose, promote, endorse, support, uphold, patronize.
n.
☞ 倡议者 defender, supporter, upholder, champion, campaigner, pleader, vindicator, proponent, promoter, speaker, spokesperson.

affair n.
☞ 业务 business, transaction, operation, proceeding, undertaking, activity, project, concern, matter, issue, subject, topic, happening, occurrence, incident, episode, event.
☞ 暧昧关系 relationship, liaison, intrigue, love, affair, romance, amour.

affect v.
☞ 假装 adopt, assume, put on, feign, simulate, imitate, fake, counterfeit, sham, pretend, profess, aspire to.
☞ 影响，改变 influence, alter, modify, change, relate to, concern.

affectation n.
☞ 装模作样 airs, artificiality, pretentiousness, mannerism, pose, act, show, appearance, facade, pretence, sham, simulation, imitation, insincerity.

affected adj.
☞ 假装的 assumed, put-on, feigned, simulated, artificial,

fake, counterfeit, sham, phoney, contrived, studied, precious, mannered, pretentious, pompous, stiff, unnatural, insincere.

affection *n*.
☞ 情爱 fondness, attachment, devotion, love, tenderness, care, warmth, feeling, kindness, friendliness, goodwill, favour, liking, partiality, inclination, penchant, passion, desire.

affirm *v*.
☞ 断言 confirm, corroborate, endorse, ratify, certify, witness, testify, swear, maintain, state, assert, declare, pronounce.

affirmative *adj*.
☞ 肯定的 agreeing, concurring, approving, assenting, positive, confirming, corroborative, emphatic.

afflict *v*.
☞ 使……痛苦 strike, visit, trouble, burden, oppress, distress, grieve, pain, hurt, wound, harm, try, harass, beset, plague, torment, torture.

affliction *n*.
☞ 痛苦 distress, grief, sorrow, misery, depression, suffering, pain, torment, disease, illness, sickness, plague, curse, cross, ordeal, trial, tribulation, trouble, hardship, adversity, misfortune, calamity, disaster.

afford *v*.
☞ 有充裕的 have enough for, spare, allow, manage, sustain, bear.
☞ 供给 provide, supply, furnish, give, grant, offer, impart, produce, yield, generate.

affront *v*.
☞ 冒犯 offend, insult, abuse, snub, slight, provoke, displease, irritate, annoy, anger, vex, incense, outrage.

afraid *adj*.
☞ 害怕的 frightened, scared, alarmed, terrified, fearful, timorous, daunted, intimidated, faint-hearted.

after *prep*.
☞ 在……之后 following, subsequent to, in consequence of, as a result of, behind, below.

again *adv*.
☞ 又,再 once more, once again, another time, over again, afresh, anew, encore.

against *prep*.
☞ 与……相对 opposite to, facing, fronting, in the face of, confronting, opposing, versus, opposed to, in opposition to, hostile to, resisting, in defiance of, in contrast to.
☞ 靠着 abutting, adjacent to, close up to, touching, in contact with, on.

age *n*.
☞ 年代 era, epoch, day, days, generation, date, time, period, duration, span, years, aeon.
☞ 老年 oldage, maturity, elderliness, seniority, dotage, senility, decline.

agency n.
- 作用 means, medium, instrumentality, power, force, influence, effect, intervention, action, activity, operation, mechanism, workings.
- 机构 bureau, office, department, organization, business, work.

agent n.
- 代理人 substitute, deputy, delegate, envoy, emissary, representative, rep, broker, middleman, go-between, intermediary, negotiator, mover, doer, performer, operator, operative, functionary, worker.

aggression n.
- 侵略 antagonism, provocation, offence, injury, attack, offensive, assault, onslaught, raid, incursion, invasion, intrusion.
- 敌意 aggressiveness, militancy, belligerence, combativeness, hostility.

aggressive adj.
- 攻击的 argumentative, quarrelsome, contentious, belligerent, hostile, offensive, provocative, intrusive, invasive, bold, assertive, pushy, go-ahead, forceful, vigorous, zealous, ruthless, destructive.

aggrieved adj.
- 受委屈的 wronged, offended, hurt, injured, insulted, maltreated, illused, resentful, pained, distressed, saddened, unhappy, upset, annoyed.

agree v.
- 同意 concur, see eye to eye, get on, settle, accord, match, suit, fit, tally, correspond, conform.
- 答应 consent, allow, permit, assent, accede, grant, admit, concede, yield, comply.

agreeable adj.
- 令人愉快的 pleasant, congenial, likable, attractive, delightful, enjoyable, gratifying, satisfying, palatable, suitable, fitting, in accord, consistent.

agreement n.
- 合同 settlement, compact, covenant, treaty, pact, contract, deal, bargain, arrangement, understanding.
- 一致 concurrence, accord, concord, unanimity, union, harmony, sympathy, affinity, compatibility, similarity, correspondence, consistency, conformity, compliance, adherence, acceptance.

ahead adv.
- 向前 forward, onward, leading, at the head, in front, in the lead, winning, at an advantage, advanced, superior, to the fore, in the forefront, in advance, before, earlier on.

aid v.
- 协助 help, assist, rally round, relieve, support, subsidize, sustain, second, serve, oblige, accommodate, favour, promote, boost, encourage, expedite, facilitate, ease.

n.
- 援助 help, assistance, prop,

support, relief, benefit, subsidy, donation, contribution, funding, grant, sponsorship, patronage, favour, encouragement, service.

ailing *adj*.
☞ 不适的 unwell, ill, sick, poorly, indisposed, out of sorts, under the weather, off-colour, suffering, languishing, sickly, diseased, invalid, infirm, unsound, frail, weak, feeble, failing.

ailment *n*.
☞ 不适 illness, sickness, complaint, malady, disease, infetion, disorder, affliction, infirmity, disability, weakness.

aim *v*.
☞ 以……为目标 point, direct, take aim, level, train, sight, zero in on, target.
☞ 决心做 aspire, want, wish, seek, resolve, purpose, intend, propose, mean, plan, design, strive, try, attempt, endeavour.
n.
☞ 宗旨,目标 aspiration, ambition, hope, dream, desire, wish, plan, design, scheme, purpose, motive, end, intention, object, objective, target, mark, goal, direction, course.

aimless *adj*.
☞ 无目标的 pointless, purposeless, unmotivated, irresolute, directionless, rambling, undirected, unguided, stray, chance, random, haphazard, erratic, unpredictable, wayward.

air *n*.
☞ 空气 atmosphere, oxygen, sky, heavens, breath, puff, waft, draught, breeze, wind, blast.
☞ 气质,外表 appearance, look, aspect, aura, bearing, demeanour, manner, character, effect, impression, feeling.
v.
☞ 换空气,通风 ventilate, aerate, freshen.
☞ 夸示,宣扬 utter, voice, express, give vent to, make known, communicate, tell, declare, reveal, disclose, divulge, expose.

aisle *n*.
☞ 过道 gangway, corridor, passage, passageway, alleyway, walkway, path, lane.

alarm *v*.
☞ 警告 frighten, scare, startle, put the wind up, terrify, panic, ennerve, daunt, dismay, distress, agitate.
n.
☞ 警报 fright, scare, fear, terror, panic, horror, shock, consternation, dismay, distress, anxiety, nervousness, apprehension, trepidation, uneasiness.
☞ 警鸣 danger signal, alert, warning, distress signal, siren, bell, alarm-bell.

alcohol *n*.
☞ 酒精饮品 drink, liquor, spirits, intoxicant.

alcoholic *adj*.
☞ 含酒精的 intoxicating, brewed, fermented, distilled,

strong, hard.
n.
☞ 醉汉 drunk, drunkard, inebriate, hard drinker.

alert *adj.*
☞ 警觉的 attentive, wide-awake, watchful, vigilant, on the lookout, sharp-eyed, observant, on the lookout, sharp-eyed, observant, perceptive, sharp-witted, on the ball, active, lively, spirited, quick, brisk, agile, nimble, ready, prepared, careful, heedful, circumspect, wary.
v.
☞ 警示 warn, forewarn, notify, inform, tip off, signal, alarm.

alike *adj.*
☞ 相似的 similar, resembling, comparable, akin, analogous, corresponding, equivalent, equal, the same, identical, duplicate, parallel, even, uniform.
adv.
☞ 一样地,相同地 similarly, equally.

all right *adj.*
☞ 令人满意的 satisfactory, passable, unobjectionable, acceptable, allowable, adequate, fair, average, ok.
☞ 身体好 well, healthy, unhurt, uninjured, unharmed, unimpaired, whole, sound, safe, secure.
adv.
☞ 可以,好吧 satisfactory, well enough, passably, unobjectionable, acceptably, suitably, appropriately, adequately, reasonably, ok.

alliance *n.*
☞ 联盟 confederation, federation, association, affiliation, coalition, league, bloc, cartel, conglomerate, consortium, syndicate, guild, union, partnership, marriage, agreement, compact, bond, pact, treaty, combination, connection.

all-out *adj.*
☞ 全力以赴的 complete, full, total, undivided, comprehensive, exhaustive, thorough, intensive, thoroughgoing, wholesale, vigorous, powerful, full-scale, no-holds-barred, maximum, utmost, unlimited, unrestrained, resolute, determined.

allow *v.*
☞ 允许 permit, let, enable, authorize, sanction, approve, tolerate, put up with, endure, suffer.
☞ 承认 admit, confess, own, acknowledge, concede, grant.
☞ 留有,配给 allot, allocate, assign, apportion, afford, give, provide.

allow for
☞ 考虑到 take into account, make provision for, make allowances for, provide for, foresee, plan for, arrange for, bear in mind, keep in mind, consider, include.

allowance *n.*
☞ 分配额,限额 allotment, lot, amount, allocation, portion, share, ration, quota.

☞折扣 rebate, reduction, dediction, discount, concession, subsidy, weighting.
☞零用钱,津贴 payment, remittance, pocket money, grant, maintenance, stipend, pension, annuity.

alloy n.
☞合金,熔合 blend, compound, composite, amalgam, combination, mixture, fusion, coalescence.

ally n.
☞联盟 confederate, associate, leaguer, consort, partner, sidekick, colleague, coworker, collaborator, helper, helpmate, accomplice, accessory, friend.
v.
☞联合 confederate, affiliate, league, associate, collaborate, join forces, band, together, team up, fraternize, side, join, connect, link, marry, unite, unify, amalgamate, combine.

almighty adj.
☞万能的 omnipotent, all powerful, supreme, absolute, great, invincible.
☞巨大的 enormous, severe, intense, overwhelming, overpowering, terrible, awful, desperate.

almost adv.
☞几乎 nearly, well-nigh, practically, virtually, just, about, as good as, all but, close to, not for from, approaching, nearing, not quite, about, approximately, .

alone adj.
☞单独的 only, sole, single, unique, solitary, separate, detached, unconnected, isolated, apart, by oneself, by itself, on one's own, lonely, lonesome, deserted, abandoned, forsaken, forlorn, desolate, unaccompanied, unescorted, unattended, solo, single-handed, unaided, unassisted, mere.

aloof adj.
☞矜持的 distant, remote, offish, standoffish, haughty, supercilious, unapproachable, inaccessible, detached, forbidding, cool, chilly, cold, sympathetic, unresponsive, indifferent, uninterested, reserved, unfriendly, unsociable, formal.

aloud adv.
☞大声的 out loud, audibly, intelligibly, clearly, plainly, distinctly, loudly, resoundingly, sonorously, noisily, vociferously.

also adv.
☞也 too, as well, and, plus, along with, including, as well as, additionally, in addition, besides, further, furthermore, moreover.

alter v.
☞改变 change, vary, diversify, modify, qualify, shift, transpose, adjust, adapt, convert, turn, transmute, transform, reform, reshape, remodel, recast, revise, amend, emend.

alteration n.
☞变动 change, variation, variance, difference, diversification, shift,

transposition, modification, adjustment, adaptation, conversion, transformation, transfiguration, metamorphosis, reformation, reshaping, remodelling, revision, amendment.

alternate n.
☞ 交替，选择 option, choice, selection, preference, other, recourse, substitute, backup.

adj.
☞ 替代的 substitute, in rotation, successive, another, other, different, fringe, alternating.

altitude n.
☞ 高度 height, elevation, loftiness, tallness, stature.

altogether adv.
☞ 全部 totally, completely, entirely, wholly, fully, utterly, absolutely, quite, perfectly, thoroughly, in all, all told, in total, all in all, as a whole, on the whole, generally, in general.

always adv.
☞ 总是 every time, consistently, invariably, without exception, unfailingly, regularly, repeatedly, continually, constantly, perpetually, unceasingly, eternally, endlessly, evermore, forever, ever.

amateur n.
☞ 业余爱好者 non-professional, layman, ham, dilettante, dabbler, enthusiast, fancier, buff.

adj.
☞ 业余的 non-professional, lay, unpaid, unqualified, untrained, amateurish, inexpert, unprofessional.

amaze v.
☞ 令人吃惊 surprise, startle, astonish, astound, stun, stupefy, daze, stagger, floor, dumbfound, flabbergast, shock, dismay, disconcert, confound, bewilder.

amazement n.
☞ 惊讶 surprise, astonishment, shock, dismay, confusion, perplexity, bewilderment, admiration, wonderment, wonder, marvel.

ambassador n.
☞ 大使 emissary, envoy, legate, diplomat, consul, plenipotentiary, deputy, representative, agent, minister, apostle.

ambiguity n.
☞ 含混不清 double meaning, equivocality, equivocation, enigma, puzzle, confusion, obscurity, unclearness, vagueness, woolliness, dubiousness, doubt, doubtfulness, uncertainty.

ambiguous adj.
☞ 模棱两可的 double-meaning, equivocal, multivocal, double-edged, back-handed, cryptic, enigmatic, puzzling, confusing, obscure, unclear, vague, indefinite, woolly, confused, dubious, doubtful, uncertain, inconclusive, indeterminate.

ambition n.

☞ 雄心 aspiration, aim, goal, target, objective, intent, purpose, design, object, ideal, dream, hope, wish, desire, yearning, longing, hankering, craving, hunger.
☞ 动力 enterprise, drive, push, thrust, striving, eagerness, commitment, zeal.

ambitious *adj.*
☞ 有雄心的 aspiring, hopeful, desirous, intent, purposeful, pushy, bold, assertive, go-ahead, enterprising, driving, energetic, enthusiastic, eager, keen, striving, industrious, zealous.
☞ 有奢望的 formidable, hard, difficult, arduous, strenuous, demanding, challenging, exacting, impressive, grandiose, elaborate.

ambivalent *adj.*
☞ 有矛盾心理的 contradictory, conflicting, clashing, warring, opposed, inconsistent, mixed, confused, fluctuating, vacillating, wavering, hesitant, irresolute, undecided, unresolved, unsettled, uncertain, unsure, doubtful, debatable, inconclusive.

amend *v.*
☞ 修正 revise, correct, rectify, emend, fix, repair, mend, remedy, redress, reform, change, alter, adjust, modify, qualify, enhance, improve, ameliorate, better.

amendment *n.*
☞ 修正 revision, correction, corrigendum, rectification, emendation, repair, remedy, reform, change, alteration, adjustment, modification, clarification, addendum, qualification, clarification, addendum, addition, adjunct, improvement.

amends *n.*
☞ 赔偿 atonement, expiation, requital; satisfaction, recompense, compensation, indemnification, indemnity, reparation, redress, restoration, restitution.

amid *prep.*
☞ 在……之中 amidst, midst, in the midst of, in the thick of, among, amongst, in the middle of, surrounded by.

among *prep.*
☞ 在……之中 amongst, between, in the middle of, surrounded by, amid, amidst, midst, in the midst of, in the thick of, with, together with.

amount *n.*
☞ 总量 quantity, number, sum, total, sum total, whole, entirety, aggregate, lot, quota, supply, volume, mass, bulk, measure, magnitude, extent, expanse.

amount to
☞ 总计 add up to, total, aggregate, come to, make, equal, mean, be tantamount to, be equivalent to, approximate to, become, grow.

ample *adj.*
☞ 宽大的 large, big, extensive, expansive, broad, wide, full, voluminous, roomy, spacious,

commodious, roomy, spacious, commodious, great, considerable, substantial, handsome, generous, bountiful, munificent, liberal, lavish, copious, abundant, plentiful, plenty, unrestricted, profuse, rich.

amplify v.
☞扩大 enlarge, magnify, expand, dilate, fill out, bulk out, add to, supplement, augment, increase, extend, lengthen, widen, broaden, develop, elaborate, enhance, boost, intensify, strengthen, deepen, heighten, raise.

amuse v.
☞使人高兴 entertain, divert, regale, make laugh, tickle, crease, slay, cheer, gladden, enliven, please, charm, delight, enthral, engross, absorb, interest, occupy, recreate, relax.

amusement n.
☞娱乐 entertainment, diversion, distraction, fun, enjoyment, pleasure, delight, merriment, mirth, hilarity, laughter, joke, prank, game, sport, recreation, hobby, pastime, interest.

amusing adj.
☞好玩的 funny, humorous, hilarious, comical, laughable, ludicrous, droll, witty, facetious, jocular, jolly, enjoyable, pleasant, charming, delightful, entertaining, intersting.

analyse v.
☞分析 break down, separate, divide, take apart, dissect, anatomize, reduce, resolve, sift, investigate, study, examine, scrutinize, review, interpret, test, judge, evaluate, estimate, consider.

analysis n.
☞分析 breakdown, separation, division, dissection, reduction, resolution, sifting, investigation, enquiry, study, examination, scrutiny, review, exposition, explication, explanation, interpretation, test, judgement, opinion, evaluation, estimation, reasoning.

analytic adj.
☞分析的 analytical, dissecting, detailed, in-depth, searching, critical, questioning, enquiring, inquisitive, investigative, diagnostic, systematic, methodical, logical, rational, interpretative, explanatory, expository, studious.

anarchic adj.
☞无政府主义的 lawless, ungoverned, anarchistic, libertarian, nihilist, revolutionary, rebellious, mutinous, riotous, chaotic, disordered, confused, disorganized.

anarchist n.
☞无政府主义者 revolutionary, rebel, insurgent, libertarian, nihilist, terrorist.

ancestor n.
☞祖先 forebear, forefather, progenitor, predecessor, forerunner, precursor, antecedent.

ancestral adj.
- 祖先的 familial, parental, genealogical, lineal, hereditary, genetic.

anchor v.
- 泊于 moor, berth, tie up, make fast, fasten, attach, affix, fix.

ancient adj.
- 古老的 old, aged, time-worn, age-old, antique, antediluvian, prehistoric, fossilized, primeval, immemorial.
- 过时的 old-fashioned, out-of-date, antiquated, archaic, obsolete, bygone, early, original.

anecdote n.
- 轶闻 story, tale, yarn, sketch, reminiscence.

angel n.
- 亲爱的人 darling, treasure, saint, paragon, ideal.
- 天使 archangel, cherub, seraph, divine messenger, principality.

anger n.
- 生气 annoyance, irritation, antagonism, displeasure, irritability, temper, pique, vexation, ire, rage, fury, wrath, exasperation, outrage, indignation, gall, bitterness, rancour, resentment.
  v.
- 惹怒 annoy, irritate, aggravate wind up, vex, irk, rile, miff, needle, nettle, bother, ruffle, provoke, antagonize, offend, affront, gall, madden, enrage, incense, infuriate, exasperate, outrage.

angle n.
- 角度 corner, nook, bend, flexure, hook, crook, elbow, knee, crotch, edge, point.
- 方面 aspect, outlook, facet, side, approach, direction, position, standpoint, viewpoint, point of view, slant, perspective.

angry adj.
- 生气的 annoyed, cross, irritated, aggravated, displeased, uptight, irate, mad, enraged, incensed, infuriated, furious, raging, passionate, heated, hot, exasperated, outraged, indignant, bitter, resentful.

animal n.
- 动物 creature, mammal, beast, brute, barbarian, savage, monster, cur, pig, swine.
  adj.
- 野兽的 bestial, brutish, inhuman, savage, wild, instinctive, bodily, physical, carnal, fleshly, sensual.

animate adj.
- 活的 alive, living, live, breathing, conscious.

animated adj.
- 活跃的 lively, spirited, buoyant, vibrant, ebullient, vivacious, alive, vital, quick, brisk, vigorous, energetic, active, passionate, impassioned, vehement, ardent, fervent, glowing, radiant, excited, enthusiastic, eager.

announce v.

☞宣称 declare, proclaim, report, state, reveal, disclose, divulge, make known, notify, intimate, promulgate, propound, publish, broadcast, advertise, publicize, blazon.

annoucement n.
☞宣称 declaration, proclamation, report, statement, communique, dispatch, bulletin, notification, intimation, revelation, disclosure, divulgence, publication, broadcast, advertisement.

announcer n.
☞发布者 broadcaster, newscaster, newsreader, commentator, compere, master of ceremonies, MC, town crier, herald, messenger.

annoy v.
☞打扰 irritate, rile, aggravate, displease, anger, vex, irk, madden, exasperate, tease, provoke, ruffle, trouble, disturb, bother, pester, plague, harass, molest.

annoyance n.
☞打扰 nuisance, pest, disturbance, bother, trouble, bore, pain, headache, tease, provocation.
☞激怒 irritation, aggravation, displeasure, anger, vexation, exasperation, harassment.

annoyed adj.
☞生气的 irritated, cross, displeased, angry, vexed, piqued, exasperated, provoked, harassed.

annoying adj.
☞令人气恼的 irritating, aggravating, vexatious, irksome, troublesome, bothersome, tiresome, trying, maddening, exasperating, galling, offensive, teasing, provoking, harassing.

anonymous adj.
☞匿名的 unnamed, nameless, unsigned, unacknowledged, unspecified, unknown, incognito, faceless, impersonal, nondescript, unexceptional.

answer n.
☞回答 reply, acknowledgement, response, reaction, rejoinder, retort, riposte, comeback, retaliation, rebuttal, vindication, defence, plea.
☞答案 solution, explanation.
v.
☞回答 reply, acknowledge, respond, react, retort, retaliate, refute, solve.
☞满足 fulfil, fill, meet, satisfy, match up to, correspond, correlate, conform, agree, fit, suit, serve, pass.

answer back
☞反诘 talk back, retort, riposte, retaliate, contradict, disagree, argue, dispute, rebut.

antagonism n.
☞对立,对抗 hostility, opposition, rivalry, antipathy, ill feeling, ill-will, animosity, friction, discord, dissension, contention, conflict.

antagonist n.
☞对抗者 opponent, adversary, enemy, foe, rival, competitor, contestant, contender.

antagonistic adj.
- 有敌意的 conflicting, opposed, adverse, at variance, incompatible, hostile, belligerent, contentious, unfriendly, ill-disposed, averse.

anticipate v.
- 先发制人 forestall, pre-empt, intercept, prevent, obviated, preclude.
- 预料 expect, foresee, predict, forecast, look for, await, look forward to, hope for, bank on, count upon.

antique adj.
- 古旧的 antiquarian, ancient, old, veteran, vintage, quaint, antiquated, old-fashioned, outdated, archaic, obsolete.

n.
- 古物 antiquity, relic, bygone, period piece, heirloom, curio, museum piece, curiosity, rarity.

antiquity n.
- 古代 ancient times, time immemorial, distant past, olden days, age, old age, oldness, agedness.

anxiety n.
- 焦虑 worry, concern, care, distress, nervousness, apprehension, dread, foreboding, misgiving, uneasiness, restlessness, fretfulness, impatience, suspence, tension, stress.

anxious adj.
- 焦急的 worried, concerned, nervous, apprehensive, afraid, fearful, uneasy, restless, fretful, impatient, in suspense, on tenterhooks, tense, taut, distressed, disturbed, troubled, tormented, tortured.

apart adv.
- 分离地 separately, independently, individually, singly, alone, on one's own, by oneself, privately, aside, to one side, away, afar, distant, aloof, excluded, isolated, cut off, separated, divorced, separate, distinct.
- 拆卸 to pieces, to bits, into parts, in pieces, in bits, piecemeal.

ape v.
- 模仿 copy, imitate, echo, mirror, parrot, mimic, take off, caricature, parody, mock, counterfeit, affect.

n.
- 猿, 猴 monkey, chimpanzee, gibbon, gorilla, baboon, orang-utan.

apologetic adj.
- 道歉的 sorry, repentant, penitent, contrite, remorseful, conscience-stricken, regretful, rueful.

apology n.
- 道歉 acknowledgement, confession, excuse, explanation, justification, vindication, defence, plea.

appal v.
- 令人可怕 horrify, shock, outrage, disgust, dismay, disconcert, daunt, intimidate, unnerve, alarm, scare, frighten, terrify.

appalling adj.
- 可怕的 horrifying, horrific, shocking, disgusting, awful, dreadful, frightful, terrible, ghastly, horrible, horrid, loathsome, daunting, intimidating, alarming, frightening, terrifying.

apparatus n.
- 设备 machine, appliance, gadget, device, contraption, equipment, gear, tackle, outfit, tools, implements, utensils.

apparent adj.
- 明显的 seeming, outward, visible, evident, noticeable, perceptible, plain, clear, distinct, obvious, manifest, open, declared.

apparently adv.
- 明显地,显然地 seemingly, ostensibly, outwardly, superficially, plainly, clearly, obviously, manifestly.

appeal n.
- 请求 request, application, petition, suit, solititation, plea, entreaty, supplication.
- 感染力 attraction, allure, interest, fascination, enchantment, charm, attractiveness, beauty, charisma, magnetism.

v.
- 请求,呼吁 ask, request, call, apply, address, petition, sue, solicit, plead, beg, beseech, implore, entreat, supplicate, call upon.
- 引起兴趣 attract, draw, allure, lure, tempt, entice, invite, interest, engage, fascinate, charm, please.

appear v.
- 出现 arrive, enter, turn up, attend, develop, show(up), come into sight, come into view, loom, rise, surface, arise, occur, crop up, come to light, come out, emerge, issue, be published.
- 好像,似乎 seem, look, turn out.

appearance n.
- 出现 appearing, arrival, advent, coming, rise, emergence, debut, introduction.
- 外表,外观 look, expression, face, aspect, air, bearing, demeanour, manner, looks, figure, form, show, front, guise, illusion, impression, image.

appendix n.
- 附录 addition, appendage, adjunct, addendum, supplement, epilogue, postscript, rider.

appetite n.
- 食欲,欲望 hunger, stomach, relish, zest, taste, propensity, inclination, liking, desire, longing, yearning, craving, eagerness.

applaud v.
- 赞成,称赞 clap, cheer, acclaim, compliment, congratulate, approve, commend, praise, laud.

applause n.
- 赞成,称赞 ovation, clapping, cheering, cheers, acclaim, acclamation, accolade,

congratulation, approval, commendation, praise.

appliance n.
☞ 装置,设备 machine, device, contrivance, contraption, gadget, tool, implement, instrument, apparatus, mechanism.

applicant n.
☞ 请求者,申请人 candidate, interviewee, contestant, competitor, aspirant, suitor, petitioner, inquirer.

application n.
☞ 申请 request, appeal, petition, suit, claim, inquity.
☞ 应用 relevance, pertinence, function, purpose, use, value.
☞ 专心,努力 deligence, industry, assiduity, effort, commitment, dedication, perseverance, keenness, attentiveness.

apply v.
☞ 申请 request, ask for, requistition, put in for, appeal, petition, solicit, sue, claim, inquire.
☞ 使用 put on, spread on, lay on, cover with, paint, anoint, smear, rub.

appoint v.
☞ 任命 name, nominate, elect, install, choose, select, engage, employ, take on, commission, delegate, assign, allot, designate, command, direct, charge, detail.
☞ 决定,安排 decide, determine, arrange, settle, fix, set, establish, ordain, decree, destine.

appointment n.
☞ 安排 arrangement, engagement, date, meeting, rendezvous, interview, consultation.
☞ 职位 job, position, situation, post, office, place.
☞ 任命 naming, nomination, election, choosing, choice, selection, commissioning, delegation.

appraisal n.
☞ 估价,评价 valuation, rating, survey, inspection, review, examination, once-over, evaluation, assessment, estimate, estimation, judgement, reckoning, opinion, appreciation.

appreciate v.
☞ 珍惜,感激 enjoy, relish, savour, prize, treasure, value, cherish, admire, respect, regard, esteem, like, welcome, take kindly to.
☞ 评价,欣赏,鉴赏 understand, comprehend, perceive, realize, recognize, acknowledge, sympathize with, know.

appreciation n.
☞ 珍惜,感激 enjoyment, relish, admiration, respect, regard, esteem, gratitude, gratefulness, thankfulness, indebtedness, obligation, liking, sensitivity, responsiveness, valuation, assessment, estimation, judgement.
☞ (价格)上涨 growth, increase, rise, inflation, gain, improvement, enhancement.
☞ 评价,欣赏 understanding,

comprehension, perception, awareness, realization, recognition, acknowledgement, sympathy, knowledge.

appreciative *adj*.
☞ 感激的 grateful, thankful, obliged, indebted, pleased.
☞ 尊重的,欣赏的 admiring, encouraging, enthusiastic, respectful, sensitive, responsive, perceptive, knowledgeable, conscious, mindful.

apprehension *n*.
☞ 忧虑 dread, foreboding, misgiving, qualm, anxiety, worry, concern, disquiet, alarm, fear, doubt, suspicion, mistrust.

apprehensive *adj*.
☞ 忧虑的,担心的 nervous, anxious, worried, concerned, uneasy, doubtful, suspicious, mistrustful, distrustful, alarmed, afraid.

approach *v*.
☞ 接近,走进 advance, move towards, draw near, near, gain on, catch up, reach, meet.
☞ 向……提出请求 apply to, appeal to, sound out, commence, set about, undertake, introduce, mention.
☞ 接近,近似 resemble, be like, compare with, approximate, come close.
n.
☞ 通路 access, road, avenue, way, passage, entrance, doorway, threshold.
☞ 方法 attitude, manner, style, technique, procedure, method, means.

☞ 临近 advance, coming, advent, arrival.

appropriate *adj*.
☞ 适宜的 applicable, relevant, pertinent, to the point, well-chosen, apt, fitting, suitable, fit, befitting, becoming, proper, right, correct, well-timed, timely, seasonable, opportune.
v.
☞ 私占 seize, take, expropriate, commandeer, requisition, confiscate, impound, assume, usurp.
☞ 盗用 steal, pocket, filch, pilfer, purloin, embezzle, misappropriate.

approval *n*.
☞ 赞成 admiration, esteem, regard, respect, good opinion, liking, appreciation, approbation, favour, recommendation, praise, commendation, acclaim, acclamation, honour, applause.
☞ 同意,批准 agreement, concurrence, assent, consent, permission, leave, sanction, authorization, licence, mandate, go-ahead, green light , blessing, ok , certification, retification, validation, confirmation, support.

approve *v*.
☞ 赞成 admire, esteem, regard, like, appreciate, favour, recommend, praise, commend, acclaim, applaud.
☞ 同意,批准 agree to, assent to, consent to, accede to, allow, permit, pass, sanction,

authorize, mandate, bless, countenance, ok, ratify, rubber-stamp, validate, endorse, support, uphold, second, back, accept, adopt, confirm.

approximate *adj.*
☞ 近似的 estimated, guessed, rough, inexact, loose, close, near, like, similar, relative.
v.
☞ 接近,近似 approach, border on, verge on, be tantamount to, resemble.

approximately *n.*
☞ 近似 roughly, around, about, circa, more or less, loosely, approaching, close to, nearly, just about.

apt *adj.*
☞ 适当的 relevant, applicable, apposite, appropriate, fitting, suitable, fit, seemly, proper, correct, accurate, spot-on, timely, seasonable.
☞ 伶俐的 clever, gifted, talented, skilful, expert, intelligent, quick, sharp.
☞ 可能的 liable, prone, given, disposed, likely, ready.

arbitrate *v.*
☞ 仲裁,公断 judge, adjudicate, referee, umpire, mediate, settle, decide, determine.

arbitration *n.*
☞ 公断 judge, adjudicator, arbiter, referee, umpire, moderator, mediator, negotiator, intermediary, go-between.

arch *n.*

☞ 拱形,桥洞 archway, bridge, span, dome, vault, concave, bend, curve, curvature, bow, arc, semicircle.
v.
☞ 拱起 bend, curve, bow, arc, vault, camber.

archaic *adj.*
☞ 古代的,古风的 antiquated, old-fashioned, outmoded, old hat, passe, outdated, out-of-date, obsolete, old, ancient, antique, quaint, primitive.

architect *n.*
☞ 建筑师 designer, planner, master builder, prime mover, originator, founder, creator, author, inventor, engineer, maker, constructor, shaper.

archives *n.*
☞ 档案 records, annals, chronicles, memorials, papers, documents, deeds, ledgers, registers, roll.

ardent *adj.*
☞ 热心的,热情的 fervent, fiery, warm, passionate, impassioned, fierce, vehement, intense, spirited, enthusiastic, eager, keen, dedicated, devoted, zealous.

arduous *adj.*
☞ 费力的,艰巨的 hard, difficult, tough, rigorous, severe, harsh, formidable, strenuous, tiring, taxing, fatiguing, exhausting, backbreaking, punishing, gruelling, uphill, laborious, onerous.

area *n.*

- 面积,地区 locality, neighbourhood, environment, environs, patch, terrain, district, region, zone, sector, department, province, domain, realm, territory, sphere, field, range, scope, compass, size, extent, expanse, width, breadth, stretch, tract, part, portion, section.

argue v.
- 辩论,说明 quarrel, squabble, bicker, row, wrangle, haggle, remonstrate, join issue, fight, feud, fall out, disagree, dispute, question, debate, discuss.
- 表示,证明 reason, assert, contend, hold, maintain, claim, plead, exhibit, display, show, manifest, demonstrate, indicate, denote, prove, evidence, suggest, imply.

argument n.
- 争论 quarrel, squabble, row, wrangle, controversy, debate, discussion, dispute, disagreement, clash, conflict, fight, feud.
- 论点,论证 reasoning, reason, logic, assertion, contention, claim, demonstration, defence, case, synopsis, summary, theme.

arise v.
- 发生,出现 originate, begin, start, commence, derive, stem, spring, proceed, flow, emerge, issue, appear, come to light, crop up, occur, happen, result, ensue, follow.
- 升起 rise, get up, stand up, go up, ascend, climb, mount, lift, soar, tower.

aristocracy n.
- 贵族阶级 upper class, gentry, nobility, peerage, ruling class, gentility, elite.

aristocrat n.
- 贵族 noble, patrician, nobleman, noblewoman, peer, peeress, lord, lady.

aristocratic adj.
- 贵族的 upper-class, highborn, well-born, noble, patrician, blue-blooded, titled, lordly, courtly, gentle, thoroughbred, elite.

arm[1] n.
- 胳膊 limb, upper, limb, appendage, bough, branch, projection, extension, offshoot, section, division, detachment, department.

arm[2] v.
- 武装,装备 provide, supply, furnish, issue, equip, rig, outfit, ammunition, prime, prepare, forearm, gird, steel, brace, reinforce, strengthen, fortify, protect.

arms n.
- 武器 weapons, weaponry, firearms, guns, artillery, instruments of war, armaments, ordnance, munitions, ammunition.
- 纹章 coat-of-arms, armorial bearings, insignia, heraldic device, escutcheon, shield, crest, heraldry, blazonry.

army n.
- 军队,大队,群 armed force,

military, militia, land forces, soldiers, troops, legions, cohorts, multitude, throng, host, horde.

around prep.
- 环绕 surrounding, round, encircling, encompassing, enclosing, on all sides of, on every side of.
- 大约 approximately, roughly, about, circa, more or less.

adv.
- 到处 everywhere, all over, in all directions, on all sides, about, here and there, to and fro.
- 接近 close, close by, near, nearby, at hand.

arouse v.
- 醒来 rouse, startle, wake up, waken, awaken, instigate, summon up, call forth, spark, kindle, inflame, whet, sharpen, quicken, animate, excite, prompt, provoke, stimulate, galvanize, goad, spur, incite, agitate, stir up, whip up.

arrange v.
- 安排 order, tidy, range, array, marshal, dispose, distribute, position, set out, lay out, align, group, class, classify, categorize, sort (out), sift, file, systematize, methodize, regulate, adjust.
- 调解 organize, co-ordinate, prepare, fix, plan, project, design, devise, contrive, determine, settle.
- 调整,改编 adapt, set, score, orchestrate, instrument, harmonize.

arrangement n.
- 安排 order, array, display, disposition, layout, line-up, grouping, classification, structure, system, method, set-up, organization, preparation, planning, plan, scheme, design, schedule.
- 协议 agreement, settlement, contract, terms, compromise.
- 调整,改编 adaptation, version, interpretation, setting, score, orchestration, instrumentation, harmonization.

array n.
- 排列,整理,列阵 arrangement, display, show, exhibition, exposition, assortment, collection, assemblage, muster, order, formation, line-up, parade.

v.
- 排列 arrange, order, range, dispose, group, line up, align, draw up, marshal, assemble, muster, parade, display, show, exhibit.
- 装束 clothe, dress, robe, deck, adorn, decorate.

arrest v.
- 阻止 stop, stem, check, restrain, inhibit, halt, interrupt, stall, delay, slow, retard, block, obstruct, impede, hinder.
- 逮捕 capture, catch, seize, nick, run in, apprehend, detain.

arrival n.
- 到达 appearance, entrance, advent, coming, approach, occurrence.

arrive v.
☞ 到达 reach, get to, appear, materialize, turn up, show up, roll up, enter, come, occur, happen.

arrogant adj.
☞ 傲慢的,自大的 haughty, supercilious, disdainful, scornful, contemptuous, superior, condescending, patronizing, high and mighty, lordly, overbearing, high-handed, imperious, self-important, presumptuous, assuming, insolent, pround, conceited, boastful.

art n.
☞ 艺术,美术 fine art, painting, sculpture, drawing, artwork, craft, artistry, draughtsmanship, craftsmanship.
☞ 技术 skill, knack, technique, method, aptitude, facility, dexterity, finesse, ingenuity, mastery, expertise, profession, trade.
☞ 人工,人为 artfulness, cunning, craftiness, slyness, guile, deceit, trickery, astuteness, shrewdness.

artful adj.
☞ 狡猾的 cunning, crafty, sly, foxy, wily, tricky, scheming, designing, deceitful, devious, subtle, sharp, shrewd, smart, clever, masterly, ingenious, resourceful, skilful, dexterous.

article n.
☞ 条款 item, thing, object, commodity, unit, part, constituent, piece, portion, division.
☞ 文章,冠词 feature, report, story, account, piece, review, commentary, composition, essay, paper.

articulate adj.
☞ 发生清楚的,关节相连的 distinct, well-spoken, clear, lucid, intelligible, comprehensible, understandable, coherent, fluent, vocal, expressive, meaningful.

v.
☞ 说话清楚 say, utter, speak, talk, express, voice, vocalize, verbalize, state, pronounce, enunciate, breathe.

articulation n.
☞ 发音清楚 saying, utterance, speaking, talking, expression, voicing, vocalization, verbalization, pronunciation, enunciation, diction, delivery.

artificial adj.
☞ 人工的,模拟的,假的 false, fake, bogus, counterfeit, spurious, pseudo, specious, sham, insincere, assumed, affected, mannered, forced, contrived, made-up, feigned, pretended, imitation, mock, synthetic, plastic, man-made, manufactured, non-natural, unnatural.

artistic adj.
☞ 美感的,艺术的 aesthetic, decorative, beautiful, exquisite, elegant, stylish, graceful, harmonious, sensitive, tasteful, refined, cultured, cultivated, skilled, talented, creative, imaginative.

artistry n.
- ☞ 艺术技巧 craftsmanship, workmanship, skill, craft, talent, brilliance, genius, finesse, style, mastery, expertise, proficiency, accomplishment, deftness, touch, sensitivity, creativity.

as conj., prep.
- ☞ 当 while, when.
- ☞ 例如 such as, for example, for instance, like, in the manner of.
- ☞ 因为 because, since, seeing that, considering that, inasmuch as, being.

as for
- ☞ 至于，关于 with reference to, as regards, with regard to, on the subject of, in connection with, in relation to, with relation to, with respect to.

ascend v.
- ☞ 上升，登 rise, take off, lift off, go up, move up, slope upwards, climb, scale, mount, tower, float up, fly up, soar.

ascent n.
- ☞ 登高 ascending, ascension, climb, climbing, scaling, escalation, rise, rising, mounting.
- ☞ 上升 slope, gradient, incline, ramp, hill, elevation.

ascertain v.
- ☞ 调查，查明 find out, learn, discover, determine, fix, establish, settle, locate, detect, identify, confirm, make certain.

ascribe v.
- ☞ 归于，归因于 attribute, credit, accredit, put down, assign, impute, charge, chalk up to.

ashamed adj.
- ☞ 惭愧的 sorry, apologetic, remorseful, contrite, guilty, conscience-stricken, sheepish, embarrassed, blushing, red-faced, mortified, humiliated, abashed, humbled, crestfallen, distressed, discomposed, confused, reluctant, hesitant, shy, self-conscious, bashful, modest, prudish.

aside adv.
- ☞ 在……一边 apart, on one side, in reserve, away, out of the way, separately, in isolation, alone

ask v.
- ☞ 请求，要求 request, appeal, petition, sue, plead, beg, entreat, implore, clamour, pray, supplicate, crave, demand, order, bid, require, seek, solicit, invite, summon.
- ☞ 问 inquire, query, question, interrogate, quiz, press.

asleep adj.
- ☞ 睡着的，麻木的 sleeping, napping, snoozing, fast asleep, sound asleep, dormant, resting, inactive, inert, unconscious, numb, dozing.

aspect n.
- ☞ 面貌，样子，方向 angle, direction, elevation, side, facet, feature, face, expression, countenance, appearance, look, air, manner, bearing, attitude, condition, situation, position, standpoint, point of view, view,

outlook, prospect, scene.

aspiration n.
- 渴望,志向 aim, intent, purpose, endeavour, object, objective, goal, ambition, hope, dream, ideal, wish, desire, yearning, longing, craving, hankering.

aspire v.
- 渴望 aim, intend, purpose, seek, pursue, hope, dream, wish, desire, yearn, long, crave, hanker.

aspiring adj.
- 渴望的 would-be, aspirant, striving, endeavouring, ambitious, enterprising, keen, eager, hopeful, optimistic, wishful, longing.

assassin n.
- 刺客,暗杀者 murderer, killer, slayer, cut-throat, executioner, hatchet man, gunman, liquidator.

assassinate v.
- 刺杀 murder, kill, slay, dispatch, eliminate, liquidate.

assault n.
- 冲击,冲突 attack, offensive, onslaught, strike, raid, invasion, incursion, storm, storming, charge.
- 伤害 battery, grievous bodily harm, rape, abuse.
  v.
- 冲突 attack, charge, invade, strike, hit, set upon, fall on, beat up, rape, molest, abuse.

assemble v.
- 集合 gather, congregate, muster, rally, convene, meet, join up, flock, group, collect, accumulate, amass, bring together, round up, marshal, mobilize.
- 装配 construct, build, put together, piece together, compose, make, fabricate, manufacture.

assembly n.
- 会议 gathering, rally, meeting, convention, conference, convocation, congress, council, group, body, company, congregation, flock, crowd, multitude, throng, collection, assemblage.
- 装配 construction, building, fabrication, manufacture.

assert v.
- 认定,断言,辩护 affirm, attest, swear, testify to, allege, claim, contend, insist, stress, protest, defend, vindicate, uphold, promote, declare, profess, state, pronounce, lay down, advance.

assertion n.
- 断言,主张,声明 affirmation, attestation, word, allegation, claim, contention, insistence, vindication, declaration, profession, statement, pronouncement.

assertive adj.
- 自信的,断言的 bold, confident, self-assured, forward, pushy, insistent, emphatic, forceful, firm, decided, strong-willed, dogmatic, opinionated, presumptuous, assuming, overbearing, domineering,

aggressive.

assess v.
☞ 估计 gauge, estimate, evaluate, review, judge, consider, weigh, size up, compute, determine, fix, value, rate, tax, levy, impose, demand.

assessment n.
☞ 评价,评定 gauging, estimation, estimate, evaluation, review, judgement, opinion, consideration, calculation, determination, valuation, rating, taxation.

assets n.
☞ 财富,资产 estate, property, possessions, goods, holdings, securities, money, wealth, capital, funds, reserves, resources, means.

assign v.
☞ 分配,指派 allocate, apportion, grant, give, dispense, distribute, allot, consign, delegate, name, nominate, designate, appoint, choose, select, determine, set, fix, specify, stipulate.
☞ 把……归功于 attribute, accredit, ascribe, put down.

assignment n.
☞ 分配,分派,任务,作业 commission, errand, task, project, job, position, post, duty, responsibility, charge, appointment, delegation, designation, nomination, selection, allocation, consignment, grant, distribution.

assist v.
☞ 协助,援助 help, aid, abet, rally round, co-operate, collaborate, back, second, support, reinforce, sustain, relieve, benefit, serve, enable, facilitate, expedite, boost, further, advance.

assistant n.
☞ 协助者,援助者 helper, helpmate, aide, right-hand man, auxiliary, ancillary, subordinate, backer, second, supporter, accomplice, accessory, abettor, collaborator, colleague, partner, ally, confederate, associate.

associate v.
☞ 联合 affiliate, confederate, ally, league, join, amalgamate, combine, unite, link, connect, correlate, relate, couple, pair, yoke.
☞ 交往 socialize, mingle, mix, fraternize, consort, hang around.

n.
☞ 同伴,同僚 partner, ally, confederate, affiliate, collaborator, co-worker, mate, colleague, peer, compeer, fellow, comrade, companion, friend, assistant, follower.

association n.
☞ 协会 organization, corporation, company, partnership, league, alliance, coalition, confederation, confederacy, federation, affiliation, consortium, cartel, syndicate, union, society, club, fraternity, fellowship, clique,

group, band.
- 关联,联合 bond, tie, connection, correlation, relation, relationship, involvement, intimacy, friendship, companionship, familiarity.

assume v.
- 假定 presume, surmise, accept, take for granted, expect, understand, deduce, infer, guess, postulate, suppose, think, believe, imagine, fancy.
- 假装 affect, take on, feign, counterfeit, simulate, put on, pretend.
- 承担 undertake, adopt, embrace, seize, arrogate, commandeer, appropriate, usurp, take over.

assumed adj.
- 假定的 false, bogus, counterfeit, fake, phone, sham, affected, feigned, simulated, pretended, made-up, fictitious, hypothetical.

assumption n.
- 假定 presumption, surmise, inference, supposition, guess, conjecture, theory, hypothesis, premise, postulate, idea, notion, belief, fancy.

assurance n.
- 保证 assertion, declaration, affirmation, guarantee, pledge, promise, vow, word, oath.
- 自信,信任 confidence, self-confidence, aplomb, boldness, audacity, courage, nerve, conviction, sureness, certainty.

assure v.
- 确信 affirm, guarantee, warrant, pledge, promise, vow, swear, tell, convince, persuade, encourage, hearten, reassure, soothe, comfort, boost, strengthen, secure, ensure, confirm.

assured adj.
- 确信的 sure, certain, indisputable, irrefutable, confirmed, positive, definite, settled, fixed, guaranted, secure.
- 自信的 self-assured, confident, self-confident, self-possessed, bold, audacious, assertive.

astonish v.
- 使……惊讶 surprise, startle, amaze, astound, stun, stupefy, daze, stagger, floor, dumbfound, flabbergast, shock, confound, bewilder.

astonishment n.
- 惊讶 surprise, amazement, shock, dismay, consternation, confusion, bewilderment, wonder.

athlete n.
- 体育家,运动员 sportsman, sportswoman, runner, gymnast, competitor, contestant, contender.

athletic adj.
- 运动的,体育的 fit, energetic, vigorous, active, sporty, muscular, sinewy, brawny, strapping, robust, sturby, strong, powerful, well-knit, well-proportioned, wiry.

athletics n.
- 竞技,运动,体育 sports,

games, races, track events, field events, exercises, gymnastics.

atmosphere n.
- ☞ 空气, 大气 air, sky, aerospace, heavens, ether.
- ☞ 气氛 ambience, environment, surroundings, aura, feel, feeling, mood, spirit, tone, tenor, character, quality, flavour.

atom n.
- ☞ 原子, 微粒 molecule, particle, bit, morsel, crumb, grain, spot, speck, mite, shred, scrap, hint, trace, scintilla, jot, iota, whit.

attach v.
- ☞ 附加 affix, stick, adhere, fasten, fix, secure, tie, bind, weld, join, unite, connect, link, couple, add, annex.
- ☞ 依附 ascribe, attribute, impute, assign, put, place, associate, relate to, belong.

attachment n.
- ☞ 附加, 爱慕 accessory, fitting, fixture, extension, appendage, extra, supplement, addition, tenderness, love, liking, partiality, loyalty, devotion, friendship, affinity, attraction, bond tie, link.

attack n.
- ☞ 攻击 offensive, blitz, bombardment, invasion, incursion, foray, raid, strike, charge, rush, onslaught, assault, battery, aggression, criticism, censure, abuse.
- ☞ 发作 seizure, fit, convulsion, paroxysm, spasm, stroke.

v.
- ☞ 攻击 invade, raid, strike, storm, charge, assail, assault, set about, set upon, fall on, lay into.
- ☞ 谴责 criticize, censure, blame, denounce, revile, malign, abuse.

attacker n.
- ☞ 攻击者 assailant aggressor, invader, raider, critic, detractor, reviler, abuser, persecutor.

attain v.
- ☞ 取得, 达到 accomplish, achieve, fulfil, complete, effect, realize, earn, reach, touch, arrive at, grasp, get, acquire, obtain, procure, secure, gain, win, net.

attainment n.
- ☞ 达到 accomplishment, achievement, feat, fulfilment, completion, consummation, realization, success, ability, capability, competence, proficiency, skill, art, talent, gift, aptitude, facility, mastery.

attempt n.
- ☞ 企图 try, edeavour, go, stab, effort, struggle, bid, undertaking, venture, trial, experiment.

v.
- ☞ 试图做 try, endeavour, have a go , aspire, seek, strive, undertake, tackle, venture, experiment.

attend v.
- ☞ 出席 be present, go to, frequent, visit.
- ☞ 护理 escort, chaperon, accompany, usher, follow,

guard, look after, take care of, care for, nurse, tend, minister to, help, serve, wait on.
☞ 注意 pay attention, listen, hear, heed, mind, mark, note, notice, observe.

attend to
☞ 处理, 照顾 deal with, see to, take care of, look after, manage, direct, control, oversee, supervise.

attendant n.
☞ 服务员, 出席者 aide, helper, assistant, auxiliary, steward, waiter, servant, page, retainer, guide, marshal, usher, escort, companion, follower, guard, custodian.
adj.
☞ 伴随的 accompanying, attached, associated, related, incidental, resultant, consequent, subsequent.

attention n.
☞ 注意 alertness, vigilance, concentration, heed, notice, observation, regard, mindfulness, awareness, recognition, thought, contemplation, consideration, concern, care, treatment, service.

attentive adj.
☞ 注意的 alert, awake, vigilant, watchful, observant, concentrating, heedful, observant, concentrating, heedful, mindful, careful, conscientious.
☞ 殷勤的 considerate, thoughtful, kind, obliging, accommodating, polite, courteous, devoted.

attitude n.
☞ 姿势, 态度 feeling, disposition, mood, aspect, manner, bearing, pose, posture, stance, position, point of view, opinion, view, outlook, perspective, approach.

attract v.
☞ 吸引, 引起 pull, draw, lure, allure, entice, seduce, tempt, invite, induce, incline, appeal to, interest, engage, fascinate, enchant, charm, bewitch, captivate, excite.

attraction n.
☞ 吸引(力) pull, draw, magnetism, lure, allure, bait, enticement, inducement, seduction, temptation, invitation, appeal, interest, fascination, enchantment, charm, captivation.

attractive adj.
☞ 有吸引力的, 诱人的 pretty, fair, fetching, good-looking, handsome, beautiful, gorgeous, stunhing, glamorous, lovely, pleasant, pleasing, agreeable, appealing, winsome, winning, enticing, seductive, tempting, inviting, interesting, engaging, fascinating, charming, cativating, magnetic.

attribute v.
☞ 归咎于 ascrible, accredit, credit, impute, assign, put down, blame, charge, refer, apply.
n.
☞ 属性, 标志 property, quality, virtue, point, aspect, facet,

feature, trait, characteristic, idiosyncrasy, peculiarity, quirk, note, mark, sign, symbol.

audience n.
☞ 听众,观众 spectators, onlookers, house, auditorium, listeners, viewers, crowd, turnout, gathering, assembly, congregation, fans, devotees, regulars, following, public.

audit n.
☞ 审计,查账 examination, inspection, check, verification, investigation, scrutiny, analysis, review, statement, balancing.

authentic adj.
☞ 可靠的,真实的 genuine, true, real, actual, certain, bona fide, legitimate, honest, valid, originual, pure, factual, accurate, true-to-life, faithful, reliable, trustworthy.

authenticity n.
☞ 可靠,真实 genuineness, certainty, authoritativeness, validity, truth, veracity, truthfulness, honesty, accuracy, correctness, faithfulness, fidelity, reliability, dependability, trustworthiness.

author n.
☞ 作者 writer, novelist, dramatist, playwright, composer, pen, penman, penwoman.
☞ 创始人 creator, founder, originator, initiator, parent, prime mover, mover, inventor, designer, architect, planner, maker, producer.

authority n.
☞ 权力 sovereignty, supremacy, rule, sway, control, dominion, influence, power, force, government, administration, officialdom.
☞ 威信 authorization, permission, sanction, permit, warrant, licence, credentials, right, prerogative.
☞ 权威 expert, pundit, connoisseur, specialist, professional, master, scholar.

authorize v.
☞ 授权,核审 legalize, validate, ratify, confirm, license, entitle, accredit, empower, enable, commission, warrant, permit, allow, consent to, sanction, approve, give the go-ahead.

autocracy n.
☞ 独裁,专制 absolutism, totalitarianism, dictatorship, despotism, tyranny, authoritarianism, fascism.

autocrat n.
☞ 独裁者 absolutist, totalitarian, dicator, despot, tyrant, authoritarian, (little) Hitler, fascist.

autocratic adj.
☞ 专制的 absolute, all-powerful, totalitarian, despotic, tyrannical, authoritraian, domineering, overbearing, imperious.

automatic adj.
☞ 自动的 automated, self-activating, mechanical, mechanized, programmed, self-regulating, computerized, push-button, robotic, self-propelling, unmanned.
☞ 无意识的 spontaneous,

reflex, involuntary, unwilled, unconscious, unthinking, natural, instinctive, routine, necessary, certain, inevitable, unavoidable, inescapable.

autonomy n.
☞ 自治(权),自主(性) self-government, self-rule, home rule, sovereignty, independence, self-determination, freedom, free will.

available adj.
☞ 能得到的,可用的 free, vacant, to hand, within reach, at hand, accessible, handy, convenient, on hand, ready, on tap, obtainable.

avenge v.
☞ 代……报仇 take revenge for, take vengeance for, punish, requite, repay, retaliate.

average n.
☞ 平均,平均数 mean, midpoint, norm, standard, rule, par, medium, run.
adj.
☞ 平均的 mean, medial, median, middle, intermediate, medium, moderate, satisfactory, fair, mediocre, middling, indifferent, so-so, passable, tolerable, undistinguished, run-of-the-mill, ordinary, everyday, common, usual, normal, regular, standard, typical, unexceptional.

averse adj.
☞ 反对的,不乐意的 reluctant, unwilling, loth, disinclined, ill-disposed, hostile, opposed, antagonistic, unfavourable.

aversion n.
☞ 反对,不乐意 dislike, hate, hatred, loathing, detestation, abhorrence, abomination, horror, reluctance, unwillingness, disinclination, distaste, disgust, revulsion, repugnance, repulsion, hostility, opposition, antagonism.

avert v.
☞ 避开,防止,避免 turn away, deflect, turn aside, parry, fend off, ward off, stave off, forestall, frustrate, prevent, obviate, avoid, evade.

aviation n.
☞ 飞行,航空 aeronautics, flying, flight, aircraft industry.

avoid v.
☞ 避免,逃避 evade, elude, sidestep, dodge, shirk, duck, escape, get out of, bypass, balk, prevent, avert, shun, abstain from, refrain from, steer clear of.

avoidable adj.
☞ 避免的 escapable, preventable.

avowed adj.
☞ 公开承认的 sworn, declared, professed, self-proclaimed, self-confessed, confessed, admitted, acknowledged, open, overt.

awake v.
☞ 叫醒,觉醒 awaken, waken, wake, wake up, rouse, arouse.
adj.
☞ 醒着的 wakeful, wide-awake, aroused, alert, vigilant, watchful, observant, attentive, conscious, aware, sensitive,

award v.
☞ 授予 give, present, distribute, dispense, bestow, confer, accord, endow, gift, grant, allot, apportion, assign, allow, determine.

n.
☞ 奖品 prize, trophy, decoration, bestowal, conferral, endowment, gift, grant, allotment, allowance, adjudication, judgment, decision, order.

aware adj.
☞ 知道的,意识到的 conscious, alive to, sensitive, appreciative, sentient, familiar, conversant, acquainted, informed, enlightened, knowing, knowledgeable, cognizant, mindful, heedful, attentive, observant, sharp, alert, on the ball, shrewd, sensible.

awe n.
☞ 敬畏 wonder, veneration, reverence, respect, admiration, amazement, astonishment, fear, terror, dread, apprehension.

awe-inspiring adj.
☞ 令人敬畏的 overwhelming, breathtaking, impressive, majestic, awesome, formidable, daunting, intimidating, fearsome.

awful adj.
☞ 可怕的,威严的 terrible, dreadful, fearful, frightful, ghastly, unpleasant, nasty, horrible, hideous, ugly, gruesome, dire, abysmal, atrocious, horrific, shocking, appalling, alarming, spine-chilling.

awkward adj.
☞ 难使用的,笨拙的 clumsy, gauche, inept, inexpert, unskilful, bungling, ham-fisted, unco-ordinated, ungainly, graceless, ungraceful, inelegant, cumbersome, unwieldy, inconvenient, difficult, fiddly, delicate, troublesome, perplexing.
☞ 难应付的,棘手的 obstinate, stubborn, unco-operative, irritable, touchy, prickly, rude, unpleasant.
☞ 难堪的 uncomfortable, ill at ease, embarrassed.

axe n.
☞ 斧子 hatchet, chopper, cleaver, tomahawk, battle-axe.
v.
☞ 砍,劈 cut (down), hew, chop, cleave, split.

B

babble v.
☞ 唠叨 chatter, gabble, jabber, cackle, prate, mutter, mumble, murmur.

n.
☞ 无意义的话 chatter, gabble, clamour, hubbub, burble, murmur.

baby n.
- ☞ 小孩,婴儿 babe, infant, suckling, child, tiny, toddler.

adj.
- ☞ 小的 miniature, small-scale, mini, small, little, tiny.

babyish *adj.*
- ☞ 孩子气的 childish, juvenile, puerile, infantile, silly, foolish, soft, sissy, baby, young, immature, naive.

back n.
- ☞ 背,背脊 read, stern, end, tail, tail end, hind part, hindquarters, backside, reverse.

v.
- ☞ 退后 go backwards, reverse, recede, regress, backtrack, retreat, retire, withdraw, back, away, recoil.
- ☞ 支援 support, sustain, assist, side with, champion, advocate, encourage, promote, boost, favour, sanction, countenance, endorse, second, countersign, sponsor, finance, subsidize, underwrite.

backbone n.
- ☞ 脊骨 spine, spinal column, vertebrae, vertebral column, mainstay, support, core.
- ☞ 骨气 courage, mettle, pluck, nerve, determination, resolve, tenacity, steadfastness, toughness, stamina, strength, power.

background n.
- ☞ 背景 setting, surroundings, environment, context, circumstances.

backward *adj.*
- ☞ 倒退 retrograde, retrogressive, regressive.
- ☞ 不情愿的 shy, bashful, reluctant, unwilling, hesitant, hesitating, wavering, slow, behind, behindhand, late, immature, retarded, subnormal.

bad *adj.*
- ☞ 不利的,严重的 unpleasant, disagreeable, nasty, undesirable, unfortunate, distressing, adverse, detrimental, harmful, damaging, injurious, serious, grave, severe, harsh.
- ☞ 恶的 evil, wicked, sinful, criminal, corrupt, immoral, vile.
- ☞ 可怜的,没用的 poor, inferior, substandard, imperfect, faulty, defective, deficient, unsatisfactory, useless.
- ☞ 腐坏的 rotten, mouldy, decayed, spoilt, putrid, rancid, sour, off, tainted, contaminated.
- ☞ 淘气的 naughty, mischievous, ill-behaved, disobedient.

badge n.
- ☞ 证章 identification, emblem, device, insignia, sign, mark, token, stamp, brand, trademark, logo.

badly *adv.*
- ☞ 极大地,非常地 greatly, extremely, exceedingly, intensely, deeply, acutely, bitterly, exceedingly, painfully, seriously, desperately, severely, critically, crucially.
- ☞ 可恶地 wickedly, criminally, immorally, unfairly.

☞ 不好地 wrong, incorrectly, improperly, defectively, faultily, imperfectly, inadequately, unsatisfactorily, poorly, incompetently, negligently, carelessly.
☞ 不幸地 unfavourably, adversely, unfortunately, unsuccessfully.

bad-tempered *adj.*
☞ 坏脾气的 irritable, cross, crotchety, crabbed, crabby, snappy, grumpy, querulous, petulant, fractious.

bag *v.*
☞ 猎获 catch, capture, trap, land, kill, shoot.
☞ 得到 obtain, acquire, get, gain, corner, take, grab, appropriate, commandeer, reserve.
n.
☞ 书包 container, sack, case, suitcase, grip, carrier, hold-all, handbag, shoulder, haversack, pack.

baggage *n.*
☞ 行李 luggage, suitcases, bags, belongings, things, equipment, gear, paraphernalia.

baggy *adj.*
☞ 宽松的 loose, slack, roomy, ill-fitting, billowing, bulging, floppy, sagging, droopy.

bail *n.*
☞ 保证金 security, surety, pledge, bond, guarantee, warranty.

bail out[1]
☞ 保释出来 help, aid, assist, relieve, rescue, finance.

bail out[2], **bale out**
☞ 放弃,跳伞 withdraw, retreat, quit, back out, escape.

bait *n.*
☞ 诱饵 lure, incentive, inducement, bride, temptation, enticement, allurement, attraction.
v.
☞ 诱惑 tease, provoke, goad, irritate, annoy, irk, needle, harass, persecute, torment.

balance *v.*
☞ 使平衡 steady, poise, stabilize, level, square, equalize, equate, match, counterbalance, counteract, neutralize, offset, adjust.
☞ 衡量 compare, consider, weigh, estimate.
n.
☞ 平衡 equilibrium, steadiness, stability, evenness, symmetry, equality, parity, equity, equivalence, correspondence.
☞ 平静 composure, self-possession, poise, equanimity.
☞ 节余,余款 remainder, rest, residue, surplus, difference.

balcony *n.*
☞ 阳台,楼厅 terrace, veranda, gallery, upper circle, gods.

bald *adj.*
☞ 秃头的 bald-headed, hairless, smooth, uncovered.
☞ 光秃的 bare, naked, unadorned, plain, simple, severe, stark, barren, treeless.
☞ 单调的 forthright, direct, straight, outright, downright, straightforward.

bale n.
- 包,捆 bundle, truss, pack, package, parcel.

balk, baulk v.
- 不肯前进 flinch, recoil, shrink, jib, boggle, hesitate, refuse, resist, dodge, evade, shirk.
- 阻挠 thwart, frustrate, foil, forestall, disconcert, baffle, hinder, obstruct, check, stall, bar, prevent, defeat, counteract.

ball[1] n.
- 球,球状物 sphere, globe, orb, globule, drop, conglomeration, pellet, pill, shot, bullet, slug.

ball[2] n.
- 舞会 dance, dinner-dance, party, soiree, masquerade, carnival, assembly.

ban v.
- 禁止 forbid, prohibit, disallow, proscribe, bar, exclude, ostracize, outlaw, banish, suppress, restrict.

n.
- 禁止,禁令 prohibition, embargo, veto, boycott, stoppage, restriction, suppression, censorship, outlawry, condemnation, curse, denunciation, taboo.

band[1] n.
- 带条 strip, belt, ribbon, tape, bandage, binding, tie, ligature, bond, strap, cord, chain.

band[2] n.
- 一帮 troop, gang, crew, group, herd, flock, party, body, association, company, society, club, clique.
- 乐队 group, orchestra, ensemble.

v.
- 联合 group, gather, join, unite, ally, collaborate, consolidate, amalgamate, merge, affiliate, federate.

bandage n.
- 绷带 dressing, plaster, compress, ligature, tourniquet, swathe, swaddle.

v.
- 上绷带 bind, dress, cover, swathe, swaddle.

bandit n.
- 匪徒,土匪 robber, thief, brigand, marauder, outlaw, highwayman, pirate, buccaneer, hijacker, cowboy, gunman, desperado, gangster.

bang n.
- 猛击 blow, hit, knock, bump, crash, collision, smack, punch, thump, wallop, stroke, whack.
- 砰的一声 explosion, boom, detonation, pop, clap, peal, clang, clash, thud, thump, slam, noise, report, shot.

v.
- 猛击 strike, hit, bash, knock, bump, rap, drum, hammer, pound, thump, stamp.
- 砰的响一下 explode, burst, detonate, boom, echo, resound, crash, slam, clatter, clang, peal, thunder.

banish v.

☞驱逐出境,排除 expel, eject, evict, deport, transport, exile, outlaw, ban, bar, debar, exclude, shut out, ostracize, excommunicate, dismiss, oust, dislodge, remove, get rid of, discard, dispel, eliminate, eradicate.

bank[1] *n*.

☞河岸,沙滩 accumulation, fund, pool, reservoir, depository, repository, treasury, savings, reserve, store, stock, stockpile, hoard, cache.

v.

☞堆积 heap, pile, stack, mass, amass, accumulate, mound, drift.

☞倾斜 slope, incline, pitch, slant, tilt, tip.

bank[2] *n*.

☞银行 heap, pile, mass, mound, earthwork, ridge, rampart, embankment, side, slope, tilt, edge, shore.

v.

☞存 deposit, save, keep, store, accumulate, stockpile.

bankrupt *adj*.

☞破产的 insolvent, in liquidation, ruined, failed, beggared, destitute, impoverished, broke, spent, exhausted, depleted, lacking.

n.

☞破产者 insolvent, debtor, pauper.

banner *n*.

☞旗帜,标识(题) standard, flag, colours, ensign, streamer, pennant, banderole.

banquet *n*.

☞宴会 feast, dinner, meal, treat.

banter *n*.

☞玩弄,戏弄 joking, jesting, pleasantry, badinage, repartee, word play, chaff, chaffing, kidding, derision, mockery, ridicule.

bar *n*.

☞酒吧 public house, pub, inn, tavern, saloon, lounge, counter.

☞横木 slab, block, lump, chunk, wedge, ingot, nugget.

☞棒条 rod, stick, shaft, pole, stake, stanchion, batten, crosspiece, rail, railing, paling, barricade.

☞障碍物 obstacle, impediment, hindrance, obstruction, barrier, stop, check, deterrent.

v.

☞阻碍 exclude, debar, ban, forbid, prohibit, prevent, preclude, hinder, obstruct, restrain.

☞闩 barricade, lock, bolt, latch, fasten, secure.

barbarian *n*.

☞野蛮人 savage, brute, ruffian, hooligan, vandal, lout, oaf, boor, philistine, ignoramus, illiterate.

barbaric *adj*.

☞粗鲁的,没教养的 barbarous, primitive, wild, savage, fierce, ferocious, cruel, inhuman, brutal, brutish, uncivilized, uncouth, vulgar, coarse, crude, rude.

barbarity *n*.

☞ 野蛮性,残暴 barbarousness, wildness, savagery, ferocity, viciousness, cruelty, inhumanity, brutality, brutishness, rudeness.

bare *adj.*
☞ 裸露的,空的 naked, nude, unclothed, undressed, stripped, denuded, uncovered, exposed.
☞ 简朴的,无装饰的 plain, simple, unadorned, unfurnished, empty, barren, bald, stark, basic, essential.

barely *adv.*
☞ 几乎不 hardly, scarcely, only just, just, almost.

bargain *n.*
☞ 契约,合同 deal, transaction, contract, treaty, pact, pledge, promise, agreement, understanding, arrangement, negotiation.
☞ 折扣 discount, reduction, snip, giveaway, special offer.
v.
☞ 讨价还价 negotiate, haggle, deal, trade, traffic, barter, buy, sell, transact, promise, agree.

bargain for
☞ 预期,预料 expect, anticipate, plan for, include, reckon on, look for, foresee, imagine, contemplate, consider.

bark *n.*
☞ 咆哮 yap, woof, yelp, snap, snarl, growl, bay, howl.
v.
☞ 咆哮 yap, woof, yelp, snarl, growl, bay, howl.

barrage *n.*
☞ 轰击 bombardment, shelling, gunfire, broadside, volley, salvo, burst, assault, attack, onset, onslaught, deluge, torrent, stream, storm, hail, rain, shower, mass, profusion.

barrier *n.*
☞ 关卡,栅栏 wall, fence, railing, blockade, boom, rampart, fortification, ditch, frontier, boundary, bar, check.
☞ 障碍物 obstacle, hurdle, stumbling-block, impediment, obstruction, hindrance, handicap, limitation, restriction, drawback, difficulty.

bartender *n.*
☞ 服务员 barman, barmaid, barkeeper, publican.

base *n.*
☞ 基座 bottom, foot, pedestal, plinth, stand, rest, support, foundation, bed, groundwork.
☞ 根据地 basis, fundamental, essential, principal, key, heart, core, essence, root, origin, source.
☞ 基地 headquarters, centre, post, station, camp, settlement, home, starting point.
v.
☞ 以……为基础 establish, found, ground, locate, station, build, construct, derive, depend, hinge.

baseless *adj.*
☞ 无根据的,无原因的 groundless, unfounded, unconfirmed, uncalled-for, gratuitous.

bashful *adj.*
☞ 害羞的 adj, shy, retiring,

backward, reticent, reserved, unforthcoming, hesitant, shrinking, nervous, timid, coy, diffident, modest, inhibited, self-conscious, embarrassed, blushing, abashed, shamefaced, sheepish.

basic *adj*.
☞ 基础的,基本的 fundamental, elementary, primary, root, underlying, key, central, inherent, intrinsic, essential, indispensable, vital, necessary, important.

basically *adv*
☞ 基础地 fundamentally, at bottom, at heart, inherently, intrinsically, essentially, principally, primarily.

basics *n*.
☞ 基础,主要成分 fundamentals, rudiments, principles, essentials, necessaries, practicalities, brass tacks, grass roots, bedrock, rock bottom, core, facts.

basin *n*.
☞ 脸盆,盆地 bowl, dish, sink, crater, cavity, hollow, depression, dip.

basis *n*.
☞ 基础 base, bottom, footing, support, foundation, ground, groundwork, fundamental, premise, principle, essential, heart, core, thrust.

bask *v*.
☞ 晒太阳 sunbathe, lie, lounge, relax, laze, wallow, revel, delight in, enjoy, relish, savour.

basket *n*.
☞ 篮子 hamper, creel, pannier, bassinet.

bass *adj*.
☞ 低音的 deep, low, low-toned, grave, resonant.

bastion *n*.
☞ 堡垒 stronghold, citadel, fortress, defence, bulwark, mainstay, support, prop, pillar, rock.

batch *n*.
☞ 一伙,一批 lot, consignment, parcel, pack, bunch, set, assortment, collection, assemblage, group, amount, quantity.

bath *n*.
☞ 澡盆,洗澡 wash, scrub, soak, shower, douche, tub.

bathe *v*.
☞ 洗澡,充满,笼罩 swim, wet, moisten, immerse, wash, cleanse, rinse, soak, steep, flood, cover, suffuse.
n.
☞ 洗澡,游泳 swim, dip, paddle, wash, rinse, soak.

battle *n*.
☞ 战役 war, warfare, hostilities, action, conflict, strife, combat, fight, engagement, encounter, attack, fray, skirmish, clash, struggle, contest, campaign, crusade, row, disagreement, dispute, debate, controversy.
v.
☞ 战斗 fight, combat, war, feud, contend, struggle, strive, campaign, crusade, agitate,

clamour, contest, argue, dispute.

battle-cry n.
☞ 战歌 war cry, war song, slogan, motto, watchword, catchword.

bay[1] n.
☞ 湾,海湾 gulf, bight, arm, inlet, cove.

bay[2] v.
☞ 狂吠 howl, roar, bellow, bell, bawl, cry, holler, bark.

bazaar n.
☞ 集市,市场,百货商店 market, marketplace, mart, exchange, sale, fair, fete, bring-and-buy.

beach n.
☞ 海滨 sand, sands, shingle, shore, strand, seashore, seaside, water's edge, coast, seaboard.

bead n.
☞ 水珠 drop, droplet, drip, globule, glob, blob, dot, bubble, pearl, jewel, pellet.

beam n.
☞ 一束 ray, shaft, gleam, glint, glimmer, glow.
☞ 梁 plank, board, timber, rafter, girder, spar, boom, bar, support.
v.
☞ 发光 emit, broadcast, transmit, radiate, shine, glare, glitter, glow, glimmer.
☞ 微笑 smile, grin.

bear v.
☞ 携带,负荷 carry, convey, transport, move, take, bring.
☞ 支持 hold, support, shoulder, uphold, sustain, maintain, harbour, cherish.
☞ 生产,生育 give birth to, breed, propagate, beget, engender, produce, generate, develop, yield, bring forth, give up.
☞ 忍耐 tolerate, stand, put up with, endure, abide, suffer, permit, allow, admit.

bear on
☞ 与……有关 refer to, relate to, affect, concern, involve.

bear out
☞ 证实 confirm, endorse, support, uphold, prove, demonstrate, corroborate, substantiate, vindicate, justify.

bear up
☞ 坚忍不屈 persevere, soldier on, carry on, suffer, endure, survive, withstand.

bear with
☞ 容忍,忍耐 tolerate, put up with, endure suffer, forbear, be patient with, make allowances for.

bearable adj.
☞ 忍得住的 tolerable, endurable, sufferable, supportable, sustainable, acceptable, manageable.

bearded adj.
☞ 长胡须的 unshaven, bristly, whiskered, tufted, hairy, hirsute, shaggy, bushy.

bearer n.
☞ 送信人 carrier, conveyor, porter, courier, messenger, runner, holder, possessor.

bearing n.
☞ 关系 relevance, significance,

connection, relation, reference.
☞ 举止 demeanour, manner, mien, air, aspect, attitude, behaviour, comportment, poise, deportment, carriage, posture.

bearings n.
☞ 方向感 orientation, position, situation, location, whereabouts, course, track, way, direction, aim.

beast n.
☞ 四足兽 animal, creature, brute, monster, savage, , pig, swine, devil, fiend.

beat v.
☞ 打击 whip, flog, lash, tan, cane, strap, thrash, lay into, hit, punch, strike, swipe, knock, bang, wham, bash, pound, hammer, batter, buffet, plet, bruise.
☞ 跳动 pulsate, pulse, throb, thump, race, palpitate, flutter, vibrate, quiver, tremble, shake, quake.
☞ 击败 defeat, trounce, best, worst, hammer , conquer, overcome, overwhelm, vanquish, subdue, surpass, excel, outdo, outstrip, outrun.
n.
☞ 跳动 pulsation, pulse, stroke, throb, thump, palpitation, flutter.
☞ 拍子 rhythm, time, tempo, metre, measure, rhyme, stress, accent.
☞ 巡逻区 round, rounds, territory, circuit, course, journey, way, path, route.

beautiful adj.
☞ 美丽的,动人的 attractive, fair, pretty, lovely, good-looking, handsome, gorgeous, radiant, ravishing, stunning , pleasing, appealing, alluring, charming, delightful, fine, exquisite.

beautify v.
☞ 使……美丽,装饰,美化 embellish, enhance, improve, grace, gild, garnish, decorate, ornament, deck, bedeck, adorn, array, glamorize .

beauty n.
☞ 美人 attractiveness, fairness, prettiness, loveliness, (good) looks, handsomeness, glamour, appeal, allure, charm, grace, elegance, symmetry, excellence.

because adj.
☞ 因为 as, for, since, owing to, on account of, by reason of, thanks to.

become v.
☞ 变成 turn, grow, get, change into, develop into.

bed n.
☞ 床 divan, couch, bunk, berth, cot, mattress, pallet.
☞ 基座,底层 layer, stratum, substratum, matrix, base, bottom, foundation, groundwork, watercourse, channel.

bedclothes n.
☞ 床上用品 bedding, bed-linen, sheets, pillowcases, pillowships, covers, blankets, bedspreads, coverlets, quilts, eiderdowns, pillows.

before adv.
☞ 在……之前 ahead, in front,

in advance, sooner, earlier, formerly, previously.

beforehand *adv.*
☞ 事先, 预先 in advance, preliminarily, already, before, previously, earlier, sooner.

beg *v.*
☞ 祈求, 肯求 request, require, desire, crave, beseech, plead, entreat, implore, pray, supplicate, petition, solicit, cadge, scrounge, sponge.

beggar *n.*
☞ 乞求者 mendicant, supplicant, pauper, down-and-out, tramp, vagrant, cadger, scrounger, sponger.

begin *v.*
☞ 开始 start, commence, set about, embark on, set in motion, activate, originate, initiate, introduce, found, institute, instigate, arise, spring, emerge, appear.

beginner *n.*
☞ 初学者 novice, tiro, starter, leaner, trainee, apprentice, student, freshman, fresher, recruit, cub, tenderfoot, fledgling.

beginning *n.*
☞ 起初, 起源 start, commencement, onset, outset, opening, preface, prelude, introduction, initiation, establishment, inauguration, inception, starting point, birth, dawn, origin, source, fountainhead, root, seed, emergence, rise.

behalf *n.*
☞ 名义 sake, account, good, interest, benefit, advantage, profit, name, authority, side, support.

behave *v.*
☞ 行为, 举止, 表现 act, react, respond, work, function, run, operate, perform, conduct oneself, acquit oneself, comport oneself (*fml*).

behaviour *n.*
☞ 行为, 举止, 态度 conduct, manner, manners, actions, doings, dealings, ways, habits, action, reaction, response, functioning, operation, performance.

behead *v.*
☞ 砍头, 斩首 decapitate, execute, guillotine.

behind *prep.*
☞ 在……后 following, after, later than, causing, responsible for, instigating, initiating.
adv.
☞ 落后于 after, following, next, subsequently, behindhand, late, overdue, in arrears, in debt.

beige *adj.*
☞ 灰棕色的 buff, fawn, mushroom, camel, sandy, khaki, coffee, neutral.

being *n.*
☞ 生存 existence, actuality, reality, life, animation, essence, substance, nature, soul, spirit.
☞ 生物 creature, animal, beast, human, being, mortal, person, individual, thing, entity.

belch *v.*

☞ 打嗝,打咽 burp, hiccup, emit, discharge, disgorge, spew.

belief n.
☞ 信任 conviction, persuasion, credit, trust, reliance, confidence, assurance, certainty, sureness, presumption, expectation, feeling, intuition, impression, notion, theory, view, opinion, judgement.
☞ 信仰 ideology, faith, creed, doctrine, dogma, tenet, principle.

believable adj.
☞ 可信的 credible, imaginable, conceivable, acceptable, plausible, possible, likely, probable, authoritative, reliable, trustworthy.

believe v.
☞ 相信 accept, wear, swallow, credit, trust, count on, depend on, rely on, swear by, hold, maintain, postulate, assume, presume, gather, speculate, conjecture, guess, imagine, think, consider, reckon, supporter, upholder.

belittle v.
☞ 轻视,贬低 minimize, play down, dismiss, underrate, undervalue, underestimate, lessen, diminish, detract from, deprecate, decry, disparage, run down, deride, scorn, ridicule.

belong v.
☞ 属于,适合 fit, go with, be part of, attach to, link up with, tie up with, be connected with, relate to.

belongings n.
☞ 所有物,动产 possessions, property, chattels, goods, effects, things, stuff, gear, paraphernalia.

beloved adj.
☞ 受热爱的 loved, adored, cherished, treasured, prized, precious, pet, favourite, dearest, dear, darling, admired, revered.

below adv.
☞ 向下 beneath, under, underneath, down, lower, lower down.
prep.
☞ 在……下面 under, underneath, beneath.
☞ 低于 inferior to, lesser than, subordinate to, subject to.

belt n.
☞ 带,皮带 sash, girdle, waistband, girth, strap.
☞ 地带 strip, band, swathe, stretch, tract, area, region, district, zone, layer.

bench n.
☞ 长凳,条凳,工作台 seat, form, settle, pew, ledge, counter, table, stall, workbench, worktable.
☞ 法官席 court, courtroom, tribunal, judiciary, judicature, judge, magistrate.

bend v.
☞ 弯曲,屈服 curve, turn, deflect, swerve, veer, diverge, twist, contort, flex, shape, mould, buckle, bow, incline, lean, stoop, crouch.
n.

☞ 变曲处 curvature, curve, arc, bow, loop, hook, crook, elbow, angle, corner, turn, twist, zigzag.

beneath *adv*.
☞ 在……下方 below, under, underneath, lower, lower down.
prep.
☞ 在……下面 under, underneath, below, lower than.
☞ 不值得 unworthy of, unbefitting.

benefactor *n*.
☞ 恩人,帮助者,支持者 philanthropist, patron, sponsor, angel, backer, supporter, promoter, donor, contributor, subscriber, provider, helper, friend, well-wisher.

beneficial *adj*.
☞ 有利的,有益的 advantageous, favourable, useful, helpful, profitable, rewarding, valuable, improving, edifying, wholesome.

beneficiary *n*.
☞ 受益人 payee, receiver, recipient, inheritor, legatee, heir, heiress, successor.

benefit *n*.
☞ 利益,好处 advantage, good, welfare, interest, favour, help, aid, assistance, service, use, avail, gain, profit, asset, blessig.
v.
☞ 帮助 help, aid, assist, serve, avail.

berth *n*.
☞ 床位 bed, bunk, hammock, billet.
☞ 下锚处 mooring, anchorage, quay, wharf, dock, harbour, port.

beside *prep*.
☞ 在……旁边 alongside, abreast of, next to, adjacent, abutting, bordering, neighbouring, next door to, close to, near, overlooking.

besides *adv*.
☞ 此外,而且 also, as well, too, in addition, additionally, further, furthermore, moreover.
prep.
☞ 除……之外 apart from, other than, in addition to, over and above.

besiege *v*.
☞ 围困 blockade, surround, encircle, confine.
☞ 困扰 trouble, bother, importune, assail, beset, beleaguer, harass, pester, badger, nag, hound, plague.

best *adj*.
☞ 最好的,最大的 optimum, optimal, first, foremost, leading, unequalled, unsurpassed, matchless, incomparble, supreme, greatest, highest, largest, finest, excellent, outstanding, superlative, first-rate, firs-class, perfect.
adv.
☞ 最好地 greatly, extremely, exceptionally, excellently, superlatively.
n.
☞ 最好的东西 finest, cream, prime, elite, top, first, pick,

choice, favourite.

bet n.
- 赌钱 wager, flutter, gamble, speculation, risk, venture, stake, ante, bid, pledge.

v.
- 赌钱 wager, gamble, punt, speculate, risk, hazard, chance, venture, lay, stake, bid, pledge.

betray v.
- 背叛 inform on, sell(out), double-cross, desert, abandon, forsake.
- 露出……迹象 disclose, give away, tell, divulge, expose, reveal, show, manifest.

betrayal n.
- 出卖,背叛 treachery, treason, sell-out, disloyalty, unfaithfulness, double-dealing, duplicity, deception, trickery, falseness.

betrayer n.
- 叛徒 traitor, Judas, informer, double-crosser, deceiver, conspirator, renegade, apostate.

better adj.
- 优秀的,较好的 superior, bigger, larger, longer, greater, worthier, finer, surpassing, preferable.
- 渐好的 improving, progressing, on the mend, recovering, fitter, healthier, stronger, recovered, restored.

v.
- 提高 improve, ameliorate, enhance, raise, further, promote, forward, reform, mend, correct.
- 改良,优于,胜过 surpass, top, beat, outdo, outstrip, overtake.

between prep.
- 在……之间 mid, amid, amidst, among, amongst.

beverage n.
- 饮料 drink, draught, liquor, liquid, refreshment.

beware v.
- 注意,当心 watch out, look out, mind, take heed, steer clear of, avoid, shun, guard, against.

bewilder v.
- 使……迷惑,为难 confuse, muddle, disconcert, confound, bamboozle, baffle, puzzle, perplex, mystify, daze, stupefy, disorient.

bewildered adj.
- 迷惑的,为难的 confused, muddled, uncertain, disoriented, nonplussed, bamboozled, baffled, puzzled, perplexed, mystified, bemused, surprised, stunned.

beyond prep.
- 在……一边,超过,出乎意料 past, further than, apart from, away from, remote from, out of range of, out of reach of, above, over, superior to.

bias n.
- 偏见,偏爱 slant, angle, distortion, bent, leaning, inclination, tendency, partiality, prejudice, one-sidedness, unfairness, bigotry, intolerance.

biased adj.
- 偏见的,倾斜的 slanted, angled, distorted, warped,

twisted, loaded, weighted, influenced, swayed, partial, predisposed, prejudiced, one-sided, unfair, bigoted, blinkered, jaundiced.

bid *v.*
- 请求,企图 ask, request, desire, instruct, direct, command, enjoin, require, charge, call, summon, invite, solicit.
- 出价 offer, proffer, tender, submit, propose.

n.
- 出价 offer, tender, sum, amount, price, advance, submission, proposal.
- 企图 attempt, effort, try, go, endeavour, venture.

big *adj.*
- 大的 large, great, sizable, considerable, substantial, huge, enormous, immense, massive, colossal, gigantic, mammoth, burly, bulky, extensive, spacious, vast, voluminous.
- 重要的 important, significant, momentous, serious, main, principal, eminent, prominent, influential.
- 大方的 generous, magnanimous, gracious, unselfish.

bill *n.*
- 账单,钞票 invoice, statement, account, charges, reckoning, tally, score.
- 广告,传单 circular, leaflet, handout, bulletin, handbill, broadsheet, advertisement, notice, poster, placard, playbill, programme.
- 议案 proposal, measure, legislation.

v.
- 给……开帐单 invoice, charge, debit.

bind *v.*
- 捆扎 attach, fasten, secure, clamp, stick, tie, lash, truss, strap, bandage, cover, dress, wrap.
- 约束 oblige, force, compel, constrain, necessitate, restrict, confine, restrain, hamper.

binding *adj.*
- 约束的 obligatory, compulsory, mandatory, necessary, requisite, permanent, conclusive, unalterable, indissoluble, unbreakable, strict.

n.
- 装订 border, edging, trimming, tape, bandage, covering, wrapping.

biography *n.*
- 传记 life story, life history, autobiography, memoirs, recollections, curriculum vitae, account, record.

birth *n.*
- 出生 childbirth, parturition, confinement, delivery, nativity.
- 开始 beginning, rise, emergence, origin, source, derivation.
- 出身 ancestry, family, parentage, descent, line, lineage, genealogy, pedigree, blood, stock, race, extraction, background, breeding.

birthplace *n.*
- 出生地,故乡 place of origin, native town, native country,

fatherland, mother country, roots, source, fount.

bit n.
☞ 一小部分 fragment, part, segment, piece, slice, crumb, morsel, scrap, atom, mite, whit, jot, iota, grain, speck.

bit by bit
☞ 越来越,一点一点 gradually, little by little, step by step, piecemeal.

bite v.
☞ 咬叮 chew, masticate, munch, gnaw, nibble, champ, crunch, crush.
☞ 咬 nip, pierce, wound, tear, rend.
☞ 上钩 smart, sting, tingle.
☞ 抓住 grip, hold, seize, pinch, take effect.
n.
☞ 咬 nip, wound, sting, smarting, pinch.

biting adj.
☞ 刺骨的 cold, freezing, bitter, harsh, severe.
☞ 尖锐的 cutting, incisive, piercing, penetrating, raw, stinging, sharp, tart, caustic, scathing, cynical, hurtful.

bitter adj.
☞ 苦的 sour, tart, sharp, acid, vinegary, unsweetened.
☞ 怀恨的 resentful, embittered, jaundiced, cynical, rancorous, acrimonious, acerbic, hostile.
☞ 难受的 intense, severe, harsh, fierce, cruel, savage, merciless, painful, stinging, biting, freezing, raw.

black adj.
☞ 黑的 jet-black, coal-black, jet, ebony, sable, inky, sooty, dusky, swarthy.
☞ 暗的 dark, unlit, moonless, starless, overcast, dingy, gloomy, sombre, funereal.
☞ 脏的 filthy, dirty, soiled, grimy, grubby.

blackmail n.
☞ 讹诈 extortion, hush money, intimidation, protection, pay-off, ransom.
v.
☞ 敲诈 extort, bleed, milk, squeeze, hold to ransom, threaten, lean on, force, compel, coerce, demand.

blackout n.
☞ 封锁 suppression, censorship, cover-up, concealment, secrecy.
☞ 中断 faint, unconsciousness, oblivion.
☞ 停电 power failure, power cut.

blade n.
☞ 刀口,叶片 edge, knife, dagger, sword, scalpel, razor, vane.

blame n.
☞ 责备,谴责 censure, criticism, reprimand, reproof, reproach, recrimination, condemnation, accusation, charge, incrimination, guilt, culpability, fault, responsibility, accountability, liability, onus.
v.
☞ 责备 accuse, charge, tax, reprimand, chide, reprove, upbraid, reprehend, admonish, rebuke, reproach, censure, criticize, find fault with, disapprove, condemn.

blameless adj.
- 没有过失的 innocent, guiltless, clear, faultless, perfect, unblemished, stainless, virtuous, sinless, upright, above reproach, irreproachable, unblamable, unimpeachable.

blank adj.
- 空白的 empty, unfilled, void, clear, bare, unmarked, plain, clean, white.
- 空虚的 expressionless, deadpan, poker-faced, impassive, apathetic, glazed, vacant, uncomprehending.

n.
- 空白 space, gap, break, void, emptiness, vacancy, vacuity, nothingness, vacuum.

blanket n.
- 毯子 covering, coating, coat, layer, film, carpet, rug, cloak, mantle, cover, sheet, envelope, wrapper, wrapping.

v.
- 覆盖 cover, coat, eclipse, hide, conceal, mask, cloak, surround, muffle, deaden, obscure, cloud.

blast n.
- 一阵风 explosion, detonation, bang, crash, clap, crack, volley, burst, outburst, discharge.
- 一股 draught, gust, gale, squall, storm, tempest.
- 管乐声 sound, blow, blare, roar, boom, peal, hoot, wail, scream, shriek.

v.
- 爆炸 explode, blow up, burst, shatter, destroy, demolish, ruin, assail, attack.

blaze n.
- 火焰,火光 fire, flames, conflagration, bonfire, flare-up, explosion, blast, burst, outburst, radiance, brilliance, glare, flash, gleam, glitter, glow, light, flame.

v.
- 燃烧,照耀 burn, flame, flare (*up*), erupt, explode, burst, fire, flash, gleam, glare, beam, shine, glow.

bleach v.
- 漂白 whiten, blanch, decolorize, fade, pale, lighten.

bleak adj.
- 暗淡 gloomy, sombre, leaden, grim, dreary, dismal, depressing, joyless, cheerless, comfortless, hopeless, discouraging, disheartening.
- 冷的,寒冷的 cold, chilly, raw, weather-beaten, unsheltered, windy, windswept, exposed, open, barren, bare, empty, desolate, gaunt.

bleed v.
- 放血 gush, spurt, flow, run, exude, weep, ooze, seep, trickle.
- 使……出血 drain, suck dry, exhaust, squeeze, milk, sap, reduce, deplete.

blend v.
- 混合 merge, amalgamate, coalesce, compound, synthesize, fuse, unite, combine, mix, mingle.
- 调合 harmonize, complement, fit, match.

n.

☞混合物 compound, composite, alloy, amalgam, amalgamation, synthesis, fusion, combination, union, mix, mixture, concoction.

bless v.
☞赐福 anoint, sanctify, consecrate, hallow, dedicate, ordain.
☞赞美,感谢 praise, extol, magnify, glorify, exalt, thank.
☞献给神 approve, countenance, favour, grace, bestow, endow, provide.

blessed adj.
☞祝福 holy, sacred, hallowed, sanctified, revered, adored, divine.
☞幸福的,保估的 happy, contented, glad, joyful, joyous, lucky, fortunate, prosperous, favoured, endowed.

blessing n.
☞祝福 consecration, dedication, benediction, grace, thanksgiving, invocation.
☞值得感谢的事 benefit, advantage, favour, godsend, windfall, gift, gain, profit, help, service.

blind adj.
☞瞎 sightless, unsighted, unseeing, eyeless, purblind, partially, sighted.
☞盲目的,轻率的 impetuous, impulsive, hasty, rash, reckless, wild, mad, indiscriminate, careless, heedless, mindless, unthinking, unreasoning, irrational.
☞无视的 ignorant, oblivious, unaware, unconscious, unobservant, inattentive, neglectful, indifferent, insensitive, thoughtless, inconsiderate.
☞无出口的,隐蔽的 closed, obstructed, hidden, concealed, obscured.

n.
☞瞎、盲、无判断力 screen, cover, clock, mask, camouflage, masquerade, front, facade, distraction, smokescreen, cover-up.

bliss n.
☞福气 blissfulness, euphoria, rapture, joy, happiness, gladness, blessedness, paradise, heaven.

blissful adj.
☞快乐的 ecstatic, euphoric, elated, enraptured, rapturous, delighted, enchanted, joyful, joyous, happy.

blizzard n.
☞大风雪 snowstorm, squall, storm, tempest.

block n.
☞木块,石块 piece, lump, mass, chunk, hunk, square, cube, brick, bar.
☞障碍 obstacle, barrier, bar, jam, blockage, stoppage, resistance, obstruction, impediment, hindrance, let, delay.

v.
☞防碍,阻碍 choke, clog, plug, stop up, dam up, close, bar, obstruct, impede, hinder, stonewall, stop, check, arrest, halt, thwart, scotch, deter.

blockage n.

☞ 防碍,阻碍 blocking, obstruction, stoppage, occlusion, block, clot, jam, log-jam, congestion, hindrance, impediment.

blond, blonde adj.
☞ 金发碧眼的 fair, golden, fair-haired, golden-haired, light-coloured, bleached.

blood n.
☞ 血统 extraction, birth, descent, lineage, family, kindred, relations, ancestry, descendants, kinship, relationship.

bloodcurdling adj.
☞ 血腥的,残忍的 horrifying, chilling, spine-chilling, hair-raising, terrifying, frightening, scary, dreadful, fearful, horrible, horrid, horrendous.

bloodshed n.
☞ 掠杀 killing, murder, slaughter, massacre, blood-bath, butchery, carnage, gore, bloodletting.

bloodthirsty adj.
☞ 极残忍的 murderous, homicidal, warlike, savage, barbaric, barbarous, brutal, ferocious, vicious, cruel, inhuman, ruthless.

bloody adj.
☞ 流血的,血腥的 bleeding, bloodstained, gory, sanguinary, murderous, savage, brutal, ferocious, fierce, cruel.

bloom n.
☞ 花 blossom, flower, bud.
☞ 旺盛 prime, heyday, perfection, blush, flush, glow, beauty, radiance, lustre, health, vigour, freshness.
v.
☞ 开花 bud, sprout, grow, wax, develop, mature, blossom, flower, blow, open.

blossom n.
☞ 开花 bloom, flower, bud.
v.
☞ 发展,开花 develop, mature, bloom, flower, blow, flourish, thrive, prosper, succeed.

blow v.
☞ 吹 breathe, exhale, pant, puff, waft, fan, flutter, float, flow, stream, rush, whirl, whisk, wave, fling, buffet, drive, blast.
☞ 吹响(乐器) play, sound, pipe, trumpet, toot, blare.
n.
☞ 吹 puff, draught, flurry, gust, blast, wind, gale, squall, tempest.

blow over
☞ 吹灭,风停 die down, subside, end, finish, cease, pass, vanish, disappear, dissipate, fizzle out, peter out.

blow up
☞ 爆炸 explode, go off, detonate, burst, blast, bomb.
☞ 发怒 lose one's temper, blow one's toperupt, hit the roof, rage, go mad.
☞ 吹胀,膨胀 inflat, pump up, swell, fill (out), puff up, bloat, distend, dilate, expand, enlarge, magnify, exaggerate, overstate.

blue adj.
☞ 蓝的 azure, sapphire, cobalt,

ultramarine, navy, indigo, aquamarine, turquoise, cyan.
- 无精打彩的 depressed, low, down in the dumps, dejected, downcast, dispirited, down-hearted, despondent, gloomy, glum, dismal, sad, unhappy, miserable, melancholy, morose, fed up.

blueprint n.
- 设计图,蓝图 archetype, prototype, model, pattern, design, outline, draft, sketch, pilot, guide, plan, scheme, project.

blunt adj.
- 钝的 unsharpened, dull, worn, pointless, rounded, stubbed.
- 直率的 frank, candid, direct, forthright, unceremonious, explicit, plain-spoken, honest, downright, outspoken, tactless, insensitive, rude, impolite, uncivil, brusque, curt, abrupt.

v.
- 使钝 dull, take the edge off, dampen, soften, deaden, numb, anaesthetize, alleviate, allay, abate, weaken.

blur v.
- 变污,模糊 smear, smudge, mist, fog, befog, cloud, becloud, blear, dim, darken, obscure, mask, conceal, soften.

n.
- 污点,模糊 smear, smudge, blotch, haze, mist, fog, cloudiness, indistinctness, muddle, confusion, dimness, obscurity.

blurred adj.
- 不清晰的 out of focus, fuzzy, unclear, indistinct, vague, ill-defined, faint, hazy, misty, foggy, cloudy, bleary, dim, obscure, confused.

blush v.
- 脸红,惭愧 flush, redden, colour, glow.

n.
- 脸红,害羞 flush, reddening, rosiness, ruddiness, colour, glow.

blushing adj.
- 惭愧的 flushed, red, rosy, glowing, confused, embarrassed, ashamed, modest.

board n.
- 木板,甲板 sheet, panel, slab, plank, beam, timber, slat.
- 委员会 committee, council, panel, jury, commission, directorate, directors, trustees, advisers.
- 伙食 meals, food, provisions, rations.

v.
- 上(船,车等) get on, embark, mount, enter, catch.

boast v.
- 自夸,以……自豪 brag, crow, swank, claim, exaggerate, talk big, bluster, trumpet, vaunt, strut, swagger, show off, exhibit, possess.

n.
- 夸耀的事物 brag, swank, claim, vaunt, pride, joy, gem, treasure.

boastful adj.
- 自夸的,自豪的 proud,

conceited, vain, swollen-headed, big-headed, puffed up, bragging, crowing, swanky, cocky, swaggering.

bodily *adj*.
☞ 身体的 physical, corporeal, carnal, fleshly, real, actual, tangible, substantial, concrete, material.
adv.
☞ 整体上 altogether, collectively, as a whole, completely, fully, wholly, entirely, totally.

body *n*.
☞ 本体 anatomy, physique, build, figure, trunk, torso.
☞ 身体 corpse, cadaver, carcase.
☞ 组织,团体 company, association, society, corporation, confederation, bloc, syndicate.
☞ 稠度,密度 consistency, density, solidity.

bodyguard *n*.
☞ 保镖 guard, protector, minder.

boil *v*.
☞ 沸腾 simmer, stew, seethe, brew, gurgle, bubble, fizz, effervesce, froth, foam, steam.
☞ 愤怒 erupt, explode, rage, rave, storm, fulminate, fume.

boil down
☞ 浓缩 reduce, concentrate, distil, condense, digest, abstract, summarize, abridge.
n.
☞ 沸点 pustule, abscess, gumboil, ulcer, tumour, pimple, carbuncle, blister, inflammation.

boiling *adj*.
☞ 沸腾的 turbulent, gurgling, bubbling, steaming.
☞ 炙手的 hot, baking, roasting, scorching, blistering.
☞ 生气的 angry, indignant, incensed, infuriated, enraged, furious, fuming, flaming.

bold *adj*.
☞ 大胆的,鲁莽的 fearless, dauntless, daring, audacious, brave, courageous, valiant, heroic, gallant, intrepid, adventurous, venturesome, enterprising, plucky, spirited, confident, outgoing.
☞ 醒目的 eye-catching, striking, conspicuous, prominent, strong, pronounced, bright, vivid, colourful, loud, flashy, showy, flamboyant.
☞ 冒失的 brazen, brash, forward, shameless, unabashed, cheeky, impudent, insolent.

bomb *n*.
☞ 炸弹 atom bomb, petrol bomb, shell, bombshell, explosive, charge, grenade, mine, torpedo, rocket, missile, projectile.
v.
☞ 轰炸 bombard, shell, torpedo, attack, blow up, destroy.

bombard *v*.
☞ 轰击,攻击 attack, assault, assail, pelt, pound, strafe, blast, bomb, shell, blitz, besiege, hound, harass, pester.

bombardment *n*.
☞ 轰击 attack, assault, air-raid, bombing, shelling, blitz,

barrage, cannonade, fusillade, salvo, fire, flak.

bond n.
☞ 联结,粘合 connection, relation, link, tie, union, affiliation, attachment, affinity.
☞ 契约,合同 contract, covenant, agreement, pledge, promise, word, obligation.
☞ 锁住,束缚 fetter, shackle, manacle, chain, cord, band, binding.
v.
☞ 联结 connect, fasten, bind, unite, fuse, glue, gum, paste, stick, seal.

bonus n.
☞ 奖金,红利 advantage, benefit, plus, extra, perk, perquisite, commission, dividend, premium, prize, reward, honorarium, tip, gratuity, gift, hand out.

bony adj.
☞ 骨瘦如柴的 thin, lean, angular, lanky, gawky, gangling, skinny, scrawny, emaciated, rawboned, gaunt, drawn.

book n.
☞ 书,册,卷 volume, tome, publication, work, booklet, tract.
v.
☞ 登记,订座 reserve, bag, engage, charter, procure, order, arrange, organize, schedule, programme.

boom v.
☞ 隆隆响 bang, crash, roar, thunder, roll, rumble, resound, reverberate, blast, explode.
☞ 繁茂,繁荣,兴旺 flourish, thrive, prosper, succeed, develop, grow, increase, gain, expand, swell, escalate, intensify, strengthen, explode.
n.
☞ 发出声响,隆隆声 bang, clap, crash, roar, thunder, rumble, reverberation, blast, explosion, burst.
☞ 迅速发展 increase, growth, expansion, gain, upsurge, jump, spurt, boost, upturn, improvement, advance, explosion.

boost n.
☞ 提高,改善 improvement, enhancement, expansion, increase, rise, jump.
v.
☞ 增加,提高 raise, elevate, improve, enhance, develop, enlarge, expand, emplify increase.

boot n.
☞ 皮靴 gumboot, galosh, overshoe, walking-boot, riding-boot, top-boot.

booth n.
☞ 货摊,摊位 kiosk, stall, stand, hut, box, compartment, cubicle, carrel.

booty n.
☞ 战利品 loot, plunder, pillage, spoils, haul, gains, takings, pickings, winnings.

border n.
☞ 边界 boundary, frontier, bound, bounds, confine, confines, limit.
☞ 加边,镶边 trimming, frill, valance, skirt, hem, frieze.

border on
☞ 临近,邻接 adjoin, abut, touch, impinge, join, connect, communicate with.
☞ 相似 resemble, approximate, approach, verge on.

bore¹ v.
☞ 钻,开洞 drill, mine, pierce, perforate, penetrate, sink, burrow, tunnel, undermine, sap.

bore² v.
☞ 令人厌烦 tire, weary, fatigue, jade, trouble, bother, worry, irritate, annoy, vex, irk.
n.
☞ 使人讨厌的人 nuisance, bother, bind, drag, pain, headache.

boredom n.
☞ 厌倦,无聊 tedium, tediousness, monotony, dullness, apathy, listlessness, weariness, world-weariness.

boring adj.
☞ 无聊的,令人厌烦的 tedious, monotonous, routine, repetitious, uninteresting, unexciting, uneventful, dull.

borrow v.
☞ 借用,擅自取走 steal, pilfer, filch, lift, plagiarize, crib, copy, imitate, mimic, echo, take, draw, derive, obtain, adopt, use, scrounge, cadge, sponge, appropriate, usurp.

bosom n.
☞ 胸部 bust, breasts, chest, breast.

boss n.
☞ 老板,雇主 employer, governor, master, owner, captain, head, chief, leadersupervisor.

boss around
☞ 支配,统治 order around, order about, domineer, tyrannize, bully, bulldoze, browdeat, push around, dominate.

bossy adj.
☞ 喜欢发号施令的 authoritarian, autocratic, tyrannical, despotic, dictatorial, domineering, overbearing.

bother v.
☞ 打扰,烦扰 disturb, inconvenience, harass, hassle, pester, plague, nag, annoy, irritate, irk, molest, trouble, worry, concern, alarm, dismay, distress, upset, vex.
n.
☞ 麻烦,焦虑 inconvenience, trouble, problem, difficulty, hassle, fuss, bustle, flurry, nuisance, pest, annoyance, irritation, aggravation, vexation, worry, strain.

bottle up v.
☞ 抑制,控制 hide, conceal, restrain, curb, hold, back, suppress, inhibit, restrict, enclose, contain.

bottle-neck n.
☞ 狭道,进展的阻碍 hold-up, traffic jam, snarl-up, congestion, clogging, blockage, obstruction, clogging, blockage, obstruction, block, obstaele.

bottom n.
☞ 底,底部 underside,

underneath, sole, base, foot, plinth, pedestal, support, foundation, substructure, ground, floor, bed, depths, nadir.
☞ 尾部 rump, rear, behind, posterior, buttocks, seat, backside, butt, tail.

bottomless *adj.*
☞ 很深的,无底的 deep, profound, fathomless, unfathomed, unplumbed, immeasurable, measureless, infinite, boundless, limitless, unlimited, inexhaustible.

bounce *v.*
☞ 弹起,跳起 spring, jump, leap, bound, bob, ricochet, robound, recoil.
n.
☞ 弹回,跳起 spring, bound, spinginess, elasticity, give, resilience, rebound, recoil.
☞ 活泼,顽皮 ebullience, exuberance, vitality, vivacity, energy, vigour, go, zip, animation, liveliness.

bound¹ *adj.*
☞ 被束缚的 fastened, secured, fixed, tied (up), chained, held, restricted, bandaged.
☞ 责任的,义务的 liable, committed, duty-bound, obliged, required, forced, compelled, constrained, destined, fated, doomed, sure, certain.

bound² *v.*
☞ 跳,跃 jump, leap, vault, hurdle, spring, bounce, bob, hop, skip, frisk, gambol, frolic, caper, prance.
n.
☞ 跳,跃 jump, leap, vault, spring, bounce, bob, hop, skip, gambol, frolic, caper, dance, prance.

boundary *n.*
☞ 界线,界限 border, frontier, barrier, line, borderline, bounds, confines, limits, margin, fringe, verge, brink, edge, perimeter, extremity, termination.

boundless *adj.*
☞ 无限的,无穷的 unbounded, limitless, unlimited, unconfined, countless, untold, incalculable, vast, immense, measureless, immeasurable, infinite, endless, unending, interminable, inexhaustible, unflagging, indefatigable.

bounds *n.*
☞ 止境,界限 confines, limits, borders, marches, margins, fringes, periphery, circumference, edges, extremities.

bouquet *n.*
☞ 花束 bunch, posy, nosegay, spray, corsage, buttonhole, wreath, garland.
☞ 芳香 aroma, smell, odour, scent, perfume, fragrance.

bourgeois *adj.*
☞ 资产阶级的 middle-class, materialistic, conservative, traditional, conformist, conventional, hide-bound, unadventurous, dull, humdrum, banal, commonplace, trite, unoriginal, unimaginative.

bout n.
- ☞ (拳击)比赛 fight, battle, engagement, encounter, struggle, set-to, match, contest, competition, round, heat.
- ☞ 回合 period, spell, time, stint, turn, go, term, stretch, run, course, session, spree, attack, fit.

bow v.
- ☞ 鞠躬 incline, bend, nod, bob, curtsy, genuflect, kowtow, salaam, stoop.
- ☞ 同意,赞许 yield, give in, consent, surrender, capitulate, submit, acquiesce, concede, accept, comply, defer.

n.
- ☞ 弯腰,鞠躬 inclination, bending, nod, bob, curtsy, kowtow, salaam, obeisance, salutation, acknowledgment.

bow out
☞ 告退,辞职 withdraw, pull out, desert, abandon, defect, back out, chickenout, retire, resign, quit, stand down, step down, give up.

bowels n.
- ☞ 肠 intestines, viscera, entrails, guts, insides, innards.
- ☞ 内部 depths, interior, inside, middle, centre, core, heart.

bowl¹ n.
☞ 碗 receptacle, container, vessel, dish, basin, sink.

bowl² v.
☞ 滚,投球 throw, hurl, fling, pitch, roll, spin, whirl, rotate, revolve.

bowl over
☞ 吃惊,撞倒 surprise, amaze, astound, astonish, stagger, stun, dumbfound, flabbergast, floor.

box¹ n.
☞ 箱子 container, receptacle, case, crate, carton, packet, pack, package, present, chest, coffer, trunk, coffin.

v.
☞ 装箱 case, encase, package, pack, wrap.

box² v.
☞ 拳击 fight, spar, punch, hit, strike, slap, buffet, cuff, clout, wallop, whack.

boxer n.
☞ 拳击运动员 pugilist, fighter, prizefighter, sparring partner, flyweight, featherweight, lightweight, welterweight, middleweight, heavyweight.

boxing n.
☞ 拳击 pugilism, prizefighting, fisticuffs, sparring.

boy n.
☞ 男孩 son, lad, youngster, kid, nipper, stripling, youth, fellow.

boyfriend n.
☞ 男朋友,情郎 young man, man, fellow, bloke, admirer, date, sweetheart, lover, fiance.

brace n.
☞ 一双,一对 pair, couple, twosome, duo.

v.
☞ 使稳固 strengthen, reinforce, fortify, bolster, buttress, prop, shore (up), support, steady,

tighten, fasten, tie, strap, bind, bandage.

bracing adj.
☞ 兴奋的,爽快的 fresh, crisp, refreshing, reviving, strengthening, fortifying, tonic, rousing, stimulating, exhilarating, invigorating, enlivening, energizing, brisk, energetic, vigorous.

brain n.
☞ 脑 cerebrum, grey matter, head, mind, intellect, nous, brains, intelligence, wit, reason, sense, common sense, shrewdness, understanding.
☞ 智囊 mastermind, intellectual, highbrow, egghead, scholar, expert, genius, prodigy.

brainy adj.
☞ 聪明的 intellectual, intelligent, clever, smart, bright, brilliant.

brake n.
☞ 刹闸 curb, rein, restraint, control, restriction, constraint, drag.
v.
☞ 刹住 slow, decelerate, retard, drag, slacken, moderate, check, halt, stop, pull up.

branch n.
☞ 树枝,分支 bough, limb, sprig, shoot, offshoot, arm, wing, prong.
☞ 分公司 department, office, part, section, division, subsection, subdivision.

branch out
☞ 扩展,多样化 diversify, vary, develop, expand, enlarge, extend, broaden out, increase, multiply, proliferate, ramify.

brand n.
☞ 商标,牌子 make, brand-name, tradename, trademark, logo, mark, symbol, sign, label, stamp, hallmark, grade, quality, class, kind, type, sort, line, variety, species.
v.
☞ 打上,烙印 mark, stamp, label, type, stigmatize, burn, scar, stain, taint, disgrace, discredit, denounce, censure.

brash adj.
☞ 无礼的,粗鲁的 brazen, forward, impertinent, impudent, insolent, rude, cocky, assured, bold, audacious.
☞ 草率的,鲁莽的 reckless, rash, impetuous, impulsive, hasty, precipitate, foolhardy, incautious, indiscreet.

bravado
☞ 虚张声势,逞威风 swagger, boasting, bragging, bluster, bombast, talk, boast, vaunting, showing off, parade, show, pretence.

brave adj.
☞ 勇敢的 courageous, plucky, unafraid, fearless, dauntless, undaunted, bold, audacious, daring, intrepid, stalwart, hardy, stoical, resolute, stout-hearted, valiant, gallant, heroic, indomitable.
v.
☞ 勇敢面对 face, confront, defy, challenge, dare, stand up to, face up to, suffer, endure, bear, withstand.

bravery n.
- ☞ 勇敢,大胆 courage, pluck, guts, fearlessness, dauntlessness, boldness, audacity, daring, intrepidity, stalwartness, hardiness, fortitude, resolution, stout-heartedness, valiance, valour, gallantry, heroism, grit, mettle, spirit.

breach n.
- ☞ 违反 violation, contravention, infringement, trespass, disobedience, offence, transgression, lapse, disruption.
- ☞ 破裂,失和 quarrel, disagreement, dissension, difference, variance, schism, rift, rupture, split, division, separation, parting, estrangement, alienation, disaffection, dissociation.
- ☞ 破裂 break, crack, rift, rupture, fissure, cleft, crevice, opening, aperture, gap, space, hole, chasm.

bread n.
- ☞ 面包 loaf, roll, food, provisions, diet, fare, nourishment, nutriment, sustenance, subsistence, necessities.

breadth n.
- ☞ 宽度,阔度 width, broadness, wideness, latitude, thickness, size, magnitude, measure, scale, range, reach, scope, compass, span, sweep, extent, expanse, spread, comprehensiveness, extensiveness, vastness.

break v.
- ☞ 折断,打破 fracture, crack, snap, split, sever, separate, divide, rend, smash, disintegrate, splinter, shiver, shatter, ruin, destroy, demolish.
- ☞ 违反 violate, contravene, infringe, breach, disobey, flout.
- ☞ 停止,中断 pause, halt, stop, discontinue, interrupt, suspend, rest.
- ☞ 征服 subdue, tame, weaken, enfeeble, impair, undermine, demoralize.
- ☞ 发布 tell, inform, impart, divulge, disclose, reveal, announce.

n.
- ☞ 裂缝,破损,破晓 fracture, crack, split, rift, rupture, schism, separation, tear, gash, fissure, cleft, crevice, opening, gap, hole, breach.
- ☞ 暂停,休息 interval, intermission, interlude, interruption, pause, halt, lull, let-up, respite, rest, breather, time out, holiday.
- ☞ 机会,运气 opportunity, chance, advantage, fortune, luck.

break away
- ☞ 脱离,逃脱 separate, split, part company, detach, secede, leave, depart, quit, run away, escape, flee, fly.

break down
- ☞ 发生故障 fail, stop, pack up, seize up, give way, collapse, crack up.
- ☞ 分解,分析 analyse, dissect, separate, itemize, detail.

break in
- 打断,插嘴 interrupt, butt in, interpose, interject, intervene, intrude, encroach, impinge.
- 闯入,强行进入 burgle, rob, raid, invade.

break off
- 分开 detach, snap off, sever, separate, part, divide, disconnect.
- 打断 pause, interrupt, suspend, discontinue, halt, stop, cease, end, finish, terminate.

break out
- 突然发生 start, begin, commence, arise, emerge, happen, occur, erupt, flare up, burst out.
- 逃脱,脱离 escape, abscond, bolt, flee.

break through
- 突破,违章 discovery, find, finding, invention, innovation, advance, progress, headway, step, leap, development, improvement.

break up
- 分裂 dismantle, take apart, demolish, destroy, disintegrate, splinter, sever, divide, split, part, separate, divorce.
- 结束,解散 disband, disperse, dissolve, adjourn, suspend, stop, finish, terminate.

breakable adj.
- 脆的,会破的 brittle, fragile, delicate, flimsy, insubstantial, frail.

breath n.
- 呼吸,一息 air, breathing, respiration, inhalation, exhalation, sigh, gasp, pant, gulp.
- 风,微风 breeze, puff, waft, gust.
- 气味 aroma, smell, odour, whiff.
- 示意,迹象 hint, suggestion, suspicion, undertone, whisper, murmur.

breathe v.
- 呼气 respire, inhale, exhale, expire, sigh, gasp, pant, puff.
- 低语,表达 say, utter, express, voice, articulate, murmur, whisper, impart, tell.
- 灌输,使浸透 instill, imbue, infuse, inject, inspire.

breathless adj.
- 气喘的 short-winded, out of breath, panting, puffing, puffed, exhausted, winded, gasping, wheezing, choking.
- 紧张的 expectant, impatient, eager, agog, excited, feverish, anxious.

breathtaking adj.
- 惊人的 awe-inspiring, impressive, magnificent, overwhelming, amazing, astonishing, stunning, exciting, thrilling, stirring, moving.

breed v.
- 繁殖,育种 reproduce, procreate, multiply, propagate, hatch, bear, bring forth, rear, raise, bring up, educate, train, instruct.
- 生产 produce, create, originate, arouse, cause, occasion, engender, generate, make, foster, nurture, nourish, cultivate, develop.

n.
- 品种 species, strain, variety, family, ilk, sort, kind, type, stamp, stock, race, progeny, line, lineage, pedigree.

breeding *n.*
- 繁殖,生育 reproduction, procreation, nurture, development, rearing, raising, upbringing, education, training, background, ancestry, lineage, stock.
- 教养 manners, politeness, civility, gentility, urbanity, refinement, culture, polish.

breeze *n.*
- 微风,和风 wind, gust, flurry, waft, puff, breath, draught, air.

breezy *adj.*
- 有风的 windy, blowing, fresh, airy, gusty, blustery, squally.
- 轻松自在的,怡然的 animated, lively, vivacious, juanty, buoyant, blithe, debonair, carefree, cheerful, easy-going, casual, informal, light, bright, exhilarating.

brevity *n.*
- 短,短暂 briefness, shortness, terseness, conciseness, succinctness, pithiness, crispness, incisiveness, abruptness, curtness, impermanence, ephemerality, transience, transitoriness.

brew *v.*
- 酿造 infuse, stew, boil, seethe, prepare, soak, steep, mix, cook.
- 设计,计划 plot, scheme, plan, project, devise, contrive, concoct, hatch, excite, foment, build up, gather, develop.

n.
- 酝酿物 infusion, drink, beverage, liquor, potion, broth, gruel, stew, mixture, blend, concoction, preparation, fermentation, distillation.

bribe *n.*
- 贿赂 incentive, inducement, allurement, enticement, backhander, kickback, payola, refresher, protection money.

v.
- 行贿 corrupt, suborn, buy off, reward.

bribery *n.*
- 贿赂行为 corruption, palm-greasing, inducement, lubrication.

bric-a-brac *n.*
- 珍品,古玩 knick-knacks, ornaments, curios, antiques, trinkets, baubles.

bridal *adj.*
- 新娘的,新婚的 wedding, nuptial, marriage, matrimonial, marital, conjugal.

bridge *n.*
- 桥 arch, span, causeway, link, connection, bond, tie.

v.
- 跨过,联接 span, cross, traverse, fill, link, connect, couple, join, unite, bind.

bridle *v.*
- 抑制,控制 check, curb, restrain, control, govern, master, subdue, moderate, repress, contain.

brief adj.
- 短暂的 short, terse, succinct, concise, pithy, crisp, compressed, thumbnail, laconic, abrupt, sharp, brusque, blunt, curt, surly.
- 简短(洁)的 short-lived, momentary, ephemeral, transient, fleeting, passing, transitory, temporary, limited, cursory, hasty, quick, swift, fast.

n.
- 指示 orders, instructions, directions, remit, mandate, directive, advice, briefing, data, information.
- 摘要 outline, summary, precis, dossier, case, defence, argument.

v.
- 下达简令,最后指令 instruct, direct, explain, guide, advise, prepare, prime, inform, fill in.

briefing n.
- 情况介绍 meeting, conference, preparation, priming, filling-in, information, advice, guidance, directions, instructions, orders.

bright adj.
- 发亮的 luminous, illuminated, radiant, shining, beaming, flashing, gleaming, glistening, glittering, sparkling, twinkling, shimmering, glowing, brilliant, resplendent, glorious, splendid, dazzling, glaring, blazing, intense, vivid.
- 欢快的 happy, cheerful, glad, joyful, merry, jolly, lively, vivacious.
- 清澈的 clear, transparent, translucent, lucid.
- 晴朗的 fine, sunny, cloudless, unclouded.
- 有希望的 promising, propitious, auspicious, favourable, rosy, optimistic, hopeful, encouraging.
- 聪明的 clever, brainy, smart, intelligent, quick-witted, quick, sharp, acute, keen, astute, perceptive.

brighten v.
- (使)发光,发亮 light up, illuminate, lighten, clear up, polish, burnish, rub up, shine, gleam, glow.
- 使活跃 cheer up, gladden, hearten, encourage, enliven, perk up.

brilliance n.
- 才能 talent, virtuosity, genius, greatness, distinction, excellence, aptitude, cleverness.
- 光辉 radiance, brightness, sparkle, dazzle, intensity, vividness, gloss, lustre, sheen, glamour, glory, magnificence, splendour.

brilliant adj.
- 有才气的 gifted, talented, accomplished, expert, skilful, masterly, exceptional, outstanding, superb, illustrious, famous, celebrated.
- 光辉的 sparkling, glittering, scintillating, dazzling, glaring, blazing, intense, vivid, bright, shining, glossy, showy, glorious, magnificent, splendid.
- 聪明的 clever, brainy, intelligent, quick, astute.

brim n.
- 边 rim, perimeter, circumference, lip, edge, margin, border, brink, verge, top, limit.

bring v.
- 带来,拿来 carry, bear, convey, transport, fetch, take, deliver, escort, accompany, usher, guide, conduct, lead.
- 产生,引起 cause, produce, engender, create, prompt, provoke, force, attract, draw.

bring about
- 引起 cause, occasion, create, produce, generate, effect, accomplish, achieve, fulfil, realize, manage, engineer, manoeuvre, manipulate.

bring in
- 获利,赚 earn, net, gross, produce, yield, fetch, return, accrue, realize.

bring off
- 办成功 achieve, accomplish, fulfil, execute, discharge, perform, succeed, win.

bring on
- 引起,导致 cause occasion, induce, lead to, give rise to, generate, inspire, prompt, provoke, precipitate, expedite, accelerate, advance.

bring out
- 使显露 emphasize, stress, highlight, enhance, draw out.
- 出版 publish, print, issue, launch, introduce.

bring up
- 教育,养育 rear, raise, foster, nurture, educate, teach, train, form.
- 呕吐 vomit, regurgitate, throw up.
- 提出,引出 introduce, broach, mention, submit, propose.

brink n.
- 边缘 verge, threshold, edge, margin, fringe, border, boundary, limit, extremity, lip, rim, brim, bank.

brisk adj.
- 轻快的 energetic, vigorous, quick, snappy, lively, spirited, active, busy, bustling, agile, nimble, alert.
- 凉爽的 invigorating, exhilarating, stimulating, bracing, refreshing, fresh, crisp.

broad adj.
- 阔的,宽的 wide, large, vast, roomy, spacious, capacious, ample, extensive, widespread.
- 广泛的 wide-ranging, far-reaching, encyclopedic, eclectic, all-embracing, inclusive, comprehensive, general, sweeping, universal, unlimited.

broadcast v.
- 传播 air, show, transmit, beam, relay, televise, report, announce, publicize, advertise, publish, circulate, promulgate, disseminate, spread.

n.
- 广播节目 transmission, programme, show.

broaden v.
- 放宽 widen, thicken, swell, spread, enlarge, expand, extend, stretch, increase, augment, develop, open up,

branch out, diversify.

broad-minded *adj.*
☞ 宽宏大量的 liberal, tolerant, permissive, enlightened, free-thinking, open-minded, receptive, unbiased, unprejudiced.

brochure *n.*
☞ 小册子 leaflet, booklet, pamphlet, prospectus, broadsheet, handbill, circular, handout, folder.

broke *adj.*
☞ 破了产的 insolvent, penniless, bankrupt, bust, ruined, impoverished, destitute.

broken *adj.*
☞ 碎了的 fractured, burst, ruptured, severed, separated, faulty, defective, out of order, shattered, destroyed, demolished.
☞ 折断的,损坏的 disjointed, disconnected, fragmentary, discontinuous, interrupted, spasmodic, erratic, hesitating, stammering, halting, imperfect.
☞ 颓丧的 beaten, defeated, crushed, demoralized, down, weak, feeble, exhausted, tamed, subdued, oppressed.

broken-down *adj.*
☞ 毁坏的 dilapidated, worn-out, ruined, collapsed, decayed, inoperative, out of order.

broken-hearted *adj.*
☞ 心碎的 heartbroken, inconsolable, devastated, grief-stricken, desolate, despairing, miserable, wretched, mournful, sorrowful, sad, unhappy, dejected, despondent, crestfallen, disappointed.

brood *v.*
☞ 考虑,沉思 ponder, ruminate, meditate, muse, mull over, go over, rehearse, dwell on, agonize, fret, mope.
n.
☞ 一窝(鸡雏)等 clutch, chicks, hatch, litter, young, offspring, issue, progeny, children, family.

brook *n.*
☞ 小河,溪流 stream, rivulet, beck, burn, watercourse, channel.

brother *n.*
☞ 兄弟 sibling, relation, relative, comrade, friend, mate, partner, colleague, associate, fellow, companion, monk, friar.

brotherhood *n.*
☞ 兄弟关系,团体 fraternity, association, society, league, confederation, confederacy, alliance, union, guild, fellowship, community, clique.

brown *adj.*
☞ 褐色的 mahogany, chocolate, coffee, russet, bay, chestnut, umber, sepia, tan, tawny, russet, rust, rusty, brunette, dark, dusky, sunburnt, tanned, bronzed, browned, toasted.

browse *v.*
☞ 浏览 leaf through, flick through, dip into, skim, survey, scan, peruse.
☞ 进食 graze, pasture, feed, eat, nibble.

bruise v.
- 擦伤 discolour, blacken, mark, blemish, pound, pulverize, crush, hurt, injure, insult, offend, grieve.

n.
- 伤痕,损伤 contusion, discoloration, black eye, mark, blemish, injury.

brush n.
- 刷子 broom, sweeper, besom.

v.
- 刷 clean, sweep, flick, burnish, polish, shine.
- 擦,拂 touch, contact, graze, kiss, stroke, rub, scrape.

brush aside
- 漠视,刷去 dismiss, pooh-pooh, belittle, disregard, ignore, flout, override.

brush off
- 拒绝,不理睬 disregard, ignore, slight, snub, cold-shoulder, rebuff, spurn, reject, repulse, disown.

brush up
- 复习 revise, relearn, improve, polish up, study, read up, swot.
- 重温 refresh, freshen up, clean, tidy.

brutality n.
- 兽性,野蛮 savagery, bloodthirstiness, viciousness, ferocity, cruelty, inhumanity, violence, atrocity, ruthlessness, callousness, roughness, coarseness, barbarism, barbarity.

brute n.
- 畜生 animal, beast, swine, creature, monster, ogre, devil, fiend, savage, sadist, bully, lout.

bubble n.
- 气泡 blister, vesicle, globule, ball, drop, droplet, bead.

v.
- 起泡,沸腾 effervesce, fizz, sparkle, froth, foam, seethe, boil, burble, gurgle.

bubbly adj.
- 起泡的 effervescent, fizzy, sparkling, carbonated, frothy, foaming, sudsy.
- 活跃的 lively, bouncy, happy, merry, elated, excited.

bucket n.
- 水桶 pail, can, bail, scuttle, vessel.

bud n.
- 芽,蓓蕾 shoot, sprout, germ, embryo.

v.
- 发芽 shoot, sprout, burgeon, develop, grow.

budding adj.
- 萌芽的 potential, promising, embryonic, burgeoning, developing, growing, flowering.

budget n.
- 预算 finances, funds, resources, means, allowance, allotment, allocation, estimate.

v.
- 安排开支 plan, estimate, allow, allot, allocate, apportion, ration.

buffet n.
- 打击,冲击 snack-bar, counter, cafe, cafeteria.

v.

☞ 打击 batter, hit, strike, knock, bang, bump, push, shove, pound, pummel, beat, thump, box, cuff, clout, slap.

bug n.
☞ 病菌,(臭)虫 virus, bacterium, germ, microbe, micro-organism, infection, disease.
☞ 缺陷 fault, defect, flaw, blemish, imperfection, failing, error, gremlin.
v.
☞ 烦忧,使苦恼 annoy, irritate, vex, irk, needle, bother, disturb, harass, badger.

build v.
☞ 建立 erect, raise, construct, fabricate, make, form, constitute, assemble, knock, together, develop, enlarge, extend, increase, augment, escalate, intensify.
☞ 建造 base, found, establish, institute, inaugurate, initiate, begin.
n.
☞ 体格,体型 physique, figure, body, form, shape, size, frame, structure.

build up
☞ 增进,加强 strengthen, reinforce, fortify, extend, expand, develop, amplify, increase, escalate, intensify, heighten, boost, improve, enhance, publicize, advertise, promote, plug.

building n.
☞ 建筑物,大楼 edifice, dwelling, erection, construction, fabrication, structure, architecture.

build-up n.
☞ 加强 enlargement, expansion, development, increase, gain, growth, escalation, publicity, promotion, plug.
☞ 积累 accumulation, mass, load, heap, stack, store, stockpile.

bulge n.
☞ 凸出 swelling, bump, lump, hump, distension, protuberance, projection.
☞ 鼓起 rise, increase, surge, upsurge, intensification.
v.
☞ 凸出 swell, puff out, bulb, hump, dilate, expand, enlarge, distend, protrude, project.

bulk n.
☞ 巨大的体积,大量 size, magnitude, dimensions, extent, amplitude, bigness, largeness, immensity, volume, mass, weight, substance, body, preponderance, majority, most.

bulky adj.
☞ 庞大的 substantial, big, large, huge, enormous, immense, massive, colossal, hulking, hefty, heavy, weighty, unmanageable, unwieldy, awkward, cumbersome.

bullet n.
☞ 子弹 shot, pellet, ball, slug, missile, projectile.

bulletin n.
☞ 公告,告示 report, newsflash, dispatch, communique, statement, announcement, notification, communicatoin,

message.
bully n.
- 暴徒 persecutor, browbeater, intimidator, bully-boy, ruffian, tough.

v.
- 欺侮,威吓 persecute, torment, terroirze, bulldoze, coerce, browbeat, bullyrag, intimidate, cow, tyrannize, domineer, overbear, oppress, push around.

bump v.
- 碰撞 hit, strike, knock, bang, crash, collide (with).
- 颠簸 jolt, jerk, jar, jostle, rattle, shake, bounce.

n.
- 撞 blow, hit, knock, bang, thump, thud, smash, crash, collision, impact, jolt, jar, shock.
- 肿块 lump, swelling, bulge, hump, protuberance.

bump into
- 碰,撞 meet, encounter, run into, chance upon, come across.

bump off
- 谋杀 kill, murder, assassinate.

bunch n.
- 捆 bundle, sheaf, tuft, clump, cluster, batch, lot, heap, pile, stack, mass, number, quantity, collection, assortment.
- 一束 bouquet, posy, spray.
- 一群 gang, band, troop, crew, team, party, gathering, flock, swarm, crowd, mob, multitude.

v.
- 捆成束 group, bundle, cluster, collect, assemble, congregate, gather, flock, herd, crowd, mass, pack, huddle.

burden n.
- 载重量 cargo, load, weight, dead-weight, encumbrance, millstone, onus, responsibility, obligation, duty, strain, stress, worry, anxiety, care, trouble, trial, affliction, sorrow.

v.
- 使负载 load, weigh down, encumber, handicap, bother, worry, tax, strain, overload, lie, heavy on, oppress, overwhelm.

bureau n.
- 办公处 service, agency, office, branch, department, division, counter, desk.

bureaucracy n.
- 官僚 administration, government, ministry, civil service, the authorities, the system, officialdom, red tape, regulations.

burglar n.
- 小偷,窃贼 housebreaker, robber, thief, pilferer, trespasser.

burglary n.
- 盗窃 housebreaking, break-in, robbery, theft, stealing, trespass.

burial n.
- 葬礼,埋葬 burying, interment, entombment, funeral, obsequies.

burn v.
- 燃烧 flame, blaze, flare,

flash, glow, flicker, smoulder, smoke, fume, simmer, seethe.
☞ 使……着火 ignite, light, kindle, incinerate, cremate, consume, corrode.
☞ 烫伤 scald, scorch, parch, shrivel, singe, char, toast, brand, sear, smart, sting, bite, hurt, tingle.

burning adj.
☞ 热烈的 ablaze, aflame, afire, fiery, flaming, blazing, flashing, gleaming, glowing, smouldering, alight, lit, illuminated.
☞ 烫手的 hot, scalding, scorching, searing, piercing, acute, smarting, stinging, prickling, tingling, biting, caustic, pungent.
☞ 强烈的 ardent, fervent, eager, earnest, intense, vehement, passionate, impassioned, frantic, frenzied, consuming.
☞ 紧急的 urgent, pressing, important, significant, crucial, essential, vital.

burst v.
☞ 爆发 puncture, rupture, tear, split, crack, break, fragment, shatter, shiver, disintegrate, explode, blow up, erupt, gush, spout, rush, run.
n.
☞ 突发 puncture, blow-out, rupture, split, crack, break, breach, explosion, blast, bang, eruption.

bury v.
☞ 埋葬 inter, entomb, lay to rest, shroud.
☞ 隐藏 sink, submerge, immerse, plant, implant, embed, conceal, hide, cover, enshroud, engulf, enclose, engross, occupy, engage, absorb.

bush n.
☞ 矮树 shrub, hedge, thicket.
☞ 灌木 scrub, brush, scrubland, backwoods, wilds.

business n.
☞ 买卖,交易 trade, commerce, industry, manufacturing, dealings, transactions, bargaining, trading, buying, selling.
☞ 公司 company, firm, corporation, establishment, organization, concern, enterprise, venture.
☞ 职业,职务 job, occupation, work, employment, trade, profession, work, employment, trade, profession, line, calling, career, vocation, duty, task, responsibility.
☞ 事务,事情 affair, matter, issue, subject, topic, question, problem, point.

businesslike adj.
☞ 事务式的,有实效的 professional, efficient, thorough, systematic, methodical, organized, orderly, well-ordered, practical, matter-of-fact, precise, correct, formal, impersonal.

businessman, businesswoman n.
☞ 商人 entrepreneur, industrialist, trader, merchant, tycoon, magnate, capitalist,

financier, employer, executive.

bust n.
- 半身像 sculpture, head, torso, statue.
- 胸部 bosom, beasts, chest, breast.

bustle v.
奔忙 dash, rush, scamper, scurry, hurry, hasten, scramble, fuss.
n.
喧闹,忙乱 activity, stir, commotion, tumult, agitation, excitement, fuss, ado, flurry, hurry, haste.

busy adj.
- 忙的 occupied, engaged, tied up, employed, working, slaving, stirring, restless, tireless, diligent, industrious, active, lively, energetic, strenuous, tiring, full, crowded, swarming, teeming, bustling, hectic, eventful.
v.
- 占用,忙于 occupy, engage, employ, engross, absorb, immerse, interest, concern, bother.

butt¹ n.
粗大的一端 stub, end, tip, tail, base, foot, shaft, stock, handle, haft.

butt² n.
目标 target, mark, object, subject, victim, laughing-stock, dupe.

butt³ v., n.
撞碰 hit, bump, knock, buffet, push, shove, ram, thrust, punch, jab, prod, poke.

butt in
插嘴,插手 interrupt, cut in, interpose, intrude, meddle, interfere.

buy v.
购买 purchase, invest in, pay for, procure, acquire, obtain, get.
n.
买 purchase, acquisition, bargain, deal.

buyer n.
采购员,买主 purchase, shopper, consumer, customer, vendee, emptor.

by prep.
在……附近 near, next to, beside, along, over, through, via, past.
adv.
附近 near, close, handy, at hand, past, beyond, away, aside.

bypass v.
绕道,回避 avoid, dodge, sidestep, skirt, circumvent, ignore, neglect, omit.
n.
辅路 ring road, detour, diversion.

by-product n.
副产品 consequence, result, side-effect, fallout, repercussion, after-effect.

bystander n.
旁观者 spectator, onlooker, looker-on, watcher, observer, witness, eye-witness, passer-by.

C

cabin n.
- 客舱 berth, quarters, compartment, room.
- 小屋 hut, shack, shanty, lodge, chalet, cottage, shed, shelter.

cabinet n.
- 橱,柜 cupboard, closet, dresser, case, locker.

cable n.
- 线 line, rope, cord, chain, wire, flex, lead.

cafe n.
- 咖啡厅 coffee shop, tea shop, tea room, coffee bar, cafeteria, snackbar, bistro, brasserie, restaurant.

cage v.
- 把……关进笼子,囚禁 encage, coop up, shut up, confine, restrain, fence in, imprison, impound, incarcerate, lock up.

  n.
- 鸟笼,兽笼 avary, coop, hutch, enclosure, pen, pound, corral.

cake v.
- 厚厚地覆盖上 coat, cover, encrust, dry, harden, solidify, consolidate, coagulate, congeal, thicken.

  n.
- 茶点 gateau, fancy, madeleine, bun, pie, flan.
- 块,条 lump, mass, bar, slab, block, loaf.

calculate v.
- 计算,数 compute, work out, count, enumerate, reckon, figure, determine, weigh, rate, value, estimate, gauge, judge, consider, plan, intend, aim.

calculating adj.
- 精明的,狡猾的 crafty, cunning, sly, devious, scheming, designing, contriving, sharp, shrewd.

calculation n.
- 计算,考虑 sum, computation, answer, result, reckoning, figuring, estimate, forecast, judgement, planning, deliberation.

call v.
- 为……取名,把……称作 name, christen, baptize, title, entitle, dub, style, term, label, designate.
- 大叫,喊 shout, yell, exclaim, cry.
- 召唤,邀请 summon, invite, bid, convene, assemble.
- 打电话 telephone, phone, ring (up), contact.

  n.
- 呼喊,喊叫 cry, exclamation, shout, yell, scream.
- 拜访 visit, ring, summons, invitation.
- 要求,命令 appeal, request, plea, order, command, claim, announcement, signal.

☞ 原因 occasion, cause, excuse, justification, reason, grounds, right.

call for
☞ 要求,需要 demand, require, need, necessitate, involve, entail, occasion, suggest.
☞ 拿取 fetch, collect, pick up.

call off
☞ 取消 cancel, drop, abandon, discontinue, break off, withdraw.

calling n.
☞ 职业,行业 mission, vocation, career, profession, occupation, job, trade, business, line, work, employment, field, province, pursuit.

calm adj.
☞ 宁静的,沉着的 composed, self-possessed, collected, cool, dispassionate, unemotional, impassive, unmoved, placid, sedate, impassive, unmoved, placid, sedate, imperturbable, unflappable, unexcitable, relaxed, unexcited, unruffled, unflustered, unperturbed, undisturbed, untroubled, unapprehensive.
☞ 平静的,无风浪的 smooth, still, windless, unclounded, mild, tranquil, serene, peaceful, quiet, uneventful, restful.
v.
☞ 使平静,平息 compose, soothe, relax, sedate, tranquillize, hush, quieten, placate, pacify.
n.
☞ 宁静,平静 calmness, stillness, tranquillity, serenity, peacefulness, peace, quiet, hush, repose.

campaign n.
☞ 战役,运动,活动 crusade, movement, promotion, drive, push, offensive, attack, battle, expedition, operation.
v.
☞ 作战,参加竞选 crusade, promote, push, advocate, fight, battle.

cancel v.
☞ 取消,撤消 call off, abort, abandon, drop, abolish, annul, quash, rescind, revoke, repeal, countermand, delete, erase, obliterate, eliminate, offset, compensate, redeem, neutralize, nullify.

cancer n.
☞ 罪恶,痼疾 evil, blight, canker, pestilence, sickness, corruption, rot.
☞ 癌 tumour, growth, malignancy, carcinoma.

candid adj.
☞ 坦白的,率直的 frank, open, truthful, honest, sincere, forthright, straightforward, ingenuous, guileless, simple, plain, clear, unequivocal, blunt, outspoken.

candidate n.
☞ 候选人 applicant, aspirant, contender, contestant, competitor, entrant, runner, possibility, nominee, claimant, pretender, suitor.

candour n.
☞ 坦白,直率 frankness, openness, truthfulness, honesty,

plain-dealing, sincerity, straightforwardness, directness, ingenuousness, guilelessness, naivety, artlessness, simplicity, plainness, unequivocalness, bluntness, outspokenness.

canyon n.
☞ 峡谷 gorge, ravine, gully, valley.

cap v.
☞ 胜过 exceed, surpass, transcend, better, beat, outdo, outstrip, eclipse, complete, finish, crown, top, cover.
n.
☞ 软帽 hat, skullcap, beret, tam-o'-shanter.
☞ 盖子 lid, top, cover.

capability n.
☞ 能力 ability, capacity, faculty, power, potential, means, facility, competence, qualification, skill, proficiency, talent.

capable adj.
☞ 能干的,有能力的 able, competent, efficient, qualified, experienced, accomplished, skilful, proficient, gifted, talented masterly, clever, intelligent, fitted, suited, apt, liable, disposed.

capacity n.
☞ 容量 volume, space, room, size, dimensions, magnitude, extent, compass, range, scope.
☞ 学习力,理解力,能量,效能 capability, ability, faculty, power, potential, competence, efficiency, skill, gift, talent, genius, cleverness, intelligence, aptitude, readiness.

☞ 身份,地位,资格 role, function, position, office, post, appointment, job.

cape¹ n.
☞ 海角,岬 headland, head, promontory, point, ness, peninsula.

cape² n.
☞ 披肩,短斗蓬 cloak, shawl, wrap, robe, poncho, coat.

capital n.
☞ 资本,资金 funds, finance, principal, money, cash, savings, investment(s), wealth, means, wherewithal, resources, assets, property, stock.

capitalize on v.
☞ 由于……而获益 profit from, take advantage of, exploit, cash in on.

captain n.
☞ 首领,军官,船长,机长 commander, master, skipper, pilot, head, chief, leader, boss, officer.

captive n.
☞ 俘虏被监禁的人 prisoner, hostage, slave, detainee, internee, convict.
adj.
☞ 被捕获的,受监禁的 imprisoned, caged, confined, restricted, secure, locked up, enchained, enslaved, ensnared.

captivity n.
☞ 囚禁,束缚 custody, detention, imprisonment, incarceration, internment, confinement, restraint, bondage, duress, slavery, servitude.

capture v.
- 捕获,俘房 catch, trap, snare, take, seize, arrest, apprehend, imprison, secure.

n.
- 捕获,俘房 catching, trapping, taking, seizure, arrest, imprisonment.

car n.
- 汽车 automobile, motor car, motor, vehicle.

care n.
- 忧虑,烦恼 worry, anxiety, stress, strain, pressure, concern, trouble, distress, affliction, tribulation, vexation.
- 谨慎,小心 carefulness, caution, prudence, forethought, vigilance, watchfulness, pains, meticulousness, attention, heed, regard, consideration, interest.
- 管理,保护 keeping, custody, guardianship, protection, ward, charge, responsibility, control, supervision.

v.
- 担心,忧虑 worry, mind, bother.

care for
- 照顾,照料 look after, nurse, tend, mind, watch over, protect, minister to, attend.
- 喜欢 like, be fond of, love, be keen on, enjoy, delight in, want, desire.

career n.
- 生涯,职业 vocation, calling, life-work, occupation, pursuit, profession, trade, job, employment, livelihood.

v.
- 急驰,飞奔 rush, dash, tear, hurtle, race, run, gallop, speed, shoot, bolt.

carefree adj.
- 快乐的,无忧无虑的 unworried, untroubled, unconcerned, blithe, breezy, happy-go-lucky, cheery, light-hearted, cheerful, happy, easy-going, laid back.

careful adj.
- 谨慎的,小心的 cautious, prudent, circumspect, judicious, wary, chary, vigilant, watchful, alert, attentive, mindful.
- 细心的,仔细的 meticulous, painstaking, conscientious, scrupulous, thorough, detailed, punctilious, particular, accurate, precise, thoughtful.

careless adj.
- 粗心的 unthinking, thoughtless, inconsiderate, uncaring, unconcerned, heedless, unmindful, forgetful, remiss, negligent, irresponsible, unguarded.

caress v.
- 亲吻,爱抚 stroke, pet, fondle, cuddle, hug, embrace, kiss, touch, rub.

n.
- 爱抚,接吻 stroke, pat, fondle, cuddle, hug, embrace, kiss.

caretaker n.
- 管理人,看理人 janitor, porter, watchman, keeper, custodian, curator, warden, superintendent.

cargo n.

☞ 货物 freight, load, pay-load, lading, tonnage, consignment, contents, goods, merchandise, baggage.

carriage n.
☞ 马车 coach, wagon car, vehicle.
☞ 仪态,举止 deportment, posture, bearing, air, manner, mien, demeanour, behaviour, conduct.
☞ 运输,运费 carrying, conveyance, transport, transportation, postage, delivery, postage.

carry v.
☞ 搬运 bring, convey, transport, haul, move, transfer, relay, release, conduct, take, fetch.
☞ 支持 bear, shoulder, support, underpin, maintain, uphold, sustain, suffer, stand.

carry on
☞ 进行,继续 continue, proceed, last, endure, maintain, keep on, persist, persevere.
☞ 操作,管理 operate, run, manage, administer.

carry out
☞ 做出,实现 do, perform, undertake, discharge, conduct, execute, implement, fulfil, accomplish, achieve, realize, bring off.

cart n.
☞ 大车,手推车 barrow, handcart, wheel-barrow, wagon, truck.
v.
☞ 移动,装运 move, convey, transport, haul, lug, hump, bear, carry.

carton n.
☞ 木盒 box, packet, pack, case, container, package, parcel.

cartoon n.
☞ 漫画,动画片 comic strip, animation, sketch, drawing, caricature, parody.

carve v.
☞ 刻,雕,切 cut, slice, hack, hew, chisel, chip, sculpt, sculpture, shape, form, fashion, mould, etch, engrave, incise, indent.

case[1] n.
☞ 盒子,箱子 container, receptacle, holder, suitcase, trunk, crate, box, carton, caket, chest, cabinet, showcase, casing, cartridge, shell, capsule, sheath, cover, jacket, wrapper.

case[2] n.
☞ 情形,情况 circumstances, context, state, condition, position, situation, contingency, occurrence, occasion, contingency, occurrence, occasion, event, specimen, example, instance, illustration, point.
☞ 案件,理由 lawsuit, suit, trial, proceedings, action, process, cause, argument, dispute.

cash n.
☞ 现金,钱 money, hard money, ready money, bank-notes, notes, coins, change, legal tender, currency, hard

currency, bullion, funds, resources, wherewithal.
v.
☞ 把……兑现,兑换 encash, exchange, realize, liquidate.

cashier n.
☞ 出纳员 clerk, teller, treasurer, bursar, purser, banker, accountant.

cast v.
☞ 抛,投 throw, hurl, lob, pitch, fling, toss, sling, shy, launch, impel, drive, direct, project, shed, emit, diffuse, spread, scatter.
☞ 铸造 mould, shape, form, model, found.
n.
☞ 演员表,特质 company, troupe, actors, players, performers, entertainers, characters, dramatis, personae.
☞ 铸造物,模型 casting, mould, shape, form.

cast down
☞ 沮丧,不乐 depress, discourage, dishearten, deject, sadden, crush, desolate.

castle n.
☞ 城堡,房舍 stronghold, fortress, citadel, tower, chateau, palace, mansion, stately home, country house.

casual adj.
☞ 马虎的,随便的 nonchalant, blase, lackadaisical, negligent, couldn't-care-less, apathetic, indifferent, unconcerned, informal, offhand, relaxed, laid back.
☞ 偶然的 fortuitous, accidental, unintentional, unpremeditated, unexpected, unforeseen, irregular, random, occasional, incidental, superficial, cursory.

casualty n.
☞ 伤亡,死伤者 injury, loss, death, fatality, victim, sufferer, injured person, wounded, dead person.

catalogue n.
☞ 目录 list, inventory, roll, register, roster, schedule, record, table, index, directory, gazetteer, brochure, prospectus.
v.
☞ 编入目录,列入目录 list, register, record, index, classify, alphabetize, file.

catch v.
☞ 捉,搜,逮 seize, grab, take, hold, grasp, grip, clutch, capture, trap, entrap, snare, ensnare, hook, net, arrest, apprehend.
☞ 听到,了解 hear, understand, perceive, recognize.
☞ 染患,罹患 contract, get, develop, go down with.

catch up
☞ 把握 gain on, draw level with, overtake.

catching adj.
☞ 传染性的 infectious, contagious, communicable, transmittable.

catchword n.
☞ 流行语,标语 catch-phrase, slogan, motto, watchword, byword, password.

catchy adj.
☞ 流行的 memorable, haunting,

categorical adj.
☞ 无条件的,明确的 absolute, total, utter, unqualified, unreserved, unconditional, downright, positive, definite, emphatic, unequivocal, clear, explicit, express, direct.

category n.
☞ 种类,范畴 class, classification, group, grouping, sort, type, section, division, department, chapter, head, heading, grade, rank, order, list.

cater v.
☞ 供应,供给,装备 provision, victual, provide, supply, furnish, serve, indulge, pander.

cattle n.
☞ 牛 cows, bulls, oxen, livestock, stock, beasts.

cause n.
☞ 起因,起源 source, origin, beginning, root, basis, spring, originator, creator, producer, maker, agent, agency.
☞ 原因,动机 reason, motive, grounds, motivation, stimulus, incentive, inducement, impulse.
☞ 事业 object, purpose, end, ideal, belief, conviction, movement, undertaking, enterprise.

v.
☞ 导致,影响,作用,引起 begin, give rise to, lead to, result in, occasion, bring about, effect, produce, generate, create, precipitate, motivate, stimulate, provoke, incite, induce, force, compel.

caution n.
☞ 注意,小心 care, carefulness, prudence, vigilance, watchfulness, alertness, heed, discretion, forethought, deliberation, wariness.
☞ 警告,提醒注意 warning, caveat, injunction, admonition, advice, counsel.

v.
☞ 警告 warn, admonish, advise, urge.

cautious adj.
☞ 仔细的,小心的 careful, prudent, circumspect, judicious, vigilant, watchful, alert, heedful, discreet, tactful, chary, wary, cagey, guarded, tentative, softly-softly, unadventurous.

cave n.
☞ 洞穴,岩洞 cavern, grotto, hole, pothole, hollow, cavity.

cave in
☞ 塌陷,陷落 collapse, subside, give way, yield, fall, slip.

cease v.
☞ 停止 stop, desist, refrain, pack in, halt, call a halt, break off, discontinue, finish, end, conclude, terminate, fail, die.

ceaseless adj.
☞ 无穷的,不间断的 endless, unending, never-ending, eternal, everlasting, continuous, non-stop, incessant, interminable, constant, perpetual, continual, persistent, untiring, unremitting.

cede v.

☞ 放弃,让与 surrender, give up, resign, abdicate, renounce, abandon, yield, relinquish, convey, transfer, hand over, grant, allow, concede.

celebrate v.
☞ 庆祝,歌颂 commemorate, remember, observe, keep, rejoice, toast, drink to, honour, exalt, glorify, praise, extol, eulogize, commend, bless, solemnize.

celebrated adj.
☞ 著名的,知名的 famous, well-known, famed, renowned, illustrious, glorious, eminent, distinguished, notable, prominent, outstanding, popular, acclaimed, exalted, revered.

celebration n.
☞ 庆祝,庆祝会 commemoration, remembrance, observance, anniversary, jubilee, festival, gala, merrymaking, jollification, revelry, festivity, party, reve-up.

celebrity n.
☞ 名人,名望 personage, dignitary, VIP, luminary, worthy, personality, name, big name, star, superstar.

cell n.
☞ 细胞,电池 dungeon, prison, room, cubicle, chamber, compartment, cavity, unit.

cellar n.
☞ 地窖,地下室 basement, crypt, vault, storeroom, wine cellar.

central adj.
☞ 中心的,中央的 middle, mid, inner, interior, focal, main, chief, key, prinicipal, primary, fundamental, vital, essential, important.

centre n.
☞ 中心,中央 middle, mid-point, bull's-eye, heart, core, nucleus, pivot, hub, focus, crux.
v.
☞ 专心,集中 focus, concentrate, converge, gravitate, revolve, pivot, hinge.

ceremony n.
☞ 纪念,庆祝 service, rite, commemoration, observance, celebration, function, parade.
☞ 礼仪,仪式 etiquette, protocol, decorum, propriety, formality, form, niceties, ceremonial, ritual, pomp, show.

certain adj.
☞ 确定的,不容置疑的 sure, positive, assured, confident, convinced, undoubted, indubitable, unquestionable, incontrovertible, undeniable, irrefutable, plain, conclusive, absolute, convincing, true.
☞ 确信的,一定的 inevitable, unavoidable, bound, destined, fated.
☞ 某种的,特定的 specific, special, particular, individual, precise, express, fixed, established, settled, decided, definite.
☞ 可靠的,有把握的 dependable, reliable, trustworthy, constant, steady,

certainly adv.
☞ 当然地,一定,必定,当然可以 of course, naturally, definitely, for sure, undoubtedly, doubtlessly.

certainty n.
☞ 确信,事实,真理,真相 sureness, positiveness, assurance, confidence, conviction, faith, trust, truth, validity, fact, reality, inevitability.

certificate n.
☞ 证书,证明书 document, award, diploma, qualification, credentials, testimonial, guarantee, endorsement, warrant, licence, authorization, pass, voucher.

certify v.
☞ 证明,宣布 declare, attest, aver, assure, guarantee, endorse, corroborate, confirm, vouch, testify, witness, verify, authenticate, validate, authorize, license.

chain n.
☞ 铁链,联合 fetter, manacle, restraint, bond, link, coupling, union.
☞ 环节,连续 sequence, succession, progression, string, train, series, set.
v.
☞ 限制住,捆住,锁住 tether, fasten, secure, bind, restrain, confine, fetter, shackle, manacle, handcuff, enslave.

chairman, chairwoman n.
☞ 主席,领袖 chairperson, chair, president, convenor, organizer, director, master of ceremonies, MC, toastmaster, speaker.

challenge v.
☞ 挑战 dare, defy, throw, down the gauntlet, confront, brave, accost, provoke, test, tax, try.
☞ 质问 dispute, question, query, protest, object to.
n.
☞ 挑战,质问 dare, defiance, confrontation, provocation, test, trial, hurdle, obstacle, question, ultimatum.

champion n.
☞ 冠军,获胜者 winner, victor, conqueror, hero, guardian, protector, defender, vindicator, patron, backer, supporter, upholder, advocate.
v.
☞ 防守,保卫,支持 defend, stand up for, back, support, maintain, uphold, espouse, advocate, promote.

chance n.
☞ 机会,可能性,运气 ACCIDENT, fortuity, coincidence, fluke, luck, fortune. providence, fate, destiny, risk, gamble, speculation, possibility, prospect, probability, likelihood, odds.
v.
☞ 冒险,尝试 risk, hazard, gamble, wager, stake, try, venture.
☞ 碰巧,偶然发生 happen, occur.

adj.
☞ 偶然的 fortuitous, casual, accidental, inadvertent, unintentional, unintended, unforeseen, unlooked-for, random, haphazard, incidental.

change *v.*
☞ 改变,变化,代替 alter, modify, convert, reorganize, reform, remodel, restyle, transform, transfigure, metamorphose, mutate, vary, fluctuate, vacillate, shift, displace, swap, exchange, trade, switch, transpose, substitute, replace, alternate, interchange.
n.
☞ 零钱,换车,变化 alteration, modification, conversion, transformation, metamorphosis, mutation, variation, fluctuation, shift, exchange, transposition, substitution, interchange, difference, diversion, novelty, innovation, variety, transition, revolution, upheaval.

changeable *adj.*
☞ 易变的,不固定的 variable, mutable, fluid, kaleidoscopic, shifting, mobile, unsettled, uncertain, unpredictable, unreliable, erratic, irregular, inconstant, fickle, capricious, volatile, unstable, unsteady, wavering, vacillating.

channel *n.*
☞ 海峡,航道 duct, conduit, main, groove, furrow, trough, gutter, canal, flume, watercourse, waterway, strait, sound.
☞ 路线,方法 route, course, path, avenue, way, means, medium, approach, passage.
v.
☞ 通向,指向,指导 direct, guide, conduct, convey, send, transmit, force.

chant *n.*
☞ 曲调 plainsong, psalm, song, melody, chorus, refrain, slogan, warcry.
v.
☞ 唱 recite, intone, sing, chorus.

chaos *n.*
☞ 纷乱,混乱 disorder, confusion, disorganization, anarchy, lawlessness, tumult, pandemonium, bedlam.

chaotic *adj.*
☞ 乱七八糟的,混乱的 disordered, confused, disorganized, topsy-turvy, deranged, anarchic, lawless, riotous, tumultuous, unruly, uncontrolled.

chap *n.*
☞ 小伙子,家伙 fellow, bloke, guy, man, boy, person, individual, character, sort, type.

chapter *n.*
☞ (书的)章,回 part, section, division, clause, topic, episode, period, phase, stage.

character *n.*
☞ (人的)性格;特征;品质 personality, nature, disposition, temperament, temper, constitution, make-up, individuality, peculiarity,

feature, attributes, quality, type, stamp, calibre, reputation, status, position, trait.
☞ 特性,类型 letter, figure, symbol, sign, mark, type, cipher, rune, hieroglyph, ideograph.
☞ (小说,戏剧的)人物,角色 individual, person, sort, type, role, part.

characteristic adj.
☞ 特别的,特有的 distinctive, distinguishing, individual, idiosyncratic, peculiar, specific, special, typical, representative, symbolic, symptomatic.
n.
☞ 特质,特色 peculiarity, idiosyncrasy, mannerism, feature, trait, attribute, property, quality, hallmark, mark, symptom.

characterize v.
☞ 显示……的特征 typify, mark, stamp, brand, identify, distinguish, indicate, represent, portray.

charge v.
☞ 要价 ask, demand, levy, exact, debit.
☞ 使承担 accuse, indict, impeach, incriminate, blame.
☞ 冲,攻击,进攻 attack, assail, storm, rush.
n.
☞ 费用,价钱 price, cost, fee, rate, amount, expense, expenditure, outlay, payment.
☞ 控告,起诉 accusation, indictment, allegation, imputation.

☞ 攻击,进攻 attack, assault, onslaught, sortie, rush.
☞ 主管,看管 custody, keeping, care, safekeeping, guardianship, ward, trust, responsibility, duty.

charitable adj.
☞ 有点善心的,好意的 philanthropic, humanitarian, benevolent, benign, kind, compassionate, sympathetic, understanding, considerate, generous, magnanimous, liberal, tolerant, broad-minded, lenient, forgiving, indulgent, gracious.

charity n.
☞ 好意,善良,友好 generosity, bountifulness, alms-giving, beneficence, philanthropy, unselfishness, altruism, benevolence, benignness, kindness, goodness, humanity, compassion, tender-heartedness, love, affection, clemency, indulgence.
☞ 施舍,周济 alms, gift, handout, aid, relief, assistance.

charm v.
☞ 吸引,迷住 please, delight, enrapture, captivate, fascinate, beguile, enchant, bewitch, mesmerize, attract, allure, cajole, win, enamour.
n.
☞ 魅力 attraction, allure, magnetism, appeal, desirability, fascination, enchantment, spell, sorcery, magic.

charming adj.
☞ 有魅力的,迷人的 pleasing, delightful, pleasant, lovely, captivating, enchanting,

attractive, fetching, appealing, sweet, winsome, seductive, winning, irresistible.

chart n.
- 图表，蓝图 diagram, table, graph, map, plan, blueprint.

v.
- 制成图表，以图表表示 map, map out, sketch, draw, draft, outline, delineate, mark, plot, place.

chase v.
- 追逐，追求 pursue, follow, hunt, track, drive, expel, rush, hurry.

chat n.
- 闲谈，聊天 talk, conversation, natter, gossip, chinwag, tete-a-tete, heart-to-heart.

v.
- 闲谈，聊天 talk, crack, natter, gossip, chatter, rabbit (on).

cheap adj.
- 廉价的，便宜的 inexpensive, reasonable, dirt-cheap, bargain, reduced, cut-price, knock-down, budget, economy, economical.
- 不重要的，低的，穷的 tawdry, tatty, shoddy, inferior, second-rate, worthless, vulgar, common, poor, paltry, mean, contemptible, despicable, low.

cheapen v.
- 降低价格，贬低价值 devalue, degrade, lower, demean, depreciate, belittle, disparage, denigrate, downgrade.

cheat v.
- 骗取，诈取，作弊 defraud, swindle, diddle, short-change, do, fleece, con, duoble-cross, mislead, deceive, dupe, fool, trick, hoodwink, bamboozle, beguile.

n.
- 骗子，骗徒 cheater, dodger, fraud, swindler, shark, con man, extortioner, double-crosser, impostor, charlatan, deceiver, trickster, rogue.

check v.
- 检查，核对 examine, inspect, scrutinize, give the once-over, investigate, probe, test, monitor, study, research, compare, cross-check, confirm, verify.
- 控制，限制，制止 curb, bridle, restrain, control, limit, repress, inhibit, damp, thwart, hinder, impede, obstruct, bar, retard, delay, stop, arrest, halt.

n.
- 检查，考验 examination, inspection, scrutiny, once-over, check-up, investigation, audit, test, research.
- 控制，限制 curb, restraint, control, limitation, constraint, inhibition, damper, blow, disappointment, reverse, setback, frustration, hindrance, impediment, obstruction, stoppage.

cheer v.
- 欢呼，高呼 acclaim, hail, clap, applaud.
- (使)高兴,(使)振奋 comfort, console, brighten, gladden, warm, uplift, elate, exhilarate,

encourage, hearten.
n.
☞ 欢呼 acclamation, hurrah, bravo, applause, ovation.

cheer up
☞ 热情高涨 encourage, hearten, take heart, rally, buck up, perk up.

cheerful *adj.*
☞ 高兴的,爽快的,令人愉快的 happy, glad, contented, joyful, joyous, blithe, carefree, light-hearted, cheery, good-humoured, sunny, optimistic, enthusiastic, hearty, genial, jovial, jolly, merry, lively, animated, bright, chirpy, breezy, jaunty, buoyant, sparking.

cherish *v.*
☞ 珍爱,怀有 foster, care for, look after, nurse, nurture, nourish, sustain, support, harbour, shelter, entertain, hold dear, value, prize, treasure.

chest *n.*
☞ 箱子,柜子 trunk, crate, box, case, casket, coffer, strongbox.

chew *v.*
☞ 嚼,咀嚼 masticate, gnaw, munch, champ, crunch, grind.

chief *adj.*
☞ 主要的,首要的 leading, foremost, uppermost, highest, supreme, grand, arch, premier, principal, main, key, central, prime, prevailing, predominant, pre-eminent, outstanding, vital, essential, primary, major.
n.
☞ 首长,首领 ruler, chieftain, lord, master, supremo, head, principal, leader, commander, captain, governor, boss, director, manager, superintendent, superior, ringleader.

chiefly *adv.*
☞ 最为重要地,主要地 mainly, mostly, for the most part, predominantly, principally, primarily, essentially, especially, generally, usually.

child *n.*
☞ 小孩 youngster, kid, nipper, brat, baby, infant, toddler, tot, minor, juvenile, offspring, issue, progeny, descendant.

childhood *n.*
☞ 幼年时代,儿童 babyhood, infancy, boyhood, girlhood, schooldays, youth, adolescence, minority, immaturity.

childish *adj.*
☞ 天真的,幼稚的 babyish, boyish, girlish, infantile, puerile, juvenile, immature, silly, foolish, frivolous.

childlike *adj.*
☞ 自然的,单纯的 innocent, naive, ingenuous, artless, guileless, credulous, trusting, trustful, simple, natural.

chill *v.*
☞ 变冷,变寒冷 cool, refrigerate, freeze, ice.
☞ 使扫兴,寒心 frighten, terrify, dismay, dishearten, discourage, depress, dampen.
n.
☞ 冷,寒冷 coolness, cold, coldness, frigidity, rawness,

bite, nip, crispness.

chilly *adj.*
- 寒冷的,相当冷的 cold, fresh, brisk, crisp, nippy, wintry.
- 冷淡的,不欢迎的 cool, frigid, unsympathetic, unwelcoming, aloof, stony, unfriendly, hostile.

china *adj.*
- 瓷的 porcelain, ceramic, pottery, earthenware, terracotta.

chip *n.*
- 抓痕,擦伤 notch, nick, scratch, dent, flaw.
- 薄片 fragment, scrap, wafer, sliver, flake, shaving, paring.
v.
- 切成片,切开 chisel, whittle, nick, notch, gash, damage.

chirp *v, n.*
- 小声唧唧啾声 chirrup, tweet, cheep, peep, twitter, warble, sing, pipe, whistle.

choice *n.*
- 选择,挑选 option, alternative, selection, variety, pick, preference, say, decision, dilemma, election, discrimination, choosing, opting.
adj.
- 最好的,精选的 best, superior, prime, plum, excellent, fine, exquisite, exclusive, select, hand-picked, special, prize, valuable, precious.

choke *v.*
- 窒息,气闷 throttle, strangle, asphyxiate, suffocate, stifle, smother, suppress.
- 阻塞 obstruct, constrict, congest, clog, block, dam, bar, close, stop.
- 噎,塞住 cough, gag, retch.

choose *v.*
- 选择,挑选 pick, select, single out, designate, predestine, opt for, plump for, vote for, settle on, fix on, adopt, elect, prefer, wish, desire, see fit.

choosy *adj.*
- 挑三拣四的 selective, discriminating, picky, fussy, particular, exacting.

chop *v.*
- 切,劈,砍 cut, hack, hew, lop, sever, truncate, cleave, divide, split, slash.

chop up
- 分开,切开 cut (up), slice (up), divide, cube, dice, mince.

chore *n.*
- 杂事 task, job, errand, duty, burden.

chorus *n.*
- 喊出 refrain, burden, response, call, shout.
- 合唱团 choir, choristers, singers, vocalists, ensemble.

Christmas *n.*
- 圣诞节 Xmas, Noel, Yule, Yuletide.

chubby *adj.*
- 丰满的,圆胖的 plump, podgy, fleshy, flabby, stout, protly, rotund, round, tubby, paunchy.

chuckle *v.*

☞ 笑,轻声笑 laugh, giggle, titter, snigger, chortle, snort, crow.

chunk n.
☞ 块,大块 lump, hunk, mass, wodge, wedge, block, slab, piece, portion.

church
☞ 教堂,礼拜堂 chapel, house of God, cathedral, minster, abbey, temple.

cinema
☞ 电影,影片 films, picture, movies, big screen.
☞ 电影院 picture-house, picture-palace, fleapit.

circle n.
☞ 圆圈,圆 ring, hoop, loop, round, disc, sphere, globe, orb, cycle, turn, revolution, circuit, orbit, circumference, perimeter, coil, spiral.
☞ 集团,界 group, band, company, crowd, set, clique, coterie, club, society, fellowship, fraternity.

v.
☞ 环绕 ring, loop, encircle, surround, gird, encompass, enclose, hem in, circumscribe, circumnavigate.
☞ 盘旋,绕行 rotate revolve, pivot, gyrate, whirl, turn, coil, wind.

circuit n.
☞ 环行,巡回 lap, orbit, revolution, tour, journey, course, route, track, round, beat, district, area, region, circumference, boundary, bounds, limit, range, compass, ambit.

circular adj.
☞ 圆的,球形的 round, annular, ring-shaped, hoop-shaped, disc-shaped.

n.
☞ 传单,通告 handbill, leaflet, pamphlet, notice, announcement, advertisement, letter.

circulate v.
☞ 循环 go round, rotate, revolve, gyrate, whirl, swirl, flow.
☞ 传播,散布 spread, diffuse, broadcast, publicize, publish, issue, propagate, pass round, distribute.

circulation n.
☞ 循环,流动 blood-flow, flow, motion, rotation, circling.
☞ 发行,流通 spread, transmission, publication, dissemination, distribution.

circumstances n.
☞ 情况,细节 details, particulars, facts, items, elements, factors, conditions, state, state of affairs, situation, position, status, lifestyle, means, resources.

cite v.
☞ 引用,引征 quote, adduce, name, specify, enumerate, mention, refer to, advance, bring up.

citizen n.
☞ 公民,市民 city-dweller, townsman, townswoman, inhabitant, denizen, resident, householder, taxpayer, subject.

city n.

☞ 城市,都市 metropolis, town, municipality, conurbation.

civic adj.
☞ 城市的,公共的,公众的 city, urban, municipal, borough, community, local, public, communal.

civil adj.
☞ 有礼貌的,有益的 polite, courteous, well-mannered, well-bred, courtly, refined, civilized, polished, urbane, affable, complaisant, obliging, accommodating.
☞ 内部的 domestic, home, national, internal, interior, state, municipal, civic.

civility n.
☞ 礼貌,有礼貌的行为 politeness, courteousness, courtesy, breeding, refinement, urbanity, graciousness, affability, amenity.

civilization n.
☞ 开化,文化 progress, advacement, development, education, enlightenment, cultivation, culture, refinement, sophistication, urbanity.

civilize v.
☞ 教化,开化 tame, humanize, educate, enlighten, cultivate, refine, polish, sophisticate, improve, perfect.

civilized adj.
☞ 开化的,有礼貌的 advanced, developed, educated, enlightened, cultured, refined, sophisticated, urbane, polite, sociable.

claim v.
☞ 宣称,断言 allege, pretend, profess, state, affirm, assert, maintain, contend, hold, insist.
☞ 要求 ask, request, require, need, demand, exact, take, collect.
n.
☞ 断言,宣称 allegation, pretension, affirmation, assertion, contention, insistence.
☞ 要求,主张 application, petition, request, requirement, demand, call, right, privilege.

clan n.
☞ 大家族,集团 tribe, family, house, race, society, brotherhood, fraternity, confraternity, sect, faction, group, band, set, clique, coterie.

clap v.
☞ 欢呼,鼓掌 applaud, acclaim, cheer.
☞ 拍,轻拍 slap, smack, pat, wallop, whack, bang.

clarify v.
☞ 解释,使明白 explain, throw light on, illuminate, elucidate, gloss, define, simplify, resolve, clear up.
☞ 使清洁 pefine, purify, filter, clear.

clarity n.
☞ 清楚,透明 clearness, transparency, lucidity, simplicity, intelligibility, comprehensibility, explicitness, unambiguousness, obviousness, definition, precision.

clasp n.
☞ 扣钩,钩环 fastener, buckle, clip, pin, hasp, hook, catch.

☞ 紧抱,拥抱 hold, grip, grasp, embrace, hug.

v.

☞ 紧抱,拥抱 hold, grip, grasp, clutch, embrace, enfold, hug, squeeze, press.

☞ 用钩环扣住 fasten, connect, attach, grapple, hook, clip, pin.

class n.

☞ 种类,类别 category, classification, group, set, section, division, department, sphere, grouping, order, league, rank, status, caste, quality, grade, type, genre, sort, kind, species, genus, style.

☞ 课程 lesson, lecture, seminar, tutorial, course.

v.

☞ 分类,归类 categorize, classify, group, sort, rank, grade, rate, designate, brand.

classic adj.

☞ 古典的,传统的 typical, characteristic, standard, regular, usual, traditional, time-honoured, established, archetypal, model, exemplary, ideal, best, finest, first-rate, consummate, definitive, masterly, excellent, ageless, immortal, undying, lasting, enduring, abiding.

n.

☞ 名著,杰作 standard, model, prototype, exemplar, masterwork, masterpiece, piece de resistance.

classical adj.

☞ 经典的,古典的 elegant, refined, pure, traditional, excellent, well-proportioned, symmetrical, harmonious, restrained.

classification n.

☞ 分类,归类 categorization, taxonomy, sorting, grading, arrangement, systematization, codification, tabulation, cataloguing.

classify v.

☞ 分类,划分 categorize, class, group, pigeonhole, sort, grade, rank, arrange, dispose, distribute, systematize, codify, tabulate, file, catalogue.

clause n.

☞ 条款,款 article, item, part, section, subsection, paragraph, heading, chapter, passage, condition, provise, provision, specification, point.

claw n.

☞ 似爪之工具 talon, nail, pincer, nipper, gripper.

v.

☞ 抓,撕 scratch, scrabble, scrape, graze, tear, rip, lacerate, maul, mangle.

clean adj.

☞ 清洁的,干净的 washed, laundered, sterile, aseptic, antiseptic, hygienic, sanitary, sterilized, decontaminated, purified, pure, unadulterated, fresh, unpolluted, uncontaminated, immaculate, spotless, unsoptted, unstained, unsoiled, unsullied, perfect, faultless, flawless, unblemishd.

☞ 无前科的,清白的 innocent, gultless, virtuous, upright,

moral, honest, honourable, respectable, decent, chaste.
☞ 整齐的,光滑的 smooth, regular, straight, neat, tidy.
v.
☞ 刷干净,清扫 wash, bath, launder, rinse, wipe, sponge, scrub, scour, mop, swab, sweep, vacuum, dust, freshen, deodorize, cleanse, purge, purify, decontaminate, disinfect, sanitize, sterilize, clear, filter.

clear adj.
☞ 清楚的,明显的 plain, distinct, comprehensible, intelligible, coherent, lucid, explicit, precise, unambiguous, well-defined, apparent, evident, patent, obvious, manifest, conspicuous, unmistakable.
☞ 有把握的,确知的 sure, certain, positive, definite, convinced.
☞ 清澈的 transparent, limpid, crystalline, glassy, see-through, clean, unclouded, colourless.
☞ 清亮的 cloudless, unclouded, fine, bright, sunny, light, luminous, undimmed.
☞ 容易看透的 unobstructed, unblocked, open, free, empty, unhindered, unimpeded.
☞ 声响的,清晰的 audible, perceptible, pronounced, distinct, recognizable.
v.
☞ 除去,除掉 unblock, unclog, decongest, free, rid, extricate, disentangle, loosen.
☞ 清理,清除 clean, wipe, erase, cleanse, refine, filter, tidy, empty, unload.

☞ 辨清,解决 acquit, exculpate, exonerate, absolve, vindicate, excuse, justify, free, liberate, release, let go.

clear up
☞ 说明,解决 explain, clarify, elucidate, unravel, solve, resolve, answer.
☞ (使)清理,整理 tidy, order, sort, rearrange, remove.

clearance n.
☞ 许可证,批准 authorization, sanction, endorsement, permission, consent, leave, ok, go-ahead, green light.
☞ 空间,间隙 space, gap, headroom, margin, allowance.

clearing n.
☞ 空地 space, gap, opening, glade, dell.

clergy n.
☞ 教士,神父 clergymen, churchmen, clerics, the church, the cloth, ministry, priesthood.

clergyman n.
☞ 牧师 churchman, cleric, ecclesiastic, devine, man of God, minister, priest, reverend, father, vicar, pastor, padre, parson, rector, canon, dean, deacon, chaplain, curate, presbyter, rabbi.

clerical adj.
☞ 办事员的,官方的 office, secretarial, white-collar, official, administrative.
☞ 神父的,教士的 ecclesiastic (al), pastoral, ministerial, priestly, episcopal, canonical, sacerdotal.

clever adj.

☞ 聪明的,理解力强的,机灵的 intelligent, brainy, bright, smart, witty, gifted, expert, knowledgeable, adroit, apt, able, capable, quick, quick-witted, sharp, keen, shrewd, knowing, discerning, cunning, ingenious, inventive, resourceful, sensible, rational.

cliche n.
☞ 老套,陈词滥调 platitude, commonplace, banality, truism, bromide, chestnut, stereotype.

client n.
☞ 顾客 customer, patron, regular, buyer, shopper, consumer, user, patient, applicant.

cliff n.
☞ 悬崖,峭壁 bluff, face, rock-face, scar, scarp, escarpment, crag, overhang, precipice.

climate n.
☞ 情形,趋势,气候 weather, temperature, setting, milieu, environment, ambience, atmosphere, feeling, mood, temper, disposition, tendency, trend.

climax n.
☞ 顶点,高潮 culmination, height, high point, highlight, acme, zenith, peak, summit, top, head.

climb v.
☞ 攀登,升高 ascend, scale, shin up, clamber, mount, rise, soar, top.

climb down
☞ 认错,屈服 retract, eat one's words, back down, retreat.

cling v.
☞ 坚持,抓紧 clasp, clutch, grasp, grip, stick, adhere, cleave, fasten, embrace, hug.

clip¹ v.
☞ 剪短,修整齐 trim, snip, cut, prune, pare, shear, crop, dock, poll, truncate, curtail, shorten, abbreviate.

clip² v.
☞ 用夹子夹在一起 pin, staple, fasten, attach, fix, hold.

clipping n.
☞ 剪下之物 cutting, snippet, quotation, citation, passage, section, excerpt, extract, clip.

cloak n.
☞ 斗篷,遮盖物 cape, mantle, robe, wrap, coat, cover, shield, mask, front, pretext.
v.
☞ 掩藏 cover, veil, mask, screen, hide, conceal, obscure, disguise, camouflage.

close¹ v.
☞ 关闭,合上 shut, fasten, secure, lock, bar, obstruct, block, clog, plug, cork, stop up, fill, seal, fuse, join, unite.
☞ 结束,完结 end, finish, complete, conclude, terminate, wind up, stop, cease.
n.
☞ 结束,完成 end, finish, completion, conclusion, culmination, ending, finale, denouement, termination, cessation, stop, pause.

close² adj.
☞ 靠近的,接近的 near, nearby, at hand, neighbouring,

adjacent, adjoining, impending, imminent.
☞ 密切的,亲密的 intimate, dear, familiar, attached, devoted, loving.
☞ 沉闷的,窒息的 oppressive, heavy, muggy, humid, sultry, sweltering, airless, stifling, suffocating, stuffy, unventilated.
☞ 吝啬的,手紧的 miserly, mean, parsimonious, tight, stingy, niggardly.
☞ 隐藏的,秘密的 secretive, uncommunicative, taciturn, private, secret, confidential.
☞ 准确的 exact, precise, accurate, strict, literal, faithful.
☞ 严密的 fixed, concentrated, intense, keen.
☞ 严格的 dense, solid, pached, cramped.

cloth n.
☞ 布,布料 fabric, material, stuff, textile.
☞ 用作特殊用途的一块布 rag, face-cloth, flannel, dish-cloth, floorcloth, duster, towel.

clothe v.
☞ 穿衣 dress, put on, robe, attire, deck, outfit, rig, vest, invest, drape, cover.

clothes n.
☞ 衣服 clothing, garments, wear, attire, garb, gear, togs, outfit, get-up, dress, costume, wardrobe.

cloud n.
☞ 云 vapour, haze, mist, fog, gloom, darkness, obscurity.
v.
☞ 变模糊,变不清楚 mist, fog, blur, dull, dim, darken, shade, shadow, overshadow, eclipse, veil, shroud, obscure, muddle, confuse, obfuscate.

cloudy adj.
☞ 多云的,阴天的 nebulous, hazy, misty, foggy, blurred, blurry, opaque, milky, muddy, dim, indistinct, obscure, dark, murky, sombre, leaden, lowering, overcast, dull, sunless.

clown n.
☞ 小丑,丑角 buffoon, comic, comedian, joker, jester, fool, harlequin, pierrot.

club n.
☞ 俱乐部,社团 association, society, company, league, guild, order, union, fraternity, group, set, circle, clique.
☞ 球棍,棒 bat, stick, mace, bludgeon, truncheon, cosh, cudgel.
v.
☞ 用棍棒击打 hit, strike, beat, bash, clout, clobber, bludgeon, cosh, batter, pummel.

clue n.
☞ 线索 hint, tip, suggestion, idea, notion, lead, tip-off, pointer, sign, indication, evidence, trace, suspicion, inkling, intimation.

clumsy adj.
☞ 笨拙的,愚蠢的 bungling, ham-fisted, unhandy, unskilful, inept, bumbling, blundering, lumbering, gauche, ungainly, gawky, unco-ordinated, awkward, ungraceful, uncouth, rough, crude, ill-made,

cluster n.
☞ 簇, 束 bunch, clump, batch, group, knot, mass, crowd, gathering, collection, assembly.
v.
☞ 聚集, 成束 bunch, group, gather, collect, assemble, flock.

coach n.
☞ 私人教师 trainer, instructor, tutor, teacher.
v.
☞ 教育, 辅导 train, drill, instruct, teach, tutor, cram, prepare.

coarse adj.
☞ 粗糙的, 粗劣的 rough, unpolished, unfinished, uneven, lumpy, unpurified, unrefined, unprocessed.
☞ 无礼的, 粗鲁的 bawdy, ribald, earthy, smutty, vulgar, crude, offensive, foul-mouthed, boorish, loutish, rude, impolite, indelicate, improper, indecent, immodest.

coast n.
☞ 海岸, 海滨 coastline, seaboard, shore, beach, seaside.
v.
☞ 滑动, 飘行 free-wheel, glide, slide, sail, cruise, drift.

coat n.
☞ 表层, 皮 fur, hair, fleece, pelt, hide, skin.
☞ 覆盖物 layer, coating, covering.
v.
☞ 外加一层, 涂上 cover, paint, spread, smear, plaster.

shapoeless, unwieldy, heavy, bulky, cumbersome.

coating n.
☞ 薄层, 薄皮 covering, layer, dusting, wash, coat, blanket, sheet, membrane, film, glaze, varnish, finish, veneer, lamination, overlay.

code n.
☞ 法规, 准则 ethics, rules, regulations, principles, system, custom, convention, etiquette, manners.
☞ 密码 cipher, secret language.

cognition n.
☞ 认识, 认知 perception, awareness, knowledge, apprehension, discernment, insight, comprehension, understanding, intelligence, reasoning.

cohere v.
☞ 粘着, 连在一起 stick, adhere, cling, fuse, unite, bind, combine, coalesce, consolidate.
☞ 前后一致, 连贯 agree, square, correspond, harmonize, hold, hang together.

coherent adj.
☞ 连贯的 articulate, intelligible, comprehensible, meaningful, lucid, consistent, logical, reasoned, rational, sensible, orderly, systematic, organized.

coil v.
☞ 盘旋, 缠绕 wind, spiral, convolute, curl, loop, twist, writhe, snake, wreathe, twine, entwine.
n.
☞ 线圈 roll, curl, loop, ring, convolution, spiral, corkscrew,

coin v.
☞ 创造,铸造 invent, make up, think up, conceive, devise, formulate, originate, create, fabricate, produce, mint, forge.

n.
☞ 硬币 piece, bit, money, cash, change, small, change, loose change, silver, copper.

coincide v.
☞ 相致,一致 coexist, synchronize, agree, concur, correspond, square, tally, accord, harmonize, match.

coincidence n.
☞ 巧合,凑巧 chance, accident, eventuality, fluke, luck, fortuity.
☞ 同时发生,符合 coexistence, conjunction, concurrence, correspondence, correlation.

coincidental adj.
☞ 巧合的 chance, accidental, casual, unintentional, unplanned, flukey, lucky, fortuitous.
☞ 同时发生的 coincident, coexistent, concurrent, simultaneous, synchronous.

cold adj.
☞ 冷的,寒冷的 unheated, cool, chilled, chilly, chill, shivery, nippy, parky, raw, biting, bitter, wintry, frosty, icy, glacial, freezing, frozen, arctic, polar.
☞ 冷淡的 unsympathetic, unmoved, unfeeling, stony, frigid, unfriendly, distant, aloof, standoffish, reserved, undemonstrative, unresponsive, indifferent, lukewarm.

n.
☞ 寒冷 coldness, chill, chilliness, coolness, frigidity, iciness.

cold-blooded adj.
☞ 无情的 cruel, inhuman, brutal, savage, barbaric, barbarous, merciless, pitiless, callous, unfeeling, heartless.

collaborate v.
☞ 一起工作,合作 conspire, collude, work tegether, co-operate, join forces, team up, participate.

collaboration n.
☞ 合作,共事 conspiring, collusion, association, alliance, partnership, teamwork, co-operation.

collaborator n.
☞ 合作者,通敌者 co-worker, associate, partner, team-mate, colleague, assistant, accomplice, traitor, turncoat.

collapse v.
☞ 崩溃,病倒 faint, pass out, crumple.
☞ 倒塌 fall, sink, founder, fail, fold, fall apart, disintegrate, crumble, subside, cave in.

n.
☞ 倒塌,崩溃 failure, breakdown, flop, debacle, downfall, ruin, disintegration, subsidence, cave-in, faint, exhaustion.

colleague n.
☞ 同事,同僚 workmate, co-worker, team-mate, partner, collaborator, ally, associate,

confederate, confrere, comrade, companion, aide, helper, assistant, auxiliary.

collect v.
☞ 收集,搜集,聚集　gather, assemble, congregate, convene, muster, rally, converge, cluster, aggregate, accumulate, amass, heap, hoard, stockpile, save, acquire, obtain, secure.

collected adj.
☞ 镇静的,心思不乱的　composed, self-possessed, placid, serene, calm, unruffled, unperturbed, imperturbable, cool.

collection n.
☞ 募捐,收集　gathering, assembly, convocation, congregation, crowd, group, cluster, accumulation, conglomeration, mass, heap, pile, hoard, stockpile, store.
☞ 收藏品,聚集品　set, assemblage, assortment, job-lot, anthology, compilation.

collective adj.
☞ 集体的,共有的　united, combined, concerted, co-operative, joint, common, shared, corporate, democratic, composite, aggregate, cumulative.

collide v.
☞ 冲突　crash, bump, smash, clash, conflict, confront, meet.

collision n.
☞ 碰撞　impact, crash, bump, smash, accident, pile-up, clash, conflict, confrontation, opposition.

colloquial adj.
☞ 口语的,会话的,通俗的　conversational, informal, familiar, everyday, vernacular, idiomatic.

colonist n.
☞ 移民　colonial, settler, immigrant, emigrant, pioneer.

colonize v.
☞ 殖民　settle, occupy, people, populate.

colony n.
☞ 殖民地　settlement, outpost, dependency, dominion, possession, territory, province.

colossal adj.
☞ 巨大的　huge, enormous, immense, vast, massive, gigantic, mammoth, monstrous, monumental.

colour n.
☞ 颜色,色彩　hue, shade, tinge, tone, tincture, tint, dye, paint, wash, pigment, pigmentation, coloration, complexion.
☞ 彩色,亮丽　vividness, brilliance, rosiness, ruddiness, glow, liveliness, animation.
v.
☞ 上色　paint, crayon, dye, tint, stain, tinge.
☞ 变色,变红　blush, flush, redden.
☞ 歪曲,渲染　affect, bias, prejudice, distort, pervert, exaggerate, falsify.

colourful adj.
☞ 艳丽的,颜色丰富的　multicoloured, kaleidoscopic, variegated, parti-coloured,

vivid, bright, brilliant, rich, intense.
- 生动的 vivid, graphic, picturesque, lively, stimulating, exciting, interesting.

colourless adj.
- 苍白的,无色的 transparent, neutral, bleached, washed out, faded, pale, ashen, sickly, anaemic.
- 不生动的,无趣味的 insipid, lacklustre, dull, dreary, drab, plain, characterless, unmemorable, uninteresting, tame.

column n.
- 柱,柱状物 pillar, post, shaft, upright, support, obelisk.
- 专栏 list, line, row, rank, file, procession, queue, string.

comb v.
- 梳理 groom, neaten, tidy, untangle.
- 彻底搜查 search, hunt, scour, sweep, sift, screen, rake, rummage, ransack.

combat n.
- 战斗,战争 war, warfare, hostilities, action, battle, fight, skirmish, struggle, conflict, clash, encounter, engagement, contest, bout, duel.

v.
- 战斗,争斗 fight, battle, strive, struggle, contend, contest, oppose, resist, withstand, defy.

combination n.
- 混合 blend, mix, mixture, composite, amalgam, synthesis, compound.
- 联合 merger, amalgamation, unification, alliance, coalition, association, federation, confederation, confederacy, combine, consortium, syndicate, union, integration, fusion, coalescence, connection.

combine v.
- 使结合,使联合 merge, amalgamate, unify, blend, mix, integrate, incorporate, synthzise, compound, fuse, bond, bind, join, connect, link, marry, unite, pool, associate, cooperate.

come v.
- 来,出现,产生 advance, move towards, approach, near, draw near, reach, attain, arrive, enter, appear, materialize, happen, occur.

come about
- 发生 happen, occur, come to pass, transpire, result, arise.

come across
- 遇见,发现 find, discover, chance upon, happen upon, bump into, meet, encounter, notice.

come along
- 发生,进展 arrive, happen, develop, improve, progress, rally, mend, recover, recuperate.

come apart
- 撕开,分开 disintegrate, fall to bits, break, separate, split, tear.

come between
- 分开,分裂 separate, part, divide, split up, disunite, estrange, alienate.

come down
☞ 下来，下降 descend, fall, reduce, decline, deteriorate, worsen, degenerate.

come in
☞ 进来 enter, appear, show up, arrive, finish.

come off
☞ 发生，举行 happen, occur, take place, succeed.

come on
☞ 开始，进步 begin, appear, advance, proceed, progress, develop, improve, thrive, succeed.

come out
☞ 产生，发生，导致，出来 result, end, conclude, terminate.

come out with
☞ 说出，陈述，说明 say, state, affirm, declare, exclaim, disclose, divulge.

come round
☞ 承认，改变观念 yield, relent, concede, allow, grant, accede.

come through
☞ 成功渡过，复元 endure, withstand, sruvive, prevail, triumph, succeed, accomplish, achieve.

come up
☞ 发生，出现 rise arise, happen, occur, crop up.

comeback n.
☞ 回来，重现，恢复 return, reappearance, resurgence, revival, recovery.

comedian n.
☞ 喜剧演员，丑角 comic, clown, humorist, wit, joker, wag.

comedown n.
☞ 衰落，屈辱 anticlimax, letdown, disappointment, deflation, blow, reverse, decline, descent, demotion, humiliation, degradation.

comedy n.
☞ 喜剧 farce, slapstick, clowning, hilarity, drollery, humour, wit, joking, jesting, facetiousness.

comfort v.
☞ 安慰，使舒适 ease, soothe, relieve, alleviate, assuage, console, cheer, gladden, reassure, hearten, encourage, invigorate, strengthen, enliven, refresh.
n.
☞ 安慰，慰问 consolation, compensation, cheer, reassurance, encouragement, alleviation, relief, help, aid, support.
☞ 安逸，舒适 ease, relaxation, luxury, snugness, cosiness, wellbeing, satisfaction, contentment, enjoyment.

comfortable adj.
☞ 舒适的 snug, cosy, comfy, relaxing, restful, easy, convenient, pleasant, agreeable, enjoyable, delightful.
☞ 舒畅的 at ease, relaxed, contented, happy.
☞ 富裕的 affluent, well-off, well-to-do, prosperous.

comic adj.
☞ 滑稽的，使人发笑的 funny, hilarous, side-splitting, comial, droll, humorous, witty, amusing, entertaining,

diverting, joking, facetious, light, farcical, ridiculous, ludicrous, absurd, laughable, priceless, rich.

n.

☞ 喜剧演员 comedian, gagster, joker, jester, clown, buffoon, humorist, wit, wag.

coming *adj.*

☞ 未来的,将来的 next, forthcoming, impending, imminent, due, approaching, near, future, aspiring, rising, up-and-coming.

n.

☞ 到达,来到 advent, approach, arrival, accession.

command *v.*

☞ 命令 order, bid, charge, enjoin, direct, instruct, require, demand, compel.

☞ 指挥控制 lead, head, rule, reign, govern, control, dominate, manage, supervise.

n.

☞ 支配,命令 commandment, decree, edict, precept, mandate, order, bidding, charge, injunction, directive, direction, instruction, requirement.

☞ 权力 power, authority, leadership, control, domination, dominion, rule, sway, government, management.

commander *n.*

☞ 指挥官,司令员 leader, head, chief, boss, commander-in-chief, general, admiral, captain, commanding officer, officer.

commemorate *v.*

☞ 纪念,庆祝 celebrate, solemnize, remember, memorialize, mark, honour, salute, immortalize, observe, keep.

commemoration *n.*

☞ 庆祝,纪念 celebration, observance, remembrance, tribute, honouring, ceremony.

commend *v.*

☞ 称赞,赞扬 praise, compliment, acclaim, extol, applaud, approve, recommend.

☞ 信托,托保 commit, entrust, confide, consign, deliver, yield.

comment *v.*

☞ 评论 say, mention, interpose, interject, remark, observe, note, annotate, interpret, explain, elucidate, criticize.

n.

☞ 解说,评论 statement, remark, observation, note, annotation, footnote, marginal note, explanation, elucidation, illustration, exposition, commentary, criticism.

commentary *n.*

☞ 集注,集释 narration, voice-over, analysis, description, review, critique, explanation, notes, treatise.

commentator *n.*

☞ 广播评论者,评论家 sportscaster, broadcaster, reporter, narrator, commenter, critic, annotator, interpreter.

commerce *n.*

☞ 商业 trade, traffic, business, dealings, relations, dealing, trafficking, exchange, marketing, merchandizing.

commercial *adj.*
☞商业的 trade, trading, business, sales, profit-making, profitable, sellable, saleable, popular, monetary, financial, mercenary, venal.

commission *n.*
☞任务,委托 assignment, mission, errand, task, job, duty, function, appointment, employment, mandate, warrant, authority, charge, trust.
☞委员会 committee, board, delegation, deputation, representative.
v.
☞委托,请托 nominate, select, appoint, engage, employ, authorize, empower, delegate, depute, send, order, request, ask for.

commit *v.*
☞交托,交付 entrust, confide, commend, consign, deliver, hand over, give, deposit.
☞使……保证 bind, obligate, pledge, engage, involve.
☞做(坏事),犯(罪) do, perform, execute, enact, perpetrate.

commit oneself
☞承诺,负责 decide, undertake, promise, pledge, bind oneself.

commitment *n.*
☞许诺,保证 undertaking, guarantee, assurance, promise, word, pledge, vow, engagement, involvement, dedication, devotion, adherence, loyalty, tie, obligation, duty, responsibility, liability.

committee *n.*
☞委员会,全体委员 council, board, panel, jury, commission, advisory group, think-tank, working party, task force.

common *adj.*
☞普通的,一般的 familiar, customary, habitual, usual, daily, everyday, routine, regular, frequent, widespread, prevalent, general, universal, standard, average, ordinary, plain, simple, workaday, run-of-the-mill, undistinguished, unexceptional, conventional, accepted, popular, commonplace.
☞粗俗的,低级的 vulgar, coarse, unrefined, crude, inferior, low, ill-bred, loutish, plebeian.
☞公共的,共同的 communal, public, shared, mutual, joint, collective.

commonplace *adj.*
☞普通的,平凡的 ordinary, everyday, common, humdrum, pedestrian, banal, trite, widespread, frequent, hackneyed, stock, stale, obvious, worn out, boring, uninteresting, threadbare.

commonsense *adj.*
☞常识的 commonsensical, matter-of-fact, sensible, level-headed, sane, sound, reasonable, practical, down-to-earth, pragmatic, hard-headed, realistic, shrewd, astute, prudent, indicious.

communicate *v.*
☞传达,传送 announce, declare, proclaim, report, reveal,

disclose, divulge, impart, inform, acquaint, intimate, notify, publish, disseminate, spread, diffuse, transmit, convey.
☞ 通讯,联络,信息,通话 talk, converse, commune, correspond, write, phone, telephone, contact.

communication n.
☞ 信息传达 information, intelligence, intimation, disclosure, contact, connection, transmission, dissemination.

communicative adj.
☞ 好说话的,直率的 talkative, voluble, expansive, informative, chatty, sociable, friendly, forthcoming, outgoing, extrovert, unreserved, free, open, frank, candid.

community n.
☞ 团体,社会 district, locality, population, people, populace, public, residents, nation, state, colony, commune, kibbutz, society, association, fellowship, brotherhood, fraternity.

commute v.
☞ 减轻,改换 reduce, decrease, shorten, curtail, lighten, soften, mitigate, remit, adjust, modify, alter, change, exchange, alternate.
☞ 通勤 travel, journey.

compact adj.
☞ 紧密的,紧凑的 small, short, brief, terse, succinct, concise, condensed, compressed, close, dense, impenetrable, solid, firm.

companion n.
☞ 伴侣,同伴 fellow, comrade, friend, buddy, crony, intimate, confidat(e), ally, confederate, colleague, associate, partner, mate, consort, escort, chaperon, attendant, aide, assistant, accomplice, follower.

companionship n.
☞ 友谊,伴侣 fellowship, comradeship, camaraderie, esprit de corps, support, friendship, company, togetherness, conviviality, sympathy, rapport.

company n.
☞ 公司 firm, business, concern, association, corporation, establishment, house, partnership, syndicate, cartel, consortium.
☞ 人群 troupe, group, band, ensemble, set, circle, crowd, throng, body, troop, crew, party, assembly, gathering, community, society.
☞ 宾客,客人 guests, visitors, callers, society, companionship, fellowship, support, attendance, presence.

comparable adj.
☞ 可比较的,类似的 similar, alike, related, akin, cognate, corresponding, analogous, equivalent, tantamount, proportionate, commensurate, parallel, equal.

compare v.
☞ 比较,对照 liken, equate, contrast, juxtapose, balance, weigh, correlate, resemble, match, equal, parallel.

comparison n.
☞ 比较,对照 juxtaposition, analogy, parallel, correlation, relationship, likeness, resemblance, similarity, comparability, contrast, distinction.

compartment n.
☞ 小间,分隔间 section, division, subdivision, category, pigeonhole, cubbyhole, niche, alcove, bay, area, stall, booth, cubicle, locker, carrel, cell, chamber, berth, crriage.

compassion n.
☞ 同情,怜悯 kindness, tenderness, fellow-feeling, humanity, mercy, pity, sympathy, commiseration, condolence, sorrow, concern, care.

compassionate adj.
☞ 有同情心的,表示怜悯的 kind-hearted, kindly, tender-hearted, benevolent, humanitarian, humane, merciful, clement, lenient, pitying, sympathetic, understanding, supportive.

compatible adj.
☞ 相容的,适宜的 harmonious, consistent, congruous, matching, consonant, accordant, suitable, reconcilable, adaptable, conformable, sympathetic, like-minded, well-matched, similar.

compel v.
☞ 强迫,逼迫 force, make, constrain, oblige, necessitate, drive, urge, impel, coerce, pressurize, hustle, browbeat, bully, strongarm, bulldoze, press-gang, dragoon.

compelling adj.
☞ 强迫的 forceful, coercive, imperative, urgent, pressing, irresistible, overiding, powerful, cogent, persuasive, convincing, conclusive, incontrovertible, irrefutable, pripping, enthralling, spellbinding, mesmeric, compulsive.

compensate v.
☞ 补偿,赔偿 balance, counterbalance, cancel, neutralize, counteract, offset, redress, satisfy, requite, repay, refund, reimburse, indemnify, recompense, reward, remunerate, atone, redeem, make good, restore.

compensation n.
☞ 补偿,赔偿,补偿物 amends, redress, satisfaction, requital, repayment, refund, reimbursement, indemnification, indemnity, damages, reparation, recompense, reward, payment, remuneration, return, restoration, restitution, consolation, comfort.

compete v.
☞ 比赛,竞争 vie, contest, fight, battle, struggle, strive, oppese, challenge, rival, emulate, contend, participate, take part.

competent adj.
☞ 有能力的,胜任的 capable, able, adept, efficient, trained, qualified, well-qualified, skilled, experienced, proficient, expert,

masterly, equal, fit, suitable, appropriate, satisfactory, adequate, sufficient.

competition n.
☞ 比赛 contest, championship, tournament, cup, event, race, match, game, quiz.
☞ 角逐,竞争 rivalry, opposition, challenge, contention, conflict, struggle, strife, competitiveness, combativeness.

competitive adj.
☞ 竞争的 combative, contentious, antagonistic, aggressive, pushy, ambitious, keen, cut-throat.

competitor n.
☞ 竞争者,对手 contestant, contender, entrant, candidate, challenger, opponent, adversary, antagonist, rival, emulator, competition, opposition. compile v. compose, put together, collect, gather, garner, cull, accumulate, amass, assemble, marshal, organize, arrange.

complacent adj.
☞ 自满的,得意的 smug, self-satisfied, gloating, triumphant, proud, self-righteous, unconcerned, serene, self-assured, pleased, gratified, contented, satisfied.

complain v.
☞ 抱怨,诉苦 protest, grumble, grouse, gripe, beef, carp, fuss, lament, bemoan, bewail, moan, whine, groan, growl.

complaint n.
☞ 抱怨,怨言 protest, objection, grumble, grouse, gripe, beef, moan, grievance, dissatisfaction, annoyance, fault-finding, criticism, censure, accusation, charge.
☞ 疾病 ailment, illness, sickness, disease, malady, malaise, indisposition, affliction, disorder, trouble, upset.

complete adj.
☞ 全部的 utter, total, absolute, downright, out-and-out, thorough, perfect.
☞ 完成的,结束的 finished, ended, concluded, over, done, accomplished, achieved.
☞ 彻底的,完全的 unabridged, unabbreviated, unedited, unexpurgated, integral, whole, entire, full, undivided, intact.
v.
☞ 完成,结束,使完善 finish, end, close, conclude, wind up, terminate, finalize, settle, clinch, perform, discharge, execute, fulfil, realize, accomplish, achieve, consummate, crown, perfect.

completion n.
☞ 完成,完结 finish, end, close, conclusion, termination, finalization, settlement, discharge, fulfilment, realization, accomplishment, achievement, attainment, fruition, clumination, consummation, perfection.

complex adj.
☞ 复杂的,复合的 complicated, intricate, elaborate, involved, convoluted, circuitous, tortuous,

- 复合,合成物 network, structure, system, scheme, organization, establishment, institute, development.
- 恐惧,情结 fixation, obsession, preoccupation, hang-up, phobia.

complicate v.
- 复杂化,使麻烦 compound, elaborate, involve, muddle, mix up, confuse, tangle, entangle.

complicated adj.
- 错综复杂的,难解的 complex, intricate, elaborate, involved, convoluted, tortuous, difficult, problematic, puzzling, perplexing.

complication n.
- 复杂,混乱 difficulty, drawback, snag, obstacle, problem, repercussion, complexity, intricacy, elaboration, convolution, tangle, web, confusion, mixture.

compliment n.
- 称赞,致意 flattery, admiration, favour, approval, congratulations, tribute, honour, accolade, bouquet, commendation, praise, eulogy.

v.
- 恭维,称赞 flatter, admire, commend, praise, extol, congratulate, applaud, salute.

complimentary adj.
- 表示称赞的 flattering, admiring, favourable, approving, appreciative, congratulatory, commendatory, eulogistic.
- 免费赠送的 free, gratic, honorary, courtesy.

comply v.
- 遵从,依从,同意 agree, consent, assent, accede, yield, submit, defer, respect, observe, obey, fall in, conform, follow, perform, discharge, fulfil, satisfy, meet, oblige, accommodate.

component n.
- 组件,部件 part, constituent, ingredient, element, factor, item, unit, piece, bit, spare part.

compose v.
- 组成 constitute, make up, form.
- 创作 create, invent, devise, write, arrange, produce, make, form, fashion, build, construct, frame.
- 使安静,镇静 calm, soothe, quiet, still, settle, tranquillize, quell, pacify, control, regulate.

composed adj.
- 镇静的,沉着的 calm, tranquil, serene, relaxed, unworried, unruffled, level-headed, cool, collected, self-possessed, confident, imperturbable, unflappable, placid.

composition n.
- 写作,创作 making, production, formation, creation, invention, design, formulation, writing, compilation, proportion, writing,

compilation, proportion.
- 构成,组成 constitution, make-up, combination, mixture, form, structure, configuration, layout, arragement, organization, layout, arrangement, organization, harmony, consonance, balance, symmetry.
- 乐曲 work, opus, piece, study, exercise.

composure n.
- 镇静,沉着 calm, tranquillity, serenity, ease, coolness, self-possession, confidence, assurance, self-assurance, aplomb, poise, dignity, imperturbability, placidity, equanimity, dispassion, impassivity.

compound v.
- 混合,调合 combine, amalgamate, unite, fuse, coalesce, synthesize, alloy, blend, mix, mingle, intermingle.
- 加重 worsen, exacerbate, aggravate, complicate, intensify, heighten, magnify, increase, augment.

n.
- 混合物,化合物 alloy, blend, mixture, medley, composite, amalgam, synthesis, fusion, composition, amalgamation, combination.

adj.
- 复合的 composite, mixed, multiple, complex, complicated, intricate.

comprehend v.
- 理解 understand, conceive, see, grasp, fathom, penetrate, tumble tp, realize, appreciate, know, apprehend, perceive, discern, take in, assimilate.
- 包含,包括 include, comprise, encompass, embrace, cover.

comprehensible adj.
- 可以理解的 understandable, intelligible, coherent, explicit, clear, lucid, plain, simple, straightforward.

comprehension n.
- 理解,理解力 understanding, conception, grasp, realization, appreciation, knowledge, apprehension, perception, discernment, judgement, sense, intelligence.

comprehensive adj.
- 有理解力的,综合的 thorough, exhaustive, full, complete, encyclopedic, compendious, broad, wide, extensive, sweeping, general, blanket, inclusive, all-inclusive, all-embracing, across-the-board.

comprise v.
- 包括,包含,由……组成 consist of, include, contain, incorporate, embody, involve, encompass, embrace, cover.

compromise v.
- 与……妥协,和解 negotiate, bargain, arbitrate, settle, agree, concede, make concessions, meet halfway, adapt, adjust.
- 危及……的安全 weaken, undermine, expose, endanger, imperil, jeopardize, risk, prejudice.
- 受牵连,损害 dishonour, discredit, embarrass, involve,

implicate.
n.
☞ 和解,妥协 bargain, trade-off, settlement, agreement, concession, give and take, co-operation, accommodation, adjustment.

compulsive adj.
☞ 强制的,强迫的 irresistible, overwhelming, overpowering, uncontrollable, compelling, driving, urgent.

compulsory adj.
☞ 必修的,规定的 obligatory, mandatory, imperative, forced, required, requisite, set, stipulated, binding, contractual.

computer n.
☞ 计算机 personal computer, PC, mainframe, processor, world-processor, data processor, calculator, adding machine.

conceal v.
☞ 隐藏,隐蔽,隐瞒,对……保守秘密 hide, obscure, disguise, camouflage, mask, screen, veil, cloak, cover, bury, submerge, smother, suppress, keep dark, keep quiet, hush up.

concede v.
☞ 让,容许 admit, confess, acknowledge, recognize, own, grant, allow, accept.
☞ 勉强承认,让与 yield, give up, surrender, relinquish, forfeit, sacrifice.

conceited adj.
☞ 自负的,自高自大的 vain, boastful, swollen-headed, bigheaded, egotistical, self-important, cocky, self-satisfied, complacent, smug, proud, arrogant, stuck-up, toffee-nosed.

conceivable adj.
☞ 可以想象的,可以相信的 imaginable, credible, believable, thinkable, tenable, possible, likely, probable.

conceive v.
☞ 设想,构思 imagine, envisage, visualize, see, understand, comprehend, realize, appreciate, think, suppose.
☞ 想出 invent, design, devise, formulate, create, originate, form, produce, develop.

concentrate v.
☞ 集中 focus, converge, centre, cluster, crowd, congregate, gather, collect, accumulate.
☞ 专心于,注意 apply oneself, think, pay attention, attend.

concentrated adj.
☞ 浓缩的 condense, reduce, thicken, intensify.
☞ 加强的 intense, intensive, concerted, hard, deep.

concentration n.
☞ 集合 convergence, centralization, cluster, crowd, grouping, collection, accumulation, agglomeration, conglomeration.
☞ 集中,专心 attention, heed, absorption, application, single-mindedness, intensity.
☞ 浓度 reduction, consilidation, denseness, thickness.

concept n.
☞ 概念,观念 idea, notion, plan, theory, hyphothesis, thought,

abstraction, conception, conceptualization, visualization, image, picture, impression.

conception n.
☞ 计划,概念 concept, idea, notion, thought.
☞ 构思,想象 knowledge, understanding, appreciation, perception, visualization, image, picture, impression, inkling, clue.
☞ 想法,意念 invention, design, birth, beginning, origin, outset, initiation, inauguration, formation.
☞ 怀孕,受胎 impregnation, insemination, fertilization.

concern v.
☞ 使(人)关切,担心,挂念 upset, distress, trouble, disturb, bother, worry.
☞ 和……有关,牵涉到 relate to, refer to, regard, involve, interest, affect, touch.

n.
☞ 关切,担心,挂念 anxiety, worry, unease, disquiet, care, sorrow, distress.
☞ 牵连 regard, consideration, attention, heed, thought.
☞ 事务,工作 duty, responsibility, charge, job, task, field, business, affair, matter, problem, interest, involement.
☞ 营业,业务 company, firm, business, corporation, establishment, enterprise, organization.

concerned adj.
☞ 担心的,忧虑的 anxious, worried, uneasy, apprehensive, upset, unhappy, distressed, troubled, disturbed, bothered, attentive, caring.
☞ 相关的 connected, related, involved, implicated, interested, affected.

concerning prep.
☞ 关于 about, regarding, with regard to, as regards, respecting with reference to, relating to, in the matter of.

concise adj.
☞ 简明的,简练的,简要的 short, brief, terse, succinct, pithy, compendious, compact, compressed, condensed, abridged, abbreviated, summary, synoptic.

conclude v.
☞ 下结论,断定 infer, deduce, assume, surmise, suppose, reckon, judge.
☞ 结束,终结 end, close, finish, complete, consummate, cease, terminate, culminate.
☞ 决心,决定 settle, resolve, decide, establish, determine, clinch.

conclusion n.
☞ 结论 inference, deduction, assumption, opinion, conviction, judgement, verdict, decision, resolution, settlement, result.
☞ 结束,终结 end, close, finish, completion, consummation, termination, culmination, finale.

conclusive adj.
☞ 令人确信的,确定的,解除疑问的 final, ultimate, definitive, decisive, clear, convincing, definite, undeniable, irrefutable, indisputable,

incontrovertible.

concrete adj.
☞ 具体的,实物的 real, actual, factual, solid, physical, material, substantial, tangible, touchable, perceptible, visible, firm, definite, specific, explicit.

condemn v.
☞ 谴责,指责,判罪 disapprove, reprehend, reprove, upbraid, reproach, castigate, blame, disparage, revile, denounce, censure, slam, slate, damn, doom, convict.

condemnation n.
☞ 谴责,指责,定罪,宣告有罪 disapproval, reproof, reproach, castigation, blame, disparagement, denunciation, censure, thumbs-down, damnation, conviction, sentence, judgement.

condense v.
☞ 浓缩,凝缩 distil, precipitate, concentrate, evaporate, reduce, thicken, solidify, coagulate.
☞ 缩短,摘要 shorten, curtail, abbreviate, abridge, precis, summarize, encapsulate, contract, compress, compact.

condition n.
☞ 环境,情况 case, state, circumstances, position, situation, predicament, plight.
☞ 条件,情形 requirement, obligation, prerequisite, terms, stipulation, proviso, qualification, limitation, restriction, rule.
☞ 健康不良 disorder, defect, weakness, infirmity, problem, complaint, disease.

v.
☞ 限制,以……为条件 indoctrinate, brainwash, influence, mould, educate, train, groom, equip, prepare, prime, accustom, season, temper, adapt, adjust, tune.

conditional adj.
☞ 有条件的,有限制的 provisional, qualified, limited, restricted, tied, relative, dependent, contingent.

conditions n.
☞ 环境,情形 surroundings, environment, milieu, setting, atmosphere, background, context, circumstances, situation, state.

condone v.
☞ 宽恕,赦免 forgive, pardon, excuse, overlook, ignore, disregard, tolerate, brook, allow.

conduct n.
☞ 行为 behaviour, comportment, actions, ways, manners, bearing, attitude.
☞ 管理,处理 administration, management, direction, running, organization, operation, control, supervision, leadership, guidance.

v.
☞ 管理,处理 administer, manage, run, organize, orchestrate, chair, control, handle, regulate.
☞ 带领,指挥 accompany, escort, usher, lead, guide, direct, pilot, steer.
☞ 传导 convey, carry, bear, transmit.

- 举止,行为 behave, acquit, comport, act.

confer v.
- 商议,讨论 discuss, debate, deliberate, consult, talk, converse.
- 授予 bestow, award, present, give, grant, accord, impart, lend.

conference n.
- 商议,会谈,会议,讨论会 meeting, convention, congress, convocation, symposium, forum, discussion, debate, consultation.

confess v.
- 认错,承认,自首,坦白,忏悔 admit, confide, own (up), come clean, grant, concede, acknowledge, recognize, affirm, assert, profess, declare, disclose, divulge, expose.

confession n.
- 承认,供认,忏悔 admission, acknowledgement, affirmation, assertion, profession, declaration, disclosure, divulgence, revelation, unburdening.

confide v.
- 倾诉,委托,信任 confess, admit, reveal, disclose, divulge, whisper, breathe, tell, impart, unburden.

confidence n.
- 信任,心事,秘密,信心 certainty, faith, credence, trust, reliance, dependence, assurance, composure, calmness, self-possession, self-confidence, self-reliance, self-assurance, boldness, courage.

confident adj.
- 自信的,确信的 sure, certain, positive, convinced, assured, composed, self-possessed, cool, self-confident, self-reliant, self-assured, unselfconscious, bold, fearless, dauntless, unabashed.

confidential adj.
- 秘密的,亲信的 secret, top secret, classified, restricted, hush-hush, off-the-record, private, personal, intimate, privy.

confine v.
- 限制,软禁,禁闭 enclose, circumscribe, bound, limit, restrict, cramp, constrain, imprison, incarcerate, intern, cage, shut up, immure, bind, shackle, trammel, restrain, repress, inhibit.

confinement n.
- 禁闭,软禁 imprisonment, incarceration, internment, custody, detention, house arrest.
- 分娩 childbirth, birth, labour, delivery.

confines n.
- 限制,界限 limits, bounds, border, boundary, frontier, circumference, perimeter, edge.

confirm v.
- 证实,确定 endorse, back, support, reinforce, strengthen, fortify, validate, authenticate, corroborate, substantiate, verify, prove, evidence.
- 使坚定 establish, fix, settle, clinch, ratify, sanction,

approve.

confirmation n.
☞ 证实,批准 ratification, scantion, approval, assent, acceptance, agreement, endorsement, backing, support, validation, authentication, corroboration, substantiation, verification, proof, evidence, testimony.

confirmed adj.
☞ 证实的,确定的 inveterate, entrenched, dyed-in-the-wool, rooted, established, long-established, long-standing, habitual, chronic, seasoned, hardened, incorrigible, incurable.

conflict n.
☞ 斗争 difference, variance, discord, contention, disagreement, dissension, dispute, opposition, antagonism, hostility, friction, strife, unrest, confrontation.
☞ 战争,冲突 battle, war, warfare, combat, fight, contest, engagement, skirmish, set-to, fracas, brawl, quarrel, feud, encounter, clash.
v.
☞ 冲突 differ, clash, collide, disagree, contradict, oppose, contest, fight, combat, battle, war, strive, struggle, contend.

conform v.
☞ 符合,服从 agree, accord, harmonize, match, correspond, tally, square, adapt, adjust, accommodate, comply, obey, follow.

conformity n.
☞ 一致,符合 conventionality, orthodoxy, traditionalism, compliance, observance, allegiance, affinity, agreement, consonance, harmony, correspondence, harmony, correspondence, congruity, likeness, similarity, resemblance.

confound v.
☞ 使惊慌,使迷惑 confuse, bewilder, baffle, perplex, mystify, bamboozle, nonplus, surprise, amaze, astonish, astound, flabbergast, dumbfound, stupefy.
☞ 推翻 thwart, upset, defeat, overwhelm, overthrow, destroy, demolish, ruin.

confront v.
☞ 面对,面临 face, meet, encounter, accost, address, oppose, challenge, defy, brave, beard.

confrontation n.
☞ 敌对,面对 encounter, clash, collision, showdown, conflict, disagreement, fight, battle, quarrel, set-to, engagement, contest.

confuse v.
☞ 使迷惑,困惑 puzzle, baffle, perplex, mystify, confound, bewilder, disorient, disconcert, fluster, discompose, upset, embarrass, mortify.
☞ 使混淆,使混乱 muddle, mix up, mistake, jumble, disarrange, disorder, tangle, entangle, involve, mingle.

confused adj.
☞ 混同的,糊涂的 muddled,

jumbled, disarranged, disordered, untidy, disorderly, hoggledy-piggledy, nonplussed, bewildered, disorientated.

confusion n.
☞ 混乱,混淆 disorder, disarray, untidiness, mess, clutter, jumble, muddle, mix-up, disorganization, chaos, commotion, upheaval.
☞ 纷乱,杂乱 misunderstyanding, puzzlement, perplexity, mystification, bewilderment.

connect v.
☞ 连接,联系 join, link, unite, cople, combine, fasten, affix, attach, relate, associate, ally.

connected adj.
☞ 连接的,联系的 joined, linked, united, coupled, combined, related, akin, associated, affiliated, allied.

connection n.
☞ 连接,联系 junction, coupling, fastening, attachment, bond, tie, link, association, alliance, relation, relationship, literrelation, contact, communication, correlation, correspondence, relevance.

conquer v.
☞ 战胜,征服 defeat, beat, overthrow, vanquish, rout, overrun, best, worst, get the better of, overcome, surmount, win, succeed, triumph, prevail, overpower, master, crush, subdue, quell, subjugate, humble.
☞ 获得,占领 seize, take, annex, occupy, possess, acquire, obtain.

conscience n.
☞ 良心,道德心 principles, standards, morals, ethics, scruples, qualms.

conscientious adj.
☞ 有责任心的,负责的 diligent, hard-working, scrupulous, painstaking, thorough, meticulous, punctilious, particular, careful, attentive, responsible, upright, honest, faithful, dutiful.

conscious adj.
☞ 有意识的,自觉的 awake, alive, responsive, sentient, sensible, rational, reasoning, alert.
☞ 神志清醒的 aware, self-conscious, heedful, mindful, knowing, deliberate, intentional, calculated, premeditated, studied, wilful, voluntary.

consciousness n.
☞ 意识,觉悟,知觉 awareness, sentience, sensibility, knowledge, intuition, realization, recognition.

consent v.
☞ 同意,应允,答应 agree, concur, accede, assent, approve, permit, allow, grant, admit, concede, acquiesce, yield, comply.
n.
☞ 同意,应允,答应 agreement, concurrence, assent, approval, permission, go-ahead, green light, sanction, concession, acquiescence, compliance.

consequence n.
☞ 结果,后果,影响 result, outcome, issue, end, upshot, effect, side effect, repercussion.
☞ 重大,重要性 importance, significance, concern, value, weight, note, eminence, distinction.

consequent adj.
☞ 随之而来的 resultant, resulting, ensuing, subsequent, following, successive, sequential.

conservation n.
☞ 保存,保持,守恒,不变 keeping, safe-keelping, custody, saving, economy, husbandry, maintenace, upkeep, preservation, protection, safeguarding, ecology, environmentalism.

conservative adj.
☞ 保守的,守旧的,稳当的,谨慎的 tory, right-wing, hidebound, die-hard, reactionary, establishmentarian, unprogressive, conventional, traditional, moderate, middle-of-the-road, cautious, guarded, sober.
n.
☞ 保守派,保守者 tory, right-winger, die-hard, stick-in-the-mud, reactionary, traditionalist, moderate.

conserve v.
☞ 保存,保藏 keep, save, store up, hoard, maintain, preserve, protect, guard, safeguard.

consider v.
☞ 考虑,照顾 ponder, deliberate, reflect, contemplate, meditate, muse, mull over, chew over, examine, study, weigh, respect, remember, take into account.
☞ 认为,以为 regard, deem, think, believe, judge, rate, count.

considerable adj.
☞ 值得考虑的,重要的,相当大的,可观的 great, large, big, sizable, substantial, tidy, ample, plentiful, abundant, lavish, marked, noticeable, perceptible, appreciable, reasonable, tolerable, respectable, important, significant, noteworthy, distinguished, influential.

considerate adj.
☞ 体贴的,体谅的,照顾的 kind, thoughtful, caring, attentive, obliging, helpful, charitable, unselfish, altruistic, gracious, sensitive, tactful, discreet.

consideration n.
☞ 体谅,关心 thought, deliberation, reflection, contemplation, meditation, examination, analysis, scrutiny, review, attention, notice, regard.
☞ 考虑 kindness, thoughtfulness, care, attention, regard, respect.

consist of
☞ 由……组成 comprise, be composed of, contain, include, incorporate, embody, embrace, involve, amount to.

consistency n.

☞ 一致 steadiness, regularity, evenness, uniformity, sameness, identity, constancy, steadfastness.
☞ 一贯 agreement, accordance, correspondence, congruity, compatibility, harmony.

consistent adj.
☞ 一致的,始终一贯的 steady, stable, regular, uniform, unchanging, undeviating, constant, persistent, unfailing, dependable.
☞ 前后统一的 agreeing, accordant, consonant, congruous, compatible, harmonious, logical.

console v.
☞ 安慰,慰问 comfort, cheer, hearten, encourage, relieve, soothe, calm.

consolidate v.
☞ 巩固,加强,合并 reinforce, strengthen, secure, stabilize, unify, unite, join, combine, amalgamate, fuse, cement, compact, condense, thicken, harden, solidify.

conspirator n.
☞ 密谋者,阴谋者 conspirer, plotter, schemer, intriguer, traitor.

conspire v.
☞ 密谋,阴谋 plot, scheme, intrigue, manoeuvre, connive, collude, hatch, devise.

constancy n.
☞ 坚定不移,恒心 stability, steadiness, permanence, firmness, regularity, uniformity, resolution, perseverance, tenacity.
☞ 忠实 loyalty, fidelity, faithfulness, devotion.

constant adj.
☞ 不变的,经常的 continuous, unbroken, never-ending, non-stop, endless, interminable, ceaseless, incessant, eternal, everlasting, perpetual, continual, unremitting, relentless, persistent, resolute, persevering, unflagging, unwavering, changeless, immutable, invariable, unalterable, fixed, permanent, firm, even, regular, uniform.
☞ 忠心的朋友 loyal, faithful, staunch, steadfast, dependable, trustworthy, true, devoted.

constitute v.
☞ 任命,制定 represent, make up, compose, comprise, form, create, establish, set up, found.

constrain v.
☞ 强迫,强制 force, compel, oblige, necessitate, drive, impel, urge.
☞ 抑制,拘束 limit, confine, constrict, restrain, check, curb, bind.

constrained adj.
☞ 勉强的,不自然的 uneasy, embarrassed, inhibited, reticent, reserved, guarded, stiff, forced, unnatural.

constraint n.
☞ 强迫,强制 force, duress, compulsion, coercion, pressure, necessity, deterrent.
☞ 抑制,拘束 restriction, limitation, hindrace, restraint, check, curb, damper.

constrict v.
☞ 压缩,使收缩 squeeze, compress, pinch, cramp, narrow, tighten, contract, shrink, choke, stangle, inhibit, limit, restrict.

construct v.
☞ 建筑,建造 build, erect, raise, elevate, make, manufacture, fabricate, assemble, put together, compose, form, shape, fashion, model, design, engineer, create, found, establish, formulate.

construction n.
☞ 建筑,建设 building, edifice, erection, structure, fabric, form, shape, figure, model, manufacture, fabrication, assembly, composition, constituion, formation, creation.

constructive adj.
☞ 建设性的,积极的 practical, productive, positive, helpful, useful, valuable, beneficial, advantageous.

consultant n.
☞ 顾问 adviser, expert, authority, specialist.

consume v.
☞ 食,饮 eat, drink, swallow, devour, gobble.
☞ 消费,耗尽 use, absorb, spend, expend, deplete, drain, exhaust, use up, dissipate, squander, waste.
☞ 毁灭 destroy, demolish, annihilate, devastate, ravage.

consumer n.
☞ 消费者,用户 user, end-user, customer, buyer, purchaser, shopper.

consumption n.
☞ 消费,消耗 use, utilization, spending, expenditure, depletion, exhaustion, waste.

contact n.
☞ 接触,联系 touch, impact, juxtaposition, contiguity, communication, meeting, junction, union, connection, association.
v.
☞ 接触,联系 approach, apply to, reach, get hold of, get in touch with, telephone, phone, ring, call, notify.

contain v.
☞ 含括,容纳 include, comprise, incorporate, embody, involve, embrace, enclose, hold, accommodate, seat.
☞ 限制,控制 repress, stifle, restrain, control, check, curb, limit.

container n.
☞ 容器 receptable, vessel, holder.

contemplate v.
☞ 凝视,沉思 meditate, reflect on, ponder, mull over, deliberate, consider, regard, view, survey, observe, study, examine, inspect, scrutinize.
☞ 打算,计划 expect, foresee, envisage, plan, design, propose, intend, mean.

contemporary adj.
☞ 当代的 modern, current, present, present-day, recent, latest, up-to-date, fashionable,

up-to-the-minute, ultra-modern.
- ☞ 同时代的 contemporaneous, coexistent, concurrent, synchronous, simultaneous.

contempt n.
- ☞ 轻蔑,蔑视 scorn, disdain, condescension, derision, ridicule, mockery, disrespect, dishonour, disregard, neglect, dislike, loathing, detestation.

contemptible adj.
- ☞ 可鄙的 despicable, shameful, ignominious, low, mean, vile, detestable, loathsome, abject, wretched, pitiful, paltry, worthless.

contemptuous adj.
- ☞ 显示轻蔑的 scornful, disrespectful, insolent.

contend v.
- ☞ 主张,断言 maintain, hold, argue, allege, assert, declare, affirm.
- ☞ 竞争,奋斗 compete, vie, contest, dispute, clash, wrestle, grapple, struggle, strive, cope.

content v.
- ☞ 满意,满足 satisfy, humour, indulge, gratify, please, delight, appease, pacify, placate.

n.
- ☞ 内容,要义 substance, matter, essence, gist, meaning, significance, text, subject matter, ideas, contents, load, burden.
- ☞ 容积,容量 capacity, volume, size, measure.

adj.
- ☞ 满足的,满意的 satisfied, fulfilled, contented, untroubled, pleased, happy, willing.

contented adj.
- ☞ 满意的,满足的 happy, glad, pleased, cheerful, comfortable, relaxed, content, satisfied.

contents n.
- ☞ 内容 chapters, divisions, subjects, topics, themes.

contest n.
- ☞ 竞争,竞赛,论争 competition, game, match, tournament, encounter, fight, battle, set-to, combat, conflict, struggle, dispute, debate, controversy.

v.
- ☞ 争辩,争论 dispute, debate, question, doubt, challenge, oppose, argue against, litigate, deny, refute.
- ☞ 争夺,斗争 compete, vie, contend, strive, fight.

context n.
- ☞ 上下文,前后关系 setting, background, surroundings, framework, frame of reference, situation, position, circumstances, conditions.

continual adj.
- ☞ 连续的,再三的 constant, perpetual, incessant, interminable, eternal, everlasting, regular, frequent, recurrent, repeated.

continue v.
- ☞ 继续,连续 resume, go on, recommence, carry on, proceed, persevere, stick at, persist, last, endure, survive, remain, abide, stay, rest, pursue, sustain, maintain, lengthen, prolong, extend, project.

continuous adj.

☞ 连绵不断的 unbroken, uninterrupted, consecutive, non-stop, endless, ceaseless, unending, unceasing, constant, unremitting, prolonged, extended, continued, lasting.

contract v.
☞ 签合同，契约 shrink, lessen, diminish, reduce, shorten, curtail, abbreviate, abridge, condense, compress, constrict, narrow, tighten, tense, shrivel, wrinkle.
☞ 承担，承包 pledge, promise, undertake, agree, stipulate, arrange, negotiate, bargain.
n.
☞ 合同，契约 bond, deal, commitment, engagement, covenant, treaty, convention, pact, compact, agreement, transaction, bargain, settlement, arrangement, understanding.

contradict v.
☞ 反驳，驳斥 deny, disaffirm, confute, challenge, oppose, impugn, dispute, counter, negate, gainsay.

contradictory adj.
☞ 互相矛盾的 contrary, opposite, paradoxical, conflicting, discrepant, inconsistent, incompatible, antagonistic, irreconcilable, opposed, repugnant.

contrary adj.
☞ 相反的，相矛盾的 opposite, counter, reverse, conflicting, antagonistic, opposed, adverse, hostile.
☞ 不利的 perverse, awkward, obstinate, intractable, cantankerous, stroppy.
n.
☞ 反面 opposite, converse, reverse.

contrast n.
☞ 对照，对比，形成对比，相对立 difference, dissimilarity, disparity, divergence, distinction, differentiation, comparison, foil, antithesis, opposition.
v.
☞ 对照，对比，相对立 compare, differentiate, distinguish, discriminate, differ, oppose, clash, conflict.

contribute v.
☞ 捐助，贡献 donate, subscribe, chip in, add, give, bestow, provide, supply, furnish, help, lead, conduce.

contribution n.
☞ 捐献，捐款，贡献，投稿 donation, subscription, gift, gratuity, handout, grant, offering, input, addition.

contributor n.
☞ 捐助者，贡献者 donor, subscriber, giver, patron, benefactor, sponsor, backer, supporter.
☞ 投稿者 writer, journalist, reporter, correspondent, freelance.

control v.
☞ 管理，控制，支配 lead, govern, rule, command, direct, manage, oversee, supervise, superintend, run, operate.
☞ 调节 regulate, adjust, monitor, verify.
☞ 抑制 restrain, check, curb,

subdue, repress, hold back, contain.

n.
- 支配,控制 power, charge, authority, command, mastery, government, rule, direction, management, oversight, supervision, superintendence, discipline, guidance.
- 监督,抑制 restraint, check, curb, repression.
- 操作装置 instrument, dial, switch, button, knob, lever.

controversial adj.
- 引起争论的 contentious, polemical, disputed, doubtful, questionable, debatable, disputable.

controversy n.
- 论争,辩论,论战 debate, discussion, war of words, polemic, dispute, disagreement, argument, quarrel, squabble, wrangle, strife, contention, dissension.

convenience n.
- 便利,方便 accessibility, availability, handiness, usefulness, use, utility, serviceability, service, benefit, advatage, help, suitability, fitness.
- 方便条件 facility, amenity, appliance.

convenient adj.
- 便利的,方便 nearby, at hand, accessible, available, handy, useful, commodious, beneficial, helpful, labour-saving, adapted, fitted, suited, suitable, fit, appropriate, opportune, timely, well-timed.

convention n.
- 协定,公约,习俗,惯例,传统作风 custom, tradition, practice, usage, protocol, etiquette, formality, matter of form, code.
- 大会,会议 assembly, congress, conference, meeting, council, delegates, representatives.

conventional adj.
- 惯例的,传统的,规范的 traditional, orthodox, formal, correct, proper, prevalent, prevailing, accepted, received, expected, unoriginal, ritual, routine, usual, customary, regular, standard, normal, ordinary, straight, stereotyped, hidebound, pedestrian, commonplace, common, run-of-the-mill.

conversation n.
- 会话,会谈 talk, chat, gossip, discussion, discourse, dialogue, exchange, communication.

convey v.
- 搬运,传达 carry, bear, bring, fetch, move, transport, send, forward, deliver, transfer, conduct, guide, transmit, communicate, impart, tell, relate, reveal.

convince v.
- 使确信,使信服 assure, persuade, sway, win over, bring round, reassure, satisfy.

convincing adj.
- 使人信服的,有说服力的 persuasive, cogent, powerful, telling, impressive, credible,

cool adj.
- 凉,凉爽 chilly, fresh, breezy, nippy, cold, chilled, iced, refreshing.
- 冷静的,镇定的 calm, unruffled, unexcited, composed, self-possessed, level-headed, unemotional, quiet, relaxed, laid-back.
- 冷淡的,冷漠的 unfriendly, unwelcoming, cold, frigid, lukewarm, half-hearted, unenthusiastic, apathetic, uninterested, unresponsive, uncommunicative, reserved, distant, aloof, standoffish.

v.
- (使)凉 chill, refrigerate, ice, freeze, fan.
- (使)镇定,(使)冷静 moderate, lessen, temper, dampen, quiet, abate, calm, allay, assuage.

n.
- 凉,冷 coolness, calmness, collectedness, composure, poise, self-possession, self-discipline, self-control, control, temper.

co-operate v.
- 互助合作,协作 collaborate, work together, play ball, help, assist, aid, contribute, participate, combine, unite, conspire.

co-operative adj.
- 互助的 helpful, supportive, obliging, accommodating, willing.
- 合作的,合作化的 collective, joint, shared, combined, united, concerted, co-ordinated.

co-ordinate v.
- 调整,协调,配合 organize, arrange, systematize, tabulate, integrate, mesh, synchronize, harmonize, match, correlate, regulate.

cope v.
- (善于)应付,(善于)处理 manage, carry on, survive, get by, make do.

cope with
- 处理,应付 deal with, encounter, contend with, struggle with, grapple with, wrestle with, handle, manage, weather.

copy n.
- 抄本,复制品,拷贝 duplicate, carbon copy, photocopy, Photostat^R, Xerox^R, facsimile, reproduction, print, tracing, transcript, transcription, replica, model, pattern, archetype, representation, image, likeness, counterfeit, forgery, fake, imitation, borrowing, plagiarism, crib.

v.
- 抄,临摹,摹仿 duplicate, photocopy, reproduce, print, trace, transcribe, forge, counterfeit, simulate, imitate, impersonate, mimic, ape, parrot, repeat, echo, mirror, follor, emulate, borrow, plagiarize, crib.

core n.
- 果心,核心 kernel, nucleus, heart, centre, middle, nub, crux, essence, gist, nitty-gritty.

corner n.
- 角 angle, joint, crook, bend, turning.
- 偏僻处, 角落 nook, cranny, niche, recess, cavity, hole, hideout, hide-away, retreat.

corporation n.
- 团体, 社团, 公司 council, authorities, association, society, organization, company, firm, combine, conglomerate.

correct v.
- 改正, 修改 rectify, put right, right, emend, remedy, cure, debug, redness, adjust, regulate, improve, amend.
- 训戒 punish, discipline, reprimand, reprove, reform.

adj.
- 正确的 right, accurate, precise, exact, strict, true, truthful, word-perfect, faultless, flawless.
- 恰当的 proper, acceptable, ok, standard, regular, just, appropriate, fitting.

correction n.
- 改正, 修改, 修正 rectification, emendation, adjustment, alteration, modification, amendment, improvement.

correspond v.
- 符合, 相应 match, fit, answer, conform, tally, square, agree, concru, coincide, correlate, accord, harmonize, dovetail, complement.
- 通信 communicate, write.

correspondence n.
- 通信, 信件 communication, writing, letters, post, mail.
- 符合, 协调, 相应, 相当 conformity, agreement, concurrence, coincidence, correlation, relation, analogy, comparison, comparability, similarity, resemblance, congruity, equivalence, harmony, match.

correspondent n.
- 通讯员, 记者, 通信者 journalist, reporter, contributor, writer.

corresponding adj.
- 相应的 matching, complementary, reciprocal, interrelated, analogous, equivalent, similar, identical.

corridor n.
- 走廊 aisle, passageway, passage, hallway, hall, lobby.

corrode v.
- 腐蚀, 侵蚀 erode, wear away, eat away, consume, waste, rust, oxibize, tarnish, impair, deteriorate, crumble, disintegrate.

corrosive adj.
- 腐蚀的, 侵蚀的 corroding, acid, caustic, cutting, abrasive, erosive, wearing, consuming, wasting.

corrupt adj.
- 腐化的, 腐败的, 不纯洁的 rotten, unscrupulous, unprincipled, unethical, immoral, fraudulent, shady, dishonest, bent, crooked, untrustworthy, depraved, degenerate, dissolute.

v.
- 腐蚀 contaminate, pollute,

adulterate, taint, defile, debase, pervert, deprave, lead, astray, lure, bribe, suborn.

corruption n.
☞ 腐化,腐败 unscrupulousness, immorality, impurity, depravity, degeneration, degradation, perversion, distortion, dishonesty, crookedness, fraud, shadiness, bribery, extortion, vice, wickedness, iniquity, evil.

cost n.
☞ 成本,价钱 expense, outlay, payment, disbursement, expenditure, charge, price, rate, amount, figure, worth.
☞ 代价,牺牲 detriment, harm, injury, hurt, loss, deprivation, sacrifice, penalty, price.

costume n.
☞ 服装,女装 outfit, uniform, livery, robes, vestment, dress, clothing, get-up, fancy, dress.

cosy adj.
☞ 适意的,温暖的 snug, comfortable, comfy, warm, sheltered, secure, homely, intimate.

couch n.
☞ 床,睡椅,沙发 sofa, settee, chesterfield, chaise-longue, ottoman, divan, bed.

council n.
☞ 理事会,委员会 committee, panel, board, cabinet, ministry, parliament, congress, assembly, convention, conference.

counsel n.
☞ 建议,忠告 advice, suggestion, recommendation, guidance, direction, information, consultation, deliberation, consideration, forethought.
☞ 律师 lawyer, advocate, solicitor, attorney, barrister.
v.
☞ 劝告,建议 advise, warn, caution, suggest, recommend, advocate, urge, exhort, guide, direct, instruct.

count v.
☞ 数,计算 number, enumerate, list, include, reckon, calculate, compute, tell, check, add, total, tot up, score.
☞ matter, signify, qualify.
n.
☞ 计数,计算 numbering, enumeration, poll, reckoning, caculation, computation, sum, total, tally.

count on
☞ 依靠 depend on, rely on, bank on, reckon on, expect, believe, trust.

counter adv.
☞ 相反地 against, in opposition, conversely.
adj.
☞ 相反的,反对的 contrary, opposite, opposing, conflicting, contradictory, contrasting, opposed, against, adverse.
v.
☞ 反击,还击 parry, resist, offset, answer, respond, retaliate, retort, return, meet.

counteract v.
☞ 抵消,抵抗 neutralize, counterbalance, offset, countervail, act against, oppose,

counterfeit v.
☞ 伪造,假冒 fake, forge, fabricate, copy, imitate, impersonate, pretend, feign, simulate, sham.
adj.
☞ 伪造的,假冒的 fake, false, phoney, forged, copied, fraudulent, bogus, pseudo, sham, spurious, imitation, artificial, simulated, feigned, pretended.
n.
☞ 伪造品,假冒品 fake, forgery, copy, reproduction, imitation, fraud, sham.

counterpart n.
☞ 对方,配对物 equivalent, opposite number, complement, supplement, match, fellow, mate, twin, duplicate, copy.

countless adj.
☞ 无数的,数不尽的 innumerable, myriad, numberless, unnumbered, untold, incalculable, infinite, endless, immeasurable, measureless, limitless.

country n.
☞ 国家 state, nation, people, kingdom, realm, principality.
☞ 乡村,乡间 countryside, green belt, farmland, provinces, sticks, backwoods, wilds.
☞ 地方,地域 terrain, land, territory, region, area, district.
adj.
☞ 乡间的,乡下的 rural, provincial, agrarian, agricultural, pastoral, rustic, bucolic, landed.

countryside n.
☞ 乡间,农村 landscape, scenery, country, green belt, farmland, outdorrs.

county n.
☞ 郡,县 shire, province, region, area, district.

couple n.
☞ 一对,一双,配偶,夫妇 pair, brace, twosome, duo.
v.
☞ 结婚,连接 pair, match, parry, wed, unite, join, link, connect, fasten, hitch, clasp, buckle, yoke.

coupon n.
☞ 息票,券,配给 voucher, token, slip, check, ticket, certificate.

courage n.
☞ 勇气,勇敢 bravery, pluck, guts, fearlessness, dauntlessness, heroism, gallantry, valour, boldness, audacity, nerve, daring, resolution, fortitude, spirit, mettle.

courageous adj.
☞ 勇敢的,有胆量的 brave, plucky, fearless, dauntless, indomitable, heroic, gallant, valiant, lion-heated, hardy, bold, audacious, daring, intrepid, resolute.

course n.
☞ 课程,科目 curriculum, syllabus, classes, lessons, lectures, studies.
☞ 前进,连续 flow, movement,

advance, progress, development, furtherance, order, sequence, series, succession, progression.
☞ 过程 duration, time, period, term, passage.
☞ 方向,路线 direction, way, path, track, road, route, channel, trail, line, circuit, orbit, trajectory, flight path.
☞ 方针 plan, schedule, programme, policy, procedure, method, mode.

court *n.*
☞ 法庭,法院 law-court, bench, bar, tribunal, trial, session.
☞ 场地,庭院 courtyard, yard, quadrangle, square, cloister, forecourt, enclosure.

courteous *adj.*
☞ 有礼貌的,谦恭的 polite, civil, respectful, well-mannered, well-bred, ladylike, gentlemanly, gracious, obliging, considerate, attentive, gallant, courtly, unrban, debonair, refined, polished.

courtesy *n.*
☞ 礼貌,好意 politeness, civility, respect, manners, breeding, graciousness, consideration, attention, gallantry, urbanity.

courtyard *n.*
☞ 院子 yard, quadrangle, quad , area enclosure, court.

cove *n.*
☞ 小海湾 bay, bight, inlet, estuary, firth, fiord, creek.

cover *v.*
☞ 盖,覆,遮 hide, conceal, obscure, shroud, veil, screen, mask, disguise, camouflage.
☞ 涵盖,包容 deal with, treat, consider, examine, investigate, encompass, embrace, incorporate, embody, involve, include, contain, comprise.
n.
☞ 盖子,套子 coating, covering, top, lid, cup, veil, screen, mask, front, facade, jacket, wrapper, case, envelope, clothing, dress, bedspread, canopy.
☞ 遮盖物 shelter, refuge, protection, shield, guard, defence, concealment, disguise, camouflage.

cover up
☞ 包裹,隐藏 conceal, hide, whitewash, dissemble, suppress, hush up, keep, dark, repress.

covering *n.*
☞ 遮盖 layer, coat, coating, blanket, film, veneer, skin, crust, shell, casing, housing, wrapping, clothing, protection, mask, overlay, cover, top, shelter, roof.

covet *v.*
☞ 垂涎,贪图 envy, begrudge, crave, long for, yearn for, hanker for, want, desire, fancy , lust after.

coward *n.*
☞ 懦夫 craven, faint-heart, chicken , scaredy-cat, yellow-belly, wimp , renegade, deserter.

cowardice *n.*
☞ 胆小,懦弱 cowardliness,

faint-heartedness, timorousness, spinelessness.

cowardly *adj.*
☞ 胆小的,懦弱的 faint-hearted, craven, fearful, timorous, scared, unheroic, chicken-hearted, chicken-livered, chicken, spineless, weak, weak-kneed, soft.

crack *v.*
☞ 裂开,断裂 split, burst, fracture, break, snap, shatter, splinter, chip.
☞ 发出破裂声 explode, burst, pop, crackle, snap, crash, clap, slap, whack.
☞ 解决 decipher, work out, solve.
n.
☞ 破裂 break, fracture, split, rift, gap, crevice, fissure, chink, line, flaw, chip.
☞ 劈啪声 explosion, burst, pop, snap, crash, clap, blow, smack, slap, whack.
☞ 俏皮话,讽刺 joke, quip, witticism, gag, wisecrack, gibe, dig.
adj.
☞ 第一流的,高明的 first-class, first-rate, top-notch, excellent, superior, choice, hand-picked.

crack down on
☞ 处罚 clamp down on, end, stop, put a stop to, crush, suppress, check, repress, act, against.

crack up
☞ 撞坏,撞毁 go mad, go to pieces, break down, collapse.

cradle *n.*
☞ 摇篮 cot, crib, bed.
☞ 发源地,支船架 source, origin, spring, wellspring, fount, fountain-head, birthplace, beginning.
v.
☞ 轻抱 hold, support, rock, lull, nurse, nurture, tend.

craft *n.*
☞ 工艺,手艺 skill, expertise, mastery, talent, knack, ability, aptitude, dexterity, cleverness, art, handicraft, handiwork.
☞ 职业,工作 trade, business, calling, vocation, job, occupation, work, employment.
☞ 船,飞机 vessel, boat, ship, aircraft, spacecraft, spaceship.

craftsman, craftswoman *n.*
☞ 工匠,技工 artisan, technician, master, maker, wright, smith.

craftsmanship *n.*
☞ 技术,手艺 artistry, workmanship, technique, dexterity, expertse, mastery.

crafty *adj.*
☞ 狡猾的,狡诈的 sly, cunning, artful, wily, devious, subtle, scheming, calculating, designing, deceitful, fraudulent, sharp, shrewd, astuete, canny.

crash *n.*
☞ 撞击,撞坏 accident, collision, bump, smash, pile-up, smash-up, wreck.
☞ 坠落声,破裂声 BANG, clash, clatter, clang, thud, thump, boom, thunder, racket, din.
☞ 崩溃,破产,垮台 collapse, failure, ruin, downfall,

bankruptcy, depression.
v.
☞ 碰撞 collide, hit, knock, bump, bang.
☞ 砸碎,撞碎 break, fracture, smash, dash, shatter, splinter, shiver, fragment, disintegrate.
☞ 倒塌,毁掉 fall, topple, pitch, plunge, collapse, fail, fold(up), go under, go bust.

crave v.
☞ 恳求,渴求 hunger for, thirst, for, long for, yearn for, pine for, hanker, after, fancy, desire, want, need, require.

craving n.
☞ 渴望 appetite, hunger, thirst, longing, yearning, hankering, lust, desire, urge.

craze n.
☞ 狂热 fad, novelty, fashion, vogue, node, trend, rage, thing, obsession, preoccupation, mania, frenzy, passion, infatuation, enthusiasm.

crazy adj.
☞ 疯狂的,不要命的 mad, insane, lunatic, unbalanced, deranged, demented, crazed, potty, barmy, daft, silly, foolish, idiotic, senseless, unwise, imprudent, nonsensical, absurd, ludicrous, ridiculous, preposterous, outageous, half-baked, impracticable, irresponsible, wild, berserk.
☞ 狂热的,着迷的 enthusiastic, fanatical, zealous, ardent, passionate, infatuated, enamoured, smitten, mad, wild.

cream n.
☞ 奶油制品 paste, emulsion, oil, lotion, ointment, salve, cosmetic.
☞ 精华 best, pick, elite, prime.

creamy adj.
☞ 油腻的 cream-coloured, creamy, off-white, yellowish-white.
☞ 含奶油的 milky, buttery, oily, smooth, velvety, rich, thick.

crease v.
☞ 起折痕,弄皱 fold, pleat, wrinkle, pucker, crumple, rumple, crinkle, crimp, corrugage, ridge.
n.
☞ 折缝,折痕 fold, line, pleat, tuck, wrinkle, pucker, ruck, crinkle, corrugation, ridge, groove.

create v.
☞ 创造,创作 invent, coin, formulate, compose, design, devise, concoct, hatch, originate, initiate, found, establish, set up.

creation n.
☞ 创造,作品 making, formation, constitution, invention, concoction, origination, voundation, establishment, institution, production, generation, procreation, conception, birth.
☞ 成就,产物 invention, brainchild, concept, product, handiwork, chef, d'oeuvre, achievement.

creative adj.

☞ 有创造力的 artistic inventive, original, imaginative, inspited, visionary, talented, gifted, clever, ingenious, resourceful, fertile, productive.

creator n.
☞ 创造(作)者 maker, inventor, designer, architect, author, originator, initiator.

creature n.
☞ 生物 animal, beast, bird, fish, organism, being, mortal, individual, person, man, woman, body, soul.

credibility n.
☞ 可信性 integrity, reliability, trustworthiness, plausibility, probablity.

credible adj.
☞ 可信的,可靠的 believable, imaginable, conceivable, thinkable, tenable, plausible, likely, probable, possible, resonable, persuasive, convincing, sincere, honest, trustworthy, reliably, dependable.

credit n.
☞ 相信,信用 acknowledgement, recognition, thanks, approval, commendation, praise, acclaim, tribute, glory, fame, prestige, distinction, honour, reputation, esteem, estimation.
v.
☞ 相信,信任 believe, swallow, accept, subscribe, to, trust, rely on.

creditable adj.
☞ 值得表扬的 honourable, reputable, respectable, estimable, admirable, commendable, praiseworhy, good, excellent, exemplary, worthy, deserving.

credulous adj.
☞ 轻信 naive, gullible, wideeyed, trusting, unsuspecting, uncritical.

creep v.
☞ 爬,匍匐,蹑手蹑脚,蔓延 inch, edge, tiptoe, steal, sneak, slink, crawl, slither, worm, wriggle, squirm, grovel, writhe.

creepy adj.
☞ 悚然的 eerie, spooky, sinister, threatening, frightening, scary, terrifying, hair-raising, nightmarish, macabre, gruesome, horrible, unpleasant, disturbing.

crest n.
☞ 顶,上部 ridge, crown, top, peak, summit, pinnacle, apex, head.
☞ 冠毛 tuft, tassel, plume, comb, mane.
☞ 饰物 insignia, device, symbol, emblem, badge.

crew n.
☞ 全体工作人员,全体船员 team, party, squad, troop, corps, company, gang, band, bunch, crowd, mob, set, lot.

crime n.
☞ 罪(行),愚蠢行为 law-breaking, lawlessness, delinquency, offence, felony, misdemeanour, misdeed, wrongdoing, misconduct, transgression, violation, sin,

iniquity, vice, villainy, wickedness, atrocity, outrage.

criminal n.
☞ 犯罪,犯罪分子 law-beaker, crook, felon, delinquent, offender, wrongdoer, miscreant, culprit, convict, prisoner.
adj.
☞ 犯罪的,犯法的 illegal, unlawful, illicit, lawless, wrong, culpable, indictable, crooked, bent, dishonest, corrupt, wcked, scandalous, deplorable.

cripple v.
☞ 使跛,损伤 lame, paralyse, disable, handicap, injure, maim, mutilate, damage, impair, spoil, ruin, destroy, sabotage, incapacitate, weaken, debilitate.

crippled adj.
☞ 跛的 lame, paralysed, disabled, handicapped, incapacitated.

crisis n.
☞ 危机,紧急关头 emergency, extremity, crunch, catastrophe, disaster, calamity, dilemma, quandary, predicament, difficulty, trouble, problem.

crisp adj.
☞ 脆的 crispy, crunchy, brittle, crumbly, firm, hard.
☞ 清新的,明快的 bracing, invigorating, refreshing, fresh, brisk.
☞ 卷缩的 terse, pithy, snappy, brief, short, clear, incisive.

criterion n.
☞ 准绳,标准 standard, norm, touchstone, benchmark, yardstick, measure, gauge, rule, principle, canon, test.

critic n.
☞ 批评家,评论家 reviewer, commentator, analyst, pundit, authority, expert, judge, censor, caper, fault-finder, attacker, knocker.

critical adj.
☞ 关键的,危急的 crucial, vital, essential, all-important, momentous, decisive, urgent, pressing, serious, grave, dangerous, perilous.
☞ 评析的 analytical, diagnostic, penetrating, probing, discerning, perceptive.
☞ 吹毛求疵的 uncomplimentary, derogatory, disparaging, disapproving, censorious, carping, fault-finding, cavilling, nit-picking.

criticism n.
☞ 批评 condemnation, disapproval, disparagement, fault-finding, censure, blame, brickbat, flak.
☞ 评判 review, critique, assessment, evaluation, appraisal, judgement, analysis, commentary, appreciation.

criticize v.
☞ 批评,评论 condemn, slate, slan, knock, disparage, carp, find, fault, censure, blame.
☞ 评判 review, assess, evaluate, appraise, judge, analyse.

crook n.
☞ 骗子 criminal, thief, robber, swindler, cheat, shark, rogue,

villain.

crooked adj.
- ☞ 弯曲的 askew, skew-shiff, awry, lopsided, asymmetric, irregular, uneven, off-centre, tilted, slanting, bent, angled, hooked, curved, bowed.
- ☞ 拐骗的,不老实的 illegal, unlawful, illicit, criminal, nefarious, dishonest, deceitful, bent, corrupt, fraudulent, shady, shifty, underhand, treacherous, unscrupulous, unprincipled, unethical.

crop n.
- ☞ 收成,作物 growth, yield, produce, fruits, harvest, vintage, gathering.

v.
- ☞ 啃去,剪短,收获 cut, snip, clip, shear, trim, pare, prune, lop, shorten, curtail.

crop up
- ☞ 突然发生 arise, emerge, appear, arrive, occur, happen.

cross adj.
- ☞ 乖戾的,坏脾气的 irritable, annoyed, angry, vexed, shirty, bad-tempered, ill-tempered, crotchety, grumpy, grouchy, irascible, crabby, short, snappy, snappish, surly, sullen, fractious, fretful, impatient.
- ☞ 横穿过的,交叉的,相反的 transverse, crosswise, oblique, diagonal, intersecting, opposite, reciprocal.

v.
- ☞ 穿过 go across, traverse, ford, bridge, span.
- ☞ 使交叉 intersect, meet, crisscross, lace, intertwine.
- ☞ 混合 crossbreed, interbreed, mongrelize, hybridize, cross-fertilize, cross-pollinate, blend, mix.
- ☞ 反对,阻碍 thwart, frustrate, foil, hinder, impede, obstruct, block, oppose.

n.
- ☞ 痛苦,苦难 burden, load, affliction, misfortune, trouble, worry, trial, trilulation, grief, misery, woe.
- ☞ 混合 crossbreed, hybrid, mongrel, blend, misture, amalgam, combination.

crowd n.
- ☞ 人群,群众 throng, multitude, host, mob, masses, populace, people, public, riff-raff, rabble, horde, swarm, flock, herd, pack, presss, crush, squash, assembly, company, group, bunch, lot, set, circle, clique.
- ☞ 一堆,一伙人,一帮 spectators, gate, attendance, auaence.

v.
- ☞ 群集,围扰,拥挤,挤满 gather, congregate, muster, huddle, mass, throng, swarm, flock, surge, stream, push, shove, elbow, jostle, press, squeeze, bundle, pile, pack, congest, cram, compress.

croded adj.
- ☞ 充满了的,挤满了的 full, filled, packed, jammed, jam-packed, congested, cramped, overcrowded, overpopulated, busy, teeming, swarming, overflowing.

crown n.
- 王冠 coronet, diadem, tiara, circlet, wreath, garland.
- 花冠,荣誉 prize, trophy, reward, honour, laurels.
- 王权,君权 sovereign, monarch, king, queen, ruler, sovereignty, monarchy, royalty.
- 顶峰,顶点 top, tip, apex, crext, summit, pinnacle, peak, acme.

v.
- 加冕,加冠于 enthrone, anoint, adorn, festoon, honour, dignify, reward.
- 顶上有 top, cap, complete, fulfil.

crucial adj.
- 决定性的,紧要关头的,严酷的 urgent, pressing, vital, essential, key, pivotal, central, important, momentous, decisive, critical, trying, testing, searching.

crude adj.
- 天然的 raw, unprocessed, unrefined, rough, unfinished, unpolished, natural, primitive.
- 粗鲁的 vulgar, coarse, rude, indecent, obscene, gross, dirty, lewd.

cruel adj.
- 残忍的,痛苦的 fierce, ferocious, vicious, savage, barbarous, bloodthirsty, murderous, cold-blooded, sadistic, brutal, inhuman, inhumane, unkind, malevolent, spiteful, callous, heartless, unfeeling, merciless, pitiless, flinty, hard-hearted, stony-hearted, implacable, ruthless, remorseless, relentless, unrelenting, inexorable, grim, hellish, atrocious, bitter, harsh, severe, cutting, painful, excruciating.

cruelty n.
- 残忍,残酷,残酷行为 ferocity, viciousness, savagery, barbarity, bloodthirstiness, murderousness, violence, sadism, brutality, bestiality, inhumanity, spite, venom, callousness, heartlessness, hard-heartedness, mercilessness, ruthlessness, tyranny, harshness, severity.

crumple v.
- 弄皱,压皱,变皱 crush, wrinkle, pucker, crinkle, rumple, crease, fold, collapse.

crusade n.
- 奋斗,运动 campaign, drive, push, movement, cause, undertaking, expedition, holy war, jihad.

crush v.
- 压榨,压碎 squash, compress, squeeze, press, pulp, break, smash, pound, pulverize, grind, crumble, crumple, wrinkle.
- 征服,压倒 conquer, vanquish, demolish, devastate, overpower, overwhelm, overcome, qussh, quell, subdue, put, down, humiliate, shame, abash.

cry v.
- 哭,哭泣 weep, sob, blubber, wail, bwal, whimper, snivel.
- 叫喊 shout, call, exclaim, roar, bellow, yell, scream, shriek, screech.

n.
- 哭，哭声 weep, sob, blubber, wail, bawl, whimper, snivel.
- 叫喊，喊声 shout, call, plea, exclamation, roar, bellow, yell, scream, shriek.

cuddle v.
- 拥抱 hug, embrace, nestle, clasp, hold, nurse, nestle, snuggle, pet, fondle, caress.

cue n.
- 暗示，提示 signal, sign, nod, hint, suggestion, reminder, prompt, incentive, stimulus.

cult n.
- 礼拜，崇拜者，宗派 sect, denomination, school, movement, party, faction.
- 时尚 craze, fad, fashion, vogue, trend.

cultivate v.
- 耕种，种植 farm, till, work, plough, grow, sow, plant, tend, harvest,
- 培养 foster, nurture, cherish, help, aid, support, encourage, promote, further, work on, develop, train, prepare, polish, refine, improve, enrich.

cultural adj.
- 文化的 artistic, aesthetic, liberal, civilizing, humanizing, enlightening, educational, edifying, improving, enriching, elevating.

culture n.
- 文化，文明 civilization, society, lifestyle, way of life, customs, mores, the arts.
- 培育，培植 cultivation, taste, education, enlightenment, breeding, gentility, refinement, politeness, urbanity.

cumbersome adj.
- 笨重的 awkward, inconvenient, bulky, unwieldy, unmanageable, burdensome, onerous, heavy, weight.

cunning adj.
- 巧妙的，熟练的，狡猾的，诡诈的 crafty, sly, artful, wily, tricky, devious, subtle, deceitful, guileful, sharp, shrewd, astute, canny, knowing, deep, imaginative, ingenious, skilful, deft, dexterous.

n.
- 狡猾，诡诈 craftiness, slyness, artfulness, trickery, deviousness, subtlety, deceitfulness, guile, sharpness, shrewdness, astuteness, ingenuity, cleverness, adroitness.

cup n.
- 杯子 mug, tankard, beaker, goblet, chalice, trophy.

cupboard n.
- 衣柜 cabinet, locker, closet, wardrobe.

curb v.
- 控制，抑制 restrain, constrain, restrict, contain, control, check, moderate, bridle, muzzle, suppress, subdue, repress, inhibit, hinder, impede, hamper, retard.

cure v.
- 治疗，治愈 heal, remedy, correct, restore, repair, mend,

relieve, ease, alleviate, help.
☞ (用爆晒,熏腌等方法)加工保存(食物,兽皮,烟草等) preserve, dry, smoke, salt, pickle, kipper.
n.
☞ 药剂,疗法 remedy, antidote, panacea, medicine, specific, corrective, restorative, healing, treatment, therapy, alleviation, recovery.

curiosity n.
☞ 好奇 inquisitiveness, nosiness, prying, snooping, interest.
☞ 珍品,新奇的事物 curio, objett, d'art, antique, bygone, novelty, trinket, knick-knacek, rarity, freak, spectacle.

cruious adj.
☞ 好奇的,好管闲事的 inquisitive, nose, prying, meddlesome, questioning, inquiring, interested.
☞ 奇怪的,不正常的 odd, queer, funny, strange, peculiar, bizarre, mysterious, puzzling, extraaordinary, unusual, rate, unique, novel, exotic, unconventional, unorthodox, quaint.

curl v.
☞ 卷曲,弯曲 crimp, frizz, wave, ripple, bend, curve, meander, loop, turn, twistle, wind, wreathe, twine, coil, spiral, corkscrew, scroll.
n.
☞ 弯曲,卷曲 wave, kink, swirl, twist, ringlet, coil, spiral, whorl.

curly adj.
☞ 卷曲的 wavy, kinky, curling, spiralled, corkscrew, curled, crimped, permed, frizzy, fuzzy.

currency n.
☞ 货币,通货 money, legal, tender, coinage, coins, notes, bills.
☞ 流通 acceptance, publicity, popularity, vogue, circulation, prevalence, exposure.

current adj.
☞ 当今的,时下的,流通的 present, on-going, existing, contemporary, present-day, modern, fashionable, up-to-date, up-to-the-minute, trendy, popular, widexpread, prevalent, common, general, prevailing, reigning, accepted.
n.
☞ 趋势,潮流 draught, stream, jet, flow, drift, tide, course, trend, tendency, undercurrent, mood, feeling.

curse n.
☞ 诅咒,咒语 swear-word, oath, expletive, obscenity, profanity, blasphemy.
☞ 祸因 jinx, anathema, bane, evil, plague, scourge, affliction, trouble, torment, ordeal, calamity, disaster.
v.
☞ 诅咒,咒骂 swear, blaspheme, damn, condemn, denounce, fulminate.
☞ 遭受痛苦 blight, plague, scoourge, afflict, trouble, torment.

curtail v.
☞ 缩短,削减 shorten, truncate, cut, trim, abridge, abbreviate, lessen, decrease, reduce,

curtain n.
☞ (舞台的)幕,帘 blind, screen, backdrop, hanging, drapery, tapestry.

curve v.
☞ 弯曲 bend, arch, arc, bow, bulge, hook, crook, turn, wind, twist, spiral, coil.
n.
☞ 弯曲 bend, turn, arc, trajectory, lop, camber, curvature.

curved adj.
☞ 弯曲的 bent, arched, bowed, rounded, humped, convex, concave, crooked, twisted, sweeping, sinuous, serpentine.

cushion n.
☞ 垫子 pad, buffer, shock absorber, bolster, pillow, headrest, hassock.
v.
☞ 减轻,缓和 soften, deaden, dampen, absorb, muffle, stifle, suppress, lessen, mitigate, protect, bolster, buttress, support.

custom n.
☞ 习俗,风俗 tradition, usage, use, habit, routine, procedure, practice, policy, way, manner, style, form, convention, etiquette, formality, observance, ritual.

customary adj.
☞ 通常的,习惯的,惯例的 traditional, conventional, accepted, established, habitual, routine, regular, usual, normal, ordinary, everyday, familiar, common, general, popular, fashionable, prevailing.

customer n.
☞ 顾客,主顾 client, patron, regualr, punter, consumer, shopper, buyer, purchaser, prospect.

cut v.
☞ 切(割,开);割(开,破),剪(修裁),劈(开) clip, trim, crop, shear, mow, shave, pare, shop, hack, hew, slice, carve, divide, part, split, bisect, dock, lop, sever, prune, excise, incise, penetrate, pierce, stab, wound, nick, gash, slit, slash, lacerate, score, engrave, chisel, sculpt.
☞ 削减;缩短 reduce, decrease, lower, shorten, curtail, abbreviate, abridge, condense, precis, delete.
☞ 刺痛或伤害(感情) ignore, cold-shoulder, spurn, avoid, snub, slight, rebuff, insult.
n.
☞ 伤口,伤痕 incision, wound, nick, gash, slit, slash, rip, laceration.
☞ 削减,降低 reduction, decrease, lowering, cutback, saving, economy.

cut down
☞ 砍倒 fell, hew, lop, level, raze.
☞ 缩短,削减 reduce, decrease, lower, lessen, diminish.

cut in
☞ 打断,插嘴 interrupty, butt, in interject, interpose, intervene, intrude.

cut off

☞隔绝 sever, ammputate, separate, isolate, disconnect, block, obstruct, intercept.
☞停止 stop, end, halt, suspend, discontinue, disown, disinherit.

cut out
☞剪去,剪开 excise, extract, remove, delete, eliminate, exclude, debar, stop, cease, cut up, chop, dice, mince, dissect, divide, carve, slice, slash.

cutback n.
☞削减,缩短 cut, saving, economy, retrenchment, reduction, decrease, lowering, lessening.

cut-price adj.
☞廉价的 reduced, sale, discount, bargain, cheap, low-priced.

cutting adj.
☞尖刻的 sharp, keen, pointed, trenchant, incisive, penetrating, piercing, wounding, stinging, biting, mordant, caustic, acid, scathing, sarcastic, malicious, bitter, raw.

cycle n.
☞周期,循环 circle, round, rotation, revolution, series, sequence, phase, period, era, age, epoch, aeon.

D

daily adj.
☞每日,天天 regular, routine, everyday, customary, common, commonplace, ordinary.
n.
☞日报 everyday.

dam n.
☞坝,水闸 barrier, barrage, embankment, blockage, obstruction, hindrance.
v.
☞筑坝 block, confine, restrict, check, barricade, staunch, stem, obstruct.

damage n.
☞损害,损坏 harm, injury, hurt, destruction, devastation, loss, suffering, mischief, impairment, detriment.
v.
☞损害,损坏 harm, injure, hurt, spoil, ruin, impair, mar, wreck, deface, weaken, tamper with, play havoc with.

damn v.
☞咒骂 curse, swear, blast, imprecate, blaspheme.
☞指责 abuse, revile, denounce criticise, censure, slate, slam, denunciate, execrate, castigate.

damp n.
☞潮湿,湿气 dampness, moisture, clamminess, dankness, humidity, wet, dew, drizzle, fog, mist, vapour.
adj.
☞潮湿的 moist, wet, clammy, dank, humid, dewy, muggy, drizzly, misty, soggy.

dampen v.

- 使微潮 moisten, wet, spray.
- 使沮丧,使挫折 discourage, dishearten, deter, dash, dull, deaden, restrain, check, depress, dismay, reduce, lessen, moderate, decrease, diminish, muffle, stifle, smother.

dance n.
- 舞蹈,舞会 ball, hop, knees-up, social, shinding.

danger n.
- 危险性 insecurity, endangerment, jeopardy, precariousness, liability, vulnerability.
- 危险 risk, threat, peril, hazard, menace.

dangerous adj.
- 危险的 unsafe, inesceure, risky, threatening, breakneck, hairy, hazardous, perilous, precarious, reckless, treacherous, vulnerable, menacing, exposed.

dangle v.
- 摇摆,摇晃,悬摆 hang, droop, swing, sway, flap, trail.
- 引诱 tempt, entice, flaunt, flourish, lure, tantalize.

dare v.
- 敢 risk, venture, brave, hazard, adventure, endanger, stake, gamble.
- 向……挑战 challenge, goad, provoke, taunt.

n.
- 挑战 challenge, provocation, taunt, gauntlet.

daring adj.
- 大胆的,勇敢的 bold, adventurous, intrepid, fearless, brave, plucky, audacious, dauntless, reckless, rash, impulsive, valiant.

n.
- 大胆,勇敢 boldness, fearlessness, courage, bravery, nerve, audacity, guts, intrepidity, defiance, pluck, rashness, spirit, grit, gall, prowess.

dark adj.
- 黑暗的,模糊的 unlit, overcast, black, dim, unilluminated, shadowy, murky, cloudy, dusky, dingy.
- 阴暗的,邪恶的 gloomy, grim, cheerlees, dismal, bleak, forbidding, sombre, sinister, mournful, ominous, menacing, drab.
- 暗中的,秘密的 hidden, mysterious, obscure, secret, unintelligible, enigmatic, cryptic, abstruse.

n.
- 黑暗 darkness, dimness, night, night-time, nightfall, gloom, dusk, twilight, murkiness.
- 隐藏,保守秘密 concealment, secrecy, obscurity.

darken v.
- 使暗,变暗 dim, obscure, blacken, cloud (over), shadow, overshadow, eclipse.
- 使沮丧,使灰心 depress, sadden.

darling n.
- 亲爱的人 beloved, dear, dearest, favourite, sweetheart, love, pet.

dart v.
- 亲爱的 dear, beloved, adored, cherished, precious, treasurd.

dart v.
- 突进,飞奔 dash, bound, sprint, flit, flash, fly, rush, run, race, spring, tear.
- 猛掷,投射 throw, , hurl, fling, shoot, sling, launch, propel, send.

n.
- 标枪,箭 bolt, arrow, barb, shaft.

dash v.
- 猛冲,飞奔 rush, dart, hurry, race, sprint, run, bolt, tear.
- 猛掷 fling, throw, crash, hurl.
- 破灭,粉粹 discourage, disappoint, dampen, confound, blight, ruin, destroy, spoil, frustrate, smash, shatter.

n.
- 少量,少许 drop, pinch, touch, flavour, soupcon, suggestion, hint, bit, little.
- 奔,冲 sprint, dart, bolt, rush, spurt, race, run.

data n.
- 资料,材料 information, documents, facts, input, statistics, figures, details, materials.

date n.
- 年代,时期 time, age, period, era, stage, epoch.
- 约会 appointment, engagement, assignation, meeting, rendezvous.
- 对象 escort, steady, partner, friend.

out-of-date adj.
- 过时的,陈旧的 old-fashioned, unfashionable, outdated, obsolete, dated, outmoded, antiquated, passe.

up-to-date adj.
- 最新的,时新的 fashionable, modern, current, contemporary.

daunt v.
- 使气馁,使胆怯,使畏缩 discourage, disfhearten, put off, dispirit, deter.
- 吓,吓倒 intimidate, overawe, unnerve, alarm, dismay, frighten, scare.

dauntless adj.
- 勇敢的 fearless, undaunted, resolute, brave, courageous, bold, intrepid, daring, plucky, valiant.

dawn n.
- 黎明,破晓 sunrise, daybreak, morning, daylight.
- 开始 beginning, start, emergence, onset, origin, birth, advent.

v.
- 破晓 break, brighten, lighten, gleam, glimmer.
- 开始,显露,出现 begin, appear, emerge, open, develop, originate, rise.

day n.
- 白天 daytime, daylight.
- 时代,时期 age, period, time, date, era, generation, epoch.

day after day
- 日复一日 regularly, continually, endlessly, persistently, monotonously, perpetually, relentlessly.

day by day
☞ 逐渐地 gradually, progressively, slowly, but, surely, steadily.

daydream n.
☞ 幻想,白日梦 fantasy, imagining, reverie, castles, in the air, pipe, dream, vision, musing, wish, dream, figment.
v.
☞ 作白日梦,妄想 fantasize, imagine, muse, fancy, dream.

daze v.
☞ 使晕眩 stun, stupefy, shock.
☞ 使迷惑 dazzle, bewilder, blind, confuse, baffle, dumbfound, amaze, surprise, startle, perplex, astonish, flabbergast, astound, stagger.
n. bewilderment, confusion, stupor, trance, shock, distraction.

dazzle v.
☞ 使迷惑 daze, blind, confuse, blur.
☞ 耀眼,使目眩 sparkle, fascinate, impress, overwhelm, awe, overawe, scintillate, bedazzle, amaze, astonish, bewitch, stupefy.
n.
☞ 闪耀 sparkle, brilliance, magnificence, splendour, scintillation, glitter, glare.

dead adj.
☞ 死的 lifeless, deceased, inanimate, defunct, departed, late, gone.
☞ 灰暗的,麻木的 unresponsive, apathetic, dull, indifferent, insensitive, numb, cold, frigid, lukewarm, torpid.
☞ 无活动的 exhausted, tired, wornout, dead-beat.
☞ 完全的,彻底的 exact, absolute, perfect, unqualified, utter, outright, complete, entire, total, downright.

deadlock n.
☞ 僵局 standstill, stalemate, impasse, halt.

deadly adj.
☞ 致命的 lethal, fatal, dangerous, venomous, destructive, pernicious, malignant, murderous, mortal.
☞ 讨厌的,充满仇恨的 dull, boring, uninteresting, tedious, monotonous.

deaf adj.
☞ 聋的 hard of hearing, stone-deaf.
☞ 不在意的,麻木的 unconcerned, indifferent, unmoved, oblivious, heedless, unmindful.

deafening adj.
☞ 令人耳聋的 piercing, ear-splitting, booming, resounding, thunderous, ringing, roaring.

deal v.
☞ 分配,发给 apportion, distribute, share, dole out, divide, allot, dispense, assign, mete out, give, bestow.
☞ 交易,买卖 trade, negotiate, traffic, bargain, treat.
n.
☞ 买卖,交易 agreement, contract, understanding, pact, transaction, bargain, buy.
☞ 分发 round, hand, distribution.

deal with

☞ 论述,涉及,有关 attend to, concern, see to, manage, handle, cope with, treat, consider, oversee.

dealer n.
☞ 商人 trader, merchant, wholesaler, marketer, merchandizer.

dear adj.
☞ 亲爱的,可爱的 loved, beloved, treasured, valued, cherished, precious, favourite, esteemed, intimate, close, darling, familiar.
☞ 昂贵的 expensive, high-priced, costly, overpriced, pricey.
n.
☞ 亲(可)爱的人(物) beloved, loved one, precious, darling, treasure.

dearly adv.
☞ 喜爱地 fondly, affectionately, lovingly, devotedly, tenderly.
☞ 非常 greatly, extremely, profoundly.

death n.
☞ 死亡 decease, end, finish, loss, demise, departure, fatality, cessation, passing, expiration, dissolution.
☞ 消灭,毁灭 destruction, ruin, undoing, annihilation, downfall, extermination, extinction, obliteration, eradication.

deathly adj.
☞ 死一般的 ashen, grim, haggard, pale, pallid, ghastly, wan.
☞ 致死的 fatal, deadly, mortal, intense.

debatable adj.
☞ 可争辩的,成问题的 questionable, uncertain, disputable, contestable, controversial, arguable, open to question, doubtful, contentious, undecided, unsettled, problematical, dubious, moot.

debate v.
☞ 讨论,辩论 dispute, argue, discuss, contend, wrangle.
☞ 思考,考虑 consider, deliberate, ponder, reflect, meditate on, mull over, weigh.
n.
☞ 讨论,辩论 discussion, argument, controversy, disputation, deliberation, consideration, contention, dispute, reflection, polemic.

debt n.
☞ 债,欠款 indebtedness, obligation, debit, arrears, due, liability, duty, bill, commitment, claim, score.

debtor n.
☞ 债务人,借方 borrower, bankrupt, insolvent, defaulter, mortgagor.

decay v.
☞ 腐烂 rot, go bad, putrefy, decompose, spoil, perish, mortify.
☞ 衰落,衰败 decline, deteriorate, disintegrate, corrode, crumble, waste, away, degenerate, wear away, dwindle, shrivel, wither, sink.
n.
☞ 腐烂 rot, decomposition, rotting, perishing.
☞ 衰退,衰微 decline,

deterioration, disintegration, degeneration, collapse, decadence, wasting, failing, withering, fading.

decease n.
☞ 死亡 death, dying, demise, departure, passing, dissolution.

deceased adj.
☞ 去世的 dead, departed, former, late, lost, defunct, expired, gone, finished, extinct.
n.
☞ 死者 dead, departed.

deceit n.
☞ 骗局,诡计 deception, pretence, cheating, misrepresentation, fraud, duplicity, trickery, fraudulence, double-dealing, underhandedness, fake, guile, sham, subterfuge, swindle, treachery, hypocrisy.

deceitful adj.
☞ 欺骗的 dishonest, deceptive, deceiving, false, insincere, untrustworthy, double-dealing, fraudulent, two-faced, treacherous, duplicitous, guileful, tricky, underhand, hypocritical.

deceive v.
☞ 欺骗,欺诈 mislead, delude, cheat, betray, fool, take in, trick, dissemble, hoax, double-cross, dupe, swindle, impose, upon, bamboozle, two-time, lead on, outwit, hoodwink, beguile, ensnare, camouflage, abuse, befool, gull.

decency n.
☞ 礼仪,礼节 propriety, courtesy, modesty, decorum, respectability, civility, correctness, fitness, etiquette, helpfulness.

decent adj.
☞ 正当的,合乎礼仪的 respectable, proper, fitting, decorous, chaste, seemly, suitable, modest, appropriate, presentable, pure, fit, becoming, befitting, nice.
☞ 正派的 kind, obliging, courteous, helpful, generous, polite, gracious.
☞ 合适的,公平的 adequate, acceptable, satisfactory, reasonable, sufficient, tolerable, competent.

deception n.
☞ 欺骗,受骗 deceit, pretence, trick, cheat, fraud, imposture, lie, dissembling, deceptiveness, insincerity, sham, subterfuge, artifice, hypocrisy, bluff, treachery, hoax, fraudulence, duplicity, ruse, snare, stratagem, leg-pull, illusion, wile, guile, craftiness, cunning.

decide v.
☞ 决定 chose, determine, resolve, reach a decision, settle, elect, opt, judge, adjudicate, conclude, fix, purpose, decree.

decided adj.
☞ 明确的,确定的 definite, certain, undeniable, indisputable, absolute, clear-cut, undisputed, unmistable, unquestionable, positive, unambiguous, categorical, distinct, emphatic.

☞ 坚定的,果断的 resolute, decisive, determined, firm, unhesitating, deliberate, forthright.

decision n.
☞ 决定,决议 result, conclusion, outcome, verdict, finding, settlement, judgement, arbitration, ruling.
☞ 果断,决心 determination, decisiveness, firmness, resolve, purpose.

decisive adj.
☞ 决定性的 conclusive, definite, definitive, absolute, final.
☞ 果断的,坚决的 determined, resolute, decided, positive, firm, forceful, forthright, strong-minded.
☞ 显著的,确切的 significant, critical, crucial, influential, momentous, fateful.

declaration n.
☞ 宣言 affirmation, acknowledgement, assertion, statement, testimony, attestation, disclosure, prfession, revelation.
☞ 宣言书,布告 announcement, notification, pronouncement, proclamation, edict, manifesto, promulgation.

declare v.
☞ 宣言,断言 affirm, assert, claim, profess, mainatin, state, attest, certify, confess, confirm, disclose, reveal, show, aver, swear, testify, witness, validate.
☞ 宣告 announce, decree, proclaim, pronounce, broadcast.

decline v.
☞ 拒绝 refuse, reject, deny, forgo, avoid, balk.
☞ 下降 diminish, decrease, dwindle, lessen, fall, sink, wane.
☞ 衰弱,跌落 decay, worsen, deteriorate, degenerate.
☞ 下倾 descend, sink, slope, dip, slant.
n.
☞ 衰弱 deterioration, dwindling, lessening, decay, degeneration, weakening, worsening, failing, downturn, diminution, falling-off, recession, slump, abatement.
☞ 下降 descent, dip, declivity, declination, hill, slope, incline, divergence, deviation.

decorate v.
☞ 装饰,装修 ornament, adorn, beautify, embellish, trim, deck, tart, up, grace, enrich, prettify, trick, out.
☞ 油漆,裱糊 renovate, do up, paint, paper, colour, refurbish.
☞ 授勋给 honour, crown, cite, garland, bemedal.

decoration n.
☞ 装饰 ornament, frill, adornment, ornamentation, trimming, embellishment, beautification, garnish, flourish, enrichment, elaboration, scroll, bauble.
☞ 勋章 award, medal, order, badge, garland, crown, colours, ribbon, laurel, star, emblem.

decorative adj.
☞ 装饰的 ornmental, fancy, adorning, beautifying, embellishing, non-functional,

pretty, ornate, enhancing.
dedicate v.
- 奉献,献身 devote, commit, assign, give over to, pledge, present, offer, sacrifice, surrender.
- 把……奉为神圣 bless, consecrate, sanctify, set apart, hallow.
- 题献(著作给某人) inscribe, address.

dedicated adj.
- 献身于工作的,热忱的 devoted, committed, enthusiastic, single-minded, whole-hearted, sing-hearted, zealous, given over to, purposeful.

dedication n.
- 献身,奉献 commitment, devotion, single-mindedness, whole-heartedness, allegiance, attachment, adherence, faithfulness, loyalty, self-sacrifice.
- 供奉 consecration, hallowing, presentation.
- 献词 inscription, address.

deduct v.
- 扣除,减除 subtract, take away, remove, reduce, by, decrease by, knock off, withdraw.

deduction n.
- 推论 inference, result, reasoning, finding, conclusion, corollary, assumption.
- 扣除额 subtration, reduction, decrease, diminution, abatement, withdrawal, discount, allowance.

deed n.
- 行为,事迹,功绩 action, act, achievement, performance, exploit, feat, fact, truth, reality.
- 证书,契约 document, contract, record, title, transaction, indenture.

deep adj.
- 深深的 profound, bottomless, unplumbed, fathomless, yawning, immersed.
- 深奥的,难懂的 obscure, mysterious, difficult, recondite, abstruse, esoteric.
- 富有理解力的,深刻的 wise, perceptive, discerning, profound, learned, astute.
- 严重的 intense, serious, earnest, extreme.
- (声音)低沉 low, bass, resonant, booming.

deepen v.
- 使深刻,加深 intensify, grow, increase, strengthen, reinforce, magnify.
- 挖深 hollow, scoop out.

defeat v.
- 击败 conquer, beat, overpower, subdue, overthrow, worst, repel, subjugate, overwhelm, rout, ruin, thump, quell.
- 使……失败 frustrate, thwart, confound, balk, get the better of, disappoint, foil, baffle, checkmate.

n.
- 战败 conquest, beating, overthrow, rout, subjugation.
- 失败 frustration, failure, setback, reverse,

defect n.
- 过失,缺点 imperfection, fault, flaw, deficiency, failing, mistake, inadequacy, blemish, error, bug, shortcoming, want, weakness, frailty, lack, spot, absence, taint.

v.
- 变节 desert, break, faith, rebel, revolt, renegue.

defence n.
- 保护 protection, resistance, security, fortification, cover, safeguardshelter, guard, shield, deterrence, barricade, bastion, immunity, bulwark, rampart, buttress.
- 辩词 justification, explanation, excuse, argument, exoneration, plea, vindication, pleading, alibi, case.

defenceless adj.
- 无抵抗力的 unprotected, undefended, unarmed, unguarded, vulnerable, exposed, helpless, powerless.

defend v.
- 保卫 protect, guard, safeguard, shelter, fortify, secure, shield, screen, cover, contest.
- 辩护 support, stand up for, stand by, uphold, endores, vindicate, champion, argue for, speak up for, justify, plead.

defendant n.
- 被告 accused, offender, prisoner, respondent.

defender n.
- 护卫 proportor, guard, bodyguard.
- 捧场者 supporter, advocate, vindicator, champion, patron, sponsor, counsel.

defensive adj.
- 防卫性的 protective, defending, safeguarding, wary, opposing, cautious, watchful.
- 自卫性的 self-justifying, apologetic.

defiance n.
- 违抗 opposition, confrontation, resistance, challenge, disobedience, rebelliousness, contempt, insubordination, disregard, insolence.

defiant adj.
- 违抗的 challenging, resistant, antagonistic, aggressive, rebellious, insubordinate, disobedient, intransigent, bold, insolent, obstinate, uncooperative, provocative.

deficiency n.
- 缺乏 shortage, lack, inadequacy, scarcity, insufficiency, dearth, want, scantiness, absence, deficit.
- 不足,短处 imperfection, shortcoming, weakness, fault, defect, flaw, failing, frailty.

deficient adj.
- 缺乏的 inadequate, insufficient, scarce, short, lacking, wanting, meagre, scanty, skimpy, incomplete.
- 不完美的 imperfect, impaired, flawed, faulty, defective, unsatisfactory, inferior, weak.

deficit n.
☞ 不足,缺乏 shortage, shortfall, deficiency, loss, arrears, lack, default.

define v.
☞ 划界限,限定 bound, limit, delimit, demarcate, mark out.
☞ 详细说明,使清楚 explain, characterize, describe, interpret, expound, determine, designate, specify, spell out, detail.

definite adj.
☞ 确定的 certain, settled, sure, positie, fixed, decided, determined, assured, guaranteed.
☞ 明确的 clear, clear-cut, exact, precise, specific, explicit, particular, obvious, marked.

definitely adv.
☞ 肯定地,明确地 positively, surely, unquestionably, absolutely, certainly, categorically, undeniably, clearly, doubtless, unmistakably, plainly, obviously, indeed, easily.

definition n.
☞ 界限,界定 delineation, demarcation, delimitation.
☞ 确定 explanation, description, interpretation, exposition, clarification, elucidation, determination.
☞ 清晰 distinctness, clarity, precision, clearness, focus, contrast, sharpness.

deft adj.
☞ 灵巧的,熟练的 adept, handy, dexterous, nimble, skilful, adroit, agile, expert, nifty, proficient, able, neat, clever.

defy v.
☞ 向……挑战 challenge, confront, resist, dare, brave, face, repel, spurn, beard, flout, withstand, disregard, scorn, despise, defeat, provoke, thwart.

degradation n.
☞ 降低 deterioration, degeneration, decline, downgrading, demotion.
☞ 堕落,变坏 abasement, humiliation, mortification, dishonour, disgrace, shame, ignominy, decadence.

degrade v.
☞ 变坏,使堕落 dishonour, disgrace, debase, abase, shame, humiliate, humble, discredit, demean, lower, weaken, impair, deteriorate, cheapen, adulterate, corrupt.
☞ 降低 demote, depose, downgrade, deprive, cashier.

degree n.
☞ 等级,社会地位 grade, class, rank, order, position, standing, status.
☞ 幅度,范围 extent, measure, range, stage, step, level, intensity, standard.
☞ 水平,标准 level, limit, unit, mark.

delay v.
☞ 耽搁 obstruct, hinder, impede, hold up, check, hold back, set back, stop, halt, detain.
☞ 延期,推迟 defer, put off,

postpone, procrastinate, suspend, shelve, hold over, stall.
☞ 拖延 dawdle, linger, lag, loiter, dilly-dally, tarry.
n.
☞ 耽搁 obstruction, hindrance, impediment, hold-up, check, setback, stay, stoppage.
☞ 延迟 deferment, postponement, procrastination, suspension.
☞ 拖延 dawdling, lingering, tarrying.

delegate *n.*
☞ 代表 representative, agent, envoy, messenger, deputy, ambassador, commissioner.
v.
☞ 委派 authorize, appoint, depute, charge, commission, assign, empower, entrust, devolve, consign, designate, nominate, name, hand over.

delegation *n.*
☞ 代表团 deputation, commission, legation, mission, contingent, embassy.
☞ (代表的)委派 authoriaztion, commissioning, assignment.

delete *v.*
☞ 删去,清除 erase, remove, cross out, cancel, rub out, strike (out), obliterate, edit (out), blot out, efface.

deliberate *v.*
☞ 考虑,研讨,慎重衡量 consider, ponder, reflect, think, cogitate, meditate, mull over, debate, discuss, weigh, consult.
adj.
☞ 深思熟虑的 intentional, planned, calculated, prearranged, premeditated, willed, conscious, designed, considered, advised.
☞ 从容不迫的 careful, unhurried, thoughtful, methodical, cautious, circumspect, studied, prudent, slow, ponderous, measured, heedful.

deliberation *n.*
☞ 考虑,商议 consideration, reflection, thought, calculation, forethought, meditation, rumination, study, debate, discussion, consultation, speculation.
☞ 深思熟虑 care, carefulness, caution, circumspection, prudence.

delicacy *n.*
☞ 优美 daintiness, fineness, elegance, exquisiteness, lightness, precision.
☞ 敏感,灵敏 refinement, sensitivity, subtlety, finesse, discrimination, tact, niceness.
☞ 精致 titbit, dainty, taste, sweetmeat, savoury, relish.

delicate *adj.*
☞ 精美的 fine, fragile, dainty, exquisite, flimsy, elegant, graceful.
☞ 易受伤害的 frail, weak, ailing, faint.
☞ 灵敏的 sensitive, scrupulous, discriminating, careful, accurate, precise.
☞ 细软的,娇嫩的 subtle, muted, pasted, soft.

delicious *adj.*

- 美妙的,使人愉快的 enjoyable, pleasant, agreeable, delightful.
- 可口的,美味的 appetizing, palatable, tasty, delecable, scrumptious, mouth-watering, succulent, savoury.

delight n.
- 欣喜,愉快,乐趣 bliss, happiness, joy, pleasure, ecstasy, enjoyment, gladness, rapture, transport, gratification, jubilation.

v.
- 使快乐,令人喜欢 please, charm, gratify, enchant, tickle, thrill, ravish.

delight in
- 喜欢,嗜好 enjoy, relish, like, love, appreciate, revel in, take pride in, glory in, savour.

delighted adj.
- 愉快的,欣喜的 charmed, elated, happy, pleased, enchanted, captivated, ecstatic, thrilled, overjoyed, jubilant, joyous.

delightful adj.
- 令人愉快的 charming, enchanting, captivating, enjoyable, pleasant, thrilling, agreeable, pleasurable, engaging, attractive, pleasing, gratifying, entertaining, fascinating.

deliver v.
- 交付 convey, bring, send, give, carry, supply.
- 交出,放弃 surrender, hand over, relinquish, yield, transfer, grant, entrust, commit.
- 发言,陈述,发音 utter, speak, proclaim, pronounce.
- 给与打击 administer, inflict, direct.
- 释放 set free, liberate, release, emancipate.

delivery n.
- 寄托,托付 conveyance, consignment, dispatch, transmission, transfer, surrender.
- 演讲,发言 articulation, enunciation, speech, utterance, intonation, elocution.
- 分娩 childbirth, labour, confinement.

demand v.
- 要求,坚持 ask, request, call for, insist on, solicit, claim, exact, inquire, question, interrogate.
- 需要 necessitate, need, require, involve.

n.
- 要求,请求 request, question, claim, order, inquiry, desire, interrogation.
- 需要,需求 need, necessity, call.

democracy n.
- 民主政府 self-government, commonwealth, autonomy, republic.

democratic adj.
- 民主政体的 self-governing, representative, egalitarian, autonomous, popular, populist, republican.

demolish v.
- 推翻,拆除 destroy, dismantle, knock down, pull down, flatten, bulldoze, raze, tear down, level.

☞ 摧毁,打败 ruin, defeat, destroy, annihilate, wreck, overturn, overthrow.

demolition *n.*
☞ 破坏,毁坏 destruction, dismantling, levelling, razing.

demon *n.*
☞ 精力充沛的人 devil, fiend, evil spirit, fallen angel, imp.
☞ 恶魔 villain, devil, rogue, monster.

demonstrable *adj.*
☞ 显然的,可证明的 verifiable, provable, arguable, attestable, self-evident, obvious, evident, certain, clear, positive.

demonstrate *v.*
☞ 证明 show, display, prove, establish, exhibit, substantiate, manifest, testify to, indicate.
☞ 展示,示范 explain, illustrate, describe, teach.
☞ 示威,抗议 protest, march, parade, rally, picket, sit in.

demonstration *n.*
☞ 展示 dispaly, exhibition, manifestation, proof, confirmation, affirmation, substantiation, validation, evidence, testimony, expression.
☞ 说明 explanation, illustration, description, exposition, presentation, test, trial.
☞ 示威(运动) protest, march, demo, rally, picket, sit-in, parade.

den *n.*
☞ 兽穴,窝藏之地 lair, hideout, hole, retreat, study, hideaway, shelter, sanctuary, haunt.

denial *n.*
☞ 取消,否定 contradiction, negation, dissent, repudiation, disavowal, disclaimer, dismissal, renunciation.
☞ 拒绝 refusal, rebuff, rejection, prohibition, veto.

dense *adj.*
☞ 密集的,稠密的 compact, thick, compressed, condensed, close, close-knit, heavy, solid, opaque, impenetrable, packed, crowded.
☞ 愚钝的 stupid, thick, crass, dull, slow, slow-witted.

dent *n.*
☞ 缺口,凹痕 hollow, depression, dip, concavity, indentation, crater, dimple, dint, pit.
v.
☞ 弄凹,(使)有缺口 depress, gouge, push in, indent.

deny *v.*
☞ 背弃,摒弃 contradict, oppose, refute, disagree with, disaffirm, disprove.
☞ 克制,克己 disown, disclaim, renounce, repudiate, recant.
☞ 不承认,否定 refuse, turn down, forbid, reject, withhold, rebuff, veto.

depart *v.*
☞ 离开 go, leave, withdraw, exit, make off, quit, decamp, take one's leave, absent oneself, set off, remove, retreat, migrate, escape, disappear, retire, vanish.
☞ 违反 deviate, digress, differ, diverge, swerve, veer.

department n.
- 部门,秩序 division, branch, subdivision, section, sector, office, station, unit, region, district.
- 省,区域 sphere, realm, province, domain, field, area, concern, responsibility, speciality, line.

departure n.
- 分离,离开 exit, going, leave-taking, removal, withdrawal, retirement, exodus.
- 转变,改变 deviation, change, digression, divergence, shift, variation, innovation, branching (out), difference, veering.

depend v.
- 信任,信赖 relyupon, count on, bank on, calculate on, reckon on, build upon, trust in, lean on, expect.
- 视……而定 hinge on, rest on, revolve around, be contingent upon, hang on.

dependence n.
- 信赖,信任 reliance, confidence, faith, trust, need, expectation.
- 依靠 subordination, attachment, subservience, helplessness, addiction.

dependent adj.
- 依赖的,依靠的 reliant, helpless, weak, immature, subject, subordinate, vulnerable.
- 相关的 contingent, conditional, determined by, relative.

depict v.
- 用图画表示,描写 portray, illustrate, delineate, sketch, outline, draw, picture, paint, trace, describe, characterize, detail.

deplorable adj.
- 可叹的,可悲的 grievous, lamentable, pitiable, regrettable, unfortunate, wretched, distressing, sad, miserable, heartbreaking, melancholy, disastrous, dire, appalling.
- 不幸的 reprehensible, disgraceful, scandalous, shameful, dishonourable, disreputable.

deplore v.
- 痛惜 grieve for, lament, mourn, regret, bemoan, rue.
- 谴责 censure, condemn, denounce, deprecate.

deploy v.
- 开展工作 dispose, arrange, position, station, use, utilize, distribute.

deposit v.
- 存放,贮存 lay, drop, place, put, settle, dump, park, precipitate, sit, lockate.
- 储蓄 save, store, hoard, bank, amass, consign, entrust, lodge, file.

n.
- 积累 sediment, dregs, accumulation, precipitate, lees, silt.
- 定金,存款 security, stake, down payment, pledge, retainer, instalment, part payment, money.

depress v.
- 使不振,使消沉 deject, sadden, dishearten, discourage,

oppress, upset, daunt, burden, overburden.
☞ 使疲倦 weaken, impair, undermine, sap, tire, drain, exhaust, weary, reduce, lessen, press, lower, level.
☞ 降低 devalue, bring down, lower.

depressed adj.
☞ 精神不振的,忧伤的 dejected, low-spirited, melancholy, dispirited, sad, unhappy, low, down, downcast, disheartened, fed up, miserable, moody, cast down, discouraged, glum, downhearted, distressed, despondent, morose, crestfallen, pessimistic.
☞ 贫乏的,落后的 poor, disadvantaged, deprived, destitute.
☞ 中间部分下凹的,凹下的 sunken, recessed, concave, hollow, indented, dented.

depressing adj.
☞ 令人沮丧的 dejecting, dismal, bleak, gloomy, saddening, cheerless, dreary, disheartening, sad, melancholy, sombre, grey, black, daunting, discouraging, heartbreaking, distressing, hopeless.

depression n.
☞ 沮丧,消沉 dejection, despair, despondency, melancholy, low spirits, sadness, gloominess, doldrums, blues, glumness, dumps, hopelessness.
☞ 萧条时期 recession, slump, stagnation, hard times, decline, inactivity.
☞ 凹陷,凹地 indentation, hollow, dip, concavity, dent, dimple, valley, pit, sink, dint, bowl, cavity, basin, impression, dish, excavation.

deprive v.
☞ 剥夺,使丧失 dispossess, strip, divest, denude, bereave, expropriate, rob.
☞ 拒绝 deny, withhold, refuse.

deprived adj.
☞ 被剥夺的,贫穷的 poor, needy, underprivileged, disadvantaged, impoverished, destitute, lacking, bereft.

depth n.
☞ 深,深度 deepness, profoundness, extent, measure, drop.
☞ 中间,深渊 middle, midst, abyss, deep, gulf.
☞ 深奥 wisdom, insight, discernment, penetration.
☞ 浓度 intensity, strength.

deputy n.
☞ 代表,议员 repesentative, agent, delegate, proxy, substitute, second-in-command, ambassador, commissioner, lieutenant, surrogate, subordinate, assistant, locum.

derogatory adj.
☞ 抨击的,诽谤的 insulting, pejorative, offensive, disparaging, deprecitive, critical, defamatory, injurious.

descend v.
☞ 下来,下跌,落下,下降 drop, go down, fall, plummet, plunge, tumble, swoop, sink, arrive, alight, dismount, dip,

slope, subside.
- 退化,沦于 degenerate, deteriorate.
- 屈尊,惠允 condescend, deign, stoop.
- 遗传 originate, proceed, spring, stem.

descendants n.
- 后裔,后代 offspring, children, issue, progeny, successors, lineage, line, seed.

descent n.
- 下降,降落 fall, drop, plunge, dip, decline, incline, slope.
- 贬低,贬损 comedown, debasement, degradation.
- 出身,世亲 ancestry, parentage, heredity, family, tree, genealogy, lineage, extraction, origin.

describe v.
- 叙述,描写,形容,记述 portray, depict, delineate, illustrate, characterize, specify, draw, define, detail, explain, express, tell, narrate, outline, relate, recount, present, report, sketch, mark out, trace.

description n.
- 叙述,描述 portrayal, representaion, characterization, account, delineation, depiction, sketch, presentation, report, outline, explanation, exposition, narration.
- 种类 sort, type, kind, variety, specification, order.

descriptive adj.
- 叙述的,描写的 illustrative, explanatory, expressive, detailed, graphic, colourful, pictorial, vivid.

desert¹ n.
- 荒地,野外 wasteland, wilderness, wilds, void.

adj.
- 荒凉的,野外的 bare, barren, waste, wild, uninhabited, uncultivated, dry, arid, infertile, desolate, sterile, solitary.

desert² v.
- 遗弃,抛弃 abandon, forsake, leave, maroon, strand, decamp, defect, give up, renounce, reliquish, jilt, abscond, quit.

desert³ n.
- 应得的赏(或罚) due, right, reward, deserts, return, retribution, come-uppance, payment, recompense, remuneration.
- 美德,优点 worth, merit, virtue.

deserted adj.
- 孤单的,荒凉的 abandoned, forsaken, empty, derelict, desolate, godforsaken, neglected, underpopulated, stranded, isolated, bereft, vacant, betrayed, lonely, solitary, unoccupied.

deserve v.
- 应得,应受 earn, be worthy of, merit, be entitled to, warrant, justify, win, rate, incur.

deserved adj.
- 应得的 due, earned, merited, justifiable, warranted, right, rightful, well-earned, suitable, proper, fitting, fair, just,

appropriate, apt, legitimate, apposite, meet.

deserving adj.
☞ 应得支持的 worthy, estimable, exemplary, praiseworthy, admirable, commendable, laudable, righteous.

design n.
☞ 计划,设计 blueprint, draft, pattern, plan, prototype, sketch, drawing, outline, moldel, guide.
☞ 图样 style, shape, form, figure, structure, organization, arrangement, composition, construction, motif.
☞ 意欲,企图 aim, intertion, goal, purpose, plan, end, object, objective, scheme, plot, project, meaning, target, undertaking.

v.
☞ 意欲,企图 plan, plot, intend, devise, purpose, aim, scheme, shape, project, propose, tailor, mean.
☞ 打图样,起草 sketch, draft, outline, draw(up).
☞ 设计 invent, originate, conceive, create, think up, develop, construct, fashion, form, model, fabricate, make.

designation n.
☞ 名称,称呼 name, title, lable, epithet, nickname.
☞ 指明,标示 indication, specification, description, definition, calssification, category.
☞ 指派,指定 nomination, appointment, selection.

designer n.
☞ 设计者,设计家 deviser, originator, maker, stylist, inventor, creator, contriver, fashioner, architect, author.

desirable adj.
☞ 值得做的,合意的 proitable, advantageous, worthwhile, advisable, appropriate, expedient, beneficial, preferable, sensible, eligible, good. pleasing.
☞ 吸引的,迷人的 attractive, alluring, sexy, seductive, fetching, tempting.

desire v.
☞ 要求,想要 ask, request, petition, solicit.
☞ 渴望,需要 want, wish for, covet, long for, need, crave, hunger, for, yearn for, fancy, hankerafter.

n.
☞ 期望,愿望 want, longing, wish, need, yearning, craving, hankering, appctite, asiration.
☞ 激情,欲望 lust, passion, ardour.
☞ 请求 request, petition, appeal, supplication. discontinue, end, break off, give up, halt, abstain, suspend, pause, peter out, remit.

desolate adj.
☞ 荒凉的,荒废的 deserted, uninhabited, abandoned, unfrequented, barren, bare, arid, bleak, gloomy, dismal, dreary, lonely, god-forsaken, forsaken, waste, depressing.
☞ 被遗弃的,孤寂的 forlorn, bereft, depressed, dejected,

forsaken, despondent, distressed, melancholy, miserable, lonely, gloomy, disheartened, dismal, downcast, solitary, wretched.
v.
☞ 使忧伤 devastate, lay waste, destroy, despoil, spoil, wreck, denude, depopulate, ruin, waste, ravage, plunder, pillage.

desolation n.
☞ 毁灭,颓败 destruction, ruin, devastation, ravages.
☞ 孤寂,凄凉 dejection, despair, despondency, gloom, misery, sadness, melancholy, sorrow, unhappiness, anguish, grief, distress, wretchedness.
☞ 荒凉,荒芜 barrenness, bleakness, emptiness, forlornness, loneliness, isolation, solitude, wildness.

despair v.
☞ 失望 lose heart, lose hope, give up, give in, collapse, surrender.
n.
☞ 绝望,失望 despondency, gloom, hopelessness, desperation, anguish, inconsolableness, melancholy, misery, wrecthedness.

despairing adj.
☞ 绝望的 despondent, distraught, inconsolable, desolate, desperate, heart-broken, suicidal, grief-stricken, hopeless, disheartened, dejected, miserable, wretched, sorrowful, dismayed, downcast.

desperate adj.
☞ 令人绝望的,无助的 hopeless, inconsolable, wretched, despondent, abandoned.
☞ 孤注一掷的,拼命的 reckless, rash, impetuous, audacious, daring, dangerous, do-or-die, foolhardy, risky, hazardous, hasty, precipitate, wild, violent, frantic, frenzied, determined.
☞ 严重的,艰难的 critical, acute, serious, severe, extreme, urgent.

desperately adv.
☞ 严重地,绝望地 dangerously, critically, gravely, hopelessly, seriously, severely, badly, dreadfully, fearfully, frightfully.

desperation n.
☞ 绝望,失望 despair, agony, despondency, anguish, hopelessness, misery, distress, pain, sorrow, trouble, worry, anxiety.
☞ 鲁莽,疯狂 recklessness, rashness, frenzy, madness, hastiness.

despise v.
☞ 轻视,蔑视 scorn, deride, look down on, disdain, condemn, spurn, undervalue, slight, revile, deplore, dislike, detest, loathe.

despite prep.
☞ 不管,不顾 in spite of, notwithstanding, regardless of, in the face of, undeterred by, against, defying.

destination n.
☞ 目标 goal, aim, objective, object, purpose, target, end, intention, aspiration, design,

ambition.
- 目的地 journey's end, terminus, station, stop.

destined adj.
- 命中注定的 fated, doomed, inevitable, predetermined, ordained, certain, foreordained, meant, unavoidable, inescapable, intended, designed, appointed.
- 意图的 bound, directed, en route, headed, heading, scheduled, assigned, booked.

destiny n.
- 命运,天命 fate, doom, fortune, karma, predestiny, kismet.

destroy v.
- 毁坏,破坏 demolish, ruin, shatter, wreck, devastate, smash, break, crush, overthrow, sabotage, undo, dismantle, thwart, undermine, waste, gut, level, ravage, raze, torpedo, unshapge.
- 杀害 kill, annihilate, eliminate, extinguish, eradicate, dispatch, nullify.

destruction n.
- 毁灭 ruin, devastation, shattering, crushing, wreckage, demolition, defeat, downfall, overthrow, ruination, desolation, undoing, wastage, havoc, ravagement.
- 消灭 annihilation, extermination, eradication, elimination, extinction, slaughter, massacre, end, liquidation, nullification.

destructive adj.
- 有害的 devastating, damaging, catastrophic, disastous, deadly, harmful, fatal, disruptive, lethal, ruinous, detrimental, hurtful, malignant, mischievous, nullifying, slaughterous.
- 恶意的 adverse, hostile, negative, discouraging, disparaging, contrary, undermining, subversive, vicious.

detach v.
- 分离,分开 separate, disconnect, unfasten, disjoin, cut off, disengage, remove, undo, uncouple, sever, dissociate, isolate, loosen, free, unfix, unhitch, segregate, divide, disentangle, estrange.

detached adj.
- 分离的 separate, disconnected, dissociated, severed, free, loose, divided, discrete.
- 独立的 aloof, neutral, dispassionate, impersonal, impartial, independent, disinterested, objective.

detachment n.
- 公平 aloofness, remoteness, coolness, unconcern, indifference, impassivity, disinterestedness, nuetrality, impartiality, objectivity, fairness.
- 分离 separtion, disconnection, disunion, disengagement.
- 小队,小组 squad, unit, force, corps, brigade, patrol, task force.

detail n.
- 细节 particular, item, factor,

element, aspect, component, feature, point, specific, ingredient, attribute, count, respect, technicality, complication, intricacy, triviality, fact, thoroughness, elaboration, meticulousness, refinement, nicety.

v.

☞列举 list, enumerate, itemize, specify, catalogue, recount, relate.

☞派遣,分配 assign, appoint, charge, delegate, commission.

detailed *adj*.

☞详细的 comprehensive, exhaustive, full, blow-by-blow, thorough, minute, exact, specific, particular, itemized, intricate, elaborate, complex, complicated, meticulous, descriptive.

detain *v*.

☞使……延迟 delay, hold (up), hinder, impede, check, retard, slow, stay, stop.

☞扣押 confine, arrest, intern, hold, restrain, keep.

detect *v*.

☞查明 notice, ascertain, note, observe, perceive, recognize, discern, distinguish, identify, sight, spot, spy.

☞发觉,发现 uncover, discover, disclose, expose, find, track down, unmask, reveal.

detective *n*.

☞侦探 investigator, private, eye, sleuth, sleuth-hound.

detention *n*.

☞扣押 detainment, custody, confinement, imprisonment, restraint, incarceration, constraint, quarantine.

☞阻留 delay, hindrance, holding back.

determination *n*.

☞决定 resoluteness, tenacity, firmness, will-power, perseverance, persistence, purpose, backbone, guts, gril, steadfastness, single-mindedness, will, insistence, conviction, dedication, drive, fortitude.

☞判决 decision, judgement, settlement, resolution, conclusion.

determine *v*.

☞下决心 decide, settle, resolve, make up one's mind, choose, conclude, fix on, elect, clinch, finish.

☞测定,发现 discover, establish, find out, ascertain, identify, check, detect, verify.

☞使……决定 affect, influence, govern, control, dicture, direct, guide, regulate, ordain.

determined *adj*.

☞坚决的 resolute, firm, purposeful, strong-willed, single-minded, persevering, persistent, strong-minded, steadfast, tenacious, dogged, insistent, intent, fixed, convinced, decided, unflinching.

detract (from) *v*.

☞去掉,减损 diminish, subtract from, take away from, reduce, lessen, lower, devaluate, depreciate, belittle, disparage.

develop *v*.

☞前进,发展 advance, evolve,

expand, progress, foster, flourish, mature, prosper, branch out.

☞ 使成长,使发育 acquire, contract, begin, generate, create, invent.

☞ 出现,发生 result, come about, grow, ensue, arise, follow, happen.

development n.

☞ 发展,进步 growth, evolution, advance, blossoming, elaboration, furtherance, progress, unfolding, expansion, extension, spread, increase, improvement, maturity, promotion, refinement, issue.

☞ 新情况 occurrence, happening, event, change, outcome, situation, result, phenomenon.

deviate v.

☞ 脱离 diverge, veer, turn (aside), digress, swerve, vary, differ, depart, stray, yaw, wander, err, go astray, go off the rails, drift, part.

deviation n.

☞ 越轨,背离 divergence, aberration, departure, abnormality, irregularity, variance, variation, digression, alteration, disparity, discrepancy, detour, fluctuation, change, quirk, shift, freak.

device n.

☞ 设备,装置 tool, machine, implement, appliance, gadget, contrivance, contraption, apparatus, utensil, instrument.

☞ 计划,方案 scheme, ruse, strategy, plan, plot, gambit, manoeuvre, wile, trick, dodge, machination.

☞ 象征,标记 emblem, symbol, motif, logo, design, insigna, crest, badge, shield.

devil n.

☞ 魔鬼 demon, Satan, fiend, evilspirit, arch-fiend, Lucifer, imp, Evil One, Prince of Darkness, Adversary, Beelzebub, Mephistopheles, Old Nick, Old Harry.

☞ 残忍的人 brute, rogue, monster, ogre.

devious adj.

☞ 诡秘的,狡诈的 underhand, deceitful, dishonest, disingenuous, double-dealing, scheming, tricky, insidious, insincere, calculating, cunning, evasive, wily, sly, slippery, surreptitious, treacherous, misleading.

☞ 迂回的,曲折的 indirect, circuitous, rambling, roundabout, wandering, winding, tortuous, erratic.

devise v.

☞ 设计,发明,计划 invent, contrive, plan, plot, design, conceive, arrange, formulate, imagine, scheme, construct, concoct, forge, frame, project, shape, form.

devoid adj.

☞ 缺乏的,空的 lacking, wanting, without, free, bereft, destitute, deficient, deprived, barren, empty, vacant, void.

devote v.

☞ 专心从事,献身,奉献 dedicate, consecrate, commit,

give oneself, set apart, set aside, reserve, apply, allocate, allot, sacrifice, enshrine, assign, appropriate, surrender, pledge.

devoted adj.
☞ 忠实的，专心的　dedicated, ardent, committed, loyal, faithful, devout, loving, staunch, steadfast, true, constant, fond, unswerving, tireless, concerned, attentive, caring.

devotee n.
☞ 献身于……的人，信使　enthusiast, fan, fanatic, addict, aficionado, follower, supporter, zealot, adherent, admirer, disciple, buff, freak, merchant, hound.

devotion n.
☞ 奉献，献身，热爱　dedication, commitment, consecration, ardour, loyalty, allegiance, adherence, zeal, support, love, passion, fervour, fondness, attachment, adoration, affection, faithfulness, reverence, steadfastness, regard, earnestness.
☞ 虔诚　devoutness, piety, godliness, faith, holiness, spirituality.
☞ 祈祷　prayer, worship.

devour v.
☞ 吞吃　eat, consume, guzzle, gulp, gorge, gobble, bolt, wolf down, swallow, stuff, cram, polish off, gormandize, feast on, relish, revel in.
☞ 毁灭，吞没　destroy, consume, absorb, engulf, ravage, dispatch.

devout adj.
☞ 真诚的　sincere, earest, devoted, fervent, genuine, staunch, steadfast, ardent, passionate, serious, wholehearted, constant, faithful, intense, heartfelt, zealous, unswerving, deep, profound.
☞ 虔诚的　pious, godly, religious, reverent, prayerful, saintly, holy, orthodox.

diagnose v.
☞ 诊断　identify, determine, recognize, pinpoint, distinguish, analyse, explain, isolate, interpret, investigate.

diagnosis n.
☞ 诊断　identification, verdict, explanation, conclusion, answer, interpretation, analysis, opinion, investigation, examination, scrutiny.

diagram n.
☞ 图表　plan, sketch, chart, drawing, figure, representation, scfhema, illustration, outline, graph, picure, layout, table.

dial n.
☞ 刻度盘　circle, disc, face, clock, control.
v.
☞ 拨号　phone, ring, call (up).

dialect n.
☞ 方言　idiom, language, regionalism, patois, provincialism, vernacular, argot, iargon, accent, lingo, speech, diction.

dialectic adj.
☞ 合理的　dialectical, logical,

rational, argumentative, analtical, rationalistic, locistic, polemical, inductive, deductive.

n.

☞ 辩证法 dialectics, logic, reasoning, rationale, disputation, analysis, debate, argumentation, contention, discussion, polemics, induction, deduction.

dialogue *n.*
☞ 对话 conversation, interchange, discourse, communication, talk, exchange, discussion, converse, debate, conference.

☞ 对白(剧本) lines, script.

diary *n.*
☞ 日记 journal, day-book, logbook, chronicle, year-book, appointment book, engagement book.

dictate *v.*
☞ 口述 SAY, speak, utter, announce, pronounce, transmit.

☞ 命令,支配 command, order, direct, decree, instruct, rule.

n.

☞ 命令 command, decree, precept, principle, rule, direction, injunction, deict, order, ruling, statute, requirement, ordinance, law, bidding, mandate, ultimatum, word.

dictator *n.*
☞ 独裁者 despot, autocrat, tyrant, supremo, Big Brother.

dictatorial *adj.*
☞ 独裁的 tyrannical, despotic, totalitarian, authoritarian, autocratic, oppressive, imperious, domineering, bossy, absolute, repressive, overbearing, arbityary, dogmatic.

dictionary *n.*
☞ 字典 lexicon, glossary, thesaurus, vocabulary, vordbook, encyclopaedia, concordance.

die *v.*
☞ 死亡 decease, perish, pass away, expire, depart, breathe one's last, peg out, snuff it, bite the dust, kick the bucket.

☞ 消失,结束 dwindle, fade, ebb, sink, wane, wilt, wither, peter out, decline, decay, finish, lapse, end, disappear, vanish, subside.

☞ 渴望 long for, pine for, yearn, desire.

die-hard *n.*
☞ 老顽固,守旧者 reactionary, intransigent, hardliner, blimp, ultra-conservative, old fogey, stick-in-the-mud, rightist, fanatic.

diet *n.*
☞ 食物 food, nutrition, provisions, sustenance, rations, foodstuffs, subsistence.

☞ 斋戒 fast, abstinence, regimen.

v.

☞ 节食 lose weight, slim, fast, reduce, abstain, weight-watch.

differ *v.*
☞ 不同 vary, diverge, deviate, depart from, contradict, contrast.

☞ 意见不同 disagree, argue, conflict, oppose, dispute,

dissent, be at odds with, clash, quarrel, fall out, debate, contend, take, issue.

difference n.
- 差别,差距 dissimilarity, unlikeness, discrepancy, divergence, diversity, variation, variety, distinctness, distinction, deviation, differentiation, contrast, disparity, singularity, exception.
- 不和,争执 disagreement, clash, dispute, conflict, contention, controversy.
- 差额 remainder, rest.

different adj.
- 不同的,差异的 dissimila, unlike, contrasting, divergent, inconsistent, deviating, at odds, clashing, opposed.
- 各种 varied, various, diverse, miscellaneous, assorted, disparate, many, numerous, several, sundry, other.
- 与众不同的 unusual, unconventional, unique, distinct, distinctive, extraordinary, individual, original, special, strange, separate, peculiar, rare, bizarre, anomalous.

differentiate v.
- 分辨,辨别 distinguish, tell apart, discriminate, contrast, separate, mark off, individualize, particularize.

difficult adj.
- 不容易的 hard, laborious, demanding, arduous, strenuous, tough, wearisome, uphill, formidable.
- 难的,复杂的 complex, complicated, intricate, involved, abstruse, obscure, dark, knotty, thorny, problematical, perplexing, abstract, baffling, intractable.
- 难相处的,不随和的 unmanageable, perverse, troublesome, trying, uncooperative, tiresome, stubborn, obstinate, intractable.

difficulty n.
- 艰苦 hardship, trouble, labour, arduousness, painfulness, trial, tribualtion, awkwardness.
- 困境,难题 problem, predicament, dilemma, quandary, perplexity, embarrassment, plight, distress, fix, mess, jam, spot, hiccup, hang-up.
- 障碍 obstacle, hindrance, hurdle, impediment, objection, opposition, block, complication, pitfall, protest, stumbling-block.

diffidence n.
- 羞怯,不自信 unassertiveness, modesty, shyness, self-consciousness, self-effacement, timidity, insecurity, reserve, bashfulness, humility, inhibition, meekness, self-distrust, self-doubt, hesitancy, reluctance, backwardness.

diffident adj.
- 害羞的,缺乏自信的 unassertive, modest, shy, timid, self-conscious, self-effacing, insecure, bashful, abashed, meek, reserved, withdrawn, tentative,

shrinking, inhibited, hesitant, reluctant, unsure, shamefaced.

dig v.
- 挖,掘 excavate, penetrate, burrow, mine, quarry, scoop, tunnel, till, gouge, delve, pierce.
- 戳,捅 poke, prod.
- 搜寻,探索 investigate, probe, go into, research, search.

n.
- 嘲弄,嘲笑 gibe, jeer, sneer, taunt, crack, insinuation, insult, wisecrack.

dig up
- 发现 discover, unearth, uncover, disinter, expose, extricate, exhume, find, retrieve, track down.

digest v.
- 消化 absorb, assimilate, incorporate, process, dissolve.
- 领悟,理解 takein, absorb, understand, assimilate, grasp, study, consider, contemplate, meditate, ponder.
- 整理,缩短文章 shorten, summarize, condense, compress, reduce.

n.
- 摘要,文摘 summary, abridgement, abstract, precis, synopsis, resume, reduction, abbreviation, compression, compendium.

dignified adj.
- 高贵的,尊严的 stately, solemn, imposing, majestic, noble, august, lordly, lofty, exalted, formal, distinguished, grave, impressive, reserved, honourable.

dignitary n.
- 职位高的人 worthy, notable, VIP, high-up, personage, bigwig.

dignity n.
- 尊严 stateliness, propriety, solemnity, decorum, courtliness, grandeur, loftiness, majesty, honour, eminence, importance, nobility, self-respect, self-esteem, standing, poise, respectability, greatness, status, pride.

dilemma n.
- 两难 quandary, conflict, predicament, problem, catch-
- 困难 difficulty, puzzle, embarrassment, perplexity, plight.

diligent adj.
- 努力的,勤勉的 assiduous, industrious, hard-working, conscientious, painstaking, busy, attentive, tireless, careful, meticulous, persevering, persistent, studious.

dim adj.
- 暗淡的 dark, dull, dusky, cloudy, shadowy, gloomy, sombre, dingy, lack-lustre, feeble, imperfect.
- 模糊的 indistinct, blurred, hazy, ill-defined, obscure, misty, unclear, foggy, fuzzy, vague, faint, weak.
- 迟钝的 stupid, dense, obtuse, thick, doltish.

v.
- 使暗淡,使模糊 darken, dull, obscure, cloud, blur, fade, tarnish, shade.

dimension(s) n.
- 尺寸,量度 extent, measurement, measure, size, scope, magnitude, largeness, capacity, mass, scale, range, bulk, importance, greatness.

diminish v.
- 减少(小,低) decrease, lessen, reduce lower, contract, decline, dwindle, shrink, recede, taper off, wane, weaken, abate, fade, sink, subside, ebb, slacken, cut.
- 贬低 belittle, disparage, deprecate, devalue.

dine v.
- 就餐,宴请 eat, feast, sup, lunch, banquet, feed.

dinner n.
- 晚宴,宴会 meal, supper, tea, banquet, feast, spread, repast.

dip v.
- 蘸,浸 plunge, immerse, submerge, duck, dunk, bathe, douse, sink.
- 下降 descend, decline, drop, fall, subside, slump, sink, lower.

  n.
- 下沉,下降 hollow, basin, decline, hole, concavity, incline, depression, fall, slone, slump, lowering.
- 浸泡 bathe, immersion, plunge, soaking, ducking, swim, drenching, infusion, dive.

diplomat n.
- 外交家 go-between, mediator, negotiator, ambassador, envoy, conciliator, peacemaker, moderator, politician.

diplomatic adj.
- 外交的 tactful, politic, discreet, judicious, subtle, sensitive, prudent, discreet.

dire adj.
- 可怕的 disastrous, dreadful, awful, appalling, calamitous, catastrophic.
- 极度的 desperate, urgent, grave, drastic, crucial, extreme, alarming, ominous.

direct v.
- 管理 control, manage, run, administer, organize, lead, govern, regulate, superintend, supervise.
- 指挥,命令 instruct, command, order, charge.
- 指导 guide, lead, conduct, point.
- aim, point, focus, turn.

  adj.
- 直的 straight, undeviating, through, uninterrupted.
- 直率的,坦白的 straightforward, outspoken, blunt, frank, unequivocal, sincere, candid, honest, explicit.
- 直接的 immediate, first-hand, face-to-face, personal.

direction n.
- 管理,指导 control, administration, management, government, supervision, guidance, leadership.
- 路径 route, way, line, road.

directions n.
- 说明(书),指引(路)

instructions, guidelines, orders, briefing, guidance, recommendations, indication, plan.

directive n.
☞ 命令 command, instruction, order, regulation, ruling, imperative, dictate, decree, charge, mandate, injunction, ordinance, edict, fiat, notice.

directly adv.
☞ 立即 immediately, instantly, promptly, right away, speedily, forthwith, instantaneously, quickly, soon, presently, straightaway, straight.
☞ 直率地,坦诚地 frankly, bluntly, candidly, honestly.

director n.
☞ 主任(管),理(董)事,导演 manager, head, boss, chief, controller, executive, principal, governor, leader, organizer, supervisor, administrator, producer, conductor.

dirt n.
☞ 灰尘,泥土 eatrh, soil, clay, dust, mud.
☞ 污物,污点 filth, girme, muck, mire, excrement, stain, smudge, slime, tarish.
☞ 淫猥 indecency, impurity, obscenity, pornography.

dirty adj.
☞ 脏的,污秽的 filthy, grimy, grubby, mucky, soiled, unwashed, foul, messy, muddy, polluted, squalid, dull, miry, scruffy, shabby, sullied, clouded, dark.
☞ 下流的,淫猥的 indecent, obscene, filthy, scutty, sordid, salacious, vulgar, pornographic, corrupt.
v.
☞ 弄脏 pollute, soil, stain, foul, mess up, defile, smear, smirch, spoil, smudge, sully, muddy, blacken.

disability n.
☞ 残疾,丧失生活(劳动)能力, 无力 handicap, impairment, disablement, disorder, inability, incapacity, infirmity, defect, unfitness, disqualification, affliction, ailment, complaint, weakness.

disable v.
☞ 使残疾 cripple, lame, incapacitate, danmage, handicap, impair, debilitate, disqualify, weaken, immobilize, invalidate, paralyse, prostrate.

disabled adj.
☞ 残废的 handicapped, incapacitated, impaired, infirm, crippled, lame, immobilized, maimed, weak, weakened, paralysed, wrecked.

disadvantage n.
☞ 不利,短处 harm, damage, detriment, hurt, injury, loss, prejudice.
☞ 弊端 drawback, snag, hindrance, handicap, impediment, inconvenience, flaw, nuisance, weakness, trouble.

disadrangaged adj.
☞ 不利的,弊端的 deprived, underprivileged, poor, handicapped, impoverished, struggling.

disadvantageous adj.
- 不利的,有害的 harmful, detrimental, inopportune, unfavourable, prejudicial, adverse, damaging, hurtful, injurious, inconvenient, ill-timed.

disaffected adj.
- 政治上不满的,叛离的 disloyal, hostile, estranged, alienated, antagonistic, rebellious, dissatisfied, disgruntled, discontened.

disaffection n.
- 背离,叛离 disloyalty, hostility, alienation, discontentment, resentment, ill-will, dissatisfaction, animosity, coolness, unfriendliness, antagonism, disharmony, discord, disagreement, aversion, dislike.

disagree v.
- 意见不同 dissent, oppose, quarrel, argue, bicker, fall out, wrangle, fight, squabble, contend, dispute, contest, object.
- 不一致 conflict, clash, diverge, contradict, counter, differ, deviate, depart, run counter to, vary.

disagreement n.
- 意见不同 dispute, argument, conflic, altercation, quarrel, clash, dissent, falling-out, contention, strife, misunderstanding, squabble, tiff, wrangle.
- 不一致 difference, variance, unlikeness, disparity, discrepancy, deviation, discord, dissimilarity, incompatibility, divergence, diversity, incongruity.

disappear v.
- 不见,消失 vanish, wane, recede, fade, evaporate, dissolve, ebb.
- 绝迹 go, depart, withdraw, retire, flee, fly, excape, scarper, hide.
- 走失 end, expire, perish, pass.

disappearance n.
- 失踪,消失 vanishing, fading, evaporation, departure, loss, going, passing, melting, desertion, flight.

disappoint v.
- 使失望,扫兴 fail, dissatisfy, let down, disillusion, dash, dismay, disenchant, sadden, thwart, vex, frustrate, foil, dishearten, disgruntle, disconcert, hamper, hinder, deveive, defeat, delude.

disappointed adj.
- 失望的 let down, frustrated, thwarted, disllusioned, dissatisfied, miffed, upset, discouraged, disgruntled, disheartened, distressed, downhearted, saddened, despondent, depressed.

disappointment n.
- 失望 frustration, dissatisfaction, failure, disenchantment, disillusionment, displeasure, discouragement, distress, regret.
- 令人扫兴的事 failure, let-down, setback, comedown, blow, misfortune, fiasco,

disaster, calamity, washout, damp squib, swiz, swizzle.

disapproval n.
☞ 反对 censure, disapprobation, condemnation, criticism, displeasure, reproach, objection, dissatisfaction, denunciation, dislike.

disapprove of
☞ 不赞成 censure, condemn, blame, take, exception to, object to, deplore, denounce, disparage, dislike, reject, spurn.

disarm v.
☞ 解除武器,裁减军队 disable, unarm, demilitarize, demobilize, deactivate, dishand.
☞ 使息怒,使化解 appease, conciliate, in over, mollify, persuade.

disaster n.
☞ 灾难,天灾 calamity, catastrophe, misfortune, reverse, tragedy, blow, accident, act of God, cataclysm, debacle, mishap, failure, flop, fiasco, ruin, stroke, trouble, mischance, ruination.

disastrous adj.
☞ 灾难性的 calamitous, catastrophic, cataclysmic, devastating, ruinous, tragic, unfortunate, dreadful, dire, terrible, destructive, ill-fated, fatal, miserable.

disbelief n.
☞ 怀疑 unbelief, incredulity, doubt, scepticism, suspicion, distrust, mistrust, rejection.

disbelieve v.
☞ 不认为,不相信 discount, discredit, repudiate, reject, mistrust, suspect.

disc n.
☞ 圆 circle, face, plate, ring.
☞ 光盘 record, album, LP, CD.
☞ 圆盘 disk, diskette, hard disk, floppy disk, CD-ROM.

discard v.
☞ 丢弃 reject, abandon, dispose of, get rid of, jettison, dispense with, cast aside, ditch, dump, drop, scrap, shed, remove, relinquish.

discern v.
☞ 识别,看出 perceive, make out, observe, detect, recognize, see, ascertain, notice, determine, discover, descry.
☞ 辨别,分辨 discriminate, distinguish, differentiate, judge.

discernible adj.
☞ 明白的,看得出的 perceptible, noticeable, detectable, appreciable, distinct, observable, recognizable, visible, apparent, clear, obvious, plain, patent, manifest, discoverable.

discerning adj.
☞ 有眼光的,高明的 discriminating, perceptive, astute, clear-sighted, sensitive, shrewd, wise, sharp, subtle, sagacious, penetrating, acute, piercing, critical, eagle-eyed.

discharge v.
☞ 开释 liberate, free, pardon, release, clear, absolve, exonerate, acquit, relive, dismiss.

- ☞ 流出 execute, carry out, perform, fulfil, dispense.
- ☞ 解雇 fire, shoot, let off, detonate, explode. 4 emit, sack, remove, fire, expel, oust, eject.

n.
- ☞ 释放 liberation, release, acquittal, exoneration.
- ☞ 放出物 emission, secretion, ejection.
- ☞ 执行 execution, accomplishment, fulfilment.

disciple n.
- ☞ 信徒 follower, convert, proselyte, adherent, believer, devotee, supporter, learner, pupil, student.

discipline n.
- ☞ 训练 training, exercise, dirll, practice.
- ☞ 处罚 punishment, chastisement, correction.
- ☞ 纪律 strictness, restraint, regulation, self-control, orderliness.

v.
- ☞ 训练 train, instruct, drill, educate, exercise, break in.
- ☞ 管教 check, control, correct, restrain, govern.
- ☞ 惩罚 punish, chastize, chasten, penalize, reprimand, castigate.

disclaim v.
- ☞ 放弃……权利,拒绝承认 deny, disown, repudiate, abandon, renounce, reject.

disclose v.
- ☞ 表明,说出 divulge, make known, reveal, tell, confess, let slip, relate, publish, communicate, impart, leak.
- ☞ 揭露 expose, reveal, uncover, lay bare, unveil, discover.

disclosure n.
- ☞ 说出,表露 divulgence, exposure, expose, revelation, uncovering, publication, leak, discovery, admission, acknowledgement, announcement, declaration.

discomfort n.
- ☞ 不舒适 ache, pain, uneasiness, malaise, trouble, distress, disquiet, hardship, vexation, irritation, annoyance.

disconnect v.
- ☞ 使分离 cot off, disengage, uncouple, sever, separate, detach, unplug, unhook, part, divide.

discontent n.
- ☞ 不满 uneasiness, dissatisfaction, disquiet, restlessness, fretfulness, unrest, impatience, vexation, regret.

discontented adj.
- ☞ 不满意的 dissatisfied, fed up, disgruntled, unhappy, browned off, cheesed off, disaffected, miserable, exasperated, complaining.

discontinue v.
- ☞ 停止,终止 stop, end, finish, cease, break off, terminate, halt, drop, suspend, abandon, cancel, interrupt.

discord n.
- ☞ 争论,不和 dissension, disagreement, discordance, clashing, disunity, incompatibility, conflict,

difference, dispute, contention, friction, division, opposition, strife, split, wrangling.
☞ 不和谐 dissonance, disharmony, jangle, jarring, harshness.

discount¹ v.
☞ 不重视,不理会 disregard, ignore, overlook, disbelieve, gloss over.
☞ 打折扣 reduce, deduct, mark down, knock off.

discount² n.
☞ 折扣 reduction, rebate, allowance, cut, concession, deduction, mark-down.

discourage v.
☞ 使丧失勇气 dishearten, dampen, dispirit, depress, demoralize, dismay, unnerve, deject, disappoint.
☞ 阻扰,妨碍 deter, dissuade, hinder, put off, restrain, prevent.

discouragement n.
☞ 沮丧,气馁 downheartedness, despondency, pessimism, dismay, depression, dejection, despair, disappointment.
☞ 令人沮丧的人或物 deterrent, damper, setback, impediment, obstacle, opposition, hindrance, restraint, rebuff.

discourse n.
☞ 谈话,谈论 conversation, dialogue, chat, communication, talk, converse, discussion.
☞ 演讲,论述 speech, address, oration, lecture, sermon, essay, treatise, dissertation, homily.
v.
☞ 讨论,谈论 converse, talk, discuss, debate, confer, lecture.

discover v.
☞ 揭露 find, uncover, unearth, dig up, disclose, reveal, light on, locate.
☞ 发现 ascertain, determine, realize, notice, recognize, perceive, see, find out, spot, discern, learn, detect.
☞ 发明 originate, invent, pioneer.

discovery n.
☞ 发现 breakthrough, find, origination, introduction, innovation, invention, exploration.
☞ 探查 disclosure, detection, revelation, location.

discredit v.
☞ 不信任,怀疑 disbelieve, distrust, doubt, question, mistrust, challenge.
☞ 使蒙羞 disparage, dishonour, degrade, defame, disgrace, slander, slur, smear, reproach, vilify.
n.
☞ 不信任 disbelief, distrust, doubt, mistrust, scepticism, suspicion.
☞ 耻辱 dishonour, disrepute, censure, aspersion, disgrace, blame, shame, reproach, slur, smear, scahdal.

discreditable adj.
☞ 耻辱的 dishonourable, disreputable, disgraceful, reprehensible, scandalous, blameworthy, shameful,

infamous, degrading, improper.

discreet adj.
- 言行谨慎的,小心的 tactful, careful, diplomatic, politic, prudent, cautious, delicate, judicious, reserved, wary, sensible.

discretion n.
- 判断,辨别 tact, diplomacy, judiciousness, caution, prudence, wisdom, circumspection, discernment, judgement, care, carefulness, consideration, wariness.
- 倾向 choic, freedom, preference, will, wish.

discriminate v.
- 区别,辨别 distinguish, differentiate, discern, tell apart, make a distinction, segregate, separate.
- 歧视 be prejudiced, be biased, vicimize.

discriminating adj.
- 有辨别能力的,歧视的 discerning, fastidious, selective, critical, perceptive, particular, tasteful, astute, sensitive, cultivated.

discrimination n.
- 歧视 bias, prejudice, intolerance, unfairness, bigotry, favourtism, inequity, racism, sexism.
- 辨别 discernment, judgement, acumen, perception, acuteness, insight, penetration, subtlety, keenness, refinement, taste.

discuss v.
- 讨论,商议 debate, talk about, confer, argue, consider, deliberate, converse, consult, examine.

discussion n.
- 讨论,商议 debate, conference, argument, conversation, dialogue, exchange, consultation, discourse, deliberation, consideration, analysis, review, examination, scrutiny, seminar, symposium.

disdain n.
- 鄙视,轻视 scorn, contempt, arrogance, haughtiness, derision, sneering, dislike, snobbishness.

disdainful adj.
- 鄙视的,轻视的 scornful, contemptuous, derisive, haughty, aloof, arrogant, supercilious, sneering, superior, proud, insolent.

disease n.
- 疾病 illness, sickness, ill-health, infirmity, complaint, disorder, ailment, indisposition, malady, condition, affliction, infection, epidemic.

diseased adj.
- 有病的 sick, ill, unhealthy, ailing, unsound, contaminated, infected.

disentangle v.
- 解开 loose, free, extricate, disconnect, untangle, disengage, detach, unravel, separate, unfold.
- 解决 resolve, clarify, simplify.

disgrace n.
- 耻辱 shame, ignominy,

disrepute, dishonour, disfavour, humiliation, defamation, discredit, scandal, reproach, slur, stain.
v.
☞ 使出丑 shame, dishonour, abase, defame, humiliate, disavour, stain, discredit, reproach, slur, sully, taint, stigmatize.

disgraceful adj.
☞ 耻辱的 shameful, dishonourable, disreputable, ignominious, scandalous, shocking, unworthy, dreadful, appalling.

disguise v.
☞ 伪装,掩饰 conceal, cover, camouflage, mask, hide, dress up, clock, screen, veil, shroud.
☞ 假扮,假装 falsify, deceive, dissemble, misrepresent, fake, fudge.
n.
☞ 化装物,假扮物 concealment, camouflage, cloak, cover, costume, mask, front, facade, masquerade, deception, pretence, travesty, screen, veil.

disgust v.
☞ 使厌恶,使憎恶 offend, displease, nauseate, revolt, sicken, repel, outrage, put off.
n.
☞ 厌恶,恶心 revulsion, repulsion, repugnance, distaste, aversion, abhorrence, nausea, loathing, detestation, hatred.

disgusted adj.
☞ 恶心的,厌恶的 repelled, repulsed, revolted, offended, appalled, outraged.

disgusting adj.
☞ 令人厌恶的 repugnant, repellent, revolting, offensive, sickening, nauseating, odious, foul, unappetizing, unpleasant, vile, obscence, abominable, detestable, objectionable, nasty.

dish n.
☞ 碟,一道菜 plate, bowl, platter, food, recipe.

dish out
☞ 分配,分发 distribute, give out, hand out, hand round, dole out, allocate, mete out, inflict.

dish up
☞ 提出 serve, present, ladle, spoon, dispense, scoop.

dishonest adj.
☞ 不诚实的,欺诈的 untruthful, fraudulent, deceitful, false, lying, deceptive, double-dealing, cheating, crooked, treacherous, unprincipled, swindling, shady, corrupt, disreputable.

dishonesty n.
☞ 不诚实,欺诈 deceit, falsehood, falsity, fraudulence, fraud, criminality, insincerity, treachery, cheating, crookedness, corruption, unscrulousness, trickery.

dishonour v.
☞ 沾辱,使蒙羞 disgrace, shame, humiliate, debase, defile, degrade, defame, discredit, demean, debauch.
n.
☞ 耻辱 disgrace, abasement, humiliation, shame, degradation, discredit, disrepute, indignity, ignominy, disrepute, indignity, ignominy,

reproach, slight, slur, scandal, insult, disfavour, outage, aspersion, abuse, discourtesy.

disillusioned adj.
☞ 醒悟的,清醒的 disenchanted, disabused, undeceived, disappointed.

disinterest n.
☞ 公开,客观 disinterestedness, impartiality, neutrality, detachment, unbiasedness, dispassionateness, fairness.

disinterested adj.
☞ 公开的,客观的 unbiased, neutral, impartial, unprejudiced, dispassionate, detached, uninvolved, open-minded, equitable, even-handed, unselfish.

dislike n.
☞ 憎恶,反感 aversion, hatred, repugnance, hostility, distaste, disinclination, disapproval, disapprobation, displeasure, animosity, angagonism, enmity, detestation, disgust, loathing.
v.
☞ 憎恶,不喜欢 hate, detest, object to, loathe, abhor, abominate, disapprove, shun, despise, scorn.

disloyal adj.
☞ 不忠的,背叛的 treacherous, faithless, false, traitorous, two-faced, unfaithful, apostate, unpatriotic.

dismal adj.
☞ 忧愁的,阴暗的 dreary, gloomy, depressing, bleak, cheerless, dull, drab, low-spirited, melancholy, sad, sombre, lugubrious, forlorn, despondent, dark, sorrowful, long-faced, hopeless, discouraging.

dismantle v.
☞ 拆开 demolish, take apart, disassemble, strip.

dismay v.
☞ 使惊慌,使沮丧 alarm, daunt, frighten, unnerve, unsettle, scare, put off, dispirit, distress, disconcert, dishearten, discourage, disillusion, depress, horrify, disappoint.
n.
☞ 恐惧,沮丧 consternation, alarm, distress, apprehension, agitation, dread, fear, trepidation, fright, horror, terror, discouragement, disappointment.

dismiss v.
☞ 解散 discharge, free, let go, release, send sawy, remove, drop, discord, banish.
☞ 解职,开除 sack, make redundant, lay off, fire, relegate.
☞ 不理会,放开 discount, disregard, reject, repudiate, set aside, shelve, spun.

disobey v.
☞ 不服从 contravene, infringe, violate, transgress, flout, disregard, defy, ignore, resist, rebel.

disorder n.
☞ 扰乱 confusion, chaos, muddle, disarray, mess, untidiness, shambles, clutter, disorganization, jumble.

- 骚乱 disturbance, tumult, riot, confusion, commotion, uproar, fracas, brawl, fight, clamour, quarrel.
- 小病 illness, complaint, disease, sickness, disability, ailment, malady, affliction.

v.
- 使扰乱 disturb, mess up, disarrange, mix up, muddle, upset, disorganize, confuse, confound, clutter, jumble, discompose, scatter, unsettle.

disorderly adj.
- 不整齐的,混乱的 disorganized, confused, chaotic, irregular, messy, untidy.
- 秩序乱的,骚动的 unruly, undisciplined, unmanageable, obstreperous, rowdy, turbulent, rebelious, lawless.

dispatch, despatch v.
- 发送 send, express, transmit, forward, consign, expedite, accelerate.
- 做完,完成 dispose of, finish, perform, discharge, conclude.
- 处决 kill, murder, execute.

n.
- 电讯,政府公文 communication, message, report, bulletin, communique, news, letter, account.
- 迅速,准确 promptness, speed, alacrity, expedition, celerity, haste, rapidity, swiftness.

dispense v.
- 给与,分配给 distribute, give out, apportion, allot, allocate, assign, share, mete out.
- 施行,让……有 administer, apply, implement, enforce, discharge, execute, operate.

dispense with
- 免除,省却 dispose of, get rid of, abolish, discard, omit, disregard, cancel, forgo, ignore, waive.

disperse v.
- 弄散,驱散,解散 scatter, dispel, spread, distribute, diffuse, dissolve, break up, dismiss, separate.

displace v.
- 赶走,取代 dislodge, move, shift, misplace, disturb, dislocate.
- 移位,重放 depose, oust, remove, replace, dismiss, discharge, supplant, eject, evict, succeed, supersede.

display v.
- 陈列,展览 show, present, demonstrate, exhibit.
- 显示 betray, disclose, reveal, show, expose.
- 炫耀 show off, flourish, parade, flaunt.

n.
- 陈列,展览 show, exhibition, demonstration, presentation, parade, spectacle, revelation.

disposal n.
- 丢掉,销毁 arrangement, grouping, order.
- 配置 control, direction, command.
- 清理,去掉 removal, riddance, discarding, jettisoning.

disposed adj.
- 愿意的 liable, inclined, predisposed, prone, likely, apt,

disposition n.
☞ 配置,气质 character, nature, temperament, inclination, make-up, bent, leaning, predisposition, constitution, habit, spirit, tendency, proneness.

minded, subject, ready, willing.

disproportionate adj.
☞ 不相称的,不均衡的 unequal, uneven, incommensurate, excessive, unreasonable.

disprove v.
☞ 反驳,证明(某事)不成立 refute, rebut, confute, discredit, invalidate, contradict, expose.

dispute v.
☞ 争论,争吵 argue, debate, question, contend, challenge, discuss, doubt, contest, contradict, deny, quarrel, clash, wrangle, squabble.
n.
☞ 争论,争端,争吵 argument, debate, disagreement, controversy, conflict, contention, quarrel, wrangle, feud, strife, squabble.

disregard v.
☞ 不管,藐视 ignore, overlook, discount, neglect, pass over, disobey, make light of, turn a blind eye to, brush aside.
☞ 忽视,不注意 slight, snub, despise, disdain, disparage.
n.
☞ 忽视,不在意 neglect, negligence, inattention, oversight, disrespect, contempt, disdain, brush-off.

disreputable adj.
☞ 名声不好的,不体面的 disgraceful, discreditable, dishonourable, unrespectable, notorious, scandalous, shameful, shady, base, contemptible, low, mean, shocking.
☞ 衣衫褴褛的,破旧的 scruffy, shabby, seedy, unkempt.

disrespectful adj.
☞ 不礼貌的 rude, discourteous, impertinent, impolite, impudent, insolent, uncivil, unmannerly, cheeky, insulting, irreverent, contemptuous.

disrupt v.
☞ 分裂,瓦解,搞垮 disturb, disorganize, confuse, interrupt, break up, unsettle, intrude, upset.

dissatisfaction n.
☞ 不满 discontent, displeasure, dislike, discomfort, disappointment, frustration, annoyance, irritation, exasperation, regret, resentment.

dissension n.
☞ 冲突,争论,纠纷 disagreement, discord, dissent, dispute, contention, conflict, strife, friction, quarrel.

dissent v.
☞ 不同意 disagree, dirrer, protest, object, refuse, quibble.
n.
☞ 异议,不同意 disagreement, difference, dissension, discord, resistance, opposition, objection.

dissident adj.
☞ (对政府或权力机构)有异议

的 disagreeing, differing, dissenting, discordant, nonconformist. heterodox.
n.
☞持异议者 dissenter, protestor, noncomformist, reble, agitator, revolutionary, schismatic, recusant.

dissimilar adj.
☞不同的,不相似的 unlike, different, divergent, disparate, unrelated, incompatible, mismatched, diverse, various, heterogenous.

dissolute adj.
☞放荡的,荒淫的 dissipated, debauched. degenerate, depraved, wanton, abandoned, corrupt, immoral, licentious, lewd, wild.

dissolution n.
☞分散,解散(组织机构) disintegration, decomposition, separation, resolution, division.
☞解除(契约,条约婚约) ending, termination, conclusion, finish, discontinuation, divorce, dismissal, dispersal, destruction, overthrow.
☞消失 evaporation, disappearance.

dissolve v.
☞溶解 evaporate, disintegrate, liquefy, melt.
☞解散,分散 decompose, disintegrate, disperse, break up, disappear, crumble.
☞解除,分开 end, terminate, separate, sever, divorce.

dissuade v.
☞劝阻,劝止 deter, discourage, put off, disincline.

distance n.
☞距离,(社会地位,时间,空间)差异,间隔 space, interval, gap, extent, range, reach, length, width.
☞疏远,冷淡 aloofness, reserve, coolness, coldness, remoteness.

distant adj.
☞在远处,久远的 far, faraway, far-flung, out-of-the-way, remote, outlying, abroad, dispersed.
☞疏远的,冷淡的 aloof, cool, reserved, stand-offish, formal, cold, restrained, stiff.

distaste n.
☞厌恶 dislike, aversion, repugnance, disgust, revulsion, loathing, abhorrence.

distasteful adj.
☞讨厌的,乏味的 disagreeable, offensive, unpleasant, objectionable, repulsive, obnoxious, repugnant, unsavoury, loathsome, abhorrent.

distinct adj.
☞个别的,不同的 separate, different, detached, individual, dissimilar.
☞清楚的,明白(显)的 lear, plain, evident, obvious, apparent, marked, definite, noticeable, recognizable.

distinction n.
☞区别 differentiation, discrimination, discernment, separation, difference, dissimilarity, contrast.
☞特点 characteristic, peculiarity, individuality,

feature, quality, mark.
- 名望,声誉,优秀,卓越,荣誉 renown, fame, celebrity, prominence, eminence, importance, reputation, greatness, honour, prestige, repute, superiority, worth, merit, excellence, quality.

distinctive adj.
- 有特色的 characteristic, distinguishing, individual, peculiar, different, unique, singular, special, original, extraordinary, idiosyncratic.

distinguish v.
- 区别 differentiate, tell apart, discriminate, determine, categorize, characterize, classify.
- 识别,认出,看清楚 discern, perceive, identify, ascertain, make out, recognize, see, discriminate.

distinguished adj.
- 著名的,卓越的,杰出的,高贵的 famous, eminent, celebrated, well-known, acclaimed, illustrious, notable, noted, renowned, famed, honoured, outstanding, striking, marked, extraordinary, conspicuous.

distort v.
- 弄歪,扭曲,使变形 deform, contort, bend, misshape, disfigure, twist, warp.
- 歪曲,曲解 falsify, misrepresent, pervert, slant, colour, garble.

distract v.
- 轻移 divert, sidetrack, deflect.
- 使分心 confuse, disconcert, bewilder, confound, disturb, perplex, puzzle.
- 占用时间,使全神贯注 amuse, occupy, divert, engross.

distress n.
- 烦恼,痛苦 anguish, grief, misery, sorrow, heartache, affiction, suffering, torment, wretchedness, sadness, worry, anxiety, desolation, pain, agony.
- 穷困,危难,不幸 adversity, hardship, poverty, need, privation, destitution, misfortune, trouble, difficulties, trial.

v.
- 使痛苦,使烦恼 upset, afflict, grieve, disturb, trouble, sadden, worry, torment, harass, harrow, pain, agonize, bother.

distribute v.
- 分配,批发 dispense, allocate, dole out, dish out, share, deal, divide, apportion.
- 散布,散播 deliver, hand out, spread, issue, circulate, diffuse, disperse, scatter.

distribution n.
- 分配 allocation, apportionment, division, sharing.
- 散布,传播 circulation, spreading, scattering, delivery, dissemination, supply, dealing, handling.
- 分类,整理 characteristic, grouping, classification, organization.

district n.

☞ 地区,行政区,区域 region, area, quarter, neighbourhood, locality, sector, precinct, parish, locale, community, vicinity, ward.

distrust v.
☞ 不信任,怀疑 mistrust, doubt, dibelieve, suspect, question.
n.
☞ 怀疑 mistrust, doubt, disbelief, suspicion, misgiving, wariness, scepticism, question, qualm.

disturb v.
☞ 打扰,使不安 disrupt, interrupt, distract.
☞ 弄乱 agitate, unsettle, upset, distress, worry, fluster, annoy, bother.
☞ 扰乱 disarrange, disorder, confuse, upse.

disturbance n.
☞ 打扰,扰乱 disruption, agitation, interruption, intrusion, upheaval, upset, confusion, annoyance, bother, trouble, hindrance.
☞ 混乱,无秩序,动乱 disorder, uproar, commotion, tumult, turmoil, fracas, fray, brawl, riot.

ditch n.
☞ 沟,渠道 trench, dyky, channel, gully, furrow, moat, drain, level, watercourse.

dive v.
☞ 跳水,潜水,俯冲 plunge, plummet, dip, submerge, jump, leap, nose-dive, fall, drop, swoop, descend, pitch.
n.

☞ 跳水,潜水,俯冲 plunge, lunge, header, jump, leap, nose-dive, swoop, dash, spring.
☞ 低级餐室,下流场所 bar, club, saloon.

diverge v.
☞ 分开,分歧 divide, branch, fork, separate, spread, split.
☞ 脱离 deviate, digress, stray, wander.
☞ 不一样 differ, vary, disagree, dissent, conflict.

diverse adj.
☞ 不同的,种种的 various, varied, varying, sundry, different, differing, assorted, dissimilar, miscellaneous, discrete, separate, several, distinct.

diversify v.
☞ 使……变化 vary, change, expand, branch out, spread out, alter, mix, assort.

diversion n.
☞ 脱离,背离 deviation, detour.
☞ 娱乐 amusement, entertainment, distraction, pastime, recreation, relaxation, paly, game.
☞ 转换 alteration, change.

diversity n.
☞ 歧异,多样 variety, dissimilarity, difference, variance, assortment, range, medley.

divert v.
☞ 改变,交换 deelect, redirect, reroute, side-track, avert, distract, switch.
☞ 娱乐,消遣 amuse, entertain, occupy, distract, interest.

divide v.
- 分,划分 split, separate, part, cut, break up, detach, bisect, disconnect.
- 分配 distribute, share, allocate, deal out, allot, apportion.
- 隔开 disunite, separate, estrange, alienate. 4 classify, group, sort, grade, segregate.

divine adj.
- 上帝的,神的 godlike, superhuman, supernatural, celestial, heavenly, angelic, spiritual.
- 极好的 holy, sacred, sanctified, consecrated, transcendent, exalted, glorious, religious, supreme.

division n.
- 部分,片段 separation, detaching, parting, cutting, disunion.
- 意见不合,分裂,异议 breach, rupture, split, schism, disunion, estrangement, disagreement, feud.
- 分开,分配 distribution, sharing, allotment, apportionment.
- 部门 section, sector, segment, part, department, category, class, compartment, branch.

divorce n.
- 离婚,分离 dissolution, annulment, break-up, split-up, rupture, separation, breach, disunion.

v.
- 使分离 separate, part, annul, split up, sever, dissolve, divide, dissociate.

dizzy adj.
- 使头晕眩的 giddy, faint, light-headed, woozy, shaky, reeling.
- 糊涂的 confused, bewildered, dazed, muddled.

do v.
- 执行 perform, carry out, execute, accomplish, achieve, fulfil, implement, complete, undertake, work, put on, present, conclude, end, finish.
- 做 behave, act, conduct oneself.
- 整理 fix, prepare, organize, arrange, deal with, look after, manage, produce, make, create, cause, proceed.
- 服务 suffice, satisfy, serve.

n.
- 大宴会 function, affair, event, gathering, party, occasion.

do away with
- 除掉,废除 get rid of, dispose of, exterminate, eliminate, abolish, discontinue, remove, destroy, discard, kill, murder.

do up
- 打领带 fasten, tie, lace, pack.
- 修理 renovate, restore, decorate, redecorate, modernize, repair.

do without
- 没有……也行 dispense with, abstain from, forgo, give up, relinquish.

docile adj.
- 听话的,温驯的 tractable, co-operative, manageable,

dock¹ n.
- 码头,船坞 harbour, wharf, quay, boat-yard, pier, waterfront, marina.

v.
- 驶入码头 anchor, moor, drop anchor, land, berth, put in, tie up.

dock² v.
- 剪短 crop, clip, cut, shorten, curtail, deduct, reduce, lessen, withhold, decrease, subtract, diminish.

doctor n.
- 博士,医生 physician, general, practitioner, GP, medic, medical officer, consultant, clinician.

v.
- 为……治病 alter, tamper with, falsify, misrepresent, pervert, adulterate, change, disguise, dilute.
- 修理 repair, fix, patch up.

doctrine n.
- 教义,教旨 dogma, creed, belief, tenet, principle, teaching, precept, conviction, opinion, canon.

document n.
- 文件 paper, certificate, deed, record, report, form, instrument.

v.
- 记录 record, report, chronicle, list, detail, cite.
- 证明 support, prove, corroborate, verify.

dodge v.

submissive, obedient, amenable, controlled, obliging.
- 闪开,避开 avoid, elude, evade, swerve, side-step, shirk, shift.

n.
- 闪避,躲避 trick, ruse, ploy, wile, scheme, stratagem, machination, manoeuvre.

dog n.
- 窝囊废,恶棍,地痞 hound, cur, mongrel, canine, puppy, pup, bitch, mutt, pooch.

v.
- 尾随,缠住 pursue, follow, trail, track, tail, hound, shadow, plague, harry, haunt, trouble, worry.

dogged adj.
- 顽强的,坚韧不拔的 determined, resolute, persistent, persevering, intent, tenacious, firm, steadfast, staunch, single-minded, indefatigable, steady, unshakable, stubborn, obstinate, relentless, unyielding.

dogma n.
- 教义,教训 doctrine, creed, belief, precept, principle, article (of faith), crdeo, tenet, conviction, teaching, opinion.

dogmatic adj.
- 教条的 opinionated, assertive, authoritative, positive, doctrinaire, dictatorial, doctrinal, categorical, emphatic, overbearing, arbitrary.

domain n.
- 统治 dominion, kingdom, realm, territory, region, empire, lands, province.
- 版图,地域 field, area, speciality, concern, department, sphere, discipline, jurisdiction.

domestic adj.
- 家庭的 home, family, household, home-loving, stay-at-home, homely, pet, house-trained, tame, private.
- 国内的 internal, indigenous, native.

n.
- 佣人 servant, maid, charwoman, char, daily help, daily, au pair.

domesticate v.
- 驯养 tame, house-train, break, train, accustom, familiarize.

dominant adj.
- 命令式的,权威性的 authoritative, controlling, governing, ruling, powerful, assertive, influential.
- 主要的 principal, main, outstanding, chief, important, predominant, primary, prominent, leading, pre-eminent, prevailing, prevalent, commanding.

dominate v.
- 控制 control, domineer, govern, rule, direct, monopolize, master, lead, overrule, prevail, overbear, tyrannize.
- 遮蔽 overshadow, eclipse, dwarf.

dominion n.
- 统治 power, authority, domination, command, control, rule, sway, jurisdiction, government, lordship, mastery, supremacy, sovereignty.
- 领域,领土 domain, country, territory, province, colony, realm, kingdom, empire.

donate v.
- 提供 give, contribute, present, bequeath, cough up, fork out, subscribe.

donation n.
- 赠品,礼品 gift, present, offering, grant, gratuity, largess(e), contribution, presentation, subscription, alms, bequest.

done adj.
- 完成的 finished, over, accomplished, completed, ended, concluded, settled, realized, executed.
- 正常的 conventional, acceptable, proper.
- 煮熟的 cooked, ready.

donor n.
- 捐赠者 giver, donator, benefactor, contributor, philanthropist, provider, fairy godmother.

doom n.
- 命运 fate, fortune, destiny, portion, lot.
- 死亡 destruction, catastrophe, downfall, ruin, death, death-knell.
- 判决 condemnation, judgement, sentence, verdict.

v.
- 判决 condemn, damn, consign, judge, sentence, destine.

doomed adj.
- 注定的 condemned, damned, fated, ill-fated, ill-omened, cursed, destined, hopeless, luckless, ill-starred.

door n.

☞门 opening, entrance, entry, exit, doorway, portal, hatch.

dose n.
☞一剂，一服 measure, dosage, amount, portion, quantity, draught, potion, prescription, shot.
v.
☞叫……吃药 medicate, administer, prescribe, dispense, treat.

dot n.
☞一点 point, spot, speck, mark, fleck, circle, pin-point, atom, decimal point, full stop, iota, jot.
v.
☞点缀 spot, sprinkle, stud, dab, punctuate.

dote on
☞宠爱 adore, idolize, treasure, admire, indulge.

double adj.
☞双倍的 dual, twofold, twice, duplicate, twin, paired, doubled, coupled.
v.
☞加倍 duplicate, enlarge, increase, repeat, multiply, fold, magnify.
n.
☞两倍 twin, duplicate, copy, clone, replica, doppelganger, lookalike, spitting image, ringer, image, counterpart, impersonator.

at the double
☞立即 immediately, at once, quickly, without delay.

double-cross v.
☞欺骗 cheat, swindle, defraud, trick, con, hoodwink, betray, wto-time, mislead.

doubt v.
☞怀疑 distrust, mistrust, query, question, suspect, fear.
☞不相信 be uncertain, be dubious, hesitate, vacillate, waver.
n.
☞疑惑 distrust, suspicion, mistrust, scepticism, reservation, misgiving, incredulity, apprehension, hesitation.
☞难处 uncertainty, difficulty, confusion, ambiguity, problem, indecision, perplexity, dilemma, quandary.

doubtful adj.
☞迷茫的 uncertain, unsure, undecided, suspicious, irresolute, wavering, hesitant, vacillating, tentative, sceptical.
☞不可靠的 dubious, questionable, unclear, ambiguous, vague, obscure, debatable.

doubtless adv.
☞确定 certainly, without doubt, undoubtedly, unquestionably indisputably, no doubt, clearly, surely, of course, truly, precisely.
☞多半,很可能 probably, presumably, most likely, seemingly, supposedly.

douse, dowse v.
☞用水浸 soak, saturate, steep, submerge, immerse, immerge, dip, duck, drench, dunk, plunge.
☞弄熄 extinguish, put out, blow out, smother, snuff.

down v.
- 放下，打倒 knock down, fell, floor, prostrate, throw, topple.
- 吞下 swallow, drink, gulp, swig, knock back.

down and out
- 贫穷的 destitute, impoverished, penniless, derelict, ruined.

downcast adj.
- 垂头丧气的 dejected, depressed, despondent, sad, unhappy, miserable, down, low, disheartened, dispirited, blue, fed up, discouraged, disappointed, crestfallen, dismayed.

downfall n.
- 毁灭 fall, ruin, failure, collapse, destruction, disgrace, debacle, undoing, overthrow.

downgrade v.
- 降级 degrade, demote, lower, humble.
- 向下 disparage, denigrate, belittle, run down, decry.

downhearted adj.
- 意志消沉的 depressed, dejected, despondent, sad, downcast, discouraged, disheartened, low-spirited, unhappy, gloomy, glum, dismayed.

downpour n.
- 大雨 cloudburs, deluge, rainstorm, flood, inundation, torrent.

downright adj., adv.
- 百分之百的(地)，十足的(地) absolute(ly), outright, plain(ly), utter(ly), clear(ly), complete(ly), out-and-out, frank(ly), explicit(ly).

down-trodden adj.
- 被征服的 oppressed, subjugated, subservient, exploited, trampled on, aboused, tyrannized, victimized, helpless.

downward adj.
- 下降的，向下的 descending, declining, downhill, sliding, slipping.

doze v.
- 打瞌睡 sleep, nod off, drop off, snooze, kip, zizz.

n.
- 小睡 nap, catnap, siesta, snooze, forty winks, kip, shut-eye, zizz.

draft¹ v.
- 起草 draw (up), outline, sketch, plan, design, formulate, compose.

n.
- 草案 outline, sketch, plan, delineation, abstract, rough, blueprint, protocol.

draft² n.
- 汇票 bill of exchange, cheque, money order, letter of credit, postal order.

drag v.
- 拖，拉 draw, pull, haul, lug, tug, trail, tow.
- 慢吞吞地走 go slowly, creep, crawl, lag.

n.
- 困恼，麻烦 bore, annoyance, nuisance, pain, bother.

drain v.
- 喝尽 empty, remove,

evacuate, draw off, strain, dry, milk, bleed.
☞ 排出 discharge, trickle, flow out, leak, ooze.
☞ 耗尽 exhaust, consume, sap, use up, deplete, drink up, swallow.
n.
☞ 水管 channel, conduit, culvert, duct, outlet, trench, ditch, pipe, sewer.
☞ 坑道 depletion, exhaustion, sap, strain.

drama *n.*
☞ 戏剧 play, acting, theatre, show, spectacle, stage-craft, scene, melodrama.
☞ 戏剧性事件 excitement, crisis, turmoil.

dramatic *adj.*
☞ 刺激的,令人兴奋的 exciting, striking, stirring, thrlling, marked, significant, expressive, impressive.
☞ 戏剧性的 histrionic, exaggerated, melodramatic, flamboyant.

draw
☞ 吸引 attract, allure, entice, bring in, influence, persuade, elicit.
☞ 拖拉 pull, drag, haul, tow, tug.
☞ 描绘 delineate, map out, sketch, portray, trace, pencil, depict, design.
☞ 打成平局 tie, be equal, be even.
n.
☞ 诱饵 attraction, enticement, lure, appeal, bait, interest.
☞ 平局,和局 tie, stalemate, dead-heat.

draw out
☞ 变长,拉长,拖长 protract, extend, prolong, drag out, spin out, elongate, stretch, lengthen, string out.

draw up
☞ 写出 draft, compose, formulate, prepare, frame, write out.
☞ 停止 pull up, stop, halt, run in.

drawback *n.*
☞ 阻碍,不平的 disadvantage, snag, hitch, obstacle, impediment, hindrance, diffculty, flaw, fault, flv in the ointment, catch, stumbling block, nuisance, trouble, defect, handicap, deficiency, imperfection.

drawing *n.*
☞ 图样,图画,素描 sketch, picture, outline, representation, delineation, portrayal, illustration, cartoon, graphic, portrait.

dread *v.*
☞ 惧怕,担心 fear, shrink from, quail, cringe at, flinch, shy, shudder, tremble.
n.
☞ 害怕,担心 fear, apprehension, misgiving, trepidaton, dismay, alarm, horror, terror, fright, disquiet, worry, quietly, qualm.

dreadful *adj.*
☞ 令人担心的,令人担忧的 awful, terrible, frightful, horrible, appalling, dire, shocking, ghastly, horrendous,

tragic, grievous, hideous, tremendous.

dream n.
- 梦 vision, illusion, reverie, trance, fantasy, daydream, nightmare, hallucination, delusion, imagination.
- 梦想,空想 aspiration, wish, hope, ambition, desire, pipe-dream, ideal, goal, design, speculation.

v.
- 做梦,梦见,梦到 imagine, envisage, fancy, fantasize, daydream, hallucinate, conceive, visualize, conjure up, muse.

dream up
- 凭空想出 invent, devise, conceive, think up, imagine, concoct, hatch, create, spin, contrive.

dreamer n.
- 做梦的人,空想家 idealist, visionary, fantasizes, romancer, daydreamer, star-gazer, theorizer.

dreamy adj.
- 神情恍惚的 fantastic, unreal, imaginary, shadowy, vague, misty.
- 美妙的 impractical, fanciful, daydreaming, romantic, visionary, faraway, absent, musing, pensive.

dreary adj.
- 无聊的 boring, tedious, uneventful, dull, humdrum, routine, monotonous, wearisome, commonplace, colourless, lifeless.
- 阴沉的 gloomy, depressing, drab, dismal, bleak, sombre, sad, mournful.

drench v.
- 使淋透 soak, saturate, steep, wet, douse, souse, immerse, inundate, duck, flood, imbue, drown.

dress n.
- 长袍,长服 frock, gown, robe.
- 服装 clothes, clothing, garment(s), outfit, costume, garb, get-up, gear, togs.

v.
- 穿(衣) clothe, put on, garb, rig, robe, wear, don, decorate, deck, garnish, trim, adorn, fit, drape.
- 准备 arrange, adjust, dispose, prepare, groom, straighten.
- 敷裹伤口 bandage, tend, treat.

dress up
- 化妆 beautify, adorn, embellish, improve, deck, doll up, tart up, gild, disguise.

drift v.
- 漂流 wander, waft, stray, float, freewheel, coast.
- 聚集,堆起 gather, accumulate, pile up, drive.

n.
- 积累,积聚 accumulation, mound, pile, bank, mass, heap.
- 动向,趋向 trend, tendency, course, direction, flow, movement, current, rush, sweep.
- 大概,意念,要旨 meaning, intention, implication, gist, tenor, thrust, significance, aim, design, scope.

drill v.
- 操练,训练 teach, train, instruct, coach, practise, school, rehearse, exercise, discipline.
- 钻 bore, pierce, penetrate, puncture, perforate.

n.
- 操练,训练 instruction, training, practice, coaching, exercise, repetition, tuition, preparation, discipline.
- 钻,钻头 borer, wal, bit, gimlet.

drink v.
- 饮,喝 imbibe, swallow, sip, drain, down, gulp, swig, knock back, sup, quaff, absorb, guzzle, partake of, swill.
- 饮酒,喝酒 gef drunk, booze, tipple, indulge, carouse, revel, tank up.

n.
- 饮料 beverage, liquid, refreshment, draught, sip, swallow, swig, gulp.
- 酒 alcohol, spirits, booze, liquor, tot, the bottle, stiffener

drip v.
- (使)滴下 drop, dribble, trickle, plop, perculate, drizzle, splash, sprinkle, weep.

n.
- 水滴 drop, trickle, dribble, leak, bead, tear.
- 无用的人 weakling, wimp, softy, bore, wet, ninny.

drive v.
- 控制 direct, control, manage, operate, run, handle, motivate.
- 强迫 force, compel, impel, coerce, constrain, press, push, urge, dragoon, gpad, guide, oblige.
- 赶,驱 steer, motor, propel, ride, travel.

n.
- 雄心,事业心,野心 energy, enterprise, ambition, initiative, get-up-and-go, givour, motivation, determination.
- 运动 campaign, crusade, appeal,, effort, action.
- 旅行 excursion, outing, journey, ride, spin, trip, jaunt, urge, instinct, impulse, need, desire.

drive at
- 意指,意欲 imply, allude to, intimate, mean, suggest, hint, get at, intend, refer to, signify, insinuate, indicate.

driving adj.
- 猛冲的,有干劲的 compelling, forceful, vigorous, dynamic, energetic, forthright, heavy, violent, sweeping.

drizzle n.
- 蒙蒙细雨 mist, mizzle, rain, spray, shower.

v.
- 下蒙蒙细雨 spit, spray, sprinkle, rain, spot, shower.

droop v.
- 低垂,下垂 hang (down), dangle, sag, bend.
- 衰退,枯萎 languish, decline, flag, falter, slump, lose heart, wilt, wither, drop, faint, fall down, fade, slouch.
- 下沉,倒下 sink.

drop n.

- 点滴 droplet, bead, tear, drip, bubble, globule, trickle.
- 一点,少量 dash, pinch, spot, sip, trace, dab.
- 落下,降落 fall, decline, falling-off, lowering, downturn, decrease, reduction, slump, plunge, deterioration.
- 下坡 descent, precipice, slope, chasm, abyss.

v.
- 滴下,落下 fall, sink, decline, plunge, plummet, tumble, dive, descend, lower, droop, depress, diminish.
- 抛弃,放下,丢下 abandon, forsake, desert, give up, relinquish, reject, jilt, leave, renounce, throw over, repudiate, cease, discontinue, quit.

drop off
- 睡着 nod off, doze, snooze, have forty winks.
- 减少 decline, fall off, decrease, dwindle, lessen, diminish, slacken.
- 离开 deliver, set down, leave.

drop out
- 抛弃,离队 back out, abandon, cry off, withdraw, forsake, leave, quit.

drought n.
- 干旱,旱灾 dryness, aridity, parchedness, dehydration, desiccation, shortage, want.

drove n.
- 人群 herd, horde, gathering, crowd, multitude, swarm, throng, flock, company, mob, press.

drown v.
- 溺死,淹死 submerge, immerse, inundate, go under, flood, sink, deluge, engulf, drench.
- 淹没 overwhelm, overpower, overcome, swamp, wipe out, extinguish.

drowsy adj.
- 想睡的,困倦的 sleepy, tired, lethargic, nodding, dreamy, dozy, somnolent.

drug n.
- 药品 medication, medicine, remedy, potion.

v.
- 吸毒 medicate, sedate, tranquillize, dope, anaesthetize, dose, knock out, stupefy, deaden, numb.

drum v.
- 打鼓 beat, pulsate, tap, throb, thrum, tattoo, reverberate, rap.

drum up
- 收集,获得 obtain, round up, collect, gather, solicit, canvass, petition, attract.

drunk adj.
- 喝醉的 inebriated, intoxicated, under the influence, drunken, paralytic, sloshed, merry, tight, tipsy, tanked up, tiddly, plastered, loaded.

drunkard n.
- 醉汉,酒鬼 drunk, inebriate, alcoholic, dipsomaniac, boozer, wino, tippler, soak, lush, sot.

dry adj.
- 干燥的,干旱的 arid, parched, thirsty, dehydrated,

desiccated, barren.
☞ 枯燥的 boring, dull, dreary, tedious, monotonous.
v.
☞ 使干燥, 使枯萎 dehydrate, parch, desiccate, drain, shrivel, wither.

dual adj.
☞ 双的, 二元的 double, twofold, duplicate, duplex, binary, combined, paired, twin, matched.

dubious adj.
☞ 怀疑的, 不确信的 doubtful, uncertain, undecided, unsure, wavering, unsettled, suspicious, sceptical, hesitant.
☞ 可疑的 questionable, debatable, unreliable, ambiguous, suspect, obscure, fishy, shady.

duck v.
☞ 蹲下, 闪避 crouch, stoop, bob, bend.
☞ 避免 avoid, dodge, evade, shirk, sidestep.
☞ 潜入水中 dip, immerse, plunge, dunk, dive, submerge, douse, souse, wet, lower.

due adj.
☞ 应付的 owed, owing, payable, unpaid, outstanding, in arrears.
☞ 适当的 rightful, fitting, appropriate, proper, merited, deserved, justified, suitable.
☞ 预期的 adequate, enough, sufficient, ample, plenty of. 4 expected, scheduled.
adv.
☞ 正向地, 直接地 exactly, direct(ly), precisely, straight, dead.

duel n.
☞ 决斗 affair of honour, combat, contest, fight, clash, competition, revalry, encounter.

dull adj.
☞ 单调的, 黯淡的 boring, uninteresting, unexciting, flat, dreary, monotonous, tedious, uneventful, humdrum, unimaginative, dismal, lifeless, plain, insipid, heavy.
☞ 无光彩的, 阴暗的 dark, gloomy, drab, murky, indistinct, grey, cloudy, lack-lustre, opaque, dim, overcast.
☞ 迟钝的 unintelligent, dense, dim, dimwitted, thick, stupid, slow.
v.
☞ 使钝, 减轻 blunt, alleviate, mitigate, moderate, lessen, relieve, soften.
☞ 消除 deaden, numb, paralyse.
☞ 使泄气 discourage, dampen, subdue, sadden.
☞ 暗淡 dim, obscure, fade.

dumb adj.
☞ 哑的, 沉默的 silent, mute, soundless, speechless, tongue-tied, inarticulate, mum.

dumbfounded adj.
☞ 使惊讶的 astonished, amazed, astounded, overwhelmed, speechless, taken aback, thrown, startled, overcome, confounded, flabbergasted, staggered, confused, bowled over, dumb, floored, paralysed.

dummy n.
☞ 模仿, 复制 copy, duplicate,

imitation, counterfeit, substitute.
☞ 模型,假人 model, lay-figure, mannequin, figure, form.
☞ 奶头 teat, pacifier.

adj.
☞ 假的 artificial, fake, imitation, false, bogus, mock, sham, phoney.
☞ 假装的 simulated, practice, trial.

dump *v.*
☞ 倾倒,倾卸 deposit, drop, offload, throw down, let fall, unload, empty out, discharge, park.
☞ 倾销 get rid of, scrap, throw away, dispose of, ditch, tip, jettison.

n.
☞ 垃圾堆 rubbish-tip, junk-yard, rubbish-heap, tip.
☞ 简陋小屋 hovel, slum, shack, shanty, hole, joint, pigsty, mess.

duplicate *adj.*
☞ 完全相同的,副的 identical, matching, twin, twofold, corresponding, matched.

n.
☞ 复本,副本,复制品 copy, replica, reproduction, photocopy, carbon (copy), match, facsimile.

v.
☞ 复写,复制,加倍 copy, reproduce, repeat, photocopy, double, clone, echo.

durable *adj.*
☞ 耐久的,耐用的 lasting, enduring, long-lasting, abiding, hard-wearing, strong, sturdy, tough, unfading, substantial, sound, reliable, dependable, stable, resistant, persistent, constant, permanent, firm, fixed, fast.

dusk *n.*
☞ 黄昏 twilight, sunset, nightfall, evening, sundown, gloaming, darkness, dark, gloom, shadows, shade.

dust *n.*
☞ 灰尘,尘土 powder, particles, dirt, earth, soil, ground, grit, grime.

dusty *adj.*
☞ 脏的 dirty, grubby, filthy.
☞ 粉末状的 powdery, granular, crumbly, chalky, sandy.

dutiful *adj.*
☞ 忠于职守的,孝顺的 obedient, respectful, conscientious, devoted, filial, reverential, submissive.

duty *n.*
☞ 责任服务 obligation, responsibility, assignment, calling, charge, role, task, job, business, function, work, office, service.
☞ 尊重 obedience, respect, loyalty.
☞ 税 tax, toll, tariff, levy, customs, excise.

on duty
☞ 值日,值班 at work, engaged, busy.

dwarf *n.*
☞ 矮子 person of restricted growth, midget, pygmy, Tom Thumb, Lilliputian.
☞ 妖怪 gnome, goblin.

adj.
- 矮小的 miniature, small, tiny, pocket, mini, diminutive, petite, Lilliputian, baby.

v.
- 阻碍……发展 stunt, retard, check.
- 使……相形见绌 overshadow, tower over, dominate.

dwell v.
- 居住 live, inhabit, reside, stay, settle, populate, people, lodge, rest, abide.

dye n.
- 染料 colour, colouring, stain, pigment, tint, tinge.

v.
- 染,着色 colour, tint, stain, pigment, tinge, imbue.

dying adj.
- 垂死的,临终的 moribund, passing, final, going, mortal, not long for this world, perishing, failing, fading, vanishing.

dynamic adj.
- 动力的 forceful, powerful, energetic, vigorous, go-ahead, high-powered, driving, self-starting, spirited, vital, lively, active.

dynasty n.
- 朝代 house, line, succession, dominion, regime, government, rule, empire, sovereignty.

E

eager adj.
- 热心的 keen, enthusiastic, fervent, intent, earnest, zealous.
- 渴望的 longing, yearning.

ear n.
- 留意 aattention, heed, notice, regard.
- 听力 perception, sensitivity, appreciation, hearing, skill.

early adj.
- 早期的 forward, advanced, premature, untimely, undeveloped.
- 古老的 primitive, ancient, primeval.

adv
- 早先 ahead of time, in good time, beforehand, in adavance, prematurely.

earn v.
- 获得 receive, obtain, make, get, draw, bring in, gain, realize, gross, reap.
- 博得,争取 deserve, merit, warrant, win, rate.

earnest adj.
- 热情的 resolute, devoted, ardent, conscientious, intent, keen, fervent, firm, fixed, eager, enthusiastic, steady.
- 真挚的 serious, sincere, solemn, grave, heartfelt.

earth n.
- 地球 world, planet, globe, sphere.
- 陆地 land, ground, soil, clay, loam, sod, humus.

earthenware n.
- 陶器 pottery, cearmics, crockery, pots.

ease n.
- 安心,安逸 facility, effortlessness, skilfulness, deftness, dexterity, naturalness, cleverness.
- 放松 comfort, contentment, peace, affluence, repose, leisure, relaxation, rest, quiet, happiness.

v.
- 减轻,放松 alleviate, moderate, lessen, lighten, relieve, mitigate, abate, relent, allay, assuage, relax, comfort, calm, soothe, facilitate, smooth.
- 缓缓滑入 inch, steer, slide, still.

easily adv.
- 舒适地 effortlessly, comfortably, readily, simply.
- 无疑地 by far, undoubtedly, indisputably, definitely, certainly, doubtlessly, clearly, far and away, undeniably, simply, surely, probably, well.

easy adj.
- 容易的 effortless, simple, uncomplicated, undemanding, straightforward, manageable, cushy.
- 舒适的 relaxed, carefree, easy-going, comfortable, informal, calm, natural, leisurely.

easy-going adj.
- 平易近人的 tolerant, amenable, happy-go-lucky, carefree, even-tempered, serence.

eat v.
- 吃 consume, feed, swallow, devour, chew, scoff, munch, dine.
- 腐蚀,蛀 corrode, erode, wear away, decay, rot, crumble, dissolve.

eatable adj.
- 可吃的 edible, palatable, good, wholesome, digestible, comestible, harmless.

eavesdrop v.
- 偷听 listen in, spy, overhear, snoop, tap, bug, monitor.

eccentric adj.
- 古怪的 odd, peculiar, abnormal, unconventional, strage, quirky, weird, way-out, queer, outlandish, idiosyncratic, bizarre, freakish, erratic, singular, dotty.

n.
- 古怪 nonconformist, oddball, oddity, crank, freak, character.

eccentricity n.
- 异常,古怪 unconventionality, strangeness, peculiarity, nonconformity, abnormality, oddity, weirdness, idiosyncrasy, singularity, quirk, freakishness, aberration, anomaly, capriciousness.

echo v.
- 响应 reverberate, resound, repeat, reflect, reiterate, ring.
- 模拟 imitate, copy, reproduce, mirror, resemble, mimic.

n.

☞ 回声,反响 reverberation, reiteration, repetition, reflection.

☞ 模拟 imitation, copy, reproduction, mirror image, image, parallel.

eclipse v.
☞ 遮蔽 blot out, obscure, cloud, veil, darken, dim.
☞ 失色 outdo, overshadow, outshine, surpass, transcend.

n.
☞ 食,蚀(天文) obscuration, overshadowing, darkening, shading, dimming.
☞ 丧失 decline, failure, fall, loss.

economic adj.
☞ 经济的 commercial, business, industrial.
☞ 经济学的 financial, budgetary, fiscal, monetary.
☞ 有利可图的 profitable, profit-making, money-making, productive, cost-effective, viable.

economical adj.
☞ 节约的 thrifty, careful, prudent, saving, sparing, frugal.
☞ 便宜的 cheap, inexpensive, low-priced, reasonable, cost-effective, modest, efficient.

economy n.
☞ 经济,节约 thrift, saving, restraint, prudence, frugality, parsimony, providence, husbandry.

edge n.
☞ 锋刃,边缘 border, rim, boundary, limit, brim, threshold, brink, fringe, margin, outline, side, verge, line, perimeter, periphery, lip.
☞ 锐利 sharpness, acuteness, keenness, incisiveness, pungency, zest.

v.
☞ 向前移动 creep, inch, ease, sidle.

edgy adj.
☞ 紧张的 on edge, nervous, tense, anxious, ill at ease, keyed-up, touchy, irritable.

edit v.
☞ 编辑 correct, emend, revise, rewrite, reorder, rearrange, adapt, check, compile, rephrase, select, polish, annotate, censor.

edition n.
☞ 版本 copy, volume, impression, printing, issue, version, number.

educate v.
☞ 教育,培养 teach, train, instruct, tutor, coach, school, inform, cultivate, edify, drill, improve, discipline, develop.

educated adj.
☞ 受教育的 learned, taught, schooled, trained, knowledgeable, informed, instructed, lettered, cultured, civilized, tutored, refined, well-bred.

education n.
☞ 教育 teaching, training, schooling, tuition, tutoring, coaching, guidance, instruction, cultivation, culture, scholarship, improvement, enlightenment, knowledge, nurture,

development.

effect n.
- 结果 outcome, result, conclusion, consequence, upshot, aftermath, issue.
- 作用,影响 power, force, impact, efficacy, impression, strength.
- 印象 meaning, significance, import.

v.
- 引起,进行 cause, execute, create, achieve, accomplish, perform, produce, make, initiate, fulfil, complete.

In effect
- 实际上 in fact, actually, really, in reality, to all intents and purposes, for all practical purposes, essentially, effectively, virtually.

take effect
- 生效 be effective, become operative, come into force, come into operation, be implemented, begin, work.

effective adj.
- 有效的 efficient, efficacious, productive, adequate, capable, useful.
- 被实施的 operative, in force, functioning, current, active.
- 给人深刻印象的 striking, impressive, forceful, cogent, powerful, persuasive, convincing, telling.

effects n.
- 动产,家产 belongings, possessions, property, goods, gear, movables, chattels, things, trappings.

efficiency n.
- 效率 effectiveness, competence, proficiency, skill, expertise, skilfulness, capability, ability, productivity.

efficient adj.
- 有效的 effective, competent, proficient, skilful, capable, able, productive, well-organized, businesslike, powerful, well-conducted.

effort n.
- 运用,精力 exertion, strain, application, struggle, trouble, energy, toil, striving, pains, travail.
- 努力,尽力 attempt, try, go, endeavour, shot, stab.
- 成果 achievement, accomplishment, feat, exploit, production, creation, deed, product, work.

eject v.
- 逐出 emit, expel, discharge, spout, spew, evacuate, vomit.
- 喷射 oust, evict, throw out, drive out, turn out, expel, remove, banish, deport, dismiss, exile, kick out, fire, sack.

elaborate adj.
- 煞费苦心的 detailed, careful, thorough, exact, extensive, painstaking, precise, perfected, minute, laboured, studied.
- 复杂的 intricate, complex, complicated, involved, ornamental, ornate, fancy, decorated, ostentatious, showy, fussy.

v.
- 精心制成 amplify, develop, enlarge, expand, flesh out,

polish, improve, refine, devise, explain.

elapse v.
- 逝去(时间) pass, lapse, go by, slip away.

elastic adj.
- 弹性的 pliable, flexible, stretchable, supple, resilient, yielding, springy, rubbery, pliant, plastic, bouncy, buoyant.
- 有伸缩性的,适应的 adaptable, accommodating, flexible, tolerant, adjustable.

elasticity n.
- 弹性 pliability, flexibility, resilience, stretch, springiness, suppleness, give, plasticity, bounce, buoyancy.
- 伸缩性 adaptability, flexibility, telerance, adjustability.

elated adj.
- 得意的 exhilarated, excited, euphoric, ecstatic, exultant, jubilant, everjoyed, joyful.

elbow v.
- 挤 jostle, nudge, push, , shove, bump, crowd, knock, shoulder.

elder adj.
- 年长的 older, senior, first-born, ancient.

elderly adj.
- 年长的 aging, aged, old, hoary, senile.

elect v.
- 选举 choose, pick, opt for, select, vote for, prefer, adopt, designate, appoint, determine.
- adj.
- 当选的 choice, elite, chosen designated, designate, picked, prospective, selected, to be, preferred, hand-picked.

election n.
- 选择,选举 choice, selection, voting, ballot, poll, appointment, determination, decision, preference.

elector n.
- 选举人 selector, voter, constituent.

electric adj.
- 电的 electrifying, exciting, stimulating, thrilling, charged, dynamic, stirring, tense, rousing.

electrify v.
- 起电,使带电 thrill, excite, shock, invigorate, animate, stimulate, stir, rouse, fire, jolt, galvanize, amaze, astonish, astound, stagger.

elegant adj.
- 文雅的,优美的 stylish, chic, fashionable, modish, smart, refined, polished, genteel, smooth, tasteful, fine, exquisite, beautiful, graceful, handsome, delicate, neat, artistic.

element n.
- 元素 factor, component, constituent, ingredient, member, part, piece, fragment, feature, trace.

elementary adj.
- 初级的,基本的 basic, fundamental, rudimentary, principal, primary, clear, easy, introductory, straightforward,

uncomplicated, simple.

elements n.
- 自然力 basics, fundamentals, foundations, principles, rudiments, essentials.

elevate v.
- 提高 lift, raise, hoist, heighten, intensify, magnify.
- 提升 exalt, advance, promote, aggrandize, upgrade.
- 举起 uplift, rouse, boost, brighten.

elevated adj.
- 高尚的 raised, lofty, exalted, high, grand, noble, dignified, sublime.

elevation n.
- 举起, 提高 rise, promotion, advancement, preferment, aggrandizement.
- (地位)高尚 exaltation, loftiness, grandeur, eminence, nobility.
- 高地 height, altitude, hill, rise.

elicit v.
- 引出, 引起 evoke, draw out, derive, extract, obtain, exact, extort, cause.

eligible adj.
- 合格的, 适应的 qualified, fit, appropriate, suitable, acceptable, worthy, proper, desirable.

eliminate v.
- 删除, 除去 remove, get rid of, cut out, take out, exclude, delete, dispense with, rub out, omit, reject, disregard, dispose of, drop, do away with, eradicate, expel, extinguish, stamp out, exterminate, knock out, kill, murder.

elite n.
- 精华 best, elect, aristocracy, upper classes, nobility, gentry, creme de la creme, establishment, high society.

adj.
- 优秀的, 精选的 choice, best, exclusive, selected, first-class, aristocratic, noble, upper-class.

elongate adj.
- 延长的, 拉长的 lengthened, extended, prolonged, protracted, stretched, long.

eloquent adj.
- 雄辩的, 有口才的 articulate, fluent, well-expressed, glib, expressive, vocal, voluble, persuasive, moving, forceful, graceful, plausible, stirring, vivid.

elude v.
- 逃避 avoid, escape, evade, dodge, shirk, duck, flee.
- 难住, 使困难 puzzle, frustrate, baffle, confound, thwart, stump, foil.

elusive adj.
- 难记的 indefinable, intangible, unanalysable, subtle, puzzling, baffling, transient, transitory.
- 逃避的, 躲闪的 evasive, shifty, slippery, tricky.

emancipate v.
- 解放 free, liberate, release, set free, enfranchise, deliver, discharge, loose, unchain, unshackle, unfetter.

embankment n.

☞堤 causeway, dam, rampart, levee, earthwork.

embargo n.
☞禁运 restriction, ban, prohibition, restraint, proscription, bar, barrier, impediment, check, hindrance, blockage, stoppage, seizure.

embark v.
☞乘船 board (ship), go aboard, take ship.

embark on
☞开始 begin, start, commence, set about, launch, undertake, enter, initiate, engage.

embarrass v.
☞使困窘 disconcert, mortify, show up, discompose, fluster, humiliate, shame, distress.

embarrassment n.
☞窘迫 discomposure, self-consciousness, chagrin, mortification, humiliation, shame, awkwardness, confusion, bashfulness.
☞困难 difficulty, constraint, predicament, distress, discomfort.

embellish v.
☞装璜,修饰 adorn, ornament, decorate, deck, dress up, beautify, gild, garnish, festoon, elaborate, embroider, enrich, exaggerate, enhance, varnish, grace.

embellishment n.
☞修饰 adornment, ornament, ornamentation, decoration, elaboration, garnish, trimming, gilding, enrichment, embroidery, enhancement, embroidery, exaggeration.

embezzle v.
☞侵吞,盗用 appropriate, misappropriate, steal, pilfer, filch, pinch.

embezzlement n.
☞侵吞,盗用 appropriation, misappropriation, pilfering, fraud, stealing, theft, filching.

embodiment n.
☞体现 incarnation, personification, exemplification, expression, epitome, example, incorporation, realization, representation, manifestation, concentration.

embody v.
☞具体,体现 personify, exemplify, represent, stand for, symbolize, incorporate, express, manifest.
☞包括 include, contain, integrate.

embrace v.
☞拥抱 hug, clasp, cuddle, hold, grasp, squeeze.
☞包容,涵盖 include, encompass, incorporate, contain, comprise, cover, involve.
☞接受 accept, take up, welcome.
n.
☞拥抱 hug, cuddle, clasp, clinch.

emerge v.
☞浮现,显露 arise, rise, surface, appear, develop, crop up, transpire, turn up, materialize.
☞出现 emanate, issue,

procceed.

emergence n.
☞ 出现 appearance, rise, advent, coming, dawn, development, arrival, disclosure, issue.

emergency n.
☞ 事变 crisis, danger, difficulty, predicament, plight, pinch, strait, quandary.

emigrate n.
☞ 移住国外 migrate, relocate, move, depart.

eminence n.
☞ 高位,显职 distinction, fame, pre-eminence, prominence, renown, reputation, greatness, importance, esteem, note, prestige, rank.

eminent adj.
☞ 杰出的,优质的 distinguished, famous, prominent, illustrious, outstanding, notable, pre-eminent, prestigious, celebrated, renowned, noteworthy, conspicuous, esteemed, important, well-known, elevated, respected, great, high-ranking, grand, superior.

emission n.
☞ 发射,放射,发行 discharge, issue, ejection, emanation, ejaculation, diffusion, transmission, exhalation, radiation, release, exudation, vent.

emit v.
☞ 发出,放射(光,热,水) discharge, issue, eject, emanate, exude, give out, give off, diffuse, radiate, release, shed, vent.

emotion n.
☞ 情绪,情感 feeling, passion, sensation, sentiment, ardour, fervour, warmth, reaction, vehemence, excitement.

emotional adj.
☞ 情绪的 feeling, passionate, sensitive, responsive, ardent, tender, warm, roused, demonstrative, excitable, enthusiastic, fervent, impassioned, moved, sentimental, zealous, hot-blooded, heated, tempestuous, overcharged, temperamental, fiery.
☞ 易激动的 emotive, moving, poignant, thrilling, touching, stirring, heart-warming, exciting, pathetic.

emphasis n.
☞ 强调,重点 stress, weight, significance, importance, priority, underscoring, accent, force, power, prominence, pre-eminence, attention, intensity, strength, urgency, positiveness, insistence, mark, moment.

emphasize v.
☞ 强调,着重 stress, accentuate, underline, highlight, accent, feature, dwell on, weight, point up, spotlight, play up, insist on, press home, intensify, strengthen, punctuate.

emphatic adj.
☞ 语势强的,强调的 forceful, positive, insistent, certain, definite, decided, unequivocal, absolute, categorical, earnest,

marked, pronounced, significant, strong, striking, vigorous, distinct, energetic, forcible, important, impressive, momentous, powerful, punctuated, telling, vivid, praphic, direct.

empire n.
- 统治 supremacy, sovereignty, rule, authority, command, government, jurisdiction, control, power, sway.
- 帝国 domain, dominion, kingdom, realm, commonwealth, territory.

employ v.
- 雇 engage, hire, take on, recruit, enlist, commission, retain, fill, occupy, take up.
- 使用 use, utilize, make use of, apply, bring to bear, ply, exercise.

employee n.
- 雇工 worker, member of staff, job-holder, hand, wage-earner.

employer n.
- 雇主 boss, proprietor, owner, manager, gaffer, management, company, firm, business, establishment.

employment n.
- 工作 job, work, occupation, situation, business, calling, profession, line, vocation, trade, pursuit, craft.
- 雇用 enlistment, employ, engagement, hire.

empower v.
- 传授 authorize, warrant, enable, license, sanction, permit, entitle, commission, delegate, qualify.

emptiness n.
- 空 vacuum, vacantness, void, hollowness, hunger, bareness, barrenness, desolation.
- 无用,无益 futility, meaninglessness, worthlessness, aimlessness, ineffectiveness, unreality.

empty adj.
- 空的 vacant, void, unoccupied, uninhabited, unfilled, deseted, bare, hollow, desolate, blank, clear.
- 无用的 futile, aimless, meaningless, senseless, trivial, vain, worthless, useless, insubstantial, ineffective, insincere.
- 空洞的 vacuous, inane, expressionless, blank, vacant.

v.
- 变空,清掉 drain, exhaust, discharge, clear, evacuate, vacate, pour out, unload, void, gut.

empty-headed adj.
- 傻的,没头脑的 inane, silly, frivolous, scatter-brained, feather-brained.

emulate v.
- 竞赛 match, copy, mimic, follow, imitate, echo, compete with, contend with, rival, vie with.

enable v.
- 使能够 equip, qualify, empower, authorize, sanction, warrant, allow, permit, prepare, fit, facilitate, license, commission, endue.

enact v.
- 制定 decree, ordain, order, authorize, command, legislate, sanction, ratify, pass, establish.
- 扮演 act (out), perform, play, portray, represent, depict.

enchant v.
- 使陶醉 captivate, charm, fascinate, enrapture, attract, allure, appeal, delight, thrill.
- 迷惑 entrance, enthral, bewitch, spellbind, hypnotize, mesmerize.

enclose v.
- 围住 encircle, encompass, surround, fence, hedge, hem in, bound, encase, embrace, envelop, confine, hold, shut in, wrap, pen, cover, circumscribe, incorporate, include, insert, contain, comprehend.

enclosure n.
- 包围,围绕 pen, pound, compound, paddock, fold, stockade, sty, arena, corral, court, ring, cloister.

encounter v.
- 遇见(偶然) meet, come, across, run into, happen on, chance upon, run across, confront, face, experience.
- 遭遇(敌人) fight, clash with, combat, cross swords with, engage, grapple with, struggle, strive, contend.

n.
- 遇见 meeting, brush, confrontation.
- 遭遇战 clash, fight, combat, conflict, contest, battle, set-to, buoy up, cheer, urge, rouse, comfort, console.

encourage v.
- 鼓励 hearten, exhort, stimulate, spur, reassure, rally, inspire, incite, egg on, buoy up, cheer, urge, rouse, comfort, console.
- 助长,帮助 promote, advance, aid, boost, forward, further, foster, support, help, strengthen.

encouragement n.
- 鼓励 reassurance, inspiration, cheer, exhortation, incitement, pep talk, urging, stimulation, consolation, succour.
- 帮助,支持 promotion, help, aid, boost, shot in the arm, incentive, support, stimulus.

encouraging adj.
- 鼓励的,鼓舞的 heatening, promising, hopeful, reassuring, stimulating, uplifting, auspicious, cheering, comforting, bright, rosy, cheerful, satiafactory.

encumber v.
- 防碍 burden, overload, weigh down, saddle, oppress, handicap, hamper, hinder, impede, slow down, obstruct, inconvenience, prevent, retard, cramp.

encumbrance n.
- 防碍 burden, cumbrance, load, cross, millstone, albatross, difficulty, handicap, impediment, obstruction, obstacle, inconvenience, hindrance, liability.

end n.
- 结束 finish, conclusion, termination, close, completion, cessation, close, completion, cessation, culmination, denouement.
- 端,尽头 extremity, boundary, edge, limit, tip.
- 残片,剩余 remainder, tip, butt, left-over, remnat, stub, scrap, fragment.
- 目的 aim, object, objective, purpose, intention, goal, point, reason, design.
- 结局,结果 result, outcome, consequence, upshot.
- 死亡 death, demise, destruction, extermination, downfall, doom, ruin, dissolution.

v.
- 结束 finish, close, cease, conclude, stop, terminate, complete, culminate, wind up.
- 绝灭 destroy, annihilate, exterminate, extinguish, ruin, abolish, dissolve.

endanger v.
- 危害 imperil, hazard, jeopardize, risk, expose, threaten, compromise.

endearing adj.
- 受喜欢的 lovable, charming, appealing, attractive, winsome, delightful, enchanting.

endeavour n.
- 尽力,努力 attempt, effort, go, try, shot, stab, undertaking, enterprise, aim, venture.

v.
- 尽力,努力 attempt, try, strive, aim, aspire, undertake, venture, struggle, labour, take, pains.

ending n.
- 终止,末尾 end, close, finish, completion, termination, conclusion, culmination, climax, resolution, consummation, denouement, finale, epilogue.

endless adj.
- 无限的 infinite, boundless, unlimited, measureless.
- 连续的,不间断的 everlasting, ceaseless, perpetual, constant, continual, continuous, undying, eternal, interminable, monotonous.

endorse v.
- 保证,支持 approve, sanction, authorize, support, back, affirm, ratify, confirm, vouch for, advocate, warrant, recomment, subscribe to, sustain, adopt.
- 批注 sign, countersign.

endorsement n.
- 保证,支持 approval, sanction, authorization, support, backing, affirmation, ratification, confirmation, advocacy, warrant, recommendation, commendation, seal of approval, testimonial, ok.
- 签名 signature, countersignature.

endow v.
- 捐助 bestow, bequeath, leave, will, give, donate, endue, confer, grant, present, award, finance, fund, support, make over, furnish, provide,

supply.

endowment n.
- 捐赠 bequest, legacy, award, grant, fund, gift, provision, settlement, donation,, bestowal, benefaction, dowry, income, revenue.
- 天才 talent, attribute, faculty, gift, ability, quality, flair, genius, qualification.

endurance n.
- 忍耐,忍受 fortitude, patience, staying, power, stamina, resignation, stoicism, tenacity, perseverance, resolution, kstability, persistence, strength, toleration.

endure v.
- 持久,忍受 bear, stand, put up with, tolerate, weather, brave, cope with, face, go through, experience, submit to, suffer, sustain, swallow, undergo, withstand, stick, stomach, allow, permit, support.
- 持续 last, abide, rival, antagonist, the opposition, competitor, opposer, other side.

energetic adj.
- 充满活力的 lively, vigorous, active, animated, dynamic, spirited, tireless, zestful, brisk, strong, forceful, potent, powerful, strenuous, high-powered.

energy n.
- 精力,活力 liveliness, vigour, activity, animation, drive, dynamism, get-up-and-go , life, spirit, verve, vivacity, vitality, zest, zeal, ardour, fire, efficiency, force, forcefulness, zip , strength, power, intensity, exertion, stamina.

enforce v.
- 实施,执行,加强 impose, administer, implement, apply, execute, discharge, insist on, compel, oblige, urge, carryout, constrain, require, coerce, prosecute, reinforce.

engage v.
- 从事,占用 participate, take, part, embark on, take up, practise, involve.
- 吸引 attract, allure, draw, captivate, charm, catch.
- 忙于,从事 occupy, engross, absorb, busy, tie up, grip.
- 雇用 employ, hire, appoint, take on, enlist, enrol, commission, recruit, contract.
- 加入 interlock, mesh, interconnect, join, interact, attach.
- 交战 fight, battle with, attack, take on, encounter, assail, combat.

engaged adj.
- 从事的 occupied, busy, engrossed, immersed, absorbed, preoccupied, involved, employed.
- 订婚的 promised, betrothed , pledged, spoken for, committed.

engagement n.
- 会议,协定 appointment, meeting, date, arrangement, assignation, fixture, rendezvous.
- 约定 promise, pledge, commitment, obligation, assurance, vow.

☞ 交战 fight, battle, combat, conflict, action, encounter, confrontation, contest.

engaging adj.
☞ 动人的,可爱的,引人注意的 charming, attactive, appealing, captivating, pleasing, delightful, winsome, lovable, likable, pleasant, fetching, fascinating, agreeable.

engine n.
☞ 发动机 motor, machine, mechanism, appliance, contraption, apparatus, device, instrument, tool, locomotive, dynamo.

engineer n.
☞ 技师,技工 mechanic, technician, engine, driver.
☞ 工程师 designer, originator, planner, inventor, deviser, mastermind, architect.
v.
☞ 指导,策划 plan, contrive, devise, manoeuvre, cause, manipulate, control, bring about, mastermind, originate, orchestrate, effect, plot, scheme, manage, create, rig.

engrave v.
☞ 刻上,铭记 inscribe, cut, carve, chisel, etch, chase.
☞ 牢记,铭记 imprint, impress, fix, stamp, lodge, ingrain.

engraving n.
☞ 雕刻品 print, impression, inscription, carving, etching, woodcut, plate, block, cutting, chiselling, mark.

enhance v.
☞ 提高,抬高 heighten, intensify, increase, improve, elevate, magnify, swell, exalt, raise, lift, boost, strengthen, reinforce, embellish.

enjoy v.
☞ 喜欢 take pleasure in, delight in, appreciate, like, relish, revel in, rejoice in, savour.

enjoy oneself
☞ 过得快乐 have a good-time, have fun, make merry.

enjoyable adj.
☞ 使人快乐的 pleasant, agreeable, delightful, pleasing, gratifying, entertaining, amusing, fun, delicious, good, satisfying.

enjoyment n.
☞ 享受 pleasure, delight, amusement, gratification, entertainment, relish, joy, fun, happiness, diersion, lindulgence, recreation, zest, satisfaction.
☞ 利益 possession, use, advantage, benefit.

enlarge v.
☞ 扩大,放大 increase, expand, augment, add to, grow, extend, magnify, inflate, swell, wax, stretch, multiply, develop, amplify, blow up, widen, broaden, lengthen, heighten, elaborate.

enlighten v.
☞ 启发 instruct, edify, educate, inform, illuminate, teach, counsel, apprise, advise.

enlightened adj.
☞ 启蒙的 informed, aware, knowledgeable, educated, civilized, cultivated, refined,

sophisticated, conversant, wise, reasonable, liberal, open-minded, literate.

enormous *adj*.
☞ 巨大的,庞大的 huge, immense, vast, gigantic, massive, colossal, gross, gargantuan, monstrous, mammoth, jumbo, tremendous, prodigious.

enough *adj*.
☞ 足够的 sufficient, adequate, ample, plenty, abundant.
n.
☞ 充足 sufficiency, adequacy, plenty, abundance.
adv.
☞ 足够地 sufficiently, adequately, reasonably, tolerably, passably, moderately, fairly, satisfactorily, amply.

enrich *v*.
☞ 改进 endow, enhance, improve, refine, develop, cultivate, augment.
☞ 使丰富 adorn, ornament, beautify, embellish, decorate, grace.

enrol *v*.
☞ 登记,注册 register, enlist, sign on, sign up, join up, recruit, engage, admit.
☞ 记录 record, list, note, inscribe.

enrolment *n*.
☞ 登记,注册 registration, recruitment, enlistment, admission, acceptance.

enslave *v*.
☞ 奴役 subjugate, subject, dominate, bind, enchain, yoke.

ensure *v*.
☞ 保证 certify, guarantee, warrant.
☞ 保护 protect, guard, safeguard, secure.

enter *v*.
☞ 进入 come in, go in, arrive, insert, introduce, board, penetrate.
☞ 登记 record, log, note, register, take down, inscribe.
☞ 参加,加入 join, embark upon, enrol, enlist, set about, sign up, participate, commence, start, begin.

enterprise *n*.
☞ 方案,实施 undertaking, venture, project, plan, effort, operation, programme, endeavour.
☞ 事业心,进取心 initiative, resourcefulness, drive, adventurousness, boldness, get-up-and-go, push, energy, enthusiasm, spirit.
☞ 事业,企业 business, company, firm, establishment, concern.

enterprising *adj*.
☞ 有事业心的 venturesome, adventurous, bold, daring, go-ahead, imaginative, resourceful, self-reliant, enthusiastic, energetic, keen, ambitious, aspiring, spirited, active.

entertain *v*.
☞ 娱乐 amuse, divert, please, delight, cheer.
☞ 招待 receive, have, guests, accommodate, put up, treat.
☞ 怀有(希望) harbour, countenance, contemplate,

consider, imagine, conceive.

entertaining adj.
☞ 令人愉快的 amusing, diverting, fun, delightful, interesting, pleasant, pleasing, humorous, witty.

entertainment n.
☞ 招待 amusement, diversion, recreation, enjoyment, play, pastime, fun, sport, distraction, pleasure.
☞ 表演 show, spectacle, performance, extravaganza.

enthusiasm n.
☞ 热心,热情 zeal, ardour, fervour, passion, keenness, eagerness. vehemence, warmth, frenzy, excitement, earnestness, relish, spirit, devotion, craze, mania, rage.

enthusiastic adj.
☞ 热心的,热情的 keen, ardent, eager, fervent, vehement, passionate, warm, whole-hearted, zealous, vigorous, spirited, earnest, devoted, avid, excited, exuberant.

entire adj.
☞ 全体的,完全的 complete, whole, total, full, intact, perfect.

entirely adv.
☞ 完全地,全然 competely, wholly, totally, fully, utterly, unreservedly, absolutely, in toto, thoroughly, altogether, perfectly, solely, exclusively, every inch.

entitle v.
☞ 给予权利〔条件,资格〕 authorize, qualify, empower, enable, allow, permit, license, warrant.
☞ 给……题名 name, call, term, title, style, christen, dub, label, designate.

entity n.
☞ 存在,实在 being, existence, thing, body, creature, individual, organism, substance.

entrance[1] n.
☞ 入口 access, admission, admittance, entry, entree.
☞ 进入 arrival, appearance, debut, initiation, introduction, start.
☞ 门口 openning, way in, door, doorway, gate.

entrance[2] v.
☞ 使迷惑,使出神 charm, enchant, enrapture, captivate, bewitch, spellbind, fascinate, delight, ravish, transport, hypnotize, mesmerize.

entrust v.
☞ 委托,信托 trust, commit, confide, consign, authorize, charge, assign, turn over, commend, depute, invest, delegate, deliver.

entry n.
☞ 入场 entrance, appearance, admittance, admission, access, entree, introduction.
☞ 入口 opening, entrance, door, doorway, access, threshold, way in, passage, gate.
☞ 登记 record, item, minute, note, memorandum, statement, account.
☞ 上场,进入 entrant,

competitor, contestant, candidate, participant, player.

envelop v.
☞ 包,封 wrap, enfold, enwrap, encase, cover, swathe, shroud, engulf, enclose, encircle, encompass, surround, cloak, veil, blanket, conceal, obscure, hide.

envelope n.
☞ 信封 wrapper, wrapping, cover, case, casing, sheath, covering, shell, skin, jacket, coating.

enviable adj.
☞ 令人羡慕的,可羡慕的 desirable, privileged, favoured, blessed, fortunate, lucky, advantageous, sought-after, excellent, fine.

envious adj.
☞ 嫉妒的,羡慕的 covetous, jealous, resentful, green (with envy), dissatisfied, grudging, jaundiced, green-eyed.

environment n.
☞ 周围,环境 surroundings, conditions, circumstances, milieu, atmosphere, habitat, situation, element, medium, background, ambience, setting, context, territory, domain.

envisage v.
☞ 正视,展望 visualize, imagine, picture, envision, conceive of, preconceive, predict, anticipate, foresee, image, see, contemplate.

envy n.
☞ 嫉妒,羡慕 covetousness, jealousy, resenfulness, resentment, dissatisfaction, grudge, ill-will, malice, spite.
v.
☞ 嫉妒,羡慕 covet, resent, begrudge, grudge, crave.

epidemic adj.
☞ 流行病的,流行性的 widespread, prevalent, rife, rampant, pandemic, sweeping, wide-ranging, prevailing.
n.
☞ 流行病,传染病 plague, outbreak, spread, rash, upsurge, wave.

episode n.
☞ 事情,经历 incident, event, occurrence, happening, occasion, circumstance, experience, adventure, matter, business.
☞ 插曲 instalment, part, chapter, passage, section, scene.

epoch n.
☞ 时代,纪元 age, era, period, time, date.

equal adj.
☞ 平等的 identical, the same, alike, like, equivalent, corresponding, commensurate, comparable.
☞ 相当的 even, uniform, regular, unvarying, balanced, matched.
☞ 胜任的 competent, able, adequate, fit, capable, suitable.
n.
☞ 相等物 peer, counterpart, equivalent, coequal, match, parallel, twin, fellow.
v.
☞ 等于 match, parallel,

correspond to, balance, square with, tally with, equalize, equate, rival, level, even.

equality *n.*
☞ 平等 uniformity, evenness, equivalence, correspondence, balance, parity, sameness, likeness.
☞ 同等 impartiality, fairness, justice, agalitarianism.

equalize *v.*
☞ 使平等,使相等 level, even up, match, equal, equate, draw level, balance, square, standardize, compensate, smooth.

equip *v.*
☞ 装备 provide, fit out, supply, furnish, prepare, arm, fit up, kit out, stock, endow, rig, dress, array, deck out.

equipment *n.*
☞ 设备,装备 apparatus, gear, supplies, tackle, rig-out, tools, material, furnishings, baggage, outfit, paraphernalia, stuff, things, accessories, furniture.

equivalence *n.*
☞ 相等,相当 identity, parity, correspondence, agreement, likeness, interchangeability, similarity, substitutability, correlation, parallel, conformity, sameness.

equivalent *adj.*
☞ 相等的 equal, same, similar, substitutable, corresponding, alike, comparable, interchangeable, even, tantamount, twin.

era *n.*
☞ 时代 age, epoch, period, date, day, days, time, aeon, stage, century.

erase *v.*
☞ 消除,抹去 obliterate, rub out, expunge, delete, blot out, cancel, efface, get rid of, remove, eradicate.

erect *adj.*
☞ 直立的 upright, straight, vertical, upstanding, standing, raised, rigid, stiff.
v.
☞ 竖立,建造 build, construct, put up, establish, set up, elevate, assemble, found, form, institute, initiate, raise, rear, lift, mount, pitch, create.

erode *v.*
☞ 侵蚀,腐蚀 wear away, eat away, wear down, corrode, abrade, consume, grind down, disintegrate, deteriorate, spoil.

erosion *n.*
☞ 侵蚀,腐蚀 wear, corrosion, abrasion, attrition, denudation, disintegration, deterioration, destruction, undermining.

err *v.*
☞ 犯错误 make a mistake, be wrong, miscalculate, mistake, misjudge, slip up, blunder, misunderstand.
☞ 做错 do wrong, sin, misbehave, go astray, offend, transgress, deviate.

error *n.*
☞ 错误 mistake, inaccuracy, slip, slip-up, blunder, howler, gaffe, fauxpas, solecism, lapse, miscalculation,

misunderstanding, misconception, misapprehension, misprint, oversight, omission, fallacy, flaw, fault, wrong.

erudite *adj.*
- 博学的 learned, scholarly, well-educated, knowledgeable, lettered, educated, well-read, literate, academic, cultured, wise, highbrow, profound.

erupt *v.*
- 爆发,突发 break out, explode, belch, discharge, burst, gush, spew, spout, eject, expel, emit, flare up, vomit, break.

eruption *n.*
- 喷发 outnirst, discharge, ejection, emission, explosion, flare-up.
- 爆发 rash, outbreak, inflammation.

escalate *v.*
- 逐级上升 increase, intensify, grow, accelerate, rise, step up, heighten, raise, spiral, magnify, enlarge, expand, extend, mount, ascend, climb, amplify.

escape *v.*
- 逃跑 get away, break free, run away, bolt, abscond, flee, fly, decamp, break loose, break out, do a bunk, flit, slip away, shake off, slip.
- 避免 avoid, evade, elude, dodge, skip, shun.
- 漏出,流出 leak, seep, flow, drain, gush, issue, discharge, ooze, trickle, pour forth, pass.
n.
- 逃脱 getaway, flight, bolt, flit, break-out, decampment, jail-break.
- 避免 avoidance, evasion.
- 流出,漏出 leak, seepage, leakage, outflow, gush, drain, discharge, emission, spurt, outpour, emanation.
- 没注意 escapism, diversion, distraction, recreation, relaxation, pastime, safety-valve.

escort *n.*
- 护送者,保护者 companion, chaperon(e), partner, attendant, aide, squire, guide, bodyguard, protector.
- 护卫(队) entourage, company, retinue, suite, train, guard, convoy, cortege.

v.
- 护卫 accompany, partner, chaperon(e), guide, lead, usher, conduct,. guard, protect.

especially *adv.*
- 特别,尤其重要地 chiefly, mainly, principally, primarily, pre-eminently, above all.
- 特别地,显著地 particularly, specially, markedly, notably, exceptionally, outstandingly, expressly, supremely, uniquely, unusually, strikingly, very.

essay *n.*
- 散文,短文 composition, dissertation, paper, article, assignment, thesis, piece, commentary, critique, discoure, treatise, review, leader, tract.

essence *n.*
- 本质,实质 nature, being, quintessence, substance, soul,

spirit, core, centre, heart, meaning, quality, significance, life, entity, crux, kernel, marrow, pith, character, characteristics, arrtibutes, principle.
☞ 精华　concentrate, extract, distillation, spirits.

essential *adj.*
☞ 本质的,实质的　fundamental, basic, intrinsic, inherent, principal, main, key, characteristic, definitive, typical, constituent.
☞ 必须的,重要的　crucial, indispensable, necessary, vital, requisite, required, needed, important.
n.
☞ 本质,要素　necessity, prerequisite, must, requisite, sine qua non, requirement, basic, fundamental, necessary, principle.

establish *v.*
☞ 建立　set up, found, start, form, institute, create, organize, inaugurate, introduce, install, plant, settle, secure, lodge, base.
☞ 使认同,确立　prove, substantiate, demonstrate, authenticate, ratify, verify, validate, certify, confirm, affirm.

establishment *n.*
☞ 建立　formation, setting up, founding, creation, foundation, installation, institution, inauguration.
☞ 机构,公司　business, company, firm, institute, organization, concern, institution, enterprise.
☞ 统治阶级　ruling class, the system, the authorities, the powers, that be.

estate *n.*
☞ 财产　possessions, effects, assets, belongings, holdings, property, goods, lands.
☞ 地产　area, development, land, manor.
☞ 情况　status, standing, situation, position, class, place, condition, state, rank.

estimate *v.*
☞ 估计,估量　assess, reckon, evaluate, calculate, gauge, guess, value, conjecture, consider, judge, think, number, count, compute, believe.
n.
☞ 估计,预算　reckoning, valuation, judgement, guess, approximation, assessment, estimation, evaluation, computation, opinion.

estimation *n.*
☞ 估计　judgement, opinion, belief, consideration, estimate, view, evaluation, assessment, reckoning, conception, calculation, computation.
☞ 尊重　respect, regard, appreciation, esteem, credit.

eternal *adj.*
☞ 永恒的,永久的　unending, endless, ceaseless, everlasting, never-ending, infinite, limitless, immortal, undying, imperishable.
☞ 永恒的　unchanging, timeless, enduring, lasting, perennial,

abiding.
- 持续的 constant, continuous, perpetual, incessant, interminable.

eternity n.
- 永远 everlastingness, endlessness, everlasting, imperishability, infinity, timelessness, perpetuity, immutability, ages, age, aeon.
- 无穷 after-life, hereafter, immortality, heaven, paradise, next, world, world to come.

ethical adj.
- 伦理的,道德的 moral, principled, just, right, proper, virtuous, honourable, fair, upright, righteous, seemly, honest, good, correct, commendable, fitting, noble, meet.

ethics n.
- 伦理学 moral values, morality, priniciples, standards, code, moral philosophy, rules, beliefs, propriety, conscience, equity.

ethnic adj.
- 人种的,种族的 racial, native, indigenous, traditional, tribal, folk, cultural, national, aboriginal.

evade v.
- 逃避 elude, avoid, escape, dodge, shirk, steer clear of, shun, sidestep, duck, balk, skive, fend off, chicken out, cop out.

evaluate v.
- 估价,评价 value, assess, appraise, estimate, reckon, calculate, gauge, judge, rate, size up, weigh, compute, rank.

evaluation n.
- 估价,评价 valuation, appraisal, assessment, estimation, estimate, judgement, reckoning, calculation, opinion, computation.

evasion n.
- 逃避,回避 avoidance, escape, dodge, equivocation, excuse, prevarication, put-off, trickery, subterfuge, shirking.

evasive adj.
- 逃避的 equivocating, indirect, prevaricating, devious, shifty, unforthcoming, slippery, misleading, deceitful, deceptive, cagey, oblique, secretive, trickly, cunning.

eve n.
- 前夕,前夜 day before, verge, brink, edge, threshold.

even adj.
- 平的 level, flat, smooth, horizontal, flush, parallel, plane.
- 有规律的,固定的 steady, unvarying, constant, regular, uniform.
- 均等的 equal, balanced, matching, same, similar, like, symmetrical, fifty-fifty, level, side by side, neck and neck.
- 平静的 even-tempered, calm, placid, serene, tranquil, composed, unruffled.
- 公平的 even-handed, balanced, equitable, fair, impartial.

v.

☞使平,使平等 smooth, flatten, level, match, regularize, balance, euqlize, align, square, stabilize, steady, straighten.

evening n.
☞傍晚 happening, occurrence, incident, occasion, affair, circumstance, eventuality, episode, experience, matter, case, adventure, business, fact, possibility, milestone.
☞晚会 game, match, competition, contest, tournament, engagement.

even-tempered adj.
☞平静的 calm, level-headed, placid, stable, tranquil, serence, placid, stable, tranquil, serene, composed, cool, steady, peaceful, peaceable.

eventual adj.
☞最后的 final, ultimate, resulting, concluding, ensuing, future, later, subsequent, prospective, projected, planned, impending.

eventually adv.
☞最后,终于 finally, ultimately, at last, in the end, at length, subsequently, after all, sooner or later.

ever adv.
☞总是 always, evermore, for ever, perpetually, constantly, at all times, continually, endlessly.
☞任何时候 at any time, in any case, in any circumstances, at all, on any account.

everlasting adj.
☞永久的,持久的 eternal, undying, never-ending, endless, immortal, infinite, imperishable, constant, permanent, perpetual, indestructible, timeless.

everyday adj.
☞每天的 ordinary, common, commonplace, day-to-day, familiar, run-of-the-mill, regular, plain, routine, usual, workaday, common-or-garden, normal, customary, stock, accustomed, conventional, daily, habitual, monotonous, frequent, simple, informal.

everyone pron.
☞每人,人人 everybody, one and all, each one, all and sundry, the whole world.

everywhere adv.
☞到处,处处 all around, all over, throughout, far and near, far and wide, high and low, ubiquitous, left, right and centre.

evidence n.
☞证物 proof, verification, confirmation, affirmation, grounds, substantiation, documentation, data.
☞证词 testimony, declaration.
☞迹象 indication, manifestation, suggestion, sign, mark, hint, demonstration, token.

evident adj.
☞明显的,显然的 clear, obvious, manifest, apparent, plain, patent, visible, conspicuous, noticeable, clear-cut, unmistakable, perceptible, distinct, discernible, tangible, incontestable, indisputable,

incontrovertible.

evidently adv.
☞ 明显地,显然地 clearly, apparently, plainly, patently, manifestly, obviously, seemingly, undoubtedly, doubtless(ly), indisputably.

evil adj.
☞ 邪恶的 wicked, wrong, sinful, bad, immoral, vicious, vile, malevolent, iniquitous, cruel, base, corrupt, heinous, malicious, malignant, devilish, depraved, mischievous.
☞ 有害的 harmul, pernicious, destructive, deadly, detrimental, hurtful, poisonous.
☞ 灾难的 disastrous, ruinous, calamitous, catastrophic, adverse, dire, inauspicious.
☞ 讨厌的 offensive, noxious, foul.

n.
☞ 邪恶 wickedness, wrongdoing, wrong, immorality, badness, sin, sinfulness, vice, viciousness, iniquity, depravity, baseness, corruption, malignity, mischief, heinousness.
☞ 恶事,灾祸 adversity, affliction, calamity, disaster, misfortune, suffering, sorrow, ruin, catastrophe, blow, curse, distress, hurt, harm, ill, injury, misery, woe.

evoke v.
☞ 唤起,引起 summon (up), call, elicit, invoke, arouse, stir, raise, stimulate, call forth, call up, conjure up, awaken, provoke, excite, recall.

evolution n.
☞ 发展,渐进 development, growth, progression, progress, expansion, increase, ripening, derivation, descent.

evolve v.
☞ 开展,发展 develop, grow, increase, mature, progress, unravel, expand, enlarge, emerge, descend, derive, result, elaborate.

exact adj.
☞ 精确的,正确的 precise, accurate, correct, faithful, literal, flawless, faultless, right, true, veracious, definite, explicit, detailed, specific, strict, unerring, right, true, veracious, definite, explicit, detailed, specific, strict, unerring, close, factual, identical, express, word-perfect, blow-by-blow.
☞ 精密的,严谨的 careful, scrupulous, particular, rigorous, methodical, meticulous, orderly, painstaking.

v.
☞ 强求,需求 extort, extract, claim, insist on, wrest, wring, compel, demand, command, force, impose, require, squeeze, milk.

exacting adj.
☞ 严格的 demanding, difficult, hard, laborious, arduous, rigorous, taxing, tough, harsh, painstaking, severe, strict, unsparing.

exactly adv.
☞ 恰好,正 precisely, accurately, literally, faithfully, correctly, specifically, rigorously,

scrupulously, veraciously, verbatim, carefully, faultlessly, unerringly, strictly, to the letter, particularly, methodically, explicitly, expressly, dead.
☞ 完全 absolutely, definitely, precisely, indeed, certainly, truly, quite, just, unequivocally.

exaggerate v.
☞ 夸大,夸张 overstate, overdo, magnify, overemphasize, emphasize, embellish, embroider, enlarge, amplify, oversell, pile it on.

examination n.
☞ 检查 inspection, enquiry, scrutiny, study, survey, search, analysis, exploration, investigation, probe, appraisal, observation, research, review, scan, once-over, perusal, check, chech-up, audit, critique.
☞ 考试 test, exam, quiz, questioning, cross-examination, cross-questioning, trial, inquisition, interrogation, viva.

examine v.
☞ 检查 inspect, investigate, scrutinize, study, survey, analyse, explore, enquire, consider, probe, review, scan, check (out), ponder, pore over, sift, vet, weigh up, appraise, assay, audit, peruse, case.
☞ 考试 test, quiz, question, cross-examine, cross-question, interrogate, grill, catechize.

example n.
☞ 例子 instance, case, case in point, illustration, exemplification, sample, speciment, model, pattern, ideal, archetype, prototype, standard, type, lesson, citation.

exceed v.
☞ 大于,多于 surpass, outdo, outstrip, beat, better, pas, overtake, top, outshine, eclipse, outreach, outrun, transcend, cap, overdo, overstep.

excel v.
☞ 优于 surpass, outdo, beat, outclass, outperform, outrank, eclipse, better.
☞ 擅长,杰出 be excellent, succeed, shine, stand out, predominate.

excellence n.
☞ 优秀,杰出 superiority, pre-eminence, distinction, merit, supremacy, quality, worth, fineness, eminence, goodness, greatness, virtue, perfection, purity.

excellent adj.
☞ 优秀的 superior, first-class, first-rate, prime, superlative, unequalled, outstanding, surpassing, remarkable, distinguished, great, good, exemplary, select, superb, admirable, commendable, top-notch, splendid, noteworthy, notable, fine, wonderful, worthy.

except prep.
☞ 除……外 excepting, but, apart from, other than, save, omitting, not counting, leaving

out, excluding, except for, besides, bar, minus, less.
v.
☞ 除去,删除 leave out, omit, bar, exclude, reject, rule out.

exception n.
☞ 除外,例外 oddity, anomaly, deviation, abnormality, irregularity, peculiarity, inconsistency, rarity, special, case, quirk.

exceptional adj.
☞ 例外的 abnormal, unusual, anomalous, strange, odd, irregular, extraordinary, peculiar, special, rare, uncommon.
☞ 不平常的,杰出的 outstanding, remarkable, phenomenal, prodigious, notable, noteworthy, superior, unequalled, marvellous.

excerpt n.
☞ 选录,引述 extract, passage, portion, section, selection, quote, quotation, part, citation, scrap, fragment.

excess n.
☞ 超过,过度 surfeit, overabundance, glut, plethora, superfluity, superabundance, surplus, overflow, overkill, remainder, left-over.
☞ 无节制 pveromdilgemce, dissipation, immoderateness, intemperance, extravagance, unrestraint, debauchery.
adj.
☞ 过量的,过分的 extra, surplus, spare, redundant, remaining, residual, left-over, additional, superfluous, supernumerary.

excessive adj.
☞ 过分的,极端的 immoderate, inordinate, extreme, undue, uncalled-for, disproportionate, unnecessary, unneeded, superfluous, unreasonable, exorbitant, extravagant, steep.

exchange v.
☞ 交换,调换 barter, change, trade, swap, switch, replace, interchange, convert, commute, substitute, reciprocate, bargain, bandy.
n.
☞ 交流,讨论 conversation, discussion, chat.
☞ 交易所 trade, commerce, dealing, market, traffic, barter, bargain.
☞ 交换 interchange, swap, switch, replacement, substitution, reciprocity.

excitable adj.
☞ 易激动的,易兴奋的 temperamental, volatile, passionate, emotional, highly-strung, fiery, hot-headed, hasty, nervous, hot-tempered, irascible, quick-tempered, sensitive, susceptible.

excite v.
☞ 激动,使兴奋 move, agitate, disturb, upset, touch, stir up, thrill, elate, turn on, impress.
☞ 唤起 arouse, rouse, animate, awaken, fire, inflame, kindle, motivate, stimulate, engender, inspire, instigate, incite, induce, ignite, galvanize, generate, provoke, sway, quicken, evoke.

excited adj.
☞ 激动的,兴奋的 aroused, roused, stimulated, stirred, thrilled, elated, enthusiastic, eager, moved, high, worked up, wrought-up, overwrought, restless, frantic, frenzied, wild.

excitement n.
☞ 使人兴奋的事件,活动 unrest, ado, action, activity, commotion, fuss, tumult, flurry, furore, adventure.
☞ 刺激,兴奋 discomposure, agitation, passion, thrill, animation, elation, enthusiasm, restlessness, kicks, ferment, fever, eagerness, stimulation.

exciting adj.
☞ 令人兴奋的 stimulating, stirring, intoxicating, exhilarating, thrilling, rousing, moving, enthralling, electrifying, nail-biting, cliff-hanging, striking, sensational, provocative, inspiring, interesting.

exclaim v.
☞ 大叫 cry (out), declare, blurt (out), call, yell, shout, proclaim, utter.

exclamation n.
☞ 叫喊 cry, call, yell, shout, expletive, interjection, ejaculation, outcry, utterance.

exclude v.
☞ 拒绝 ban, bar, prohibit, disallow, veto, proscribe, forbid, blacklist.
☞ 排除 omit, leave out, keep out, refuse, reject, ignore, shut out, rule out, ostracize, eliminate.
☞ 开除 expel, eject, evict, excommunicate.

exclusive adj.
☞ 孤高的 sole, single, unique, only, undivided, unshared, whole, total, peculiar.
☞ 排他的,排外的 restricted, limited, closed, private, narrow, restrictive, choice, select, discriminative, cliquey, chic, classy, elegant, fashionable, posh, snobbish.

excursion n.
☞ 短途,旅行 outing, trip, jaunt, expedition, day trip, journey, tour, airing, breather, junket, ride, drive, walk, ramble.

excuse v.
☞ 原谅 forgive, pardon, overlook, absolve, indulge.
☞ 免除 release, free, discharge, liberate, let off, relieve, spare, exempt.
☞ 辨解 condonge, explain, mitigate, justify, vindicate, defend, apologize for.
n.
☞ 原谅 justification, explanation, grounds, defence, plea, alibi, reason, apology, pretext, pretence, exoneration, evasion, cop-out, shift, substitute.

execute v.
☞ 处决 put to death, kill, liquidate, hang, electrocute, shoot, guillotine, decapitate, behead.
☞ 执行,实行 carry out, perform, do, accomplish, achieve, fulfil, complete,

discharge, effect, enact, deliver, enforce, finish, implement, administer, consummate, realize, dispatch, expedite, validate, serve, render, sign.

execution n.
☞处死 death penalty, capital punishment, killing, hanging, electrocution, firing squad, shooting, guillotining, decapitation, beheading.
☞执行,成功 accomplishment, operation, performance, completion, achievement, administration, effect, enactment, implementation, realization, discharge, dispatch, consummation, eforcement.
☞演奏,技巧 style, technique, rendition, delivery, performance, manner, mode.

executive n.
☞行政部门 administration, management, government, leadership, hierarchy.
☞执行者,经理 administrator, manager, organizer, leader, controller, director, governor, official, controlling, supervisory, regulating, decision-making, governing, organizing, directing, directorial, organizational, leading, guiding.

exemplary adj.
☞示范性的,典型的 model, ideal, perfect, admirable, excellent, faultless, flawless, correct, good, commendable, praiseworthy, worthy, laudable, estimable, honourable.
☞惩戒性的 cautionary, warning.

exemplify v.
☞例证,示范 illustrate, demonstrate, show, instance, represent, typify, manifest, embody, epitomize, exhibit, depict, display.

exempt v.
☞免除 excuse, release, relieve, let off, free, absolve, discharge, dismiss, liberate, spare.
adj.
☞免除的 excused, not liable, immune, released, spared, absolved, discharged, excluded, free, liberated, clear.

exercise v.
☞运用,利用 use, utilize, employ, apply, exert, practise, wield, try, discharge.
☞运动,训练 train, drill, practise, work out, keep fit.
☞使烦恼 worry, disturb, trouble, upset, burden, distress, vex, annoy, agitate, afflict.
n.
☞运动 training, drill, practice, effort, exertion, task, lesson, work, discipline, activity, physical jerks, work-out, aerobics, labour.
☞运用,练习 use, utilization, employment, application, emplementation, practice, operation, discharge, assignment, fulfilment, accomplishment.

exert v.
☞尽力,发挥,运用 use, utilize, employ, apply, exercise, bring to bear, wield, expend.

exert oneself
☞ 努力,尽力 strive, struggle, strain, make and effort, take pains, toil, labour, work, sweat, endeavour, apply oneself.

exertion n.
☞ 努力,行使 effort, industry, labour, toil, work, struggle, diligence, assiduousness, perseverance, pains, endeavour, attempt, strain, travail, trial.
☞ 运用 use, utilization, employment, application, exercise, eperation, action.

exhaust v.
☞ 用尽,耗尽 consume, empty, deplete, drain, sap, spend, waste, squander, dissipate, impoverish, use up, finish, dry, bankrupt.
☞ 精疲力尽 tire (out), weary, fatigue, tax, strain, weaken, overwork, wear out.
n.
☞ 排出 emission, exhalation, discharge, fumes.

exhausted adj.
☞ 排空的 empty, finished, depleted, spent, used up, drained, dry, worn out, void.
☞ 耗尽的 tired(out), dead tried, dead-beat, all in, done (in), fatigued, weak, washed-out, whacked, knackered, jaded.

exhausting adj.
☞ 耗尽的 tiring, strenuous, taxing, gruelling, arduous, hard, laborious, backbreaking, draining, severe, testing, punishing, formidable, debilitatin.

exhaustion n.
☞ 耗尽,竭尽 fatigue, tiredness, weariness, debility, feebleness, jet-lag.

exhaustive adj.
☞ 详尽的,彻底的 comprehensive, all-embracing, all-inclusive, far-reaching, complete, extensive, encyclopedic, full-scale, thorough, full, in-depth, intensive, detailed, definitive, all-out, sweeping.

exhibit v.
☞ 展览 display, show, present, demonstrate, manifest, expose, parade, reveal, express, disclose, indicate, air, flaunt, offer.
n.
☞ 展览品 display, exhibition, show, illustration, model.

exhibition n.
☞ 展览,表演,显示 display, show, demonstration, exhibit, presentation, manifestation, spectacle, exposition, expo, showing, fair, performance, airing, representation, showcase.

exile n.
☞ 放逐,充军 banishment, deportation, expatriation, expulsion, ostracism, transportation.
☞ 流犯 expatriate, refugee, emigre, deportee, outcast.
v.
☞ 放逐,充军 banish, expel, deport, expatriate, drive out, ostracize, oust.

exist v.
- 生存 be, live, abide, continue, endure, have one's being, breathe, prevail.
- 存在 subsist, survive.
- 产生 be present, occur, happen, be available, remain.

existence n.
- 生活 being, life, reality, actuality, continuance, continuation, endurance, survival, breath, subsistence.
- 产生,存在 creation, the world.
- 生物 entity, creature, thing.

exit n.
- 退出 departure, going, retreat, withdrawal, leave-taking, retirement, farewell, exodus.
- 出口 door, way out, doorway, gate, vent.

v.
- 退出 depart, leave, go, retire, withdraw, take one's leave, retreat, issue.

expand v.
- 张开,展开 stretch, swell, widen, lengthen, thicken, magnify, multiply, inflate, broaden, blow up, open out, fill out, fatten.
- 扩大,发展 increase, grow, extend, enlarge, develop, amplify, spread, branch out, diversify, elaborate.

expanse n.
- 宽阔的区域 extent, space, area, breadth, range, stretch, sweep, field, plain, tract.

expansive adj.
- 扩张性的 friendly, genial, outgoing, open, affable, sociable, talkative, warm, communicative, effusive.
- 宽阔的 extensive, broad, comprehensive, wide-ranging, all-embracing, thorough.

expect v.
- 期望 anticipate, await, look forward to, hope for, look for, bank on, bargain for, envisage, predict, forecast, contemplate, project, foresee.
- 坚持,要求 require, want, wish, insist on, demand, rely on, count on.
- 以为 suppose, surmise, assume, believe, think, presume, imagine, reckon, guess, trust.

expectant adj.
- 期待的 awaiting, anticipating, hopeful, in suspense, ready, apprehensive, anxious, watchful, eager, curious.

expedition n.
- 远征 journey, excursion, trip, voyage, tour, exploration, trek, safari, hike, sail, ramble, raid, quest, pilgrimage, mission, crusade.
- 敏捷 promtness, speed, alacrity, haste.

expel v.
- 驱逐,逐出 drive out, eject, evict, banish, throw out, ban, bar, oust, exile, expatriate.

expend v.
- 花费,耗费 spend, pay, fork out.
- 使用 consume, use (up), dissipate, exhaust, employ.

expenditure n.
☞ 消费，支出 spending, expense, outlay, outgoings, payment, output.

expense n.
☞ 花费，代价 spending, expenditure, outlay, payment, loss, cost, charge.

expensive adj.
☞ 昂贵的 dear, hight-priced, costly, exorbitant, extortionate, steep, extravagant, lavish.

experience n.
☞ 经验 knowledge, familiarity, know-how, involvement, participation, practice, understanding.
☞ 经历 incident, event, episode, happening, encounter, occurrence, adventure.
v.
☞ 经历，体验 undergo, go through, live through, suffer, feel, endure, encounter, face, meet, know, try, perceive, sustain.

experienced adj.
☞ 有经验的 practised, knowledgeable, familiar, capable, competent, well-versed, expert, accomplished, qualified, skilled, tried, trained, professional.
☞ 老练的 mature, seasoned, wise, veteran.

experiment n.
☞ 实验 trial, test, investigation, experimentation, research, examination, trial run, venture, trial and error, attempt, procedure, proof.
v.
☞ 做实验 try, test, investigate, examine, research, sample, verify.

experimental adj.
☞ 实验的 trial, test, exploratory, tentative, provisional, speculative, pilot, preliminary, trial-and-error.

expert n.
☞ 专家，能手 specialist, connoisseur, authority, professional, pro, dab hand, maestro, virtuoso.
adj.
☞ 熟练的，老练的 proficient, adept, skilled, skilful, knowledgeable, experienced, able, practised, professional, masterly, specialist, qualified, virtuoso.

expertise n.
☞ 专长，鉴别 expertness, proficiency, skill, skilfulness, know-how, knack, knowledge, mastery, dexterity, virtuosity.

explain v.
☞ 解释，说明，讲解 interpret, clarify, describe, define, make clear, elucidate, simplify, resolve, solve, spell out, translate, unfold, unravel, untangle, illustrate, demonstrate, disclose, expound, teach.
☞ 为……辩解 justify, excuse, account for, rationalize.

explanation n.
☞ 说明 interpretation, clarification, definition, elucidation, illustration, demonstration, account,

description.
- ☞ 解释 justification, excuse, warrant, rationalization, answer, meaning, motive, reason, key, sense, significance.

explanatory *adj*.
- ☞ 解释的,说明的 descriptive, interpretive, explicative, demonstrative, justifying.

explicit *adj*.
- ☞ 清晰的 clear, distinct, exact, categorical, absolute, certain, positive, precise, specific, unambiguous, express, difinite, declared, detailed, stated.
- ☞ 明确的 open, direct, frank, outspoken, straightforward, unreserved, plain.

explode *v*.
- ☞ 爆炸 blow up, burst, go off, set off, detonate, discharge, blast, erupt.
- ☞ 揭穿 discredit, disprove, give the lie to, debunk, invalidate, refute, rebut, repudiate.

exploit *n*.
- ☞ 功绩,行为 deed, feat, adventure, achievement, accomplishment, attainment, stunt.

v.
- ☞ 利用 use, utilize, capitalize on, profit by, turn to account, take advatage of, cash in on, make capital out of.
- ☞ 剥削 misuse, abuse, oppress, ill-treat, impose on, manipulate, rip off, fleece.

exploration *n*.
- ☞ 探查 investigation, examination, enquiry, research, scrutiny, study, inspection, analysis, probe.
- ☞ 勘探 expedition, survey, reconnaissance, search, trip, tour, voyage, travel, safari.

explore *v*.
- ☞ 检查 investigate, examine, inspect, research, scrutinize, probe, analyse.
- ☞ 勘探 travel, tour, search, reconnoitre, prospect, scout, survey.

explosion *n*.
- ☞ 爆炸,爆发 detonation, blast, burst, outburst, discharge, eruption, bang, outbreak, clap, crack, fit, report.

explosive *adj*.
- ☞ 易爆炸的 unstable, volatile, sensitive, tense, fraught, charged, touchy, overwrought, dangerous, hazardous, perilous, stormy.

expose *v*.
- ☞ 暴露 reveal, show, exhibit, display, disclose, uncover, bring, to light, present, manifest, detect, divulge, unveil, unmask, denouce.
- ☞ 使危险 endanger, jeopardize, imperil, risk, hazard.

exposed *adj*.
- ☞ 暴露的 bare, open, revealed, laid bare, unprotected, vulnerable, exhibited, on display, on show, on view, shown, susceptible.

exposure *n*.
- ☞ 暴露 revelation, uncovering, disclosure, expose, showing, unmasking, unveiling, display, airing, exhibition, presentation,

☞ 危险 jeopardy, danger, hazard, risk, vulnerability.

express v.
☞ 表示,表达 articulate, verbalize, utter, voice, say, speak, state, communicate, pronounce, tell, assert, declare, put, across, formulate, intimate, testify, convey.
☞ 展示 show, manifest, exhibit, disclose, divulge, reveal, indicate, denote, depict, embody.
☞ 象征 symbolize, stand for, represent, signify, designate.

adj.
☞ 明白的,明确的 specific, explicit, exact, definite, clear, categorical, precise, distinct, clear-cut, certain, plain, manifest, particular, stated, unambiguous.
☞ 特快的 fast, speedy, rapid, quick, high-speed, non-stop.

expression n.
☞ 表情 look, air, aspect, countenance, appearance.
☞ 展示 representation, manifestation, demonstration, indication, exhibition, embodiment, show, sign, symbol, style.
☞ 表达,发表 utterance, verbalization, communication, articulation, statement, assertion, announcement, declaration, pronouncement, speech.
☞ 语调 tone, intonation, delivery, diction, enunciation, modulation, wording.
☞ 表达方式 phrase, term, turn of phrase, saying, set phrase, idiom.

expressive adj.
☞ 有表现力的 eloquent, meaningful, forceful, telling, revealing, informative, indicative, communicative, demonstrative, emphatic, moving, poignant, lively, striking, suggestive, significant, thoughtful, vivid, sympathetic.

exquisite adj.
☞ 优美的 beautiful, attractive, dainty, delicate, charming, elegant, delightful, lovely, pleasing.
☞ 完美的 perfect, flawless, fine, excellent, choice, precious, rare, outstanding.
☞ 精巧的 refined, discriminating, meticulous, sensitive, impeccable.
☞ 敏锐的 intense, keen, sharp, poignant.

extend v.
☞ 展开 spread, stretch, reach, continue.
☞ 延长 enlarge, increase, expand, develop, amplify, lengthen, widen, elongate, draw out, protract, prolong, spin out, unwind.
☞ 给予 offer, give, grant, hold out, impart, present, bestow, confer.

extension n.
☞ 伸长,展开 enlargement, increase, stretching, broadening, widening, lengthening, expansion,

elongation, development, enhancement, protraction, continuation.
- 增加 addition, supplement, appendix, annexe, addendum.
- 延长 delay, postponement.

extensive adj.
- 辽阔的 broad, comprehensive, far-reaching, large-scale, thorough, widespread, universal, extended, all-inclusive, general, pervasive, prevalent.
- 广大的 large, huge, roomy, spacious, vast, voluminous, long, lengthy, wide.

extent n.
- 范围 demension(s), amount, magnitude, expanse, size, area, bulk, degree, breadth, quantity, spread, stretch, volume, width, measure, duration, term, time.
- 程度 limit, bounds, lengths, range, reach, scope, compass, sphere, play, sweep.

exterior n.
- 外表 outside, surface, covering, coating, face, facade, shell, skin, finish, externals, appearance.

adj.
- 外表的,外部的 outer, outside, outermost, surface, external, superficial, surrounding, outward, peripheral, extrinsic.

external adj.
- 外表的,外部的 outer, surface, outside, exterior, superficial, outward, outermost, apparent, visible, extraneous, extrinsic, extramural, independent.

extinct adj.
- 灭绝的 defunct, dead, gone, obsolete, ended, exterminated, terminated, vanished, lost, abolished.
- 熄灭的 extinguished, quenched, inactive, out.

extinction n.
- 消灭,灭绝 annihilation, extermination, death, eradication, obliteration, destruction, abolition, excision.

extinguish v.
- 熄灭 put out, blow out, snuff out, stifle, smother, douse, quench.
- 使……灭绝 annihilate, exterminate, eliminate, destroy, kill, eradicate, erase, expunge, abolish, remove, end, suppress.

extra adj.
- 额外的 additional, added, auxiliary, supplementary, new, more, further, ancillary, fresh, other.
- 备用的 excess, spare, superfluous, supernumerary, surplus, unused, unneeded, leftover, reserve, redundant.

n.
- 附加物 addition, supplement, extension, accessory, appendage, bonus, complement, adjunct, attachment.

adv.
- 额外,特别 especially, exceptionally, extraordinarily, particularly, unusually, remarkably, extremely.

extract v.

☞ 拔出,抽出 remove, take out, draw out, exact, uproot, withdraw.
☞ 提取 derive, draw, distil, obtain, get, gather, glean, wrest, wring, elicit.
☞ 选择 choose, select, cull, abstract, cite, quote.
n.
☞ 精华,汁 distillation, essence, juice.
☞ 选录 excerpt, passage, selection, clip, cutting, quotation, abstract, citation.

extraordinary *adj.*
☞ 非常的,格外的 remarkable, unusual, exceptional, notable, noteworthy, outstanding, unique, special, strange, peculiar, rare, surprising, amazing, wonderful, unprecedented, marvellous, fantastic, significant, particular.

extravagance *n.*
☞ 浪费 overspending, profligacy, squandering, waste.
☞ 放肆的言行 excess, immoderation, recklessness, profusion, outrageousness, folly.

extravagant *adj.*
☞ 浪费的,奢侈的 profligate, prodigal, spendthrift, thriftless, wasteful, reckless.
☞ 过度的 immoderate, flamboyant, preposterous, outrageous, ostentatious, pretentious, lavish, ornate, flashy, fanciful, fantastic, wild.
☞ 昂贵的 overpriced, exorbitant, expensive, excessive, costly.

extreme *adj.*
☞ 极端的 intense, great, immoderate, inordinate, utmost, utter, out-and-out, maximum, acute, downright, extraordinary, exceptional, greatest, higest, unreasonable, remarkable.
☞ 最远的 farthest, far-off, faraway, distant, endmost, outermost, remotest, uttermost, final, last, terminal, ultimate.
☞ 急进的 radical, zealous, extremist, fanatical.
☞ 激烈的 drastic, dire, uncompromising, stern, strict, rigid, severe, harsh.
n.
☞ 极端,末端 extremity, limit, maximum, ultimate, utmost, excess, top, pinnacle, peak, height, end, climax, depth, edge, termination.

extremity *n.*
☞ 末端,极度 extreme, limit, boundary, brink, verge, bound, border, apex, height, tip, top, edge, excess, end, acme, termination, peak, pinnacle, margin, terminal, terminus, ultimate, pole, maximum, minimum, frontier, depth.
☞ 危机 crisis, danger, emergency, plight, hardship.

eye *n.*
☞ 眼,目 appreciation, discrimination, discernment, perception, recognition.
☞ 视力 viewpoint, opinion, judgement, mind.
☞ 看 watch, observation, lookout.

v.
- 看, 注视 look at, watch, regard, observe, stare at, gaze at, glance at, view, scrutinize, scan, examine, peruse, study, survey, inspect, contemplate.

eyesight *n.*
- 视力 vision, sight, perception, observation, view.

eye-witness *n.*
- 见证人, 目击者 witness, observer, spectator, looker-on, onlooker, bystander, viewer, passer-by.

F

fable *n.*
- 寓言, 传说 allegory, parable, story, tale, yarn myth, legend, fiction, fabrication, invention, lie, untruth, falsehood, tall story, old wives'tale.

fabric *n.*
- 织品 cloth, material, textile, stuff, web, texture.
- 组织, 结构 structure, framework, construction, make-up, constitution, organization, infrastructure, foundations.

fabricate *v.*
- 捏造, 伪造 fake, falsify, forge, invent, make up, trump up, concoct.
- 建造 make, manufacture, construct, assemble, build, erect, form, shape, fashion, create, devise.

fabulous *adj.*
- 极好的, 难以置信的 wonderful, marvellous, fantastic, superb, breathtaking, spectacular, phenomenal, amazing, astounding, unbelievable, incredible, inconceivable.
- 传说上的 mythical, legendary, fabled, fantastic, fictitious, invented, imaginary.

face *n.*
- 脸 features, countenance, visage, physiognomy.
- 表情 expression, look, appearance, air.
- 脸色 grimace, frown, scowl, pout.
- 外表 exterior, outside, surface, cover, front, facade, aspect, side.

v.
- 面对 be opposite, give on to, front, overlook.
- 勇敢面对 confront, face up to, deal with, cope with, tackle, brave, defy, oppose, encounter, meet, experience.
- 盖 cover, coat, dress, clad, overlay, veneer.

face to face
- 面对面 opposite, eye to eye, eyeball to eyeball, in confrontation.

face up to
- 勇敢对付 accept, come to terms with, acknowledge, recognize, cope with, deal with, confront, meet head-on, stand

up to.

facet n.
☞ 刻面 surface, plane, side, face, aspect, angle, point, feature, characteristic.

facilitate v.
☞ 促使 ease, help, assist, further, promote, forward, expedite, speed up.

facilities n.
☞ 设备,便利 amenities, services, conveniences, resources, prerequisites, equipment, mod cons, means, opportunities.

facility n.
☞ 灵巧,熟练 ease, effortlessness, readiness, quickness, fluency, proficiency, skill, skilfulness, talent, gift, knack, ability.

fact n.
☞ 实情 reality, actuality, truth.
☞ 事实 information, datum, detail, particular, specific, point, item, circumstance, event incident, occurrence, happening, act, deed, fait accompli.

in fact
☞ 事实上,实际上 actually, in actual fact, in point of fact, as a matter of fact, in reality, really, indeed.

faction n.
☞ 宗派,集团 splinter group, ginger group, minority, division, contingent, party, camp, set, clique, coterie, cabal, junta, lobby, pressure group.

factor n.
☞ 因素 cause, influence, circumstance, contingency, consideration, element, ingredient, component, part, point, aspect, fact, item, detail.

factory n.
☞ 工厂 works, plant, mill, shop floor, assembly line, manufactory.

faculty n.
☞ 才能,能力 ability, capability, capacity, power, facility, knack, gift, talent, skill, aptitude, bent.

fad n.
☞ 风尚,狂热 craze, rage, mania, fashion, mode, vogue, trend, whim, fancy, affectation.

fade v.
☞ 枯萎,褪色 discolour, bleach, blanch, blench, pale, whiten, dim, dull.
☞ 消失 decline, fall, diminish, dwindle, ebb, wane, disapear, vanish, flag, weaken, droop, wilt, wither, shrivel, perish, die.

fail v.
☞ 失败,不成功 go wrong, miscarry, misfire, flop, miss, flunk, fall through, come to grief, collapse, fold, go bankrupt, go bust, go under, founder, sink, decline, fall, weaken, dwindle, fade, wane, peter out, cease, die.
☞ 忘记 omit, neglect, forget.
☞ 使失望 let down, disappoint,

leave, desert, abandon, forsake.

failing n.
☞ 缺点,弱点 weakness, foible, fault, defect, imperfection, flaw, blemish, drawback, deficiency, shortcoming, failure, lapse, error.

failure n.
☞ 失败 miscarriage, flop, wash out , fiasco, disappointment, loss, defeat, downfall, decline, decay, deterioration, ruin, bankruptcy, crash, collapse, breakdown, stoppage.
☞ 疏忽,不足 omission, slip-up , neglect, negligence, failing, shortcoming, deficiency.

faint adj.
☞ 软弱的,无力的 slight, weak, feeble, soft, low, hushed, muffled, subdued, faded, bleached, light, pale, dull, dim, hazy, indistinct, vague.
☞ 头晕的 dizzy, giddy, woozy , light-headed, weak, feeble, exhausted.
v.
☞ 昏倒,昏晕 black out, pass out, swoon, collapse, flake out , keel over , drop.
n.
☞ 昏晕 blackout, swoon, collapse, unconsciousness.

fair¹ adj.
☞ 公平的 just, equitable, square, even-handed, dispassionate, impartial, objective, disinterested, unbiased, unprejudiced, right, proper, lawful, legitimate, honest, trustworthy, upright, honourable.

☞ 中等的 average, moderate, middling, not bad, all right, ok, satisfactory, adequate, acceptable, tolerable, reasonable, passable, mediocre, so-so.
☞ 晴朗的 fine, dry, sunny, bright, clear, cloudless, unclouded.

fair² n.
☞ 庙会,集市,展览会 show, exhibition, exposition, expo, market, bazaar, fete, festival, carnival, gala.

faith n.
☞ 信任 belief, credit, trust, reliance, dependence, conviction, confidence, assurance.
☞ 信仰 religion, denomination, persuasion, church, creed, dogma.
☞ 忠诚,忠实 faithfulness, fidelity, loyalty, allegiance, honour, sincerity, honesty, truthfulness.

faithful adj.
☞ 忠诚的,准确的 loyal, devoted, staunch, steadfast, constant, trusty, reliable, dependable, true.
☞ 忠实的 accurate, precise, exact, strict, close, true, truthful.

fake v.
☞ 伪造,假冒 forge, fabricate, counterfeit, copy, imitate, simulate, feign, sham, pretend, put on, affect, assume.
n.
☞ 假货 forgery, copy, reproduction, replica, imitation,

simulation, sham, hoax, fraud, phoney, impostor, charlatan.

adj.

☞ 假的, 伪造的 forged, counterfeit, false, spurious, phoney, pseudo, bogus, assumed, affected, sham, artificial, simulated, mock, imitation, reproduction.

fall *v.*

☞ 落下 tumble, stumble, trip, topple, keel over, collapse, slump, crash.

☞ 倒下 descend, go down, drop, slope, incline, slide, sink, dive, plunge, plummet, nose-dive, pitch.

☞ 减少, 降低 decrease, lessen, decline, diminish, dwindle, fall off, subside.

n.

☞ 落下, 降落 tumble, descent, slope, incline, dive, plunge, decrease, reduction, lessening, drop, decline, dwindling, slump, crash.

☞ 颠覆 defeat, conquest, overthrow, downfall, collapse, surrender, capitulation.

fall apart

☞ 分裂, 崩溃 break, go to pieces, shatter, disintegrate, crumble, decompose, decay, rot.

fall asleep

☞ 熟睡 drop off, doze off, nod off.

fall back on

☞ 求助于, 投靠 resort to, have recourse to, use, turn to, look to.

fall behind

☞ 落后 lag, trail, dropo back.

fall in

☞ 集合 cave in, come down, collapse, give way, subside, sink.

fall in with

☞ 与……偶遇, 同意 agree with, assent to, go along with, accept, comply with, co-operate with.

fall off

☞ 落下 decrease, lessen, drop, slump, decline, deteriorate, worsen, slow, slacken.

fall out

☞ 争吵 quarrel, argue, squabble, bicker, fight, clash, disagree, differ.

fall through

☞ 归于失败 come to nothing, fail, miscarry, founder, collapse.

false *adj.*

☞ 错误的, 不正确的 wrong, incorrect, mistaken, erroneous, inaccurate, inexact, misleading, faulty, fallacious, invalid.

☞ 虚伪的, 假的 unreal, artificial, synthetic, imitation, simulated, mock, fake, counterfeit, forged, feigned, pretended, sham, bogus, assumed, fictitious.

☞ 不讲义气的 disloyal, unfaithful, faithless, lying, deceitful, insincere, hypocritical, two-faced, double-dealing, treacherous, unreliable.

falsehood *n.*

☞ 谎话 untruth, lie, fib, story, fiction, fabrication, perjury, untruthfulness, deceit, deception, dishonesty.

falsify v.
- 伪造 alter, cook, tamper with, doctor, distort, pervert, misrepresent, misstate, forge, counterfeit, fake.

fame n.
- 名声,声望 renown, celebrity, stardom, prominence, eminence, illustriousness, glory, honour, esteem, reputation, name.

familiar adj.
- 熟悉的 everyday, routine, household, common, ordinary, well-known, recognizable.
- 亲近的 intimate, close, confidential, friendly, informal, free, free-and-easy, relaxed.

familiarity n.
- 亲近 intimacy, liberty, closeness, friendliness, sociability, openness, naturalness, informality.
- 熟悉情况 awareness, acquaintance, experience, knowledge, understanding, grasp.

familiarize v.
- 使熟悉 accustom, acclimatize, school, train, coach, instruct, prime, brief.

family n.
- 家属,家族 relatives, relations, kin, kindred, kinsmen, people, folk, ancestors, forebears, children, offspring, issue, progeny, descendants.
- 部族 clan, tribe, race, dynasty, house, pedigree, ancestry, parentage, descent, line, lineage, extraction, blood, stock, birth.
- 类别 class, group, classification.
- 世系,祖先 ancestry, pedigree, genealogy, line, lineage, extraction.

famine n.
- 饥荒 starvation, hunger, destitution, want, scarcity, death.

famous adj.
- 著名的 well-known, famed, renowned, celebrated, noted, great, distinguished, illustrious, eminent, honoured, acclaimed, glorious, legendary, remarkable, notable, prominent, signal.

fan[1] v.
- 扇 cool, ventilate, air, air-condition, air-cool, blow, refresh.
- 煽动 increase, provoke, stimulate, rouse, arouse, excite, agitate, stir up, work up, whip up.

n.
- 扇子 extractor fan, ventilator, air-conditioner, blower, propeller, vane.

fan[2] n.
- 爱好者,迷 enthusiast, admirer, supporter, follower, adherent, devotee, lover, buff, fiend, freak.

fanatic n.
- 狂热者 zealot, devotee, enthusiast, addict, fiend, freak, maniac, visionary, bigot, extremist, militant, activist.

fanatical adj.
- 盲信的,狂热的 overenthusiastic, extreme, passionate, zealous, fervent, burning, mad, wild, frenzied, rabid, obsessive, single-minded, bigoted, visionary.

fancy v.
- 喜欢,爱好 like, be attracted to, take a liking to, take to, go for, prefer, favour, desire, wish for, long for, yearn for.
- 想象,设想 think, conceive, imagine, dream of, picture, conjecture, believe, suppose, reckon, guess.

n.
- 嗜好,爱好 desire, craving, hankering, urge, liking, fondness, inclination, preference.
- 想象力 notion, thought, impression, imagination, dream, fantasy.

adj.
- 悦目的,花样的 elaborate, kornate, decorated, ornamented, rococo, baroque, elegant, extravagant, fantastic, fanciful, far-fetched.

fantastic adj.
- 奇异的 wonderful, marvellous, sensational, superb, excellent, first-rate, tremendous, terrific, great, incredible, unbelievable, overwhelming, enormous, extreme.
- 不能实现的,荒谬的 strange, weird, odd, exotic, outlandish, fanciful, fabulous, imaginative, visionary.

fantasy n.
- 幻想,幻想作品 dream, daydream, reverie, pipe-dream, nightmare, vision, hallucination, illusion, mirage, apparition, invention, fancy, flight of fancy, delusion, misconception, imagination, unreality.

far adv.
- 遥远,远地 a long way, a good way, miles, much, greatly, considerably, extremely, decidedly, incomparable.

adj.
- 远远的 distant, far-off, faraway, far-flung, cutlving, remote, out-of-the-way, god-forsaken, removed, far-removed, further, opposite, other.

fare n.
- 车费 charge, cost, price, fee, passage.
- 伙食,饮食 food, eatables, provisions, rations, sustenance, meals, diet, menu, board, table.

far-fetched adj.
- 牵强的 implausible, improbable, unlikely, dubious, incredible, unbelievable, fantastic, preposterous, crazy, unrealistic.

farm n.
- 农场 ranch, farmstead, grange, homestead, station, land, holding, acreage, acres.

v.
- 耕作,租 cultivate, till, work the land, plant, operate.

farmer n.
☞ 农场主 agriculturist, crofter, smallholder, husbandman, yeoman.

farming n.
☞ 农业,耕作 agriculture, cultivation, husbandry, crofting.

far-reaching adj.
☞ 影响深远的 broad, extensive, widespread, sweeping, important, significant, momentous.

fascinate v.
☞ 使着迷,使吓呆 absorb, engross, intrigue, delight, charm, captivate, spellbind, enthral, rivet, transfix, hypnotize, mesmerize.

fascination n.
☞ 迷惑,着迷 interest, attraction, lure, magnetism, pull, charm, enchantment, spell, sorcery, magic.

fashion n.
☞ 方式,方法 manner, way, method, mode, style, shape, form, pattern, line, ctu, look, appearance, type, sort, kind.
☞ 风尚,风气 vogue, trend, mode, style, fad, craze, rage, latest, custom, convention.
v.
☞ 形成,创造 create, form, shape, mould, model, design, fit, tailor, alter, adjust, adapt, suit.

fashionable adj.
☞ 流行的,时髦的 chic, smart, elegant, stylish, modish, a la mode, in vogue, trendy, in, all the rage, popular, prevailing,
current, latest, up-to-the-minute, contemporary, modern, up-to-date.

fast¹ adj.
☞ 快的,迅速的 quick, swift, rapid, brisk, accelerated, speedy, nippy, hasty, hurried, flying.
☞ 坚固的 fastened, secure, fixed, immovable, immobile, firm, tight.
adv.
☞ 快地,迅速地 quickly, swiftly, rapidly, speedily, like a flash, like a shot, hastily, hurriedly, apace, presto.

fast² v.
☞ 禁食,斋戒 go hungry, diet, starve, abstain.
n.
☞ 禁食,斋戒(期) fasting, diet, starvation, abstinence.

fasten v.
☞ 使牢固 fix, attach, clamp, grip, anchor, river, nail, seal, close, shut, lock, bolt, secure, tie, bind, chain, link, interlock, connect, join, unite, do up, button, lace, buckle.

fat adj.
☞ 胖的,厚的,满的 plump, obese, tubby, stout, corpulent, portly, round, rotund, paunchy, pot-bellied, overweight, heavy, beefy, solid, chubby, podgy, fleshy, flabby, gross.
n.
☞ 脂肪,肥肉 fatness, obesity, overweight, corpulence, paunch, pot (belly), blubber,

flab.

fatal adj.
- 致命的 deadly, lethal, mortal, killing, incurble, malignant, terminal, final, destructive, calamitous, catastrophic, disatrous.

fatality n.
- 死亡,灾祸 death, mortality, loss, casualty, deadliness, lethality, disaster.

fate n.
- 命运,死祸 destiny, providence, chance, future, fortune, horoscope, stars, lot, doom, end, outcome, ruin, destruction, death.

fated adj.
- 命中注定的 destined, predestined, preordained, foreordained, doomed, unavoidable, inevitable, inescapable, certain, sure.

fateful adj.
- 关系重大的,决定的 crucial, critical, decisive, important, momentous, significant, fatal, lethal, disastrous.

father n.
- 父亲 parent, begetter, procreator, progenitor, sire, papa, dad, daddy, old man, patriarch, elder, forefather, ancestor, forebear, predecessor.
- 创造者 founder, creator, originator, inventor, maker, architect, author, patron, leader, prime mover.
- 神父 priest, padre, abbe, cure.

v.
- 产生,生产 beget, procreate, sire, produce.

fatigue n.
- 疲劳 tiredness, weariness, exhaustion, lethargy, listlessness, lassitude, weakness, debility.

v.
- 使疲劳 tire, wear out, weary, exhaust, drain, weaken, debilitate.

fatten v.
- 养肥,长肥,使肥沃 feed, nourish, build up, overfeed, cram, stuff, blost, swell, fill out, spread, expand, thicken.

fatty adj.
- 像脂肪的,含脂肪的 fat, greasy, oily.

fault n.
- 缺点,毛病,故障 defect, flaw, blemish, imperfection, deficiency, shortcoming, weakness, failing, foible, negligence, omission, oversight.
- 错误,过失 error, mistake, blunder, slip-up, slip, lapse, misdeed, offence, wrong, sin.
- 责备 responsibility, accountability, liability, culpability.

v.
- 挑剔 find fault with, pick holes in, criticize, knock, impugn, censure, blame, call to account.

at fault
- 有错 (in the) wrong, blameworthy, to blame, responsible, guilty, culpable.

faultless adj.
- 无过失的,完善的 perfect,

flawless, unblemished, spotless, immaculate, unsullied, pure, blameless, exemplary, model, correct, accurate.

faulty *adj.*
- 有过失的,有缺点的 imperfect, defective, flawed, blemished, damaged, impaired, out of order, broken, wrong.

favour *n.*
- 好意,关心,支持 approval, esteem, support, backing, sympathy, goodwill, patronage, favouritism, preference, partiality.
- 帮忙 kindness, service, good turn, courtesy.

v.
- 偏爱 prefer, choose, opt for, like, approve, support, back, advocate, champion.
- 赞助,照顾 help, assist, aid, benefit, promote, encourage, pamper, spoil.

in favour of
- 赞同,支持 for, supporting, on the side of.

favourable *adj.*
- 有利的,好意的 beneficial, advantageous, helpful, fit, suitable, convenient, timely, opportune, good, fair, promising, auspicious, hopeful, positive, encouraging, complimentary, enthusiastic, friendly, amicable, well-disposed, kind, sympathetic, understanding, ressuring.

favourite *adj.*
- 喜爱的 preferred, favoured, pet, best-loved, dearest, beloved, esteemed, chosen.

n.
- 宠儿 preference, choice, pick, pet, blue-eyed boy, teacher's pet, the apple of one's eye, darling, idol.

fear *n.*
- 恐惧,害怕,担忧 alarm, fright, terror, horror, panic, agitation, worry, anxiety, consternation, concern, dismay, distress, uneasiness, qualms, misgivings, apprehension, trepidation, dread, foreboding, awe, phobia, nightmare.

v.
- 惧怕,担忧 take fright, shrink from, dread, shudder at, tremble, worry, suspect, anticipate, expect, foresee, respect, venerate.

fearful *adj.*
- 担心的,恐惧的 frightened, afraid, scared, alarmed, nervous, anxious, tense, uneasy, apprehensive, hesitant, nervy, panicky.
- 可怕的 terrible, fearsome, dreadful, awful, frightful, atrocious, shocking, appalling, monstrous, gruesome, hideous, ghastly, horrible.

feasible *adj.*
- 可行的,办得通的 practicable, practical, workable, achievable, attainable, realizable, viable, reasonable, possible, likely.

feast *n.*
- 宴会 banquet, dinner, spread, binge, beano, junket.
- 节日 festival, holiday, gala, fete, celebration, revels.

v.

☞ 设宴,参加宴会 gorge, eat one's fill, wine and dine, treat, entertain.

feature n.

☞ 特点,特色 aspect, facet, point, factor, attribute, quality, property, trait, lineament, characteristic, peculiarity, mark, hallmark, speciality, highlight.

☞ 特写 column, article, report, story, piece, item, comment.

v.

☞ 描写……特征 emphasize, highlight, spotlight, play up, promote, show, present.

☞ 由……主演 appear, figure, participate, act, perform, star.

fee n.

☞ ……费(学费,会费,手续费) charge, terms, bill, account, pay, remuneration, payment, retainer, subscription, reward, recompense, hire, toll.

feed v.

☞ 喂,饲养,供给(原料) nourish, cater for, provide for, supply, sustain, suckly, nurture, foster, strengthen, fuel, graze, pasture, eat, dine.

n.

☞ 食物 food, fodder, forage, pasture, siage.

feed on

☞ 以……为食 eat, consume, devour, live on, exist on.

feel v.

☞ 觉得,感到 exoeruebce, go throuth, undergo, suffer, endure, enjoy.

☞ 触摸 touch, finger, handle, manipulate, hold, stroke, caress, fondle, paw, fumble, grope.

☞ 以为 think, believe, consider, reckon, judge.

☞ 感知 sense, perceive, notice, observe, know.

n.

☞ 感觉 texture, surface, finsih, touch, knack, sense, impression, feeling, quality.

feel for

☞ 同情 pity, sympathize (with), commiserate (with), be sorry for.

feel like

☞ 喜欢 fancy, want, desire.

feeling n.

☞ 知觉 sensation, perception, sense, instinct, hunch, suspicion, inking, impression, idea, notion, opinion, view, point of view.

☞ 感觉,感情 emotion, passion, intersity, warmth, compassion, sympathy, understanding, pity, concern, affection, fondness, sentiment, sentimentality, susceptibility, sensibility, sensitivity, appreciation.

☞ 气氛 air, aura, atmosphere, mood, quality.

fell v.

☞ 砍倒,打倒 cut down, , hew, knock down, strike down, floor, level, flatten, raze, demolish.

fellow n.

☞ 人,家伙,小伙子 person, man, boy, chap, bloke, guy, individual, character.

☞ 同事,伙伴 peer, compeer,

equal, parther, associate, colleague, co-worker, companion, comrade, friend, counterpart, match, mate, twin, double.
adj.
☞ 有关的 co-, associate, associated, related, like, similar.

fellowship n.
☞ 交情,友谊 companionship, camaraderie, communion, familiarity, intimacy.
☞ 联谊会,团体 association, league, guild, society, club, fraternity, brotherhood, sisterhood, order.

female *adj.*
☞ 女性的,妇女的 feminine, she-, girlish, womanly.

feminism n.
☞ 女权主义 women's movement, women's lib (eration), female emancipation, women's rights.

fence n.
☞ 栅栏,篱笆 barrier, railing, paling, wall, hedge, windbreak, guard, defence, barricade, stockade, rampart.
v.
☞ 围以栅栏 surround, encircle, bound, hedge, wall, enclose, pen, coop, confine, restrict, separate, protect, guard, defend, fortify.
☞ 避开 parry, dodge, evade, hedge, equivocate, quibble, pussyfoot, stonewall.

fend for
☞ 照顾 look after, take care of, shift for, support, maintain, sustain, provide for.

fend off
☞ 躲开 ward off, beat off, parry, deflect, avert, resist, repel, repulse, hold at bay, keep off, shut out.

ferry n.
☞ 渡口,渡船 ferry-boat, car ferry, ship, boat, vessel.
v.
☞ 摆渡,空运 transport, ship, convey, carry, take, shuttle, taxi, drive, run, move, shift.

fertile *adj.*
☞ 肥沃的,富饶的,多产的 fruitful, productive, generative, yielding, prolific, teeming, abundant, plentiful, rich, lush, luxuriant, fat.

fertilize v.
☞ 使……肥沃,使多产 impregnate, inseminate, pollinate.

festival n.
☞ 节日,节期,庆祝 celebration, commemoration, anniversary, jubilee, holiday, feast, gala, fete, carnival, fiesta, party, merrymaking, entertainment, festivities.

festive *adj.*
☞ 宴庆的,喜庆的 celebratory, festal, holiday, gala, carnival, happy, joyful, merry, hearty, cheery, jolly, jovial, cordial, convivial.

fetch v.
☞ 获得,拿来 get, collect, bring, carry, transport, deliver, escort.
☞ 卖得 sell for, go for, bring

in, yield, realize, make, earn.

fetching adj.
- 有吸引力的 attractive, pretty, sweet, cute, charming, enchanting, fascinating, captivating.

feud n.
- 宿仇 vendetta, quarrel, row, argument, disagreement, dispute, conflict, strife, discord, animosity, ill will, bitterness, enmity, hostility, antagonism, rivalry.

fever n.
- 发热,发烧 feverishness, (high) temperature, deliriumm.
- 热,极度兴奋 excitement, agitation, turmoil, unrest, restlessness, heat, passion, ecstasy.

feverish adj.
- 发烧的 delirious, hot, burning, flushed.
- 狂热的 excited, impatient, agitated, restless, nervous, overwrought, frenzied, frantic, hectic, hasty, hurried.

few adj.
- 几乎没有的,很少的 scarce, rare, uncommon, sporadic, infrequent, sparse, thin, scant, scanty, meagre, inconsiderable, inadequate, insufficient, in short supply.

pron.
- 几乎没有 not many, hardly any, one or two, a couple, scattering, sprinkling, handful, some.

fibre n.
- 纤维,纤维组织 FILAMENT, strand, thread, nerve, sinew, pile, texture.
- 性格 character, calibre, backbone, strength, stamina, toughness, courage, resolution, determination.

fickle adj.
- 易变的,反复无常的 inconstant, disloyal, unfaithful, faithless, treacherous, unreliable, unpredictable, changeable, capricious, mercurial, irresolute, vacillating.

fiction n.
- 虚构的事物 fantasy, fancy, imagination, figment, invention, fabrication, concoction, improvisation, story-telling.
- 小说 novel, romance, story, tale, yarn, fable, parable, legend, myth, lid.

fictional adj.
- 虚构的 literary, invented, made-up, imaginary, make-believe, legendary, mythical, mythological, fabulous, non-existent, unreal.

fictitious adj.
- 虚假的 false, untrue, invented, made-up, fabricated, apocryphal, imaginary, non-existent, bogus, counterfeit, spurious, assumed, supposed.

fiddle v.
- 瞎搞,乱动 play, tinker, toy, trifle, tamper, mess around, meddle, interfere, fidget.
- 欺骗 cheat, swindle, diddle, cook the books, juggle, manoeuvre, racketeer, graft.

n.
- 假货 swindle, con, rip-off,

fraud, racket, sharp practice, graft.

fidelity n.
☞ 忠实,忠诚 faithfulness, loyalty, allegiance, devotion, constancy, reliability.
☞ 准确性 accuracy, exactness, precision, closeness, adherence.

field n.
☞ 原野,旷野 grassland, meadow, pasture, paddock, playing-field, ground, pitch, green, lawn.
☞ 范围 range, scope, bounds, limits, confines, territory, area, province, domain, sphere, environment, department, discipline, speciality, line, forte.

fiend n.
☞ 恶魔 evil sprit, demon, devil, monster.
☞ 热心家,热衷者 enthusiast, fanatic, addict, devotee, freak, nut.

fiendish adj.
☞ 魔鬼似的,凶恶的 devilish, diabolical, infernal, wicked, malevolent, cunning, crule, inhuman, savage, monstrous, unspeakable.

fierce adj.
☞ 凶猛的,残忍的 ferocious, vicious, savage, cruel, brutal, merciless, aggressive, dangerous, murderous, frightening, menacing, threatening, stern, grim, relentless, raging, wild, passionate, intense, strong, powerful.

fiery adj.
☞ 燃烧的,火热的 burning, afire, flaming, aflame, blazing, ablaze, red-hot, glowing, aglow, flushed, hot, torrid, sultry.
☞ 激烈的 passionate, inflamed, ardent, fervent, impatient, excitable, impetuous, impulsive, hot-headed, fierce, violent, heated.

fight v.
☞ 打仗,作战,战斗,斗争 wrestle, box, fence, joust, brawl, scrap, scuffle, tussle, skimish, combat, battle, do battle, war, wage war, clash, cross swords, engage, grapple, struggle, strive, contend.
☞ 争论 quarrel, argue, dispute, squabble, bicker, wrangle.
☞ 对抗,对立,反抗 oppose, contest, campaign against, resist, withstand, defy, stand up to.

n.
☞ 战斗,斗争 bout, contest, duel, combat, action, battle, war, hostilities, brawl, scrap, scuffle, tussle, struggle, skirmish, set-to, clash, engagement, brush, encounter, conflict, fray, free-for-all, fracas, riot.
☞ 论战 quarrel, row, argument, dispute, dissension.

fight back
☞ 报复,反抗 retaliate, defend oneself, resist, put up a fight, retort, reply.

fight off
☞ 挡住,不使接近 hold off,

fighter n.
- 战士 combatant, contestant, conterder, disputant, boxer, wrestler, pugilist, prizefighter, soldier, trouper, mercenary, warrior, man-at-arms, swordsman, gladiator.

figure n.
- 数字 number, numeral, digit, integer, sum, amount.
- 外形,轮廓 shape, form, outline, silhouette, body, frame, build, physique.
- 公众形象 dignitary, celebrity, personality, character, person.
- 图案,图画 diagram, illustration, picture, drawing, sketch, image, representation, symbol.

v.
- 想象 reckon, guess, estimate, judge, think, believe.
- 扮演,出现 feature, appear, crop up.

figure out
- 算出,理解,弄清楚 work out, calculate, compute, reckon, puzzle out, resolve, fathom, understand, see, make out, decipher.

file¹ v.
- 挫 rub (down), sand, abrade, scour, scrape, grate, rasp, hone, whet, shave, plane, smooth, polish.

file² n.
- 文件夹,卷宗 folder, dossier, portfolio, binder, case, record, keep at bay, ward off, stave off, resist, repel, rebuff, beat off, rout, put to flight.

documents, data, information.

v.
- 归(档),存卷,保存 record, register, note, enter, process, store, classify, categorize, pigeonhole, catalogue.

file³ n.
- 行列 line, queue, column, row, procession, cortege, train, string, stream, trail.

v.
- 排成纵队,行进 march, troop, parade, stream, trail.

fill v.
- 再装满,补充 replenish, stock, supply, furnish, satisfy, pack, crowd, cram, stuff, congest, block, clong, plug, bung, cork, stop, close, seal.
- 弥漫,渗透,遍及 pervade, imbue, permeate, soak, impregnate.
- 占领,占据 take up, hold, occupy, discharge, fulfil.

fill in
- 填空 complete, fill out, answer.
- 代替 stand in, deputize, understudy, substitute, replace, represent, act for.
- 简要介绍 brief, inform, advise, acquaint, bring up to date.

filling n.
- 填充物 contents, inside, stuffing, padding, wadding, filler.

film n.
- 电影,影片 motion, picture, movie, video, feature film, short, documentary.
- 层,分层,薄片 layer,

covering, dusting, coat, coating, glaze, skin, membranne, tissue, sheet, veil, screen, cloud, mist, haze.
v.
☞录制 photograph, shoot, video, videotape.

filter v.
☞过滤,滤除 strain, seeve, sift, screen, refine, purify, clarify, percolate, ooze, seep, leak, trickle, dribble.
n.
☞过滤器,滤色光(器) strainer, sieve, sifter, colander, mesh, gauze, membrane.

filth n.
☞肮脏,污物 dirt, grime, muck, dung, excrement, faeces, sewage, refuse, rubbish, garbage, trash, slime, sludge, effluent, pollution, contamination, corruption, impurity, uncleanness, foulness, sordidness, squalor.
☞下流话,猥亵语 obscenity, pornography, smut, indecency, vulgarity, coarseness.

filthy adj.
☞不干净的,肮脏的 dirty, soiled, unwahed, grimy, grubby, mucky, muddy, slimy, sooty, unclean, impure, foul, gross, sordid, squalid, vile, low, mean, base, contemptible, despicable.
☞淫秽的,下流的 obscene, pornographic, smutty, bawdy, suggestive, indecent, offensive, foul-mouthed, vulgar, coarse, corrupt, depraved.

final adj.
☞最终的,终了的,定了的,确定的 last, latest, closing, concluding, finishing, end, ultimate, terminal, dying, last-minute, eventual, conclusive, definitive, decisive, definite, incontrovertible.

finale n.
☞终曲,乐曲最后一部分 climax, denouement, culmination, crowning glory, end, conclusion, close, curtain, epilogue.

finalize v.
☞完成,作最后决定 conclude, finish, complete, round off, resolve, settle, agree, decide, close, clinch, sew up, wrap up

finally adv.
☞最后,最终 lastly, in conclusion, ultimately, eventually, at last, at length, in the end, conclusively, once and for all, for ever, irreversibly, irrevocably, definitely.

finance n.
☞财政学,提供的经费(资金) economics, money management, accounting, banking, investment, stock market, business, commerce, trade, money, funding, sponsorship, subsidy.
v.
☞供资金给 pay for, fund, sponsor, back, support, underwrite, guarantee, subsidize, capitalize, float, set up.

finances n.
☞财富,资金 accounts, affairs,

budget, bank account, income, revenue, liquidity, resources, assets, capital, wealth, money, cash, funds, wherewithal.

financial adj.
☞ 财政的 monetary, money, pecuniary, economic, fiscal, budgetary, commercial.

financier n.
☞ 银行家,投资者 financialist, banker, stockbroker, money-maker, investor, speculator.

find v.
☞ 发现,遇到,观察,懂得 discover, locate, track down, trace, retrieve, recover, unearth, uncover, expose, reveal, come across, chance on, stumble on, meet, encounter, detect, recognize, notice, observe, perceive, realize, learn.
☞ 赢,到达,得到 attain, achieve, win, reach, gain, obtain, get.
☞ 认为 consider, think, judge, declare.

find out
☞ 发现,观察,意识到 learn, ascertain, discover, detect, note, observe, perceive.
☞ 露出,揭露,抓住 unmask, expose, show up, uncover, reveal, disclose, catch, suss out, rumble, tumble to.

finding n.
☞ 发现,突破 find, discovery, breakthrough.
☞ 结论,判断,奖赏 decision, conclusion, judgement, verdict, pronouncement, decree, recommendation, award.

fine¹ adj.
☞ 辉煌的,华丽的,优良的 excellent, outstanding, exceptional, superior, exquisite, splendid, magnificent, brilliant, beautiful, handsome, attractive, elegant, lovely, nice, good.
☞ 苗条的,纯粹的 thin, slender, sheer, gauzy, powdery, flimsy, fragile, delicate, dainty.
☞ 能接受的,好的 satisfactory, acceptable, all right, OK.
☞ 晴朗的 bright, sunny, clear, cloudless, dry, fair.

fine² n.
☞ 惩罚,伤害 penalty, punishment, forfeit, forfeiture, damages.

finger v.
☞ 触摸,感觉 touch, handle, manipulate, feel, stroke, caress, fondle, paw, fiddle with, toy with, play about with, meddle with.

finish v.
☞ 完成,停止,对付 end, terminate, stop, cease, complete, accomplish, achieve, fulfil, discharge, deal with, do, conclude, close, wind up, settle, round off, culminate, perfect.
☞ 除去,击败 destroy, ruin, exterminate, get rid of, annihilate, defeat, overcome, rout, overthrow.
☞ 用完 use (up), consume, devour, eat, drink, exhaust, drain, empty.

n.

- 结束,完成,结论 end, termination, completion, conclusion, close, ending, finale, culmination.
- 外表,闪耀 surface, appearance, texture, grain, polish, shine, gloss, lustre, smoothness.

finite *adj.*
- 有限的,固定的 limited, restricted, bounded, demarcated, terminable, definable, fixed, measurable, calculable, countable, numbered.

fire *n.*
- 火焰 flames, blaze, bonfire, conflagration, inferno, burning, combustion.
- 热情,激情,激怒 passion, feeling, excitement, enthusiasm, spirt, intensity, heat, radiance, sparkle.

v.
- 射击,发射 ignite, light, kindle, set fire to, set on fire, set alight.
- 起飞,开始,发起 shoot, launch, set off, let off, detonate, explode.
- 激发,释放,解除 dismiss, discharge, sack, eject.
- 刺激 excite, whet, enliven, galvanize, electrify, stir, arouse, rouse, stimulate, inspire, incite, spark off, trigger off.

on fire
- 着火 burning, alight, ignited, flaming, in flames, aflame, blazing, ablaze, fiery.

firm¹ *adj.*
- 坚硬的,坚固的 dense, compressed, compact, concentrated, set, solid, hard, unyielding, stiff, rigid, inflexible.
- 稳固的 fixed, embedded, fast, tight, secure, fastened, anchored, immovable, motionless, stationary, steady, stable, sturdy, strong.
- 坚定的,稳定的(信念) adamant, unshakable, resolute, determined, dogged, unwavering, strict, constant, steadfast, staunch, dependable, true, sure, convinced, definite, settled, committed.

firm² *n.*
- 商行,商号,公司 company, corporation, business, enterprise, concern, house, establishment, institution, organization, association, partnership, syndicate, conglomerate.

first *adj.*
- 初级的,初等的 initial, opening, introductory, preliminary, elementary, primary, basic, fundamental.
- 早期的,在……之前的 original, earliest, earlier, prior, primitive, primeval, oldest, eldest, senior.
- 等级最高的,主要的,重要的 chief, main, kdy, cardinal, principal, head, leading, ruling, sovereign, highest, uppermost, paramount, prime, predominant, pre-eminent.
- 首先的,最初的 initially, to begin with, to start with, at the

first-rate adj.

☞ 优越的,极好的,辉煌的,一流的 first-class, Al, second-to-none, matchless, peerless, top, top-notch, top-flight, leading, supreme, superior, prime, excellent, outstanding, superlative, exceptional, splendid, superb, fine, admirable.

fish v.

☞ 捕鱼,诱捕 angle, trawl, delve, hunt, seek, invite, solicit.

fish out

☞ 摸出,掏出 produce, take out, extract, find, come up with, dredge up, haul up.

fishing n.

☞ 渔业 angling, trawling.

fit^1 adj.

☞ 正确的,适合的,适当的 suitable, appropriate, apt, fitting, correct, right, proper, ready, prepared, able, capable, competent, qualified, eligible, worthy.

☞ 健康的,强健的 healthy, well, able-bodied, in good form, in good shape, sound, sturdy, strong, robust, hale and hearty.

v.

☞ 适合,合适于,使重合 match, correspond, conform, follow, agree, concur, tally, suit, harmonize, go, belong, dovetail, interlock, join, meet, arrange, place, position, accommodate.

☞ 使适合,使适应 alter, modify, change, adjust, adapt, tailor, shape, fashion.

fit out

☞ 装备,供应 equip, rig out, kit out, outfit, provide, supply, furnish, prepare, arm.

fit^2 n.

☞ 发作 seizure, convulsion, spasm, paroxysm, attack, outbreak, bout, spell, burst, surge, outburst, eruption, explosion.

fitful adj.

☞ 不定的 sporadic, intermittent, occasional, spasmodic, erratic, irregular, uneven, broken, disturbed.

fitted adj.

☞ 装备的,设备的 equipped, rigged out, provided, furnished, appointed, prepared, armed.

☞ 合身的,适合的 suited, right, suitable, fit, qualified.

fitting adj.

☞ 适当的,适合的 apt, appropriate, suitable, fit, correct, right, proper, seemly, meet, desirable, deserved.

n.

☞ 连接,附物,连接物 connection, attachment, accessory, part, component, piece, unit, fitment.

fittings n.

☞ 装备,设备 equipment, furnishings, furniture, fixtures, installations, fitments, accessories, extras.

fix v.

☞ 使固定,使安装,坐落,建立 fasten, secure, tie, bind,

attach, join, connect, link, couple, anchor, pinnail, rivet, stick, glue, cement, set, harden, solidify, stiffen, stabilize, plant, root, implant, embed, establish, install, place, locate, position.
☞ 修理,修补调节 mend, repair, correct, rectify, adjust, restore.
☞ 安排,规定,限定 arrange, set, specify, define, agree on, decide, determine, settle, resolve, finalize.
n.
☞ 困境 dilemma, quandary, predicament, plight, difficulty, hole, corner, spot, mess, muddle.

fix up
☞ 安排,组织,解决 arrange, organize, plan, lay on, provide, supply, furnish, equip, settle, sort out, produce, bring about.

fixed adj.
☞ 坚固的,不动的,计划的,安排的 decided, settled, established, definite, arranged, planned, set, firm, rigid, inflexible, steady, secure, fast, rooted, permanent.

flabby adj.
☞ 松弛的,不结实 fleshy, soft, yielding, flaccid, limp, floppy, drooping, hanging, sagging, slack, loose, lax, weak, feeble.

flag[1] v.
☞ 衰退,减弱,减少 lessen, diminish, decline, fall (off), abate, subside, sink, slump, dwindle, peter out, fade, fail, weaken, slow, falter, tire, weary, wilt, droop, sag, flop, faint, die.

flag[2] n.
☞ 旗,旗帜 ensign, jack, pennant, colours, standard, banner, streamer.
v.
☞ 示意,表示 signal, wave, salute, motion.
☞ 暗示 mark, indicate, label, tag, note.

flamboyant adj.
☞ 艳丽的,浮华的 showy, ostentatious, flashy, gaudy, colourful, brilliant, dazzling, striking, extravagant, rich, elaborate, ornate, florid.

flame v.
☞ 燃烧 burn, flare, blaze, glare, flash, beam, shine, glow, radiate.
n.
☞ 火,烧 fire, blaze, light, brightness, heat, warmth.
☞ 热情,激情,爱好 passion, ardour, fervour, enthusiasm, zeal, intensity, radiance.

flaming adj.
☞ 燃烧的,明亮的 burning, alight, aflame, blazing, fiery, brilliant, scintillating, red-hot, glowing, smouldering.
☞ 激发的,热烈的,强烈的 intense, vivid, aroused, impassioned, hot, raging, frenzied.

flammable adj.
☞ 易燃,容易着火的 inflammable, ignitable, combustible.

flap v.

☞飘动,拍打,吹动 flutter, vibrate, wave, agitate, shake, wag, swing, swish, thrash, beat.

n.

☞褶(层),边 fold, fly, lapel, tab, lug, tag, tail, skirt, aileron.

☞惊慌,恐慌 panic, state, fuss, commotion, fluster, agitation, flutter, dither, tizzy.

flash v.

☞闪光,闪烁,盯住,使发光 beam, shine, light up, flare, blaze, glare, gleam, glint, flicker, twinkle, sparkle, glitter, shimmer.

☞猛冲,突飞 streak, fly, dart, race, dash.

n.

☞闪光,爆发 beam, ray, shaft, spark, blaze, flare, burst, streak, gleam, glint, flicker, twinkle, sparkle, shimmer.

flashy adj.

☞浮华的,华而不实的,便宜的 showy, ostentatious, flamboyant, glamorous, bold, loud, garish, gaudy, jazzy, flash, tawdry, cheap, vulgar, tasteless.

flat¹ adj.

☞平坦的,平直的 level, plane, even, smooth, uniform, unbroken, horizontal, outstretched, prostrate, prone, recumbent, reclining, low.

☞弱的,扁的,无生气的 dull, boring, montonous, tedious, uninteresting, unexciting, stale, lifeless, dead, spiritless, lacklustre, vapid, insipid, weak, watery, empty, pointless.

☞全部的,绝对的 absolute, utter, total, unequivocal, categorical, positive, unconditional, unqualified, point-blank, direct, straight, explicit, plain, final.

☞爆炸的,爆破的 punctured, burst, deflated, collapsed.

flat out

☞最高的,全速的 at top speed, at full speed, all out, for all one is worth.

flat² n.

☞公寓 apartment, penthouse, maisonnette, tenement, flatlet, rooms, suite, bed-sit(ter).

flatten v.

☞使平,变平 smooth, iron, press, roll, crush, squash, compress, level, even out.

☞拆除,撞倒,击翻 knock down, prostrate, floor, fell, demolish, raze, overwhelm, subdue.

flatter v.

☞谄媚,奉承,使得意 praise, compliment, sweet-talk, adulate, fawn, butter up, wheedle, humour, play up to, court, curry favour with.

flattery n.

☞奉承,谄媚,恭维 adulation, eulogy, sweet talk, soft soap, flannel, blarney, cajolery, fawning, toadyism, sycophancy, ingratiation, servility.

flavour n.

☞味觉,味道,鉴赏 taste, tang, smack, savour, relish, zest,

zing, aroma, odour.
☞ 质量,性格,品质,特性 quality, property, character, style, aspect, feeling, feel, atmosphere.
☞ 暗示,示意 hint, suggestion, touch, tinge, tone.
v.
☞ 加味于,调味 season, spice, ginger up, infuse, imbue.

flavouring n.
☞ 香料,调味品 seasoning, zest, essence, extract, additive.

flaw n.
☞ 缺点,瑕疵 defect, imperfection, fault, blemish, spot, mark, speck, crack, crevice, fissure, cleft, split, rift, break, fracture, weakness, shortcoming, failing, fallacy, lapse, slip, error, mistake.

flawed adj.
☞ 不完美的,有缺点的 imperfect, defective, faulty, blemished, marked, damaged, spoilt, marred, cracked, chipped, broken, unsound, fallcious, erroneous.

flawless adj.
☞ 完美的,毫无缺点的 perfect, faultless, unblemished, spotless, immaculate, stainless, sound, intact, whole, unbroken, undamaged.

flee v.
☞ 逃跑,逃走 run away, bolt, fly, take flight, take off, make off, cut and run, escape, get away, decamp, abscond, leave, depart, withdraw, retreat, vanish, disappear.

fleet n.
☞ 海军,舰队 flotilla, armada, navy, task force, squadron.

fleeting adj.
☞ 短暂的,飞逝的 short, brief, flying, short-lived, momentary, ephemeral, transient, transitory, passing, temporary.

flesh n.
☞ 肉,果肉,亲人,骨肉 body, tissue, fat, muscle, brawn, skin, meat, pulp, substance, matter, physicality.

flex v.
☞ 伸屈 bend, bow, curve, angle, ply, double up, tighten, contract.
n.
☞ 绳索,绳,线 cable, wire, lead, cord.

flexible adj.
☞ 易弯曲的,可弯曲的 bendable, bendy, pliable, pliant, plastic, malleable, mouldable, elastic, stretchy, springy, yielding, supple, lithe, limber, double-jointed, mobile.
☞ 有弹性的,可变的,灵活的 adaptable, adjustable, amenable, accommodating, variable, open.

flight¹ n.
☞ 航班,坐飞机旅行 elying, aviation, aeronautics, air transport, air travel.
☞ 旅行,航程 journey, trip, voyage.

flight² n.
☞ 逃亡,逃跑 fleeing, escape, gateway, breakaway, exit, departure, exodus, retreat.

flinch v.

☞ 畏缩,退缩 wince, start, cringe, cower, quail, tremble, shake, quake, shudder, shiver, shrink, recoil, draw back, balk, shy away, duck, shirk, withdraw, retreat, flee.

fling v.
☞ 投掷,抛扔 throw, hurl, pitch, lob, toss, chuck, cast, sling, catapult, launch, propel, send, let fly, heave, jerk.

flirt v.
☞ 挑逗,调情 chat up, make up to, lead on, philander, dally.

flirt with
☞ 玩弄 consider, entertain, toy with, play with, trifle with, dabble in, try.

flit v.
☞ 轻快地飞 dart, speed, flash, fly, wing, flutter, whisk, skim, slip, pass, bob, dance.

float v.
☞ 漂浮 glide, sail, swim, bob, drift, waft, hover, hang.
☞ 创立 launch, initiate, set up, promote.

floating adj.
☞ 漂浮的 afloat, buoyant, unsinkable, sailing, swimming, bobbing, drifting.
☞ 流动的,不定的 variable, fluctuating, movable, migratory, transitory, wandering, unattached, free, uncommitted.

flock v.
☞ 群聚,群集,聚集 herd, swarm, troop, converge, mass, bunch, cluster, huddle, crowd, throng, group, gather, collect, congregate.
n.
☞ 人群,聚在一起 herd, pack, crowd, throng, multitude, mass, bunch, cluster, group, gathering, assembly, congregation.

flood v.
☞ 泛滥,淹没 deluge, inundate, soak, drench, saturate, fill, overflow, immerse, submerge, engulf, swamp, overwhelm, drown.
☞ 冲进,涌进 flow, pour, stream, rush, surge, gush.
n.
☞ 洪水 deluge, inundation, downpour, torrent, flow, tide, stream, rush, spate, outpouring, overflow, glut, excess, abundance, profusion.

floor n.
☞ 地板,楼层 flooring, ground, base, basis.
☞ 楼层,甲板 storey, level, stage, landing, deck, tier.
v.
☞ 打倒,击败 defeat, overwhelm, beat, stump, frustrate, confound, perplex, baffle, puzzle, bewilder, disconcert, throw.

flop v.
☞ 扑抱,猛然落下 droop, hang, dangle, sag, drop, fall, topple, tumble, slump, collapse.
☞ 失败 fall, misfire, fall flat.
n.
☞ 下落,惨败 failure, non-starter, fiasco, debacle, wash-out, disaster.

floppy adj.

☞ 松软的 droopy, hanging, dangling, sagging, limp, loose, baggy, soft, flabby.

florid adj.
☞ 华丽的 flowery, ornate, elaborate, fussy, overelaborate, baroque, rococo, flamboyant, grandiloquent.
☞ 红润的 ruddy, red, purple.

flourish v.
☞ 红火,繁荣,茂盛 thrive, grow, wax, increase, flower, blossom, bloom, develop, progress, get on, do well, prosper, succeed, boom.
☞ 挥舞,挥动 brandish, wave, shake, twirl, swing, display, wield, flaunt, parade, vaunt.
n.
☞ 夸耀,炫耀 display, parade, show, gesture, wave, sweep, fanfare, ornament, decoration, panache, pizzazz.

flourshing adj.
☞ 夸耀的,炫耀的 thriving, bloming, prosperous, successful, booming.

flow v.
☞ 流,流动 circulate, ooze, trickle, ripple, bubble, well, spurt, squirt, gush, spill, run, pour, cascade, rush, stream, teem, flood, overflow, surge, sweep, move, drift, slip, slide, glide, roll, swirl.
☞ 来自,结果 arise, spring, emerge, issue, result, proceed, emanate.
n.
☞ 流水,流动 course, flux, tide, current, drift, outpouring, stream, deluge, cascade, spurt, gush, flood, spate, abundance, plenty.

flower n.
☞ 花,花草 bloom, blossom, bud, floret.
☞ 精华 best, cream, pick, choice, elite.

fluent adj.
☞ 流利的,流畅的 flowing, smooth, easy, effortless, articulate, eloquent, voluble, glib, ready.

fluid adj.
☞ 流体的,流动的 liquid, liquefied, aqueous, watery, running, runny, melted, molten.
☞ 变动的 variable, changeable, unstable, inconstant, shifting, mobile, adjustable, adaptable, flexible, open.
☞ 顺利的 flowing, smooth, graceful.

flush¹ v.
☞ 脸红,惭愧 blush, go red, redden, crimson, colour, burn, glow, suffuse.
☞ 冲洗,清除 cleanse, wash, rinse, hose, swab, clear, empty, evacuate.
adj.
☞ 富裕的,富有的 abundant, lavish, generous, full, overflowing, rich, wealthy, moneyed, prosperous, well-off, well-heeled, well-to-do.
☞ 齐平的,同高的 level, even, smooth, flat, plane, square, true.

flush² v.
☞ 揭开,扰乱 start, rouse,

fly v.
- 飞,飞行,盘旋 take off, rise, ascend, mount, soar, glide, float, hover, flit, wing
- 飞越,冲刺 race, sprint, dash, tear, rush, hurry, speed, zoom, shoot, dart, career.

fly at
- 攻击,抨击 attack, go for, fall upon.

foam n.
- 泡沫,汗沫 froth, lather, suds, head, bubbles, effervescence.

v.
- 吐泡沫,起泡沫 froth, lather, bubble, effervesce, fizz, boil, seethe.

fob off
- 搪塞,以骗术脱手 foist, pass off, palm off, get rid of, dump, unload, inflict, impose, deceive, put off.

focus n.
- 中心点,焦点 focal point, target, centre, heart, core, nucleus, kernel, crux, hub, axis, linchpin, pivot, hinge.

v.
- 使聚焦,对准焦距 converge, meet, join, centre, concentrate, aim, direct, fix, spotlight, home in, zoom in, zero in.

fog n.
- 云霭,雾 mist, haze, cloud, gloom, murkiness, smog, pea-souper.
- 迷惑 perplexity, puzzlement, confusion, bewilderment, daze, trance, vagueness, obscurity.

v.
- 变得模糊不清 mist, steam up, cloud, dull, dim, darken, obscure, blur, confuse, muddle.

foggy adj.
- 有雾的,多雾的 misty, hazy, smoggy, cloudy, murky, dark, shadowy, dim, indistinct, obscure.

foil¹ v.
- 阻挠,挫败 defeat, outwit, frustrate, thwart, baffle, counter, nullify, stop, check, obstruct, block, circumvent, elude.

foil² n.
- 陪衬者,衬托物 setting, background, relief, contrast, complement, balance.

fold v.
- 折叠,对折 bend, ply, double, overlap, tuck, pleat, crease, crumple, crimp, crinkle.
- 使败 fail, go bust, shut down, collapse, crash.
- 围抱 enfold, embrace, hug, clasp, envelop, wrap (up), enclose, entwine, intertwine.

n.
- 褶,褶层 bend, turn, layer, ply, overlap, tuck, pleat, crease, knife-edge, line, wrinkle, furrow, corrugation.

folder n.
- 文件夹,纸夹 file, binder, folio, portfolio, envelope, holder.

folk n.
- 人,人们 people, society,

nation, race, tribe, clan, family, kin, kindred.
adj.
☞ 民间的，民俗的 ethnic, national, traditional, native, indigenous, tribal, ancestral.

follow v.
☞ 跟随，接着 come after, succeed, come next, replace, supersede, supplannt.
☞ 追赶，追捕 chase, pursue, go after, hunt, track, trail, shadow, tail, hound, catch.
☞ 伴随 accompany, go (along) with, escort, attend.
☞ 结果，效果 result, ensue, develop, emanate, arise.
☞ 服从，执行 obey, comply with, adhere to, heed, mind, observe, conform to, carry out, practise.
☞ 理解，掌握 grasp, understand, comprehend, fathom.

follow through
☞ 贯彻执行，贯彻到底 continue, pursue, see through, finish, complete, conclude, fulfil, implement.

follower n.
☞ 追随者,崇拜者 attendant, retainer, helper, companion, sidekick, apostle, disciple, pupil, imitator, emulator, adherent, hanger-on, believer, convert, backer, supporter, admirer, fan, devotee, freak, buff.

following *adj.*
☞ 随后的，其次的 subsequent, next, succeeding, successive, resulting, ensuing, consequent, later.
n.
☞ 下一个，下一列，追随者 followers, suite, retinue, entourage, circle, fans, supporters, support, backing, patronage, clientele, audience, public.

folly n.
☞ 愚笨，愚蠢 foolishness, stupidity, senselessness, rashness, recklessness, irresponsibility, indiscretion, craziness, madness, lunacy, insanity, idiocy, imbecility, silliness, absurdity, nonsense.

fond *adj.*
☞ 深情的，温柔的，溺爱的，盲目轻信的 affectionate, warm, tender, caring, loving, adoring, devoted, doting, indulgent.

fond of
☞ 喜欢,爱好 partial to, attached to, enamoured of, keen on, addicted to, hooked on.

fondle v.
☞ 爱抚，抚弄 caress, stroke, pat, pet, cuddle.

food n.
☞ 食料,养料,食品,固体食物 foodstuffs, comestibles, eatables, provisions, stores, rations, eats, refreshment, sustenance, nourishment, nutrition, nutriment, subsistence, feed, fodder, diet, fare, cooking, cuisine, menu, board, table, larder.

fool n.
☞ 傻子 blockhead, fat-head, nincompoop, ass, chump, ninny, clot, dope, twit,

nitwit, nit, dunce, dimwit, simpleton, halfwit, idiot, imbecile, moron, dupe, sucker, mug, stooge, clown, buffoon, jester.

v.
☞ 欺骗,愚弄,鬼混,开玩笑
deceive, take in, delude, mislead, dupe, gull, hoodwink, put one over on, trick, hoax, con, cheat, swindle, diddle, string along, have, on, kid, tease, joke, jest.

fool about
☞ 闲逛,干蠢事 lark about, play about, mess about, mess around.

foolhardy *adj.*
☞ 鲁莽的,有勇无谋的 rash, reckless, imprudent, ill-advised, irresponsible.

foolish *adj.*
☞ 不懂事的,傻的,可笑的
stupid, senseless, unwise, ill-advised, ill-considered, short-sighted, half-baked, daft, crazy, mad, insane, idiotic, moronic, hare-brained, half-witted, simple-minded, simple, unintelligent, inept, inane, silly, absurd, ridiculous, ludicrous, nonsensical.

foolproof *adj.*
☞ 安全的,错不了的,容易懂的
idiot-proof, infallible, fail-safe, sure, certain, sure-fire, guaranteed.

footing *n.*
☞ 立足点,关系 base, foundation, basis, ground, relations, relationship, terms, conditions, state, standing, status, grade, rank, position, balance, foothold, purchase.

footprint *n.*
☞ 脚印 footmark, track, trail, trace, vestige.

forbid *v.*
☞ 禁止,不许 prohibit, disallow, ban, proscribe, interdict, veto, refuse, deny, outlaw, debar, exclude, rule out, preclude, prevent, block, hinder, inhibit.

forbidden *adj.*
☞ 禁忌的,忌讳的 prohibited, banned, proscribed, taboo, vetoed, outlawed, out of bounds.

forbidding *adj.*
☞ 令人生畏的,可怕的,凶恶的
stern, formidable, awesome, daunting, off-putting, uninviting, menacing, threatening, ominous, sinister, frightening.

force *n.*
☞ 影响,支配力 compulsion, impulse, influence, coercion, constraint, pressure, duress, violence, aggression.
☞ 力,力量 power, might, strength, intensity, effort, energy, vigour, dirve, dynamism, stress, emphasis.
☞ 部队,武装力量,兵力 army, troop, body, corps, regiment, squadron, battalion, division, unit, detachment, patrol.

v.
☞ 强迫,迫使 compel, make, oblige, necessitate, urge, coerce, constrain, press, pressurize, lean on, press-gang, bulldoze, drive, propel, push,

thrust.
- 强夺,夺取 prise, wrench, wrest, extort, exact, wring.

forced adj.
- 强迫的,被迫的 unnatural, stiff, wooden, stilted, laboured, strained, false, artificial, contrived, feigned, affected, insincere.

forceful adj.
- 强有力的,坚强的 strong, mighty, powerful, potent, effective, compelling, convincing, persuasive, cogent, telling, weighty, urgent, emphatic, vehement, forcible, dynamic, energetic, vigorous.

forecast v.
- 预报,预测 predict, prophesy, foretell, foresee, anticipate, expect, estimate, calculate.
n.
- 预测 prediction, prophecy, expectation, prognosis, outlook, projection, guess, guesstimate.

foreign adj.
- 外国的 alien immigrant, imported, international, external, outside, overseas, exotic, faraway, distant, remote, strange, unfamiliar, unknown, uncharacteristic, incongruous, extraneous, borrowed.

foreigner n.
- 外国人 alien, immigrant, incomer, stranger, newcomer, visitor.

foremost adj.
- 最先的,主要的 first, leading, front, chief, main, principal, primary, cardinal, paramount, central, highest, uppermost, supreme, prime, pre-eminent.

forerunner n.
- 先锋 predecessor, ancestor, antecedent, precursor, harbinger, herald, envoy, sign, token.

foresee v.
- 预示 envisage, anticipate, expect, forecast, predict, prophesy, prognosticate, foretell, forebode, divine.

foresight n.
- 先见之明,先见 anticipation, planning, forethought, far-sightedness, vision, caution, prudence, circumspection, care, readiness, preparedness, provision, precaution.

forethought n.
- 先见,未雨绸缪 preparation, planning, forward planning, provision, precaution, anticipation, foresight, far-sightedness, circumspection, prudence, caution.

forever adv.
- 永远地 continually, constantly, persistently, incessantly, perpetually, endlessly, eternally, always, evermore, for all time, permanently.

foreword n.
- 前言,序 preface, introduction, prologue.

forge v.
- 制作,打制 make, mould, cast, shape, form, fashion, beat out, hammer out, work,

create, invent.
☞ 复制,捏造,伪造 fake, counterfeit, falsify, copy, imitate, simulate, feign.

forgery n.
☞ 伪造,伪造品 fake, counterfeit, copy, replica, reproduction, imitation, dud, phoney, sham, fraud.

forget v.
☞ 忽视,忽略,忘却 omit, fail, neglect, let slip, overlook, disregard, ignore, lose sight of, dismiss, think no more of, unlearn.

forgetful adj.
☞ 健忘的,疏忽的,心不在焉的 absent-minded, dreamy, inattentive, oblivious, negligent, lax, heedless.

forgive v.
☞ 原谅,宽恕 pardon, absolve, excuse, exonerate, exculpate, acquit, remit, let off, overlook, condone.

forgiveness n.
☞ 宽恕,原谅 pardon, absolution, exoneration, acquittal, remission, amnesty, mercy, clemency, leniency.

forgiving adj.
☞ 宽恕的,仁慈的 merciful, clement, lenient, tolerant, forbearing, indulgent, kind, humane, compassionate, soft-hearted, mild.

forgo v.
☞ 放弃,抛弃 give up, yield, surrender, relinquish, sacrifice, forfeit, waive, renounce, abandon, resign, pass up, do without, abstain from, refrain from.

fork v.
☞ 分盆,成盆形 split, divide, part, separate, diverge, branch (off).

form v.
☞ 使形成,制作 shape, mould, model, fashion, make, manufacture, produce, create, found, establish, build, construct, assemble, put together, arrange, organize.
☞ 构成,组成 comprise, constitute, make up, compose.
☞ 形成,出现,做成 appear, take shape, materialize, crystallize, grow, develop.
n.
☞ 形状,外形,安排 appearance, shape, mould, cast, cut, outline, silhouette, figure, build, frame, structure, format, model, pattern, design, arrangement, organization, system.
☞ 等级 class, year, grade, stream.
☞ 种类,方式 type, kind, sort, order, species, variety, genre, style, manner, nature, character, description.
☞ 态度,举止行为 etiquette, protocol, custom, convention, ritual, behaviour, manners.
☞ 表格 questionnaire, document, paper, sheet.

formal adj.
☞ 官方的,正式的 official, ceremonial, stately, solemn, conventional, orthodox, correct, fixed, set, regular.

☞ 拘谨的, 刻板的 prim, starchy, stiff, strict, rigid, precise, exact, punctilious, ceremonious, stilted, reserved.

formality n.
☞ 拘泥形式, 遵守礼节, 风俗 custom, convention, ceremony, ritual, procedure, matter of form, bureaucracy, red tape, protocol, etiquette, form, correctness, propriety, decorum, politeness.

formation n.
☞ 组成, 形成, 队形 structure, construction, composition, constitution, configuration, format, organization, arrangement, grouping, pattern, design, figure.
☞ 构成方式, 创造, 建告, 建立 creation, generation, production, manufacture, appearance, development, establishment.

former adj.
☞ 早期的, 前任的 past, ex-, one-time, sometime, late, departed, old, old-time, ancient, bygone, earlier, prior, previous, preceding, antecedent, fioregoing, above.

formerly adv.
☞ 以前, 从前 once, previously, earlier, before, at one time, lately.

formidable adj.
☞ 可怕的, 令人生畏的, 困难的, 难以克服的 daunting, challenging, intimidating, threatening, frightening, terrifying, terrific, frightful, fearful, great, huge, tremendous, prodigious, impressive, awesome, overwhelming, staggering.

formula n.
☞ 配方, 公式, 规则, 方法 recipe, prescription, proposal, blueprint, code, wording, rubric, rule, principle, form, procedure, technique, method, way.

formulate v.
☞ 用公式……表示, 设计, 规划 create, invent, originate, found, form, devise, work out, plan, design, draw up, frame, define, express, state, specify, detail, develop, evolve.

forsake v.
☞ 遗弃, 放弃 desert, abandon, jilt, throw over, discard, jettison, reject, disown, leave, quit, give up, surrender, relinquish, renounce, forgo.

fort n.
☞ 要塞, 保垒, 城保 fortress, castle, tower, citadel, stronghold, fortification, garrison, station, camp.

forthcoming adj.
☞ 即将出现的, 即将发生的 impending, imminent, approaching, coming, future, prospective, projected, expected.
☞ 友善的, 热心的, 现成的 communicative, talkative, chatty, conversational, sociable, informative, expansive, open, frank, direct.

forthright adj.
☞ 坦白的, 直率的 direct,

fortunate adj.
☞ 幸运的,吉祥的 lucky, providential, happy, felicitous, prosperous, successful, well-off, timely, well-timed, opportune, convenient, propitious, advantageous, favourable, auspicious.

fortune n.
☞ 财富,财产 wealth, riches, treasure, mint, pile, income, means, assets, estate, property, possessions, affluence, prosperity, success.
☞ 命运,运气,未来 luck, chance, accident, providence, fate, destiny, doom, lot, portion, life, history, future.

forward adj.
☞ 面前的,前部的 first, head, front, fore, foremost, leading, onward, progressive, go-ahead, forward-looking, enterprising.
☞ 进取的 confident, assertive, pushy, bold, audacious, brazen, brash, barefaced, cheeky, impudent, impertinent, familiar, presumptuous.
☞ 早到的,早的 early, advance, precocious, premature, advanced, well-advanced, well-developed.
adv.
☞ 前方,前部,提前,往前 forwards, ahead, on, onward, out, into view.
v.
☞ 转寄,转递 advance, promote, further, foster, encourage, support, back, favour, help, assist, aid, facilitate, accelerate, speed, hurry, hasten, expedite, dispatch, send (on), post, transport, ship.

foster v.
☞ 激发,鼓励,照顾,抚育 raise, rear, bring up, nurse, care for, take care of, nourish, feed, sustain, support, promote, advance, encourage, stimulate, cultivate, nurture, cherish, entertain, harbour.

foul adj.
☞ 不干净的,恶臭的,污染的 dirty, filthy, unclean, tainted, polluted, contaminated, rank, fetid, stinking, smelly, putrid, rotten, nauseating, offensive, repulsive, revolting, disgusting, squalid.
☞ 邪恶的,残酷的,羞耻的 nasty, disagreeable, wicked, vicious, vile, base, abhorrent, disgraceful, shameful.
☞ 粗鲁的 obscene, lewd, smutty, indecent, coarse, vulgar, gross, blasphemous, abusive.
☞ 恶劣的,有暴风雨的 bad, unpleasant, rainy, wet, stormy, rough.
v.
☞ 弄脏,使污染 dirty, soil, stain, sully, defile, taint, pollute, contaminate.
☞ 阻挡,犯规 block, obstruct, clog, choke, foul up.
☞ 拧,扭 entangle, catch, snarl, twist, ensnare.

found v.
☞ 建立,开创 start, originate,

create, initiate, institute, inaugurate, set up, establish, endow, organize.
☞ 创办,设立 base, ground, bottom, rest, settle, fix, plant, raise, build, erect, construct.

foundation n.
☞ 基础,基地 base, foot, bottom, ground, bedrock, substance, basis, footing.
☞ 建立,创立,创建 setting up, establishment, institution, inauguration, endowment, organization, groundwork.

founder¹ n.
☞ 创建者,建立者 originator, initiator, father, mother, benefactor, creator, author, architect, designer, inventor, maker, builder, constructor, organizer.

fountain n.
☞ 人造喷泉,喷水池 spray, jet, spout, spring, well, wellspring, reservoir, waterworks.
☞ 起源,由来 source, origin, fount, font, fountainhead, wellhead.

fragile adj.
☞ 易碎的,易坏的,虚弱的,衰弱的 brittle, breakable, frail, delicate, flimsy, dainty, fine, slight, insubstantial, weak, feeble, infirm.

fragment n.
☞ 碎片 piece, bit, part, portion, fraction, particle, crumb, morsel, scrap, remnant, shred, chip, splinter, shiver, sliver, shard.
v.
☞ 打成碎片 break, shatter, splinter, shiver, crumble, disintegrate, come to pieces, come apart, break up, divide, split (up), disunite.

fragmentary adj.
☞ 碎的,不完整的 bitty, piecemeal, scrappy, broken, disjointed, disconnected, separate, scattered, sketchy, partial, incomplete.

fragrance n.
☞ 芳香,芬芳 perfume, scent, smell, odour, aroma, bouquet.

fragrant adj.
☞ 芳香的,芬芳的 perfumed, scented, sweet-smelling, sweet, balmy, aromatic, odorous.

frail adj.
☞ 虚弱的,衰弱的 delicate, brittle, breakable, fragile, flimsy, insubstantial, slight, puny, weak, feeble, infirm, vulnerable.

frailty n.
☞ 弱点,脆弱 weakness, foible, failing, deficiency, shortcoming, fault, defect, flaw, blemish, imperfection, fallibility, susceptibility.

frame v.
☞ 建立,构思,表达 compose, formulate, conceive, devise, contrive, concoct, cook up, plan, map out, sketch, draw up, draft, shape, form, model, fashion, mould, forge, assemble, put together, build, construct, fabricate, make.
☞ 包围,围住 surround, enclose, box in, case, mount.

n.
- 构思,表达 structure, fabric, framework, skeleton, caracase, shell, casing, chassis, construction, bodywork, body, build, form.
- 登上,爬上 mount, mounting, setting, surround, border, edge.
- 态度,情绪 state of mind, mood, humour, temper, disposition, spirit, outlook, attitude.

framework *n.*
- 骨架,框架 structure, fabric, bare bones, skeleton, shell, frame, outline, plan, foundation, groundwork.

frank *adj.*
- 老实的,坦诚的 honest, truthful, sincere, candid, blunt, open, free, plain, direct, forthright, straight, straightforward, downright, outspoken.

frankly *adv.*
- 直率地,老实地 to be frank, to be honest, in truth, honestly, candidly, bluntly, openly, freely, plainly, directly, straight.

frantic *adj.*
- 非常激动的,高兴的,害怕的 agitated, overwrought, fraught, desperate, beside oneself, furious, raging, mad, wild, raving, frenzied, berserk, hectic.

fraud *n.*
- 欺诈,欺骗 deceit, deception, guile, cheating, swindling, double-dealing, sharp practice, fake, counterfeit, forgery, sham, hoax, trick.
- 骗子,行骗者 charlatan, impostor, pretender, phoney, bluffer, hoaxer, cheat, swindler, double-dealer, con man.

free *adj.*
- 自由的,无约束的 at liberty, at large, loose, unattached, unrestrained, liberated, emancipated, independent, democratic, self-governing.
- 空的 spare, available, idle, unemployed, unoccupied, vacant, empty.
- 免费 gratis, without charge, free of charge, complimentary, on the house.
- 无碍的 clear, unobstructed, unimpeded, open.
- 解放的,自由的 generous, liberal, open-handed, lavish, charitable, hospitable.

v.
- 释放,使自由,移开,松开,使解脱 release, let go, loose, turn loose, set free, untie, unbind, unchain, unleash, liberate, emancipate, rescue, deliver, save, ransom, disentangle, disengage, extricate, clear, rid, relieve, unburden, exempt, absolve, acquit.

free of
- 摆脱了……的 lacking, devoid of, without, unaffected by, immune to, exempt from, safe from.

freedom *n.*
- 自由 liberty, emancipation,

deliverance, release, exemption, immunity, impunity.
- ☞ 独立 independence, autonomy, self-government, home rule.
- ☞ 回旋余地 range, scope, play, leeway, latitude, licence, privilege, power, free rein, free hand, opportunity, informality.

freely *adv.*
- ☞ 情愿地,坦然地 readily, willingly, voluntarily, spontaneously, easily.
- ☞ 欣然地 generously, liberally, lavishly, extravagantly, amply, abundantly.
- ☞ 坦然地,直率地 frankly, candidly, unreservedly, openly, plainly.

freeze *v.*
- ☞ 硬化,僵化 ice over, ice up, glaciate, congeal, solidify, harden, stiffen.
- ☞ 使变冷,变凉 deep-freeze, ice, refrigerate, chill, cool.
- ☞ 决定,同意 stop, suspend, fix, immobilize, hold.

n.
- ☞ 霜降,霜冻 frost, freeze-up.
- ☞ 冻结 stoppage, halt, standstill, shutdown, suspension, interruption, postponement, stay, embargo, moratorium.

freezing *adj.*
- ☞ 寒冷入骨的,寒冷的 icy, frosty, glacial, arctic, polar, Siberian, wintry, raw, bitter, biting, cutting, penetrating, numbing, cold, chilly.

freight *n.*
- ☞ 货运,运输,货物 cargo, load, lading, pay-load, contents, goods, merchandise, consignment, shipment, transportation, conveyance, carriage, haulage.

frenzied *adj.*
- ☞ 狂乱的,忙乱的,疯狂的 frantic, frenetic, hectic, feverish, desperate, furious, wild, uncontrolled, mad, demented, hysterical.

frenzy *n.*
- ☞ 狂暴狂乱,疯猛 turmoil, agitation, distraction, derangement, madness, lunacy, mania, hysteria, delirium, fever.
- ☞ 发作 burst, fit, spasm, paroxysm, convulsion, seizure, outburst, transport, passion, rage, fury.

frequent *adj.*
- ☞ 连续的,不断的,重复的 numerous, countless, incessant, constant, continual, persistent, repeated, recurring, regular.
- ☞ 普通的,一般的,平常的 common, commonplace, everyday, familiar, usual, customary.

v.
- ☞ 常去,时常出席 visit, patronize, attend, haunt, hang out at, associate with, hang about with, hang out with.

fresh *adj.*
- ☞ 额外的,附加的 additional, supplementary, extra, more, further, other.
- ☞ 新的,最近的 new, novel, innovative, original, different, unconventional, modern, up-to

☞ 清爽的 refreshed, bracing, invigorating, brisk, crisp, keen, cool, fair, bright, clear, pure.
☞ 天然的,未加工的 raw, natural, unprocessed, crude.
☞ 心旷神怡的 refreshed, revived, restored, renewed, rested, invigorated, energetic, vigorous, lively, alert.
☞ 大胆的 pert, saucy, cheeky, disrespectful, impudent, insolent, bold, brazen, forward, familiar, presumptuous.

freshen v.
☞ 使纯净 air, ventilate, purify.
☞ 使振作,新鲜 refresh, restore, revitalize, reinvigorate, liven, enliven, spruce up, tart up.

friction n.
☞ 冲突 disagreement, dissension, dispute, disharmony, conflict, antagonism, hostility, opposition, rivalry, animosity, ill feeling, bad blood, resentment.
☞ 摩擦 rubbing, chafing, irritation, abrasion, scraping, grating, rasping, erosion, wearing away, resistance.

friend n.
☞ 朋友 mate, pal, chum, buddy, crony, intimate, confidant(e), bosom friend, soul mate, comrade, ally, partner, associate, companion, playmate, pen-friend, acquaintance, well-wisher, supporter.

friendly adj.
☞ 友好的,慷慨的,善良的 amiable, affable, genial, kind, kindly, neighbourly, helpful, sympathetic, fond, affectionate, familiar, intimate, close, matey, pally, chummy, companionable, receptive, comradely, amicable, peaceable, well-disposed, favourable.
☞ 怡人的 convivial, congenial, cordial, welcoming, warm.

friendship n.
☞ 友谊,友情 closeness, intimacy, familiarity, affinity, rapport, attachment, affection, fondness, love, harmony, concord, goodwill, friendliness, alliance, fellowship, comradeship.

fright n.
☞ 惊吓,恐怖,发抖 shock, scare, alarm, consternation, dismay, dread, apprehension, trepidation, fear, terror, horror, panic.

frighten v.
☞ 使吃惊,惊吓 alarm, daunt, unnerve, dismay, intimidate, terrorize, scare, startle, scare stiff, terrify, petrify, horrify, appal, shock.

frightening adj.
☞ 惊吓的,恐怖的 alarming, daunting, formidable, fearsome, scary, terrifying, hair-raising, bloodcurdling, spine-chilling, petrifying, traumatic.

frightful adj.
☞ 可怕的,惊人的,恐怖的 unpleasant, disagreeable, awful, dreadful, terrible, appalling, shocking, harrowing, unspeakable, dire, grim, ghastly, hideous, horrible,

horrid, grisly, macabre, gruesome.

frigid *adj.*
☞ 寒冷的,冷淡的,无生气的 unfeeling, unresponsive, passionless, unloving, cool, aloof, passive, lifeless.
☞ 冰冷的,冷淡的 frozen, icy, frosty, glacial, arctic, cold, chill, chilly, wintry.

front *n.*
☞ 前面,正面,前部 at the front, face, aspect, frontage, facade, outside, exterior, facing, cover, obverse, top, head, lead, vanguard, forefront, front line, foreground, forepart, bow.
☞ 态度,模样,表情 pretence, show, air, appearance, look, expression, manner, facade, cover, mask, disguise, pretext, cover-up.
adj.
☞ 前面的,在前面的 fore, leading, foremost, head, first.

in front
☞ 在前面,在正面,在最重要的位置 ahead, leading, first, in advance, before, preceding.

frontier *n.*
☞ 边境(界) border, boundary, borderline, limit, edge, perimeter, confines, marches, bounds, verge.

frown *v.*
☞ 皱眉,表不满 scowl, glower, lour, glare, grimace.
n.
☞ 不满意,皱眉 scowl, glower, dirty look, glare, grimace.

frown on
☞ 不同意,不赞同 disapprove of, object to, dislike, discourage.

frozen *adj.*
☞ 冰冻的,寒冷的 iced, chilled, icy, icebound, ice-covered, arctic, ice-cold, frigid, freezing, numb, solidified, stiff, rigid, fixed.

frugal *adj.*
☞ 节俭的,节省的,少量的,花钱少的,经济的 thrifty, penny-wise, parsimonious, careful, provident, saving, economical, sparing, meagre.

fruitful *adj.*
☞ 丰收的,富裕的 fertile, rich, teeming, plentiful, abundant, prolific, productive.
☞ 成功的,有用的 rewarding, profitable, advantageous, beneficial, worthwhile, well-spent, useful, successful.

fruitless *adj.*
☞ 不成功的,徒劳的 unsuccessful, abortive, useless, futile, pointless, vain, idle, hopeless, barren, sterile.

frustrate *v.*
☞ 击败,挫败 thwart, foil, balk, baffle, block, check, spike, defeat, circumvent, forestall, counter, nullity, neutralize, inhibit.
☞ 使沮丧,使丧气 disappoint, discourage, dishearten, depress.

fuel *n.*
☞ 燃料 combustible, propellant, motive power.
☞ 激励 provocation, incitement, encouragement, ammunition,

material.

v.

☞加油,加燃料 incite, inflame, fire, encourage, fan, feed, nourish, sustain, stoke up.

fugitive n.

☞逃亡,逃跑,难民 escapee, runaway, deserter, refugee.

adj.

☞逃亡的,简短的 fleeting, transient, transitory, passing, short, brief, flying, temporary, ephemeral, elusive.

fulfil v.

☞完成 complete, finish, conclude, consummate, perfect, realize, achieve, accomplish, perform, execute, discharge, implement, carry out, comply with, observe, keep, obey, conform to, satisfy, fill, answer.

fulfilment n.

☞实践,实现,实行,满足 completion, perfection, consummation, realization, achievement, accomplishment, success, performance, execution, discharge, implementation, observance, satisfaction.

full adj.

☞满的 filled, loaded, packed, crowded, crammed, stuffed, jammed.

☞全部的,整个的 entire, whole, intact, total, complete, unabridged, unexpurgated.

☞彻底的,完全的 thorough, comprehensive, exhaustive, all-inclusive, broad, vast, extensive, ample, generous, abundant, plentiful, copious, profuse.

full-grown adj.

☞成熟的 adult, grown-up, of age, mature, ripe, developed, full-blown, full-scale.

fully adv.

☞完全地,彻底地 completely, totally, utterly, wholly, entirely, thoroughly, altogether, quite, positively, without reserve, perfectly.

fun n.

☞娱乐,玩耍,嘲笑 enjoyment, pleasure, amusement, entertainment, diversion, distraction, recreation, play, sport, game, foolery, tomfoolery, horseplay, skylarking, romp, merrymaking, mirth, jollity, jocularity, joking, jesting.

make fun of

☞取笑,嘲笑 rag, jeer at, ridicule, laugh at, mock, taunt, tease.

function n.

☞功能,工作,职责,任务 role, part, office, duty, charge, responsibility, concern, job, task, occupation, business, activity, purpose, use.

☞典礼,聚会,晚餐 reception, party, gathering,, affair, do, dinner, luncheon.

v.

☞运作,运行 work, operate, run, go, serve, act, perform, behave.

functional adj.

☞实用的,运作的 working, operational, practical, useful,

utilitarian, utility, plain, hard-wearing.

fund n.
☞ 基金,专款 pool, kitty, treasury, repository, storehouse, store, reserve, stock, hoard, cache, stack, mine, well, source, supply.
v.
☞ 提供资金,为……提供经费 finance, capitalize, endow, subsidize, underwrite, sponsor, back, support, promote, float.

fundamental adj.
☞ 基本的,根本的,中心的,重要的 basic primary, first, rudimentary, elementary, underlying, integral, central, principal, cardinal, prime, main, key, essential, indispensable, vital, necessary, crucial, important.

funds n.
☞ 资金,钱 money, finance, backing, capital, resources, savings, wealth, cash.

funeral n.
☞ 丧礼,葬礼 burial, interment, entombment, cremation, obsequies, wake.

funny adj.
☞ 有趣的,可笑的 humorous, amusing, entertaining, comic, comical, hilarious, witty, facetious, droll, farcical, laughable, ridiculous, absurd, silly.
☞ 古怪的,离奇的,想不到的 odd, strange, peculiar, curious, queer, weird, unusual, remarkable, puzzling, perplexing, mysterious, suspicious, dubious.

furnish v.
☞ 配置,布置,供应 equip, fit out, decorate, rig, stock, provide, supply, afford, grant, give, offer, present.

funiture n.
☞ 家具,装置 equipment, appliances, furnishings, fittings, fitments, household goods, movables, possessions, effects, things.

further adj.
☞ 更多的,更进一步的 more, additional, supplementary, extra, fresh, new, other.
v.
☞ 帮助,促进 advance, forward, promote, champion, push, encourage, foster, help, aid, assist, ease, facilitate, speed, hasten, accelerate, expedite.

furthermore adv.
☞ 此外,再者 moreover, what's more, in addition, further, besides, also, too, as well, additionally.

furthest adj.
☞ 最远的 farthest, furthermost, remotest, outermost, outmost, extreme, ultimate, utmost, uttermost.

furtive adj.
☞ 偷偷摸摸的,鬼鬼祟祟的 surreptitious, sly, stealthy, secretive, underhand, hidden, covert, secret.

fusion n.
☞ 熔解,熔合 melting, smelting, welding, union, synthesis, blending, coalescence,

fuss n.
☞ 大惊小怪,小题大作,大吵大闹,引起骚动 bother, trouble, hassle, palaver, to-do, hoo-ha, furore, squabble, row, commotion, stir, fluster, confusion, upset, worry, agitation, flap, excitement, bustle, flurry, hurry.
v.
☞ 小题大作,忙乱,大惊小怪 complain, grumble, fret, worry, flap, take pains, bother, bustle, fidget.

fussy adj.
☞ 烦躁的,神经质的,大惊小怪的 particular, fastidious, scrupulous, finicky, pernickety, difficult, hard to please, choosy, discriminating.
☞ fancy, elaborate, ornate, cluttered.

futile adj.
☞ 徒劳的,无效的,无用的 pointless, useless, worthless, vain, idle, wasted, fruitless, profitless, unavailing, unsuccessful, abortive, unprofitable, unproductive, barren, empty, hollow, forlorn.

futility n.
☞ 无用,徒劳 pointlessness, uselessness, worthlessness, vanity, emptiness, hollowness, aimlessness.

future n.
☞ 前途,未来,以后,将来 hereafter, tomorrow, outlook, prospects, expectations.
adj.
☞ 未来的,将来的 prospective, designate to be, fated, destined, to come, forthcoming, in the offing, impending, coming, approaching, expected, planned, unborn, later, subsequent, eventual.

fuzzy adj.
☞ 似绒毛的 frizz, fluffy, furry, woolly, fleecy, downy, velvety, napped.
☞ 模糊的,不清晰的 blurred, unfocused, ill-defined, unclear, vague, faint, hazy, shadowy, woolly, muffled, distorted.

G

gain v.
☞ 获得 earn, make, produce, gross, net, clear, profit, yield, bring in, reap, harvest, win, capture, secure, net, obtain, acquire, procure.
☞ 达到 reach, arrive at, come to, get to, attain, achieve, realize.
☞ 增加 increase, pick up, gather, collect, advance, progress, improve.
n.
☞ 收获,赢利 earnings, proceeds, income, revenue, winnings, profit, return, yield,

dividend, growth, increase, increment, rise, advance, progress, headway, improvement, advantage, benefit, attainment, achievement, acquisition.

gain on
- 缩短差距　close with, narrow the gap, approach, catch up, level with, overtake, outdistance, leave behind.

gallant *adj.*
- 举止得体的;勇敢的　chivalric, gentlemanly, courteous, polite, gracious, courtly, noble, dashing, heroic, valiant, brave, courageous, fearless, dauntless, bold, daring.

gallery *n.*
- 廊　art gallery, museum, arcade, passage, walk, balcony, circle, gods, spectators.

gallop *v.*
- 跳跃,快走,跑　bolt, run, sprint, race, career, fly, dash, tear, speed, zoom, shoot, dart, rush, hurry, hasten.

gamble *v.*
- 赌博　bet, wager, have a flutter, try one's luck, punt, play, game, stake, chance, take a chance, risk, hazard, venture, speculate, back.

n.
- 赌博　bet, wager, flutter, punt, lottery, chance, risk, venture, speculation.

gambler *n.*
- 赌徒,赌博的人　better, punter.

game *n.*
- 游戏　recreation, play, sport, pastime, diversion, distraction, entertainment, amusement, fun, frolic, romp, joke, jest.
- 比赛　competition, contest, match, round, tournament, event, meeting.
- 猎物　game birds, animals, meat, flesh, prey, quarry, bag, spoils.

adj.
- 愿意的　willing, inclined, ready, prepared, eager.
- 胆大的　bold, daring, intrepid, brave, courageous, fearless, resolute, spirited.

gang *n.*
- 伙,群　group, band, ring, pack, herd, mob, crowd, circle, clique, coterie, set, lot, team, crew, squad, shift, party.

gangster *n.*
- 坏人,恶棍　mobster, desperado, hoodlum, ruffian, rough, tough, thug, heavy, racketeer, bandit, brigand, robber, criminal, crook.

gap *n.*
- 沟壑　space, blank, void, hole, opening, crack, chink, crevice, cleft, breach, rift, divide, divergence, difference.
- 间断　interruption, break, recess, pause, lull, interlude, intermission, interval.

gape *v.*
- 吃惊地,盯着看　stare, gaze, gawp, goggle, gawk.
- 分开,分离　open, yawn, part, split, crack.

gaping *adj.*
☞ 有鸿沟的 open, yawning, broad, wide, vast, cavernous.

garage *n.*
☞ 车库 lock-up, petrol station, service station.

garden *n.*
☞ 花园 yard, backyard, plot, allotment, orchard, park.

garments *n.*
☞ 长袍 clothes, clothing, wear, attire, gear, togs, outfit, get-up, dress, costume, uniform.

gasp *v.*
☞ 喘气 pant, puff, blow, breathe, wheeze, choke, gulp.
☞ 喘气, 屏息 pant, puff, blow, breath, gulp, exclamation.

gate *n.*
☞ 大门 barrier, door, doorway, gateway, opening, entrance, exit, access, passage.

gather *v.*
☞ 收集 congregate, convene, muster, rally, round up, assemble, collect, group, amass, accumulate, hoard, stockpile, heap, pile up, build.
☞ 推断, 推测 infer, deduce, conclude, surmise, assume, understand, learn, hear.
☞ 皱, 缩 fold, pleat, tuck, pucker.
☞ 采集 pick, pluck, cull, select, reap, harvest, glean.

gathering *n.*
☞ 聚集, 集会 assembly, convocation, convention, meeting, round-up, rally, get-together, jamboree, party,
group, company, congregation, mass, crowd, throng, turnout.

gay *adj.*
☞ 快乐的, 快活的 happy, joyful, jolly, merry, cheerful, blithe, sunny, carefree, debonair, fun-loving, pleasure-seeking, vivacious, lively, animated, playful, light-hearted.
☞ 同性恋的 homosexual, lesbian.
☞ 华美的, 花哨的 vivid, rich, bright, brilliant, sparkling, festive, colourful, gaudy, garish, flashy, showy, flamboyant.
n.
☞ 同性恋者 homosexual, lesbian.

gaze *v.*
☞ 盯, 注视 stare, contemplate, regard, watch, view, look, gape, wonder.
n.
☞ 盯, 注视 stare, look.

gear *n.*
☞ 工具 equipment, kit, outfit, tackle, apparatus, tools, instruments, accessories.
☞ 齿轮 gearwheel, cogwheel, cog, gearing, mechanism, machinery, works.
☞ 财产 belongings, possessions, things, stuff, baggage, luggage, paraphernalia.
☞ 衣服 clothes, clothing, garments, attire, dress, garb, togs, get-up.

gel (**jell**) *v.*
☞ 胶化, 结冻 set, congeal, coagulate, crystallize, harden, thicken, solidify, materialize,

come together, finalize, form, take shape.

gem n.
- 宝石 gemstone, precious stone, jewel, treasure, prize, masterpiece, piece de resistance.

general adj.
- 总的 broad, sweeping, blanket, all-inclusive, comprehensive, universal, global, total, across-the-board, widespread, prevalent, extensive, overall, panoramic.
- 泛泛的 vague, ill-defined, indefinite, imprecise, inexact, approximate, loose, unspecific.
- 一般的 usual, regular, normal, typical, ordinary, everyday, customary, conventional, common, public.

generally adv.
- 一般地 usually, normally, as a rule, by and large, on the whole, mostly, mainly, chiefly, broadly, commonly, universally.

generate v.
- 产生 produce, engender, whip up, arouse, cause, bring about, give rise to, create, originate, initiate, make, form, breed, propagate.

generation n.
- 代 age group, age, era, epoch, period, time.
- 产生 production, creation, origination, formation, genesis, procreation, reproduction, propagation, breeding.

generosity n.
- 慷慨, 大方 liberality, munificence, open-handedness, bounty, charity, magnanimity, philanthropy, kindness, big-heartedness, benevolence, goodness.

generous adj.
- 宽大的 liberal, free, bountiful, open-handed, unstinting, unsparing, lavish.
- 大方的 magnanimous, charitable, philanthropic, public-spirited, unselfish, kind, big-hearted, benevolent, good, high-minded, noble.
- 丰富的 ample, full, plentiful, abundant, copious, overflowing.

genius n.
- 天才 virtuoso, maestro, master, past master, expert, adept, egghead, intellectual, mastermind, brain, intellect.
- 才智 intelligence, brightness, brilliance, ability, aptitude, gift, talent, flair, knack, bent, inclination, propensity, capacity, faculty.

gentle adj.
- 温和的 kind, kindly, amiable, tender, soft-hearted, compassionate, sympathetic, merciful, mild, placid, calm, tranquil.
- 平静的 soothing, peaceful, serene, quiet, soft, balmy.
- 和缓的 gradual, slow, easy, smooth, moderate, slight, light, imperceptible.

genuine adj.
- 真正的 real, actual, natural, pure, original, authentic, veritable, true, bonafide,

legitimate, honest, sincere, frank, candid, earnest.

germ n.
☞ 细菌 micro-organism, microbe, bacterium, bacillus, virus, bug.

☞ 根源 beginning, start, origin, source, cause, spark, rudiment, nucleus, root, seed, embryo, bud, sprout.

gesture n.
☞ 手势 act, action, movement, motion, indication, sign, signal, wave, gesticulation.

v.
☞ 打手势 indicate, sign, motion, beckon, point, signal, wave, gesticulate.

get v.
☞ 得到 obtain, acquire, procure, come by, receive, earn, gain, win, secure, achieve, realize.

☞ 变得 become, turn, go, grow.

☞ 到, 抵 move, go, come, reach, arrive.

☞ 取 fetch, collect, pick up, take, catch, capture, seize, grab.

☞ 使产生(某种结果) contract, catch, pick up, develop, come down with.

☞ 使, 让 persuade, coax, induce, urge, influence, sway.

get across
☞ 使人了解 communicate, transmit, convey, impart, put across, bring home to.

get ahead
☞ 进步, 获得成功 advance, progress, get on, go places, thrive, flourish, prosper, succeed, make good, make it, get there.

get along
☞ 过日子 cope, manage, get by, survive, fare, progress, develop.

☞ 相处融洽 agree, harmonize, get on, hit if off.

get at
☞ 到达, 了解 reach, attain, find, discover.

☞ 收买 bribe, suborn, corrupt, influence.

☞ 意指 mean, intend, imply, insinuate, hint, suggest.

☞ 攻击, 挖苦 criticize, find fault with, pick on, attack, make fun of.

get away
☞ 逃走 escape, get out, break out, break away, run away, flee, depart, leave.

get back
☞ 恢复 recover, regain, recoup, repossess, retrieve.

get down
☞ 使沮丧 depress, sadden, dishearten, dispirit.

☞ 落下, 下车 descend, dismount, disembark, alight, get off.

get in
☞ 进入 enter, penetrate, infiltrate, arrive, come, land, embark.

get off
☞ 下(车) alight, disembark, dismount, descend.

☞ 去掉 remove, detach, separate, shed, get down.

get on

- 上(车) board, embark, mount, ascend.
- 过日子,成功 cope, manage, fare, get along, make out, prosper, succeed.
- 继续 continue, proceed, press on, advance, progress.

get out
- 逃脱,脱离 escape, flee, break out, extricate oneself, free oneself, leave, quit, vacate, evacuate, clear out, clear off.
- 走开,泄露 go away, become known, leak.

get over
- 痊愈 recover from, shake off, survive.
- 克服 surmount, overcome, defeat, deal with.
- 使了解 communicate, get across, convey, put over, impart, explain.

get round
- 逃避 circumvent, bypass, evade, avoid.
- 说服 persuade, win over, talk round, coax, prevail upon.

get together
- 聚集 assemble, collect, gather, congregate, rally, meet, join, unite, collaborate.

get up
- 起来 stand(up), arise, rise, ascend, climb, mount, scale.

ghost n.
- 鬼魅 spectre, phantom, spook, apparition, visitant, spirit, wraith, soul, shade, shadow.

ghostly adj.
- 鬼一样的 eerie, spooky, creepy, supernatural, unearthly, ghostlike, spectral, wraith-like, phantom, illusory.

giant n.
- 巨人 monster titan, colossus, Goliath, Hercules.

adj.
- 巨大的 gigantic, colossal, titanic, mammoth, jumbo, king-size, huge, enormous, immense, vast, large.

gift n.
- 礼物 present, offering, donation, contribution, bounty, largess, gratuity, tip, bonus, legacy, bequest, endowment.
- 天赋 talent, genius, flair, aptitude, bent, knack, power, faculty, attribute, ability, capability, capacity.

gifted adj.
- 有天赋的 talented, adept, skilful, expert, masterly, skilled, accomplished, able, capable, clever, intelligent, bright, brilliant.

gigantic adj.
- 巨大的 huge, enormous, immense, vast, giant, colossal, titanic, mammoth, gargantuan, Brobdingnagian.

giggle v., n.
- 格格地笑 titter, snigger, chuckle, chortle, laugh.

gilded adj.
- 镀金的 gilt, gold, golden, gold-plated.

girl n.
- 女孩子 lass, young woman, girlfriend, sweetheart, daughter.

give v.

☞ 给 present, award, confer, offer, lend, donate, contribute, provide, supply, furnish, grant, bestow, endow, gift, make over, hand over, deliver, entrust, commit, devote.
☞ 让出 concede, allow, admit, yield, give way, surrender.
☞ 发布 communicate, transmit, impart, utter, announce, declare, pronounce, publish, set forth.
☞ 引起 cause, occasion, make, produce, do, perform.

give away
☞ 泄露 betray, inform on, expose, uncover, divulge, let slip, disclose, reveal, leak, let out.

give in
☞ 屈服 surrender, capitulate, submit, yield, give way, concede, give up, quit.

give off
☞ 放出 emit, discharge, release, give out, send out, throw out, pour out, exhale, exude, produce.

give out
☞ 分发 distribute, hand out, dole out, deal.
☞ 发布 announce, declare, broadcast, publish, disseminate, communicate, transmit, impart, notify, advertise.

give up
☞ 停止 stop, cease, quit, resign, abandon, renounce, relinquish, waive.
☞ 放弃 surrender, capitulate, give in.

given adj.
☞ 确定的 specified, particular, definite.
☞ 可能的 inclined, disposed, likely, liable, prone.

glad adj.
☞ 高兴的 pleased, delighted, gratified, contented, happy, joyful, merry, cheerful, cheery, bright.
☞ 愿意的 willing, eager, keen, ready, inclined, disposed.

glance v.
☞ 瞟一眼 peep, peek, glimpse, view, look, scan, skim, leaf, flip, thumb, dip, browse.
n.
☞ 瞟一眼 peep, peek, glimpse, look.

glare v.
☞ 瞪眼 glower, look daggers, frown, scowl, stare.
☞ 耀眼 dazzle, blaze, flame, flare, shine, reflect.
n.
☞ 瞪眼 black look, dirty look, frown, scowl, stare, look.
☞ 闪亮 brightness, brilliance, blaze, flame, dazzle, spotlight.

glaring adj.
☞ 突出的 blatant, flagrant, open, conspicuous, manifest, patent, obvious, outrageous, gross.

glib adj.
☞ 善辩的 fluent, easy, facile, quick, ready, talkative, plausible, insincere, smooth, slick, suave, smooth-tongued.

glide v.
☞ 滑动 slide, slip, skate, skim, fly, float, drift, sail, coast,

roll, run, flow.

glimmer v.
- 闪光 glow, shimmer, glisten, glitter, sparkle, twinkle, wink, blink, flicker, gleam, shine.

n.
- 闪光 glow, shimmer, sparkle, twinkle, flicker, glint, gleam.
- 暗示 trace, hint, suggestion, grain.

glimpse n.
- 一瞥 peep, peek, squint, glance, look, sight, sighting, view.

v.
- 瞥见 spy, espy, spot, catch sight of, sight, view.

global adj.
- 全球性的 universal, worldwide, international, general, all-encompassing, total, thorough, exhaustive, comprehensive, all-inclusive, wide-ranging.

globe n.
- 球体 world, earth, planet, sphere, ball, orb, round.

gloom n.
- 低沉 depression, low spirits, despondency, dejection, sadness, unhappiness, glumness, melancholy, misery, desolation, despair.
- 阴暗 dark, darkness, shade, shadow, dusk, twilight, dimness, obscurity, cloud, cloudiness, dullness.

gloomy adj.
- 低沉的 depressed, down, low, despondent, dejected, downcast, dispirited, down-hearted, sad, miserable, glum, morose, pessimistic, cheerless, dismal, depressing.
- 阴暗的,单调的 dark, sombre, shadowy, dim, obscure, overcast, dull, dreary.

glorious adj.
- 辉煌的 illustrious, eminent, distinguished, famous, renowned, noted, great, noble, splendid, magnificent, grand, majestic, triumphant.
- 华丽的 fine, bright, radiant, shining, brilliant, dazzling, beautiful, gorgeous, superb, excellent, wonderful, marvellous, delightful, heavenly.

glory n.
- 荣誉 fame, renown, celebrity, illustriousness, greatness, eminence, distinction, honour, prestige, kudos, triumph.
- 赞誉 praise, homage, tribute, worship, veneration, adoration, exaltation, blessing, thanksgiving, gratitude.
- 壮丽 brightness, radiance, brilliance, beauty, splendour, resplendence, magnificence, grandeur, majesty, dignity.

glow n.
- 光热 light, gleam, glimmer, radiance, luminosity, brightness, vividness, brilliance, splendour.
- 激情 ardour, fervour, intensity, warmth, passion, enthusiasm, excitement.
- 发红 flush, blush, redness, burning.

v.
☞ 发光 shine, radiate, gleam, glimmer, burn, smoulder.
☞ 发红 flush, blush, colour, redden.

glowing *adj.*
☞ 热情的 bright, luminous, vivid, vibrant, rich, warm, flushed, red, flaming.

glue *n.*
☞ 胶 adhesive, gum, paste, size, cement.
v.
☞ 粘贴 stick, affix, gum, paste, seal, bond, cement, fix.

glut *n.*
☞ 过量 surplus, excess, superfluity, surfeit, overabundance, superabundance, saturation, overflow.

gnarled *adj.*
☞ 多瘤节的 gnarly, knotted, knotty, twisted, contorted, distorted, rough, rugged, weather-beaten.

gnaw *v.*
☞ 咬,啃,啮 bite, nibble, munch, chew, eat, devour, consume, erode, wear, haunt.
☞ 使……苦恼 worry, niggle, fret, trouble, plague, nag, prey.

go *v.*
☞ 走 move, pass, advance, progress, proceed, make for, travel, journey, start, begin, depart, leave, take one's leave, retreat, withdraw, disappear, vanish.
☞ 起作用 operate, function, work, run, act, perform.
☞ 延伸 extend, spread, stretch, reach, span, continue, unfold.
☞ 流逝 pass, elapse, lapse, roll on.
n.
☞ 精力 energy, get-up-and-go, vitality, life, spirit, dynamism, effort.
☞ 尝试 attempt, try, shot, bash, stab, turn.

go about
☞ 从事 approach, begin, set about, address, tackle, attend to, undertake, engage in, perform.

go ahead
☞ 进步,前进 begin, proceed, carry on, continue, advance, progress, move.

go away
☞ 离去,走开 depart, leave, clear of, withdraw, retreat, disappear, vanish.

go back
☞ 返回 return, revert, backslide, retreat.

go by
☞ 过去,走过 pass, elapse, flow.
☞ 遵守 observe, follow, comply with, heed.

go down
☞ 沉没 descend, sink, set, fall, drop, decrease, decline, deteriorate, degenerate, fail, founder, go under, collapse, fold.

go for
☞ 喜欢,赞许 choose, prefer, favour, like, admire, enjoy.
☞ 攻击 attack, assail, set about,

lunge at.

go in for
☞ 从事,爱好 enter, take part in, participate in, engage in, take up, embrace, adopt, undertake, practise, pursue, follow.

go into
☞ 探究 discuss, consider, review, examine, study, scrutinize, investigate, inquire into, check out, probe, delve into, analyle, dissect.

go off
☞ 离开 depart, leave, quit, abscond, vanish, disappear.
☞ 爆炸 explode, blow up, detonate.
☞ 变坏 deteriorate, turn, sour, go bad, rot.

go on
☞ 继续 continue, carry on, proceed, persist, stay, endure, last.
☞ 漫谈 chatter, rabbit, witter, ramble on.
☞ 发生 HAPPEN, occur, take place.

go out
☞ 离开 exit, depart, leave.

go over
☞ 检查 examine, peruse, study, revise, scan, read, inspect, check, review, repeat, rehearse, list.

go through
☞ 经受 suffer, undergo, experience, bear, tolerate, endure, withstand.
☞ 调查 investigate, check, examine, look, search, hunt, explore.

☞ 耗费 use, consume, exhaust, spend, squander.

go together
☞ 般配 match, harmonize, accord, fit.

go with
☞ 和睦 match, harmonize, coordinate, blend, complement, suit, fit, correspond.
☞ 陪伴 accompany, escort, take, usher.

go without
☞ 缺乏 abstain, forgo, do without, manage without, lack, want.

go-ahead n.
☞ 允许 permission, authorization, clearance, green light, sanction, assent, consent, ok(infml), agreement.
adj.
☞ 有进取心的 enterprising, pioneering, progressive, ambitious, up-and-coming, dynamic, energetic.

goal n.
☞ 目标 target, mark, objective, aim, intention, object, purpose, end, ambition, aspiration.

go-between n.
☞ 中介 intermediary, mediator, liaison, contact, middleman, broker, dealer, agent, messenger, medium.

God n.
☞ 上帝 Supreme Being, Creator, Providence, Lord, Almighty, Holy One, Jehovah, Yahweh, Allah, Brahma, Zeus.

god, goddess n.
☞ 神 deity, divinity, idol, spirit, power.

golden adj.
- 金色的 gold, gilded, gilt, yellow, blond(e), fair, bright, shining, lustrous, resplendent.
- 贵重的,好的,极好的 prosperous, successful, glorious, excellent, happy, joyful, favourable, auspicious, promising, rosy.

good adj.
- 好的 acceptable, satisfactory, pleasant, agreeable, nice, enjoyable, pleasing, commendable, excellent, great, super, first-class, first-rate, superior, advantageous, beneficial, favourable, auspicious, helpful, useful, worthwhile, profitable, appropriate, suitable, fitting.
- 胜任的 competent, proficient, skilled, expert, accomplished, professional, skilful, clever, talented, gifted, fit, able, capable, dependable, reliable.
- 善良的 kind, considerate, gracious, benevolent, charitable, philanthropic.
- 楷模的 virtuous, exemplary, moral, upright, honest, trustworthy, worthy, righteous.
- 有教养的 well-behaved, obedient, well-mannered.
- 全面的 thorough, complete, whole, substantial, considerable.

n.
- 美德 virtue, morality, goodness, righteousness, right.
- 好处 use, purpose, avail, advantage, profit, gain, worth, merit, usefulness, service.
- 利益 welfare, wellbeing, interest, sake, behalf, benefit, convenience.

good-bye n.
- 再见 farewell, adieu, valediction, leave-taking, parting.

good-humoured adj.
- 愉快的,亲切的 cheerful, happy, jovial, genial, affable, amiable, friendly, congenial, pleasant, good-tempered, approachable.

good-looking adj.
- 好看的 attractive, handsome, beautiful, fair, pretty, personable, presentable.

good-natured adj.
- 善良的 king, kindly, king-hearted, sympathetic, benevolent, helpful, neighbourly, gentle, good-tempered, approachable, friendly, tolerant, patient.

goodness n.
- 美德 virtue, uprightness, rectitude, honesty, probity, kingness, compassion, graciousness, goodwill, benevolence, unselfishness, generosity, friendliness, helpfulness.

goods n.
- 所有物 property, chattels, effects, possessions, belongings, paraphernalia, stuff, things, gear.
- 货物 merchandise, wares, commodities, stock, freight.

goodwill n.
- 亲切,善意 benevolence, kindness, generosity, favour,

gorge n.
- ☞ 峡谷 canyon, ravine, gully, defile, chasm, abyss, cleft, fissure, gap, pass.

v.
- ☞ 狼吞虎咽 feed, guzzle, gobble, devour, bolt, wolf, gulp, swallow, cram, stuff, fill, sate, surfeit, glut, overeat.

gorgeous adj.
- ☞ 华丽灿烂的 magnificent, splendid, grand, glorious, superb, fine, rich, sumptuous, luxurious, brilliant, dazzling, showy, glamorous, attractive, beautiful, handsome, good-looking, delightful, pleasing, lovely, enjoyable, good.

gossip n.
- ☞ 说闲话 idle talk, prattle, chitchat, tittle-tattle, rumour, hearsay, report, scandal.
- ☞ 私语 gossip-monger, scandalmonger, whisperer, prattler, babbler, chatterbox, nosey marker, busybody, talebearer, tell-tale, tattler.

v.
- ☞ 聊天 talk, chat, natter, chatter, gabble, prattle, tattle, tell tales, whisper, rumour.

govern v.
- ☞ 统治权 rule, reign, direct, manage, superintend, supervise, oversee, preside, lead, head, command, influence, guide, conduct, steer, pilot.
- ☞ 支配 dominate, master, control, regulate, curb, check, restrain, contain, quell, subdue, tame, discipline.

friendliness, friendship, zeal.

government n.
- ☞ 行政机关 administration, executive, ministry, establishment, authorities, powers that be, state, regime.
- ☞ 统治权 rule, sovereignty, sway, direction, management, superintendence, supervision, surveillance, command, charge, authority, guidance, conduct, domination, dominion, control, regulation, restraint.

governor n.
- ☞ 统治者 ruler, commissioner, administrator, executive, director, manager, leader, head, chief, commander, superintendent, supervisor, overseer, controller, boss.

gown n.
- ☞ 长外衣 robe, dress, frock, dressing-gown, habit, costume.

grab v.
- ☞ 抓, 握 seize, snatch, take, nab, pluck, grip, catch, bag, capture, collar, commandeer, appropriate, usurp, annex.

grace n.
- ☞ 优美 gracefulness, poise, beauty, attractiveness, loveliness, shapeliness, elegance, tastefulness, refinement, polish, breeding, manners, etiquette, decorum, decency, courtesy, charm.
- ☞ 仁慈 kindness, kindliness, compassion, consideration, goodness, virtue, generosity, charity, benevolence, goodwill, favour, forgiveness, indulgence, mercy, leniency, pardon, reprieve.

☞ 祈祷 blessing, benediction, thanksgiving, prayer.

v.

☞ 使增光荣 favour, honour, dignify, distinguish, embellish, enhance, set off, trim, garnish, decorate, ornament, adorn.

graceful adj.
☞ 优美的 easy, flowing, smooth, supple, agile, deft, natural, slender, fine, tasteful, elegant, beautiful, charming, suave.

gracious adj.
☞ 亲切的 elegant, refined, polite, courteous, well-mannered, considerate, sweet, obliging, accommodating, kind, compassionate, kindly, benevolent, generous, magnanimous, charitable, hospitable, forgiving, indulgent, lenient, mild, clement, merciful.

grade n.
☞ 倾斜 rank, status, standing, station, place, position, level, stage, degree, step, rung, notch, mark, brand, quality, standard, condition, size, order, group, class, category.

v.

☞ 分级 sort, arrange, categorize, order, group, class, rate, size, rank, range, classify, evaluate, assess, value, mark, brand, label, pigeonhole, type.

gradual adj.
☞ 渐次的 slow, leisurely, unhurried, easy, gentle, moderate, regular, even, measure, steady, continuous, progressive, step-by-step.

gradually adv.
☞ 逐渐地 little by little, bit by bit, imperceptibly, inch by inch, step by step, progressively, by degrees, piecemeal, slowly, gently, cautiously, gingerly, moderately, evenly, steadily.

graduate v.
☞ 毕业 pass, qualify.

☞ 标上刻度;分等级 calibrate, mark off, measure out, proportion, grade, arrange, range, order, rank, sort, group, classify.

grain n.
☞ 颗粒;少许 bit, piece, fragment, scrap, morsel, crumb, granule, particle, molecule, atom, jot, iota, mite, speck, modicum, trace.

☞ 谷物 seed, kernel, corn, cereals.

☞ 纹 texture, fibre, weave, pattern, marking, surface.

grand adj.
☞ 显要的 majestic, regal, stately, splendid, magnificent, glorious, superb, sublime, fine, excellent, outstanding, first-rate, impressive, imposing, striking, monumental, large, noble, lordly, lofty, pompous, pretentious, grandiose, ambitious.

☞ 雄伟的 supreme, pre-eminent, leading, head, chief, arch, highest, senior, great, illustrious.

grandeur n.

grant v.
☞ 给予 give, donate, present, award, confer, bestow, impart, transmit, dispense, apportion, assign, allot, allocate, provide, supply.
☞ 允许 admit, acknowledge, concede, allow, permit, consent to, agree to, accede to.
n.
☞ 补助 allowance, subsidy, concession, award, bursary, scholarship, gift, donation, endowment, bequest, annuity, pension, honorarium.

☞ 崇高 majesty, stateliness, pomp, state, dignity, splendour, magnificence, nobility, greatness, illustrious, importance.

graph n.
☞ 图 diagram, chart, table, grid.

graphic adj.
☞ 生动的 vivid, descriptive, expressive, striking, telling, lively, realistic, explicit, clear, lucid, specific, detailed, blow-by-blow, visual, pictorial, diagrammatic, illustrative.

grasp v.
☞ 抓住 hold, clasp, clutch, grip, grapple, seize, snatch, grab, catch.
n.
☞ 控制 grip, clasp, hold, embrace, clutches, possession, control, power.
☞ 领会 understanding, comprehension, apprehension, mastery, familiarity, knowledge.

grasping adj.
☞ 能理解的 avaricious, greedy, rapacious, acquisitive, mercenary, mean, selfish, miserly, close-fisted, tight-fisted, parsimonious.

grass n.
☞ 草 turf, lawn, green, grassland, field, meadow, pasture, prairie, pampas, savanna, steppe.

grateful adj.
☞ 感谢的 thankful, appreciative, indebted, obliged, obligated.

gratitude n.
☞ 感谢 gratefulness, thankfulness, thanks, appreciation, acknowledgement, recognition, indebtedness, obligation.

grave¹ n.
☞ 墓地 burial-place, tomb, vault, crypt, sepulchre, mausoleum, pit, barrow, tumulus, cairn.

grave² adj.
☞ 重大的 important, significant, weighty, momentous, serious, critical, vital, crucial, urgent, acute, severe, dangerous, hazardous.
☞ 严肃的 solemn, dignified, sober, sedate, serious, thoughtful, pensive, grim, long-faced, quiet, reserved, subdued, restrained.

graveyard n.
☞ 墓地 cemetery, burial-ground, churchyard.

gravity n.
☞ 重要性 importance,

significance, seriousness, urgency, acuteness, severity, danger.
☞ 庄重 solemnity, dignity, sobriety, seriousness, thoughtfulness, sombreness, reserve, restraint.
☞ 重力 gravitation, attraction, pull, weight, heaviness.

graze v.
☞ 磨擦 scratch, scrape, skin, abrade, rub, chafe, shave, brush, skim, touch.
n.
☞ 擦痕 scratch, scrape, abrasion.

grease n.
☞ 油脂 oil, fatty, lardy, buttery, smeary, slimy, slippery, smooth, waxy.

great adj.
☞ 巨大 large, big, huge, enormous, massive, colossal, gigantic, mammoth, immense, vast, impressive.
☞ 非常的 considerable, pronounced, extreme, excessive, inordinate.
☞ 伟大的 famous, renowned, celebrated, illustrious, eminent, distinguished, prominent, noteworthy, outstanding, grand, glorious, fine.
☞ 重要的 important, significant, serious, major, principal, primary, main, chief, leading.
☞ 极好的 excellent, first-rate, superb, wonderful, marvellous, tremendous, terrific, fantastic, fabulous.

greed n.
☞ 欲望 hunger, ravenousness, gluttony, voracity, insatiability.
☞ 贪欲 acquisitiveness, covetousness, desire, craving, longing, eagerness, avarice, selfishness.

greedy adj.
☞ 贪吃的 hungry, starving, ravenous, gluttonous, gormandizing, voracious, insatiable.
☞ 渴望的 acquisitive, covetous, desirous, craving, eager, impatient, avaricious, grasping, selfish.

green adj.
☞ 未成熟的 grassy, leafy, verdant, unripe, unseasoned, tender, fresh, budding, blooming, flourishing.
☞ 嫉妒的 envious, covetous, jealous, resentful.
☞ 无经验的 immature, naive, unsophisticated, ignorant, inexperienced, untrained, raw, new, recent, young.
☞ 环保的 ecological, environmental, eco-friendly, environmentally aware.
n.
☞ 草 common, lawn, grass, turf.

greenhouse n.
☞ 温室 glasshouse, hothouse, conservatory, pavilion, vinery, orangery.

greet v.
☞ 问候 hail, salute, acknowledge, address, accost, meet, receive, welcome.

greeting n.
- 致敬 salutation, acknowledgement, wave, hallo, the time of day, address, reception, welcome.

greetings n.
- 致意 regards, respects, compliments, salutations, best wishes, good wishes, love.

gregarious adj.
- 群居的,爱交际的 sociable, outgoing, extrovert, friendly, affable, social, convivial, cordial, warm.

grey adj.
- 灰色的 neutral, colourless, pale, ashen, leaden, dull, cloudy, overcast, dim, dark, murky.
- 阴沉的 gloomy, dismal, cheerless, depressing, dreary, bleak.

grief n.
- 悲痛 sorrow, sadness, unhappiness, depression, dejection, desolation, distress, misery, woe, heartbreak, mourning, bereavement, heartache, anguish, agony, pain, suffering, affliction, trouble, regret, remorse.

grieve v.
- (使)悲痛 sorrow, mope, lament, mourn, wail, cry, weep.
- (使)伤心 sadden, upset, dismay, distress, afflict, pain, hurt, wound.

grim adj.
- 可怕的 unpleasant, horrible, horrid, ghastly, gruesome, grisly, sinister, frightening, fearsome, terrible, shocking.
- 冷酷的 stern, severe, harsh, dour, forbidding, surly, sullen, morose, gloomy, depressing, unattractive.

grimace n.
- 愁眉苦脸 frown, scowl, pout, smirk, sneer, face.

v.
- 面部的歪扭 make a face, pull a face, frown, scowl, pout, smirk, sneer.

grind v.
- 磨碎 crush, pound, pulverize, powder, mill, grate, scrape, gnash, rut, abrade, sand, file, smooth, polish, sharpen, whet.

grip n.
- 控制 hold, grasp, clasp, embrace, clutches, control, power.

v.
- 抓住 hold, grasp, clasp, clutch, seize, grab, catch.
- 使着迷 fascinate, thrill, enthral, spellbind, mesmerize, hypnotize, rivet, engross, absorb, involve, engage, compel.

groan n.
- 呻吟声 moan, sigh, cry, whine, wail, lament, complaint, objection, protest, outcry.

v.
- 呻吟 moan, sigh, cry, whine, wail, lament, complain, object, protest.

grope v.
- 摸索 fell, fumble, scrabble, flounder, cast about, fish,

gross adj.
- ☞ 严重的 serious, grievous, blatant, flagrant, glaring, obvious, plain, sheer, utter, outright, shameful, shocking.
- ☞ 粗俗的 obscene, lewd, improper, indecent, offensive, rude, coarse, crude, vulgar, tasteless.
- ☞ 肥大的 fat, obese, overweight, big, large, huge, colossal, hulking, bulky, heavy.
- ☞ 全部的 inclusive, all-inclusive, total, aggregate, entire, complete, whole.

ground n.
- ☞ 土地 bottom, foundation, surface, land, terrain, dry land, terra firma, earth, soil, clay, loam, dirt, dust.
- ☞ 场地 field, pitch, stadium, arena, park.

v.
- ☞ 建基础于 base, found, establish, set, fix, settle.
- ☞ 教导 prepare, introduce, initiate, familiarize with, acquaint with, inform, instruct, teach, train, drill, coach, tutor.

groundless adj.
- ☞ 无根据地 baseless, unfounded, unsubstantiated, unsupported, empty, imaginary, false, unjustified, unwarranted, unprovoked, uncalled-for.

grounds^1 n.
- ☞ 陆地 land, terrain, holding, estate, property, territory, domain, gardens, park, campus, surroundings, fields, acres.

grounds^2 n.
- ☞ 理由 base, foundation, justification, excuse, vindication, reason, motive, inducement, cause, occasion, call, score, account, argument, principle, basis.

group n.
- ☞ 群 band, gang, pack, team, crew, troop, squad, detachment, party, faction, set, circle, clique, club, society, association, organization, company, gathering, crowd, collection, bunch, clump, cluster, conglomeration, constellation, batch, lot, combination, formation, grouping, class, classification, category, genus, species.

v.
- ☞ 成群 gather, collect, assemble, congregate, mass, cluster, clump, bunch.
- ☞ 分类 sort, range, arrange, marshal, organize, order, class, classify, categorize, band, link, associate.

grow v.
- ☞ 发展 increase, rise, expand, enlarge, swell, spread, extend, stretch, develop, proliferate, mushroom.
- ☞ 发生 originate, arise, issue, spring, germinate, shoot, sprout, bud, flower, mature, develop, progress, thrive, flourish, prosper.
- ☞ 栽种 cultivate, farm, produce, propagate, breed,

raise.
☞ 变得 become, get, go, turn.

grown-up *adj.*
☞ 已长成的 adult, mature, of age, full-grown, fully-fledged.
n.
☞ 成人 adult, man, woman.

growth *n.*
☞ 增加 increase, rise, extension, enlargement, expansion, spread, proliferation, development, evolution, progress, advance, improvement, success, prosperity.
☞ 生物 tumour, lump, swelling, protuberance, outgrowth.

guarantee *n.*
☞ 保证 warranty, insurance, assurance, promise, word of honour, pledge, oath, bond, security, collateral, surety, endorsement, testimonial.
v.
☞ 保证 assure, promise, pledge, swear, vouch for, answer for, warrant, certify, underwrite, endorse, secure, protect, insure, ensure, make sure, make certain.

guard *v.*
☞ 保护 protect, safeguard, save, preserve, shield, screen, shelter, cover, defend, patrol, police, escort, supervise, oversee, watch, look out, mind, beware.
n.
☞ 防卫物 protector, defender, custodian, warder, escort, bodyguard, watchman, lookout, sentry, picket, patrol, security.
☞ 戒备 protection, safeguard, defence, wall, barrier, screen, shield, bumper, buffer, pad.

guardian *n.*
☞ 监护人 trustee, curator, custodian, keeper, warden, protector, preserver, defender, champion, guard, warder, escort, attendant.

guess *v.*
☞ 推测 speculate, conjecture, predict, estimate, judge, reckon, work out, suppose, assume, surmise, think, believe, imagine, fancy, feel, suspect.
n.
☞ 猜测 prediction, estimate, speculation, conjecture, supposition, assumption, belief, fancy, idea, notion, theory, hypothesis, opinion, feeling, suspicion, intuition.

guesswork *n.*
☞ 推测 speculation, conjecture, estimation, reckoning, supposition, assumption, surmise, intuition.

guest *n.*
☞ 客人 visitor, caller, boarder, lodger, resident, patron, regular.

guidance *n.*
☞ 指导 leadership, direction, management, control, teaching, instruction, advice, counsel, counselling, help, instructions, directions, guidelines, indications, pointers, recommendations.

guide *v.*

- **引导** lead, conduct, direct, navigate, point, steer, pilot, manoeuvre, usher, escort, accompany, attend, control, govern, manage, oversee, supervise, superintend, advise, counsel, influence, educate, teach, instruct, train.

n.
- **引导者** leader, courier, navigator, pilot, helmsman, steersman, usher, escort, chaperon, attendant, companion, adviser, counsellor, mentor, guru, teacher, instructor.
- **指南(书)** manual, handbook, guidebook, catalogue, directory.
- **指导,原则** guideline, example, model, standard, criterion, indication, pointer, signpost, sign, marker.

guilt *n.*
- **罪过** culpability, responsibility, blame, disgrace, dishonour.
- **内疚** guilty conscience, conscience, shame, self-condemnation, self-reproach, regret, remorse, contrition.

guilty *adj.*
- **有罪的** culpable, responsible, blamable, blameworthy, offending, wrong, sinful, wicked, criminal, convicted.
- **内疚的** conscience-stricken, ashamed, shamefaced, sheepish, sorry, regretful, remorseful, contrite, penitent, repentant.

gulf *n.*
- **海湾** bay, bight, basin, gap, opening, separation, rift, split, breach, cleft, chasm, gorge, abyss, void.

gulp *v.*
- **吞** swallow, swig, swill, knock back, bolt, wolf, gobble, guzzle, devour, stuff.

n.
- **吞咽** swallow, swig, draught, mouthful.

gum *n.*
- **树胶** adhesive, glue, paste, cement.

v.
- **粘合** stick, glue, paste, fix, cement, seal, clog.

gun *n.*
- **枪** firearm, handgun, pistol, revolver, rifle, shotgun, bazooka, howitzer, cannon.

gust *n.*
- **阵风** blast, burst, rush, flurry, blow, puff, breeze, wind, gale, squall.

H

habit *n.*
- **习惯,习性** custom, usage, practice, routine, rule, second, nature, way, manner, mode, wont, inclination, tendency, bent, mannerism, quirk, addiction, dependence, fixation, obsession, weakness.

habitat n.
☞ 产地 home, abode, domain, element, environment, surroundings, locality, territory, terrain.

habitual adj.
☞ 习惯性的 customary, traditional, wonted, routine, usual, ordinary, common, natural, normal, standard, regular, recurrent, fixed, established, familiar.

hail¹ n.
☞ 雹 barrage, bombardment, volley, torrent, shower, rain, storm.
v.
☞ 下降,猛烈地降 pelt, bombard, shower, rain, batter, attack, assail.

hail² v.
☞ 欢迎,欢呼 greet, address, acknowledge, salute, wave, signal to, flag down, shout, call, acclaim, cheer, applaud, honour, welcome.

hair n.
☞ 毛发,头发 locks, tresses, shock, mop, mane.

hairdresser n.
☞ 理发师 hairstylist, stylist, barber, coiffeur, coiffeuse.

hairless adj.
☞ 无毛发的 bald, bald-headed, shorn, tonsured, shaven, clean-shaven, beardless.

hairstyle n.
☞ 发式 style, coiffure, hairdo, cut, haircut, set, perm.

half n.
☞ 半,一半 fifty percent, bisection, hemisphere, semicircle, section, segment, portion, share, fraction.
adj.
☞ 一半的 semi-, halved, divided, fractional, part, partial, incomplete, moderate, limited.
adv.
☞ 部分地 partly, partially, incompletely, moderately, slightly.

half-hearted adj.
☞ 消极的,冷淡的 lukewarm, cool, weak, feeble, passive, apathetic, uninterested, indifferent, neutral.

halfway adv.
☞ 半路上 midway, in the middle, centrally.
adj.
☞ 中间,半途 middle, central, equidistant, mid, midway, intermediate.

hall n.
☞ 门厅,大厅,礼堂 hallway, corridor, passage, passageway, entrance-hall, foyer, vestibule, lobby, concert-hall, auditorium, chamber, assembly room.

halt v.
☞ 停止,停住 stop, draw up, pull up, pause, wait, rest, break off, discontinue, cease, desist, quit, end, terminate, check, stem, curb, obstruct, impede.
n.
☞ 止步,停止 stop, stoppage, arrest, interruption, break, pause, rest, standstill, end, close, termination.

halting *adj.*
☞ 犹豫的,踌躇的 hesitant, stuttering, stammering, faltering, stumbling, broken, imperfect, laboured, awkward.

halve *v.*
☞ 对分,平摊 bisect, cut in half, split in two, divide, split, share, cut down, reduce, lessen.

hammer *v.*
☞ 敲击,锤打 hit, strike, beat, drum, bang, bash, pound, batter, knock, drive, shape, form, make.

hammer out
☞ 解决,辛苦地做成 settle, sort out, negotiate, thrash out, produce, bring about, accomplish, complete, finish.

hamper *v.*
☞ 妨碍,阻碍 hinder, impede, obstruct, slow down, hold up, frustrate, thwart, prevent, handicap, hamstring, shackle, cramp, restrict, curb, restrain.

hand *n.*
☞ 手 fist, palm, paw, mitt.
☞ 人手,职工 worker, employee, operative, workman, labourer, farm-hand, hireling.
☞ 帮助 help, aid, assistance, support, participation, part, influence.
v.
☞ 递交,送交 give, pass, offer, submit, present, yield, deliver, transmit, conduct, convey.

at hand
☞ 在近处,在手边 near, close, to hand, handy, accessible, available, ready, imminent.

hand down
☞ 传递 bequeath, will, pass on, transfer, give, grant.

hand out
☞ 分配 distribute, deal out, give out, share out, dish out, mete out, dispense.

hand over
☞ 交出,交给 yield, relinquish, surrender, turn over, deliver, release, give, donate, present.

handbook *n.*
☞ 手册,指南 manual, instruction book, guide, guidebook, companion.

handful *n.*
☞ 一把,少数 few, sprinkling, scattering, smattering.

handicap *n.*
☞ 不利条件 obstacle, block, barrier, impediment, stumbling-block, hindrance, drawback, disadvantage, restriction, limitation, penalty, disability, impairment, defect, shortcoming.
v.
☞ 妨碍,使……不利 impede, hinder, disadvantage, hold back, retard, hamper, burden, encumber, restrict, limit, disable.

handicraft *n.*
☞ 手艺 craft, art, craftwork, handwork, handiwork.

handiwork *n.*
☞ 手工,手工制品 work, doing, responsibility, achievement, product, result, design, invention, creation, production, skill, workmanship, craftsmanship, artisanship.

handle n.
- 拉手,把柄 grip, handgrip, knob, stock, shaft, hilt.

v.
- 触,摸 touch, finger, feel, fondle, pick up, hold, grasp.
- 处理,解决 tackle, treat, deal with, manage, cope with, control, supervise.

handout n.
- 施舍的,救济品 charity, alms, dole, largess(e), share, issue, free sample.
- 讲义,传单 leaflet, circular, bulletin, statement, press release, literature.

hands n.
- 管理,监护 care, custody, possession, charge, authority, command, power, control, supervision.

handsome adj.
- 漂亮的 good-looking, attractive, fair, personable, elegant.
- 可观的,慷慨的 generous, liberal, large, considerable, ample.

handwriting n.
- 笔迹,手迹 writing, script, hand, fist, penmanship, calligraphy.

handy adj.
- 手边的,便利的 available, to hand, ready, at hand, near, accessible, convenient, practical, useful, helpful.
- 熟练的 skilful, proficient, expert, skilled, clever, practical.

hang v.
- 悬挂 suspend, dangle, swing, drape, drop, flop, droop, sag, trail.
- 固定 fasten, attach, fix, stick.
- 悬浮 float, drift, hover, linger, remain, cling.

hang about
- 闲荡,游逛 hang around, linger, loiter, dawdle, waste time, associate, with, frequent, haunt.

hang back
- 犹豫 hold back, demur, hesitate, shy away, recoil.

hang on
- 坚忍 wait, hold on, remain, hold out, endure, continue, carry on, persevere, persist.
- 紧握 grip, grasp, hold fast.
- 以……而定 depend on, hinge on, turn on.

hanger-on n.
- 跟班 follower, minion, lackey, toady, sycophant, parasite, sponger, dependant.

hang-up n.
- 困难 inhibition, difficulty, problem, obsession, preoccupation, thing, block, mental, block.

hanker for
- 希望 hanker after, crave, hunger for, thirst for, want, wish for, desire, covet, yearn for, long for, pine for, itch for.

hankering n.
- 渴望的 craving, hunger, thirst, wish, desire, yearning, longing, itch, urge.

happen v.
- 发生 occur, take place, arise,

crop up, develop, materialize, come about, result, ensue, follow, turn out, transpire.

happening *n.*

☞发生之事 occurrence, phenomenon, event, incident, episode, occasion, adventure, experience, accident, chance, circumstance, case, affair.

happiness *n.*

☞高兴,快乐 joy, joyfulness, gladness, cheerfulness, contentment, pleasure, delight, glee, elation, bliss, ecstasy, euphoria.

happy *adj.*

☞高兴的 joyful, jolly, merry, cheerful, glad, pleased, delighted, thrilled, elated, satisfied, content, contented.

☞幸运的 lucky, fortunate, felicitous, favourable, appropriate, apt, fitting.

harass *v.*

☞使……困扰,不断侵扰 pester, badger, harry, plague, torment, persecute, exasperate, vex, annoy, irritate, bother, disturb, hassle, trouble, worry, stress, tire, wear out, exhaust, fatigue.

harbour *n.*

☞港口 port, dock, quay, wharf, marina, mooring, anchorage, haven, shelter.

v.

☞隐匿 hide, conceal, protect, shelter.

☞心怀 hold, retain, cling to, entertain, foster, nurse, nurture, cherish, believe, imagine.

hard *adj.*

☞硬的,坚硬的 solid, firm, unyielding, tough, strong, dense, impenetrable, stiff, rigid, inflexible.

☞困难的,复杂的 difficult, arduous, strenuous, laborious, tiring, exhausting, backbreaking, complex, complicated, involved, knotty, baffling, puzzling, perplexing.

☞艰苦的,艰难的 harsh, severe, strict, callous, unfeeling, unsympathetic, cruel, pitiless, merciless, ruthless, unrelenting, distressing, painful, unpleasant.

adv.

☞努力地,猛烈地 industriously, diligently, assiduously, doggedly, steadily, laboriously, strenuously, earnestly, keenly, intently, strongly, violently, intensely, energetically, vigorously.

hard up

☞缺少 poor, broke, penniless, impoverished, in the red, bankrupt, bust, short, lacking.

harden *v.*

☞使变硬,坚固 solidify, set, freeze, bake, stiffen, strengthen, reinforce, fortify, buttress, brace, steel, nerve, toughen, season, accustom, train.

hard-headed *adj.*

☞冷静的,脚踏实地的 shrewd, astute, businesslike, level-headed, clear thinking, sensible, realistic, pragmatic, practical, hard-boiled, tough, unsentimental.

hard-hearted adj.
☞ 冷酷的,无感觉的 callous, unfeeling, cold, hard, stony, heartless, unsympathetic, cruel, inhuman, pitiless, merciless.

hardly adv.
☞ 仅,才,几乎不 barely, scarcely, just, only just, not quite, not at all, by no means.

hardship n.
☞ 苦难,困苦 misfortune, adversity, trouble, difficulty, affliction, distress, suffering, trial, tribulation, want, need, privation, austerity, poverty, destitution, misery.

hard-working adj.
☞ 努力工作的,勤勉的 industrious, diligent, assiduous, conscientious, zealous, busy, energetic.

hardy adj.
☞ 强壮的,耐劳的 strong, tough, sturdy, robust, vigorous, fit, sound, healthy.

harm n.
☞ 损害,危害 damage, loss, injury, hurt, detriment, ill, misfortune, wrong, abuse.
v.
☞ 伤害,危害 damage, impair, blemish, spoil, mar, ruin, hurt, injure, wound, ill-treat, maltreat, abuse, misuse.

harmful adj.
☞ 有害的,有毒的 damaging, detrimental, pernicious, noxious, unhealthy, unwholesome, injurious, dangerous, hazardous, poisonous, toxic, destructive.

harmless adj.
☞ 无害的 safe, innocuous, nontoxic, inoffensive, gentle, innocent.

harmonious adj.
☞ 和谐的 melodious, tuneful, musical, sweet-sounding.
☞ 协调的 matching, co-ordinated, balanced, compatible, like-minded, agreeable, cordial, amicable, friendly, sympathetic.

harmonize v.
☞ 和谐,协调 match, co-ordinate, balance, fit in, suit, tone, blend, correspond, agree, reconcile, accommodate, adapt, arrange, compose.

harmony n.
☞ 和谐 tunefulness, tune, melody, euphony.
☞ 和睦 agreement, unanimity, accord, concord, unity, compatibility, like-mindedness, peace, goodwill, rapport, sympathy, understanding, amicability, friendliness, co-operation, co-ordination, balance, symmetry, correspondence, conformity.

harvest n.
☞ 收获季节,收获 harvest-time, ingathering, reaping, collection.
☞ 成果 crop, yield, return, produce, fruits, result, consequence.
v.
☞ 收获,收割 reap, mow, pick, gather, collect, accumulate, amass.

haste n.

☞ 匆忙,急速 hurry, rush, hustle, bustle, speed, velocity, rapidity, swiftness, quickness, briskness, urgency, rashness, recklessness, impetuosity.

hasten v.
☞ 赶快,催促 hurry, rush, make haste, run, sprint, dash, tear, race, fly, bolt, accelerate, speed (up), quicken, expedite, dispatch, precipitate, urge, press, advance, step up.

hasty adj.
☞ 仓促的,匆忙的 hurried, rushed, impatient, headlong, rash, reckless, heedless, thoughtless, impetuous, impulsive, hot-headed, fast, quick, rapid, swift, speedy, brisk, prompt, short, brief, cursory.

hate v.
☞ 不喜欢,恨 dislike, despise, detest, loathe, abhor, abominate, execrate.
n.
☞ 憎恨,恨 hatred, aversion, dislike, loathing, abhorrence, abomination.

hatred n.
☞ 仇恨,敌意 hate, aversion, dislike, detestation, loathing, repugnance, revulsion, abhorrence, abomination, animosity, ill-will, antagonism, hostility, enmity, antipathy.

haughty adj.
☞ 傲慢的 lofty, imperious, high and mighty, supercilious, cavalier, snooty, contemptuous, disdainful, scornful, superior, snobbish, arrogant, proud, stuck-up, conceited.

haul v.
☞ 抢走,运送 pull, heave, tug, draw, tow, drag, trail, move, transport, convey, carry, cart, lug, hump.
n.
☞ 收获物,战利品 loot, booty, plunder, swag, spoils, takings, gain, yield, find.

haunt v.
☞ 出没,常到 frequent, patronize, visit.
☞ 折磨,困扰 plague, torment, trouble, disturb, recur, prey on, beset, obsess, possess.
n.
☞ 出没之地 resort, hangout, stamping-ground, den, meeting-place, rendezvous.

haunting adj.
☞ 不易忘怀的 memorable, unforgettable, persistent, recurrent, evocative, nostalgic, poignant.

have v.
☞ 有,占有 own, possess, get, obtain, gain, acquire, procure, secure, receive, accept, keep, hold.
☞ 经历,感觉 feel, experience, enjoy, suffer, undergo, endure, put up with.
☞ 包括,包含 contain, include, comprise, incorporate, consist of.
☞ 养,生 give birth to, bear.

have to
☞ 不得不,必须 must, be forced to, be compelled to, be obliged to, be required, ought, should.

havoc n.
- 混乱, 破坏 chaos, confusion, disorder, disruption, damage, destruction, ruin, wreck, rack and ruin, devastation, waste, desolation.

haze n.
- 雾 mist, fog, cloud, steam, vapour, film, mistiness, smokiness, dimness, obscurity.

hazy adj.
- 雾蒙蒙的, 朦胧的 misty, foggy, smoky, clouded, cloudy, milky, fuzzy, blurred, ill-defined, veiled, obscure, dim, faint, unclear, indistinct, vague, indefinite, uncertain.

head n.
- 头脑, 头 skull, cranium, brain, mind, mentality, brains, intellect, intelligence, understanding, thought.
- 头顶, 顶峰 top, peak, summit, crown, tip, apex, height, climax, front, fore, lead.
- 首脑 leader, chief, captain, commander, boss, director, manager, superintendent, principal, head teacher, ruler.

adj.
- 领头的 leading, front, foremost, first, chief, main, prime, principal, top, highest, supreme, premier, dominant, pre-eminent.

v.
- 领导 lead, rule, govern, command, direct, manage, run, superintend, oversee, supervise, control, guide, steer.

head for
- 向……方向前进 make for, go towards, direct towards, aim for, point to, turn for, steer for.

head off
- 拦截, 防止 forestall, intercept, intervene, interpose, deflect, divert, fend off, ward off, avert, prevent, stop.

heading n.
- 标题, 题目 title, name, headline, rubric, caption, section, division, category, class.

headquarters n.
- 司令部, 指挥部 hq, base (camp), head office, nerve, centre.

heal v.
- 治愈, 愈合 cure, remedy, mend, restore, treat, soothe, salve, settle, reconcile, patch up.

health n.
- 健康, 卫生 fitness, constitution, form, shape, trim, fettle, condition, tone, state, healthiness, good condition, wellbeing, welfare, soundness, robustness, strength, vigour.

healthy adj.
- 健康的 well, fit, good, fine, in condition, in good, shape, in fine fettle, sound, sturdy, robust, strong, vigorous, hale and hearty, blooming, flourishing, thriving.
- 营养均衡的 wholesome, nutritious, nourishing, bracing, invigorating, healthful.

heap n.

☞ 堆,大量许多　pile, stack, mound, mountain, lot, mass, accumulation, collection, hoard, stockpile, store.
v.
☞ 堆,堆积,装满　pile, stack, mound, bank, build, amass, accumulate, collect, gather, hoard, stockpile, store, load, burden, shower, lavish.

hear v.
☞ 听,听到,得知　listen, catch, pick up, overhear, eavesdrop, heed, pay attention.
☞ 检查,审讯　judge, try, examine, investigate.

hearing n.
☞ 听力　earshot, sound, range, reach, ear, perception.
☞ 审讯　trial, inquiry, investigation, inquest, audition, interview, audience.

hearsay n.
☞ 道听途说,谣言　rumour, word of mouth, talk, gossip, tittle-tattle, report, buzz.

heart n.
☞ 心脏,心,内心　soul, mind, character, disposition, nature, temperament, feeling, emotion, sentiment, love, tenderness, compassion, sympathy, pity.
☞ 中心,要点　centre, middle, core, kernel, nucleus, nub, crux, essence.
☞ 勇气,决心　courage, bravery, boldness, spirit, resolution, determination.

by heart
☞ 逐字的,用心的　by rote, parrot-fashion, pat, off pat, word for word, verbatim.

heartbreaking adj.
☞ 令人心碎的,令人伤心的　distressing, sad, tragic, harrowing, heart-rending, pitiful, agonizing, grievous, bitter, disappointing.

heartbroken adj.
☞ 心碎的,伤心的　broken-hearted, desolate, sad, miserable, dejected, despondent, downcast, crestfallen, disappointed, dispirited, grieved, crushed.

heartless adj.
☞ 无情的,残酷的　unfeeling, uncaring, cold, hard, hard-hearted, callous, unkind, cruel, inhuman, brutal, pitiless, merciless.

heat n.
☞ 热量　1 hotness, warmth, sultriness, closeness, high temperature, fever.
☞ 热烈,激烈　ardour, fervour, fieriness, passion, intensity, vehemence, fury, excitement, impetuosity, earnestness, zeal.
v.
☞ 把……加热,变热　warm, boil, toast, cook, bake, roast, reheat, warm up, inflame, excite, animate, rouse, stimulate, flush, glow.

heated adj.
☞ 激烈的　angry, furious, raging, passionate, fiery, stormy, tempestuous, bitter, fierce, intense, vehement, violent, frenzied.

heaven n.
☞ 天空,天　sky, firmament,

next world, hereafter, after-life, paradise, utopia, ecstasy, rapture, bliss, happiness, joy.

heavenly adj.
- 美好的 blissful, wonderful, glorious, beautiful, lovely, delightful, out of this world.
- 天空的,天的 celestial, unearthly, supernatural, spiritual, divine, godlike, angelic, immortal, sublime, blessed.

heavy adj.
- 重的,稠而粘的 weighty, hefty, ponderous, burdensome, massive, large, bulky, solid, dense, stodgy.
- 繁重的,大量的 hard, difficult, tough, arduous, laborious, strenuous, demanding, taxing, harsh, severe.

hedge n.
- 树篱,篱笆 hedgerow, screen, windbreak, barrier, fence, dike, boundary.

v.
- (用树篱)围住 surround, enclose, hem in, confine, restrict, fortify, guard, shield, protect, safeguard, cover.
- 避免直接回答 stall, temporize, equivocate, dodge, sidestep, evade, duck.

heed v.
- 留心,注意 listen, pay attention, mind, note, regard, observe, follow, obey.

height n.
- 高度,高处 highness, altitude, elevation, tallness, loftiness, stature.
- 顶点,离地 top, summit, peak, pinnacle, apex, crest, crown, zenith, apogee, culmination, climax, extremity, maximum, limit, ceiling.

heighten v.
- 增长,提高,加高 raise, elevate, increase, add to, magnify, intensify, strengthen, sharpen, improve, enhance.

hell n.
- 痛苦 suffering, anguish, agony, torment, ordeal, nightmare, misery.
- 地狱 underworld, hades, inferno, lower regions, nether world, abyss.

help v.
- 帮助 aid, assist, lend a hand, serve, be of use, collaborate, co-operate, back, stand by, support.
- 援助,促进 improve, ameliorate, relieve, alleviate, mitigate, ease, facilitate.

n.
- 帮助,支持 aid, assistance, collaboration, co-operation, support, advice, guidance, service, use, utility, avail, benefit.

helper n.
- 助手,协助者 assistant, deputy, auxiliary, subsidiary, attendant, right-hand man, PA, mate, partner, associate, colleague, collaborator, accomplice, ally, supporter, second.

helpful adj.
- 有用的,有益的 useful, practical, constructive, worthwhile, valuable, beneficial,

advantageous.
☞ 有帮助的　co-operative, obliging, neighbourly, friendly, caring, considerate, kind, sympathetic, supportive.

helping *n.*
☞ 支援,援助　serving, portion, share, ration, amount, plateful, piece, dollop.

helpless *adj.*
☞ 无助的,没用的　weak, feeble, powerless, dependent, vulnerable, exposed, unprotected, defenceless, abandoned, friendless, destitute, forlorn, incapable, incompetent, infirm, disabled, paralysed.

hem *n.*
☞ 边　edge, border, margin, fringe, trimming.

hem in
☞ 围住,包围　surround, enclose, box in, confine, restrict.

henpecked *adj.*
☞ 惧内的　dominated, subjugated, browbeaten, bullied, intimidated, meek, timid.

herald *n.*
☞ 通报者,使者　messenger, courier, harbinger, forerunner, precursor, omen, token, signal, sign, indication.
v.
☞ 预告　announce, proclaim, broadcast, advertise, publicize, trumpet, pave the way, precede, usher in, show, indicate, promise.

herd *n.*
☞ 群,兽群,牛群　drove, flock, swarm, pack, press, crush, mass, horde, throng, multitude, crowd, mob, the masses, rabble.
v.
☞ 集群　flock, congregate, gather, collect, assemble, rally.
☞ 带领　lead, guide, shepherd, round up, drive, force.

heresy *n.*
☞ 异教,异论　heterodoxy, unorthodoxy, free-thinking, apostasy, dissidence, schism, blasphemy.

heretic *n.*
☞ 异教者,异端者　free-thinker, nonconformist, apostate, dissident, dissenter, revisionist, separatist, schismatic, sectarian, renegade.

heretical *adj.*
☞ 异教的,异端的　heterodox, unorthodox, free-thinking, rationalistic, schismatic, impious, irreverent, iconoclastic, blasphemous.

heritage *n.*
☞ 遗产　inheritance, legacy, bequest, endowment, lot, portion, share, birthright, due.
☞ 传统　history, past, tradition, culture.

hermit *n.*
☞ 隐士　recluse, solitary, monk, ascetic, anchorite.

hero *n.*
☞ 英雄,勇士　protagonist, lead, celebrity, star, superstar, idol, paragon, goody, champion, conqueror.

heroic *adj.*

☞ 英雄的,英勇的 brave, courageous, fearless, dauntless, undaunted, lion-hearted, stout-hearted, valiant, bold, daring, intrepid, adventurous, gallant, chivalrous, noble, selfless.

heroism n.
☞ 英雄主义 bravery, courage, valour, boldness, daring, intrepidity, gallantry, prowess, selflessness.

hesitant adj.
☞ 犹豫的 hesitating, reluctant, half-hearted, uncertain, unsure, indecisive, irresolute, vacillating, wavering, tentative, wary, shy, timid, halting, stammering, stuttering.

hesitate v.
☞ 犹豫,踌躇 pause, delay, wait, by reluctant, be unwilling, think twice, hold back, shrink from, scruple, boggle, demur, vacillate, waver, be uncertain, dither, shilly-shally, falter, stumble, halt, stammer, stutter.

hesitation n.
☞ 犹豫,迟疑,含糊 pause, delay, reluctance, unwillingness, hesitance, scruple(s), qualm(s), misgivings, doubt, second thoughts, vacillation, uncertainty, indecision, irresolution, faltering, stumbling, stammering, stuttering.

hew v.
☞ 砍,伐,砍成 cut, fell, axe, lop, chop, hack, sever, split, carve, sculpt, sculpture, fashion, model, form, shape, make.

heyday n.
☞ 全盛期 peak, prime, flush, bloom, flowering, golden age, boom time.

hidden adj.
☞ 隐藏的 concealed, covered, shrouded, veiled, disguised, camouflaged, unseen, secret.
☞ 秘密的,模糊的 obscure, dark, occult, secret, covert, close, cryptic, mysterious, abstruse, mystical, latent, ulterior.

hide¹ v.
☞ 隐藏,潜伏 conceal, cover, cloak, shroud, veil, screen, mask, disguise, camouflage, obscure, shadow, eclipse, bury, stash, secrete, withhold, keep dark, suppress.
☞ 躲藏,隐瞒 take cover, shelter, lie low, go to ground, hole up.

hide² n.
☞ 牛皮,兽皮 skin, pelt, fell, fur, leather.

hiding¹ n.
☞ 鞭打 beating, flogging, whipping, caning, spanking, thrashing, walloping.

hiding² n.
☞ 隐匿 concealment, cover, veiling, screening, disguise, camouflage.

hiding-place n.
☞ 隐藏处 hide-away, hideout, lair, den, hole, hide, cover, refuge, haven, sanctuary, retreat.

hierarchy n.

统治集团,等级制度 pecking order, ranking, grading, scale, series, ladder, echelons, strata.

high adj.
- 高,高的 tall, lofty, elevated, soaring, towering.
- 高度的,强烈的 great, strong, intense, extreme.
- 高级的,重要的 important, influential, powerful, eminent, distinguished, prominent, chief, leading, senior.
- 尖锐的,极度的 high-pitched, soprano, treble, sharp, shrill, piercing.
- 昂贵的 expensive, dear, costly, exorbitant, excessive.

high-class adj.
- 上层的 upper-class, posh, classy, top-class, top flight, high-quality, quality, de luxe, superior, excellent, first-rate, choice, select, exclusive.

highlight n.
- 最精彩部分,最显著部分 high point, high spot, peak, climax, best, cream.

v.
- 使显著,使精彩加强 underline, emphasize, stress, accentuate, play up, point up, spotlight, illuminate, show up, set off, focus on, feature.

highly adv.
- 高度地,非常 very, greatly, considerably, decidedly, extremely, immensely, tremendously, exceptionally, extraordinarily, enthusiastically, warmly, well.

hike v.
- 徒步,旅行 ramble, walk, trek, tramp, trudge, plod.

n.
- 远足 ramble, walk, trek, tramp, march.

hill n.
- 小山 knoll, mound, prominence, eminence, elevation, foothill, down, fell, mountain, height.

hinder v.
- 妨碍,阻碍 hamper, obstruct, impede, encumber, handicap, hamstring, hold up, delay, retard, slow down, hold back, check, curb, stop, prevent, frustrate, thwart, oppose.

hindrance n.
- 阻止,妨碍 obstruction, impediment, handicap, encumbrance, obstacle, stumbling-block, barrier, bar, check, restraint, restriction, barrier, bar, check, restraint, restriction, limitation, difficulty, drag, snag, hitch, drawback, disadvantage, inconvenience, deterrent.

hint n.
- 提示,显示 tip, advice, suggestion, help, clue, inkling, suspicion, tip-off, reminder, indication, sign, pointer, mention, allusion, intimation, insinuation, implication, innuendo.
- 暗示 touch, trace, tinge, taste, dash, soupcon, speck.

v.
- 提示,暗示,显示 suggest, prompt, tip off, indicate, imply, insinuate, intimate,

allude, mention.

hire v.
☞ 雇用,租用 rent, let, lease, charter, commission, book, reserve, employ, take on, sign up, engage, appoint, retain.

n.
☞ 租金,工钱 rent, rental, fee, charge, cost, price.

hiss v.
☞ 嘶嘶声 whistle, shrill, whizz, sizzle.
☞ 嘲弄 jeer, mock, ridicule, deride, boo, hoot.

historic adj.
☞ 历史性的,有历史意义的 momentous, consequential, important, significant, epoch-making, notable, remarkable, outstanding, extraordinary, celebrated, renowned, famed, famous.

historical adj.
☞ 历史的,历史上的 real, actual, authentic, factual, documented, recorded, attested, verifiable.

history n.
☞ 历史 past, olden days, days of old, antiquity.
☞ 履历,经历 chronicle, record, annals, archives, chronology, account, narrative, story, tale, saga, biography, life, autobiography, memoirs.

hit v.
☞ 击,击中 1 strike, knock, tap, smack, slap, thrash, whack, bash, thump, clout, punch, belt, wallop, beat, batter.

☞ 撞碰,打击 bump, collide with, bang, crash, smash, damage, harm.

n.
☞ 打击,击中 stroke, shot, blow, knock, tap, slap, smack, bash, bump, collision, impact, crash, smash.
☞ 成功,完成 success, triumph.

hit back
☞ 反击 retaliate, reciprocate, counter-attack, strike back.

hit on
☞ 偶然发现,偶遇 chance on, stumble on, light on, discover, invent, realize, arrive at, guess.

hit out
☞ 打击 lash out, assail, attack, rail, denounce, condemn, criticize.

hobby n.
☞ 癖好,嗜好 pastime, diversion, recreation, relaxation, pursuit, sideline.

hold v.
☞ 抓住,拿住,握住 grip, grasp, clutch, clasp, embrace, have, own, possess, keep, retain.
☞ 举行 conduct, carry on, continue, call, summon, convene, assemble.
☞ 认为,把握 consider, regard, deem, judge, reckon, think, believe, maintain.
☞ 包含,容纳 bear, support, sustain, carry, comprise, contain, accommodate.
☞ 逮捕 imprison, detain, stop, arrest, check, curb, restrain.
☞ 占有 cling, stick, adhere, stay.

n.

☞ 抓住,握住 grip, grasp, clasp, embrace.

☞ 掌握,占有 influence, power, sway, mastery, dominance, authority, control, leverage.

hold back
☞ 阻止,阻碍 control, curb, check, restrain, suppress, stifle, retain, withhold, repress, inhibit.

☞ 犹豫 hesitate, delay, desist, refrain, shrink, refuse.

hold forth
☞ 高谈阔论 speak, talk, lecture, discourse, orate, preach, declaim.

hold off
☞ 保持距离 fend off, ward off, stave off, keep off, repel, rebuff.

☞ 推迟 put off, postpone, defer, delay, wait.

hold up
☞ 支持 support, sustain, brace, shore up, lift, raise.

☞ 阻滞,阻碍 delay, detain, retard, slow, hinder, impede.

hold with
☞ 同意,赞成 agree with, go along with, approve of, countenance, support, subscribe to, accept.

holder n.
☞ 所有人,持有人 bearer, owner, possessor, proprietor, keeper, custodian, occupant, incumbent.

☞ 容器 container, receptacle, case, housing, cover, sheath, rest, stand.

hold-up n.
☞ 阻滞,困难 delay, wait, hitch, setback, snag, difficulty, trouble, obstruction, stoppage, (traffic)jam, bottle-neck.

☞ 抢劫案 robbery.

hole n.
☞ 洞,穴,孔,窟窿 aperture, opening, orifice, pore, puncture, perforation, eyelet, tear, split, vent, outlet, shaft, slot, gap, breach, break, crack, fissure, fault, defect, flaw, dent, dimple, depression, hollow, cavity, crater, pit, excavation, cavern, cave, chamber, pocket, niche, recess, burrow, nest, lair, retreat.

holiday n.
☞ 假日,节日,休假 vacation, recess, leave, time off, day off, break, rest, half-term, bank-holiday, feast-day, festival, celebration, anniversary.

holiness n.
☞ 神圣,圣洁 sacredness, sanctity, spirituality, divinity, piety, devoutness, godliness, saintliness, virtuousness, righteousness, purity.

hollow adj.
☞ 中空的,空虚的 concave, indented, depressed, sunken, deep, cavernous, empty, vacant, unfilled.

☞ 人造的,空洞的,不真实的 false, artificial, deceptive, insincere, meaningless, empty, vain, futile, fruitless, worthless.

n.
☞ 洞,坑 hole, pit, well, cavity, crater, excavation, cavern, cave, depression, concavity,

basin, bowl, cup, dimple, dent, indentation, groove, channel, trough, valley.
v.
☞挖空,凿空 dig, excavate, burrow, tunnel, scoop, gouge, channel, groove, furrow, pit, dent, indent.

holy adj.
☞神圣的,圣洁的 scared, hallowed, consecrated, sanctified, dedicated, blessed, venerated, revered, spiritual, divine, evangelical.
☞宗教的,上帝的 pious, religious, devout, godly, god-fearing, saintly, virtuous, good, righteous, faithful, pure, perfect.

home n.
☞家,家乡 residence, domicile, dwelling-place, abode, base, house, pied-a-terre, hearth, fireside, birthplace, home town, home ground, territory, habitat, element.
adj.
☞家的,家乡的 domestic, household, family, internal, local, national, inland.

at home
☞在家,放松 comfortable, relaxed, at ease.
☞熟悉的 familiar, knowledgeable, experienced, skilled.

homeland n.
☞祖国,家乡 native land, native country, fatherland, motherland.

homeless adj.
☞无家可归的 itinerant, travelling, nomadic, wandering, vagrant, rootless, unsettled, displaced, dispossessed, evicted, exiled, outcast, abandoned, forsaken, destitute, down-and-outs, squatters.

homosexual n.
☞同性恋 gay, lesbian.

honest adj.
☞诚实的 truthful, sincere, frank, candid, blunt, outspoken, direct, straight, outright, forthright, straightforward, plain, simple, open, above-board, legitimate, legal, lawful, on the level, fair, just, impartial, objective.
☞有道德的,正直的 law-abiding, virtuous, upright, ethical, moral, high-minded, scrupulous, honourable, reputable, respectable, reliable, trustworthy, true, genuine, real.

honestly adv.
☞诚实地,正直地 truly, really, truthfully, sincerely, frankly, directly, outright, plainly, openly, legitimately, outright, plainly, openly, legitimately, legally, lawfully, on the level, fairly, justly, objectively, honourably, in good faith.

honesty n.
☞正直 truthfulness, sincerity, frankness, candour, bluntness, outspokenness, straightforwardness, plain-speaking, explicitness, openness, legitimacy, legality, equity, fairness, justness, objectivity, even-handedness.

☞ 诚实,实在,坦诚 virtue, uprightness, honour, integrity, morality, scrupulousness, trustworthiness, genuineness, veracity.

honour n.
☞ 荣誉,名誉 reputation, good name, repute, renown, distinction, esteem, regard, respect, credit, dignity, self-respect, pride, integrity, morality, decency, rectitude, probity.

☞ 光荣,赞誉 award, accolade, commendation, acknowledgement, recognition, tribute, privilege.

☞ 敬意 praise, acclaim, homage, admiration, reverence, worship, adoration.

v.
☞ 称赞,尊敬 praise, acclaim, exalt, glorify, pay homage to, decorate, crown, celebrate, commemorate, remember, admire, esteem, respect, revere, worship, prize, value.

☞ 遵守 keep, observe, respect, fulfil, carry out, discharge, execute, perform.

honourable adj.
☞ 光荣的,荣誉的 great, eminent, distinguished, renowned, respected, worthy, prestigious, trusty, reputable, respectable, virtuous.

hook n.
☞ 钩 crook, sickle, peg, barb, trap, snare, catch, fastener, clasp, hasp.

v.
☞ 弯曲 bend, crook, curve, curl.

☞ 钩住 catch, capture, bag, grab, trap, snare, ensnare, entangle.

hooligan n.
☞ 流氓,强盗 ruffian, rowdy, hoodlum, mobster, thug, tough, lout, vandal, delinquent.

hoop n.
☞ 圈 ring, circle, round, loop, wheel, band, girdle, circlet.

hop v.
☞ 跳跃 jump, leap, spring, bound, vault, skip, dance, prance, frisk, limp, hobble.

n.
☞ 跳跃 jump, leap, spring, bound, vault, bounce, step, skip, dance.

hope n.
☞ 希望,期望 hopefulness, optimism, ambition, aspiration, wish, desire, longing, dream, expectation, anticipation, prospect, promise, belief, confidence, assurance, conviction, faith.

v.
☞ 希望,愿望 aspire, wish, desire, long, expect, await, look forward, anticipate, contemplate, foresee, believe, trust, rely, reckon on, assume.

hopeful adj.
☞ 有信心的,怀有希望的 optimistic, bullish, confident, assured, expectant, sanguine, cheerful, buoyant.

☞ 有希望的 encouraging, heartening, reassuring, favourable, auspicious, promising rosy, bright.

hopeless adj.
☞ 悲观的,无希望的 pessimistic, defeatist, negative, despairing, demoralized, downhearted, dejected, despondent, forlorn, wretched.
☞ 绝症,不可救药的 unattainable, unachievable, impracticable, impossible, vain, foolish, futile, useless, pointless, worthless, poor, lost, irremediable, irreparable, incurable.

horizon n.
☞ 地平线 skyline, vista, prospect, compass, range, scope, perspective.

horrible adj.
☞ 可怕的,讨厌的 unpleasant, disagreeable, nasty, unkind, horrid, disgusting, revolting, offensive, repulsive, hideous, grim, ghastly, awful, dreadful, frightful, fearful, terrible, abominable, shocking, appalling, horrific.

horrific adj.
☞ 可怕的 horrifying, shocking, appalling, awful, dreadful, ghastly, gruesome, terrifying, frightening, scary, harrowing.

horrify v.
☞ 使……恐惧 shock, outrage, scandalize, appal, disgust, sicken, dismay, alarm, startle, scare, frighten, terrify.

horror n.
☞ 战栗 shock, outrage, disgust, revulsion, repugnance, abhorrence, loathing, dismay, consternation, alarm, fright, fear, terror, panic, dread, apprehension.
☞ 可怕 ghastliness, awfulness, frightfulness, hideousness.

horseman, horsewoman n.
☞ 骑手 equestrian, rider, jockey, cavalryman, hussar.

hospitable adj.
☞ 好客的 friendly, sociable, welcoming, receptive, cordial, amicable, congenial, convivial, genial, kind, gracious, generous, liberal.

hospitality n.
☞ 好客,殷勤 friendliness, sociability, welcome, accommodation, entertainment, conviviality, warmth, cheer, generosity, open-handedness.

host¹ n.
☞ 节目主持人 compe(gr)re, master of ceremonies, presenter, announcer, anchorman, anchorwoman, linkman.
☞ 地主,主人,老板 publican, innkeeper, landlord, proprietor.
v.
☞ 主持 present, introduce, compere.

host² n.
☞ 群,批 multitude, myriad, array, army, horde, crowd, throng, swarm, pack, band.

hostage n.
☞ 人质 prisoner, captive, pawn, surety, security, pledge.

hostel n.
☞ 旅店,招待所 youth hostel, residence, boarding-house, guest-house, hotel, inn.

hostile adj.

☞ 敌意的，敌方的 belligerent, warlike, ill-disposed, unsympathetic, unfriendly, inhospitable, inimical, antagonistic, opposed, adverse, unfavourable, contrary, opposite.

hostilities n.
☞ 战事行动 war, warfare, battle, fighting, conflict, strife, bloodshed.

hostility n.
☞ 敌意，进攻 opposition, aggression, belligerence, enmity, estrangement, antagonism, animosity, ill-will, malice, resentment, hate, hatred, dislike, aversion, abhorrence.

hot adj.
☞ 热的，炎热的 warm, heated, fiery, burning, scalding, blistering, scorching, roasting, baking, boiling, steaming, sizzling, sweltering, sultry, torrid, tropical.
☞ 辣的，激烈的 spicy, peppery, piquant, sharp, pungent, strong.

hotel n.
☞ 旅馆 boarding-house, guest-house, pension, motel, inn, public house, pub, hostel.

hound v.
☞ 追猎，紧追 chase, pursue, hunt (down), drive, goad, prod, chivvy, nag, pester, badger, harry, harass, persecute.

house n.
☞ 房屋，住宅 building, dwelling, residence, home.
☞ 家庭 dynasty, family, clan, tribe.
v.
☞ 留宿 lodge, quarter, billet, board, accommodate, put up, take in, shelter, harbour.
☞ 藏有 hold, contain, protect, cover, sheathe, place, keep, store.

household n.
☞ 家务，家庭，住户 family, family circle, house, home, menage, establishment, set-up.
adj.
☞ 家庭的 domestic, home, family, ordinary, plain, everyday, common, familiar, well-known, established.

housing n.
☞ 住房，房屋 accommodation, houses, homes, dwellings, habitation, shelter.
☞ 住宅 casing, case, container, holder, covering, cover, sheath, protection.

hover v.
☞ 盘旋 hang, poise, float, drift, fly, flutter, flap.
☞ 徘徊，彷徨 pause, linger, hang about, hesitate, waver, fluctuate, seesaw.

however conj.
☞ 然而 nevertheless, nonetheless, still, yet, even so, notwithstanding, though, anyhow.

hue n.
☞ 色度 colour, shade, tint, dye, tinge, nuance, tone, complexion, aspect, light.

hug v.
☞ 搂,抱 embrace, cuddle, squeeze, enfold, hold, clasp, clutch, grip, cling to, enclose.
n.
☞ 紧抱,搂 embrace, cuddle, squeeze, clasp, hold, clinch.

huge adj.
☞ 大的,巨大的 immense, vast, enormous, massive, colossal, titanic, giant, gigantic, mammoth, monumental, tremendous, great, big, large, bulky, unwieldy.

hum v.
☞ 嗡嗡叫,哼 buzz, whirr, purr, drone, thrum, croon, sing, murmur, mumble, throb, pulse, vibrate.
n.
☞ 嗡嗡声 buzz, whirr, purring, drone, murmur, mumble, throb, pulsation, vibration.

human adj.
☞ 通人情的 mortal, fallible, susceptible, reasonable, rational.
☞ 人的 kind, considerate, understanding, humane, compassionate.
n.
☞ 人类 human being, mortal, homo sapiens, man, woman, child, person, individual, body, soul.

humane adj.
☞ 人道的 kind, compassionate, symthetic, understanding, kind-hearted, good-natured, gentle, tender, loving, mild, lenient, merciful, forgiving, forbearing, kindly, benevolent, charitable, humanitarian, good.

humanitarian adj.
☞ 人道主义的 benevolent, charitable, philanthropic, public-spirited, compassionate, humane, altruistic, unselfish.
n.
☞ 人道主义 philanthropist, benefactor, do-gooder, altruist.

humanity n.
☞ 人类 human race, humankind, mankind womankind, mortality, people.
☞ 人性,人情 humaneness, kindness, compassion, fellow-feeling, understanding, tenderness, benevolence, generosity, goodwill.

humanize v.
☞ 使……具有人的属性 domesticate, tame, civilize, cultivate, educate, enlighten, edify, improve, better, polish, refine.

humble adj.
☞ 恭顺的,谦卑的 1 meek, submissive, unassertive, self-effacing, polite, respectful, deferential, servile, subservient, sycophantic, obsequious.
☞ 低下的,卑贱的 lowly, low, mean, insignificant, unimportant, common, commonplace, ordinary, plain, simple, modest, unassuming, unpretentious, unostentatious, unostentatious.
v.
☞ 使……低下,使……耻辱 bring down, lower, bring low, abase, demean, sink, discredit, disgrace, shame, humiliate, mortify, chasten, crush,

deflate, subdue.

humid adj.
- 湿的 damp, moist, dank, clammy, sticky, muggy, sultry, steamy.

humiliate v.
- 使……丢脸,使羞辱 mortify, embarrass, confound, crush, break, deflate, chasten, shame, disgrace, discredit, degrade, demean, humble, bring low.

humiliation n.
- 羞辱 mortification, embarrassment, shame, disgrace, dishonour, ignominy, abasement, deflation, put-down, snub, rebuff, affront.

humility n.
- 谦逊 meekness, submissiveness, deference, self-abasement, servility, humbleness, lowliness, modesty, unpretentiousness.

humorist n.
- 谈话幽默者 wit, satirist, comedian, comic, joker, wag, jester, clown.

humorous adj.
- 幽默的 funny, amusing, comic, entertaining, witty, satirical, jocular, facetious, playful, waggish, droll, whimsical, comical, farcical, zany, ludicrous, absurd, hilarious, side-splitting.

humour n.
- 幽默 wit, drollery, jokes, jesting, badinage, repartee, facetiousness, satire, comedy, farce, fun, amusement.
- 心情 mood, temper, frame of mind, spirits, disposition, temperament.

v.
- 迁就,使满足 go along with, comply with, accommodate, gratify, indulge, pamper, spoil, favour, please, mollify, flatter.

humourless adj.
- 无幽默感 boring, tedious, dull, dry, solemn, serious, glum, morose.

hunger n.
- 饥饿 hungriness, emptiness, starvation, malnutrition, famine, appetite, ravenousness, voracity, greed, greediness.
- 渴望 desire, craving, longing, yearning, itch, thirst.

v.
- 渴望 stvrve, want, with, desire, crave, hanker, long, yearn, pine, ache, itch, thirst.

hungry adj.
- 饿的,饥饿的 starving, underfed, undernourished, peckish, empty, hollow, famished, ravenous, greedy.
- 渴望的 desirous, craving, longing, aching, thirsty, eager, avid.

hunt v.
- 打猎,狩猎 chase, pursue, hound, dog, stalk, track, trail.
- 寻找,搜索 seek, look for, search, scour, rummage, forage, investigate.

n.
- 搜索,寻找 chase, pursuit, search, quest, investigation.

hurried adj.
- 匆忙的,慌忙的 rushed, hectic, hasty, precipitate,

speedy, quick, swift, rapid, passing, brief, short, cursory, superficial, shallow, careless, slapdash.

hurry v.
☞ 赶紧,急赶 rush, dash, fly, get a move on, hasten, quicken, speed up, hustle, push.
n.
☞ 急忙,匆忙 rush, haste, quickness, speed, urgency, hustle, bustle, flurry, commotion.

hurt v.
☞ 疼痛 ache, pain, throb, sting.
☞ 伤害,损伤 injure, wound, maltreat, ill-treat, bruise, cut, burn, torture, maim, disable.
☞ 损害 damage, impair, harm, mar, spoil.
☞ 伤……感情 upset, sadden, grieve, distress, afflict, offend, annoy.
n.
☞ 损伤,伤害 pain, soreness, discomfort, suffering, injury, wound, damage, harm, distress, sorrow.
adj.
☞ 受伤的 injured, wounded, bruised, grazed, cut, scarred, maimed.
☞ 伤心的 upset, sad, saddened, distressed, aggrieved, annoyed, offended, affronted.

hurtful adj.
☞ 造成伤害的 upsetting, wounding, vicious, cruel, mean, unkind, nasty, malicious, spiteful, catty, derogatory, scathing, cutting.
☞ 有害的 harmful, damaging, injurious, pernicious, destructive.

husband n.
☞ 丈夫 spouse, partner, mate, better half, hubby, groom, married man.

hush v.
☞ 沉默,静寂 quieten, silence, still, settle, compose, calm, soothe, subdue.
n.
☞ 沉默 quietness, silence, peace, stillness, repose, calm, calmness, tranquillity, serenity.
interj.
☞ 嘘,别响 quiet, hold your tongue, shut up, not another word.

hush up
☞ 秘而不宣 keep dark, suppress, conceal, cover up, stifle, gag.

hut n.
☞ 小屋,棚屋 cabin, shack, shanty, booth, shed, lean-to, shelter, den.

hypocrisy n.
☞ 伪善,虚伪 insincerity, double-talk, double-dealing, falsity, deceit, deception, pretence.

hypocritical adj.
☞ 伪善的,虚伪的 insincere, two-faced, self-righteous, double-dealing, false, hollow, deceptive, spurious, deceitful, dissembling, pharisaic(a).

hypothesis n.
☞ 假说,假设 theory, thesis, premise, postulate, proposition,

supposition, conjecture, speculation.

hypothetical adj.
☞ 假定的,假设的 theoretical, imaginary, supposed, assumed, proposed, conjectural, speculative.

hysteria n.
☞ 歇斯底里症 agitation, frenzy, panic, hysterics, neurosis, mania, madness.

hysterical adj.
☞ 歇斯底里症引起的 frantic, frenzied, berserk, uncontrollable, mad, raving, crazed, demented, overwrought, neurotic.
☞ 歇斯底里的 hilarious, uproarious, side-splitt, spriceless, rich.

I

ice n.
☞ 冰 frost, rime, icicle, glacier, iciness, frostiness, coldness, chill.
v.
☞ 冷冻 freeze, refrigerate, chill, cool, frost, glaze.

icy adj.
☞ 冰的,冷的 ice-cold, arctic, polar, glacial, freezing, frozen, raw, bitter, biting, cold, chill, chilly.
☞ 冰的,结冰的 frosty, slippery, glassy, frozen, icebound, frostbound.
☞ 冷淡的 hostile, cold, stony, cool, indifferent, aloof, distant, formal.

idea n.
☞ 意见,看法 thought, concept, notion, theory, hypothesis, guess, conjecture, belief, opinion, view, viewpoint, judgement, conception, vision, image, impression, perception, interpretation, understanding, inkling, suspicion, clue.
☞ 念头,想法 brainwave, suggestion, proposal, proposition, recommendation, plan, scheme, point, object.

ideal n.
☞ 理想 perfection, epitome, acme, paragon, exemplar, example, model, pattern, archetype, prototype, type, image, criterion, standard.
adj.
☞ 完美的,理想的 perfect, dream, utopian, best, optimum, optimal, supreme, highest, model, archetypal.
☞ 唯心的,空想的 unreal, imaginary, theoretical, hypothetical, unattainable, impractical, idealistic.

idealist n.
☞ 理想主义者 perfectionist, romantic, visionary, dreamer, optimist.

identical adj.
☞ 完全相同的,同样的 same, self-same, indistinguishable, interchangeable, twin,

duplicate, like, alike, corresponding, matching, equal, equivalent.

identification n.
- 认出,识别 recognition, detection, diagnosis, naming, labelling, classification.
- 等同,同一,迭合 empathy, association, involvement, rapport, relationship, sympathy, fellow-feeling.
- 身份,鉴别 identity card, documents, papers, credentials.

identity n.
- 本身,本体 individuality, particularity, singularity, uniqueness, self, personality, character, existence.
- 同一,完全相同 sameness, likeness.

ideology n.
- 思想方式,意识形态 philosophy, world-view, ideas, principles, tenets, doctrine(s), convictions, belief(s), faith, creed, dogma.

idiom n.
- 成语,惯用语 phrase, expression, colloquialism, language, turn of phrase, phraseology, style, usage, jargon, vernacular.

idiot n.
- 白痴 fool, blockhead, ass, nitwit, dimwit, halfwit, imbecile, moron, cretin, simpleton, dunce, ignoramus.

idle adj.
- 未用的,无工作的 inactive, inoperative, unused, unoccupied, unemployed, jobless, redundant.
- 懒惰的,不愿工作的 lazy, work-shy, indolent.
- 无价值的,无用的 empty, trivial, casual, futile, vain, pointless, unproductive.

v.
- 懒散 do nothing, laze, lounge, take it easy, kill time, potter, loiter, dawdle, fritter, waste, loaf, slack, skive.

ignite v.
- 点燃 set fire to, set alight, catch fire, flare up, burn, conflagrate, fire, kindle, touch off, spark off.

ignorance n.
- 不知,无知 unintelligence, illiteracy, unawareness, unconsciousness, oblivion, unfamiliarty, inexperience, innocence, naivety.

ignorant adj.
- 无知识的,不知道的 uneducated, illiterate, unread, untaught, untrained, inexperienced, stupid, clueless, uninitiated, unenlightened, uninformed, ill-informed, unwitting, unaware, unconscious, oblivious.

ignore v.
- 不理,忽视 disregard, take no notice of, shut one's eyes to, overlook, pass over, neglect, omit, reject, snub, cold-shoulder.

ill adj.
- 生病的 sick, poorly, unwell, indisposed, laid up, ailing, off-colour, out of sorts, under the weather, seedy, queasy,

☞ diseased, unhealthy, infirm, frail.
☞ 恶劣的,破的 bad, evil, damaging, harmful, injurious, detrimental, adverse, unfavourable, inauspicious, unpromising, sinister, ominous, threatening, unlucky, unfortunate, difficult, harsh, severe, unkind, unfriendly, antagonistic.

illegal adj.
☞ 不合法的,违法的 unlawful, illicit, criminal, wrong, forbidden, prohibited, banned, counter, black-market, unconstitutional, wrongful.

illegible adj.
☞ 难读的,无法辨认的 unreadable, indecipherable, scrawled, obscure, faint, indistinct.

illness n.
☞ 不健康,疾病 disease, disorder, complaint, ailment, sickness, ill health, ill-being, indisposition, infirmity, disability, affliction.

illogical adj.
☞ 不合理的,不合逻辑的 irrational, unreasonable, unscientific, invalid, unsound, faulty, fallacious, specious, sophistical, inconsistent, senseless, meaningless, absurd.

ill-treat v.
☞ 虐待 maltreat, abuse, injure, harm, damage, neglect, mistreat, mishandle, misuse, wrong, oppress.

illusion n.
☞ 幻想,错视 apparition, mirage, hallucination, figment, fantasy, fancy, delusion, misapprehension, misconception, error, fallacy.

illustrate v.
☞ 图解,说明 draw, sketch, depict, picture, show, exhibit, demonstrate, exemplify, explain, interpret, clarify, elucidate, illuminate, decorate, ornament, adorn.

illustration n.
☞ 插图,图解 picture, plate, half-tone, photograph, drawing, sketch, figure, representation, decoration.
☞ 例证 example, specimen, instance, case, analogy, demonstration, explanation, interpretation.

ill-will n.
☞ 敌意,怨恨 hostility, antagonism, bad blood, enmity, unfriendliness, malevolence, malice, spite, animosity, ill-feeling, resentment, hard feelings, grudge, dislike, aversion, hatred.

image n.
☞ 概念 idea, notion, concept, impression, perception.
☞ 像,肖像 representation, likeness, picture, portrait, icon, effigy, figure, statue, idol, reflection.

imagination n.
☞ 想象 imaginativeness, creativity, inventiveness, inspiration, insight, ingenuity, resourcefulness, enterprise, wit, vision, mind's eye, fancy,

illusion.

imaginative adj.
- 想象的,有想象力的 creative, inventive, innovative, original, inspired, visionary, ingenious, clever, resourceful, enterprising, fanciful, fantastic, vivid.

imagine v.
- 设想,想象 picture, visualize, envisage, conceive, fancy, fantasize, pretend, make believe, conjure up, dream up, think up, invent, devise, create, plan, project.
- 认为,认定 think, believe, judge, suppose, guess, conjecture, assume, take it, gather.

imbalance n.
- 不均匀,不公平 unevenness, inequality, disparity, disproportion, unfairness, partiality, bias.

imitate v.
- 仿做 copy, emulate, follow, ape, mimic, impersonate, take off, caricature, parody, send up, spoof, mock, parrot, repeat, echo, mirror, duplicate, reproduce, simulate, counterfeit, forge.

imitation n.
- 模仿,仿造 mimicry, impersonation, impression, take-off, caricature, parody, send-up, spoof, mockery, travesty.
- 仿造品,赝品 copy, duplicate, reproduction, replica, simulation, counterfeit, fake, forgery, sham, likeness, resemblance, reflection, dummy.

imitative adj.
- 模仿的,摹拟的 copying, mimicking, parrot-like, unoriginal, derivative, plagiarized, second-hand, simulated, mock.
- 仿制的 artificial, synthetic, man-made, ersatz, fake, phoney, mock, pseudo, reproduction, simulated, sham, dummy.

immeasurable adj.
- 不能衡量的 vast, immense, infinite, limitless, unlimited, boundless, unbounded, endless, bottomless, inexhaustible, incalculable, inestimable.

immediate adj.
- 立刻的,即时的 instant, instantaneous, direct, prompt, swift, current, present, existing, urgent, pressing.
- 直接的,最近的 nearest, next, adjacent, near, close, recent.

immediately adv.
- 马上,立刻 now, straight away, right away, at once, instantly, directly, forthwith, without delay, promptly, unhesitatingly.

immense adj.
- 巨大的 vast, great, huge, enormous, massive, giant, gigantic, tremendous, monumental.

immigrant n.
- 移民 incomer, settler, newcomer, alien.

immoral adj.
- 不朽的,永生的 unethical,

wrong, bad, sinful, evil, wicked, unscrupulous, unprinciple, dishonest, corrupt, depraved, degenerate, dissolute, lewd, indecent, pornographic, obscene, impure.

impact n.
☞ 影响,效果 effect, consequences, repercussions, impression, power, influence, significance, meaning.
☞ 撞击,碰撞 collision, crash, smash, bang, bump, blow, knock, contact, jolt, shock, brunt.

impartial adj.
☞ 公正的,无私的 objective, dispassionate, detached, disinterested, neutral, non-partisan, unbiased, unprejudiced, open-minded, fair, just, equitable, even-handed, equal.

impasse n.
☞ 死路,绝境 deadlock, stalemate, dead end, cul-de-sac, blind alley, halt, standstill.

impede v.
☞ 阻碍,妨碍 hinder, hamper, obstruct, block, clog, slow, retard, hold up, delay, check, curb, restrain, thwart, disrupt, stop, bar.

impediment n.
☞ 妨碍物 hindrance, obstacle, obstruction, barrier, bar, block, stumbling-block, snag, difficulty, handicap, check, curb, restraint, restriction.

impending adj.
☞ 逼近的,即将发生的 imminent, forthcoming, approaching, coming, close, near, looming, menacing, threatening.

imperfect adj.
☞ 不完善的,不完全的 faulty, flawed, defective, damaged, broken, chipped, deficient, incomplete.

imperial adj.
☞ 帝国的,皇帝的 sovereign, supreme, royal, regal, majestic, grand, magnificent, great, noble.

implement n.
☞ 工具 tool, instrument, utensil, gadget, device, appartus, appliance.
v.
☞ 行使 enforce, effect, bring about, carry out, execute, discharge, perform, do, fulfil, complete, accomplish, realize.

implication n.
☞ 含义,暗示 inference, insinuation, suggestion, meaning, significance, ramification.
☞ 牵连 involvement, entanglement, incrimination, connection, association.

implicit adj.
☞ 暗示的,含蓄的 implied, inferred, insinuated, indirect, unsaid, unspoken, tacit, understood.
☞ 不置疑的 unquestioning, utter, total, full, complete, absolute, unqualified, unreserved, wholehearted.

imply v.

☞ 暗示 suggest, insinuate, hint, intimate, mean, signify, point to, indicate, involve, require.

importance n.
☞ 重要,重大 momentousness, significance, consequence, substance, matter, concern, interest, usefulness, value, worth, weight, influence, mark, prominence, eminence, distinction, esteem, prestige, status, standing.

important adj.
☞ 重要的 momentous, noteworthy, significant, meaningful, relevant, material, salient, urgent, vital, essential, key, primary, major, substantial, valuable, seminal, weighty, serious, grave, far-reaching.
☞ 显著的,位尊的 leading, foremost, high-level, high-ranking, influential, powerful, pre-eminent, prominent, outstanding, eminent, noted.

impose v.
☞ 强使,加……于 introduce, institute, enforce, promulgate, exact, levy, set, fix, put, place, lay, inflict, burden, encumber, saddle.
☞ 介入,迫使 intrude, butt in, encroach, trespass, obtrude, force oneself, presume, take liberties.

imposing adj.
☞ 壮丽的,堂皇的 impressive, striking, grand, stately, majestic, dignified.

imposition n.
☞ 强加之事物 introduction, infliction, exaction, levying.
☞ 征税,课税 intrusion, encroachment, liberty, burden, constraint, charge, duty, task, punishment.

impossible adj.
☞ 不可能的 hopeless, impracticable, unworkable, unattainable, unachievable, unobtainable, insoluble, unreasonable, unacceptable, inconceivable, unthinkable, preposterous, absurd, ludicrous, ridiculous.

impress v.
☞ 影响,使……铭记 strike, move, touch, affect, influence, stir, inspire, excite.
☞ 压印,盖 stamp, imprint, mark, indent, instil, inculcate.

impression n.
☞ 观念,印象 feeling, awareness, consciousness, sense, illusion, idea, notion, opinion, belief, conviction, suspicion, hunch, memory, recollection.
☞ 印记 stamp, mark, print, dent, outline.
☞ 模仿 impersonation, imitation, take-off, parody, send-up.
☞ 影响 effect, impact, influence.

imprison v.
☞ 把……关进监狱 jail, incarcerate, intern, detain, send down, put away, lock up, cage, confine, shut in.

imprisonment n.
☞ 下狱 internment, detention, custody, confinement.

improve v.
☞ 提高,改善 better, ameliorate, enhance, polish, touch up, mend, rectify, correct, amend, reform, upgrade, increase, rise, pick up, develop, look up, advance, progress, get better, recover, recuperate, rally, perk up, mend one's ways, turn over a new leaf.

improvement n.
☞ 提高,改善 betterment, amelioration, enhancement, rectification, correction, amendment, reformation, increase, rise, upswing, gain, development, advance, progress, furtherance, recovery, rally.

impulse n.
☞ 冲击,冲动 urge, wish, desire, inclination, whim, notion, instinct, feeling, passion.
☞ 刺激 impetus, momentum, force, pressure, drive, thrust, push, incitement, stimulus, motive.

impulsive adj.
☞ 冲击的 impetuous, rash, reckless, hasty, quick, spontaneous, automatic, instinctive, intuitive.

impure adj.
☞ 脏的 unrefined, adulterated, diluted, contaminated, polluted, tainted, infected, corrupt, debased, unclean, dirty, foul.
☞ 猥亵的 obscene, indecent, immodest.

impurity n.
☞ 混杂物 adulteration, contamination, pollution, infection, corruption, dirtiness, contaminant, dirt, filth, foreign body, mark, spot.

inability n.
☞ 无能力 incapability, incapacity, powerlessness, impotence, inadequacy, weakness, handicap, disability.

inadequacy n.
☞ 不充足 insufficiency, lack, shortage, dearth, want, deficiency, scantiness, meagreness, defectiveness, ineffectiveness, inability, incompetence.
☞ fault, defect, imperfection, weakness, failing, shortcoming.

inadequate adj.
☞ 不充分的 insufficient, short, wanting, deficient, scanty, sparse, meagre, niggardly.
☞ 不适当的 incompetent, incapable, unequal, unqualified, ineffective, faulty, defective, imperfect, unsatisfactory.

incentive n.
☞ 刺激 bait, lure, enticement, carrot, reward, encouragement, inducement, reason, motive, impetus, spur, stimulus, motivation.

incident n.
☞ 事情 occurrence, happening, event, episode, adventure, affair, occasion, instance.
☞ 事件 confrontation, clash, fight, skirmish, commotion, disturbance, scene, upset, mishap.

incidental *adj.*
☞ 偶然的 accidental, chance, random, minor, non-essential, secondary, subordinate, subsidiary, ancillary, supplementary, accompanying, attendant, related, contributory.

incite *v.*
☞ 鼓动，激励 prompt, instigate, rouse, foment, stir up, whip up, work up, excite, animate, provoke, stimulate, spur, goad, impel, drive, urge, encourage, egg on.

incitement *n.*
☞ 鼓动，激励 prompting, instigation, agitation, provocation, spur, goad, impetus, stimulus, motivation, encouragement, inducement, incentive.

inclination *n.*
☞ 意愿 liking, fondness, taste, predilection, preference, partiality, bias, tendency, trend, disposition, propensity, leaning.
☞ 倾斜 angle, slope, gradient, incline, pitch, slant, tilt, bend, bow, nod.

incline *v.*
☞ 倾向，爱好 dispose, influence, persuade, affect, bias, prejudice.
☞ 倾斜 lean, slope, slant, tilt, tip, bend, bow, tend, veer.
n.
☞ 斜坡 slope, gradient, ramp, hill, rise, ascent, acclivity, dip, descent, declivity.

inclined *adj.*
☞ 喜爱的 liable, likely, given, apt, disposed, of a mind, willing.

include *v.*
☞ 包括 comprise, embody, comprehend, contain, enclose, embrace, encompass, cover, subsume, take in, add, allow for, take into account, involve, rope in.

inclusion *n.*
☞ 包括 incorporation, involvement, addition, insertion.

inclusive *adj.*
☞ 包含的 comprehensive, full, all-in, all-inclusive, all-embracing, blanket, across-the-board, general, catch-all, overall, sweeping.

incoherent *adj.*
☞ 语无伦次的，不连贯的 unintelligible, incomprehensible, inarticulate, rambling, stammering, stuttering, unconnected, disconnected, broken, garbled, scrambled, confused, muddled, jumbled, disordered.

income *n.*
☞ 收入 revenue, returns, proceeds, gains, profits, interest, takings, receipts, earnings, pay, salary, wages, means.

incoming *adj.*
☞ 进来的 arriving, entering, approaching, coming, homeward, returning, ensuing, succeeding, next, new.

incomparable *adj.*
☞ 不能比较的 matchless,

unmatched, unequalled, unparalleled, unrivalled, peerless, supreme, superlative, superb, brilliant.

incompatible adj.
☞ 不相容的 irreconcilable, contradictory, conflicting, at variance, inconsistent, clashing, mismatched, unsuited.

incompetent adj.
☞ 无能力的 incapable, unable, unfit, inefficient, inexpert, unskillful, bungling, stupid, useless, ineffective.

incomplete adj.
☞ 不完全的 deficient, lacking, short, unfinished, abridged, partial, part, fragmentary, broken, imperfect, defective.

inconvenience n.
☞ 不方便 awkwardness, difficulty, annoyance, nuisance, hindrance, drawback, bother, trouble, fuss, upset, disturbance, disruption.
v.
☞ 困扰 bother, disturb, disrupt, put out, trouble, upset, irk.

inconvenient adj.
☞ 烦扰的 awkward, ill-timed, untimely, inopportune, unsuitable, difficult, embarrassing, annoying, troublesome, unwieldy, unmanageable.

incorporate v.
☞ 结合 include, embody, contain, subsume, take in, absorb, assimilate, integrate, combine, unite, merge, blend, mix, fuse, coalesce, consolidate.

increase v.
☞ 增加 raise, boost, add to, improve, enhance, advance, step up, intensify, strengthen, heighten, grow, develop, build up, wax, enlarge, extend, prolong, expand, spread, swell, magnify, multiply, proliferate, rise, mount, soar, escalate.
n.
☞ 增加量 rise, surge, upsurge, upturn, gain, boost, addition, increment, advance, step-up, intensification, growth, development, enlargement, extension, expansion, spread, proliferation, escalation.

incredible adj.
☞ 难以相信的 unbelievable, improbable, implausible, far-fetched, preposterous, absurd, impossible, inconceivable, unthinkable, unimaginable, extraordinary, amazing, astonishing, astounding.

incur v.
☞ 招致 suffer, sustain, provoke, arouse, bring upon oneself, expose oneself to, meet with, run up, gain, earn.

indebted adj.
☞ 负债的,感激的 obliged, grateful, thankful.

indeed adv.
☞ 的确 really, actually, in fact, certainly, positively, truly, undeniably, undoubtedly, to be sure.

indefinite adj.
☞ 不确定的 unknown,

uncertain, unsettled, unresolved, undecided, undetermined, undefined, unspecified, unlimited, ill-defined, vague, indistinct, unclear, obscure, ambiguous, imprecise, inexact, loose, general.

indefinitely adv.
☞ 无限定地 for ever, eternally, endlessly, continually, ad infinitum.

independence n.
☞ 自治 autonomy, self-government, self-determination, self-rule, home rule, sovereignty, freedom, liberty, individualism, separation.

independent adj.
☞ 独立自主的 autonomouse, self-governing, self-determining, sovereign, absolute, non-aligned, neutral, impartial, unbiased.
☞ 独立的 free, liberated, unconstrained, individualistic, unconventional, self-sufficient, self-supporting, self-reliant, unaided.
☞ 个人的 individual, self-contained, separate, unconnected, unrelate.

index n.
☞ 索引 table, key, list, catalogue, directory, guide.
☞ 指示物 indicator, pointer, needle, hand, sign, token, mark, indication, clue.

indicate v.
☞ 指出 register, record, show, reveal, display, manifest, point to, designate, specify, point out, mark, signify, mean, denote, express, suggest, imply.

indication n.
☞ 指示 mark, sign, manifestation, evidence, symptom, signal, warning, omen, intimation, suggestion, hint, clue, note, explanation.

indicator n.
☞ 指示者 pointer, needle, marker, sign, symbol, token, signal, display, dial, gauge, meter, index, guide, signpost.

indifference n.
☞ 不感兴趣 apathy, unconcern, coldness, coolness, inattention, disregard, negligence, neutrality, disinterestedness.

indifferent adj.
☞ 漠不关心的 uninterested, unenthusiastic, unexcited, apathetic, unconcerned, unmoved, uncaring, unsympathetic, cold, cool, distant, aloof, detached, uninvolved, neutral, disinterested.
☞ 质量不高的 mediocre, average, middling, passable, moderate, fair, ordinary.

indirect adj.
☞ 间接的 roundabout, circuitous, wandering, rambling, winding, meandering, zigzag, tortuous.

indispensable adj.
☞ 不可缺少的 vital, essential, basic, key, crucial, imperative, required, requisite, needed, necessary.

individual *n.*
☞ 人 person, being, creature, party, body, soul, character, fellow.
adj.
☞ 个别的, 个人的 distinctive, characteristic, idiosyncratic, peculiar, singular, unique, exclusive, special, personal, own, proper, respective, several, separate, distinct, specific, personalized, particular, single.

individuality *n.*
☞ 个性 character, personality, distinctiveness, peculiarity, singularity, uniqueness, separateness, distinction.

induce *v.*
☞ 招致 cause, effect, bring about, occasion, give rise to, lead to, incite, instigate, prompt, provoke, produce, generate.
☞ 引诱 coax, prevail upon, encourage, press, persuade, talk into, move, influence, draw tempt.

inducement *n.*
☞ 诱因 lure, bait, attraction, enticement, encouragement, incentive, reward, spur, stimulus, motive, reason.

indulge *v.*
☞ 放纵 gratify, satisfy, humour, pander to, go along with, give in to, yield to, favour, pet, cosset, mollycoddle, pamper, spoil, treat, regale.

indulgence *n.*
☞ 沉溺 extravagance, luxury, excess, immoderation, intemperance, favour, tolerance.

indulgent *adj.*
☞ 纵容的 tolerant, easy-going, lenient, permissive, generous, liberal, kind, fond, tender, understanding, patient.

industrialist *n.*
☞ 实业家 manufacturer, producer, magnate, tycoon, baron, captain of industry, capitalist, financier.

industrious *adj.*
☞ 勤勉的 busy, productive, hard-working, diligent, assiduous, conscientious, zealous, active, energetic, tireless, persistent, persevering.

industry *n.*
☞ 工业, 产业 business, trade, commerce, manufacturing, production.
☞ 勤奋 industriousness, diligence, application, effort, labour, toil, persistence, perseverance, determination.

inevitable *adj.*
☞ 不可避免的 unavoidable, inescapable, necessary, definite, certain, sure, decreed, ordained, destined, fated, automatic, assured, fixed, unalterable, irrevocable, inexorable.

inexpensive *adj.*
☞ 廉价的 cheap, low-priced, reasonable, modest, bargain, budget, low-cost, economical.

infancy *n.*
☞ 幼年 babyhood, childhood,

youth.
初期
beginning, start, commencement, inception, outset, birth, dawn, genesis, emergence, origins, early stages.

infant n.
婴儿
baby, toddler, tot, child, babe, babe in arms.
adj.
新生的
newborn, baby, young, youthful, juvenile, immature, growing, developing, rudimentary, early, initial, new.

infer v.
推论
derive, extrapolate, deduce, conclude, assume, presume, surmise, gather, understand.

inference n.
推断,结论
deduction, conclusion, corollary, consequence, assumption, presumption, surmise, conjecture, extrapolation, construction, interpretation, reading.

inferior adj.
较低的,下级的
lower, lesser, minor, secondary, junior, subordinate, subsidiary, second-class, low, humble, menial.
劣等的
substandard, second-rate, mediocre, bad, poor, unsatisfactory, slipshod, shoddy.
n.
下级,部下
subordinate, junior, underling, minion, vassal, menial.

inferiority n.
下级
subordination, subservience, humbleness, lowliness, meanness, insignificance.
劣质
mediocrity, imperfection, inadequacy, slovenliness, shoddiness.

infinite adj.
无限的
limitless, unlimited, boundless, unbounded, endless, never-ending, inexhaustible, bottomless, innumerable, numberless, uncountable, countless, untold, incalculable, inestimable, immeasurable, unfathomable, vast, immense, enormous, huge, absolute, total.

infinity n.
无限
eternity, perpetuity, limitlessness, boundlessness, endlessness, inexhaustibility, countlessness, immeasurableness, vastness, immensity.

inflate v.
膨胀
blow up, pump up, blow out, puff out, swell, distend, bloat, expand, enlarge, increase, boost, exaggerate.

inflation n.
通货膨胀
expansion, increase, rise, escalation, hyprinflation.

inflexible adj.
坚定的
rigid, stiff, hard, solid, set, fixed, fast, immovable, firm, strict, stringent, unbending, unyielding, adamant, resolute,

relentless, implacable, uncompromising, stubborn, obstinate, intransigent, entrenched, dyed-in-the-wool.

influence n.
☞ 影响 power, sway, rule, authority, domination, mastery, hold, control, direction, guidance, bias, prejudice, pull, pressure, effect, impact, weight, importance, prestige, standing.
v.
☞ 影响,感化 dominate, control, manipulate, direct, guide, manoeuvre, change, alter, modify, affect, impress, move, stir, arouse, rouse, sway, persuade, induce, incite, instigate, prompt, motivate, dispose, incline, bias, prejudice, predispose.

influential adj.
☞ 有权势的 dominant, controlling, leading, authoritative, charismatic, persuasive, convincing, compelling, inspiring, moving, powerful, potent, effective, telling, strong, weighty, momentous, important, significant, instrumental, guiding.

influx n.
☞ 注入 inflow, inrush, invasion, arrival, stream, flow, rush, flood, inundation.

inform v.
☞ 报告 tell, advise, notify, communicate, impart, leak, tip off, acquaint, fill in, brief, instruct, enlighten, illuminate.

inform on
☞ 背叛 betray, incriminate, tell on, blab, denounce.

informal adj.
☞ 非正式的 unofficial, unceremonious, casual, relaxed, easy, free, natural, simple, unpretentious, familiar, colloquial.

information n.
☞ 通知报告 facts, data, input, gen, intelligence, news, report, bulletin, communique, message, word, advice, notice, briefing, instrouction, knowledge, dossier, database, databank, clues, evidence.

informative adj.
☞ 有教益的,增进知识的 educational, instructive, edifying, enlightening, illuminating, revealing, forthcoming, communicative, chatty, gossipy, newsy, helpful, useful, constructive.

informed adj.
☞ 熟悉的 familiar, conversant, acquainted, enlightened, briefed, primed, posted, up to date, abreast, au fait, in the know.
☞ 有见识的 well-informed, authoritative, expert, versed, well-read, erudite, learned, knowledgeable, well-researched.

ingredient n.
☞ 成份 constituent, element, factor, component, part.

inhabit v.
☞ 居住 live, dwell, reside, occupy, possess, colonize,

settle, people, populate, stay.

inhabitant n.
☞ 居民 resident, dweller, citizen, native, occupier, occupant, inmate, tenant, lodger.

inherent adj.
☞ 与生俱来的 inborn, inbred, innate, inherited, hereditary, native, natural, inbuilt, built-in, intrinsic, ingrained, essential, fundamental, basic.

inherit v.
☞ 遗传,继承 succeed to, accede to, assume, come into, be left, receive.

inheritance n.
☞ 遗产 legacy, bequest, heritage, birthright, heredity, descent, succession.

inheritor n.
☞ 遗产继承人 heir, heiress, successor, beneficiary, recipient.

initial adj.
☞ 创始的 first, beginning, opening, introductory, inaugural, original, primary, early, formative.

initially adv.
☞ 首要地 at first, at the beginning, to begin with, to start with, originally, first, firstly, first of all.

initiate v.
☞ 开始 begin, start, commence, originate, pioneer, institute, set up, introduce, launch, open, inaugurate, instigate, activate, trigger, prompt, stimulate, cause.

initiation n.
☞ 开始着手 admission, reception, entrance, entry, debut, introduction, enrolment, induction, investiture, installation, inauguration, inception.

initiative n.
☞ 发端 energy, drive, dynamism, get-up-and-go, ambition, enterprise, resourcefulness, invertiveness, originality, innovativness.
☞ 主动 suggestion, recommendation, action, lead, first move, first step.

injure v.
☞ 伤害 hurt, harm, damage, impair, spoil, mar, ruin, disfigure, deface, mutilate, wound, cut, break, fracture, maim, disable, cripple, lame, ill-treat, maltreat, abuse, offend, wrong, upset, put out.

injury n.
☞ 伤处 wound, cut, lesion, fracture, trauma, hurt, mischief, ill, harm, damage, impairment, ruin, disfigurement, mutilation, ill-treatment, abuse, insult, offence, wrong, injustice.

injustice n.
☞ 不公正的 unfairness, inequality, disparity, discrimination, oppression, bias, prejudice, one-sideness, partisanship, partiality, favouritism, wrong, iniquity.

inn n.
☞ 小旅馆 public house, pub, local, tavern, hostelry, hotel.

inner adj.
☞ 在内的 internal, interior, inside, inward, innermost, central, middle, concealed, hidden, secret, private, personal, intimate, mental, psychological, spiritual, emotional.

innocence n.
☞ 无罪 guiltlessness, blamelessness, honesty, virtue, righteousness, purity, chastity, virginity, incorruptibility, harmlessness, innocuousness.
☞ 天真 artlessness, guilelessness, naiveness, inexperience, ignorance, naturalness, simplicity, unsophisitication, unworldliness, credulity, gullibility, trustfulness.

innocent adj.
☞ 无罪的 guiltless, blameless, irreproachable, unimpeachable, honest, upright, virtuous, righteous, sinless, faultless, impeccable, stainless, spotless, immaculate, unsullied, untainted, uncontaminated, pure, chaste, virginal, incorrupt, inoffensive, harmless, innocuous.
☞ 天真的 artless, guileless, ingenuous, naive, green, inexperienced, fresh, natural, simple, unsophisticated, unworldly, childike, credulous, gullible, trusting.

innovation n.
☞ 革新 newness, novelty, neologism, modernization, progress, reform, change, alteration, variation, departure.

innovative adj.
☞ 富有创造性的 new, fresh, original, creative, imaginative, inventive, resourceful, enterprising, go-ahead, progressive, reforming, bold, daring, adventurous.

inquire, enquire v.
☞ 询问 ask, question, quiz, query, investigate, look into, probe, examine, inspect, scrutinize, search, explore.

inquiry, enquiry n.
☞ 调查 question, query, investigation, inquest, hearing, inquisition, examination, inspection, scrutiny, study, survey, poll, search, probe, exploration.

insane adj.
☞ 疯狂的 mad, crazy, mentally ill, lunatic, mental, demented, deranged, unhinged, disturbed.
☞ 愚蠢的 foolish, stupid, senseless, impractical.

insanity n.
☞ 疯狂 madness, craziness, lunacy, mental illness, neurosis, psychosis, mania, dementia, derangement, folly, stupidity, senselessness, irresponsibility.

insensible adj.
☞ 麻木的 numb, anaesthetized, dead, cold, insensitive, unresponsive, blind, deaf, unconscious, unaware, oblivious, unmindful.

insensitive adj.
☞ 感觉迟钝的, 不灵敏的 hardened, immune,

insert v.
☞ 插入 put, place, put in, stick in, push in, introduce, implant, embed, engraft, set, inset, let in, interleave, intercalate, interpolate, interpose.

n.
☞ 插入物 insertion, enclosure, inset, notice, advertisement, supplement, addition.

inside n.
☞ 内部 interior, content, contents, middle, centre, heart, core.

adv.
☞ 在内部 within, indoors, internally, inwardly, secretly, privately.

adj.
☞ 内部的 interior, internal, inner, innermost, inward, secret, classified, confidential, private.

insides n.
☞ 内脏,肠胃 entrails, guts, intestines, bowels, innards, organs, viscera, belly, stomach.

insight n.
☞ 见识 awareness, knowledge, comprehension, understanding, grasp, apprehension, perception, intuition, sensitivity, discernment, judgement, acumen, penetration, observation, vision, wisdom, intelligence.

insist v.
☞ 坚持 demand, require, urge, stress, emphasize, repeat, reiterate, dwell on, harp on, assert, maintain, claim, contend, hold, vow, swear, persist, stand firm.

insistence n.
☞ 坚持,主张 demand, entreaty, exhortation, urging, stress, emphasis, repetition reiteration, assertion, claim, contention, persistence, determination, resolution, firmness.

insistent adj.
☞ 坚持的 demanding, importunate, emphatic, forceful, pressing, urgent, dogged, tenacious, persistent, persevering, relentless, unrelenting, unremitting, incessant.

inspect v.
☞ 检查 check, vet, look over, examine, search, investigate, scrutinize, study, scan, survey, superintend, supervise, oversee, visit.

inspection n.
☞ 检查,视察 check, check-up, examination, scrutiny, scan, study, search, investigation, supervision, visit.

inspector n.
☞ 检查员 supervisor, superintendent, overseer, surveyor, controller, scrutineer, checker, tester, examiner, investigator, reviewer, critic.

inspiration n.
☞ 灵感,启发 creativity, imagination, genius, muse, influence, encouragement, stimulation, motivation, spur,

inspire v.
☞ 鼓舞,激励 encourage, hearten, influence, impress, animate, enliven, quicken, galvanize, fire, kindle, stir, arouse, trigger, spark off, prompt, spur, motivate, provoke, stimulate, excite, exhilarate, thrill, enthral, enthuse, imbue, infuse.

inspiring adj.
☞ 令人鼓舞的 encouraging, heartening, uplifting, invigorating, stirring, rousing, stimulating, exciting, exhilarating, thrilling, enthralling, moving, affecting, memorable, impressive.

install v.
☞ 安装,装置 fix, fit, lay, put, place, position, locate, site, situate, station, plant, settle, establish, set up, introduce, institute, inaugurate, invest, induct, ordain.

instant n.
☞ 瞬间 flash, twinkling, trice, moment, tick, split second, second, minute, time, occasion.
adj.
☞ 立即的 instantaneous, immediate, on-the-spot, direct, prompt, urgent, unhesitating, quick, fast, rapid, swift.

instead adv.
☞ 代替 alternatively, preferably, rather.

instead of
☞ 代替,而不 in place of, in lieu of, on behalf of, in preference to, rather than.

instinct n.
☞ 本能 intuition, sixth sense, gut reaction, impulse, urge, feeling, hunch, flair, knack, gift, talent, feel, faculty, ability, aptitude, predisposition, tendency.

instinctive adj.
☞ 本能的,天性的 natural, native, inborn, innate, inherent, intuitive, impulsive, involuntary, automatic, mechanical, reflex, spontaneous, immediate, unthinking, unpremeditated, gut, visceral.

institute v.
☞ 设立 originate, initiate, introduce, enact, begin, start, commence, create, establish, set up, organize, found, inaugurate, open, launch, appoint, install, invest, induct, ordain.
n.
☞ 学院 school, college, academy, conservatory, foundation, institution.

institution n.
☞ 制度 custom, tradition, usage, practice, ritual, convention, rule, law.
☞ 机构 organization, association, society, guild, concern, corporation, foundation, establishment, institute, hospital, home.
☞ 建立,设立 initiation, introduction, enactment, inception, creation,

(introductory section: a 灵机,妙想 idea, brainwave, insight, illumination, revelation, awakening.)

stimulus.

establishment, formation, founding, foundation, installation.

instruct v.
- 指导 teach, educate, tutor, coach, train, drill, ground, school, discipline.
- 命令 order, command, direct, mandate, tell, inform, notify, advise, counsel, guide.

instruction n.
- 指令 direction, recommendation, advice, guidance, information, order, command, injunction, mandate, directive, ruling.
- 教导 education, schooling, lesson(s), tuition, teaching, training, coaching, drilling, grounding, preparation.

instructive adj.
- 有教导性的 informative, educational, edifying, enlightening, illuminating, helpful, useful.

instructor n.
- 导师 teacher, master, mistress, tutor, coach, trainer, demonstrator, exponent, adviser, mentor, guide, guru.

instrument n.
- 工具 tool, implement, utensil, appliance, gadget, contraption, device, contrivance, apparatus, mechanism.
- 方法, 手段 agent, agency, vehicle, organ, medium, factor, channel, way, means.

instrumental adj.
- 用作工具或手段的 active, involved, contributory, conducive, influential, useful, helpful, auxiliary, subsidiary.

insult v.
- 侮辱 abuse, call names, disparage, revile, libel, slander, slight, snub, injure, affront, offend, outrage.

n.
- 侮辱 abuse, rudeness, insolence, defamation, libel, slander, slight, snub, affront, indignity, offence, outrage.

insurance n.
- 保险 cover, protection, safeguard, security, provision, assurance, indemnity, guarantee, warranty, policy, premium.

insure v.
- 确保 cover, protect, assure, underwrite, indemnify, guarantee, warrant.

intact adj.
- 完整的 unbroken, all in one piece, whole, complete, integral, entire, perfect, undamaged, unhurt, uninjured.

intangible adj.
- 捉摸不定的 insubstantial, imponderable, elusive, fleeting, airy, shadowy, vague, indefinite, abstract, unreal, invisible.

integral adj.
- 不可分开的 intrinsic, constituent, elemental, basic, fundamental, necessary, essential, indispensable.
- 整个的 complete, entire, full, whole, undivided.

integrate v.
☞ 使并入,使完整 merge, join, unite, combine, amalgamate, incorporate, coalesce, fuse, knit, mesh, mix, blend, harmonize.

integrity n.
☞ 正直 honesty, uprightness, probity, incorruptibility, purity, morality, principle, honour, virtue, goodness, righteousness.
☞ 完整 completeness, wholeness, unity, coherence, cohesion.

intellect n.
☞ 智力 mind, brain(s), brainpower, intelligence, genius, reason, understanding, sense, wisdom, judgement.

intellectual adj.
☞ 智力的 academic, scholarly, intelligent, studious, thoughtful, cerebral, mental, highbrow, cultural.
n.
☞ 学者 thinker, academic, highbrow, egghead, mastermind, genius.

intelligence n.
☞ 智力 intellect, reason, wit(s), brain(s), brainpower, cleverness, brightness, aptitude, quickness, alertness, discernment, perception, understanding, comprehension.
☞ 情报 information, facts, data, knowledge, findings, news, report, warning, tip-off.

intelligent adj.
☞ 聪明的 clever, bright, smart, brainy, quick, alert, quick-witted, sharp, acute, knowing, knowledgeable, well-informed, thinking, rational, sensible.

intend v.
☞ 意指,打算 aim, have a mind, contemplate, mean, propose, plan, project, scheme, plot, design, purpose, resolve, determine, destine, mark out, earmark, set apart.

intense adj.
☞ 非常的 great, deep, profound, strong, powerful, forceful, fierce, harsh, severe, acute, sharp, keen, eager, earnest, ardent, fervent, fervid, passionate, vehement, energetic, violent, intensive, concentrated, heightened.

intensify v.
☞ 加强,加剧 increase, step up, escalate, heighten, hot up, fire, boost, fuel, aggravate, add to, strengthen, reinforce, sharpen, whet, quicken, deepen, concentrate, emphasize, enhance.

intensive adj.
☞ 强烈的 concentrated, thorough, exhaustive, comprehensive, detailed, in-depth, thoroughgoing, all-out, intense.

intent adj.
☞ 热心的 concentrated, thorough, exhaustive, comprehensive, detailed, in-depth, thoroughgoing, all-out, intense.
☞ 专心的 determined, resolved, resolute, set, bent, concentrated, eager, earnest, committed, steadfast, fixed,

alert, attentive, concentrating, preoccupied, engrossed, wrapped up, absorbed, occupied.

intention n.
☞ 意图 aim, purpose, object, end, point, target, goal, objective, idea, plan, design, view, intent, meaning.

interest n.
☞ 兴趣 importance, significance, note, concern, care, attention, notice, curiosity, involvement, participation.
☞ 消遣 activity, pursuit, pastime, hobby, diversion, amusement.
☞ 利益 advantage, benefit, profit, gain.
v.
☞ 关心,感兴趣 concern, involve, touch, move, attract, appeal to, divert, amuse, occupy, engage, absorb, engross, fascinate, intrigue.

interested adj.
☞ 感兴趣的 attentive, curious, absorbed, engrossed, fascinated, enthusiastic, keen, attracted.
☞ 关心的 concerned, involved, affected.

interesting adj.
☞ 有趣的,有吸引力的 attractive, appealing, entertaining, engaging, absorbing, engrossing, fascinating, intriguing, compelling, gripping, stimulating, thought-provoking, curious, unusual.

interfere v.
☞ 干预,干涉 intrude, poke one's nose in, pry, butt in, interrupt, intervene, meddle, tamper.
☞ 阻碍,妨碍 hinder, hamper, obstruct, block, impede, handicap, cramp, inhibit, conflict, clash.

interference n.
☞ 干涉,干扰 intrusion, prying, interruption, intervention, meddling.
☞ 妨碍 obstruction, opposition, conflict, clashing.

interim adj.
☞ 暂时的,临时的 temporary, provisional, stopgap, makeshift, improvised, stand-in, acting, caretaker.
n.
☞ 期间,间隔 meantime, meanwhile, interval.

interior adj.
☞ 内部的,里面的 internal, inside, inner, central, inward, mental, spiritual, private, secret, hidden.
☞ 国内的,内地的 home, domestic, inland, up-country, remote.
n.
☞ 内部,内地 inside, centre, middle, core, heart, depths.

internal adj.
☞ 内部的,国内的 inside, inner, interior, inward, intimate, private, personal, domestic, in-house.

international adj.
☞ 国际的,世界的 global, worldwide, intercontinental, cosmopolitan, universal, general.

interpret v.
☞ 解释,翻译,说明,阐明 explain, expound, elucidate, clarify, throw light on, define, paraphrase, translate, render, decode, decipher, solve, make sense of, understand, construe, read, take.

interpretation n.
☞ 解释,说明,翻译 explanation, clarification, analysis, translation, rendering, version, performance, reading, understanding, sense, meaning.

interrogate v.
☞ 质问 question, quiz, examine, cross-examine, grill, give the third degree, pump, debrief.

interrogation n.
☞ 质问,审问,讯问 questioning, cross-questioning, examination, cross-examination, grilling, third degree, inquisition, inquiry, inquest.

interrupt v.
☞ 打断 intrude, barge in, butt in, interject, break in, heckle, disturb, disrupt, interfere, obstruct, check, hinder, hold up, stop, halt, suspend, discontinue, cut off, disconnect, punctuate, separate, divide, cut, break.

interruption n.
☞ 打断,中断 intrusion, interjection, disturbance, disruption, obstruction, impediment, obstacle, hitch, pause, break, half, stop, stoppage, suspension, discontinuance, disconnection, separation, division.

intersect v.
☞ 贯穿,和……交叉 cross, criss-cross, cut across, bisect, divide, meet, converge.

intersection n.
☞ 交叉路口 junction, interchange, crossroads, crossing.

interval n.
☞ 间歇,休息 interlude, intermission, break, rest, pause, delay, wait, interim, meantime, meanwhile, gap, opening, space, distance, period, spell, time, season.

intervene v.
☞ 介入,干涉 step in, mediate, arbitrate, interfere, interrupt, intrude.
☞ 发生 occur, happen, elapse, pass.

intervention n.
☞ 干涉,介入 involvement, interference, intrusion, mediation, agency, intercession.

interview n.
☞ 接见,会见 audience, consultation, talk, dialogue, meeting, conference, press conference, oral examination, viva.
v.
☞ 询问 question, interrogate, examine, vet.

intimacy n.
☞ 亲密,密切 friendship, closeness, familiarity, confidence, confidentiality, privacy.

intimate[1] v.

☞宣布,明白表示 hint, insinuate, imply, suggest, indicate, communicate, impart, tell, state, declare, announce.

intimate² adj.
☞亲密的,密切的 friendly, informal, familiar, cosy, warm, affectionate, dear, bosom, close, near, confidential, secret, private, personal, internal, innermost, deep, penetrating, detailed, exhaustive.

n.
☞密友 friend, bosom friend, confidant(e), associate.

intolerable adj.
☞无法忍受的 unbearable, unendurable, insupportable, unacceptable, insufferable, impossible.

intolerant adj.
☞偏狭的,不宽容的 impatient, prejudiced, bigoted, narrow-minded, small-minded, opinionated, dogmatic, illiberal, uncharitable.

intrigue n.
☞密谋,诡计 plot, scheme, conspiracy, collusion, machination, manoeuvre, stratagem, ruse, wile, trickery, double-dealing, sharp practice.
☞私通 romance, liaison, affair, amour, intimacy.

v.
☞引起……兴趣 fascinate, rivet, puzzle, tantalize, attract, charm, captivate.
☞策划阴谋 plot, scheme, conspire, connive, machinate, manoeuvre.

introduce v.
☞介绍,引进 institute, begin, start, commence, establish, found, inaugurate, launch, open, bring in, announce, present, acquaint, familiarize, initiate.
☞提出 put forward, advance, submit, offer, propose, suggest.

introduction n.
☞开始,序曲 institution, beginning, start, commencement, establishment, inauguration, launch, presentation, debut, initiation.
☞引言,序言 foreword, preface, preamble, prologue, preliminaries, overture, prelude, lead-in, opening.

introductory adj.
☞介绍的,导引的 preliminary, preparatory, opening, inaugural, first, initial, early, elementary, basic.

intrude v.
☞闯入,强行进入 interrupt, butt in, meddle, interfere, violate, infringe, encroach, trespass.

intruder n.
☞入侵者,闯入者 trespasser, prowler, burglar, raider, invader, infiltrator, interloper, gatecrasher.

intrusion n.
☞闯入,入侵 interruption, interference, violation, infringement, encroachment, trespass, invasion.

intuition n.

☞直觉 instinct, sixth sense, perception, discernment, insight, hunch, feeling, gut feeling.

intuitive *adj.*
☞本能的 instinctive, spontaneous, involuntary, innate, untaught.

invade *v.*
☞侵入 enter, penetrate, infiltrate, burst in, descend on, attack, raid, seize, occupy, overrun, swarm over, infest, pervade, encroach, infringe, violate.

invalid¹ *adj.*
☞有病的 sick, ill, poorly, ailing, sickly, weak, feeble, frail, infirm, disabled, bedridden.
n.
☞病人 patient, convalescent.

invalid² *adj.*
☞错误的 false, fallacious, unsound, ill-founded, unfounded, baseless, illogical, irrational, unscientific, wrong, incorrect.
☞无效的 illegal, null, void, worthless.

invaluable *adj.*
☞无价的 priceless, inestimable, incalculable, precious, valuable, useful.

invariable *adj.*
☞不变的 fixed, set, unvarying, unchanging, unchangeable, permanent, constant, steady, unwavering, uniform, rigid, inflexible, habitual, regular.

invariably *adv.*

☞习惯地 always, witout exception, without fail, unfailingly, consistently, regularly, habitually.

invasion *n.*
☞侵犯 attack, offensive, onslaught, raid, incursion, foray, breach, penetration, infiltration, intrusion, encroachment, infringement, violation.

invent *v.*
☞发明 conceive, think up, design, discover, create, originate, formulate, frame, devise, contrive, improvise, fabricate, make up, concoct, cook up, trump up, imagine, dream up.

invention *n.*
☞发明 design, creation, brainchild, discovery, development, device, gadget.
☞虚构 lie, falsehood, deceit, fabrication, fiction, tall story, fantasy, figment.
☞创造力 inventiveness, imagination, creativity, innovation, originality, ingenuity, inspiration, genius.

inventor *n.*
☞发明者 designer, discoverer, creator, originator, author, architect, maker, scientist, engineer.

invest *v.*
☞投资 spend, lay out, put in, sink.
☞授权予 provide, supply, endow, vest, empower, authorize, sanction.

investigate v.
☞ 调查 inquire into, look into, consider, examine, study, inspect, scrutinize, analyze, go into, probe, explore, search, sift.

investigation n.
☞ 调查 inquiry, inquest, hearing, examination, study, research, survey, review, inspection, scrutiny, analysis, probe, exploration, search.

investigator n.
☞ 调查者 examiner, researcher, detective, sleuth, private detective, private eye.

investment n.
☞ 投资,投资额 asset, speculation, venture, stake, contribution, outlay, expenditure, transaction.

invisible adj.
☞ 看不见的 unseen, out of sight, hidden, concealed, disguised, inconspicuous, indiscernible, imperceptible, infinitesimal, microscopic, imaginary, non-existent.

invitation n.
☞ 邀请 request, solicitation, call, summons, temptation, enticement, allurement, come-on, encouragement, inducement, provocation, incitement, challenge.

invite v.
☞ 恳请 ask, call, summon, welcome, encourage, lead, draw, attract, tempt, entice, allure, bring on, provoke, ask for, request, solicit, seek.

inviting adj.
☞ 诱惑的,动人的 welcoming, appealing, attractive, tempting, seductive, enticing, alluring, pleasing, delightful, captivating, fascinating, intriguing, tantalizing.

invoke v.
☞ 祈求 call upon, conjure, appeal to, petition, solicit, implore, entreat, beg, beseech, supplicate, pray.

involuntary adj.
☞ 不知不觉的 spontaneous, unconscious, automatic, mechanical, reflex, instinctive, conditioned, impulsive, unthinking, blind, uncontrolled, unintentional.

involve v.
☞ 包括 require, necessitate, mean, imply, entail, include, incorporate, embrace, cover, take in, affect, concern.
☞ 牵涉 implicate, incriminate, inculpate, draw in, mix up, embroil, associate.
☞ 专心于 engage, occupy, absorb, engross, preoccupy, hold, grip, rivet.

involved adj.
☞ 与某事某人有关连 concerned, implicated, mixed up, caught, participating.
☞ 复杂的 complicated, complex, intricate, elaborate, tangled, knotty, tortuous, confusing.

involvement n.
☞ 关联 concern, interest, responsibility, association, connection, participation,

implication, entanglement.

inward adj.
☞ 内部的 incoming, entering, inside, interior, internal, inner, innermost, inmost, personal, private, secret, confidential.

iron adj.
☞ 铁一样的 rigid, inflexible, adamant, determined, hard, steely, tough, strong.
v.
☞ 熨平 press, smooth, flatten.

iron out
☞ 消除 resolve, settle, sort out, straighten out, clear up, put right, reconcile, deal with, get rid of, eradicate, eliminate.

ironic adj.
☞ 讽刺 ironical, sarcastic, sardonic, scornful, contemptuous, derisive, sneering, scoffing, mocking, satirical, wry, paradoxical.

irony n.
☞ 反语 sarcasm, mockery, satire, paradox, contrariness, incongruity.

irrational adj.
☞ 不理智的 unreasonable, unsound, illogical, absurd, crazy, wild, foolish, silly, senseless, unwise.

irregular adj.
☞ 不整齐的 rough, bumpy, uneven, crooked.
☞ 不规则的 variable, fluctuating, wavering, erratic, fitful, intermittent, sporadic, spasmodic, occasional, random, haphazard, disorderly, unsystematic.
☞ 非正式的 abnormal, unconventional, unorthodox, improper, unusual, exceptional, anomalous.

irrelevant adj.
☞ 无关的，跑题的 immaterial, beside the point, inapplicable, inappropriate, unrelated, unconnected, inconsequent, peripheral, tangential.

irresponsible adj.
☞ 无责任感的 unreliable, untrustworthy, careless, negligent, thoughtless, heedless, ill-considered, rash, reckless, wild, carefree, light-hearted, immature.

irrigate v.
☞ 灌溉 water, flood, inundate, wet, moisten, dampen.

irritable adj.
☞ 过敏的，易怒的 cross, bad-tempered, ill-tempered, crotchety, crusty, cantankerous, crabby, testy, short-tempered, snappish, snappy, short, impatient, touchy, edgy, thin-skinned, hypersensitive, prickly, peevish, fretful, fractious.

irritate v.
☞ 激怒 annoy, get on one's nerves, aggravate, bother, harass, rouse, provoke, rile, anger, enrage, infuriate, incense, exasperate, peeve, put out.
☞ 使感不适 inflame, chafe, rub, tickle, itch.

irritation n.
☞ 刺激物 displeasure, dissatisfaction, annoyance,

aggravation, provocation, anger, vexation, indignation, fury, exasperation, irritability, crossness, testiness impatience.

isolate v.
☞ 隔离 set apart, sequester, seclude, keep apart, segregate, quarantine, insulate, cut off, detach, remove, disconnect, separate, divorce, alienate, shut out, ostracize, exclude.

isolated adj.
☞ 隔离的,孤立的 remote, separate, detached, cut off, lonely, solitary, single, unique, alone.

isolation n.
☞ 孤独 quarantine, solitude, solitariness, loneliness, remoteness, seclusion, retirement, withdrawal, exile, segregation, insulation, separation, detachment, disconnection, dissociation, alienation.

issue n.
☞ 问题 matter, affair, concern, problem, point, subject, topic, question, debate, argument, dispute, controversy.
☞ 发行 publication, release, distribution, supply, delivery, circulation, promulgation, broadcast, announcement.
☞ (报刊)期,号,版 copy, number, installment, edition, impression, printing.
v.
☞ 发行 publish, release, distribute, supply, deliver, give out, deal out, circulate, promulgate, broadcast, announce, put out, emit, produce.
☞ 发生 originate, stem, spring, rise, emerge, burst forth, gush, flow, proceed, emanate, arise.

itch v.
☞ 发痒 tickle, irritate, tingle, prickle, crawl.
n.
☞ 痒 itchiness, tickle, irritation, prickling.
☞ 渴望 eagerness, keenness, desire, longing, yearning, hankering, craving.

item n.
☞ 条款,一则 object, article, thing, piece, component, ingredient, element, factor, point, detail, particular, aspect, feature, consideration, matter.
☞ 一则新闻 article, piece, report, account, notice, entry, paragraph.

J

jab v.
☞ 戳,刺 poke, prod, dig, nudge, stab, push, elbow, lunge, punch, tap, thrust.

jail, gaol n.
☞ 监狱 prison, jailhouse, custody, lock-up, penitenrtiary, guardhouse, inside, nick, clink.
v.

☞ 监禁 imprison, incarcerate, lock up, put away, send down, confine, detain, intern, impound, immure.

jailer, gaoler n.
☞ 监狱看守,看守人 prison officer, warden, warder, guard, screw, keeper, captor.

jam¹ v.
☞ 拥挤,挤入 cram, pack, wedge, squash, squeeze, press, crush, crowd, congest, ram, stuff, confine, force.
☞ 阻塞,发生故障 block, obstruct, stall, stick.
n.
☞ 拥挤的人群 crush, crowd, press, congestion, pack, mob, throng, bottle-neck, traffic jam.
☞ 困境 predicament, trouble, quandary, plight, fix.

jam² n.
☞ 果酱 conserve, preserve, jelly, spread, marmalade.

jangle v.
☞ 发出尖锐的声音 clank, clash, jar, clatter, jingle, chime, rattle, vibrate.
n.
☞ 铿锵刺耳声 clang, clash, rattle, jar, cacophony, dissonance, din, discord, racket, reverberation.

jar n.
☞ 广口瓶,坛子 pot, container, vessel, receptacle, crock, pitcher, urn, vase, flagon, jug, mug.
v.
☞ 震动 jolt, agitate, rattle, shake, vibrate, jangle, rock, disturb, discompose.
☞ 使苦恼,刺激 annoy, irritate, grate, nettle, offend, upset, irk.
☞ 不和,吵架 bicker, quarrel, cant, argot, vernacular, idiom.
☞ 乱语 nonsense, gobbledygook, mumbo-jumbo, gibberish.

jaw v.
☞ 闲谈,对……唠叨 chat, chatter, gossip, natter, talk, rabbit (on), gabble, babble.
n.
☞ 闲谈,唠叨 talk, gossip, chat, conversation, discussion, chinwag, natter.

jealous adj.
☞ 嫉妒的,羡慕的 envious, covetous, grudging, resentful, green, green-eyed.
☞ 怀疑的 suspicious, wary, distrustful, anxious, possessive, protective.

jealousy n.
☞ 妒忌 envy, covetousness, grudge, resentment, spite, ill-will.
☞ 怀疑 suspicion, distrust, mistrust, possessiveness.

jeer v.
☞ 嘲弄,嘲笑 mock, scoff, taunt, jibe, ridicule, sneer, deride, make fun of, chaff, barrack, twit, knock, heckle, banter.
n.
☞ 嘲弄 mockery, derision, ridicule, taunt, jibe, sneer, scoff, abuse, catcall, dig, hiss, hoot.

jeopardize v.
☞ 使冒危险 endanger, imperil, risk, hazard, venture, gamble.

chance, threaten, menace, expose, stake.

jeopardy n.
- 危险 danger, peril, risk, hazard, endangerment, venture, vulnerability, precariousness, insecurity, exposure, liability.

jerk n.
- 急拉,猛扯 jolt, tug, twitch, jar, jog, yank, wrench, pull, pluck, lurch, throw, thrust, shrug.

v.
- 猛,拉扯 jolt, tug, twich, jog, yank, wrench, pull, jiggle, lurch, pluck, thrust, shrug, throw, bounce.

jerky adj.
- 急动的,痉挛性的 fitful, twitchy, spasmodic, jumpy, jolting, convulsive, disconnected, bumpy, bouncy, shaky, rough, unco-ordinated, uncontrolled, incoherent.

jet n.
- 喷射,喷气发动机 gush, spurt, spout, spray, spring, sprinkler, sprayer, fountain, flow, stream, squirt.

jewel n.
- 宝石 gem, precious stone, gemstone, ornament, rock.
- 珠宝 treasure, find, prize, rarity, paragon, pearl.

jilt v.
- 遗弃,抛弃 abandon, reject, desert, discard, brush off, ditch, drop, spurn, betray.

jingle v.
- 使发出叮当声 clink, tinkle, ring, chime, chink, jangle, clatter, rattle.

n.
- 叮当声 clink, tinkle, ringing, clang, rattle, clangour.
- 音,韵,押韵 rhyme, verse, song, tune, ditty, doggerel, melody, poem, chant, chorus.

job n.
- 工作 work, employment, occupation, position, post, situation, profession, career, calling, vocation, trade, metier, capacity, business, livelihood.
- 任务 task, chore, duty, responsibility, charge, commission, mission, activity, affair, concern, proceeding, project, enterprise, office, pursuit, role, undertaking, venture.

jobless adj.
- 无工作的,失业的 unemployed, out of work, laid off, on the dole, inactive, redundant.

join v.
- 连结 unite, connect, combine, conjoin, attach, link, amalgamate, fasten, merge, marry, couple, yoke, tie, splice, knit, cement, add, adhere, annex.
- 碰头,相会 abut, adjoin, border (on), verge on, tough, meet, coincide, march with.
- 参加 associate, affiliate, accompany, ally, enlist, enroll, enter, sign up, team.

joint n.
- 连接处,关节 junction, connection, union, juncture, intersection, hinge, knot,

articulation, seam.
adj.
☞ 连接的,联合的 combined, common, communal, joined, shared, united, collective, amalgamated, mutual, co-operative, co-ordinated, consolidated, concerted.

joke *n.*
☞ 笑话,恶作剧 jest, quip, crack, gag, one-liner, pun, hoot, whimsy, yarn.
☞ 诡计,戏法 trick, jape, lark, prank, spoof, fun.
v.
☞ 开玩笑,戏弄 jest, quip, clown, fool, pun, wisecrack, kid, tease, banter, mock, laugh, frolic, gambol.

joker *n.*
☞ 逗笑的人 comedian, comic, wit, humorist, jester, trickster, wag, clown, buffoon, kidder, droll, card, character, sport.

journal *n.*
☞ 杂志,日报 newspaper, periodical, magazine, paper, publication, review, weekly, monthly, register, chronicle, diary, gazette, daybook, log, record.

journalist *n.*
☞ 新闻记者 reporter, news-writer, hack, correspondent, editor, columnist, feature-writer, commentator, broadcaster, contributor.

journey *n.*
☞ 旅程,路程 voyage, trip, travel, trek, expedition, passage, tour, ramble, outing, wanderings, safari, progress.
v.
☞ 旅行,旅游 travel, voyage, go, trek, tour, roam, rove, proceed, wander, tramp, ramble, range, gallivant.

joy *n.*
☞ 喜悦,快乐 happiness, gladness, delight, pleasure, bliss, ecstasy, elation, joyfulness, exultation, gratification, rapture.

joyful *adj.*
☞ 十分喜悦的,高兴的 happy, pleased, delighted, elated, ecstatic, triumphant.

judge *n.*
☞ 法官,评判员 justice, law lord, magistrate, arbiter, adjudicator, arbitrator, mediator, referee, umpire, beak.
☞ 鉴别家,技术顾问 connoisseur, authority, expert, evaluator, assessor, critic.
v.
☞ 审判,判决 adjudicate, arbitrate, try, referee, umpire, decree, mediate, examine, sentence, review, rule, find.
☞ 鉴别,判断 ascertain, determine, decide, assess, appraise, evaluate, estimate, value, distinguish, discern, reckon, believe, think, consider, conclude, rate.
☞ 判罪,判决 condemn, criticize, doom.

judgement *n.*
☞ 判决,判断 verdict, sentence, ruling, decree, conclusion, decision, arbitration, finding, result, mediation, order.

- 认识,识别 discernment, discrimination, understanding, wisdom, prudence, common sense, sense, intelligence, taste, shrewdness, penetration, enlightenment.
- 意见,看法 assessment, evaluation, appraisal, estimate, opinion, view, belief, diagnosis.
- 判罪 conviction, damnation, punishment, retribution, doom, fate, misfortune.

judicial *adj.*
- 司法的,法定的 legal, judiciary, magistral, forensic, official, discriminating, critical, impartial.

judicious *adj.*
- 明智的,有判断力的 wise, prudent, careful, cautious, astute, discerning, informed, shrewd, thoughtful, reasonable, sensible, sound, well-judged, well-advised, considered.

juice *n.*
- 液,汁,浆 liquid, fluid, extract, essence, sap, secretion, nectar, liquor.

juicy *adj.*
- 汁液多的 succulent, moist, lush, watery.
- 有趣的 interesting, colourful, sensational, racy, suggestive, lurid.

jump *v.*
- 使跳过 leap, spring, bound, vault, clear, bounce, skip, hop, prance, frolic, gambol.
- 暴涨 rise, increase, gain, appreciate, ascend, escalate, mount, advance, surge, spiral.

n.
- 跳跃 leap, spring, bound, vault, hop, skip, bounce, prance, frisk, frolic, pounce.
- 中断 break, gap, interruption, lapse, omission, interval, breach, switch.
- 猛增 rise, increase, escalation, boost, advance, increment, upsurge, upturn, mounting.
- 障碍物 hurdle, fence, gate, hedge, barricade, obstacle.

junction *n.*
- 汇合处,交叉处 joint, join, joining, connection, juncture, union, intersection, linking, coupling, meeting-point, confluence.

junior *adj.*
- 年少的,低一级的 younger, minor, lesser, lower, subordinate, secondary, subsidiary, inferior.

junk *n.*
- 垃圾 rubbish, refuse, trash, debris, garbage, waste, scrap, litter, clutter, oddments, rummage, dregs, wreckage.

jurisdiction *n.*
- 权限 power, authority, control, influence, dominion, province, sovereignty, command, domination, rule, prerogative, sway, orbit, bounds, area, field, scope, range, reach, sphere, zone.

just *adj.*
- 公平的 fair, equitable, impartial, unbiased, unprejudiced, fair-minded, even-handed, objective, righteous, upright, virtuous, honourable,

good, honest, irreproachable.
☞ 应得的,理所当然的 deserved, merited, fitting, well-deserved, appropriate, suitable, due, proper, reasonable, rightful, lawful, legitimate.

justice n.
☞ 正义,公道 fairness, equity, impartiality, objectivity, equitableness, justness, legitimacy, honesty, right, rightfulness, rightness, justifiableness, reasonableness, rectitude.
☞ 合法,正当 legality, law, penalty, recompense, reparation, satisfaction.
☞ 评判 judge, justice of the peace, JP, magistrate.

justifiable adj.
☞ 正当的,无可非议的 defensible, excusable, warranted, reasonable, justified, lawful, legitimate, acceptable, explainable, forgivable, pardonable, understandable, valid, well-founded, right, proper, explicable, fit, tenable.

justification n.
☞ 辩护,理由 defence, plea, mitigation, apology, explanation, excuse, vindication, warrant, rationalization, reason, grounds.

justify v.
☞ 证明……有理 vindicate, exonerate, warrant, substantiate, defend, acquit, absolve, excuse, forgive, explain, pardon, validate, uphold, sustain, support, maintain, establish.

K

keen adj.
☞ 强烈的,渴望的 eager, avid, fervent, enthusiastic, earnest, devoted, diligent, industrious.
☞ 敏锐的,聪明的 astute, shred, clever, perceptive, wise, discerning, quick, deep, sensitive.
☞ 锐利的 sharp, piercing, penetrating, incisive, acute, pointed, intense, pungent, trenchant.

keep v.
☞ 保存,保藏 retain, hold, preserve, hold on to, hang on to, store, stock, possess, amass, accumulate, collect, stack, conserve, deposit, heap, pile, place, maintain, furnish.
☞ 保持下去,维持原状 carry on, keep on, continue, persist, remain.
☞ 留意,照看 look after, tend, care for, have charge of, have custody of, maintain, provide for, subsidize, support, sustain, be responsible for, foster, mind, protect, shelter, guard, defend, watch (over), shield, safeguard, feed, nurture, manage.
☞ 使延迟,耽搁 detain, delay,

retard, check, hinder, hold (up), impede, obstruct, prevent, block, curb, interfere with, restrain, limit, inhibit, deter, hamper, keep back, control, constrain, arrest, withhold.
☞ 认识,服从 observe, comply with, respect, obey, fulfil, adhere to, recognize, keep up, keep faith with, commemorate, celebrate, hold, maintain, perform, perpetuate, mark, honour.
n.
☞ 生计,生活必需 subsistence, board, livelihood, living, maintenance, support, upkeep, means, food, nourishment, nurture.
☞ 城堡,堡垒 fort, fortress, tower, castle, citadel, stroghold, dungeon.

keep back
☞ 保留 restrain, check, constrain, curb, impede, limit, prohibit, retard, stop, control, delay.
☞ 阻止,阻挡 hold back, restrict, suppress, withhold, conceal, censor, hide, hush up, stifle, reserve, retain.

keep in
☞ 阻止,抑制 repress; keep back, inhibit, bottle up, conceal, stifle, suppress, hide, control, restrain, quell, stop up.
☞ 限制 confine, detain, shut in, coop up.

keep on
☞ 继续,保持 continue, carry on, endure, persevere, persist, keep at it last, remain, stay, stay the corse, soldier on, hold on, retain, maintain.

keep up
☞ 保持,维持,继续 keep pace, equal, contend, compete, vie, rival, match, emulate, continue, maintain, persevere, support, sustain, preserve.

keeper *n.*
☞ 保管员,看守人 guard, custodian, curator, caretaker, attendant, guardian, overseer, steward, warder, jailer, gaoler, warden, supervisor, minder, inspector, conservator, defender, governor, superintendent, surveyor.

key *n.*
☞ 答案,钥匙,关键 clue, cue, indicator, pointer, explanation, sign, answer, solution, interpretation, means, secret.
☞ 向导,图例 guide, glossary, translation, legend, code, table, index.
adj.
☞ 主要的,关键的 important, essential, vital, crucial, necessary, principal, decisive, central, chief, main, major, leading, basic, fundamental.

kick *v.*
☞ 踢 boot, hit, strike, jolt
☞ 放弃,踢退 give up, quit, stop, leave off, abandon, desist from, break.
n.
☞ 踢 blow, recoil, jolt, striing
☞ 刺激,兴奋 stimulation, thrill, excitement.

kick off
☞ (足球比赛)开球 begin, commence, start, open, get under way, open the proceedings, set the ball rolling, introduce, inaugurate, initiate.

kick out
☞ 踢出,解雇 eject, expel, oust, remove, chuck out, discharge, dismiss, get rid of, sack, throw out, reject.

kid¹ n.
☞ 小孩儿 child, youngster, youth, juvenile, infant, girl, boy, teenager, lad, nipper, tot.

kid² v.
☞ 开玩笑 tease, joke, have on, hoax, fool, pull someone's leg, pretend, trick, delude, dupe, con, jest, hoodwink, humbug, bamboozle.

kidnap v.
☞ 绑架,绑架 abduct, capture, seize, hold to ransom, snatch, hijack, steal.

kill v.
☞ 杀死 slaughter, murder, slay, put to death, exterminate, assassinate, do to death, do in, bump off, finish off, massacre, smite, execute, eliminate, destroy, dispatch, do away with, butcher, annihialte, liquidate, knock off, rub out.
☞ 抑制 stifle, deaden, smother, quash, quell, suppress.

killer n.
☞ 凶手,杀人者 murderer, assassin, executioner, destroyer, slaughterer, exterminator, butcher, cut-throat, gunman.

killing n.
☞ 杀戮,屠宰 slaughter, murder, massacre, homicide, assassintion, execution, slaying, manslaughter, extermination, carnage, bloodshed, elimination, fatality, liquidation.
☞ 赚大笔钱 gain, fortune, windfall, profit, lucky break, coup, clean-up, success, stroke of luck, bonanza, hit, big hit.
adj.
☞ 滑稽的,热闹的 funny, hilarious, comical, amusing, side-splitting, ludicrous.
☞ 使人疲惫的 exhausting, hard, taxing, arduous.

kind n.
☞ 种类 sort, type, class, category, set, variety, character, genus, genre, style, brand, family, breed, race, nature, persuasion, description, species, stamp, temperament, manner.
adj.
☞ 亲切的 benevolent, kind-hearted, kindly, good-hearted, good-natured, helpful, obliging, humane, generous, compassionate, charitable, amiable, friendly, congenial, soft-hearted, thoughtful, warm, warm-hearted, considerate, courteous, sympathetic, tender-hearted, understanding, lenient, mild, hospitable, gentle, indulgent, neighbourly, tactful, giving, good, loving, gracious.

kindle v.
☞ 点燃的 ignite, light, set alight, set on fire.

☞ 使人兴奋,激动 inflame, fire, stir, thrill, stimulate, rouse, arouse, awaken, excite, fan, incite, inspire, induce, provoke.

kindly *adj*.
☞ 亲切地,礼善地 benevolent, kind, compassionate, charitable, good-natured, helpful, warm, generous, cordial, favourable, giving, indulgent, pleasant, sympathetic, tender, gentle, mild, patient, polite.

kindness *n*.
☞ 怜悯,友好的行为 benevolence, kindliness, charity, magnanimity, compassion, generosity, hospitality, humanity, loving-kindness, courtesy, friendliness, good will, goodness, grace, indulgence, tolerance, understanding, gentleness.
☞ 仁慈,亲切 favour, good turn, assistance, help, service.

king *n*.
☞ 国王,君主 monarch, ruler, sovereign, majesty, emperor, chief, chieftain, prince, supremo, leading light.

kingdom *n*.
☞ 王国,国土 monarchy, sovereignty, reign, realm, empire, dominion, commonwealth, nation, principality, state, country, domain, dynasty, province, sphere, territory, land, division.

kinship *n*.
☞ 家族关系,血缘关系,家属关系 kin, blood, relation
☞ 相似 affinity, similarity, association, alliance, connection, correspondence, relationship, tie, community, conformity.

kiss *v*.
☞ 接吻 caress, peck, smooch, neck, snog.
☞ 轻拂,轻触 touch, graze, glance, brush, lick, scrape, fan.

knife *v*.
☞ 用刀切,用刀刺 cut, rip, slash, stab, pierce, wound.

knit *v*.
☞ 结合,接合 join, unite, secure, connect, tie, fasten, link, mend, interlace, intertwine
☞ 编织,编结 knot, loop, crotchet, weave.
☞ 皱纹 wrinkle, furrow.

knock *v*.
☞ 打击 hit, strike, rap, thump, pound, slap, smack.
n.
☞ 敲击声 blow, box, rap, thump, cuff, clip, pounding, hammering, slap, smack.

knock about
☞ 流浪,漫走 wander, travel, roam, rove, saunter, traipse, ramble, range.
☞ 粗暴地对待,敲击 beat up, batter, abuse, mistreat, hurt, hit, bash, damage, maltreat, manhandle, bruise, buffet.

knock down
☞ 打倒 demolish, destroy, fell, floor, level, wreck, raze, pound, batter, clout, smash, wallop.

knock off
☞ 停止工作 finish, cease, stop,

pack (it) in, clock off, clock out, terminate.
☞偷,窃取 steal, rob, pilfer, pinch, nick, filch.
☞减去 deduct, take away.
☞杀死,处理 kill, murder, slay, assassinate, do away with, bump off, do in, waste.

knot v.
☞打结,包扎 tie, secure, bind, entangle, tangle, knit, entwine, ravel, weave.
n.
☞结 tie, bond, joint, fastening, loop, splice, hitch.
☞帮,(树)节 bunch, cluster, clump, group.

know v.
☞知道,理解 understand, comprehend, apprehend, perceive, notice, be aware, fathom, experience, realize, see, undergo.
☞对……熟悉,认识 be acquainted with, be familiar with, recognize, identify.
☞识别,辨明 distinguish, discriminate, discern, differentiate, make out, tell.

knowledge n.
☞知识,学问 learning, scholarship, erudition, education, schooling, instruction, tuition, information, enlightenment, know-how.
☞认识 acquaintance, familiarity, awareness, cognizance, intimacy, consciousness.
☞知道,了解 understanding, comprehension, cognition, apprehension, recognition, judgement, discernment, ability, grasp, wisdom, intelligence.

knowledgeable adj.
☞博识的 educated, scholarly, learned, well-informed, lettered, intelligent.
☞有见识的 aware, acquainted, conscious, familiar, au fait, in the know, conversant, experienced.

known adj.
☞知道的,出名的 acknowledged, recognized, well-known, noted, obvious, patent, plain, admitted, familiar, avowed, commonplace, published, confessed, celebrated, famous.

kowtow v.
☞磕头,奉承 defer, cringe, fawn, grovel, pander, suck up, toady, flatter, kneel.

L

label n.
☞标签 tag, ticket, docket, mark, marker, sticker, trademark.
☞说明 description, categorization, identification, characterization, classification, badge, brand.
v.
☞作记号,贴标签 tag, mark,

stamp.
☞ 命名,指为 define, describe, classify, categorize, characterize, identify, class, designate, brand, call, dub, name.

labour n.
☞ 劳动,工作 work, task, job, chore, toil, effort, exertion, drudgery, grind, slog, sweat.
☞ 工人,劳动力 workers, employees, workforce, labourers.
☞ 分娩 childbirth, birth, delivery, labour pains, contractions.
v.
☞ 工作,劳动 work, toil, drudge, slave, strive, endeavour, struggle, grind, sweat, plod, travail.

lace n.
☞ 网织品,花边 netting, mesh work, open-work, tatting, crochet.
☞ 带,系带 string, cord, thong, tie, shoelace, bootlace.
v.
☞ 系 tie, do up, fasten, thread, close, bind, attach, string, intertwine, interweave.
☞ 搀 add to, mix in, spike, fortify.

lack n.
☞ 缺乏,需要 need, want, scarcity, shortage, insufficiency, dearth, deficiency, absence, scantiness, vacancy, void, privation, deprivation, destitution, emptiness.
v.
☞ 需要 need, want, require, miss.

lacking adj.
☞ 需要的,缺乏的 needing, wanting, without, short of, missing, minus, inadequate, deficient, defective, flawed.

lad n.
☞ 少年,小伙子 boy, youth, youngster, kid, schoolboy, chap, guy, fellow.

lag v.
☞ 落后,耽搁,延迟 dawdle, loiter, hang back, linger, straggle, trail, saunter, delay, shuffle, tarry, idle.

lake n.
☞ 湖 lagoon, reservoir, loch, mere, tarn.

lame adj.
☞ 跛的,瘸的 disabled, handicapped, crippled, limping, hobbling.
☞ 虚弱的,不能令人满意的 weak, feeble, flimsy, inadequate, unsatisfactory, poor.

land n.
☞ 陆地,土壤 earth, ground, soil, terra firma
☞ 庄园,地产 property, grounds, estate, real estate, country, countryside, farmland, tract.
☞ 国家 country, nation, region, territory, province.
v.
☞ 着陆,登陆 alight, disembark, bock, berth, touch down, come to rest, arrive, deposit, wind up, end up, drop, settle, turn up.

☞ 获得，取得 obtain, secure, gain, get, acquire, net, capture, achieve, win.

landlord n.
☞ 地主，旅店主 owner, proprietor, host, publican, innkeeper, hotelier, restaurateur, hotel-keeper, freeholder.

landmark n.
☞ 界标，陆标 feature, monument, signpost, turning-point, watershed, milestone, beacon, cairn.

landscape n.
☞ 风景，风景画 scene, scenery, view, panorama, outlook, vista, prospect, countryside, aspect.

landslide n.
☞ 山崩 landslip, earthfall, rock-fall, avalanche.
adj.
☞ 压倒性的 overwhelming, decisive, emphatic, runaway.

language n.
☞ 语言 speech, vocabulary, terminology, parlance.
☞ 谈话 talk, conversation, discourse.
☞ 措辞 wording, style, phraseology, phrasing, expression, utterance, diction.

languish v.
☞ 凋萎，苦恼 wilt, droop, fade, fail, flag, wither, waster away, weaken, sink, faint, decline, mope, waste, grieve, sorrow, sigh, sicken.
☞ 渴望 pine, yearn, want, long, desire, hanker, hunger.

lap¹ v.
☞ 舔食 drink, sip, sup, lick.

lap² n.
☞ 一周，一圈 circuit, round, orbit, tour, loop, course, circle, distance.
v.
☞ 包裹 wrap, fold, envelop, enfold, swathe, surround, cover, swaddle, overlap.

lapse n.
☞ 过失 error, slip, mistake, negligence, omission, oversight, fault, failing, indiscretion, aberration, backsliding, relapse.
☞ 堕落 fall, descent, decline, drop, deterioration.
☞ 间歇 break, gap, interval, lull, interruption, intermission, pause.
v.
☞ 失足 decline, fall, sink, drop, deteriorate, slide, slip, fail, worsen, degenerate, backslide.
☞ 终止，失效 expire, run out, end, stop, terminate.

large adj.
☞ 巨大的 big, huge, immense, massive, vast, sizable, great, giant, gigantic, bulky, enormous, king-sized, broad, considerable, monumental, substantial.
☞ 开阔的，慷慨的 full, extensive, generous, liberal, roomy, plentiful, spacious, grand, sweeping, grandiose.

at large
☞ 逍遥法外的 free, at libety, on the loose, on the run, independent.

largely adv.

☞ 主要地,大部分地 mainly, principally, chiefly, generally, primarily, predominantly, mostly, considerably, by and large, widely, extensively, greatly.

lash n.
☞ 鞭打 blow, whip, stroke, swipe, hit.

v.
☞ 鞭挞 whip, flog, beat, hit, thrash, strike, scourge.
☞ 责骂 attack, criticize, lay into, scold.

last¹ adj.
☞ 最后的 final, ultimate, closing, latest, rearmost, terminal, furthest, concluding, remotest, utmost, extreme, conclusive, definitive.

adv.
☞ 最后地,最终地 finally, ultimately, behind, after.

at last
☞ 最后 eventually, finally, in the end, in due course, at length.

last² v.
☞ 延续,延伸 continue, endure, remain, persist, keep (on), survive, hold out, carry on, wear, stay, hold on, stand up, abide.

lasting adj.
☞ 持久的,永远的 enduring, unchanging, unceasing, unending, continuing, permanent, perpetual, lifelong, long-standing, long-term.

latch n.
☞ 门锁 fastening, catch, bar, bolt, lock, hook, hasp.

late adj.
☞ 迟的 overdue, behind, behind-hand, slow, unpunctual, delayed, last-minute.
☞ 前任的 former, previous, departed, dead, deceased, past, preceding, old.
☞ 最近的 recent, up-to-date, current, fresh, new.

lately adv.
☞ 最近地 recently, of late, latterly.

later adv.
☞ 接下来 next, afterwards, subsequently, after, successively.

lateral adj.
☞ 侧面的,旁边的 sideways, side, oblique, sideward, edgeways, marginal, flanking.

laugh v.
☞ 笑 chuckle, giggle, guffaw, snigger, titter, chortle, split one's sides, fall about, crease up.

n.
☞ 笑 giggle, chuckle, snigger, titter, guffaw, chortle, lark, scream, hoot, joke.

laugh at
☞ 嘲笑 mock, ridicule, deride, jeer, make fun of, scoff at, scorn, taunt.

laughable adj.
☞ 愉悦的,可笑的 funny, amusing, comical, humorous, hilarious, droll, farcical, diverting.
☞ 滑稽的 ridiculous, absurd, ludicrous, preposterous,

nonsensical, derisory, derisive.

laughing-stock
- 笑柄 figure of fun, butt, victim, target, fair game.

laughter n.
- 笑声 laughing, giggling, chuckling, chortling, guffawing, tittering, hilarity, amusement, merriment, mirth, glee, convulsions.

launch v.
- 发射 propel, dispatch, discharge, send off, project, float, set in motion, throw, fire.
- 开动 begin, commence, start, embark on, establish, found, open, initiate, inaugurate, introduce, instigate.

lavatory v.
- 洗澡间 toilet, WC, bathroom, cloakroom, washroom, water-closet, public convenience, ladies, gents, bog, urinal, powder-room.

law n.
- 法规,规定 rule, act, decree, edict, order, statute, regulation, command, ordinance, charter, constitution, enactment.
- 法典 principle, axiom, criterion, standard, precept, formula, code, canon.
- 法律,法令 jurisprudence, legislation, litigation.

  law-abiding adj.
  - 守法的 obedient, upright, orderly, lawful, honest, honourable, decent, good.

lawyer n.
- 律师 solicitor, barrister, advocate, attorney, counsel, QC.

lay¹ v.
- 摆放 put, place, deposit, set down, settle, lodge, plant, set, establish, leave.
- 安排 arrange, position, set out, locate, work out, devise, prepare, present, submit.

lay into
- 指责,痛斥 attack, assail, pitch into, set about, tear into, let fly at.

lay off
- 让……走 dismiss, discharge, make redundant, sack, pay off, let go.
- 放弃 give up, drop, stop, quit, cease, desist, leave off, leave alone, let up.

lay out
- 陈列 display, set out, spread out, exhibit, arrange, plan, design.
- 击倒 knock out, fell, flatten, demolish.
- 花,用 spend, pay, shell out, fork out, give, invest.

lay up
- 储存 store up, hoard, accumulate, amass, keep, save, put away.

lay² adj.
- 凡俗的 laic, secular.
- 非专业的 amateur, non-professional, non-specialist.

layer n.
- 层,表面 cover, coating, coat, covering, film, blanket, mantle, sheet, lamina.

laze v.
☞ 懒散 idle, loaf, lounge, sit around, lie around, loll.

lazy adj.
☞ 懒惰的 idle, slothful, slack, work-shy, inactive, lethargic.

lead v.
☞ 指导 guide, conduct, escort, steer, pilot, usher.
☞ 统治 rule, govern, head, preside over, direct, supervise.
☞ 影响,左右 influence, persuade, incline.
☞ 领先 surpass, outdo, excel, outstrip, transcend.

n.
☞ 领先 priority, precedence, first place, start, van, vanguard, advantage, edge, margin.
☞ 领导 leadership, guidance, direction, example, model.

lead off
☞ 开始,出发 begin, commence, open, get going, start (off), inaugurate, initiate, kick off, start the ball rolling.

lead on
☞ 唆使,诱使 entice, lure, seduce, tempt, draw on, beguile, persuade, string along, deceive, trick.

lead to
☞ 导致 cause, result in, produce, bring about, bring on, contribute to, tend towards.

lead up to
☞ 带领,导致 prepare (the way) for, approach, introduce, make overtures, pave the way.

leader n.
☞ 领导者 head, chief, director, ruler, principal, commander, captain, boss, superior, chieftain, ringleader, guide, conductor.

leadership n.
☞ 领导,指挥 direction, control, command, management, authority, guidance, domination, pre-eminence, premiership, administration, sway, directorship.

leading adj.
☞ 有领导能力的,英明的 main, principal, chief, primary, first, supreme, outstanding, foremost, dominant, ruling, superior, greatest, highest, governing, pre-eminent, number one.

leaflet n.
☞ 传单,活页 pamphlet, booklet, brochure, circular, handout.

league n.
☞ 同盟,联盟 association, confederation, alliance, union, federation, confederacy, coalition, combination, band, syndicate, guild, consortium, cartel, combine, parnership, fellowship, compact.
☞ 类型,范畴 category, class, level, group.

in league
☞ 联合的 allied, collaborating, conspiring.

leak n.
☞ 漏洞 crack, hole, opening, puncture, crevice, chink.
☞ 渗漏 leakage, leaking, seepage, drip, oozing, percolation.

☞ 泄漏 disclosure, divulgence.

v.
☞ 使漏 seep, drip, ooze, escape, spill, trickle, percolate, exude, discharge.
☞ 泄露 divulge, disclose, reveal, let slip, make known, make public, tell, give away, pass on.

leaky *adj.*
☞ 有漏洞的 leaking, holey, perforated, punctured, split, cracked, porous, permeable.

lean¹ *v.*
☞ 倾斜 slant, slope, bend, tilt, list, tend.
☞ 偏向 recline, prop, rest.
☞ 依赖 incline, favour, prefer.

lean² *adj.*
☞ 瘦的 thin, skinny, bony, gaunt, lank, angular, slim, scraggy, scrawny, emaciated.
☞ 贫乏的 scanty, inadequate, bare, barren.

leaning *n.*
☞ 倾向,倾斜 tendency, inclination, propensity, partiality, liking, bent, bias, disposition, aptitude.

leap *v.*
☞ 使跳过,跃过 jump (over), bound, spring, vault, clear, skip, hop, bounce, caper, gambol.
☞ 上升 soar, surge, increase, rocket, escalate, rise.

n.
☞ 跳跃 jump, bound, spring, vault, hop, skip, caper.
☞ 增加 increase, upsurge, upswing, surge, rise, escalation.

learn *v.*
☞ 掌握,学会 grasp, comprehend, understand, master, acquire, pick up, gather, assimilate, discern.
☞ 记住 memorize, learn by heart.
☞ 发现,获悉 discover, find out, ascertain, hear, detect, determine.

learned *adj.*
☞ 充分理解的,精通的 scholarly, erudite, well-informed, well-read, cultured, academic, lettered, literate, intellectual, versed.

learner *n.*
☞ 初学者 novice, beginner, student, trainee, pupil, scholar, apprentice.

learning *n.*
☞ 学习 scholarship, erudition, education, schooling, knowledge, information, letters, study, wisdom, tuition, culture, edification, research.

lease *v.*
☞ 租借 let, loan, rent, hire, sublet, charter.

least *adj.*
☞ 最小的 smallest, lowest, minimum, fewest, slightest, poorest.

leave¹ *v.*
☞ 出发,离开 depart, go, go away, set out, take off, decamp, exit, move, quit, retire, withdraw, disappear, do a bunk.
☞ 留下 abandon, desert,

forsake, give up, drop, relinquish, renounce, pull out, surrender, desist, cease.

leave off
☞ 中断,打断 stop, cease, discontinue, desist, abstain, refrain, lay off, quit, terminate, break off, end, halt, give over.

leave out
☞ 忽略 omit, exclude, overlook, ignore, except, disregard, pass over, count out, cut (out), eliminate, neglect, reject, cast aside, bar.

leave² n.
☞ 许可 permission, authorization, consent, allowance, sanction, concession, indulgence, liberty, freedom.
☞ 请假 holiday, time off, vacation, sabbatical, furlough.

lecture n.
☞ 演讲 discourse, address, lesson, speech, talk, instruction.
☞ 教训,训斥 reprimand, rebuke, reproof, scolding, harangue, censure, chiding, telling-off, talking-to, dressing-down.
v.
☞ 说话,演讲 talk, teach, hold forth, speak, expound, address.
☞ 责诉 reprimand, reprove, scold, admonish, harangue, chide, censure, tell off.

left adj.
☞ 左,左边的 left-hand, port, sinistral.
☞ 左派的 left-wing, socialist, radical, progressive, revolutionary, liberal, communist, red.

left-overs n.
☞ 剩余物 leavings, remainder, remains, remnants, residue, surplus, scraps, sweepings, refuse, dregs, excess.

leg n.
☞ 肢,腿 limb, member, shank, pin, stump.
☞ 支柱 support, prop, upright, brace.

legacy n.
☞ 遗产 bequest, endowment, gift, heritage, inheritance, birthright, estate, heirloom.

legal adj.
☞ 合法的 lawful, legitimate, permissible, sanctioned, allowed, authorized, allowable, legalized, constitutional, valid, warranted, above-board, proper, rightful.
☞ 法律上承认的 judicial, forensic.
☞ 适用于法律的 judiciary.

legalize v.
☞ 使合法,使正当 legitimize, license, permit, sanction, allow, authorize, warrant, validate, approve.

legend n.
☞ 传奇,故事 myth, story, tale, folk-tale, fable, fiction, narrative.
☞ 刻字,铭文 inscription, caption, key, motto.

legendary adj.
☞ 传说的 mythical, fabulous, story-book, fictitious, traditional.
☞ 著名的 famous, celebrated,

legible *adj.*
☞ 易读的 readable, intelligible, decipherable, clear, distinct, neat.

legislate *v.*
☞ 立法 enact, ordain, authorize, codify, constitutionalize, prescribe, establish.

leisure *n.*
☞ 空闲,闲时 relaxation, rest, spare time, time off, ease, freedom, liberty, recreation, retirement, holiday, vacation.

leisurely *adj.*
☞ 从容的,慢慢的 unhurried, slow, relaxed, comfortable, easy, unhasty, tranquil, restful, gentle, carefree, laid-back, lazy, loose.

lend *v.*
☞ 伸出,借给 loan, advance.
☞ 给予 give, grant, bestow, provide, furnish, confer, supply, impart, contribute.

length *n.*
☞ 长度 extent, distance, measure, reach, portion, section, segment.
☞ 时期 duration, period, term, stretch, space, span.

lengthen *v.*
☞ 延长,使变长 stretch, extend, elongate, draw out, prolong, protract, spin out, eke (out), pad out, increase, expand, continue.

lessen *v.*
☞ 减少 decrease, reduce, diminish, lower, ease, abate, contract, die down, dwindle, lighten, slow down, weaken, shrink, abridge, de-escalate, erode, minimize, narrow, moderate, slack, flag, fail, deaden, impair.

lesser *adj.*
☞ 较低的,较不重要的 lower, secondary, inferior, smaller, subordinate, slighter, minor.

lesson *n.*
☞ 课程,课时 class, period, instruction, lecture, tutorial, teaching, coaching.
☞ 练习,技能 assignment, exercise, homework, practice, task, drill.
☞ 教训 example, model, warning, deterrent.

let *v.*
☞ 让,允许 permit, allow, give leave, give permission, authorize, consent to, agree to, sanction, grant, ok, enable, tolerate.
☞ 租借 lease, hire, rent.

let in
☞ 使……进入 admit, accept, receive, take in, include, incorporate, welcome.

let off
☞ 原谅 excuse, absolve, pardon, exempt, forgive, acquit, exonerate, spare, ignore, liberate, release.
☞ 释放 discharge, detonate, fire, explode, emit.

let out
☞ 放出 free, release, let go, discharge, leak.
☞ 泄漏 reveal, disclose, make known, utter, betray, let slip.

let up
☞ 减少，减轻 abate, subside, ease (up), moderate, slacken, diminish, decrease, stop, end, cease, halt.

let-down n.
☞ 失望 anticlimax, disappointment, disillusionment, set-back, betrayal, desertion, wash-out.

letter n.
☞ 信笺，便条 note, message, line, missive, epistle, dispatch, communication, chit, acknowledgement.
☞ 字母 character, symbol, sign, grapheme.

level adj.
☞ 平坦的 flat, smooth, even, flush, horizontal, aligned, plane.
☞ 同等的 equal, balanced, even, on a par, neck and neck, matching, uniform.

v.
☞ 损毁 demolish, destroy, devastate, flatten, knock down, raze, pull down, bulldoze, tear down, lay low.
☞ 使平 even out, flush, plane, smooth, equalize.
☞ 瞄准 direct, point.

n.
☞ 高度 height, elevation, altitude.
☞ 级别 postion, rank, status, class, degree, grade, standard, standing, plane, echelon, layer, stratum, storey, stage, zone.

liable adj.
☞ 易受影响的 inclined, likely, apt, disposed, prone, tending, susceptible.
☞ 有责任的 responsible, answerable, accountable, amenable.

liaison n.
☞ 联络 contact, connection, go-between, link.
☞ 沟通，私通 love affair, affair, romance, intrigue, amour, entanglement.

liar n.
☞ 说谎者 falsifier, perjurer, deceiver, fibber.

liberal adj.
☞ 心胸宽大的 broad-minded, open-minded, tolerant, lenient.
☞ 自由的 progressive, reformist, moderate.
☞ 大方的 generous, ample, bountiful, lavish, plentiful, handsome.

liberate v.
☞ 释放，解放 free, emancipate, release, let loose, let go, let out, set free, deliver, unchain, discharge, rescue, ransom.

liberty n.
☞ 自由 freedom, emancipation, release, independence, autonomy.
☞ 许可 licence, permission, sanction, right, authorization, dispensation, franchise.
☞ 随便 familiarity, disrespect, overfamiliarity, presumption, impertinence, impudence.

at liberty
☞ 不受约束的 free, unconstrained, unrestricted, not confined.

licence n.

license v.
- ☞ 许引,特许 permission, permit, leave, warrant, authorization, authority, certificate, charter, right, imprimatur, entitlement, privilege, dispensation, carte blanche, freedom, liberty, exemption, independence.
- ☞ 放肆 abandon, dissipation, excess, immoderation, indulgence, lawlessness, unruliness, anarchy, disorder, debauchery, dissoluteness, impropriety, irresponsibility.

license v.
- ☞ 特准 permit, allow, authorize, certify, warrant, entitle, empower, sanction, commission, accredit.

lick v.
- ☞ 舔,吃 tongue, touch, wash, lap, taste, dart, flick, flicker, play over, smear, brush.

lie¹ v.
- ☞ 说谎 perjure, misrepresent, fabricate, falsify, fib, invent, equivocate, prevaricate, forswear oneself.

  n.
- ☞ 谎言 falsehood, untruth, falsification, fabrication, invention, fiction, deceit, fib, falsity, white lie, prevarication, whopper.

lie² v.
- ☞ 位于 be, exist, dwell, belong, extend, remain.

lie down
- ☞ 躺下 repose, rest, recline, stretch out, lounge, couch, laze.

life n.
- ☞ 生命 being, existence, animation, breath, viability, entity, soul.
- ☞ 寿命 duration, course, span, career.
- ☞ 活力 liveliness, vigour, vitality, vivacity, verve, zest, energy, elan, spirit, sparkle, activity.

lifeless adj.
- ☞ 无生气的 dead, deceased, defunct, cold, unconscious, inanimate, insensible, stiff.
- ☞ 慢慢腾腾的 lethargic, listless, sluggish, dull, apathetic, passive, insipid, colourless, slow.
- ☞ 空虚的,单调的 barren, bare, empty, desolate, arid.

lifelong adj.
- ☞ 毕生的 lifetime, long-lasting, long-standing, persistent, lasting, enduring, abiding, permanent, constant.

lift v.
- ☞ 举起 raise, elevate, hoist, upraise.
- ☞ 提高,振奋 uplift, exalt, buoy up, boost.
- ☞ 解除 revoke, cancel, relax.

light¹ n.
- ☞ 光,光线 illumination, brightness, brilliance, luminescence, radiance, glow, ray, shine, glare, gleam, glint, lustre, flash, blaze.
- ☞ 灯 lamp, lantern, lighter, match, torch, candle, bulb, beacon.
- ☞ 白天 day, daybreak, daylight,

daytime, dawn, sunrise.
☞ 启发 enlightenment, explanation, elucidation, understanding.
v.
☞ 点燃 ignite, fire, set alight, set fire to, kindle.
☞ 照亮 illuminate, light up, lighten, brighten, animate, cheer, switch on, turn on, put on.
adj.
☞ 明亮的 illuminated, bright, brilliant, luminous, glowing, shining, well-lit, sunny.
☞ 淡的 pale, pastel, fair, blond, blonde, bleached, faded, faint.

light² adj.
☞ 轻的 weightless, insubstantial, delicate, airy, buoyant, flimsy, feathery, slight.
☞ 不值得的 trivial, inconsiderable, trifling, inconsequential, worthless.
☞ 高兴的 cheerful, cheery, carefree, lively, merry, blithe.
☞ 有趣的 entertaining, amusing, funny, humorous, frivolous, witty, pleasing.

lighten¹ v.
☞ 照亮 illuminate, illumine, brighten, light up, shine.

lighten² v.
☞ 减轻 ease, lessen, unload, lift, relieve, reduce, mitigate, alleviate.
☞ 使快乐,使轻松 brighten, cheer, encourage, hearten, inspirit, uplift, gladden, revive, elate, buoy up, inspire.

likable adj.
☞ 可爱的 loveable, pleasing, appealing, agreeable, charming, engaging, winsome, pleasant, amiable, congenial, attractive, sympathetic.

like¹ adj.
☞ 相似的 similar, resembling, alike, same, identical, equivalent, akin, corresponding, related, relating, parellel, allied, analogous, approximating.

like² v.
☞ 喜爱 enjoy, delight in, care for, admire, appreciate, love, adore, hold dear, esteem, cherish, prize, relish, revel in, approve, take (kindly) to.

likelihood n.
☞ 可能 likeliness, probability, possibility, chance, prospect, liability.

likely adj.
☞ 可能的 probable, possible, anticipated, expected, liable, prone, tending, predicatable, odds-on, inclined, foreseeable.
☞ 有原因的 credible, believable, plausible, feasible, reasonable.
☞ 有希望的 promising, hopeful, pleasing, appropriate, proper, suitable.
adv.
☞ 可能地 probably, presumably, like as not, in all probability, no doubt, doubtlessly.

likewise adv.
☞ 而且 moreover, furthermore, in addition, similarly, also, further, besides, by the same token, too.

limit n.

☞限度 boundary, bound, border, frontier, confines, edge, brink, threshold, verge, brim, end, perimeter, rim, compass, termination, ultimate, utmost, terminus, extent.
☞限定 check, curb, restraint, restriction, limitation, ceiling, maximum, cut-off point, saturation point, deadline.

v.
☞限制,限定 check, curb, restrict, restrain, constrain, confine, demarcate, delimit, bound, hem in, ration, specify, hinder.

limitation n.
☞限制 check, restriction, curb, control, constraint, restraint, delimitation, demarcation, block.
☞局限性 inadequacy, shortcoming, disadvantage, drawback, condition, qualification, reservation.

limited adj.
☞有限的,缺乏创业的 restricted, circumscribed, constrained, controlled, confined, checked, defined, finite, fixed, minimal, narrow, inadequate, insufficient.

limitless adj.
☞无限制的 unlimited, unbounded, boundless, undefined, immeasurable, incalculable, infinite, countless, endless, never-ending, unending, inexhaustible, untold, vast.

line n.
☞划线 stroke, band, bar, stripe, mark, strip, rule, dash, strand, streak, underline, score, scratch.
☞排列 row, rank, queue, file, column, sequence, series, procession, chain, trail.

lineage n.
☞血统,世家,家族 ancestry, descent, extraction, genealogy, family, line, pedigree, race, stock, birth, breed, house, heredity, ancestors, forebears, descendants, offspring, succession.

lined adj.
☞规定的 ruled, feint.
☞有皱的 wrinkled, furrowed, wizened, worn.

line-up n.
☞排列 array, arrangement, queue, row, selection, cast, team, bill.

linger v.
☞磨蹭 loiter, delay, dally, tarry, wait, remain, stay, hang on, lag, procrastinate, dawdle, dilly-dally, idle, stop, endure, hold out, last, persist, survive.

link n.
☞连接物 connection, bond, tie, association, joint, relationship, tie-up, union, knot, liaison, attachment, communication.

v.
☞连接 connect, join, couple, tie, fasten, unite, bind, amalgamate, merge, associate, ally, bracket, identify, relate, yoke, attach, hook up, join forces, team up.

lip n.

☞ 嘴唇 edge, brim, border, brink, rim, margin, verge.

liquid n.
☞ 液体,流体 liquor, fluid, juice, drink, sap, solution, lotion.
adj.
☞ 液体的 fluid, flowing, liquefied, watery, wet, runny, melted, molten, thawed, clear, smooth.

liquidate v.
☞ 除去,清理 annihilate, terminate, do away with, dissolve, kill, murder, massacre, assassinate, destroy, dispatch, abolish, eliminate, exterminate, remove, finish off, rub out.
☞ 清偿 pay (off), close down, clear, discharge, wind up, sell.

liquor n.
☞ 酒精,药汁 alcohol, intoxicant, strong drink, spirits, drink, hard stuff, booze.

list¹ n.
☞ 目录 catalogue, roll, inventory, register, schedule, index, listing, record, file, directory, table, tabulation, tally, series, syllabus, invoice.
v.
☞ 列表 enumerate, register, itemize, catalogue, index, tabulate, record, file, enroll, enter, note, bill, book, set down, write down.

list² v.
☞ 倾斜 lean, incline, tilt, slope, heel (over), tip.

literal *adj.*
☞ 原本的 verbatim, word-for-word, strict, close, actual, precise, faithful, exact, accurate, factual, true, genuine, unexaggerated.
☞ 不夸张的 prosaic, unimaginative, uninspired, matter-of-fact, down-to-earth, humdrum.

literature n.
☞ 文学 writings, letters, paper(s).
☞ 著作,文献 information, leaflet(s), pamphlet(s), circular(s), brochure(s), hand-out(s).

litter n.
☞ 混乱 rubbish, debris, refuse, waste, mess, disorder, clutter, confusion, disarray, untidiness, junk, muck, jumble, fragments, shreds.
☞ 同窝小息 offspring, young, progeny, brood, family.
v.
☞ 使散乱 strew, scatter, mess up, disorder, clutter.

little *adj.*
☞ 小的,短的 small, short, tiny, wee, minute, teeny, diminutive, miniature, infinitesimal, mini, microscopic, petite, pint-size(d), slender.
☞ 短时间的 short-lived, brief, fleeting, passing, transient.
☞ 徽量的 insignificant, inconsiderable, negligible, trivial, petty, trifling, unimportant.
adv.
☞ 稍微 barely, hardly, scarcely, rarely, seldom, infrequently, not much.

n.
- 少许 bit, dash, pinch, spot, trace, drop, dab, speck, touch, taste, particle, hint, fragment, modicum, trifle.

live¹ v.
- 活着 be, exist, breathe, draw breath.
- 生存 last, endure, continue, remain, persist, survive.
- 居住 dwell, inhabit, reside, lodge, abide.
- 经历 pass, spend, lead.

live² adj.
- 活的 alive, living, existent.
- 充满生命力的 lively, vital, active, energetic, dynamic, alert, vigorous.

livelihood n.
- 生活 occupation, employment, job, living, means, income, maintenance, work, support, subsistence, sustenance.

lively adj.
- 活泼的 animated, alert, active, energetic, spirited, vivacious, vigorous, sprightly, spry, agile, nimble, quick, keen.
- 热烈的 cheerful, blithe, merry, frisky, perky, breezy, chirpy, frolicsome.
- 热闹的 busy, bustling, brisk, crowded, eventful, exciting, buzzing.
- 闪亮的 vivid, bright, colourful, stimulating, stirring, invigorating, racy, refreshing, sparkling.

liven (up)
- 使高兴,使活泼 enliven, vitalize, put life into, rouse, invigorate, animate, energize, brighten, stir (up), buck up, pep up, perk up, hot up.

livid adj.
- 青黑色的 leaden, black-and-blue, bruised, discoloured, greyish, purple.
- 苍白的 pale, pallid, ashen, blanched, bloodless, wan, waxy, pasty.
- 愤怒的 angry, furious, infuriated, irate, outraged, enraged, raging, fuming, indignant, incensed, exasperated, mad.

living adj.
- 活的,生动的 alive, breathing, existing, live, current, extant, operative, strong, vigorous, active, lively, vital, animated.

n.
- 生计 being, life, animation, existence.
- 收入 livelihood, maintenance, support, income, subsistence, sustenance, work, job, occupation, profession, benefice, way of life.

load n.
- 负担 burden, onus, encumbrance, weight, pressure, oppression, millstone.
- 装载 cargo, consignment, shipment, goods, lading, freight.

v.
- 装载 burden, weigh down, encumber, overburden, oppress, trouble, weight, saddle with.

loaded adj.

☞ 载重的 burdened, charged, laden, full, weighted.

oafer n.
☞ 游手好闲的人 idler, shirker, skiver, sluggard, wastrel, lounger, ne'er-do-well, lazybones.

loan n.
☞ 贷款,借债 advance, credit, mortgage, allowance.
v.
☞ 借贷 lend, advance, credit, allow.

loathe v.
☞ 厌恶,憎恨 hate, detest, abominate, abhor, despise, dislike.

loathing n.
☞ 厌恶,憎恨 hatred, detestation, abhorrence, abomination, revulsion, repulsion, dislike, disgust, aversion, horror.

loathsome adj.
☞ 讨厌的 detestable, abhorrent, odious, repulsive, abominable, hateful, repugnant, repellent, offensive, horrible, disgusting, vile, revolting, nasty.

lobby v.
☞ 游说,通过议案 campaign for, press for, demand, persuade, call for, urge, push for, influence, solicit, pressure, promote.
n.
☞ 接待室,休息室 vestibule, foyer, porch, anteroom, hall, hallway, waiting-room, entrance hall, corridor, passage.
☞ 游说团 pressure group, campaign, ginger group.

local adj.
☞ 地方的,当地的 regional, provincial, community, district, neighbourhood, parochial, vernacular, small-town, limited, narrow, restricted, parish (pump).
n.
☞ 当地人 inhabitant, citizen, resident, native.
☞ 本地小酒店 pub.

locality n.
☞ 位置,地点 neighbourhood, vicinity, district, area, locale, region, position, place, site, spot, scene, setting.

locate v.
☞ 寻找 find, discover, unearth, run to earth, track down, detect, lay one's hands on, pinpoint, identify.
☞ 定位 situate, settle, fix, establish, place, put, set, seat.

location n.
☞ 地点,位置 position, situation, place, locus, whereabouts, venue, site, locale, bearings, spot, point.

lock n.
☞ 锁 fastening, bolt, clasp, padlock.
v.
☞ 上锁 fasten, secure, bolt, latch, seal, shut.
☞ 连接 join, unite, engage, link, mesh, entangle, entwine, clench.
☞ 封锁 clasp, hug, embrace, grasp, encircle, enclose, clutch, grapple.

lock out

☞拒之门外 shut out, refuse admittance to, keep out, exclude, bar, debar.

lock up
☞关进监狱 imprison, jail, confine, shut in, shut up, incarcerate, secure, cage, pen, detain, close up.

lodge n.
☞门房,传达室 hut, cabin, cottage, chalet, shelter, retreat, den, gatehouse, house, hunting-lodge, meeting-place, club, haunt.
v.
☞寄宿 accommodate, put up, quarter, board, billet, shelter.
☞逗留 live, stray, reside.
☞混合 fix, imbed, implant, get stuck.
☞提供住处 deposit, place, put, submit, register.

lodger n.
☞房客 boarder, paying guest, resident, tenant, roomer, inmate, guest.

lodgings n.
☞寓所 accommodation, digs, dwelling, quarters, billet, abode, boarding-house, rooms, pad, residence.

log n.
☞木头 timber, trunk, block, chunk.
☞航海或飞行日志 record, diary, jounal, logbook, daybook, account, tally.
v.
☞行进,记录 record, register, write up, note, book, chart, tally.

logic n.
☞逻辑,论理学 reasoning, reason, sense, deduction, rationale, argumentation.

logical adj.
☞逻辑的 reasonable, rational, reasoned, coherent, consistent, valid, sound, well-founded, clear, sensible, deducible, methodical, well-orgnized.

lone adj.
☞单独的 single, sole, one, only, isolated, solitary, separate, separated, unattached, unaccompanied, unattended.

loneliness n.
☞寂寞,凄凉 aloneness, isolation, lonesomeness, solitariness, solitude, seclusion, desolation.

lonely adj.
☞孤独的 alone, friendless, lonesome, solitary, abandoned, forsaken, companionless, unaccompanied, destitute.
☞偏僻的 isolated, uninhabited, remote, out-of-the-way, unfrequented, secluded, abandoned, deserted, forsaken, desolate.

long adj.
☞长的 lengthy, extensive, extended, expanded, prolonged, protracted, stretched, spread out, sustained, expansive, far-reaching, long-drawn-out, interminable, slow.

long for
☞希望,想要 yearn for, crave, want, wish, desire, dream of, hanker for, pine, thirst for, lust after, covet, itch for, yen for.

longing n.
☞ 渴望 craving, desire, yearning, hungering, hankering, yen, thirst, wish, urge, coveting, aspiration, ambition.

long-lasting adj.
☞ 长期的 permanent, imperishable, enduring, unchanging, unfading, continuing, abiding, long-standing, prolonged, protracted.

long-standing adj.
☞ 持久的,永久的 established, long-established, long-lived, long-lasting, enduring, abiding, time-honoured, traditional.

look v.
☞ 看 watch, see, observe, view, survey, regard, gaze, study, stare, examine, inspect, scrutinize, glance, contemplate, scan, peep, gawp.
☞ 显示 seem, appear, show, exhibit, display.

n.
☞ 看,视 view, survey, inspection, examination, observation, sight, review, once-over, glance, glimpse, gaze, peek.
☞ 表面现象 appearance, aspect, manner, semblance, mien, expression, bearing, face, complexion.

look after
☞ 照顾 take care of, mind, care for, attend to, take charge of, tend, keep an eye on, watch over, protect, supervise, guard.

look down on
☞ 瞧不起 despise, scorn, sneer at, hold in contempt, disdain, look down one's nose at, turn one's nose up at.

look forward to
☞ 希望做某事 anticipate, await, expect, hope for, long for, envisage, envision, count on, wait for, look for.

look into
☞ 调查,窥视 investigate, probe, research, study, go into, examine, enquire about, explore, check out, inspect, scrutinize, look over, plumb, fathom.

look out
☞ 注意,朝外看 pay attention, watch out, beware, be careful, keep an eye out.

look over
☞ 过目,检查 inspect, examine, check, give a once-over, cast an eye over, look through, scan, view.

look up
☞ 寻找,检寻 search for, research, hunt for, find, track down.

look up to
☞ 尊崇,崇敬 admire, esteem, respect, revere, honour, have a high opinion of.

look-out n.
☞ 守卫,门卫 guard, sentry, watch, watch-tower, watchman, sentinel, tower, post.
☞ 小心 concern, responsibility, worry, affair, business, problem.

loom v.
☞ 出现,显现 appear, emerge, take shape, menace, threaten,

impend, hang over, dominate, tower, overhang, rise, soar, overshadow, overtop.

loop n.
☞ 环绕 hoop, ring, circle, noose, coil, eyelet, loophole, spiral, curve, curl, kink, twist, whorl, twirl, turn, bend.
v.
☞ 使成圈环 coil, encircle, roll, bend, circle, curve, round, turn, twist, spiral, connect, join, knot, fold, braid.

loose adj.
☞ 自由的 free, unfastened, untied, movable, unattached, insecure, wobbly.
☞ 松散的 slack, lax, baggy, hanging.
☞ 不严谨的 imprecise, vague, inexact, ill-defined, indefinite, inaccurate, indistinct.

loosen v.
☞ 松散 ease, relax, loose, slacken, undo, unbind, untie, unfasten.
☞ 使自由 free, set free, release, let go, let out, deliver.

lose v.
☞ 忘记, 丢失 mislay, misplace, forget, miss, forfeit.
☞ 浪费 waste, squander, dissipate, use up, exhaust, expend, drain.
☞ 失败 fail, fall short, suffer defeat.

loser n.
☞ 失败者 failure, also-ran, runner-up, flop, no-hoper.

loss n.
☞ 失败 deprivation, disadvantage, defeat, failure, losing, bereavement, damage, destruction, ruin, hurt.
☞ 损失 waste, depletion, disappearance, deficiency, deficit.

lost adj.
☞ 遗失的, 毁灭的 mislaid, missing, vanished, disappeared, misplaced, astray.
☞ 迷惘的 confused, disoriented, bewildered, puzzled, baffled, perplexed, preoccupied.
☞ 浪费的 wasted, squandered, ruined, destroyed.

lot n.
☞ 许多 collection, batch, assortment, quantity, group, set, crowd.
☞ 一组, 一份 share, portion, allowance, ration, quota, part, piece, parlel.

loud adj.
☞ 喧哗的, 吵闹的 noisy, deafening, booming, resounding, ear-piercing, ear-splitting, piercing, thundering, blaring, clamorous, vociferous.
☞ 华丽的 garish, gaudy, glaring, flashy, brash, showy, ostentatious, tasteless.

lounge v.
☞ 懒散, 闲逛 relax, loll, idle, laze, waste time, kill time, lie about, take it easy, sprawl, recline, lie back, slump.
n.
☞ 起居室, 卧室 sitting-room, living-room, drawing-room, day-room, parlour.

lovable adj.
☞ 可爱的 adorable, endearing,

winsome, captivating, charming, engaging, attractive, fetching, sweet, lovely, pleasing, delightful.

love v.
☞ 爱 adore, cherish, dote on, treasure, hold dear, idolize, worship.
☞ 喜爱 like, take pleasure in, enjoy, delight in, appreciate, desire, fancy.

n.
☞ 爱情 adoration, affection, fondness, attachment, regard, liking, amorousness, ardour, devotion, adulation, passion, rapture, tenderness, warmth, inclination, infatuation, delight, enjoyment, weakness, taste, friendship.

love affair n.
☞ 爱情 affair, romance, liaison, relationship, love, passion.

lovely adj.
☞ 可爱的 beautiful, charming, delightful, attractive, enchanting, pleasing, pleasant, pretty, adorable, agreeable, enjoyable, sweet, winning, exquisite.

lover n.
☞ 情人 beloved, admirer, boyfriend, girlfriend, sweetheart, suitor, mistress, fiance(e), flame.

loving adj.
☞ 爱的，钟爱的 amorous, affectionate, devoted, doting, fond, ardent, passionate, warm, warm-hearted, tender.

low adj.
☞ 短小的，低的 short, small, squat, stunted, little, shallow, deep, depressed, sunken.
☞ 贫穷的 inadequate, deficient, poor, sparse, meagre, paltry, scant, insignificant.
☞ 低沉的 unhappy, depressed, downcast, gloomy.
☞ 基础的 base, coarse, vulgar, mean, contemptible.
☞ 低价的 cheap, inexpensive, reasonable.

lower adj.
☞ 较低的 inferior, lesser, subordinate, secondary, minor, second-class, low-level, lowly, junior.

v.
☞ 降下 drop, depress, sink, descend, let down.
☞ 减少 reduce, decrease, cut, lessen, diminish.

lowly adj.
☞ 卑下的，位低的 humble, low-born, obscure, poor, plebeian, plain, simple, modest, ordinary, inferior, meek, mild, mean, submissive, subordinate.

loyal adj.
☞ 忠实的 true, faithful, steadfast, staunch, devoted, trustworthy, sincere, patriotic.

loyalty n.
☞ 忠诚，忠实 allegiance, faithfulness, fidelity, devotion, steadfastness, constancy, trustworthiness, reliability, patriotism.

luck n.
☞ 运气，机会 chance, fortune, accident, fate, fortuity, fluke, destiny.

luck n.
☞ 好运 good fortune, success, break, godsend.

luckily adv.
☞ 幸运地 fortunately, happily, providentially.

lucky adj.
☞ 幸运的 fortunate, favoured, auspicious, successful, prosperous, timely.

lull v.
☞ 使缓和,使安静 soothe, subdue, calm, hush, pacify, quieten down, quiet, quell, compose.
n.
☞ 平静,间歇 calm, peace, quiet, tranquillity, stillness, let-up, pause, hush, silence.

lure v.
☞ 引诱 tempt, entice, draw, attract, allure, seduce, ensnare, lead on.
n.
☞ 诱饵 temptation, enticement, attraction, bait, inducement.

lush adj.
☞ 茂盛的 flourishing, luxuriant, abundant, prolific, overgrown, green, verdant.
☞ 奢华的 sumptuous, opulent, ornate, plush, rich.

luxurious adj.
☞ 奢侈的,浪费的 sumptuous, opulent, lavish, de luxe, plush, magnificent, splendid, expensive, costly, self-indulgent, pampered.

luxury n.
☞ 豪华 sumptuousness, opulence, hedonism, splendour, affluence, richness, magnificence, pleasure, indulgence, gratification, comfort, extravagance, satisfaction.

lying adj.
☞ 说谎的,虚伪的 deceitful, dishonest, false, untruthful, double-dealing, two-faced.
n.
☞ 说谎 dishonesty, untruthfulness, deceit, falsity, fibbing, perjury, duplicity, fabrication, double-dealing.

M

machine n.
☞ 机器 instrument, device, contrivance, tool, mechanism, engine, apparatus, appliance.
☞ 机械系统 agency, organization, structure, system.

machinery n.
☞ 机器,机件 instruments, mechanism, tools, apparatus, equipment, tackle, gear.
☞ 机关,组织 organization, channels, structure, system, procedure.

mad adj.
☞ 发疯的 insane, lunatic, unbalanced, psychotic, deranged, demented, out of one's mind, crazy, nuts,

barmy, bonkers.
- 发怒的 angry, furious, enraged, infuriated, incensed.
- 不理智 irrational, illogical, unreasonable, absurd, preposterous, foolish.
- 热情的 fanatical, enthusiastic, infatuated, ardent.

madden v.
- 使疯狂,使发怒 anger, enrage, infuriate, incense, exasperate, provoke, annoy, irritate.

madly adv.
- 发狂地 excitedly, frantically, furiously, rapidly, hastily, hurriedly.
- 狂热地 intensely, extremely, exceedingly, fervently, devotedly.

madman, madwoman n.
- 疯子 lunatic, psychotic, psychopath, maniac, loony, nutcase, fruitcake.

magazine n.
- 杂志 journal, periodical, paper, weekly, monthly, quarterly.
- 军火库 arsenal, storehouse, ammunition dump, depot, ordnance.

magic n.
- 巫法,幻术 sorcery, enchantment, occultism, black art, witchcraft, spell.
- 魔术 conjuring, illusion, sleight of hand, trickery.
- 符咒 charm, fasination, glamour, allure.

adj.
- 迷人的,充满诱惑的 charming, enchanting, bewitching, fascinating, spellbinding.

magician n.
- 魔术师,术士 sorcerer, miracle-worker, conjuror, enchanter, wizard, witch, warlock, spellbinder, wonder-worker.

magnetic adj.
- 有吸引力的 attractive, alluring, fascinating, charming, mesmerizing, seductive, irresistible, entrancing, captivating, gripping, absorbing, charismatic.

magnificent adj.
- 华丽的,豪华的 splendid, grand, imposing, impressive, glorious, gorgeous, brilliant, excellent, majestic, superb, sumptuous, noble, elegant, fine, rich.

magnify v.
- 放大,扩大 enlarge, amplify, increase, expand, intensify, boost, enhance, greaten, heighten, deepen, build up, exaggerate, dramatize, overemphasize, overplay, overstate, overdo, blow up.

magnitude n.
- 大小,宽度 size, extent, measure, amount, expanse, dimensions, mass, proportions, quantity, volume, bulk, largeness, space, strength, amplitude.
- 重要性 importance, consequence, significance, weight, greatness, moment, intensity.

maiden n.
☞ 少女，处女 girl, virgin, lass, lassie, damsel, miss.

mail n.
☞ 邮件，邮车 post, letters, correspondence, packages, parcels, delivery.
v.
☞ 邮寄 post, send, dispatch, forward.

main adj.
☞ 主要的，重要的 principal, chief, leading, first, foremost, predominant, pre-eminent, primary, prime, supreme, paramount, central, cardinal, outstanding, essential, critical, crucial, necessary, vital.
n.
☞ 主要部分，干线 pipe, duct, conduit, channel, cable, line.

mainly adv.
☞ 主要地，大体上 primarily, principally, chiefly, in the main, mostly, on the whole, for the most part, generally, in general, especially, as a rule, above all, largely, overall.

maintain v.
☞ 继续 carry on, continue, keep (up), sustain, retain.
☞ 保养 care for, conserve, look after, take care of, preserve, support, finance, supply.
☞ 坚持 assert, affirm, claim, contend, declare, hold, state, insist, believe, fight for.

maintenance n.
☞ 保持 continuation, continuance, perpetuation.
☞ 保养 care, conservation, preservation, support, repairs, protection, upkeep, running.
☞ 维持生计的方法 keep, subsistence, living, livelihood, allowance, alimony.

majestic adj.
☞ 有威严的，崇高的 magnificent, grand, dignified, noble, royal, stately, splendid, imperial, impressive, exalted, imposing, regal, sublime, superb, lofty, monumental, pompous.

majesty n.
☞ 崇高，尊严 grandeur, glory, dignity, magnificence, nobility, royalty, resplendence, splendour, stateliness, pomp, exaltedness, impressiveness, loftiness.

major adj.
☞ 较大的，主要的 greater, chief, main, larger, bigger, higher, leading, outstanding, notable, supreme, uppermost, significant, crucial, important, key, keynote, great, senior, older, superior, pre-eminent, vital, weighty.

majority n.
☞ 大多数 bulk, mass, preponderance, meet, greater part.
☞ 成人 adulthood, maturity, manhood, womanhood, years of discretion.

make v.
☞ 形成，生成 create, manufacture, fabricate, construct, build, produce, put together, originate, compose, form, shape.

- 使产生 cause, bring about, effect, accomplish, occasion, give rise to, generate, render, perform.
- 迫使 coerce, force, oblige, constrain, compel, prevail upon, pressurize, press, require.
- 任命 appoint, elect, designate, nominate, ordain, install.
- 获得 earn, gain, net, obtain, acquire.

n.
- 构造,样式 brand, sort, type, style, variety, manufacture, model, mark, kind, form, structure.

make off
- 逃跑 run off, run away, depart, bolt, leave, fly, cut and run, beat a hasty retreat, clear off.

make out
- 发现 discern, perceive, decipher, distinguish, recognize, see, detect, discover, understand, work out, grasp, follow, fathom.
- 完成 draw up, complete, fill in, write out.
- 证实 maintain, imply, claim, assert, describe, demonstrate, prove.
- 发展 manage, get on, progress, succeed, fare.

make up
- 发明,虚构 create, invent, devise, fabricate, construct, originate, formulate, dream up, compose.
- 供给 complete, fill, supply, meet, supplement.
- 形成 comprise, constitute, compose, form.
- 言归于好 be reconciled, make peace, settle differences, bury the hatchet, forgive and forget, call it quits.

make up for
- 弥补 compensate for, make good, make amends for, redress, recompense, redeem, atone for.

make-believe n.
- 假装 pretence, imagination, fantasy, unreality, play-acting, role-play, dream, charade.

maker n.
- 制造者,创造者 creator, manufacturer, constructor, builder, producer, director, architect, author.

makeshift adj.
- 临时的,代替的 temporary, improvised, rough and ready, provisional, substitute, stop-gap, expedient, make-do.

make-up n.
- 化妆 cosmetics, paint, powder, maquillage, war paint.
- 组织,构成 constitution, nature, composition, character, construction, form, format, formation, arrangement, organization, style, structure, assembly.

male adj.
- 男性的 masculine, manly, virile, boyish, he-.

malfunction n.
- 障碍,故障 fault, defect, failure, breakdown.

v.

☞发生故障 break down, go wrong, fail.

malice n.
☞恶意,怨恨 malevolence, enmity, animosity, ill-will, hatred, hate, spite, vindictiveness, bitterness.

malicious adj.
☞有恶意的 malevolent, ill-natured, malign, spiteful, venomous, vicious, vengeful, evil-minded, bitter, resentful.

malign adj.
☞有害的 malignant, malevolent, bad, evil, harmful, hurtful, injurious, destructive, hostile.
v.
☞诋毁 defame, slander, libel, disparage, abuse, run down, harm, injure.

maltreat v.
☞虐待,误用 ill-treat, mistreat, misuse, abuse, injure, harm, damage, hurt.

man n.
☞男人 male, gentleman, fellow, bloke, chap, guy.
☞人 human being, person, individual, adult, human.
☞人类,人种 humanity, humankind, mankind, human race, people, homo sapiens, mortals.
☞仆人 manservant, servant, worker, employee, hand, soldier, valet, houseman, houseboy.
v.
☞配置人员 staff, crew, take charge of, operate, occupy.

manage v.
☞产生好效果,完成 accomplish, succeed, bring about, bring off, effect.
☞指挥 administer, direct, run, command, govern, preside over, rule, superintend, supervise, oversee, conduct.
☞控制 control, influence, deal with, handle, operate, manipulate, guide.

management n.
☞管理,经理 administration, direction, control, government, command, running, superintendence, supervision, charge, care, handling.
☞资方,管理部门 managers, directors, directorate, executive, executives, governors, board, bosses, supervisors.

manager n.
☞经理,管理人 director, executive, administrator, controller, superintendent, supervisor, overseer, governor, organizer, head, boss.

manifest adj.
☞明白的,明显的 obvious, evident, clear, apparent, plain, open, patent, noticeable, conspicuous, unmistakable, visible, unconcealed.
v.
☞表明,显示 show, exhibit, display, demonstrate, reveal, set forth, expose, prove, illustrate, establish.

manifestation n.
☞表明,表示 display, exhibition, demonstration, show, revelation, exposure,

manipulate v.
- 操纵,使用 handle, control, wield, operate, use, manoeuvre, influence, engineer, guide, direct, steer, negotiate, work.
- 巧妙处理 falsify, rig, juggle with, doctor, cook, fiddle.

mankind n.
- 人类 humankind, humanity, human race, man, homo sapiens, people.

man-made adj.
- 人造的 synthetic, manufactured, simulated, imitation, artificial.

manner n.
- 方法,途径 way, method, means, fashion, style, procedure, process, form.
- 态度,举止 behaviour, conduct, bearing, demeanour, air, appearance, look, character.

manners n.
- 礼节 behaviour, conduct, demeanour, etiquette, politeness, bearing, courtesy, formalities, social graces, p's and q's.

manoeuvre n.
- 调遣,策略 move, movement, operation, action, exercise, plan, ploy, plot, ruse, strategy, machination, gambit, tactic, trick, scheme, dodge.

v.
- 练习,演习 move, manipulate, handle, guide, pilot, steer, navigate, jockey, direct, drive, exercise.
- 用计策 contrive, engineer, plot, scheme, wangle, pull strings, manipulate, manage, plan, devise, negotiate.

manual n.
- 手册 handbook, guide, guidebook, instructions, bible, vade mecum, directions.

adj.
- 手制的 hand-operated, by hand, physical, human.

manufacture v.
- 大规模制造 make, produce, construct, build, fabricate, create, assemble, mass-produce, turn out, process, forge, form.
- 创作,创造 invent, make up, concoct, fabricate, think up.

n.
- 生产 production, making, construction, fabrication, mass-production, assembly, creation, formation.

manufacturer n.
- 制造者,创造商 maker, producer, industrialist, constructor, factory-owner, builder, creator.

manure n.
- 肥料 fertilizer, compost, muck, dung.

many adj.
- 许多的,很多的 numerous, countless, lots of, manifold, various, varied, sundry, diverse, umpteen.

map n.
- 地图 chart, plan, street plan, atlas, graph, plot.

mar v.
- 损坏,损毁 spoil, impair, harm, hurt, damage, deface, disfigure, mutilate, injure, maim, scar, detract from, mangle, ruin, wreck, tarnish.

march v.
- 行军,行进 walk, stride, parade, pace, file, tread, stalk/

margin n.
- 边缘 border, edge, boundary, bound, periphery, perimeter, rim, brink, limit, confine, verge, side, skirt.
- 富裕,余地 allowance, play, leeway, latitude, scope, room, space, surplus, extra.

marginal adj.
- 边缘的 borderline, peripheral, negligible, minimal, insignificant, minor, slight, doubtful, low, small.

marine adj.
- 海的,海事的 sea, maritime, naval, nautical, seafaring, sea-going, ocean-going, salt-water.

marital adj.
- 婚姻的 conjugal, matrimonial, married, wedded, nuptial, connubial.

maritime adj.
- 航海的,海事的 marine, nautical, naval, maritime, sea, seaside, oceanic, coastal.

mark n.
- 痕迹 spot, stain, blemish, blot, blotch, smudge, dent, impression, scar, scratch, bruise, line.
- 标价 symbol, sign, indication, emblem, brand, stamp, token, characteristic, feature, proof, evidence, badge.
- 目标,目地 target, goal, aim, objective, purpose.

v.
- 做记号 stain, blemish, blot, smudge, dent, scar, scratch, bruise.
- 表示特征 brand, label, stamp, characterize, identify, distinguish.
- 注意,关心 heed, listen, mind, note, observe, regard, notice, take to heart.

marked adj.
- 醒目的 noticeable, obvious, conspicuous, evident, pronounced, distinct, decided, emphatic, considerable, remarkable, apparent, glaring.
- 被注意的 suspected, watched, doomed.

market n.
- 市场,交易 mart, marketplace, bazaar, fair, exchange, outlet.

v.
- 销售,贩卖 sell, retail, hawk, peddle.

marriage n.
- 结婚 matrimony, wedlock, wedding, nuptials.
- 结合 union, alliance, merger, coupling, amalgamation, link, association, confederation.

marry v.
- 使结婚 wed, join in matrimony, tie the knot, get hitched, get spliced.
- 使结合 unite, ally, join, merge, match, link, knit.

marsh n.

- 沼泽,低湿地 marshland, bog, swamp, fen, morass, quagmire.

marshal v.
- 排列,整顿 arrange, dispose, order, line up, align, array, rank, organize, assemble, gather, muster, group, collect, draw up, deploy.
- 引导 guide, lead, escort, conduct, usher.

marvel n.
- 令人惊奇的事物 wonder, miracle, phenomenon, prodigy, spectacle, sensation, genius.

v.
- 对……感到惊讶,惊奇 wonder, gape, gaze, be amazed at.

marvellous adj.
- 令人惊叹的 wonderful, excellent, splendid, superb, magnificent, terrific, super, fantastic.
- 绝妙的 extraordinary, amazing, astonishing, astounding, miraculous, remarkable, surprising, unbelievable, incredible, glorious.

masculine adj.
- 男性的 male, manlike, manly, mannish, virile, macho.
- 雄性的,阳性的 vigorous, strong, strapping, robust, powerful, muscular, red-blooded, bold, brave, gallant, resolute, stout-hearted.

mask n.
- 面具,面罩 disguise, camouflage, facade, front, concealment, cover-up, cover, guise, pretence, semblance, cloak, veil, blind, show, veneer, visor.

v.
- 掩饰,掩盖 disguise, camouflage, cover, conceal, cloak, veil, hide, obscure, screen, shield.

mass n.
- 团,块 heap, pile, load, accumulation, aggregate, collection, conglomeration, combination, entirety, whole, totality, sum, lot, group, batch, bunch.
- 聚群 quantity, multitude, throng, troop, crowd, band, horde, mob.
- 主体 majority, body, bulk.
- 多数 dimension, magnitude, immensity.
- 大量 lump, piece, chunk, block, hunk.

adj.
- 全部的,总的,大量的 widespread, large-scale, extensive, comprehensive, general, indiscriminate, popular, across-the-board, sweeping, wholesale, blanket.

v.
- 聚集 collect, gather, assemble, congregate, crowd, rally, cluster, muster, swarm, throng.

massacre n.
- 大屠杀 slaughter, murder, extermination, carnage, butchery, holocaust, blood bath, annihilation, killing.

v.
- 残杀,乱砍 slaughter,

butcher, murder, mow down, wipe out, exterminate, annihilate, kill, decimate.

massage n.
☞ 按摩,推拿 manipulation, kneading, rubbing, rub-down.
v.
☞ 对……施以按摩 manipulate, knead, rub (down).

massive adj.
☞ 巨大的,厚重的 huge, immense, enormous, vast, colossal, gigantic, big, bulky, monumental, solid, substantial, heavy, large-scale, extensive.

master n.
☞ 主人 ruler, chief, governor, head, lord, captain, boss, employer, commander, controller, director, manager, superintendent, overseer, principal, overlord, owner.
☞ 负责人,长官 expert, genius, virtuoso, past master, maestro, dab hand, ace, pro.
☞ 教师 teacher, tutor, instructor, schoolmaster, guide, guru, preceptor.
adj.
☞ 主要的 chief, principal, main, leading, foremost, prime, predominant, controlling, great, grand.
☞ 专业的 expert, masterly, skilled, skilful, proficient.
v.
☞ 支配,统治 conquer, defeat, subdue, subjugate, vanquish, triumph over, overcome, quell, rule, control.
☞ 掌握,精通 learn, grasp, acquire, get the hang of, manage.

masterpiece n.
☞ 杰作,极品 master-work, magnum opus, piece de resistance, chef d'oeuvre, jewel.

mastery n.
☞ 知识,优势 proficiency, skill, ability, command, expertise, virtuosity, knowledge, know-how, dexterity, familiarity, grasp.
☞ 统治权 control, command, domination, supremacy, upper hand, domination, authority.

match n.
☞ 比赛 contest, competition, bout, game, test, trial.
☞ 对手 equal, equivalent, peer, counterpart, fellow, mate, rival, copy, double, replica, look-alike, twin, duplicate.
☞ 配合 marriage, alliance, union, partnership, affiliation.
v.
☞ 对抗 equal, compare, measure up to, rival, compete, oppose, contend, vie, pit against.
☞ 使……适合 fit, go with, accord, agree, suit, correspond, harmonize, tally, co-ordinate, blend, adapt, go together, relate, tone with, accompany.
☞ 使……配合 join, marry, unite, mate, link, couple, combine, ally, pair, yoke, team.

matching adj.
☞ 同一的,相同的 corresponding, comparable, equivalent, like, identical, co-ordinating, similar, duplicate, same, twin.

matchless adj.
- 无比的,无双的 unequalled, peerless, incomparable, unmatched, unparalleled, unsurpassed, unrivalled, inimitable, unique.

mate n.
- 伙伴,朋友 friend, companion, comrade, pal, colleague, partner, fellow-worker, co-worker, associate.
- 伴侣 spouse, husband, wife.
- 助手 assistant, helper, subordinate.
- 同伴 match, fellow, twin.

v.
- 配对 couple, pair, breed, copulate.
- 结婚 join, match, marry, wed.

material n.
- 物质 stuff, substance, body, matter.
- 衣料,木料 fabric, textile, cloth.
- 资料 information, facts, data, evidence, constituents, work, notes.

adj.
- 物质的 physical, concrete, tangible, substantial.
- 重要的 relevant, significant, important, meaningful, pertinent, essential, vital, indispensable, serious.

matter n.
- 事情,问题 subject, issue, topic, question, affair, business, concern, event, episode, incident.
- 重要 importance, significance, consequence, note.
- 麻烦 trouble, problem, difficulty, worry.
- 资料 substance, stuff, material, body, content.

v.
- 要紧,有重大关系 count, be important, make a difference, mean something.

matter-of-fact adj.
- 实事求是的 emotionless, straightforward, sober, unimaginative, flat, deadpan.

mature adj.
- 成熟的,慎重的 adult, grown-up, grown, full-grown, fully fledged, complete, perfect, perfected, well-thought-out.

v.
- 长大 grow up, come of age, develop, mellow, ripen, perfect, age, bloom, fall, due.

maturity n.
- 成熟 adulthood, majority, womanhood, manhood, wisdom, experience.
- 齐备,完成 ripeness, readiness, mellowness, perfection.

maxim n.
- 格言,箴言 saying, proverb, adage, axiom, aphorism, epigram, motto, byword, precept, rule.

maximum adj.
- 最大的,最大值的 greatest, highest, largest, biggest, most, utmost, supreme.

n.
- 最大量,最高量 most, top (point), utmost, upper limit, peak, pinnacle, summit, height, ceiling, extremity,

maybe adv.
- 或许,大概 perhaps, possibly, perchance.

maze n.
- 迷惘,错综复杂 labyrinth, network, tangle, web, complex, confusion, puzzle, intricacy.

meadow n.
- 草地,多草的地方 field, grassland, pasture, lea.

mean[1] adj.
- 吝啬的 miserly, niggardly, parsimonious, selfish, tight, tight-fisted, stingy, penny-pinching.
- 坏脾气的 unkind, unpleasant, nasty, bad-tempered, cruel.
- 低级的 lowly, base, poor, humble, wretched.

mean[2] v.
- 意思指 signify, represent, denote, stand for, symbolize, suggest, indicate, imply.
- 目的是 intend, aim, propose, design.

mean[3] adj.
- 中间的 average, intermediate, middle, halfway, median, normal.

n.
- 中庸,平均 average, middle, mid-point, norm, median, compromise, middle course, middle way, happy medium, golden mean.

meaning n.
- 意思,意义 significance, sense, import, implication, gist, trend, explanation, interpretation.
- 目标 aim, intention, purpose, object, idea.

meaningful adj.
- 意味深长的 important, significant, relevant, valid, useful, worthwhile, material, purposeful, serious.
- 有目的的 expressive, speaking, suggestive, warning, pointed.

meaningless adj.
- 无意义的 senseless, pointless, purposeless, useless, insignificant, aimless, futile, insubstantial, trifling, trivial.
- 没意思的 empty, hollow, vacuous, vain, worthless, nonsensical, absurd.

means n.
- 方法,手段 method, mode, way, medium, course, agency, process, instrument, channel, vehicle.
- 财富,金钱 resources, funds, money, income, wealth, riches, substance, wherewithal, fortune, affluence.

measure n.
- 份额 portion, ration, share, allocation, quota.
- 尺寸 size, quantity, magnitude, amount, degree, extent, range, scope, proportion.
- 量度,标准 rule, gauge, scale, standard, criterion, norm, touchstone, yardstick, test, meter.
- 措施 step, course, action, deed, procedure, method, act, bill, statute.

v.
- 测量,估量 quantify, evaluate, assess, weigh, value, gauge, judge, sound, fathom, determine, calculate, estimate, plumb, survey, compute, measure out, measure out, measure off.

measured adj.
- 精确的 deliberate, planned, reasoned, slow, unhurried, steady, studied, well-thought-out, calculated, careful, considered, precise.

measurement n.
- 尺寸,大小 dimension, size, extent, amount, magnitude, area, capacity, height, depth, length, width, weight, volume.
- 衡量,测量 assessment, evaluation, estimation, computation, calculation, calibration, gauging, judgement, appraisal, appreciation, survey.

meat n.
- 肉,食用肉 flesh.
- 食物 food, rations, provisions, nourishment, sustenance, subsistence, eats.

mechanical adj.
- 机械 automatic, involuntary, instinctive, routine, habitual, impersonal, emotionless, cold, matter-of-fact, unfeeling, lifeless, dead, dull.

mechanism n.
- 机械,装置 machine, machinery, engine, appliance, instrument, tool, motor, works, workings, gadget, device, apparatus, contrivance, gears, components.
- 方法,技术 means, method, agency, process, procedure, system, technique, medium, structure, operation, functioning, performance.

meddle v.
- 干涉,扰乱 interfere, intervene, pry, snoop, intrude, butt in, tamper.

meddlesome adj.
- 好管闲事的 interfering, meddling, prying, intrusive, intruding, mischievous.

mediate v.
- 调解,和解 arbitrate, conciliate, intervene, referee, umpire, intercede, moderate, reconcile, negotiate, resolve, settle, step in.

mediator n.
- 调解者,仲裁者 arbitrator, referee, umpire, intermediary, negotiator, go-between, interceder, judge, moderator, intercessor, conciliator, peacemaker, Ombudsman.

medicinal adj.
- 医药的,治病的 therapeutic, healing, remedial, curative, restorative, medical.

medicine n.
- 医药 medication, drug, cure, remedy, medicament, prescription, pharmaceutical, panacea.

meditate v.
- 考虑 reflect, ponder, ruminate, contemplate, muse, brood, think.
- 深思 think over, consider,

deliberate, mull over, study, speculate, scheme, plan, devise, intend.

medium *adj.*
☞ 中间的，中等的 average, middle, median, mean, medial, intermediate, middling, midway, standard, fair.
n.
☞ 中间 average, middle, mid-point, middle ground, compromise, centre, happy medium, golden mean.
☞ 手段 means, agency, channel, vehicle, instrument, way, mode, form, avenue, organ.
☞ 巫术 psychic, spiritualist, spiritist, clairvoyant.

meet *v.*
☞ 遇见 encounter, come across, run across, run into, chance on, bump into.
☞ 会面，见面 experience, encounter, face, go through, undergo, endure.
☞ 聚合 gather, collect, assemble, congregate, convene.
☞ 使满足 fulfil, satisfy, match, answer, measure up to, equal, discharge, perform.
☞ 相连 join, converge, come together, connect, cross, intersect, touch, abut, unite.

meeting *n.*
☞ 会面 encounter, confrontation, rendezvous, engagement, assignation, introduction, trust.
☞ 集会 assembly, gathering, congregation, conference, convention, rally, get-together, forum, conclave, session.

☞ 汇合点 convergence, confluence, junction, intersection, union.

melancholy *adj.*
☞ 忧郁的，抑郁的，悲伤的 depressed, dejected, downcast, down, down-hearted, gloomy, low, low-spirited, heavy-hearted, sad, unhappy, despondent, dispirited, miserable, mournful, dismal, sorrowful, moody.
n.
☞ 悲伤，抑郁 depression, dejection, gloom, despondency, low spirits, blues, sadness, unhappiness, sorrow.

mellow *adj.*
☞ 甜醇的 mature, ripe, juicy, full-flavoured, sweet, tender, mild.
☞ 沉迷的 genial, cordial, affable, pleasant, relaxed, placid, serene, tranquil, cheerful, happy, jolly.
☞ 松软的，柔和的 smooth, melodious, rich, rounded, soft.
v.
☞ 使软化，使芳醇 mature, ripen, improve, sweeten, soften, temper, season, perfect.

melody *n.*
☞ 音乐，歌曲 tune, music, song, refrain, harmony, theme, air, strain.

melt *v.*
☞ 溶化，溶解 liquefy, dissolve, thaw, fuse, deliquesce.

melt away
☞ 消失 disappear, vanish, fade, evaporate, dissolve, disperse.

member *n.*

☞会员,成员 adherent, associate, subscriber, representative, comrade, fellow.

memorable *adj.*
☞值得纪念的,难忘的 unforgettable, remarkable, significant, impressive, notable, noteworthy, extraordinary, important, outstanding, momentous.

memorial *n.*
☞记载,纪念物 remembrance, monument, souvenir, memento, record, stone, plaque, mausoleum.
adj.
☞纪念的,记忆的 commemorative, celebratory.

memorize *v.*
☞心记,记录于 learn, learn by heart, commit to memory, remember.

memory *n.*
☞记忆力,记忆 recall, retention, recollection, remembrance, reminiscence, commemoration.

menace *v.*
☞恐吓,胁迫 threaten, frighten, alarm, intimidate, terrorize, loom.
n.
☞警告 intimidation, threat, terrorism, warning.
☞威胁 danger, peril, hazard, jeopardy, risk.
☞威胁性言行 nuisance, annoyance, pest.

mend *v.*
☞修理 repair, restore, refit, fix, patch, cobble, darn, heal.
☞恢复,变好 recover, get better, improve.
☞改善中,康复中 remedy, correct, rectify, reform, revise.

mental *adj.*
☞精神的,脑力的 intellectual, abstract, conceptual, cognitive, cerebral, theoretical, rational.
☞精神不正常的 mad, insane, lunatic, crazy, unbalanced, deranged, psychotic, disturbed, loony.

mentality *n.*
☞精神 intellect, brains, understanding, faculty, rationality.
☞心理 frame of mind, character, disposition, personality, psychology, outlook.

mention *v.*
☞指明,提到 refer to, speak of, allude to, touch on, name, cite, acknowledge, bring up, report, make known, impart, declare, communicate, broach, divulge, disclose, intimate, point out, reveal, state, hint at, quote.
n.
☞提到 reference, allusion, citation, observation, recognition, remark, acknowledgement, announcement, notification, tribute, indication.

merchandise *n.*
☞商品,货物 goods, commodities, stock, produce, products, wares, cargo, freight, shipment.

merchant *n.*
☞商人,生意人 trader, dealer,

broker, trafficker, wholesaler, retailer, seller, shopkeeper, vendor.

merciful *adj.*
☞ 仁慈的，宽大的 compassionate, forgiving, forbearing, humane, lenient, sparing, tender-hearted, pitying, gracious, humanitarian, kind, liberal, sympathetic, generous, mild.

merciless *adj.*
☞ 残酷的，无情的 pitiless, relentless, unmerciful, ruthless, hard-hearted, hard, heartless, implacable, inhumane, unforgiving, remorseless, unpitying, unsparing, severe, cruel, callous, inhuman.

mercy *n.*
☞ 怜悯 compassion, clemency, forgiveness, forbearance, leniency, pity, humanitarianism, kindness, grace.
☞ 仁慈，慈悲 blessing, godsend, good luck, relief.

mere *adj.*
☞ 仅仅的，只不过的 sheer, plain, simple, bare, utter, pure, absolute, complete, stark, unadulterated, common, paltry, petty.

merge *v.*
☞ 使……融合，使合并，结合 join, unite, combine, converge, amalgamate, blend, coalesce, mix, intermix, mingle, melt into, fuse, meet, meld, incorporate, consolidate.

merger *n.*
☞ 吞并，合并 amalgamation, union, fusion, combination, coalition, consolidation, confederation, incorporation.

merit *n.*
☞ 价值，优点 worth, excellence, value, quality, good, goodness, virtue, asset, credit, advantage, strong point, talent, justification, due, claim.
v.
☞ 值得，应得 deserve, be worthy of, earn, justify, warrant.

merriment *n.*
☞ 欢乐，笑闹 fun, jollity, mirth, hilarity, laughter, conviviality, festivity, amusement, revelry, frolic, liveliness, joviality.

merry *adj.*
☞ 欢乐的，愉快的 jolly, light-hearted, mirthful, joyful, happy, convivial, festive, cheerful, glad.

mess *n.*
☞ 混乱 chaos, untidiness, disorder, disarray, confusion, muddle, jumble, clutter, disorganization, mix-up, shambles.
☞ 麻烦，困难 difficulty, trouble, predicament, fix.

mess about
☞ 干涉，搅乱 mess around, fool, around, play, play around, play about, muck about, interfere, tamper, trifle.

mess up
☞ 杂乱 disarrange, jumble, muddle, tangle, dishevel, disrupt.
☞ 弄糟 botch, bungle, spoil,

muck up.

message n.
- 消息,信息 communication, bulletin, dispatch, communique, report, missive, errand, letter, memorandum, note, notice, cable.
- 启示,寓意 meaning, idea, point, theme, moral.

messenger n.
- 使者,送信者 courier, emissary, envoy, go-between, herald, runner, carrier, bearer, harbinger, agent, ambassador.

messy adj.
- 杂乱的,污浊的 untidy, unkempt, dishevelled, disorganized, chaotic, sloppy, slovenly, confused, dirty, grubby, muddled, cluttered.

metaphor n.
- 隐喻,暗喻 figure of speech, allegory, analogy, symbol, picture, image.

metaphorical adj.
- 比喻的,隐喻的 figurative, allegorical, symbolic.

method n.
- 方法,方式 way, approach, means, course, manner, mode, fashion, process, procedure, route, technique, style, plan, scheme, programme.
- 条理,秩序,组织 organization, order, structure, system, pattern, form, planning, regularity, routine.

methodical adj.
- 有方法的,有组织的 systematic, structured, organized, ordered, orderly, tidy, regular, planned, efficient, disciplined, businesslike, deliberate, neat, scrupulous, precise, meticulous, painstaking.

meticulous adj.
- 慎重的,细心的 precise, scrupulous, exact, punctilious, fussy, detailed, accurate, thorough, fastidious, painstaking, strict.

middle adj.
- 中间的,中央的 central, halfway, mean, median, intermediate, inner, inside, intervening.

n.
- 中间,中央 centre, halfway point, midpoint, mean, heart, core, midst, inside, bull's eye.

middling adj.
- 中等的,平常的 mediocre, medium, ordinary, moderate, average, unexceptional, unremarkable, run-of-the-mill, indifferent, modest, passable, tolerable, so-so, ok.

midst n.
- 中间,中央部位 middle, centre, mid-point, heart, hub, interior.

migrate v.
- 移居,迁移 move, resettle, relocate, wander, roam, rove, journey, emigrate, travel, voyage, trek, drift.

mild adj.
- 温文尔雅的 gentle, calm, peaceable, placid, tender, soft, good-natured, kind, amiable, lenient, compassionate.

militant adj.
- ☞ 挑衅的 aggressive, belligerent, vigorous, fighting, warring.

n.
- ☞ 战士 activist, combatant, fighter, struggler, warrior, aggressor, belligerent.

military adj.
- ☞ 军事的 martial, armed, soldierly, warlike, service.

n.
- ☞ 军队 army, armed forces, soldiers, forces, services.

militate against
- ☞ 对抗 oppose, counter, counteract, count against, tell against, weigh against, contend, resist.

milk v.
- ☞ 挤 drain, bleed, tap, extract, draw off, exploit, use, express, press, pump, siphon, squeeze, wring.

milky adj.
- ☞ 乳白的 white, milk-white, chalky, opaque, clouded, cloudy.

mill n.
- ☞ 作坊 factory, plant, works, workshop, foundry.
- ☞ 磨 grinder, crusher, quern, roller.

v.
- ☞ 磨 grind, pulverize, powder, pound, crush, roll, press, grate.

mince v.
- ☞ 剁碎 chop, cut, hash, dice, grind, crumble.
- ☞ 吞吞吐吐地说 diminish, suppress, play down, tone down, hold back, moderate, weaken, soften, spare.

mind n.
- ☞ 才智,思想 intelligence, intellect, brains, reason, sense, understanding, wits, mentality, thinking, thoughts, grey matter, head, genius, concentration, attention, spirit, psyche.
- ☞ 记忆 memory, remembrance, recollection.
- ☞ 想法,期望 opinion, view, point of view, belief, attitude, judgement, feeling, sentiment.
- ☞ 心胸 inclination, disposition, tendency, will, wish, intention, desire.

v.
- ☞ 介意,反对 care, object, take offence, resent, disapprove, dislike.
- ☞ 注意,服从 regard, heed, pay attention, pay heed to, note, obey, listen to, comply with, follow, observe, be careful, watch.
- ☞ 当心 look after, take care of, watch over, guard, have charge of, keep an eye on.

bear in mind
- ☞ 记住,备忘 consider, remember, note.

make up one's mind
- ☞ 下决心 decide, choose, determine, settle, resolve.

mindful adj.

- 留神的，留心的 aware, conscious, alive (to), alert, attentive, careful, watchful, wary.

mindless adj.
- 愚蠢的 thoughtless, senseless, illogical, irrational, stupid, foolish, gratuitous, negligent.
- 机械的 mechanical, automatic, tedious.

mine n.
- 坑，地洞 pit, colliery, coalfield, excavation, vein, seam, shaft, trench, deposit.
- 资源，矿藏 supply, source, stock, store, reserve, fund, hoard, treasury, wealth.

v.
- 开采，挖掘 excavate, dig for, dig up, delve, quarry, extract, unearth, tunnel, remove, undermine.

mingle v.
- 结合，调合 mix, intermingle, intermix, combine, blend, merge, unite, alloy, coalesce, join, compound.
- 混熟 associate, socialize, circulate, hobnob, rub shoulders.

minimum n.
- 最小量，最低限 least, lowest point, slightest, bottom.

adj.
- 最小的，最低的 minimal, least, lowest, slightest, smallest, littlest, tiniest.

minister n.
- 大臣，部长 offical, office-holder, politician, dignitary, diplomat, ambassador, delegate, envoy, consul, cabinet minister, agent, aide, administrator, executive.
- 牧师，修道院院长 clergyman, churchman, cleric, parson, priest, pastor, vicar, preacher, ecclesiastic, divine.

v.
- 侍候，看护 attend, serve, tend, take care of, wait on, cater to, accommodate, nurse.

ministry n.
- 内阁，政府各部 government, cabinet, department, office, bureau, administration.
- 牧师职务 the church, holy orders, the priesthood.

minor adj.
- 次要的，较小的 lesser, secondary, smaller, inferior, subordinate, subsidiary, junior, younger, insignificant, inconsiderable, negligible, petty, trivial, trifling, second-class, unclassified, slight, light.

minute¹ n.
- 分钟，瞬间 moment, second, instant, flash, jiffy, tiek.

minute² adj.
- 细微的 tiny, infinitesimal, minuscule, microscopic, miniature, inconsiderable, negligible, small.
- 详细的 detailed, precise, meticulous, painstaking, close, critical, exhaustive.

minutes n.
- 纪录 proceedings, record(s), notes, memorandum, transcript, transactions, details, tapes.

miracle n.
- 令人惊奇的人，奇迹 wonder,

marvel, prodigy, phenomenon.

miraculous adj.
☞神奇的,不可思议的 wonderful, marvellous, phenomenal, extraordinary, amazing, astounding, astonishing, unbelievable, supernatural, incredible, inexplicable, unaccountable, superhuman.

mirror n.
☞镜子 glass, looking-glass, reflector.
☞影像 reflection, likeness, image, double, copy.
v.
☞反映,反射 reflect, echo, imitate, copy, represent, show, depict, mimic.

miscellaneous adj.
☞各种的,杂务的 mixed, varied, various, assorted, diverse, diversified, sundry, motley, jumbled, indiscriminate.

miscellany n.
☞杂集,混合物 mixture, variety, assortment, collection, anthology, medley, mixed bag, jumble, diversity.

mischief n.
☞伤害,损害 trouble, harm, evil, damage, injury, disruption.
☞淘气 misbehaviour, naughtiness, impishness, pranks.

mischievous adj.
☞有害的 malicious, evil, spiteful, vicious, wicked, pernicious, destructive, injurious.
☞淘气的 naughty, impish, rascally, roguish, playful, teasing.

miser n.
☞吝啬鬼,守财奴 niggard, skinflint, penny-pincher, scrooge.

miserable adj.
☞不幸的 unhappy, sad, dejected, despondent, downcast, heartbroken, wretched, distressed, crushed.
☞忧伤的 cheerless, depressing, dreary, impoverished, shabby, gloomy, dismal, forlorn, joyless, squalid.
☞简陋的 contemptible, despicable, ignominious, detestable, disgraceful, deplorable, shameful.
☞可怜的 meagre, paltry, niggardly, worthless, pathetic, pitiful.

miserly adj.
☞吝啬的,贪婪的 mean, niggardly, tight, stingy, sparing, parsimonious, cheese-paring, beggarly, penny-pinching, mingy.

miss v.
☞失去,缺 fail, miscarry, lose, let slip, let go, omit, overlook, pass over, slip, leave out, mistake, trip, misunderstand, err.
☞错过,没中 avoid, escape, evade, dodge, forego, skip, bypass, circumvent.
☞惦念 pine for, long for, yearn for, regret, grieve for, mourn, sorrow for, want, wish, need, lament.

n.
- 失败 failure, error, blunder, mistake, omission, oversight, fault, flop, fiasco.

missile n.
- 导弹 projectile, shot, guided missile, arrow, shaft, dart, rocket, bomb, shell, flying bomb, grenade, torpedo, weapon.

missing adj.
- 失落的,缺少的 absent, lost, lacking, gone, mislaid, unaccounted-for, wanting, disappeared, astray, strayed, misplaced.

mission n.
- 使命任务 task, undertaking, assignment, operation, campaign, crusade, business, errand.
- 使命 calling, duty, purpose, vocation, raison, aim, charge, office, job, work.
- 传教活动 commission, ministry, delegation, deputation, legation, embassy.

missionary n.
- 传教士,外交官 evangelist, campaigner, preacher, proselytizer, apostle, crusader, propagandist, champion, promoter, emissary, envoy, ambassador.

mist n.
- 雾,朦胧 haze, fog, vapour, smog, cloud, condensation, film, spray, drizzle, dew, steam, veil, dimness.

mist over
- 笼罩 cloud over, fog, dim, blur, steam up, obscure, veil.

mistake n.
- 错误,误解 error, inaccuracy, slip, slip-up, oversight, lapse, blunder, boob, gaffe, fault, faux pas, solecism, indiscretion, misjudgement, miscalculation, misunderstanding, misprint, misspelling, misreading, mispronunciation, howler.

v.
- 犯错,弄错 misunderstand, misapprehend, misconstrue, misjudge, misread, miscalculate, confound, confuse, slip up, blunder, err, boob.

mistaken adj.
- 弄错的,错误的 wrong, incorrect, erroneous, inaccurate, inexact, untrue, inappropriate, ill-judged, inauthentic, false, deceived, deluded, misinformed, misled, faulty.

mistreat v.
- 虐待,恶待 abuse, ill-treat, ill-use, maltreat, harm, hurt, batter, injure, knock about, molest.

misty adj.
- 迷蒙的,含糊的 hazy, foggy, cloudy, blurred, fuzzy, murky, smoky, unclear, dim, indistinct, obscure, opaque, vague, veiled.

misunderstand v.
- 误解,误会 misapprehend, misconstrue, misinterpret, misjudge, mistake, get wrong, miss the point, mishear, get hold of the wrong end of the stick.

misunderstanding n.

- 误解,误会 mistake, error, misapprehension, misconception, misjudgement, misinterpretation, misreading, mix-up.
- 意见相左 disagreement, argument, dispute, conflict, clash, difference, breach, quarrel, discord, rift.

misuse n.
- 错用,滥用 mistreatment, maltreatment, abuse, harm, ill-treatment, misapplication, misappropriation, waste, perversion, corruption, exploitation.

v.
- 滥用,虐待 abuse, misapply, misemploy, ill-use, ill-treat, harm, mistreat, wrong, distort, injure, corrupt, pervert, waste, squander, misappropriate, exploit, dissipate.

mix v.
- 参与,混合 combine, blend, mingle, intermingle, intermix, amalgamate, compound, homogenize, synthesize, merge, join, unite, coalesce, fuse, incorporate, fold in.
- 调配 associate, consort, fraternize, socialize, mingle, join, hobnob.

n.
- 混合物 mixture, blend, amalgam, assortment, combination, conglomerate, compound, fusion, synthesis, medley, composite, mishmash.

mix up
- 搅拌,弄乱 confuse, bewilder, muddle, perplex, puzzle, confound, mix, jumble, complicate, garble, involve, implicate, disturb, upset, snarl up.

mixed adj.
- 混合的 combined, hybrid, mingled, crossbred, mongrel, blended, composite, compound, incorporated, united, alloyed, amalgamated, fused.
- 混杂的 assorted, varied, miscellaneous, diverse, diversified, motley.

mixture n.
- 混合物 mix, blend, combination, amalgamation, amalgam, compound, conglomeration, composite, coalescence, alloy, brew, synthesis, union, fusion, concoction, cross, hybrid, assortment, variety, miscellany, medley, melange, hotchpotch.

moan n.
- 呻吟,呜咽 lament, lamentation, sob, wail, howl, whimper, whine, grumble, complaint, grievance, groan.

v.
- 发出呻吟,呜咽 lament, wail, sob, weep, howl, groan, whimper, mourn, grieve.
- 抱怨 complain, grumble, whine, gripe, carp.

mob n.
- 群 crowd, mass, throng, multitude, horde, host, swarm, gathering, group, collection, flock, herd, pack, set, tribe, troop, company, crew, gang.
- 乌合之众 populace, rabble, masses, hoi polloi, plebs, riff-

raff.
v.
☞ 包围 crowd, crowd round, surround, swarm round, jostle, overrun, set upon, besiege, descend on, throng, pack, pester, charge.

mobile adj.
☞ 动的,流动性的 moving, movable, portable, peripatetic, travelling, roaming, roving, itinerant, wandering, migrant.
☞ 易变的,机动的 flexible, agile, active, energetic, nimble.
☞ 易动的 changing, changeable, ever-changing, expressive, lively.

mobilize v.
☞ 动员,使流动 assemble, marshal, rally, conscript, muster, call up, enlist, activate, galvanize, organize, prepare, ready, summon, animate.

mock v.
☞ 嘲弄,嘲笑 ridicule, jeer, make fun of, laugh at, disparage, deride, scoff, sneer, taunt, scorn, tease.
☞ 伪造,模拟 imitate, simulate, mimic, ape, caricature, satirize.
adj.
☞ 假的,虚幻的 imitation, counterfeit, artificial, sham, simulated, synthetic, false, fake, forged, fraudulent, bogus, phoney, pseudo, spurious, feigned, faked, pretended, dummy.

mockery n.
☞ 嘲弄 ridicule, jeering, scoffing, scorn, derision, contempt, disdain, disrespect, sarcasm.
☞ 伪造 parody, satire, sham, travesty.

mocking adj.
☞ 愚弄的,取笑的 scornful, derisive, contemptuous, sarcastic, satirical, taunting, scoffing, sardonic, snide, insulting, irreverent, impudent, disrespectful, disdainful, cynical.

model n.
☞ 复制品 copy, replica, representation, facsimile, imitation, mock-up.
☞ 模型 example, exemplar, pattern, standard, ideal, mould, prototype, template.
☞ 样式 design, style, type, version, mark.
☞ 模特 mannequin, dummy, sitter, subject, poser.
v.
☞ 做模型,使模仿 make, form, fashion, mould, sculpt, carve, cast, shape, work, create, design, plan.
☞ 做模特儿 display, wear, show off.

moderate adj.
☞ 中间派的,中庸的 mediocre, medium, ordinary, fair, indifferent, average, middle-of-the-road.
☞ 有节制的 reasonable, restrained, sensible, calm, controlled, cool, mild, well-regulated.
v.
☞ 主持,握持 control, regulate, decrease, lessen, soften, restrain, tone down, play

down, diminish, ease, curb, calm, check, modulate, repress, subdue, soft-pedal, tame, subside, pacify, mitigate, allay, alleviate, abate, dwindle.

moderately *adv.*
☞ 适当地,适度地 somewhat, quite, rather, fairly, slightly, reasonably, passably, to some extent.

moderation *n.*
☞ 缓和,减轻 decrease, reduction.
☞ 节制,适度 restraint, self-control, caution, control, composure, sobriety, abstemiousness, temperance, reasonableness.

modern *adj.*
☞ 现代的,前卫的 current, contemporary, up-to-date, new, fresh, latest, late, novel, present, present-day, recent, up-to-the-minute, newfangled, advanced, progressive, modernistic, innovative, inventive, state-of-the-art, go-ahead, fashionable, stylish, in vogue, in style, modish, trendy

modernize *v.*
☞ 使……现代化 renovate, refurbish, rejuvenate, regenerate, streamline, revamp, renew, update, improve, do up, redesign, reform, remake, remodel, refresh, transform, modify, progress.

modest *adj.*
☞ 谦虚的,羞怯的 unassuming, humble, self-effacing, quiet, reserved, retiring, unpretentious, discreet, bashful, shy.
☞ 适度的 moderate, ordinary, unexceptional, fair, reasonable, limited, small.

modesty *n.*
☞ 谦虚,羞怯,朴实 humility, humbleness, self-effacement, reticence, reserve, quietness, decency, propriety, demureness, shyness, bashfulness, coyness.

modify *v.*
☞ 修改,变更 change, alter, redesign, revise, vary, adapt, adjust, transform, reform, convert, improve, reorganize.
☞ 限制 moderate, reduce, temper, tone down, limit, soften, qualify.

moist *adj.*
☞ 潮湿的,多雨的 damp, clammy, humid, wet, dewy, rainy, muggy, marshy, drizzly, watery, soggy.

moisten *v.*
☞ 使潮湿,变湿 moisturize, dampen, damp, wet, water, lick, irrigate.

moisture *n.*
☞ 水分,湿气 water, liquid, wetness, wateriness, damp, dampness, dankness, humidity, vapour, dew, mugginess, condensation, steam, spray.

moment *n.*
☞ 片刻,瞬间,当前 second, instant, minute, split second, trice, jiffy, tick.

momentary *adj.*
☞ 瞬息的,顷刻的 brief, short, short-lived, temporary,

transient, transitory, fleeting, ephemeral, hasty, quick, passing.

monetary *adj*.
☞货币的,金钱的 financial, fiscal, pecuniary, budgetary, economic, capital, cash.

money *n*.
☞钱,财产,货币 currency, cash, legal tender, banknotes, coin, funds, capital, dough, dosh, riches, wealth.

monitor *n*.
☞监视器,监听器 screen, display, VDU, recorder, scanner.
☞班长,级长 supervisor, watchdog, overseer, invigilator, adviser, prefect.
v.
☞监听,监视 check, watch, keep track of, keep under surveillance, keep an eye on, follow, track, supervise, observe, note, survey, trace, scan, record, plot, detect.

monotonous *adj*.
☞单调的,无变化的 boring, dull, tedious, uninteresting, tiresome, wearisome, unchanging, uneventful, unvaried, uniform, toneless, flat, colourless, repetitive, routine, plodding, humdrum, soul-destroying.

monotony *n*.
☞单调,无趣味 tedium, dullness, boredom, sameness, tiresomeness, uneventfulness, flatness, wearisomeness, uniformity, routine, repetitiveness.

monster *n*.
☞怪物,怪形动植物 beast, fiend, brute, barbarian, savage, villain, giant, ogre, ogress, troll, mammoth.
☞讨厌的人 freak, monstrosity, mutant.
adj.
☞巨大的 huge, gigantic, giant, colossal, enormous, immense, massive, monstrous, jumbo, mammoth, vast, tremendous.

monument *n*.
☞典范,标竿 memorial, cenotaph, headstone, gravestone, tombstone, shrine, mausoleum, cairn, barrow, cross, marker, obelisk, pillar, statue, relic, remembrance, commemoration, testament, reminder, record, memento, evidence, token.

monumental *adj*.
☞留下印象的 impressive, imposing, awe-inspiring, awesome, overwhelming, significant, important, epoch-making, historic, magnificent, majestic, memorable, notable, outstanding, abiding, immortal, lasting, classic.
☞巨大的 huge, immense, enormous, colossal, vast, tremendous, massive, great.
☞纪念的 commemorative, memorial.

mood *n*.
☞心境,心情 disposition, frame of mind, state of mind, temper, humour, spirit, tenor, whim.
☞坏心情 bad temper, sulk, the sulks, pique, melancholy,

depression, blues, doldrums, dumps.

moody adj.
☞ 心情不稳的,忧郁的 changeable, temperamental, unpredictable, capricious, irritable, short-tempered, crabby, crotchety, crusty, testy, touchy, morose, angry, broody, mopy, sulky, sullen, gloomy, melancholy, miserable, downcast, doleful, glum, impulsive, fickle, flighty.

moon v.
☞ 闲荡,出神 idle, loaf, mooch, languish, pine, mope, brood, daydream, dream, fantasize.

mop n.
☞ 蓬乱的头发 head of hair, shock, mane, tangle, thatch, mass.
v.
☞ 用拖把拖洗 swab, sponge, wipe, clean, wash, absorb, soak.

moral adj.
☞ 道德的 ethical, virtuous, good, right, principled, honourable, decent, upright, upstanding, straight, righteous, high-minded, honest, incorruptible, proper, blameless, chaste, clean-living, pure, just, noble.
n.
☞ 教训,伦理 lesson, message, teaching, dictum, meaning, maxim, adage, precept, saying, proverb, aphorism, epigram.

morale n.
☞ 民心,士气 confidence, spirits, esprit de corps, self-esteem, state of mind, heart, mood.

morality n.
☞ 德行,品行 ethics, morals, ideals, principles, standards, virtue, rectitude, righteousness, decency, goodness, honesty, integrity, justice, uprightness, propriety, conduct, manners.

morals n.
☞ 道德 morality, ethics, principles, standards, ideals, integrity, scruples, behaviour, conduct, habits, manners.

more adj.
☞ 更多的,更好的 further, extra, additional, added, new, fresh, increased, other, supplementary, repeated, alternative, spare.
adv.
☞ 更,再 further, longer, again besides, moreover, better.

moreover adv.
☞ 而且,此外 furthermore, further, besides, in addition, as well, also, additionally, what is more.

morning n.
☞ 早晨,上午,白天 daybreak, daylight, dawn, sunrise, break of day, before noon.

mortal adj.
☞ 凡尘的 worldly, earthly, bodily, human, perishable, temporal.
☞ 致命的 fatal, lethal, deadly.
☞ 非常的 extreme, great, severe, intense, grave, awful.
n.
☞ 人类 human being, human,

individual, person, being, body, creature.

mortality n.
☞ 死亡 humanity, death, impermanence, perishability.
☞ 死亡率 fatality, death rate.

mostly adv.
☞ 主要地，大部分地 mainly, on the whole, principally, chiefly, generally, usually, largely, for the most part, as a rule.

mother n.
☞ 母亲 parent, procreator, progenitress, dam, mamma, mum, mummy, matriarch, ancestor, matron, old woman.
☞ 根源 origin, source.

v.
☞ 养育 bear, produce, nurture, raise, rear, nurse, care for, cherish.
☞ 溺爱 pamper, spoil baby, indulge, overprotect, fuss over.

motherly adj.
☞ 慈祥的，似母亲的 maternal, caring, comforting, affectionate, kind, loving, protective, warm, tender, gentle, fond.

motion n.
☞ 移动，活动 movement, action, mobility, moving, activity, locomotion, travel, transit, passage, passing, progress, change, flow, inclination.
☞ 姿态 gesture, gesticulation, signal, sign, wave, nod.
☞ 请求，申请 proposal, suggestion, recommendation, proposition.

v.
☞ 示意，指示 signal, gesture, gesticulate, sign, wave, nod, beckon, direct, usher.

motionless adj.
☞ 不动的，静止的 unmoving, still, stationary, static, immobile, at a standstill, fixed, halted, at rest, resting, standing, paralyied, inanimate, lifeless, frozen, rigid, stagnant.

motivate v.
☞ 激发，驱使 prompt, incite, impel, spur, provoke, stimulate, drive, lead, stir, urge, push, propel, persuade, move, inspire, encourage, cause, trigger, induce, kindle, draw, arouse, bring.

motive n.
☞ 主题，主旨，目的 ground(s), cause, reason, purpose, motivation, object, intention, influence, rationale, thinking, incentive, impulse, stimulus, inspiration, incitement, urge, encouragement, design, desire, consideration.

mount v.
☞ 安置，安装 produce, put on, set up, prepare, stage, exhibit, display, launch.
☞ 增多 increase, grow, accumulate, multiply, rise, intensify, soar, swell.
☞ 登上 climb, ascend, get up, go up, get on, clamber up, scale, get astride.

n.
☞ 骑马 horse, steed, support, mounting.

mountain n.
☞ 高山，山脉 height, elevation, mount, peak, mound, alp, tor,

massif.
- 大堆,大量 heap, pile, stack, mass, abundance, backlog.

mountainous adj.
- 多山的 craggy, rocky, hilly, high, highland, upland, alpine, soaring, steep.
- 巨大的 huge, towering, enormous, immense.

mourn v.
- 遗憾,悲悼 grieve, lament, sorrow, bemoan, miss, regret, deplore, weep, wail.

mournful adj.
- 悲痛的,凄惨的 sorrowful, sad, unhappy, desolate, grief-stricken, heavy-hearted, heartbroken, broken-hearted, cast-down, downcast, miserable, tragic, woeful, melancholy, sombre, depressed, dejected, gloomy, dismal.

mourning n.
- 悲伤,哀悼 bereavement, grief, grieving, lamentation, sadness, sorrow, desolation, weeping.

mouth n.
- 嘴,口 lips, jaws, trap, gob.
- 进入口 opening, aperture, orifice, cavity, entrance, gateway, inlet, estuary.

v.
- 说话,发表 enunciate, articulate, utter, pronounce, whisper, form.

movable adj.
- 可动的,变动的 mobile, portable, transportable, changeable, alterable, adjustable, flexible, transferable.

move v.
- 发展 stir, go, advance, budge, change, proceed, progress, make strides.
- 移动 transport, carry, transfer.
- 出发,迁移 depart, go away, leave, decamp, migrate, remove, move house, relocate.
- 驱动,煽动 prompt, stimulate, urge, impel, drive, propel, motivate, incite, persuade, induce, inspire.
- 激励 affect, touch, agitate, stir, impress, excite.

n.
- 行动 movement, motion, stratagem.
- 移动,迁居 removal, relocation, migration, transfer.

movement n.
- 动作 repositioning, move, moving, relocation, activity, act, action, agitation, stirring, transfer, passage.
- 发展 change, development, advance, evolution, current, drift, flow, shift, progress, progression, trend, tendency.
- 社会运动 campaign, crusade, drive, group, organization, party, faction.

moving adj.
- 动的,移动的 mobile, active, in motion.
- 感动的 touching, affecting, poignant, impressive, emotive, arousing, stirring, inspiring, inspirational, exciting, thrilling, persuasive, stimulating.

much adv.
- 大量地,许多地 greatly,

considerably, a lot, frequently, often.
  adj.
  ☞ 许多的 copious, plentiful, ample, considerable, a lot, abundant, great, substantial.
  n.
  ☞ 许多,大量 plenty, a lot, lots, loads, heaps, lashings.

mud *n.*
  ☞ 泥浆,污泥 clay, mire, ooze, dirt, sludge, silt.

muddle *v.*
  ☞ 使混浊 disorganize, disorder, mix up, mess up, jumble, scramble, tangle.
  ☞ 使糊涂 confuse, bewilder, bemuse, perplex.
  n.
  ☞ 混乱,杂乱 chaos, confusion, disorder, mess, mix-up, jumble, clutter, tangle.

muddy *adj.*
  ☞ 泥泞的,混浊的 dirty, foul, miry, mucky, marshy, boggy, swampy, quaggy, primy.
  ☞ 不明确的 cloudy, indistinct, obscure, opaque, murky, hazy, blurred, fuzzy, dull.

muffle *v.*
  ☞ 围住 wrap, envelop, cloak, swathe, cover.
  ☞ 使声音低沉 deaden, dull, quieten, silence, stifle, dampen, muzzle, suppress.

mug[1] *n.*
  ☞ 杯 cup, beaker, pot, tankard.

mug[2] *v.*
  ☞ 攻击 set upon, attack, assault, waylay, steal from, rob, beat up, jump (on).

multiple *adj.*
  ☞ 复合的,多样的 many, numerous, manifold, various, several, sundry, collective.

multiply *v.*
  ☞ 增加,增多 increase, proliferate, expand, spread, reproduce, propagate, breed, accumulate, intensify, extend, build up, augment, boost.

multitude *n.*
  ☞ 群众,许多 crowd, throng, horde, swarm, mob, mass, herd, congregation, host, lot, lots, legion, public, people, populace.

municipal *adj.*
  ☞ 都市的,市政的 civic, city, town, urban, borough, community, public.

murder *n.*
  ☞ 杀害 homicide, killing, manslaughter, slaying, assassination, massacre, bloodshed.
  v.
  ☞ 谋杀 kill, slaughter, slay, assassinate, butcher, massacre.

murderer *n.*
  ☞ 凶杀犯 killer, homicide, slayer, slaughterer, assassin, butcher, cut-throat.

murderous *adj.*
  ☞ 杀人的,凶恶的 homicidal, brutal, barbarous, bloodthirsty, bloody, cut-throat, killing, lethal, cruel, savage, ferocious, deadly.
  ☞ 极难的 difficult, exhausting, strenuous, unpleasant, dangerous.

murmur n.
☞ 低语 mumble, muttering, whisper, undertone, humming, rumble, drone, grumble.

v.
☞ 诉怨,低声说 mutter, mumble, whisper, buzz, hum, rumble, purr, burble.

muscular adj.
☞ 肌肉发达的,壮健的 brawny, beefy, sinewy, athletic, powerfully, built, strapping, hefty, powerful, husky, robust, stalwart, vigorous, strong.

musical adj.
☞ 音乐的 tuneful, melodious, melodic, harmonious, dulcet, sweet-sounding, lyrical.

mute adj.
☞ 沉默的 silent, dumb, voiceless, wordless, speechless, mum, unspoken, noiseless, unexpressed, unpronounced.

v.
☞ 减弱……的声音 tone down, subdue, muffle, lower, moderate, dampen, deaden, soften, silence.

mutual adj.
☞ 共同的,相互的 reciprocal, shared, common, joint, interchangeable, interchanged, exchanged, complementary.

mysterious adj.
☞ 神秘的 enigmatic, cryptic, mystifying, inexplicable, incomprehensible, puzzling, perplexing, obscure, strange, unfathomable, unsearchable, mystical, baffling, curious, hidden, insoluble, secret, weird, secretive, veiled, dark, furtive.

mystery n.
☞ 神秘事物 enigma, puzzle, secret, riddle, conundrum, question.
☞ 秘密 obscurity, secrecy, ambiguity.

mystical adj.
☞ 神秘的,不可思议的 occult, arcane, mystic, esoteric, supernatural, paranormal, transcendental, metaphysical, hidden, mysterious.

mystify v.
☞ 使困惑,使神秘 puzzle, bewilder, baffle, perplex, confound, confuse.

myth n.
☞ 神话,虚构的故事 legend, fable, fairytale, allegory, parable, saga, story, fiction, tradition, fancy, fantasy, superstition.

mythical adj.
☞ 神话的,神话式的 mythological, legendary, fabled, fairytale.
☞ 虚构的 fictitious, imaginary, made-up, invented, make-believe, non-existent, unreal, pretended, fanciful.

mythology n.
☞ 神话学 legend, myths, lore, traditoin(s), folklore, folk-tales, tales.

N

nag v.
- 抱怨,困扰,唠叨 scold, berate, irritate, annoy, pester, badger, plague, torment, harass, henpeck, harry, vex, upbraid, goad.

nail v.
- 钉住,抓住 fasten, attach, secure, pin, tack, fix, join.

n.
- 钉子 fastener, pin, tack, spike, skewer.
- 指甲 talon, claw.

naive adj.
- 天真的,自然的 unsophisticated, ingenuous, innocent, unaffected, artless, guileless, simple, natural, childlike, open, trusting, unsuspecting, gullible, credulous, wide-eyed.

naivety n.
- 无邪,天真的言语行为 ingenuousness, innocence, inexperience, naturalness, simplicity, openness, frankness, gullibility, credulity.

naked adj.
- 无遮盖的 nude, bare, undressed, unclothed, uncovered, stripped, stark-naked, disrobed, denuded, in the altogether.
- 明白无误的 open, unadorned, undisguised, unqualified, plain, stark, overt, blatant, exposed.

name n.
- 名称 title, appellation, designation, label, term, epithet, handle.
- 名誉 reputation, character, repute, renown, esteem, eminence, term, honour, distinction, note.

v.
- 命名,提出 call, christen, baptize, term, title, entitle, dub, label, style.
- 指定 designate, nominate, cite, choose, select, specify, classify, commission, appoint.

nameless adj.
- 无名的 unnamed, anonymous, unidentified, unknown, obscure.
- 难以形容的 inexpressible, indescribable, unutterable, unspeakable, unmentionable, unheard-of.

namely adv.
- 即,那就是 that is, viz, specifically, that is to say.

nap v.
- 小睡,打盹,疏忽 doze, sleep, snooze, nod (off), drop off, rest, kip.

n.
- 小睡,打盹 rest, sleep, siesta, catnap, forty winks, kip.

narrate v.
- 叙述,讲故事 tell, relate, report, recount, describe, unfold, recite, state, detail.

narrative n.
☞ 叙述 story, tale, chronicle, account, history, report, detail, statement.

narrator n.
☞ 说故事者,叙述者 storyteller, chronicler, reporter, raconteur, commentator, writer.

narrow adj.
☞ 狭窄的 tight, confined, constricted, cramped, slim, slender, thin, fine, tapering, close.
☞ 受限的 limited, restricted, circumscribed.
☞ 偏执的 narrow-minded, biased, bigoted, exclusive, dogmatic.

v.
☞ 变窄,限制 constrict, limit, tighten, reduce, diminish, simplify.

narrow-minded adj.
☞ 小心眼的,心胸狭窄的 illiberal, biased, bigoted, prejudiced, reactionary, small-minded, conservative, intolerant, insular, petty.

nasty adj.
☞ 很不愉快的,难缠的 unpleasant, repellent, repugnant, repulsive, objectionable, offensive, disgusting, sickening, horrible, filthy, foul, polluted, obscene.
☞ 恶劣的 malicious, mean, spiteful, vicious, malevolent.

nation n.
☞ 国家,民族,联盟 country, people, race, state, realm, population, community, society.

national adj.
☞ 国家的,民族的,关于国籍的 countrywide, civil, domestic, nationwide, state, internal, general, governmental, public, widespread, social.

n.
☞ 公民 citizen, native, subject, inhabitant, resident.

nationality n.
☞ 民族 race, nation, ethnic group, birth, tribe, clan.

native adj.
☞ 本土的 local, indigenous, domestic, vernacular, home, aboriginal, autochthonous, mother, original.
☞ 土生的,自然形成的 inborn, inherent, innate, inbred, hereditary, inherited, congenital, instinctive, natural, intrinsic, natal.

n.
☞ 生于某地的人,产于某地的动植物 inhabitant, resident, national, citizen, dweller, aborigine.

natural adj.
☞ 普通的 ordinary, normal, common, regular, standard, usual, typical.
☞ 天生的 innate, inborn, instinctive, intuitive, inherent, congenital, native, indigenous.
☞ 天然的 genuine, pure, authentic, unrefined, unprocessed, unmixed, real.
☞ 真诚的 sincere, unaffected, genuine, artless, ingenuous, guileless, simple, unsophisticated, open, candid, spontaneous.

naturally adv.

- 当然地 of course, as a matter of course, simply, obviously, logically, typically, certainly, absolutely.
- 自然地 normally, genuinely, instinctively, spontaneously.

nature n.
- 性质,特性 essence, quality, character, features, disposition, attributes, personality, make-up, constitution, temperament, mood, outlook, temper.
- 类型 kind, sort, type, description, category, variety, style, species.
- 大自然 universe, world, creation, earth, environment.

naughty adj.
- 淘气的 bad, badly behaved, mischievous, disobedient, wayward, exasperating, playful, roguish.
- 不道德的,邪恶的 indecent, obscene, bawdy, risque, smutty.

nausea n.
- 作呕,晕船 vomiting, sickness, retching, queasiness, biliousness.
- 厌恶 disgust, revulsion, loathing, repugnance.

nauseate v.
- 使作呕,使恶心 sicken, disgust, revolt, repel, offend, turn one's stomach.

nautical adj.
- 航海的,船舶的 naval, marine, maritime, sea-going, seafaring, sailing, oceanic, boating.

navigate v.
- 驾驶,航海,领航 steer, drive, direct, pilot, guide, handle, manoeuvre, cruise, sail, skipper, voyage, journey, cross, helm, plot, plan.

navigation n.
- 航海 sailing, steering, cruising, voyaging, seamanship, helmsmanship.

navy n.
- 海军,船队 fleet, ships, flotilla, armada, warships.

near adj.
- 接近的,附近的 nearby, close, bordering, adjacent, adjoining, alongside, neighbouring.
- 来临的 imminent, impending, forthcoming, coming, approaching.
- 亲密的 dear, familiar, close, related, intimate, akin.

nearby adj.
- 在附近 near, neighbouring, adjoining, adjacent, accessible, convenient, handy.

adv.
- 附近地 near, within reach, at close quarters, close at hand, not far away.

nearly adv.
- 几乎 almost, practically, virtually, closely, approximately, more or less, as good as, just about, roughly, well-nigh.

neat adj.
- 整洁的 tidy, orderly, smart, spruce, trim, clean, spick-and-span, shipshape.
- 灵巧的 deft, clever, adroit,

skilful, expert.
- 简洁的 undiluted, unmixed, unadulterated, straight, pure.

necessary adj.
- 必需的 needed, required, essential, compulsory, indispensable, vital, imperative, mandatory, obligatory, needful, unavoidable, inevitable, inescapable, inexorable, certain.

necessity n.
- 要求 requirement, obligation, prerequisite, essential, fundamental, need, want, compulsion, demand.
- 需要,有需要 indispensability, inevitability, needfulness.
- 困难 poverty, destitution, hardship.

need v.
- 需要 miss, lack, want, require, demand, call for, necessitate, have need of, have to, crave.

n.
- 要求 call, demand, obligation, requirement.

needless adj.
- 不必要的 unnecessary, gratuitous, uncalled-for, unwanted, redundant, superfluous, useless, pointless, purposeless.

negative adj.
- 负的 contradictory, contrary, denying, opposing, invalidating, neutralizing, nullifying, annulling.
- 不积极的 unco-operative, cynical, pessimistic, unenthusiastic, uninterested, unwilling.

n.
- 否定 contradiction, denial, opposite, refusal.

neglect v.
- 疏忽 disregard, ignore, leave alone, abandon, pass by, rebuff, scorn, disdain, slight, spurn.

n.
- 疏忽 negligence, disregard, carelessness, failure, inattention, indifference, slackness, dereliction of duty, forgetfulness, heedlessness, oversight, slight, disrespect.

negotiate v.
- 谈判,协商 confer, deal, mediate, arbitrate, bargain, arrange, transact, work out, manage, settle, consult, contract.
- 通过 get round, cross, surmount, traverse, pass.

negotiation n.
- 谈判 mediation, arbitration, debate, discussion, diplomacy, bargaining, transaction.

negotiator n.
- 谈判者 arbitrator, go-between, mediator, intermediary, moderator, intercessor, adjudicator, broker, ambassador, diplomat.

neighbourhood n.
- 附近 district, locality, vicinity, community, locale, environs, confines, surroundings, region, proximity.

neighbouring adj.
- 临近的 adjacent, bordering,

near, nearby, adjoining, connecting, next, surrounding.

neighbourly adj.
☞ 友好的 sociable, friendly, amiable, kind, helpful, genial, hospitable, obliging, considerate, companionable.

nerve n.
☞ 神经 courage, bravery, mettle, pluck, guts, spunk, spirit, vigour, intrepidity, daring, fearlessness, firmness, resolution, fortitude, steadfastness, will, determination, endurance, force.
☞ 勇气 audacity, impudence, cheek, effrontery, brazenness, boldness, chutzpah, impertinence, insolence.

nerves n.
☞ 神经质,紧张 nervousness, tension, stress, anxiety, worry, strain, fretfulness.

nervous adj.
☞ 紧张 highly-strung, excitable, anxious, agitated, nervy, on edge, edgy, jumpy, jittery, tense, fidgety, apprehensive, neurotic, shaky, uneasy, worried, flustered, fearful.

nest n.
☞ 窝 breeding-ground, roost, eyrie, lair.
☞ 隐蔽所 retreat, refuge, haunt, hideaway.

nestle v.
☞ 依偎 snuggle, huddle, cuddle, curl up.

net¹ n.
☞ 罗网 mesh, web, network, netting, open-work, lattice, lace.
v.
☞ 网捕 catch, trap, capture, bag, ensnare, entangle, nab.

net² adj.
☞ 纯(净)的 clear, after tax, final, lowest.
v.
☞ 获得 bring in, clear, earn, make, realize, receive, gain, obtain, accumulate.

network n.
☞ 网,系统 system, organization, arrangement, structure, interconnnections, complex, grid, net, maze, mesh, labyrinth, channels, circuitry, convolution, grill, tracks.

neutral adj.
☞ 中立的,无特色的 impartial, uncommitted, unbia(s)sed, non-aligned, disinterested, unprejudiced, undecided, non-partisan, non-committal, objective, indifferent, dispassionate, even-handed.
☞ 不显著的 dull, nondescript, colourless, drab, expressionless, indistinct.

never-ending adj.
☞ 无尽的,无穷的 everlasting, eternal, non-stop, perpetual, unceasing, uninterrupted, unremitting, interminable, incessant, unbroken, permanent, persistent, unchanging, relentless.

nevertheless adv.

☞ 仍然,还是 nonetheless, notwithstanding, still, anyway, even so, yet, however, anyhow, but, regardless.

new adj.
☞ 新的 novel, original, brand-new, mint, unknown, unused, virgin, newborn.
☞ 新型的,现代的 modern, contemporary, current, latest, recent, up-to-date, up-to-the-minute, topical, trendy, ultra-modern, advanced, newfangled.
☞ 更新的 changed, altered, modernized, improved, renewed, restored, redesigned.
☞ 增加的 added, additional, extra, more, supplementary.

newcomer n.
☞ 新来者,不认识的人 immigrant, alien, foreigner, incomer, colonist, settler, arrival, outsider, stranger, novice, beginner.

news n.
☞ 新闻,报导 report, account, information, intelligence, dispatch, communique, bulletin, gossip, hearsay, rumour, statement, story, word, tidings, latest, release, scandal, revelation, lowdown, expose, disclosure, gen

next adj.
☞ 接近的 adjacent, adjoining neighbouring, nearest, closest.
☞ 下一个的,紧跟的 following, subsequent, succeeding, ensuing, later.
adv.
☞ 下面 afterwards, subsequently, later, then.

nibble n.
☞ 一点,一件 bite, morsel, taste, bit, crumb, snack, piece.
v.
☞ 吃掉,吸收 bite, eat, peck, pick at, nosh, munch, gnaw.

nice adj.
☞ 好的,令人愉快的 pleasant, agreeable, delightful, charming, likable, attractive, good, kind, friendly, well-mannered, polite, respectable.
☞ 精细的 subtle, delicate, fine, fastidious,, discriminating, scrupulous, precise, exact, accurate, careful, strict.

nicety n.
☞ 精细 delicacy, refinement, subtlety, distinction, nuance.
☞ 细节 precision, accuracy, meticulousness, scrupulousness, minuteness, finesse.

niche n.
☞ 适当的地方 orner, opening, position, place, vocation, calling, metier, slot.

nickname n.
☞ 绰号,小名 pet name, sobriquet, epithet, diminutive.

nightfall n.
☞ 黄昏 sunset, dusk, twilight, evening, gloaming.

nightmare n.
☞ 恶梦 bad dream, hallucination.
☞ 可怕的经验 ordeal, horror, torment, trial.

nil n.
☞ 无,零 nothing, zero, none, nought, naught, love, duck, zilch.

nip¹ v.
- 紧紧夹住,抓住 bite, pinch, squeeze, snip, clip, tweak, catch, grip, nibble.

nip² n.
- 一点 dram, draught, shot, swallow, mouthful, drop, sip, taste, portion.

nobility n.
- 贵族,高贵 nobleness, dignity, grandeur, illustriousness, stateliness, majesty, magnificence, eminence, excellence, superiority, uprightness, honour, virtue, worthiness.
- 贵族阶级 peerage, nobles, gentry, elite, lords, high society.

noble n.
- 贵族,出身高贵的人 aristocrat, peer, lord, lady, nobleman, noblewoman.

  adj.
- 贵族的,显贵的 aristocratic, high-born, titled, high-ranking, patrician, blue-blooded.
- 高尚的,崇高的 magnificent, magnanimous, splendid, stately, generous, dignified, distinguished, eminent, grand, great, honoured, honourable, imposing, impressive, majestic, virtuous, worthy, excellent, elevated, fine, gentle.

nobody n.
- 没有人,谁也不 no-one, nothing, nonentity, menial, cipher.

nod v.
- 点头 gesture, indicate, sign, signal, salute, acknowledge.
- 表示同意 agree, assent.
- 瞌睡,打盹 sleep, doze, drowse, nap.

  n.
- 点头示意 gesture, indication, sign, signal, salute, greeting, beck, acknowledgement.

noise n.
- 噪声;吵嚷,嘈杂声 sound, din, racket, row, clamour, clash, clatter, commotion, outcry, hubbub, uproar, cry, blare, talk, pandemonium, tumult, babble.

  v.
- 哄传,谣传 report, rumour, publicize, announce, circulate.

noiseless adj.
- 无声的,静的,声音很轻的 silent, inaudible, soundless, quiet, mute, still, hushed.

noisy adj.
- 吵闹的,喧闹的 loud, deafening, ear-splitting, clamorous, piercing, vocal, vociferous, tumultuous, boisterous, obstreperous.

nominate v.
- 提名,任命 propose, choose, select, name, designate, submit, suggest, recommend, put up, present, elect, appoint, assign, commission, elevate, term.

nomination n.
- 提名,提名权,任命权 proposal, choice, selection, submission, suggestion, recommendation, designation, election, appointment.

none *pron*
☞ 没有人，一点不 no-one, not any, not one, nobody, nil, zero.

nonsense *n.*
☞ 无意义的言谈,废话 rubbish, trash, drivel, balderdash, gibberish, gobbledygook, senselessness, stupidity, silliness, foolishness, folly, rot, blather, twaddle, ridiculousness, claptrap, cobblers.

non-stop *adj.*
☞ 不停的,不断的 never-ending, uninterrupted, continuous, incessant, constant, endless, interminable, unending, unbroken, round-the-clock, on-going.

norm *n.*
☞ 标准,规范 average, mean, standard, rule, pattern, criterion, model, yardstick, benchmark, measure, reference.

normal *adj.*
☞ 正常的,正规的,垂直的 usual, standard, general, common, ordinary, conventional, average, regular, routine, typical, mainstream, natural, accustomed, well-adjusted, straight, rational, reasonable.

normality *n.*
☞ 常态 usualness, commonness, ordinariness, regularity, routine, conventionality, balance, adjustment, typicality, naturalness, reason, rationality.

normally *adv.*
☞ 正常地,通常地,一般地 ordinarily, usually, as a rule, typically, commonly, characteristically.

nosey *adj.*
☞ 好管闲事的 inquisitive, meddlesome, prying, interfering, snooping, curious, eavesdropping.

nostalgia *n.*
☞ 怀旧,怀乡,留恋过去 yearning, longing, regretfulness, remembrance, reminiscence, homesickness, pining.

nostalgic *adj.*
☞ 怀乡的,留恋过去的 yearning, longing, wistful, emotional, regretful, sentimental, homesick.

notable *adj.*
☞ 值得注意的,杰出的 noteworthy, remarkable, noticeable, striking, extraordinary, impressive, outstanding, marked, unusual, celebrated, distinguished, famous, eminent, well-known, notorious, renowned, rare.
n.
☞ 名士,贤达 celebrity, notability, vip, personage, somebody, dignitary, luminary, worthy.

notably *adv.*
☞ 显著地,值得注意地 markedly, noticeably, particularly, remarkably, strikingly, conspicuously, distinctly, especially, impressively, outstandingly, eminently.

notation *n.*

☞ 标志, 标志法, 注释 symbols, characters, code, signs, alphabet, system, script, noting, record, shorthand.

note n.
☞ 笔记, 草稿 communication, letter, message, memorandum, reminder, memo, line, jotting, record.
☞ 短笺, 便条 annotation, comment, gloss, remark.
☞ 注释 indication, signal, token, mark, symbol.
☞ 名望 eminence, distinction.
☞ 注意 heed, attention, regard, notice, observation.

v.
☞ 注意到 notice, observe, perceive, heed, detect, mark, remark, mention, see, witness.
☞ 记下 record, register, write down, enter.

noted adj.
☞ 有名望的, 著名的 famous, well-known, renowned, notable, celebrated, eminent, prominent, great, acclaimed, illustrious, distinguished, respected, recognized.

notes n.
☞ 记录 jottings, record, impressions, report, sketch, outline, synopsis, draft.

noteworthy adj.
☞ 值得注意的, 显著的 remarkable, significant, important, notable, memorable, exceptional, extraordinary, unusual, outstanding.

nothing n.
☞ 没有什么东西, 无, 零 nought, zero, nothingness, zilch, nullity, non-existence, emptiness, void, nobody, nonentity.

notice v.
☞ 注意, 评价 note, remark, perceive, observe, mind, see, discern, distinguish, mark, detect, heed, spot.

n.
☞ 布告, 通知 notification, announcement, information, declaration, communication, intelligence, news, warning, instruction.
☞ 预告, 通知 advertisement, poster, sign, bill.
☞ 短评, 简介 review, comment, criticism.
☞ 注意 attention, observation, awareness, note, regard, consideration, heed.

noticeable adj.
☞ 令人注目的, 显著的 perceptible, observable, appreciable, unmistakable, conspicuous, evident, manifest, clear, distinct, significant, striking, plain, obvious, measurable.

notification n.
☞ 通知, 通知书 announcement, information, notice, declaration, advice, warning, intelligence, message, publication, statement, communication.

notify v.
☞ 通知, 报告, 宣告 inform, tell, advise, announce, declare, warn, acquaint, alert, publish, disclose, reveal.

notion n.
☞ 意见, 看法 idea, thought,

concept, conception, belief, impression, view, opinion, understanding, apprehension.
☞ 意图 inclination, wish, whim, fancy, caprice.

notorious adj.
☞ 臭名昭著的 infamous, disreputable, scandalous, dishonourable, disgraceful, ignominious, flagrant, well-known.

nought n.
☞ 无,零 zero, nil, zilch, naught, nothing, nothingness.

nourishment n.
☞ 食品,营养品 nutrition, food, sustenance, diet.

novel adj.
☞ 新颖的,不平常的 new, original, fresh, innovative, unfamiliar, unusual, uncommon, different, imaginative, unconventional, strange.
n.
☞ (长篇)小说 fiction, story, tale, narrative, romance.

novelty n.
☞ 新颖,新奇 newness, originality, freshness, innovation, unfamiliarity, uniqueness, difference, strangeness.
☞ 新事物 gimmick, gadget, trifle, memento, knick-knack, curiosity, souvenir, trinket, bauble, gimcrack.

novice n.
☞ 新手 beginner, tiro, learner, pupil, trainee, probationer, apprentice, amateur, newcomer.

now adv.
☞ 现在,目前 immediately, at once, directly, instantly, straight away, promptly, next.
☞ 立刻,马上 at present, nowadays, these days.

nuance n.
☞ 细微差别,细腻 subtlety, suggestion, shade, hint, suspicion, gradation, distinction, overtone, refinement, touch, trace, tinge, degree, nicety.

nude adj.
☞ 裸体的,无遮盖的 naked, bare, undressed, unclothed, stripped, stark-naked, uncovered, starkers, in one's birthday suit.

numb adj.
☞ 失去知觉的,麻木的 benumbed, insensible, unfeeling, deadened, insensitive, frozen, immobilized.
v.
☞ 使……失去失觉,使……麻木,发僵 deaden, anaesthetize, freeze, immobilize, paralyse, dull, stun.

number n.
☞ 数,数字 figure, numeral, digit, integer, unit.
☞ 数目,数量 total, sum, aggregate, collection, amount, quantity, several, many, company, crowd, multitude, throng, horde.
☞ 期,册 copy, issue, edition, impression, volume, printing.
v.
☞ 给……编码,加号码 count, calculate, enumerate, reckon, total, add, compute, include.

numerous adj.

☞ 很多的,大批的 many, abundant, several, plentiful, copious, profuse, sundry.

nurse v.
☞ 看护,护理 tend, care for, look after, treat.
☞ 哺育 breast-feed, feed, suckle, nurture, nourish.
☞ 培养,怀有(希望) preserve, sustain, support, cherish, encourage, keep, foster, promote.

nurture n.
☞ 养料 food, nourishment.
☞ 培养 rearing, upbringing, training, care, cultivation, development, education, discipline.

nutrition n.
☞ 营养物,滋养物 food, nourishment, sustenance.

nutritious adj.
☞ 有营养的,营养的 nourishing, nutritive, wholesome, healthful, health-giving, good, beneficial, strengthening, substantial, invigorating.

O

oath n.
☞ 誓约,誓言 vow, pledge, promise, word, affirmation, assurance, word of honour.
☞ 诅咒 curse, imprecation, swear-word, profanity, expletive, blasphemy.

obedient adj.
☞ 服从的,顺从的 compliant, docile, acquiescent, submissive, tractable, yielding, dutiful, law-abiding, deferential, respectful, subservient, observant.

obey v.
☞ 服从,听从 comply, submit, surrender, yield, be ruled by, bow to, take orders from, defer (to), give way, follow, observe, abide by, adhere to, conform, heed, keep, mind, respond.
☞ 执行 carry out, discharge, execute, act upon, fulfil, perform.

object¹ n.
☞ 物体,实物 thing, entity, article, body.
☞ 目的 aim, objective, purpose, goal, target, intention, motive, end, reason, point, design.

object² v.
☞ 反对 protest, oppose, demur, take exception, disapprove, refuse, complain, rebut, repudiate.

objection n.
☞ 反对,异议 protest, dissent, disapproval, opposition, demur, complaint, challenge, scruple.

objectionable adj.
☞ 令人不快的,引起反对的 unacceptable, unpleasant, offensive, obnoxious, repugnant, disagreeable, abhorrent, detestable,

deplorable, despicable.

objective adj.
☞ 客观的,如实的 impartial, unbiased, detached, unprejudiced, open-minded, equitable, dispassionate, even-handed, neutral, disinterested, just, fair.
n.
☞ 目标,目的 object, aim, goal, end, purpose, ambition, mark, target, intention, design.

obligation n.
☞ 义务,责任 duty, responsibility, onus, charge, commitment, liability, requirement, bond, contract, debt, burden, trust.

obligatory adj.
☞ 义不容辞的,必须履行的 compulsory, mandatory, statutory, required, binding, essential, necessary, enforced.

oblige v.
☞ 迫使,责成 compel, constrain, coerce, require, make, necessitate, force, bind.
☞ 施恩于,请求,使满足 help, assist, accommodate, do a favour, serve, gratify, please.

obliging adj.
☞ 热心帮忙的,关心人的 accommodating, cooperative, helpful, considerate, agreeable, friendly, kind, civil.

obscure adj.
☞ 无名的,微贱的 unknown, unimportant, little-known, unheard-of, undistinguished, nameless, inconspicuous, humble, minor.
☞ 含糊的,暧昧的 incomprehensible, enigmatic, cryptic, recondite, esoteric, accrue, mysterious, deep, abstruse, confusing.
☞ 阴暗的,模糊的 indistinct, unclear, indefinite, shadowy, blurred, cloudy, faint, hazy, dim, misty, shady, vague, murky, gloomy, dusky.
v.
☞ 使昏暗,遮蔽 conceal, cloud, obfuscate, hide, cover, blur, disguise, mask, overshadow, shadow, shade, cloak, veil, shroud, darken, dim, eclipse, screen, block out.

observation n.
☞ 观测 attention, notice, examination, inspection, scrutiny, monitoring, study, watching, consideration, discernment.
☞ 评述,言论 remark, comment, utterance, thought, statement, pronouncement, reflection, opinion, finding, note.

observe v.
☞ (观)看,注视,观察 watch, see, study, notice, contemplate, keep an eye on, perceive.
☞ 陈述 remark, comment, say, mention.
☞ 遵守 abide by, comply with, honour, keep, fulfil, celebrate, perform.

observer n.
☞ 观察者 watcher, spectator, viewer, witness, looker-on, onlooker, eyewitness, commentator, bystander,

beholder.

obstructive adj.
- 引起阻碍的 hindering, delaying, blocking, stalling, unhelpful, awkward, difficult, restrictive, inhibiting.

obtain v.
- 获得,取得 acquire, get, gain, come by, attain, procure, secure, earn, achieve.
- 普及 prevail, exist, hold, be in force, be the case, stand, reign, rule, be prevalent.

obvious adj.
- 明显的,明白的 evident, self-evident, manifest, patent, clear, plain, distinct, transparent, undeniable, unmistakable, conspicuous, glaring, apparent, open, unconcealed, visible, noticeable, perceptible, pronounced, recognizable, self-explanatory, straightforward, prominent.

obviously adv.
- 明白地,清楚地 plainly, clearly, evidently, manifestly, undeniably, unmistakably, without doubt, certainly, distinctly, of course.

occasion n.
- 事件 event, occurrence, incident, time, instance, chance, case, opportunity.
- 原因,理由 reason, cause, excuse, justification, ground(s).
- 庆祝,典礼 celebration, function, affair, party.

occasional adj.
- 偶然的 periodic, intermittent, irregular, sporadic, infrequent, uncommon, incidental, odd, rare, casual.

occasionally adv.
- 有时候 sometimes, on occasion, from time to time, at times, at intervals, now and then, now and again, irregularly, periodically, every so often, once in a while, off and on, infrequently.

occupation n.
- 工作,职业 job, profession, work, vocation, employment, trade, post, calling, business, line, pursuit, craft, walk of life, activity.
- 侵略,侵犯 invasion, seizure, conquest, control, takeover.
- 占有 occupancy, possession, holding, tenancy, tenure, residence, habitation, use.

occupy v.
- 居住于 inhabit, live in, reside in, stay in, take possession of, own.
- 使全神贯注的 absorb, take up, engross, engage, hold, involve, preoccupy, amuse, busy, interest.
- 侵占 invade, seize, capture, overrun, take over.
- 派人担任,充满 fill, take up, use.

occur v.
- 发生,碰巧 happen, come about, take place, transpire, chance, come to pass, materialize, befall, develop, crop up, arise, appear, turn up, obtain, result, exist, be present, be found.

occurrence n.

- (暴力性的政治)事件 incident, event, happening, affair, circumstance, episode, instance, case, development, action.
- 发生 incidence, existence, appearance, manifestation.

odd adj.
- 不普通的,不平常的 unusual, strange, uncommon, peculiar, abnormal, exceptional, curious, atypical, different, queer, bizarre, eccentric, remarkable, unconventional, weird, irregular, extraordinary, outlandish, rarer.
- 临时的 occasional, incidental, irregular, random, casual.
- 奇数的,余的 unmatched, unpaired, single, spare, surplus, left-over, remaining, sundry, various, miscellaneous.

off-colour adj.
- (健康)不佳 indisposed, off form, under the weather, unwell, sick, out of sorts, ill, poorly.

offence n.
- 犯罪,过错 misdemeanour, transgression, violation, wrong, wrong-doing, infringement, crime, misdeed, sin, trespass.
- 公开的侮辱 affront, insult, injury.
- 怨恨 resentment, indignation, pique, umbrage, outrage, hurt, hard feelings.

offend v.
- 使受伤;冒犯 hurt, insult, injure, affront, wrong, wound, displease, snub, upset, annoy, outrage.
- 使厌恶,作呕 disgust, repel, sicken.
- 违反,违背 transgress, sin, violate, err.

offender n.
- 违反者 transgressor, wrong-doer, culprit, criminal, miscreant, guilty party, law-breaker, delinquent.

offensive adj.
- 令人不舒服的 disagreeable, unpleasant, objectionable, displeasing, disgusting, odious, obnoxious, repellent, repugnant, revolting, loathsome, vile, nauseating, nasty, detestable, rude, insulting, impertinent.

n.
- 攻击,攻打 attack, assault, onslaught, invasion, raid, sortie.

offer v.
- 赠送,给予 present, make available, advance, extend, put forward, submit, suggest, hold out, provide, sell.
- 提出,提供 proffer, propose, bid, tender.
- 自愿提出,自动提供 volunteer, come forward, show willing.

n.
- 提议 proposal, bid, submission, tender, suggestion, proposition, overture, approach, attempt, presentation.

offering n.
- 礼物 present, gift, donation, contribution, subscription.

offhand adj.
- 即席的,随便的 casual, unconcerned, uninterested, take-

it-or-leave-it, brusque, abrupt, perfunctory, informal, cavalier, careless.
adv.
☞ 当场,立即 impromptu, off the cuff, extempore, off teh top of one's head, immediately.

office n.
☞ 任务,职务 responsibility, duty, obligation, charge, commission, occupation, situation, post, employment, function, appointment, business, role, service.
☞ 工作室 workplace, workroom, bureau.

officer n.
☞ 官员,高级职员 official, office-holder, public servant, functionary, dignitary, bureaucrat, administrator, representative, executive, agent, appointee.

official adj.
☞ 授权的,正式的 authorized, authoritative, legitimate, formal, licensed, accredited, certified, approved, authenticated, authentic, bona fide, proper.
n.
☞ 公务员 office-bearer, officer, functionary, bureaucrat, executive, representative, agent.

offset v.
☞ 抵消 counterbalance, compensate for, cancel out, counteract, make up for, balance out, neutralize.

often adv.
☞ 经常地 frequently, repeatedly, regularly, generally, again and again, time after time, time and again, much.

oily adj.
☞ 用油脂润滑的,滑的 greasy, fatty.
☞ 油的,滑腻的,言词圆滑的 unctuous, smooth, obsequious, ingratiating, smarmy, glib, flattering.

old adj.
☞ 年老的 aged, elderly, advanced in years, grey, senile.
☞ 古代的,古老的 ancient, original, primitive, antiquated, mature.
☞ 长期存在的 long-standing, long-established, time-honoured, traditional.
☞ 废弃的,陈腐的 obsolete, old-fashioned, out of date, worn-out, decayed, decrepit.
☞ 以前的,从前的 former, previous, earlier, one-time, ex-.

old-fashioned adj.
☞ 过时了的,废弃了的 outmoded, out of date, outdated, dated, unfashionable, obsolete, behind the times, antiquated, archaic, passe, obsolescent.

omen n.
☞ 预兆 portent, sign, warning, premonition, foreboding, augury, indication.

ominous adj.
☞ 预兆的 portentous, inauspicious, foreboding, menacing, sinister, fateful, unpromising, threatening.

omission n.
☞ 省略,遗漏 exclusion, gap,

oversight, failure, lack, neglect, default, avoidance.

omit v.
☞ 省略 leave out, exclude, miss out, pass over, overlook, drop, skip, eliminate, forget, neglect, leave undone, fail, disregard, edit out.

once adv.
☞ 以前 formerly, previously, in the past, at one time, long ago, in times past, once upon a time, in the old days.

at once
☞ 立即 immediately, instantly, directly, right away, straightaway, without delay, now, promptly, forthwith.
☞ 同时(发生)的 simultaneously, together, at the same time.

oncoming adj.
☞ 靠近的,临近的 approaching, advancing, upcoming, looming, onrushing, gathering.

one adj.
☞ 单独的 single, solitary, lone, individual, only.
☞ 完整的 united, harmonious, like-minded, whole, entire, complete, equal, identical, alike.

one-sided adj.
☞ 不平衡,失衡的 unbalanced, unequal, lopsided.
☞ 不公平的 unfair, unjust, prejudiced, biased, partial, partisan.
☞ 一方的,单方的 unilateral, independent.

ongoing adj.
☞ 继续的 continuing, continuous, unbroken, uninterrupted, constant.
☞ 发展的,壮大的 developing, evolving, progressing, growing, in progress, unfinished, unfolding.

onlooker n.
☞ 旁观者 bystander, observer, spectator, looker-on, eye-witness, witness, watcher, viewer.

only adv.
☞ 正好,恰好 just, at most, merely, simply, purely, barely, exclusively, solely.
adj.
☞ 唯一的,单独的 sole, single, solitary, lone, unique, exclusive, individual.

onset n.
☞ 开始;根源 beginning, start, commencement, inception, outset, outbreak.
☞ 攻击 assault, attack, onslaught, onrush.

onslaught n.
☞ 攻击,攻打 attack, assault, offensive, charge, bombardment, blitz.

open adj.
☞ 敞开的 unclosed, ajar, gaping, uncovered, unfastened, unlocked, unsealed, yawning, lidless.
☞ 开阔的,空旷的 unrestricted, free, unobstructed, clear, accessible, exposed, unprotected, unsheltered, vacant, wide, available.
☞ 公开的 overt, obvious, plain, evident, manifest, noticeable,

flagrant, conspicuous.
☞ 没有结果的, 胜负未分的 undecided, unresolved, unsettled, debatable, problematic, moot.
☞ 坦白的, 直率的 frank, candid, honest, guileless, natural, ingenuous, unreserved.

v.
☞ 打开, 展开, 张开 unfasten, undo, unlock, uncover, unseal, unblock, uncork, clear, expose.
☞ 开始, 开放, 开发 begin, start, launch, inaugurate, commence.

opening n.
☞ 开, 空, 裂缝, 穴, 孔 gap, breach, aperture, orifice, hole, cleft, split, rift.
☞ 开始, 开端 beginning, start, launch, initiation, inauguration, commencement.
☞ 机会 opportunity, chance, occasion, break, place, vacancy.

adj.
☞ 开始的 beginning, commencing, starting, first, inaugural, introductory, initial, early, primary.

openly adv.
☞ 公开地 overtly, frankly, candidly, blatantly, flagrantly, plainly, unashamedly, unreservedly, glaringly, in public, in full view, shamelessly.

operate v.
☞ 运行 function, act, perform, run, work, go.
☞ 操作, 控制 control, handle, manage, use, utilize, manoeuvre.

operation n.
☞ 职责, 作用 functioning, action, running, motion, movement, performance, working.
☞ 影响力, 效果 influence, manipulation, handling, management, use, utilization.
☞ 任务, 工作 undertaking, enterprise, affair, procedure, proceeding, process, business, deal, transaction, effort.
☞ 运动 campaign, action, task, manoeuvre, exercise.

operational adj.
☞ 工作上的, 操作上的 working, in working order, usable, functional, going, viable, workable, ready, prepared, in service.

operative adj.
☞ 工作的, 能起作用的 operational, in operation, in force, functioning, active, effective, efficient, in action, workable, viable, serviceable, functional.
☞ 关键的, 基本的 key, crucial, important, relevant, significant.

opinion n.
☞ 信仰, 信念 belief, judgement, view, point of view, idea, perception, stance, theory, impression, feeling, sentiment, estimation, assessment, conception, mind, notion, way of thinking.

opponent n.
☞ 对手, 敌手 adversary, enemy, antagonist, foe, competitor, contestant, challenger, opposer,

opposition, rival, objector, dissident.

opportunity n.
☞ 机会,运气 chance, opening, break, occasion, possibility, hour, moment.

oppose v.
☞ 抵抗,抗拒 resist, withstand, counter, attack, combat, contest, stand up to, take a stand, against, take issue with, confront, defy, face, fight, hinder, obstruct, bar, check, prevent, thwart.
☞ 比较,对照 compare, contrast, match, offset, counterbalance, play off.

opposed adj.
☞ 相反的 in opposition, against, hostile, conflicting, opposing, opposite, antagonistic, clashing, contrary, incompatible, anti.

opposite adj.
☞ 相对的 facing, fronting, corresponding.
☞ 对立的 opposed, antagonistic, conflicting, contrary, hostile, adverse, contradictory, antithetical, irreconcilable, unlike, reverse, inconsistent, different, contrasted, differing.
n.
☞ 相反 reverse, converse, contrary, antithesis, contradiction, inverse.

opposition n.
☞ 对抗,敌对 antagonism, hostility, resistance, obstructiveness, unfriendliness, disapproval.
☞ 对手,敌手 opponent, antagonist, rival, foe, other side.

oppress v.
☞ 加负担于 burden, afflict, lie heavy on, harass, depress, sadden, torment, vex.
☞ 压服 subjugate, suppress, subdue, overpower, overwhelm, crush, trample, tyrannize, persecute, maltreat, abuse.

oppression n.
☞ 暴政 tyranny, subjugation, subjection, repression, despotism, suppression, injustice, cruelty, brutality, abuse, persecution, maltreatment, harshness, hardship.

oppressive adj.
☞ 憋闷的,空气不流通的 airless, stuffy, close, stifling, suffocating, sultry, muggy, heavy.
☞ 暴虐的,专制的 tyrannical, despotic, overbearing, overwhelming, repressive, harsh, unjust, inhuman, cruel, brutal, burdensome, onerous, intolerable.

oppressor n.
☞ 暴君 tyrant, bully, taskmaster, slave-driver, despot, dictator, persecutor, tormentor, intimidator, autocrat.

optimistic adj.
☞ 乐观的 confident, assured, sanguine, hopeful, positive, cheerful, buoyant, bright, idealistic, expectant.

optimum adj.
☞ 恰当的,好的 best, ideal,

perfect, optimal, superlative, top, choice.

option n.
- 选择权 choice, alternative, preference, possibility, selection.

optional adj.
- 自愿的 voluntary, discretionary, elective, free, unforced.

oral adj.
- 口头的 verbal, spoken, unwritten, vocal.

orbit n.
- 环行 circuit, cycle, circle, course, path, trajectory, track, revolution, rotation.
- 范围 range, scope, domain, influence, sphere of influence, compass.

v.
- (使)环绕,(使)旋转 revolve, circle, encircle, circumnavigate.

order n.
- 命令 command, directive, decree, injunction, instruction, direction, edict, ordinance, mandate, regulation, rule, precept, law.
- 需要 requisition, request, booking, commission, reservation, application, demand.
- 种类,分类 arrangement, organization, grouping, disposition, sequence, categorization, classification, method, pattern, plan, system, array, layout, line-up, structure.
- 治安,秩序 peace, quiet, calm, tranquillity, harmony, law and order, discipline.
- 团体 association, society, community, fraternity, brotherhood, sisterhood, lodge, guild, company, organization, denomination, sect, union.

v.
- 命令 command, instruct, direct, bid, decree, require, authorize.
- 订 request, reserve, book, apply for, requisition.
- 整理 arrange, organize, dispose, classify, group, marshal, sort out, lay out, manage, control, catalogue.

orderly adj.
- 整齐的 ordered, systematic, neat, tidy, regular, methodical, in order, well-organized, well-regulated.
- 守纪律的 well-behaved, controlled, disciplined, law-abiding.

ordinary adj.
- 通常的 common, commonplace, regular, routine, standard, average, everyday, run-of-the-mill, usual, unexceptional, unremarkable, typical, normal, customary, common-or-garden, plain, familiar, habitual, simple, conventional, modest, mediocre, indifferent, pedestrian, prosaic, undistinguished.

organic adj.
- 有机的 natural, biological, living, animate.

organization n.
- 协会 association, institution, society, company, firm,

corporation, federation, group, league, club, confederation, consortium.
☞ 组织 arrangement, system, classification, methodology, order, formation, grouping, method, plan, structure, pattern, composition, configuration, design.

organize v.
☞ 组织 structure, co-ordinate, arrange, order, group, marshal, classify, systematize, tabulate, catalogue.
☞ 建立 establish, found, set up, develop, form, frame, construct, shape, run.

orientation n.
☞ 定位 situation, bearings, location, direction, position, alignment, placement, attitude.
☞ 适应 initiation, training, acclimatization, familiarization, adaptation, adjustment, settling in.

origin n.
☞ 根源 source, spring, fount, foundation, base, cause, derivation, provenance, roots, well-spring.
☞ 起始 beginning, commencement, start, inauguration, launch, dawning, creation, emergence.
☞ 祖先,列祖 ancestry, descent, extraction, heritage, family, lineage, parentage, pedigree.

original adj.
☞ 首先的 first, early, earliest, initial, primary, archetypal, rudimentary, embryonic, starting, opening, commencing, first-hand.
☞ 新的,新颖的 novel, innovative, new, creative, fresh, imaginative, inventive, unconventional, unusual, unique.
n.
☞ 原型 prototype, master, paradigm, model, pattern, archetype, standard, type.

originate v.
☞ 起源,发生 rise, arise, spring, stem, issue, flow, proceed, derive, come, evolve, emerge, be born.
☞ 产生 create, invent, inaugurate, introduce, give birth to, develop, discover, establish, begin, commence, start, set up, launch, pioneer, conceive, form, produce, generate.

ornament n.
☞ 装饰的 decoration, adornment, embellishment, garnish, trimming, accessory, frill, trinket, bauble, jewel.
v.
☞ 装饰,修饰 decorate, adorn, embellish, garnish, trim, beautify, brighten, dress up, deck, gild.

ornamental adj.
☞ 装饰的,装璜的 decorative, embellishing, adorning, attractive, showy.

other adj.
☞ 另外的 different, dissimilar, unlike, separate, distinct, contrasting.
☞ 另外的,附加的 more, further, extra, additional, supplementary, spare,

outbreak n.
☞ 爆发 eruption, outburst, explosion, flare-up, upsurge, flash, rash, burst, epidemic.

outburst n.
☞ 爆发 outbreak, eruption, explosion, flare-up, outpouring, burst, fit, gush, surge, storm, spasm, seizure, gale, attack, fit of temper.

outcome n.
☞ 结果,后果 result, consequence, upshot, conclusion, effect, end result.

outdated adj.
☞ 过时的 out of date, old-fashioned, dated, unfashionable, outmoded, behind the times, obsolete, obsolescent, antiquated, archaic.

outdo v.
☞ 胜过,超过 surpass, exceed, beat, excel, outstrip, outshine, get the better of, overcome, outclass, outdistance.

outdoor adj.
☞ 户外,室外的 out-of-door(s), outside, open-air.

outfit n.
☞ 衣服,被褥 clothes, costume, ensemble, get-up, togs, garb.
☞ 设备,装备 equipment, gear, kit, rig, trappings, paraphernalia.

outing n.
☞ 游览 excursion, expedition, jaunt, pleasure, trip, trip, spin, picnic.

outlaw n.
☞ 匪徒,土匪 bandit, brigand, robber, desperado, highwayman, criminal, marauder, pirate, fugitive.
v.
☞ 用法律禁止 ban, disallow, forbid, prohibit, exclude, embargo, bar, debar, banish, condemn.

outlet n.
☞ 出口 exit, way out, vent, egress, escape, opening, release, safety, valve, channel.
☞ 销路,批发商店 retailer, shop, store, market.

outline n.
☞ 摘要,概要 summary, synopsis, precis, bare facts, sketch, thumbnail sketch, abstract.
☞ 外形,轮廓 profile, form, contour, shape.
v.
☞ 略图,草图 sketch, summarize, draft, trace, rough out.

outlook n.
☞ 风景,景色 view, viewpoint, point of view, attitude, perspective, frame of mind, angle, slant, standpoint, opinion.
☞ 预期,期望的事 expectations, future, forecast, prospect, prognosis.

outlying adj.
☞ 远的,远隔 distant, remote, far-off, far-away, far-flung, outer, provincial.

out-of-the-way adj.
☞ 偏远的 remote, isolated, far-flung, far-off, far-away, distant, inaccessible, little-

known, obscure, unfrequented.

output n.
- 产量 production, productivity, product, yield, manufacture, achievement.

outrage n.
- 愤怒 anger, fury, rage, indignation, shock, affront, horror.
- 残暴,暴行 atrocity, offence, injury, enormity, barbarism, crime, violation, evil, scandal.

v.
- 使发怒,使生气 anger, infuriate, affront, incense, enrage, madden, disgust, injure, offend, shock, scandalize.

outrageous adj.
- 残暴的,可恶的 atrocious, abominable, shocking, scandalous, offensive, disgraceful, monstrous, heinous, unspeakable, horrible.
- 不能容忍的,过分的 excessive, exorbitant, immoderate, unreasonable, extortionate, inordinate, preposterous.

outset n.
- 开端,开始 start, beginning, opening, inception, commencement, inauguration, kick-off.

outside adj.
- 外部的,外向的 external, exterior, outer, surface, superficial, outward, extraneous, outdoor, outermost, extreme.

n.
- 外部,外表 exterior, facade, front, surface, face, appearance, cover.

outsider n.
- 外人 stranger, intruder, alien, non-member, non-resident, foreigner, newcomer, visitor, intruder, interloper, misfit, odd man out.

outskirts n.
- 郊区,住宅区 suburbs, vicinity, periphery, fringes, borders, boundary, edge, margin.

outspoken adj.
- 直言的,坦率的 candid, frank, forthright, blunt, unreserved, plain-spoken, direct, explicit.

outstanding adj.
- 极好的,杰出的 excellent, distinguished, eminent, pre-eminent, celebrated, exceptional, superior, remarkable, prominent, superb, great, notable, impressive, striking, superlative, important, noteworthy, memorable, special, extraordinary.
- 欠着的,未付的 owing, unpaid, due, unsettled, unresolved, uncollected, pending, payable, remaining, ongoing, leftover.

outwit v.
- 以机智胜过 outsmart, outthink, get the better of, trick, better, beat, dupe, cheat, deceive, defraud, swindle.

oval adj.
- 卵形的 egg-shaped, elliptical,

ovoid, ovate.

overall *adj.*
- 总体,全体的 total, all-inclusive, all-embracing, comprehensive, inclusive, general, universal, global, broad, blanket, complete, all-over.

adv.
- 总体上,总的来说 in general, on the whole, by and large, broadly, generally speaking.

overcome *v.*
- 战胜,征服 conquer, defeat, beat, surmount, triumph over, vanquish, rise above, master, overpower, overwhelm, overthrow, subdue.

overcrowded *adj.*
- 挤满,拥塞的 congested, packed(out), jam-packed, crammed full, chock-full, overpopulated, overloaded, swarming.

overdo *v.*
- 夸张,夸大,使过大 exaggerate, go too far, carry to excess, go overboard, lay it on thick, overindulge, overstate, overact, overplay, overwork.

overdue *adj.*
- 迟的,晚的 late, behindhand, behind schedule, delayed, owing, unpunctual, slow.

overhead *adv.*
- 在上面 above, up above, on high, upward.

adj.
- 上面的 elevated, aerial, overhanging, raised.

overload *v.*
- 加负担于 burden, oppress, strain, tax, weigh down, overcharge, encumber.

overlook *v.*
- 眺望 front on to, face, look on to, look over, command a view of.
- 错过 miss, disregard, ignore, omit, neglect, pass over, let pass, let ride, slight.
- 原谅 excuse, forgive, pardon, condone, wink at, turn a blind eye to.

owing *adj.*
- 未付的,未还的 unpaid, due, owed, in arrears, outstanding, payable, unsettled, overdue.

owing to
- 因为,由于 because of, as a result of, on account of, thanks to.

own *adj.*
- 自己的,个人的 personal, individual, private, particular, idiosyncratic.

v.
- 拥有,占有 possess, have, hold, retain, keep, enjoy.

own up
- 承认 admit, confess, come clean, tell the truth, acknowledge.

owner *n.*
- 拥有人,持有人 possessor, holder, landlord, landlady, proprietor, proprietress, master, mistress, freeholder.

P

pace n.
- 一步 step, stride, walk, gait, tread, movement, motion, progress, rate, speed, velocity, celerity, quickness, rapidity, tempo, measure.
- v.
- 踱步 step, stride, walk, march, tramp.

packed adj.
- 充满的,装满的 filled, full, jam-packed, chock-a-block, crammed, crowded, congested.

packet n.
- 包,兜 pack, carton, box, bag, package, parcel, case, container, wrapper, wrapping, packing.

pad n.
- 垫子,坐垫 cushion, pillow, wad, buffer, padding, protection.
- 写字垫 writing-pad, note-pad, jotter, block.
- v.
- 充满 fill, stuff, wad, pack, wrap, line, cushion, protect.

padding n.
- 充填,填充物 filling, stuffing, wadding, packing, protection.
- 啰嗦,冗长 verbiage, verbosity, wordiness, waffle, bombast, hot air.

page n.
- 张 leaf, sheet, folio, side.
- v.
- 呼唤 call, send for, summon, bid, announce.

pain n.
- 创伤,伤害 hurt, ache, throb, cramp, spasm, twinge, pang, stab, sting, smart, soreness, tenderness, discomfort, distress, suffering, affliction, trouble, anguish, agony, torment, torture.
- 讨厌的人或事 nuisance, bother, bore, annoyance, vexation, burden, headache.
- v.
- 使受伤 hurt, afflict, torment, torture, agonize, distress, upset, sadden, grieve.

pained adj.
- 伤害的 hurt, injured, wounded, stung, offended, aggrieved, reproachful, distressed, upset, saddened, grieved.

painful adj.
- 酸痛的,痛苦的 sore, tender, aching, throbbing, smarting, stabbing, agonizing, excruciating.
- 令人厌烦的 unpleasant, disagreeable, distressing, upsetting, saddenning, harrowing, traumatic.
- 苦的,艰难的 hard, difficult, laborious, tedious.

pain-killer n.
- 止痛药 pain-free, trouble-free, effortless, easy, simple,

undemanding.
pains n.
☞ 烦恼,困境 trouble, bother, effort, labour, care, diligence.

painstaking adj.
☞ 小心的,仔细的 careful, meticulous, scrupulous, thorough, conscientious, diligent, assiduous, industrious, hardworking, dedicated, devoted, persevering.

paint n.
☞ 颜料,染料 colour, colouring, pigment, dye, tint, stain.
v.
☞ 给……着色 colour, dye, tint, stain, lacquer, varnish, glaze, apply, daub, coat, cover, decorate.
☞ 画,描绘 portray, depict, describe, recount, picture, represent.

painting n.
☞ 画 oil painting, oil, watercolour, picture, portrait, landscape, still life, miniature, illustration, fresco, mural.

pair n.
☞ 一双,一对 couple, brace, twosome, duo, twins, two of a kind.
v.
☞ 相配,使配合 match (up), twin, team, mate, marry, wed, splice, join, couple, link, bracket, put together.

palace n.
☞ 大厦 castle, chateau, mansion, stately home, basilica, dome.

pale adj.
☞ 苍白的 pallid, livid, ashen, ashy, white, chalky, pasty, pasty-faced, waxen, waxy, wan, sallow, anaemic.
☞ 淡色的 light, pastel, faded, washed-out, bleached, colourless, insipid, vapid, weak, feeble, faint, dim.
v.
☞ (使)变白 whiten, blanch, bleach, fade, dim.

palm n.
☞ 手掌 hand, paw, mitt.
v.
☞ 抓住,握 take, grab, snatch, appropriate.

palm off
☞ 把……强加于 foist, impose, fob off, offload, unload, pass off.

pamphlet n.
☞ 传单,散页印刷品 leaflet, brochure, booklet, folder, circular, handout, notice.

panic n.
☞ 恐慌 agitation, flap, alarm, dismay, consternation, fright, fear, horror, terror, frenzy, hysteria.
v.
☞ 恐慌 lose one's nerve, lose one's head, go to pieces, flap, overreact.

panic-stricken adj.
☞ 惊慌的 alarmed, frightened, horrified, terrified, petrified, scared stiff, in a cold sweat, panicky, frantic, frenzied, hysterical.

pant v.
☞ 喘气 puff, blow, gasp, wheeze, breathe, sigh, heave,

pants n.
- ☞ 男衬裤 underpants, drawers, panties, briefs, knickers, y-fronts, boxer shorts, trunks, shorts.
- ☞ 裤子 trousers, slacks, jeans.

paper n.
- ☞ 报纸 newspaper, daily, broadsheet, tabloid, rag, journal, organ.
- ☞ 公文,文件 document, credential, authorization, identification, certificate, deed.
- ☞ 文章,论文 essay, composition, dissertation, thesis, treatise, article, report.

parade n.
- ☞ 队列、队伍(列队的)行进 procession, cavalcade, motorcade, march.

v.
- ☞ 游行 march, process, file past.
- ☞ 展示 show, display, exhibit, show off, vaunt, flaunt, brandish.

paradise n.
- ☞ 天堂 heaven, Utopia, Shangri-la, Elysium, Eden, bliss, delight.

paradox n.
- ☞ 谬论 contradiction, inconsistency, incongruity, absurdity, oddity, anomaly, mystery, enigma, riddle, puzzle.

paradoxical adj.
- ☞ 自相矛盾 self-contradictory, contradictory, conflicting, inconsistent, incongruous, absurd, illogical, improbable, impossible, mysterious, enigmatic, puzzling, baffling.

paragraph n.
- ☞ 段落 passage, section, part, portion, subsection, subdivision, clause, item.

parallel adj.
- ☞ 平行的 equidistant, aligned, coextensive, alongside, analogous, equivalent, corresponding, matching, like, similar, resembling.

n.
- ☞ 相配 match, equal, twin, duplicate, analogue, equivalent, counterpart.
- ☞ 相似 similarity, resemblance, likeness, correspondence, correlation, equivalence, analogy, comparison.

v.
- ☞ 和……相配,使相称 match, echo, conform, agree, correspond, correlate, compare, liken.

paralyse v.
- ☞ 使残废,使无用 cripple, lame, disable, incapacitate, immobilize, anaesthetize, numb, deaden, freeze, transfix, halt, stop.

paralysed adj.
- ☞ 瘫痪的,麻痹的 paralytic, paraplegic, quadriplegic, crippled, lame, disabled, incapacitated, immobilized, numb.

paraphrase n.
- ☞ 改说,重写,释义 rewording, rephrasing, restatement,

version, interpretation, rendering, translation.
v.
☞ 改说,重写,释义 reword, rephrase, restate, interpret, render, translate.

parcel *n*.
☞ 包裹 package, packet, pack; box, carton, bundle.
v.
☞ 把……包成一包 package, pack, wrap, bundle, tie up.

parcel out
☞ 分几份 divide, carve up, apportion, allocate, allot, share out, distribute, dispense, dole out, deal out, mete out.

pardon *v*.
☞ 原谅,饶恕 forgive, condone, overlook, excuse, vindicate, acquit, absolve, remit, let off, reprieve, free, liberate, release.
n.
☞ 饶恕,宽恕 forgiveness, mercy, clemency, indulgence, amnesty, excuse, acquittal, absolution, reprieve, release, discharge.

parent *n*.
☞ 父母亲 father, mother, dam, sire, progenitor, begetter, procreator, guardian.

park *n*.
☞ 公园 grounds, estate, parkland, gardens, woodland, reserve, pleasure-ground.
v.
☞ 停放 put, position, deposit, leave.

parliament *n*.
☞ 立法机构 legislature, senate, congress, house, assembly, convocation, council, diet.

parliamentary *adj*.
☞ 议会的 governmental, senatorial, congressional, legislative, law-making.

part *n*.
☞ 组成部分,成分 component, constituent, element, factor, piece, bit, particle, fragment, scrap, segment, fraction, portion, territory.
☞ 作用 role, character, duty, task, responsibility, office, function, capacity.
v.
☞ 分开,隔开 separate, detach, disconnect, sever, split, tear, break, break up, take apart, dismantle, come apart, split up, divide, disunite, part company, disband, disperse, scatter, leave, depart, withdraw, go away.

part with
☞ 放弃,松手放开 relinquish, let go of, give up, yield, surrender, renounce, forgo, abandon, discard, jettison.

partial *adj*.
☞ 不完全,不完备的 incomplete, limited, restricted, imperfect, fragmentary, unfinished.
☞ 偏见的 biased, prejudiced, partisan, one-sided, discriminatory, unfair, unjust, predisposed, coloured.

partial to
☞ 喜欢,偏爱 fond of, keen on, crazy about, mad about.

partiality *n*.
☞ 爱好,喜欢 liking, fondness,

predilection, inclination, preference, predisposition.

participant n.
- 参加者 entrant, contributor, participator, member, party, cooperator, helper, worker.

participate v.
- 参加 take part, join in, contribute, engage, be involved, enter, share, partake, co-operate, help, assist.

participation n.
- 参加 involvement, sharing, partnership, co-operation, contribution, assistance.

particle n.
- 小块,一点儿 bit, piece, fragment, scrap, shred, sliver, speck, morsel, crumb, whit, jot, tittle, atom, grain, drop.

particular adj.
- 专门的 specific, precise, exact, distinct, special, peculiar.
- 例外的,不平常的 exceptional, remarkable, notable, marked, thorough, unusual, uncommon.
- 苛求的 fussy, discriminating, choosy, finicky, fastidious.

n.
- 细节,小事 detail, specific, point, feature, item, fact, circumstance.

particularly adv.
- 特殊地 especially, exceptionally, remarkably, notably, extraordinarily, unusually, uncommonly, surprisingly, in particular, specifically, explicitly,

distinctly.

parting n.
- 离去,离开 departure, going, leave-taking, farewell, goodbye, adieu.
- 分叉,分歧 divergence, separation, division, partition, rift, split, rupture, breaking.

adj.
- 分开的 departing, farewell, last, dying, final, closing, concluding.

partly adv.
- 有些,有几分 somewhat, to some extent, to a certain extent, up to a point, slightly, fractionally, moderately, relatively, in part, partially, incompletely.

partner n.
- 同事,同伴 associate, ally, confederate, colleague, team-mate, collaborator, accomplice, helper, mate, sidekick, oppo, companion, comrade, consort, spouse, husband, wife.

partnership n.
- 结盟,联姻 alliance, confederation, affiliation, combination, union, syndicate, co-operative, association, society, corporation, company, firm, fellowship, fraternity, brotherhood.
- 协作,合作 collaboration, co-operation, participation, sharing.

party n.
- 庆祝会,聚会 celebration, festivity, social, do, get-together, gathering, reunion, function, reception, at-home,

housewarming.
- 队, 组 team, squad, crew, gang, band, group, company, detachment.
- 派别, 宗派 faction, side, league, cabal, alliance, association, grouping, combination.
- (泛指的)人 person, individual, litigant, plaintiff, defendant.

pass v.
- 超过, 胜过 surpass, exceed, go beyond, outdo, outstrip, overtake, leave, behind.
- 经过 go past, go by, elapse, lapse, proceed, roll, flow, run, move, go, disappear, vanish.
- 给 give, hand, transfer, transmit.
- 通过, 批准 enact, ratify, validate, adopt, authorize, sanction, approve.
- 通过(考试) succeed, get through, qualify, graduate.

n.
- 通行证 permit, passport, identification, ticket, licence, authorization, warrant, permission.

pass away
- 死 die, pass on, expire, decease, give up the ghost.

pass off
- 假装, 伴作 feign, counterfeit, fake, palm off.
- 发生 happen, occur, take place, go off.

pass out
- 昏厥, 晕倒 faint, lose consciousness, black out, collapse, flake out, keel over, drop.
- 分发, 分配 give out, hand out, dole out, distribute, deal out, share out.

pass over
- 不顾, 漠视 disregard, ignore, overlook, miss, omit, leave, neglect.

passable adj.
- 令人满意的, 合格的 satisfactory, acceptable, allowable, tolerable, average, ordinary, unexceptional, moderate, fair, adequate, all right. ok, mediocre.
- 可通行的, 可流通的 clear, unobstructed, unblocked, open, navigable.

passage n.
- 通道, 走廊 passageway, aisle, corridor, hall, hallway, lobby, vestibule, doorway, opening, entrance, exit.
- 大道 thoroughfare, way, route, road, avenue, path, lane, alley.
- 摘录, 选录 extract, excerpt, quotation, text, paragraph, section, piece, clause, verse.
- 航行, 旅行 journey, voyage, trip, crossing.

passenger n.
- 旅行者 traveller, voyager, rider, fare, hitch-hiker.

passer-by n.
- 过路人 bystander, witness, looker-on, onlooker, spectator.

passing adj.
- 短暂的 ephemeral, transient, short-lived, temporary, momentary, fleeting, brief, short, cursory, hasty, quick,

slight, superficial, shallow, casual, incidental.

passion n.
☞ 感觉,感情 feeling, emotion, love, adoration, infatuation, fondness, affection, lust, itch, desire, craving, fancy, mania, obsession, craze, eagerness, keenness, avidity, enthusiasm, zest, fanaticism, zeal, ardour, fervour, warmth, heat, fire, spirit, intensity, vehemence, anger, indignation, wrath, fury, rage, outburst.

passionate adj.
☞ 热情的,热心的 ardent, fervent, eager, keen, avid, enthusiastic, fanatical, zealous, warm, hot, fiery, inflamed, aroused, excited, impassioned, intense, strong, fierce, vehement, violent, stormy, tempestuous, wild, frenzied.

☞ 感情上的,易激动的 emotional, excitable, hot-headed, impetuous, impulsive, quick-tempered, irritable.

☞ 爱的;充满深情的 loving, affectionate, lustful, erotic, sexy, sensual, sultry.

passive adj.
☞ 被动的 receptive, unassertive, submissive, docile, unresisting, non-violent, patient, resigned, long-suffering, indifferent, apathetic, lifeless, inert, inactive, non-participating.

past adj.
☞ 结束的,完了的 over, ended, finished, completed, done, over and done with.

☞ 以前的;从前的 former, previous, preceding, foregoing, late, recent.

☞ 过去的 ancient, bygone, olden, early, gone, no more, extinct, defunct, forgotten.

n.

☞ 过去 history, former, times, olden days, antiquity.

☞ 往事,经历 life, background, experience, track record.

paste n.
☞ 胶合剂 adhesive, glue, gum, mastic, putty, cement.

v.

☞ 粘住 stick, glue, gum, cement, fix.

pat v.
☞ 轻拍,轻叩 tap, dab, slap, touch, stroke, caress, fondle, pet.

n.

☞ 轻拍,轻叩 tap, dab, slap, touch, stroke, caress.

adv.

☞ 正好,恰恰 precisely, exactly, perfectly, flawlessly, faultlessly, fluently.

adj.

☞ 准备好的,恰好合适的 glib, fluent, smooth, slick, ready, easy, facile, simplistic.

patch n.
☞ 块,片,碎片 piece, bit, scrap, spot, area, stretch, tract, plot, lot, parcel.

v.

☞ 修补 mend, repair, fix, cover, reinforce.

patchy adj.
☞ 不规则的,补缀的 uneven, irregular, inconsistent, variable, random, fitful, erratic,

path n.
- 路径 route, course, direction, way, passage, road, avenue, lane, footpath, trail, track, walk.

pathetic adj.
- 可怜的 pitiable, poor, sorry, lamentable, miserable, sad, distressing, moving, touching, poignant, plaintive, heart-rending, heartbreaking.
- 可鄙的,可轻视的 contemptible, derisory, deplorable, useless, worthless, inadequate, meagre, feeble.

patience n.
- 耐心 calmness, composure, self-control, restraint, tolerance, forbearance, endurance, fortitude, long-suffering, submission, resignation, stoicism, persistence, perseverance, diligence.

patient adj.
- 有耐心的 calm, composed, self-possessed, self-controlled, restrained, even-tempered, mild, lenient, indulgent, understanding, forgiving, tolerant, accommodating, forbearing, long-suffering, uncomplaining, submissive, resigned, philosophical, stoical, persistent, persevering.

n.
- 病弱者,伤残者 invalid, sufferer, case, client.

patriotic adj.
- 爱国的 nationalistic, chauvinistic, jingoistic, loyal, flag-waving.

patrol n.
- 巡警 guard, sentry, sentinel, watchman.

v.
- 巡逻 police, guard, protect, defend, go the rounds, tour, inspect.

patron n.
- 恩人,捐助者 benefactor, philanthropist, sponsor, backer, supporter, sympathizer, advocate, champion, defender, protector, guardian, helper.
- 顾客,主顾 customer, client, frequenter, regular, shopper, buyer, purchaser, subscriber.

patronage n.
- 惠顾 custom, business, trade, sponsorship, backing, support.

patronize v.
- 保护,赞助 sponsor, fund, back, support, maintain, help, assist, promote, foster, encourage.
- 惠顾 frequent, shop at, buy from, deal with.

patronizing adj.
- 屈尊俯就的 condescending, stooping, overbearing, high-handed, haughty, superior, snobbish, supercilious, disdainful.

pattern n.
- 方法,方式 system, method, order, plan.
- 装饰 decoration, ornamentation, ornament, figure, motif, design, style.
- 模型 model, template, stencil, guide, original, prototype, standard, norm.

pause v.
☞ (使)停止,(使)停止,前进 halt, stop, cease, discontinue, break off, interrupt, take a break, rest, wait, delay, hesitate.
   n.
☞ 停止,止步 halt, stoppage, interruption, break, rest, breather, lull, let-up, respite, gap, interval, interlude, intermission, wait, delay, hesitation.

pay v.
☞ 汇(款) remit, settle, discharge, reward, remunerate, recompense, reimburse, repay, refund, spend, pay out.
☞ 有利,合算 benefit, profit, pay off, bring in, yield, return.
☞ 抵偿,赎罪 atone, make amends, compensate, answer, suffer.
   n.
☞ 酬劳,报酬 remuneration, wages, salary, earnings, income, fee, stipend, honorarium, emoluments, payment, reward, recompense, compensation, reimbursement.

pay back
☞ 偿还,还 repay, refund, reimburse, recompense, settle, square.
☞ 报复 get one's own back, take revenge, get even with, reciprocate, counter-attack.

pay off
☞ 清帐 discharge, settle, square, clear.
☞ 把……打发走 dismiss, fire, sack, lay off.

☞ 有回报 succeed, work.

pay out
☞ 付款 spend, disburse, hand over, fork out, shell out, lay out.

payable adj.
☞ 欠钱应该给的 owed, owing, unpaid, outstanding, in arrears, due, mature.

payment n.
☞ 付款 remittance, settlement, discharge, premium, outlay, advance, deposit, instalment, contribution, donation, allowance, reward, remuneration, pay, fee, hire, fare, toll.

peace n.
☞ 沉默无声 silence, quiet, hush, stillness, rest, relaxation, tranquillity, calm, calmness, composure, contentment.
☞ 和平 armistice, truce, cease-fire, conciliation, concord, harmony, agreement, treaty.

peaceable adj.
☞ 和平的,平和的 pacific, peace-loving, unwarlike, non-violent, conciliatory, friendly, amicable, inoffensive, gentle, placid, easy-going, mild.

peaceful adj.
☞ 安静的,平静的 quiet, still, restful, relaxing, tranquil, serene, calm, placid, unruffled, undisturbed, untroubled, friendly, amicable, peaceable, pacific, gentle.

peacemaker n.
☞ 调停人 appeaser, conciliator, mediator, arbitrator,

intercessor, peace-monger, pacifist.

peak n.
- 顶端 top, summit, pinnacle, crest, crown, zenith, height, maximum, climax, culmination, apex, tip, point.

v.
- (使)达到,顶点 climax, come to a head.

peasant n.
- 农民 rustic, provincial, yokel, bumpkin, oaf, boor, lout.

peculiar adj.
- 奇怪的 strange, odd, curious, funny, weird, bizarre, extraordinary, unusual, abnormal, exceptional, unconventional, offbeat, eccentric, way-out, outlandish, exotic.
- 特有的,独特的 characteristic, distinctive, specific, particular, special, individual, personal, idiosyncratic, unique, singular.

peculiarity n.
- 奇怪,古怪 oddity, bizarreness, abnormality, exception, eccentricity, quirk, mannerism, feature, trait, mark, quality, attribute, characteristic, distinctiveness, particularity, idiosyncrasy.

peddle v.
- 推销,兜售 sell, vend, flog, hawk, tout, push, trade, traffic, market.

pedestal n.
- 底座 plinth, stand, support, mounting, foot, base, foundation, platform, podium.

pedestrian n.
- 步行者 walker, foot-traveller.

adj.
- 单调的 dull, boring, flat, uninspired, banal, mundane, run-of-the-mill, commonplace, ordinary, mediocre, indifferent, prosaic, stodgy, plodding.

peep v.
- 偷看 look, peek, glimpse, spy, squint, peer, emerge, issue, appear.

n.
- 偷看 look, peek, glimpse, glance, squint.

peer¹ v.
- 细看 look, gaze, scan, scrutinize, examine, inspect, spy, snoop, peep, squint.

peer² n.
- 贵族的一员 aristocrat, noble, nobleman, lord, duke, marquess, marquis, earl, count, viscount, baron.
- 相同的人,相等的物 equal, counterpart, equivalent, match, fellow.

penalty n.
- 惩罚,处罚 punishment, retribution, fine, forfeit, handicap, disadvantage.

pending adj.
- 未解决的 impending, in the offing, forthcoming, imminent, undecided, in the balance.

penetrate v.
- 刺穿,穿过 pierce, stab, prick, puncture, probe, sink, bore, enter, infiltrate, permeate, seep, pervade,

suffuse.

penniless adj.
- 贫穷的 poor, poverty-stricken, impoverished, destitute, bankrupt, ruined, bust, broke, stony-broke.

pension n.
- 养老金 annuity, superannuation, allowance, benefit.

people n.
- 人 persons, individuals, humans, human beings, mankind, humanity, folk, public, general public, populace, rank and file, population, inhabitants, citizens, community, society, race, nation.

v.
- 居住于 populate, inhabit, occupy, settle, colonize.

perceive v.
- 感觉到,观察 sense, feel, apprehend, learn, realize, appreciate, be aware of, know, grasp, understand, gather, deduce, conclude.

perceptible adj.
- 可感觉的 perceivable, discernible, detectable, appreciable, distinguishable, observable, noticeable, obvious, evident, conspicuous, clear, plain, apparent, visible.

perception n.
- 感觉,领悟力 sense, feeling, impression, idea, conception, apprehension, awareness, consciousness, observation, recognition, grasp, understanding, insight, discernment, taste.

perceptive adj.
- 有眼力的 discerning, observant, sensitive, responsive, aware, alert, quick, sharp, astute, shrewd.

perch v.
- (使)登陆,(使)到达 land, alight, settle, sit, roost, balance, rest.

perfect adj.
- 无缺点的,完美的 faultless, impeccable, flawless, immaculate, spotless, blameless, pure, superb, excellent, matchless, incomparable.
- 准确的 exact, precise, accurate, right, correct, true.
- 完全的,全然的 utter, absolute, sheer, complete, entire, total.

v.
- 使……完美 fulfil, consummate, complete, finish, polish, refine, elaborate.

perfection n.
- 无缺,完美 faultlessness, flawlessness, excellence, superiority, ideal, model, paragon, crown, pinnacle, acme, consummation, completion.

perfectly adv.
- 全然 utterly, absolutely, quite, thoroughly, completely, entirely, wholly, totally, fully.
- 完美地 faultlessly, flawlessly, impeccably, ideally, exactly, correctly.

perform v.

- 做,干 do, carry out, execute, discharge, fulfil, satisfy, complete, achieve, accomplish, bring off, pull off, effect, bring about.
- 运行,活动 function, work, operate, behave, produce.
- 上演 stage, put on, present, enact, represent, act, play, appear as.

performance n.
- 上演 show, act, play, appearance, gig, presentation, production, interpretation, rendition, representation, portrayal, acting.
- 行动 action, deed, doing, carrying out, execution, implementation, discharge, fulfilment, completion, achievement, accomplishment.
- 活动 functioning, operation, behaviour, conduct.

perfume n.
- 香水 scent, fragrance, smell, odour, aroma, bouquet, sweetness, balm, essence, cologne, toilet water, incense.

perhaps adv.
- 大概,或许 maybe, possibly, conceivably, feasibly.

peril n.
- 危险 danger, hazard, risk, jeopardy, uncertainty, insecurity, threat, menace.

perilous adj.
- 引起危险的 dangerous, unsafe, hazardous, risky, chancy, precarious, insecure, unsure, vulnerable, exposed, menacing, threatening, dire.

period n.
- 时代,时期 era, epoch, age, generation, date, years, time, term, season, stage, phase, stretch, session, interval, space, span, spell, cycle.

periodic adj.
- 偶尔的,定期的 occasional, infrequent, sporadic, intermittent, recurrent, repeated, regular, periodical, seasonal.

periodical n.
- 杂志,期刊 magazine, journal, publication, weekly, monthly, quarterly.

perk n.
- 额外报酬,好处 perquisite, fringe benefit, benefit, bonus, dividend, gratuity, tip, extra, plus.

permanent adj.
- 永久的 fixed, stable, unchanging, imperishable, indestructible, unfading, eternal, everlasting, lifelong, perpetual, constant, steadfast, perennial, long-lasting, lasting, enduring, durable.

permissible adj.
- 许可的 permitted, allowable, allowed, admissible, all right, acceptable, proper, authorized, sanctioned, lawful, legal, legitimate.

permission n.
- 同意,赞成 consent, assent, agreement, approval, go-ahead, green light, authorization, sanction, leave, warrant, permit, licence, dispensation,

freedom, liberty.

permissive adj.
☞ 宽大的 liberal, broad-minded, tolerant, forbearing, lenient, easy-going, indulgent, overindulgent, lax, free.

permit v.
☞ 允许 allow, let, consent, agree, admit, grant, authorize, sanction, warrant, license.
n.
☞ 通行证 pass, passport, visa, licence, warrant, authorization, sanction, permission.

perpetual adj.
☞ 永久的,不朽的 eternal, everlasting, infinte, endless, unending, never-ending, interminable, ceaseless, unceasing, incessant, continuous, uninterrupted, constant, persistent, continual, repeated, recurrent.

perplex v.
☞ 使迷惑 puzzle, baffle, mystify, stump, confuse, muddle, confound, bewilder, dumbfound.

perseverance n.
☞ 固执,坚持 persistence, determination, resolution, doggedness, tenacity, diligence, assiduity, dedication, commitment, constancy, steadfastness, stamina, endurance, indefatigability.

persevere v.
☞ 继续 continue, carry on, stick at it, keep going, soldier on, persist, plug away, remain, stand firm, stand fast, hold on, hang on.

persist v.
☞ 坚持 remain, linger, last, endure, abide, continue, carry on, keep at it, persevere, insist.

persistent adj.
☞ 不懈的 incessant, endless, never-ending, interminable, continuous, unrelenting, relentless, unremitting, constant, steady, continual, repeated, perpetual, lasting, enduring.

person n.
☞ 人 individual, being, human being, human, man, woman, body, soul, character, type.

personal adj.
☞ 自己的,个人的 own, private, confidential, intimate, special, particular, individual, exclusive, idiosyncratic, distinctive.

personality n.
☞ 个性,性质,特征 character, nature, disposition, temperament, individuality, psyche, traits, make-up, charm, charisma, magnetism.
☞ 人名,驰名 celebrity, notable, personage, public figure, vip, star.

personnel n.
☞ 全体职员 staff, workforce, workers, employees, crew, human, resources, manpower, people, members.

perspective n.
☞ 观点,看法 aspect, angle, slant, attitude, standpoint,

persuade v.
- ☞ 说服 coax, prevail upon, lean on, cajole, wheedle, inveigle, talk into, induce, bring round, win over, convince, convert, sway, influence, lead on, incite, prompt, urge.

viewpoint, point of view, view, vista, scene, prospect, outlook, proportion, relation.

persuasion n.
- ☞ 说服 coaxing, cajolery, wheedling, enticement, pull, power, influence, conviction, conversion.
- ☞ 信念 party, faction, side, conviction, faith, belief, denomination, sect.

persuasive adj.
- ☞ 有说服力的 convincing, plausible, cogent, sound, valid, influential, forceful, weighty, effective, telling, potent, compelling, moving, touching.

pessimistic adj.
- ☞ 消极的 negative, cynical, fatalistic, defeatist, resigned, hopeless, despairing, despondent, dejected, downhearted, glum, morose, melancholy, depressed, dismal, gloomy, bleak.

pet n.
- ☞ 特别喜爱的物或人 favourite, darling, idol, treasure, jewel.

  adj.
- ☞ 喜爱的 favourite, favoured, preferred, dearest, cherished, special, particular.

  v.
- ☞ 抚摩 stroke, caress, fondle, cuddle, kiss, neck, snog.

petty adj.
- ☞ 较小的 minor, unimportant, insignificant, trivial, secondary, lesser, small, little, slight, trifling, paltry, inconsiderable, negligible.
- ☞ 心地狭窄的,自私的 small-minded, mean, ungenerous, grudging, spiteful.

phase n.
- ☞ 阶段时期 stage, step, time, period, spell, season, chapter, position, point, aspect, state, condition.

phase out:
- ☞ (钟,表)越走越慢 wind down, run down, ease off, taper off, eliminate, dispose of, get rid of, remove, withdraw, close, terminate.

phenomenal adj.
- ☞ 绝妙的,神奇的 marvellous, sensational, stupendous, amazing, remarkable, extraordinary, exceptional, unusual, unbelievable, incredible.

phenomenon n.
- ☞ 事件,发生 occurrence, happening, event, incident, episode, fact, appearance, sight.
- ☞ 奇迹 wonder, marvel, miracle, prodigy, rarity, curiosity, spectacle, sensation.

philanthropic adj.
- ☞ 慈善的 humanitarian, public-spirited, altruistic, unselfish, benevolent, kind, charitable, alms-giving, generous, liberal, open-handed.

philanthropist n.
☞ 慈善家 humanitarian, benefactor, patron, sponsor, giver, donor, contributor, altruist.

philanthropy n.
☞ 慈善 humanitarianism, public-spiritedness, altruism, unselfishness, benevolence, kind-heartedness, charity, alms-giving, patronage, generosity, liberality, open-handedness.

philosophical adj.
☞ 哲学的 metaphysical, abstract, theoretical, analytical, rational, logical, erudite, learned, wise, thoughtful.
☞ 达观的 resigned, patient, stoical, unruffled, calm, composed.

philosophy n.
☞ 哲学,人生观 metaphysics, rationalism, reason, logic, thought, thinking, wisdom, knowledge, ideology, world-view, doctrine, beliefs, convictions, values, principles, attitude, viewpoint.

phone v.
☞ 打电话 telephone, ring(up), call (up), dial, contact, gat in touch, give a buzz, give a tinkle.

phony adj.
☞ 假的 fake, counterfeit, forged, bogus, trick, false, spurious, assumed, affected, put-on, sham, pseudo, imitation.

photograph n.
☞ 照片 photo, snap, snapshot, print, shot, slide, transparency, picture, image, likeness.
v.
☞ 照像 snap, take, film, shoot, video, record.

phrase n.
☞ 词组 construction, clause, idiom, expression, saying, utterance, remark.
v.
☞ 措辞 word, formulate, frame, couch, present, put, express, say, utter, pronounce.

physical adj.
☞ 身体的,物理的 bodily, corporeal, fleshy, incarnate, mortal, earthly, material, concrete, solid, substantial, tangible, visible, real, actual.

physician n.
☞ 医生 doctor, medical practioiner, medic, general practitioner, GP, houseman, intern, registrar, consultant.

pick v.
☞ 挑选 select, choose, opt for, decide on, settle on, single out.
☞ 收集 gather, collect, pluck, harvest, cull.
n.
☞ 选择 choice, selection, option, decision, preference.
☞ 最好的东西 best, cream, flower, elite, elect.

pick on
☞ 威逼,欺凌 bully, torment, persecute, nag, get at, needle, bait.

pick out
☞ 认出,看出 spot, notice, perceive, recognize, distinguish, tell apart, separate, single out,

hand-pick, choose, select.

pick up
- ☞ 抬起,举起 lift, raise, hoist.
- ☞ 获悉 learn, master, grasp, gather.
- ☞ 改进,改善 improve, rally, recover, perk up.
- ☞ 买 buy, purchase.
- ☞ 得到,获得 obtain, acquire, gain.

pictorial *adj.*
- ☞ 图表的,图例的 graphic, diagrammatic, representational, vivid, striking, expressive, illustrated, picturesque, scenic.

picture *n.*
- ☞ 画 painting, portrait, landscape, drawing, sketch, illustration, engraving, photograph, print, representation, likeness, image, effigy.
- ☞ 描绘 depiction, portrayal, description, account, report, impression.
- ☞ 电影 film, movie, motion picture.

v.
- ☞ 想象,设想 imagine, envisage, envision, conceive, visualize, see.
- ☞ 描绘,描写 depict, describe, represent, show, portray, draw, sketch, paint, photograph, illustrate.

picturesque *adj.*
- ☞ 吸引的,诱人的 attractive, beautiful, pretty, charming, quaint, idyllic, sweet.
- ☞ 美丽如画的 descriptive, graphic, vivid, colourful, striking.

pierce *v.*
- ☞ 穿入,透过 penetrate, enter, stick into, puncture, drill, bore, probe, perforate, punch, prick, stab, lance, bayonet, run through, spear, skewer, spike, impale, transfix.

piercing *adj.*
- ☞ 尖叫的,高音的 shrill, high-pitched, loud, ear-splitting, sharp.
- ☞ (目光,问题)尖锐的 penetrating, probing, searching.
- ☞ 寒冷的 cold, bitter, raw, biting, keen, fierce, severe, wintry, frosty, freezing.
- ☞ 使痛的 painful, agonizing, excruciating, stabbing, lacerating.

piety *n.*
- ☞ 虔诚 piousness, devoutness, godliness, saintliness, holiness, sanctity, religion, faith, devotion, reverence.

pig *n.*
- ☞ 猪 swine, hog, sow, boar, animal, beast, brute, glutton, gourmand.

pigeonhole *n.*
- ☞ 分隔间(架) compartment, niche, slot, cubby-hole, cubicle, locker, box, place, section, class, category, classification.

v.
- ☞ 整齐的堆起 stack, heap, mass, amass, accumulate, build up, gather, assemble, collect, hoard, stockpile, store, load, pack, crush, crowd, flock, flood, stream, rush, charge.

pill *n.*

☞药片 tablet, capsule, pellet.

pillar n.
☞柱,支柱 column, shaft, post, mast, pier, upright, pile, support, prop, mainstay, bastion, tower of strength.

pilot n.
☞飞行员 flyer, aviator, airman.
☞导航员 navigator, steersman, helmsman, coxswain, captain, leader, director, guide.
v.
☞导航 fly, drive, steer, direct, control, handle, manage, operate, run, conduct, lead, guide, navigate.
adj.
☞实验的,试验性 experimental, trial, test, model.

pin v.
☞钉上 tack, nail, fix, affix, attach, join, staple, clip, fasten, secure, hold down, restrain, immobilize.
n.
☞大头钉 tack, nail, screw, spike, rivet, bolt, peg, fastener, clip, staple, brooch.

pin down
☞明确的指出 pinpoint, identify, determine, specify.
☞强迫 force, make, press, pressurize.

pinch v.
☞榨压,挤出 squeeze, compress, crush, press, tweak, nip, hurt, grip, grasp.
☞偷 steal, nick, pilfer, filch, snatch.
n.
☞榨出的少量东西 squeeze, tweak, nip.
☞急奔,猛冲 dash, soupcon, taste, bit, speck, jot, mite.
☞紧急情况 emergency, crisis, predicament, difficulty, hardship, pressure, stress.

pine v.
☞渴望 long, yearn, ache, sigh, grieve, mourn, wish, desire, crave, hanker, hunger, thirst.

pinnacle n.
☞尖端 peak, summit, top, cap, crown, crest, apex, vertex, acme, zenith, height, eminence.
☞塔尖 spire, steeple, turret, pyramid, cone, obelisk, needle.

pinpoint v.
☞识别出,验明 identify, spot, distinguish, locate, place, home in on, zero in on, pin down, determine, specify, define.

pioneer n.
☞开拓者,先锋 colonist, settler, frontiersman, frontierswoman, explorer, developer, pathfinder, trail-blazer, leader, innovator, inventor, discoverer, founder.
v.
☞开拓 invent, discover, originate, create, initiate, instigate, begin, start, launch, institute, found, establish, set up, develop, open up.

pipe n.
☞管,软金属管 tube, hose, piping, tubing, pipeline, line, main, flue, duct, conduit, channel, passage, conveyor.
v.
☞引导 channel, funnel, siphon,

carry, convey, conduct, transmit, supply, deliver.
☞吹哨 whistle, chirp, tweet, cheep, peep, twitter, sing, warble, trill, play, sound.

pitch v.
☞投掷 throw, fling, toss, chuck, lob, bowl, hurl, heave, sling, fire, plummet, drop, fall headlong, tumble, lurch, roll, wallow.
☞建造,竖起 erect, put up, set up, place, station, settle, plant, fix.

pitfall n.
☞危险 danger, peril, hazard, trap, snare, stumbling-block, catch, snag, drawback, difficulty.

pitiful adj.
☞可悲的 contemptible, despicable, low, mean, vile, shabby, deplorable, lamentable, woeful, inadequate, hopeless, pathetic, insignificant, paltry, worthless.
☞令人哀悯的 piteous, doleful, mournful, distressing, heart-rending, pathetic, pitiable, sad, miserable, wretched, poor, sorry.

pitiless adj.
☞残忍的 merciless, cold-hearted, unsympathetic, unfeeling, uncaring, hard-hearted, callous, uncaring, hard-hearted, callous, cruel, inhuman, brutal, cold-blooded, ruthless, relentless, unremitting, inexorable, harsh.

pity n.
☞同情 sympathy, commiseration, regret, understanding, fellow-feeling, compassion, kindness, tenderness, mercy.
v.
☞同情 feel sorry for, feel for, sympathize with, commiserate with, grieve for, weep for.

pivot n.
☞轴,轴线 axis, hinge, axle, spindle, kingpin, linchpin, swivel, hub, focal point, centre, heart.
v.
☞(使)旋转 swivel, turn, spin, revolve, rotate, swing.
☞依靠 depend, rely, hinge, hang, lie.

place n.
☞场所,位置 site, locale, venue, location, situation, spot, point, position, seat, space, room.
☞地区,地点 city, town, village, locality, neighbourhood, district, area, region.
☞住所 building, property, dwelling, residence, house, flat, apartment, home.
n.
☞放 put, set, plant, fix, position, locate, situate, rest, settle, lay, stand, deposit, leave.

out of place
☞不合适的 inappropriate, unsuitable, unfitting, unbecoming, unseemly.

take place
☞发生 happen, occur, come about.

plain adj.

☞ 简单的,朴素的 ordinary, basic, simple, unpretentious, modest, unadorned, unelaborate, restrained.

☞ 明显的 obvious, evident, patent, clear, understandable, apparent, visible, unmistakable.

☞ 坦白的 frank, candid, blunt, outspoken, direct, forthright, straightforward, unambiguous, plain-spoken, open, honest, truthful.

☞ 平常的 unattractive, ugly, unprepossessing, unlovely.

plan n.
☞ 计划 blueprint, layout, diagram, figure, map, drawing, sketch, representation, design.

☞ 主意 idea, suggestion, proposal, proposition, project, scheme, plot, system, method, procedure, strategy, programme, schedule, scenario.

v.
☞ 拟定 plot, scheme, design, invent, devise, contrive, formulate, frame, draft, outline, prepare, organize, arrange.

☞ 打算 aim, intend, propose, contemplate, envisage, foresee.

plant n.
☞ 工厂 factory, works, foundry, mill, shop, yard, workshop, machinery, apparatus, equipment, gear.

v.
☞ 种 sow, seed, bury, transplant.

☞ 插嵌 insert, put, place, set, fix, lodge, root, settle, found, establish.

plastic adj.
☞ 柔软的 soft, pliable, flexible, supple, malleable, mouldable, ductile, receptive, impressionable, manageable.

plate n.
☞ 盘碟 dish, platter, salver, helping, serving, portion.

☞ 版画 illustration, picture, print, lithograph.

v.
☞ 电镀 coat, cover, overlay, veneer, laminate, electroplate, anodize, galvanize, platinize, gild, silver, tin.

platform n.
☞ 舞台 stage, podium, dais, rostrum, stand.

☞ 政纲 policy, party line, principles, tenets, manifesto, programme, objectives.

play v.
☞ 逗笑,逗乐 amuse, oneself, have fun, enjoy oneself, revel, sport, romp, frolic, caper.

☞ 参加 participate, take part, join in, compete.

☞ 对付,反对 oppose, vie with, challenge, take on.

☞ 演奏 act, perform, portray, represent, impersonate.

n.
☞ 娱乐 fun, amusement, entertainment, diversion, recreation, sport, game, hobby, pastime.

☞ 戏剧,戏剧性事件 drama, tragedy, comedy, farce, show, performance.

☞ 行动 movement, action, flexibility, give, leeway, latitude, margin, scope, range, room, space.

play down
☞ 使减到最小,最低限度 minimize, make light of, gloss over, underplay, understate, undervalue, underestimate.

play on
☞ 开发,利用 exploit, take advantage of, turn to account, profit by, trade on, capitalize on.

playboy n.
☞ 花花公子 philanderer, womanizer, ladies'man, rake, libertine.

player n.
☞ 竞争者,参加比赛者 contestant, competitor, participant, sportsman, sportswoman.
☞ 表演者 performer, entertainer, artiste, actor, actress, musician, instrumentalist.

playful adj.
☞ 爱玩耍的 sportive, frolicsome, lively, spirited, mischievous, roguish, impish, puckish, kittenish, good-natured, jesting, teasing, humorous, tongue-in-cheek.

playwright n.
☞ 剧作家 dramatist, scriptwriter, screenwriter.

plea n.
☞ 请求 appeal, petition, request, entreaty, supplication, prayer, invocation.
☞ 申辩 defence, justification, excuse, explanation, claim.

plead v.
☞ 请求 beg, implore, beseech, entreat, appeal, petition, ask, request.
☞ 维护,声称,要求 assert, maintain, claim, allege.

pleasant adj.
☞ 令人愉快的 agreeable, nice, fine, lovely, delightful, charming, likable, amiable, friendly, affable, good-humoured, cheerful, congenial, enjoyable, amusing, pleasing, gratifying, satisfying, acceptable, welcome, refreshing.

please v.
☞ 使高兴 delight, charm, captivate, entertain, amuse, cheer, gladden, humour, indulge, gratify, satisfy, content, suit.
☞ 想要,愿意 want, will, wish, desire, like, prefer, choose, think fit.

pleased adj.
☞ 满意的 contented, satisfied, gratified, glad, happy, delighted, thrilled, euphoric.

pleasing adj.
☞ 令人满意的 gratifying, satisfying, acceptable, good, pleasant, agreeable, nice, delightful, charming, attractive, engaging, winning.

pleasure n.
☞ 愉快 amusement, entertainment, recreation, fun, enjoyment, gratification, satisfaction, contentment, happiness, joy, delight, comfort, solace.

pledge n.
☞ 诺言 promise, vow, word of honour, oath, bond, covenant, guarantee, warrant, assurance, secure.

v.
☞ 发誓,保证 promise, vow, swear, contract, engage, undertake, vouch, guarantee, secure.

plentiful adj.
☞ 充足的 ample, abundant, profuse, copious, overflowing, lavish, generous, liberal, bountiful, fruitful, productive.

plenty n.
☞ 大量,许多 abundance, profusion, plethora, lots, loads, masses, heaps (infml), piles, stacks, enough, sufficiency, quantity, mass, volume, fund, mine, store.

plight n.
☞ 困境 predicament, quandary, dilemma, extremity, trouble, difficulty, straits, state, condition, situation, circumstances, case.

plot n.
☞ 阴谋 conspiracy, intrigue, machination, scheme, plan, stratagem.
☞ 情节 story, narrative, subject, theme, storyline, thread, outline.

v.
☞ 合谋,合作 conspire, intrigue, machinate, scheme, hatch, lay, cook up, devise, contrive, plan, project, design, draft.
☞ 制图 chart, map, mark, locate, draw, calculate.

plug n.
☞ 塞子 stopper, bung, cork, spigot.
☞ 广告 advertisement, publicity, mention, puff.

v.
☞ 堵住,塞住 stop (up), bung, cork, block, choke, close, seal, fill, pack, stuff.
☞ 为……做广告 advertise, publicize, promote, push, mention.

plump adj.
☞ 肥胖的 fat, obese, dumpy, tubby, stout, round, rotund, portly, chubby, podgy, fleshy, full, ample, buxom.

plunge v.
☞ 跳水 dive, jump, nose-dive, swoop, dive-bomb, plummet, descend, go down, sink, drop, fall, pitch, tumble, hurtle, career, charge, dash, rush, tear.
☞ 浸 immerse, submerge, dip.

n.
☞ 跳水 dive, jump, swoop, descent, drop, fall, tumble, immersion, submersion.

pocket n.
☞ 袋 pouch, bag, envelope, receptacle, compartment, hollow, cavity.

adj.
☞ 小的 small, little, mini, concise, compact, portable, miniature.

v.
☞ 挪用 take, appropriate, help oneself to, lift, pilfer, filch, steal, nick, pinch.

poignant adj.

☞ 令人感动的 moving, touching, affecting, tender, distressing, upsetting, heartbreaking, heart-rending, piteous, pathetic, sad, painful, agonizing.

point n.
☞ 特征 feature, attribute, aspect, facet, detail, particular, item, subject, topic.
☞ 本质,精髓 essence, crux, core, pith, gist, thrust, meaning, drift, burden.
☞ 地点 place, position, situation, location, site, spot.
☞ 时刻 moment, instant, juncture, stage, time, period.
☞ 点 dot, spot, mark, speck, full stop.
v.
☞ 指明,指向 aim, direct, train, level.
☞ 指出,显示 indicate, signal, show, signify, denote, designate.

point of view
☞ 观点 opinion, view, belief, judgement, attitude, position, standpoint, viewpoint, outlook, perspective, approach, angle, slant.

point out
☞ 指出 show, indicate, draw attention to, point to, reveal, identify, specify, mention, bring up, allude to, remind.

pointed adj.
☞ 锋利的 sharp, keen, edged, barbed, cutting, incisive, trenchant, biting, penetrating, telling.

pointless adj.
☞ 无用的 useless, futile, vain, fruitless, unproductive, unprofitable, worthless, senseless, absurd, meaningless, aimless.

poise n.
☞ 镇静,沉着 calmness, composure, self-possession, presence of mind, coolness, equanimity, aplomb, assurance, dignity, elegance, grace, balance, equilibrium.
v.
☞ 平衡 balance, position, hover, hang, suspend.

poised adj.
☞ (举止)庄严的,平衡的 dignified, graceful, calm, composed, unruffled, collected, self-possessed, cool, self-confident, assured.
☞ 准备好的 prepared, ready, set, malignancy, contagion, contamination, corruption.

poisonous adj.
☞ 有毒的,中毒的 toxic, venomous, lethal, deadly, fatal, mortal, noxious, pernicious, malicious.

policy n.
☞ 政事 code of practice, rules, guidelines, procedure, method, practice, custom, protocol.

polish v.
☞ 磨光 shine, brighten, smooth, rub, buff, burnish, clean, wax.
☞ 改进,润饰 improve, enhance, brush up, touch up, finish, perfect, refine, cultivate.

polite adj.

彬彬有礼的 courteous, well-mannered, respectful, civil, well-bred, refined, cultured, gentlemanly, ladylike, gracious, obliging, thoughtful, considerate, tactful, diplomatic.

politician n.
政客 member of parliament, MP, minister, statesman, stateswoman, legislator.

politics n.
政治 public affairs, civics, affairs of state, statecraft, government, diplomacy, statesmanship, political science.

poll n.
选票 ballot, vote, voting, plebiscite, referendum, straw-poll, sampling, canvass, opinion poll, survey, census, count, tally.

pollute v.
污染 contaminate, infect, poison, taint, adulterate, debase, corrupt, dirty, foul, soil, defile, sully, stain, mar, spoil.

pollution n.
污染 impurity, contamination, infection, taint, adulteration, corruption, dirtiness, foulness, defilement.

pool¹ n.
水注 puddle, pond, lake, mere, tarn, watering-hole, paddling-pool, swimming-pool.

pool² n.
储备 fund, reserve, accumulation, bank, kitty, purse, pot, jackpot.
联合企业 syndicate, cartel, ring, combine, consortium, collective, group, team.
v.
共享, 贡献 contribute, chip in, combine, amalgamate, merge, share, muck in.

poor adj.
贫困的 impoverished, poverty-stricken, badly off, hard-up, broke, stony-broke, skint, bankrupt, penniless, destitute, miserable, wretched, distressed, straitened, needy, lacking, deficient, insufficient, scanty, skimpy, meagre, sparse, depleted, exhausted.
坏的 bad, substandard, unsatisfactory, inferior, mediocre, below par, low-grade, second-rate, third-rate, shoddy, imperfect, faulty, weak, feeble, pathetic, sorry, worthless, fruitless.
不幸的 unfortunate, unlucky, luckless, ill-fated, unhappy, miserable, pathetic, pitiable, pitiful.

poorly adj.
有病的 ill, sick, unwell, indisposed, ailing, sickly, off colour, below par, out of sorts, under the weather, seedy, groggy, rotten.

pop v.
爆炸 burst, explode, go off, bang, crack, snap.
n.
猛击 bang, crack, snap, burst, explosion.

popular adj.
流行的 well-liked, favourite, liked, favoured, approved, in

demand, sought-after, fashionable, modish, trendy, prevailing, current, accepted, conventional, standard, stock, common, prevalent, widespread, universal, general, household, famous, well-known, celebrated, idolized.

popularly adv.
☞ 一致地,普通地 commonly, widely, universally, generally, usually, customarily, conventionally, traditionally.

population n.
☞ 居民 inhabitants, natives, residents, citizens, occupants, community, society, people, folk.

portable adj.
☞ 可移动的,活动的 movable, transportable, compact, lightweight, manageable, handy, convenient.

portion n.
☞ 一份,份儿 share, allocation, allotment, parcel, allowance, ration, quota, measure, part, section, division, fraction, percentage, bit, fragment, morsel, piece, segment, slice, serving, helping.

portrait n.
☞ 图片 picture, painting, drawing, sketch, caricature, miniature, icon, photograph, likeness, image, representation, vignette, profile, characterization, description, depiction, portrayal.

portray v.
☞ 画 draw, sketch, paint, illustrate, picture, represent, depict, describe, evoke, play, impersonate, characterize, personify.

portrayal n.
☞ 描写 representation, characterization, depiction, description, evocation, presentation, performance, interpretation, rendering.

pose v.
☞ 做模特 model, sit, position.
☞ 作假 pretend, feign, affect, put on an act, masquerade, pass oneself off, impersonate.
☞ 设置 set, put forward, submit, present.
n.
☞ 姿势,姿态 position, stance, air, bearing, posture, attitude.
☞ 虚伪 pretence, sham, affectation, facade, front, masquerade, role, act.

poser[1] n.
☞ 难题 puzzle, riddle, conundrum, brain-teaser, mystery, enigma, problem, vexed question.

poser[2] n.
☞ 模特儿 poseur, poseuse, posturer, attitudinizer, exhibitionist, show-off, pseud, phoney.

position n.
☞ 地点 place, situation, location, site, spot, point.
☞ 姿势 posture, stance, pose, arrangement, disposition.
☞ 工作 job, post, occupation, employment, office, duty, function, role.

☞职位 rank, grade, level, status, standing.
☞意见 opinion, point of view, belief, view, outlook, viewpoint, standpoint, stand.

v.
☞安放 put, place, set, fix, stand, arrange, dispose, lay out, deploy, station, locate, situate, site.

positive adj.
☞确信的 sure, certain, convinced, confident, assured.
☞积极的 helpful, constructive, practical, useful, optimistic, hopeful, promissing.
☞肯定的 definte, decisive, conclusive, clear, unmistakable, explicit, unequivocal, express, firm, emphatic, categorical, undeniable, irrefutable, indisputable, incontrovertible.
☞绝对的,彻底的 absolute, utter, sheer, complete, perfect.

possess v.
☞拥有 own, have, hold, enjoy, be endowed with.
☞没收,占有 seize, take, obtain, acquire, take over, occupy, control, dominate, bewitch, haunt.

possession n.
☞所有 ownership, title, tenure, occupation, custody, control, hold, grip.

possessions n.
☞(个人的)财物 belongings, property, things, paraphernalia, effects, goods, chattels, movables, assets, estate, wealth, riches.

possessive adj.
☞自私自利的 selfish, clinging, overprotective, domineering, dominating, jealous, covetous, acquisitive, grasping.

possibility n.
☞可能性 likelihood, probability, odds, chance, risk, danger, hope, prospect, potentiality, conceivability, practicability, feasibility.

possible adj.
☞可能 potential, promising, likely, probable, imaginable, conceivable, practicable, feasible, viable, tenable, workable, achievable, attainable, accomplishable, realizable.

possibly adv.
☞可能 perhaps, maybe, hopefully, by any means, at all, by any chance.

post¹ n.
☞职位 office, job, employment, position, situation, place, vacancy, appointment, assignment, station, beat.

v.
☞驻扎 station, locate, situate, position, place, put, appoint, assign, second, transfer, move, send.

post² n.
☞邮政 mail, letters, dispatch, collection, delivery.

v.
☞邮递 mail, send, dispatch, transmit.

postpone v.
☞推迟 put off, defer, put back, hold over, delay,

adjourn, suspend, shelve, pigeonhole, freeze, put on ice.

postscript *n.*
☞ 附言 PS, addition, supplement, afterthought, addendum, codicil, appendix, afterword, epilogue.

postulate *v.*
☞ 假定 theorize, hypothesize, suppose, assume, propose, advance, lay down, stipulate.

posture *n.*
☞ 位置 position, stance, pose, attitude, disposition, bearing, carriage, deportment.

potential *adj.*
☞ 潜在的,有潜力的 possible, likely, probable, prospective, future, aspiring, would-be, promising, budding, embryonic, undeveloped, dormant, latent, hidden, concealed, unrealized.
n.
☞ 可能性 possibility, ability, capability, capacity, aptitude, talent, powers, resources.

pound¹ *v.*
☞ 打击 strike, thump, beat, drum, pelt, hammer, batter, bang, bash, smash.
☞ 变成粉末 pulverize, powder, grind, mash, crush.
☞ (心脏)跳动,悸动 throb, pulsate, palpitate, thump, thud.

pound² *n.*
☞ 被围的场,围绕 enclosure, compound, corral, yard, pen, fold.

pour *v.*
☞ 灌注,倒,倾泻 flow, stream, run, rush, spout, emit, issue, decant, serve, rain, teem, pelt.

poverty *n.*
☞ 贫穷 want, need, impoverishment, insolvency, bankruptcy, pennilessness, penury, destitution, distress, hardship, privation, need, necessity, want, lack, deficiency, shortage, inadequacy, insufficiency, depletion, scarcity, meagreness, paucity, dearth.

power *n.*
☞ 控制权 command, authority, sovereignty, rule, dominion, control, influence.
☞ 权力 right, privilege, prerogative, authorization, warrant.
☞ 权势,力量 potency, strength, intensity, force, vigour, energy.
☞ 能力 ability, capability, capacity, potential, faculty, competence.

powerful *adj.*
☞ 支配的,居高临下的 dominant, prevailing, leading, influential, high-powered, authoritative, commanding, potent, effective, strong, mighty, robust, muscular, energetic, forceful, telling, impressive, convincing, persuasive, compelling, winning, overwhelming.

powerless *adj.*
☞ 无能的 impotent, incapable, ineffective, weak, feeble, frail, infirm, incapacitated, disabled, paralysed, helpess, vulnerable, defenceless, unarmed.

practical adj.
☞ 实际的 realistic, sensible, commonsense, practicable, workable, feasible, down-to-earth, matter-of-fact, pragmatic, hardnosed, hard-headed, businesslike, experienced, trained, qualified, skilled, accomplished, proficient, hands on, applied.
☞ 有用的 useful, handy, serviceable, utilitarian, functional, working, everyday, ordinary.

practically adv.
☞ 几乎,差不多 almost, nearly, well-nigh, virtually, pretty well, all but, just about, in principle, in effect, essentially, fundamentally, to all intention and purposes.
☞ 现实上 realistically, sensibly, reasonably, rationally, pragmatically.

practice n.
☞ 风俗 custom, tradition, convention, usage, habit, routine, way, method, system, procedure, policy.
☞ 排练 rehearsal, run-through, dry run, dummy run, try-out, training, drill, exercise, work-out, study, experience.

practise v.
☞ 执行,实践 do, perform, execute, implement, carry out, apply, put into practive, follow, pursue, engage in, undertake.
☞ 练习 rehearse, run through, repeat, drill, exercise, train, study, perfect.

practised adj.
☞ 有经验的 experienced, seasoned, veteran, trained, qualified, accomplished, skilled, versed, knowledgeable, able, proficient, expert, masterly, consummate, finished.

pragmatic adj.
☞ 实用的 practical, realistic, sensible, matter-of-fact, businesslike, efficient, hard-headed, hardnosed, unsentimental.

praise n.
☞ 称赞 approval, admiration, commendation, congratulation, compliment, flattery, adulation, eulogy, applause, ovation, cheering, acclaim, recognition, testimonial, tribute, accolade, homage, honour, glory, worship, adoration, devotion, thanksgiving.
v.
☞ 称赞 commend, congratulate, admire, compliment, flatter, eulogize, wax lyrical, rave over, extol, promote, applaud, cheer, acclaim, hail, recognize, acknowledge, pay tribute to, honour, laud, glorify, magnify, exalt, worship, adore, bless.

praiseworthy adj.
☞ 值得表扬的 commendable, fine, excellent, admirable, worthy, deserving, honourable, reputable, estimable, sterling.

pray v.
☞ 祈求 invoke, call on, supplicate, entreat, implore, plead, beg, beseech, petition, ask, request, crave, solicit.

preach v.

- ☞ 说教 address, lecture, harangue, pontificate, sermonize, evangelize, moralize, exhort, urge, advocate.

precarious adj.
- ☞ 不安全的 unsafe, dangerous, treacherous, risky, hazardous, chancy, uncertain, unsure, dubious, doubtful, unpredictable, unreliable, unsteady, unstable, shaky, wobbly, insecure, vulnerable.

precaution n.
- ☞ 小心 safeguard, security, protection, insurance, providence, forethought, caution, prudence, foresight, anticipation, preparation, provision.

precautionary adj.
- ☞ 小心的 safety, protective, preventive, provident, cautious, prudent, judicious, preparatory, preliminary.

precede v.
- ☞ 在……之前 come before, lead, come first, go before, take precedence, introduce, herald, usher in.

precedence n.
- ☞ 优先 priority, preference, pride of place, superiority, supremacy, pre-eminence, lead, first place, seniority, rank.

precious adj.
- ☞ 珍惜的 valued, treasured, prized, cherished, beloved, dearest, darling, favourite, loved, adored, idolized.
- ☞ 贵重的 valuable, expensive, costly, dear, priceless, inestimable, rare, choice, fine.

precise adj.
- ☞ 正确的,精确的 exact, accurate, right, punctilious, correct, factual, faithful, authentic, literal, word-for-word, express, definite, explicit, unequivocal, unambiguous, clear-cut, distinct, detailed, blow-by-blow, minute, nice, particular, specific, fixed, rigid, strict, careful, meticulous, scrupulous, fastidious.

precisely adv.
- ☞ 精确地 exactly, absolutely, just so, accurately, correctly, literally, verbatim, word for word, strictly, minutely, clearly, distinctly.

precision n.
- ☞ 精确 exactness, accuracy, correctness, faithfulness, explicitness, distinctness, detail, particularity, rigour, care, meticulousness, scrupulousness, neatness.

predict v.
- ☞ 预言,预示 foretell, prophesy, foresee, forecast, prognosticate, project.

predictable adj.
- ☞ 可预料的 foreseeable, expected, anticipated, likely, probable, imaginable, foreseen, foregone, certain, sure, reliable, dependable.

prediction n
- ☞ 预言的事,预言的能力 *prophecy*, *forecast*, *prognosis*, *augury*, *divination*, *fortune-*

preface n.
☞ 前言,序言 foreword, introduction, preamble, prologue, prelude, preliminaries.
v.
☞ 以…开端,为…作序 precede, prefix, lead up to, introduce, launch, open, begin, start.

prefer v.
☞ 喜爱 favour, like better, would rather, would sooner, want, wish, desire, choose, select, pick, opt for, go for, plump for, single out, advocate, recommend, back, support, fancy, elect, adopt.

preferable adj.
☞ 更好的 better, superior, nicer, preferred, favoured, chosen, desirable, advantageous, advisable, recommended.

preference n.
☞ 最喜欢的人或物 favourite, first, choice, choice, pick, selection, option, wish, desire.
☞ 爱好,喜欢 liking, fancy, inclination, predilection, partiality, favouritism, preferential treatment.

pregnant adj.
☞ 怀孕的 expectant, expecting, with child.
☞ 富有意义的 meaningful, significant, eloquent, expressive, suggestive, charged, loaded, full.

prejudice n.
☞ 偏见 bias, partiality, partisanship, discrimination, unfairness, injustice, intolerance, narrow-mindedness, bigotry, chauvinism, racism, sexism.
☞ 损害,伤害 harm, damage, impairment, hurt, injury, detriment, disadvantage, loss, ruin.
v.
☞ 抱偏见 bias, predispose, incline, sway, influence, condition, colour, slant, distort, load, weight.
☞ 损害 harm, damage, impair, hinder, undermine, hurt, injure, mar, spoil, ruin, wreck.

prejudiced adj.
☞ 有偏见的 biased, partial, predisposed, subjective, partisan, one-sided, discriminatory, unfair, unjust, loaded, weighted, intolerant, narrow-minded, bigoted, chauvinist, racist, sexist, jaundiced, distorted, warped, influenced, conditioned.

prejudicial adj.
☞ 有害的 harmful, damaging, hurtful, injurious, detrimental, disadvantageous, unfavourable, inimical.

premature adj.
☞ 早熟 early, immature, green, unripe, embryonic, half-formed, incomplete, undeveloped, abortive, hasty, ill-considered, rash, untimely, inopportune, ill-timed.

preoccupation n.
☞ 迷住 obsession, fixation, hang-up, concern, interest, enthusiasm, hobby-horse.

☞ 分散注意 distraction, absent-mindedness, reverie, obliviousness, oblivion.

preoccupied adj.
☞ 着迷的 obsessed, intent, immersed, engrossed, engaged, taken up, wrapped up, involved.
☞ 心烦意乱的 distracted, abstracted, absent-minded, daydreaming, absorbed, faraway, heedless, oblivious, pensive.

preparation n.
☞ 准备 readiness, provision, precaution, safeguard, foundation, groundwork, spadework, basics, rudiments, preliminaries, plans, arrangements.
☞ 制剂 mixture, compound, concoction, potion, medicine, lotion, application.

preparatory adj.
☞ 预备的 preliminary, introductory, opening, initial, primary, basic, fundamental, rudimentary, elementary.

prepare v.
☞ 准备好 get ready, warm up, train, coach, study, make ready, adapt, adjust, plan, organize, arrange, pave the way.
☞ 供应 provide, supply, equip, fit out, rig out.
☞ 做 make, produce, construct, assemble, concoct, contrive, devise, draft, draw up, compose.

prepare oneself
☞ 给自己打气 brace oneself, steel oneself, gird oneself, fortify oneself.

prepared adj.
☞ 准备好的 ready, waiting, set, fit, inclined, disposed, willing, planned, organized, arranged.

presence n.
☞ 出席 attendance, company, occupancy, residence, existence.
☞ 风度 aura, air, demeanour, bearing, appearance, poise, self-assurance, personality, charisma.
☞ 近密 nearness, closeness, proximity, vicinity.

present¹ adj.
☞ 出席的 attending, here, there, near, at hand, to hand, available, ready.
☞ 现在的 current, contemporary, present-day, immediate, instant, existent, existing.

present² v.
☞ 给……看 show, display, exhibit, demonstrate, mount, stage, put on, introduce, announce.
☞ 奖给 award, confer, bestow, grant, give, donate, hand over, entrust, estend, hold out, offer, tender, submit.

present³
☞ 礼物 gift, offering, donation, grant, endowment, benefaction, bounty, largess, gratuity, tip, favour.

presentation n.
☞ 演示 show, performance, production, staging,

representation, display, exhibition, demonstration, talk, delivery, appearance, arrangement.
☞ 奖品 award, conferral, bestowal, investiture.

present-day adj.
☞ 当前的, 当代的 current, present, existing, living, contemporary, modern, up-to-date, fashionable.

presently adv.
☞ 不久 soon, shortly, in a minute, before long, by and by.
☞ 目前 currently, at present, now.

preside v.
☞ 主持 chair, officiate, conduct, direct, manage, administer, control, run, head, lead, govern, rule.

press v.
☞ 压坏, 弄皱 crush, squash, squeeze, compress, stuff, cram, crowd, push, depress.
☞ 烫平 iron, smooth, flatten.
☞ 紧抱 hug, embrace, clasp, squeeze.
☞ 力说, 强调 urge, plead, petition, campaign, demand, insist on, compel, constrain, force, pressure, pressurize, harass.
n.
☞ 人群 crowd, throng, multitude, mob, horde, swarm, pack, crush, push.
☞ 新闻界 journalists, reporters, correspondents, the media, newspapers, papers, fleet street, fourth estate.

pressing adj.
☞ 紧急的 urgent, high-priority, burning, crucial, vital, essential, imperative, serious, important.

pressure n.
☞ 压力 force, power, load, burden, weight, heaviness, compression, squeezing, stress, strain.
☞ 困难 difficulty, problem, demand, constraint, obligation, urgency.

prestige n.
☞ 名望 status, reputation, standing, stature, eminence, distinction, esteem, regard, importance, authority, influence, fame, renown, kudos, credit, honour.

prestigious adj.
☞ 受尊敬的 esteemed, respected, reputable, important, influential, great, eminent, prominent, illustrious, renowned, celebrated, exalted, imposing, impressive, up-market.

pretend v.
☞ 假装(托) affect, put on, assume, feign, sham, counterfeit, fake, simulate, bluff, impersonate, pass oneself off, act, play-act, mime, go through the motions.
☞ 自封, 自称 claim, allege, profess, purport.
☞ 想象 imagine, make believe, suppose.

pretty adj.
☞ 漂亮的 attractive, good-looking, beautiful, fair, lovely, bonny, cute, winsome,

appending, charming, dainty, graceful, elegant, fine, delicate, nice.
adv.
☞ 相当　fairly, somewhat, rather, quite, reasonably, moderately, tolerably.

prevail v.
☞ 居主导地位　predominate, preponderate, abound.
☞ 赢　win, triumph, succeed, overcome, overrule, reign, rule.
☞ 说服　persuade, talk into, prompt, induce, incline, sway, influence, convince, win over.

prevailing adj.
☞ 占优势的　predominant, preponderant, main, principal, dominant, controlling, powerful, compelling, influential, reigning, ruling, current, fashionable, popular, mainstream, accepted, established, set, usual, customary, common, prevalent, widespread.

prevalent adj.
☞ 广布的　widespread, extensive, rampant, rife, frequent, general, customary, usual, universal, ubiquitous, common, everyday, popular, current, prevailing.

prevent v.
☞ 防止　stop, avert, avoid, head off, ward off, stave off, intercept, forestall, anticipate, frustrate, thwart, check, restrain, inhibit, hinder, hamper, impede, obstruct, block, bar.

prevention n.
☞ 防止　avoidance, frustration, check, hindrance, impediment, obstruction, obstacle, bar, elimination, precaution, safeguard, deterrence.

previous adj.
☞ 在前面的　preceding, foregoing, earlier, prior, past, former, ex-, one-time, sometime, erstwhile.

previously adv.
☞ 以前　formerly, once, earlier, before, beforehand.

price n.
☞ 价值　value, worth, cost, expense, outlay, expenditure, fee, charge, levy, toll, rate, bill, assessment, valuation, estimate, quotation, figure, amount, sum, payment, reward, penalty, forfeit, sacrifice, consequences.
v.
☞ 定价值　value, rate, cost, evaluate, assess, estimate.

priceless adj.
☞ 无价的　invaluable, inestimable, incalculable, expensive, costly, dear, precious, valuable, prized, treasured, irreplaceable.
☞ 好玩的　funny, amusing, comic, hilarious, riotous, side-splitting, killing, rich.

prick v.
☞ 刺穿　pierce, puncture, perforate, punch, jab, stab, sting, bite, prickle, itch, tingle.
n.
☞ 刺，刺痕　puncture, perforation, pinhole, stab,

pang, twinge, sting, bite.

prickle n.
- 刺 thorn, spine, barb, spur, point, spike, needle.

v.
- 感到刺痛 tingle, itch, smart, sting, prick.

prickly adj.
- 多刺的 thorny, brambly, spiny, barbed, spiky, bristly, rough, scratchy.
- 易怒的,烦躁的 irritable, edgy, touchy, grumpy, short-tempered.

pride n.
- 自负,自高,自大 conceit, vanity, egotism, highheadedness, boastfulness, smugness, arrogance, self-importance, presumption, haughtiness, superciliousness, snobbery, pretentiousness.
- 自豪 dignity, self-respect, self-esteem, honour.
- 满意 satisfaction, gratification, pleasure, delight.

priest n.
- 教士 minister, vicar, padre, father, man of god, man of the cloth, clergyman, churchman.

primarily adv.
- 主要地 chiefly, principally, mainly, mostly, basically, fundamentally, especially, particularly, essentially.

primary adj.
- 初始的 first, earliest, original, initial, introductory, beginning, basic, fundamental, essential, radical, rudimentary, elementary, simple.
- 首要的 chief, principal, main, dominant, leading, foremost, supreme, cardinal, capital, paramount, greatest, highest, ultimate.

prime adj.
- 最好的 best, choice, select, quality, first-class, first-rate, excellent, top, supreme, pre-eminent, superior, senior, leading, ruling, chief, principal, main, predominant, primary.

n.
- 青春,全盛时期 height, peak, zenith, heyday, flower, bloom, maturity, perfection.

primitive adj.
- 原始的 crude, rough, unsophisticated, uncivilized, barbarian, savage.
- 早期的 early, elementary, rudimentary, primary, first, original, earliest.

principal adj.
- 主要的 main, chief, key, essential, cardinal, primary, prime, paramount, pre-eminent, supreme, highest.

n.
- 校长 head, head teacher, headmaster, headmistress, chief, leader, boss, director, manager, superintendent.

principally adv.
- 主要地 mainly, mostly, chiefly, primarily, predominantly, above all, particularly, especially.

principle n.
- 规则 rule, formula, law, canon, axiom, dictum, precept, maxim, truth, tenet, doctrine,

creed, dogma, code, standard, criterion, proposition, fundamental, essential.

print v.
☞印 mark, stamp, imprint, impress, engrave, copy, reproduce, run off, publish, issue.
n.
☞印刷 letters, characters, lettering, type, typescript, typeface, fount.
☞印痕,指纹 mark, impression, fingerprint, footprint.
☞复印件,图片,晒图 copy, reproduction, picture, engraving, lithograph, photograph, photo.

prior adj.
☞早的 earlier, preceding, foregoing, previous, former.

prior to
☞在……以前 before, preceding, earlier than.

priority n.
☞优先 right of way, precedence, seniority, rank, superiority, pre-eminence, supremacy, the lead, first place, urgency.

prison n.
☞监狱 jail, nick, clink, cooler, penitentiary, cell, lock-up, cage, dungeon, imprisonment, confinement, detention, custody.

prisoner n.
☞犯人 captive, hostage, convict, jail-bird, inmate, internee, detainee.

privacy n.
☞隐退,隐居 secrecy, confidentiality, independence, solitude, isolation, seclusion, concealment, retirement, retreat.

private adj.
☞秘密的 secret, classified, hush-hush, off the record, unofficial, confidential, intimate, personal, individual, own, exclusive, particular, special, separate, independent, solitary, isolated, secluded, hidden, concealed, reserved, withdrawn.

privilege n.
☞特权 advantage, benefit, concession, birthright, title, due, right, prerogative, entitlement, freedom, liberty, franchise, licence, sanction, authority, immunity, exemption.

privileged adj.
☞有特权的 advantaged, favoured, special, sanctioned, authorized, immune, exempt, elite, honoured, ruling, powerful.

prize n.
☞奖 reward, trophy, medal, award, winnings, jackpot, purse, premium, stake(s), honour, accolade.
adj.
☞最好的 best, top, first-rate, excellent, outstanding, champion, winning, prize-winning, award-winning.
v.
☞珍惜 treasure, value, appreciate, esteem, revere,

probability n.
☞ 可能性 likelihood, odds, chances, expectation, prospect, chance, possibility.

probable adj.
☞ 很可能的 likely, odds-on, expected, credible, believable, plausible, feasible, possible, apparent, seeming.

problem n.
☞ 麻烦 trouble, worry, predicament, quandary, dilemma, difficulty, complication, snag.
☞ 问题 question, poser, puzzle, brain-teaser, conundrum, riddle, enigma.
adj.
☞ 困难的 difficult, unmanageable, uncontrollable, unruly, delinquent.

procedure n.
☞ 过程，程序，常规 routine, process, method, system, technique, custom, practice, policy, formula, course, scheme, strategy, plan of action, move, step, action, conduct, operation, performance.

proceed v.
☞ 进行 advance, go ahead, move on, progress, continue, carry on, press on.
☞ 产生 originate, derive, flow, start, stem, spring, arise, issue, result, ensue, follow, come.

proceedings n.
☞ 记录 matters, affairs, business, dealings, transactions, report, account, minutes, records, archives, annals.
☞ 行为 events, happenings, deeds, doings, moves, steps, measures, action, course of action.

proceeds n.
☞ 收入 revenue, income, returns, receipts, takings, earnings, gain, profit, yield, produce.

process n.
☞ 方法 procedure, operation, practice, method, system, technique, means, manner, mode, way, stage, step.
☞ 过程 course, progression, advance, progress, development, evolution, formation, growth, movement, action, proceeding.
v.
☞ 加工，处理 deal with, handle, treat, prepare, refine, transform, convert, change, alter.

procession n.
☞ 游行 march, parade, cavalcade, motorcade, cortege, file, column, train, succession, series, sequence, course, run.

proclaim v.
☞ 宣布 announce, declare, pronounce, affirm, give out, publish, advertise, make known, profess, testify, show, indicate.

proclamation n.
☞ 告示 announcement, declaration, pronouncement, affirmation, publication,

promulgation, notice, notification, manifesto, decree, edict.

prodigy n.
☞ 天才 genius, virtuoso, wonder, marvel, miracle, phenomenon, sensation, freak, curiosity, rarity, child genius, wonder child, whizz kid.

produce v.
☞ 引起 cause, occasion, give rise to, provoke, bring about, result in, effect, create, originate, invent, make, manufacture, fabricate, construct, compose, generate, yield, bear, deliver.
☞ 推进 advance, put forward, present, offer, give, supply, provide, furnish, bring out, bring forth, show, exhibit, demonstrate.

n.
☞ 农产品 crop, harvest, yield, output, product.

product n.
☞ 商品 commodity, merchandise, goods, end-product, work, creation, invention, production, output, yield, produce, fruit, return.
☞ 结果 result, consequence, outcome, issue, upshot, offshoot, spin-off, by-product, legacy.

production n.
☞ 制做 making, manufacture, fabrication, construction, assembly, creation, origination, preparation, formation.

productive adj.
☞ 多产的 fruitful, profitable, rewarding, valuable, worthwhile, useful, constructive, creative, inventive, fertile, rich, teeming, busy, energetic, vigorous, efficient, effective.

productivity n.
☞ 生产力 productiveness, yield, output, work rate, efficiency.

profess v.
☞ 声称 admit, confess, acknowledge, own, confirm, certify, declare, announce, proclaim, state, assert, affirm, maintain, claim, allege, make out, pretend.

profession n.
☞ 职业 career, job, occupation, employment, business, line (of work), trade, vocation, calling, metier, craft, office, position.
☞ 声称 admission, confession, acknowledgement, statement, testimony, assertion, affirmation, claim.

professional adj.
☞ 职业的 qualified, licensed, trained, experienced, practised, skilled, expert, pasterly, proficient, competent, businesslike, efficient.

n.
☞ 专家 expert, authority, specialist, pro, master, virtuoso, dab hand.

profile n.
☞ 轮廓 side view, outline, contour, silhouette, shape, form, figure, sketch, drawing, diagram, chart, graph.
☞ 传记,传记文学 biography, curriculum vitae, thumbnail sketch, vignette, portrait,

study, analysis, examination, survey, review.

profit n.
☞ 获利,好处 gain, surplus, excess, bottom line, revenue, return, yield, proceeds, receipts, takings, earnings, winnings, interest, advantage, benefit, use, avail, value, worth.
v.
☞ 获利 gain, make money, pay, serve, avail, benefit.

profitable adj.
☞ 有利可图的 cost-effective, economic, commercial, money-making, lucrative, remunerative, paying, rewarding, successful, fruitful, productive, successful, productive, advantageous, beneficial, useful, valuable, worthwhile.

profound adj.
☞ 深奥的 deep, great, intense, extreme, heartfelt, marked, far-reaching, extensive, exhaustive.

programme n.
☞ 计划 schedule, timetable, agenda, calendar, order of events, listing, line-up, plan, scheme, project, syllabus, curriculum.
☞ 节目 broadcast, transmission, show, performance, production, presentation.

progress n.
☞ 进步 movement, progression, passage, journey, way, advance, headway, step forward, breakthrough, development, evolution, growth, increase, improvement, betterment, promotion.
v.
☞ 进步 proceed, advance, go forward, forge ahead, make progress, make headway, come on, develop, grow, mature, blossom, improve, better, prosper, increase.

progressive adj.
☞ 进步的 modern, avant-garde, advanced, forward-looking, enlightened, liberal, radical, revolutionary, reformist, dynamic, enterprising, go-ahead, up-and-coming.
☞ 向前进的 advancing, continuing, developing, growing, increasing, intensifying.

prohibit v.
☞ 禁止 forbid, ban, bar, veto, proscribe, outlaw, rule out, preclude, prevent, stop, hinder, hamper, impede, obstruct, restrict.

project n.
☞ 项目 assignment, contract, task, job, work, occupation, activity, enterprise, undertaking, venture, plan, scheme, programme, design, proposal, idea, concention.
v.
☞ 预设,规划 predict, forecast, extrapolate, estimate, reckon, calculate.
☞ 投掷(射) throw, fling, hurl, launch, propel.
☞ 凸出 protrude, stick out, bulge, jut out, overhang.

projection n.

- 突出物 protuberance, bulge, overhang, ledge, sill, shelf, ridge.
- 预料 prediction, forecast, extrapolation, estimate, reckoning, calculation, computation.

prolific adj.
- 多产的 productive, fruitful, fertile, profuse, copious, abundant.

prolong v.
- 延长 lengthen, extend, stretch, protract, draw out, spin out, drag out, delay, continue, perpetuate.

promise v.
- 答应 vow, pledge, swear, take an oath, contract, undertake, give one's word, vouch, warrant, guarantee, assure.
- 有可能 augur, presage, indicate, suggest, hint at.

  n.
- 答应 vow, pledge, oath, word of honour, bond, compact, gaurantee, assurance, undertaking, engagement, commitment.
- 潜能 potential, ability, capability, aptitude, talent.

promising adj.
- 有希望的 auspicious, propitious, favourable, rosy, bright, encouraging, hopeful, talented, gifted, budding, up-and-coming.

promote v.
- 宣传 advertise, plug, hype, popularize, market, sell, push, recommend, advocate, champion, endorse, sponsor, support, back, help, aid, assist, foster, nurture, further, forward, encourage, boost, stimulate, urge.
- 提升 upgrade, advance, move up, raise, elevate, exalt, honour.

promotion n.
- 晋升 advancement, upgrading, rise, preferment, elevation, exaltation.
- 扩大影响,增进,发扬 advertising, plugging, publicity, hype, campaign, propaganda, marketing, pushing, support, backing, furtherance, development, encouragement, boosting.

prompt¹ adj.
- 准时的 punctual, on time, immediate, instantaneous, instant, direct, quick, swift, rapid, speedy, unhesitating, willing, ready, alert, responsive, timely, early.

  adv.
- 正(指时间) promptly, punctually, exactly, on the dot, to the minute, sharp.

prompt² v.
- 使发生 cause, give rise to, result in, occasion, produce, instigate, call forth, elicit, provoke, incite, urge, encourage, inspire, move, stimulate, motivate, spur, prod, remind.

pronounce v.
- 宣言,宣告 say, utter, speak, express, voice, vocalize, sound,

enunciate, articulate, stress.
☞ 宣布 declare, announce, proclaim, decree, judge, affirm, assert.

pronounced adj.
☞ 清楚的 clear, distinct, definite, positive, decided, marked, noticeable, conspicuous, evident, obvious, striking, unmistakable, strong, broad.

pronunciation n.
☞ 发音 speech, diction, elocution, enunciation, articulation, delivery, accent, stress, inflection, intonation.

proof n.
☞ 证据 evidence, documentation, demonstration, verification, confirmation, corroboration, substantiation.

propaganda n.
☞ 宣传 advertising, publicity, hype, indoctrination, brainwashing, disinformation.

propagate v.
☞ 宣传 spread, transmit, broadcast, diffuse, disseminate, circulate, publish, promulgate, publicize, promote.
☞ 繁殖,增殖 increase, multiply, proliferate, generate, produce, breed, beget, spawn, procreate, reproduce.

proper adj.
☞ 对的 right, correct, accurate, exact, precise, true, genuine, real, actual.
☞ 合适的 accepted, correct, suitable, appropriate, fitting, decent, respectable, polite, formal.

property n.
☞ 大块房地产 estate, land, real estate, acres, premises, buildings, house(s), wealth, riches, resources, means, capital, assets, holding(s), belongings, possessions, effects, goods, chattels.
☞ 特征 feature, trait, quality, attribute, characteristic, idiosyncrasy, peculiarity, mark.

proportion n.
☞ 百分比 percentage, fraction, part, division, share, quota, amount.
☞ 比例 ratio, relationship, correspondence, symmetry, balance, distribution.

proposal n.
☞ 主张 proposition, suggestion, recommendation, motion, plan, scheme, project, design, programme, manifesto, presentation, bid, offer, tender, terms.

propose v.
☞ 建议 suggest, recommend, move, advance, put forward, introduce, bring up, table, submit, present, offer, tender.
☞ 想要 intend, mean, aim, purpose, plan, design.

proprietor, proprietress n.
☞ 地主,房东 landlord, landlady, title-holder, freeholder, leaseholder, landowner, owner, possessor.

prospect n.
☞ 希望 chance, odds, probability, likelihood,

possibility, hope, expectation, anticipation, outlook, future.

prospective *adj*.
☞ 未来的,将来的 future, -to-be, intended, designate, destined, forthcoming, approaching, coming, imminent, awaited, expected, anticipated, likely, possible, probable, potential, aspiring, would-be.

prosper *v*.
☞ (使)兴旺 boom, thrive, flourish, flower, bloom, succeed, get on, advance, progress, grow rich.

prosperity *n*.
☞ 繁荣,成功 boom, plenty, affluence, wealth, riches, fortune, well-being, luxury, the good life, success, good fortune.

prosperous *adj*.
☞ 繁荣的,成功的 booming, thriving, flourishing, blooming, successful, fortunate, lucky, rich, wealthy, affluent, well-off, well-to-do.

protect *v*.
☞ 保卫 safeguard, defend, guard, escort, cover, screen, shield, secure, watch over, look after, care for, support, shelter, harbour, keep, conserve, preserve, save.
☞ 保护 care, custody, charge, guardianship, safekeeping, conservation, preservation, safety, safeguard.
☞ 屏障 barrier, buffer, bulwark, defence, guard, shield, armour, screen, cover, shelter, refuge, security, insurance.

protective *adj*.
☞ 保护的 possessive, defensive, motherly, maternal, fatherly, paternal, watchful, vigilant, careful.

protest *n*.
☞ 抗议 objection, disapproval, opposition, dissent, complaint, protestation, outcry, appeal, demonstration.
v.
☞ 反对,抗议 object, take exception, complain, appeal, demonstrate, oppose, disapprove, disagree, argue.

protester *n*.
☞ 示威者 demonstrator, agitator, rebel, dissident, dissenter.

protocol *n*.
☞ 礼仪 procedure, formalities, convention, custom, etiquette, manners, good form, propriety.

protrude *v*.
☞ 凸出 stick out, poke out, come through, bulge, jut out, project, extend, stand out, obtrude.

proud *adj*.
☞ 自高自大的 conceited, vain, egotistical, bigheaded, boastful, smug, complacent, arrogant, self-important, cocky, presumptuous, haughty, high and mighty, overbearing, supercilious, snooty, snobbish, toffee-nosed, stuck-up.
☞ 满足的 satisfied, contented, gratified, pleased, delighted, honoured.

☞高贵的 dignified, noble, honourable, worthy, self-respecting.

prove v.
☞证明 show, demonstrate, attest, verify, confirm, corroborate, substantiate, bear out, document, certify, authenticate, validate, justify, establish, determine, ascertain, try, test, check, examine, analyie.

proverb n.
☞格言,谚语 saying, adage, aphorism, maxim, byword, dictum, precept.

proverbial adj.
☞有名的 famous, well-known, legendary, notorious, typical, archetypal.

provide v.
☞供应,供给 supply, furnish, stock, equip, outfit, prepare for, cater, serve, present, give, contribute, yield, lend, add, bring.
☞规定,指定 state, specify, stipulate, lay down, require.

providing conj.
☞假如 provided, with the proviso, given, as long as, on condition, on the understanding.

province n.
☞地区,省 region, area, district, zone, county, shire, department, territory, colony, dependency.
☞领域,部门 responsibility, concern, duty, office, role, function, field, sphere, domain, department, line.

provincial adj.
☞地区的 regional, local, rural, rustic, country, home-grown, small-town, parish-pump, parochial, insular, inward-looking, limited, narrow, narrow-minded, small-minded.

provision n.
☞准备 plan, arrangement, preparation, measure, precaution.
☞条款,规定 stipulation, specification, proviso, condition, term, requirement.

provisional adj.
☞临时的 temporary, interim, transitional, stopgap, makeshift, conditional, tentative.

provisions n.
☞食物 food, foodstuff, groceries, eatables, sustenance, rations, supplies, stocks, stores.

provoke v.
☞惹怒 annoy, irritate, rile, aggravate, offend, insult, anger, enrage, infuriate, incense, madden, exasperate, tease, taunt.
☞引起 cause, occasion, give rise to, produce, generate, induce, elicit, evoke, excite, inspire, move, stir, prompt, stimulate, motivate, incite, instigate.

psychological adj.
☞心理的 mental, cerebral, intellectual, cognitive, emotional, subjective, subconscious, unconscious, psychosomatic, irrational, unreal.

puberty n.
☞ 春青期 pubescence, adolescence, teens, youth, growing up, maturity.

public adj.
☞ 公共的 state, national, civil, community, social, collective, communal, common, general, universal, open, unrestricted.
☞ 公然的 known, well-known, recognized, acknowledged, overt, open, exposed, published.

n.
☞ 国民,公众 people, nation, country, population, populace, masses, citizens, society, community, voters, electorate, followers, supporters, fans, audience, patrons, clientele, customers, buyers, consumers.

public house
☞ 小酒店 pub, local, bar, saloon, inn, tavern.

publication n.
☞ 出版物 book, newspaper, magazine, periodical, booklet, leaflet, pamphlet, handbill.
☞ 发表,发布 announcement, declaration, notification, disclosure, release, issue, printing, publishing.

publicity n.
☞ 宣传 advertising, plug, hype, promotion, build-up, boost, attention, limelight, splash.

publish v.
☞ 宣布 announce, declare, communicate, make known, divulge, disclose, reveal, release, publicize, advertise.
☞ 出版(一部书) produce, print, issue, bring out, distribute, circulate, spread, diffuse.

puff n.
☞ 呼吸,气息 breath, waft, whiff, draught, flurry, gust, blast.

v.
☞ 呼吸 breathe, pant, gasp, gulp, wheeze, blow, waft, inflate, expand, swell.

puffy adj.
☞ 胀起的 puffed up, inflated, swollen, bloated, distended, enlarged.

pull v.
☞ 拖拉 tow, drag, haul, draw, tug, jerk, yank.
☞ 移动,搬开 remove, take out, extract, pull out, pluck, uproot, pull up, rip, tear.
☞ 吸引 attract, draw, lure, allure, entice, tempt, magnetize.
☞ (使)脱位,(使)变位 dislocate, sprain, wrench, strain.

n.
☞ 拖,拉 tow, drag, tug, jerk, yank.
☞ 吸引力 attraction, lure, allurement, drawing power, magnetism, influence, weight.

pull apart
☞ 分离,分开 separate, part, dismember, dismantle, take to pieces.

pull down
☞ 破坏,毁坏 destroy, demolish, knock down, bulldoze.

pull off
☞ 完成,实现 accomplish,

achieve, bring off, succeed, manage, carry out.
☞ 分开,拆开 detach, remove.

pull out
☞ 后退,撤走 retreat, withdraw, leave, depart, quit, move out, evacuate, desert, abandon.

pull through
☞ 恢复,康复 recover, rally, recuperate, survive, weather.

pull together
☞ 协作,合作 co-operate, work together, collaborate, team up.

pull up
☞ 停止 stop, halt, park, draw up, pull in, pull over, brake.
☞ 惩戒,谴责 reprimand, tell off, tick off, take to task, rebuke, criticize.

pulp n.
☞ 果肉 flesh, marrow, paste, puree, mash, mush, pap.
v.
☞ 压榨,压碎 crush, squash, pulverize, mash, puree, liquidize.

pulse n.
☞ 节拍 beat, stroke, rhythm, throb, pulsation, beating, pounding, drumming, vibration, oscillation.

pump v.
☞ 灌输 push, drive, force, inject, siphon, draw, drain.

pump up
☞ 充气 blow up, inflate, puff up, fill.

pun n.
☞ 双关语 play on words, double entendre, witticism, quip.

punch v.

☞ 打击,碰撞 hit, strike, pummel, jab, bash, clout, cuff, box, thump, sock, wallop.
n.
☞ 打击 blow, jab, bash, clout, thump, wallop.
☞ 活力,力量 force, impact, effectiveness, drive, vigour, verve, panache.

punctual adj.
☞ 守时的,准时的 prompt, on time, on the dot, exact, precise, early, in good time.

puncture n.
☞ 刺孔,洞 leak, hole, perforation, cut, nick.
v.
☞ 刺孔 prick, pierce, penetrate, perforate, hole, cut, nick, burst, rupture, flatten, deflate.

punish v.
☞ 惩罚,痛击 penalize, discipline, correct, chastise, castigate, scold, beat, flog, lash, cane, spank, fine, imprison.

punishment n.
☞ 惩罚 discipline, correction, chastisement, beating, flogging, penalty, fine, imprisonment, sentence, deserts, retribution, revenge.

pupil n.
☞ 学生 student, scholar, schoolboy, schoolgirl, learner, apprentice, beginner, novice, disciple, protege(e).

purchase v.
☞ 购买 buy, pay for, invest in, procure, acquire, obtain, get, secure, gain, earn, win.

n.
- 购买 acquisition, buy, investment, asset, possession, property.

purchaser n.
- 顾客 buyer, consumer, shopper, customer, client.

pure adj.
- 纯的 unadulterated, unalloyed, unmixed, undiluted, neat, solid, simple, natural, real, authentic, genuine, true.
- 洁净的 sterile, uncontaminated, unpolluted, germ-free, aseptic, antiseptic, disinfected, sterilized, hygienic, sanitary, clean, immaculate, spotless, clear.
- 总的,全部 sheer, utter, complete, total, thorough, absolute, perfect, unqualified.
- 纯洁的 chaste, virginal, undefiled, unsullied, moral, upright, virtuous, blameless, innocent.
- 纯粹的 theoretical, abstract, conjectural, speculative, academic.

purely adv.
- 完全地 utterly, completely, totally, entirely, wholly, thoroughly, absolutely.
- 只是 only, simply, merely, just, solely, exclusively.

purify v.
- 使纯净 refine, filter, clarify, clean, cleanse, decontaminate, sanitize, disinfect, sterilize, fumigate, deodorize.

purity n.
- 纯净 clearness, clarity, cleanness, cleanliness, untaintedness, wholesomeness.
- 单纯 simplicity, authenticity, genuineness, truth.
- 纯洁 chastity, decency, morality, integrity, rectitude, uprightness, virtue, innocence, blamelessness.

purpose n.
- 目的 intention, aim, objective, end, goal, target, plan, design, vision, idea, point, object, reason, motive, rationale, principle, result, outcome.
- 决心 determination, resolve, resolution, drive, single-mindedness, dedication, devotion, constancy, steadfastness, persistence, tenacity, zeal.
- 用途,效果 use, function, application, good, advantage, benefit, value.

on purpose
- 故意地 purposely, deliberately, intentionally, consciously, knowingly, wittingly, willfully.

purposeful adj.
- 有目的的 determined, decided, resolved, resolute, single-minded, constant, steadfast, persistent, persevering, tenacious, strong-willed, positive, firm, deliberate.

purse n.
- 钱包 money-bag, wallet, pouch.
- 金钱 money, means, resources, finances, funds, coffers, treasury, exchequer.

☞ 奖金 reward, award, prize.

v.
☞ 收拢 pucker, wrinkle, draw together, close, tighten, contract, compress.

pursue v.
☞ 从事 perform, engage in, practise, conduct, carry on, continue, keep on, keep up, maintain, persevere in, persist in, hold to, aspire to, aim for, strive for, try for.
☞ 追求 chase, go after, follow, track, trail, shadow, tail, dog, harass, harry, hound, hunt, seek, search for, investigate, inquire into.

pursuit n.
☞ 追击 chase, hue and cry, tracking, stalking, trail, hunt, quest, search, investigation.
☞ 从事 activity, interest, hobby, pastime, occupation, trade, craft, line, speciality, vocation.

push v.
☞ 推进 propel, thrust, ram, shove, jostle, elbow, prod, poke, press, depress, squeeze, squash, drive, force, constrain.
☞ 强力推出 promote, advertise, publicize, boost, encourage, urge, egg on, incite, spur, influence, persuade, pressurize, bully.

n.
☞ 推 knock, shove, nudge, jolt, prod, poke, thrust.
☞ 干劲 energy, vigour, vitality, go, drive, effort, dynamism, enterprise, initiative, ambition, determination.

pushy adj.
☞ 进取的 assertive, self-assertive, ambitious, forceful, aggressive, over-confident, forward, bold, brash, arrogant, presumptuous, assuming, bossy.

put v.
☞ 放,安置 place, lay, deposit, set, fix, settle, establish, stand, position, dispose, situate, station, post.
☞ 指派 apply, impose, inflict, levy, assign, subject.
☞ 表达 word, phrase, formulate, frame, couch, express, voice, utter, state.
☞ 提出 submit, present, offer suggest, propose.

put aside
☞ 收起来 put by, set aside, keep, retain, save, reserve, store, stow, stockpile, stash, hoard, salt away.

put back
☞ 延误 delay, defer, postpone, reschedule.
☞ 放回 replace, return.

put down
☞ 记录,写下 write down, transcribe, enter, log, register, record, note.
☞ 抑制,压抑 crush, quash, suppress, defeat, quell, silence, snub, slight, squash, deflate, humble, take down a peg, shame, humiliate, mortify.

put forward
☞ 提出 advance, suggest, recommend, nominate, propose, move, table, introduce, present, submit, offer, tender.

put off

- 延期 delay, defer, postpone, reschedule.
- 使……受挫 deter, dissuade, discourage, dishearten, demoralize, daunt, dismay, intimidate, disconcert, confuse, distract.

put on
- 增加 attach, affix, apply, place, add, impose.
- 装作 pretend, feign, sham, fake, simulate, affect, assume.
- 上演 stage, mount, produce, present, do, perform.

put out
- 公告 publish, announce, broadcast, circulate.
- 熄灯 extinguish, quench, douse, smother, switch off, turn off.
- 干扰,使为难 inconvenience, impose on, bother, disturb, trouble, upset, hurt, offend, annoy, irritate, irk, anger, exasperate.

put through
- 完成 accomplish, achieve, complete, conclude, finalize, execute, manage, bring off.

put up
- 建造 erect, build, construct, assemble.
- 为……提供食宿 accommodate, house, lodge, shelter.

put up to
- 促进,推动 prompt, incite, encourage, egg on, urge, goad.

put up with
- 容忍,忍受 stand, bear, abide, stomach, endure, suffer, tolerate, allow, accept, stand form, take, take lying down.

puzzle v.
- 使迷惑 baffle, mystify, perplex, confound, stump, floor, confuse, bewilder, flummox.
- 考虑 think, ponder, meditate, consider, mull over, deliberate, figure, rack one's brains.

n.
- 难题,谜 question, poser, brain-teaser, mind-bender, crossword, rebus, anagram, riddle, conundrum, mystery, enigma, paradox.

puzzle out
- 做出 solve, work out, figure out, decipher, decode, crack, unravel, untangle, sort out, resolve, clear up.

puzzled adj.
- 迷惑的 baffled, mystified, perplexed, confounded, at a loss, beaten, stumped, confused, bewildered, nonplussed, lost, at sea, flummoxed.

Q

quake v.
- 发抖 shake, tremble,

qualification n.
☞ 资格,合格性 certificate, diploma, training, skill, competence, ability, capability, capacity, aptitude, suitability, fitness, eligibility.

☞ 限制,限定 restriction, limitation, reservation, exception, exemption, condition, caveat, provision, proviso, stipulation, modification.

qualified adj.
☞ 允许的,有资格的 certified, chartered, licensed, professional, trained, experienced, practised, skilled, accomplished, expert, knowledgeable, skilful, talented, proficient, competent, efficient, able, capable, fit, eligible.

☞ 有限的,限制的 reserved, guarded, cautious, restricted, limited, bounded, contingent, conditional, provisional, equivocal.

qualify v.
☞ 授权 train, prepare, equip, fit, pass, graduate, certify, empower, entitle, authorize, sanction, permit.

☞ 节制,限制 moderate, reduce, lessen, diminish, temper, soften, weaken, mitigate, ease, adjust, modify, restrain, restrict, limit, delimit, define, classify.

quality n.
☞ 品质,特征 property, characteristic, peculiarity, attribute, aspect, feature, trait, mark.

☞ 标准,品质 standard, grade, class, kind, sort, nature, character, status, rank, value, worth, merit, condition.

☞ 优秀,杰出 excellence, superiority, preeminence, distinction, refinement.

quantity n.
☞ 数量,容量 amount, number, sum, total, aggregate, mass, lot, share, portion, quota, allotment, measure, dose, proportion, part, content, capacity, volume, weight, bulk, size, magnitude, expanse, extent, length, breadth.

quarrel n.
☞ 争吵 row, argument, slanging match, wrangle, squabble, tiff, misunderstanding, disagreement, dispute, dissension, controversy, difference, conflict, clash, contention, strife, fight, scrap, brawl, feud, vendetta, schism.

v.
☞ 争吵 row, argue, bicker, squabble, wrangle, be at loggerheads, fall out, disagree, dispute, dissent, differ, be at variance, clash, contend, fight, scrap, feud.

quarrelsome adj.
☞ 爱争吵的 argumentative, disputatious, contentious, belligerent, ill-tempered, irritable.

quarry n.
☞ 猎物 prey, victim, object,

goal, target, game, kill, prize.

quarter n.
- 地区,方面 district, sector, zone, neighbourhood, locality, vicinity, area, region, province, territory, division, section, part, place, spot, point, direction, side.

v.
- 驻,扎,供……住宿 station, post, billet, accommodate, put up, lodge, board, house, shelter.

quarters n.
- 供应膳宿,住宿 accommodation, lodgings, billet, digs, residence, dwelling, habitation, domicile, rooms, barracks, station, post.

query v.
- 询问 ask, inquire, question, challenge, dispute, quarrel with, doubt, suspect, distrust, mistrust, disbelieve.

n.
- 询问 question, inquiry, problem, uncertainty, doubt, suspicion, skepticism, reservation, hesitation.

quest n.
- 寻找,寻求,探索 search, hunt, pursuit, investigation, inquiry, mission, crusade, enterprise, undertaking, venture, journey, voyage, expedition, exploration, adventure.

question v.
- 提问题,对……表示疑问 interrogate, quiz, grill, pump, interview, examine, cross-examine, debrief, ask, inquire, investigate, probe, query, challenge, dispute, doubt, disbelieve.

n.
- 疑问,怀疑 query, inquiry, poser, problem, difficulty.
- 问题 issue, matter, subject, topic, point, proposal, proposition, motion, debate, dispute, controversy.

questionable adj.
- 有问题的;可疑的,靠不住的 debatable, disputable, unsettled, undetermined, unproven, uncertain, arguable, controversial, vexed, doubtful, dubious, suspicious, suspect, shady, fishy.

questionnaire n.
- 问题表,征求意见表,问卷 quiz, test, survey, opinion, poll.

queue n.
- 行列,长队 line, tailback, file, crocodile, procession, train, string, succession, series, sequence, order.

quick adj.
- 快的,迅速的 fast, swift, rapid, speedy, express, hurried, hasty, cursory, fleeting, brief, prompt, ready, immediate, instant, instantaneous, sudden, brisk, nimble, sprightly, agile.
- 精明的 clever, intelligent, quick-witted, smart, sharp, keen, shrewd, astute, discerning, perceptive, responsive, receptive.

quicken v.
- 使加快,加速 accelerate, speed, hurry, hasten,

precipitate, expedite, dispatch, advance.
☞ 使有生气 animate, enliven, invigorate, energize, galvanize, activate, rouse, arouse, stimulate, excite, inspire, revive, refresh, reinvigorate, reactivate.

quiet adj.
☞ 静的,肃静的,无闹声的 silent, noiseless, inaudible, hushed, soft, low.
☞ 平静的,镇静的 peaceful, still, tranquil, serene, calm, composed, undisturbed, untroubled, placid.
☞ 腼腆的 shy, reserved, reticent, uncommunicative, taciturn, retiring, withdrawn, thoughtful, subdued, meek.
n.
☞ 寂静,安静,宁静 quietness, silence, hush, peace, lull, stillness, tranquillity, serenity, calm, rest, repose.

quieten v.
☞ 使安静,使镇静 silence, hush, mute, soften, deaden, dull.
☞ 使镇静,抚慰 subdue, pacify, quell, quiet, still, smooth, calm, soothe, compose, sober.

quit v.
☞ 丢下工作离去;撒手不干 leave, depart, go, exit, decamp, desert, forsake, abandon, renounce, relinquish, surrender, give up, resign, retire, withdraw.
☞ 戒,免除 stop, cease, end, discontinue, desist, drop, give up, pack in .

quite adv.
☞ 相当的 moderately, rather, somewhat, fairly, relatively, comparatively.
☞ 完全,彻底,十分 utterly, absolutely, totally, completely, entirely, wholly, fully, perfectly, exactly, precisely.

quiz n.
☞ 回答比赛,提问,小型考试,测验 questionnaire, test, examination, competition.
v.
☞ 考问,反复盘问 question, interrogate, grill, pump, examine, cross-examine.

quizzical adj.
☞ 探询的,取笑的 questioning, inquiring, curious, amused, humorous, teasing, mocking, satirical, sardonic, skeptical.

quotation n.
☞ 引文 citation, quote, extract, excerpt, passage, piece, cutting, reference.
☞ 报价单 estimate, quote, tender, figure, price, cost, charge, rate.

quote v.
☞ 引用,引证 cite, refer to, mention, name, reproduce, echo, repeat, recite, recall, recollect.

R

race¹ n.
- 速度上的比赛,竞赛　sprint, steeplechase, marathon, scramble, regatta, competition, contest, contention, rivalry, chase, pursuit, quest.

v.
- 跑,全速行进　run, sprint, dash, tear, fly, gallop, speed, career, dart, zoom, rush, hurry, hasten.

race² n.
- 民族,种族　nation, people, tribe, clan, house, dynasty, family, kindred, ancestry, line, blood, stock, genus, species, breed.

race-course n.
- 跑道　racetrack, course, track, circuit, lap, turf, speedway.

racial adj.
- 种族的,人种的　national, tribal, ethnic, folk, genealogical, ancestral, inherited, genetic.

racism n.
- 种族主义　racialism, xenophobia, chauvinism, jingoism, discrimination, prejudice, bias.

rack n.
- 搁物架,挂物架　shelf, stand, support, structure, frame, framework.

racket n.
- 喧嚷,吵闹声　noise, din, uproar, row, fuss, outcry, clamour, commotion, disturbance, pandemonium, hurly-burly, hubbub.
- 勒索,敲诈,骗取　swindle, con, fraud, fiddle, deception, trick, dodge, scheme, business, game.

radiant adj.
- 光芒四散的　bright, luminous, shining, gleaming, glowing, beaming, glittering, sparkling, brilliant, resplendent, splendid, glorious, happy, joyful, delighted, ecstatic.

radiate v.
- 发射(光线),放射(热量)　shine, gleam, glow, beam, shed, pour, give off, emit, emanate, diffuse, issue, disseminate, scatter, spread (out), diverge, branch.

radical adj.
- 基础的　basic, fundamental, primary, essential, natural, native, innate, intrinsic, profound.
- (变革)彻底的,完全的　drastic, comprehensive, thorough, sweeping, far-reaching, thoroughgoing, complete, total, entire.
- 狂热的,激进的　fanatical, militant, extreme, extremist, revolutionary.

n.
- 激进派　fanatic, militant,

extremist, revolutionary, reformer, reformist, fundamentalist.

rage n.
☞ 盛怒,狂怒 anger, wrath, fury, frenzy, tantrum, temper.
☞ 风靡一时 craze, fad, thing, fashion, vogue, style, passion, enthusiasm, obsession.

v.
☞ 肆虐 fume, seethe, rant, rave, storm, thunder, explode, rampage.

ragged adj.
☞ 破旧的,褴褛的 frayed, torn, ripped, tattered, worn-out, threadbare, tatty, shabby, scruffy, unkempt, down-at-heel.
☞ 粗糙的 jagged, serrated, indented, notched, rough, uneven, irregular, fragmented, erratic, disorganized.

raid n.
☞ 突然袭击 attack, onset, onslaught, invasion, inroad, incursion, foray, sortie, strike, blitz, swoop, bust, robbery, break-in, hold-up.

v.
☞ 袭击 loot, pillage, plunder, ransack, rifle, maraud, attack, descend on, invade, storm.

railway n.
☞ 铁路 track, line, rails, underground, tube subway, metro.

rain n.
☞ 雨,雨水,下雨 rainfall, precipitation, raindrops, drizzle, shower, cloudburst, downpour, deluge, torrent, storm, thunderstorm, squall.

v.
☞ (使)大量降下;(使)如雨下 spit, drizzle, shower, pour, teem, pelt, bucket, deluge.

rainy adj.
☞ 多雨的 wet, damp, showery, drizzly.

raise v.
☞ 举起,提升,抬高,使向上运动 lift, elevate, hoist, jack up, erect, build, construct.
☞ 增加,提高 increase, augment, escalate, magnify, heighten, strengthen, intensify, amplify, boost, enhance.
☞ 召集,筹集 get, obtain, collect, gather, assemble, rally, muster, recruit.
☞ 饲养,养育 gring up, rear, breed, grow, cultivate, develop.

rally v.
☞ 聚合,重整旗鼓 gather, collect, assemble, convene, muster, summon, round up, unite, marshal, organize, mobilize, reassemble, regroup, reorganize.
☞ (从疾病中)恢复,(从不幸中)振作 recover, recuperate, revive, improve, pick up.

n.
☞ 大规模群众集会 gathering, assembly, convention, convocation, conference, meeting, jamboree, reunion, march, demonstration.
☞ 重新获得;找回,被找到 recovery, recuperation, revival, comeback, improvement, resurgence, renewal.

ram v.

- 撞击,猛击 hit, strike, butt, hammer, pound, drum, crash, smash, slam.
- 夯紧,锤实 force, drive, thrust, cram, stuff, pack, crowd, jam, wedge.

ramble v.
- 闲逛,漫步 walk, hike, trek, tramp, traipse, stroll, amble, saunter, straggle, wander, roam, rove, meander, wind, zigzag.
- 喋喋不休,唠叨 chatter, babble, rabbit(on), witter (on), expatiate, digress, drift.

n.
- 漫游 walk, hike, trek, tramp, stroll, saunter, tour, trip, excursion.

rambler n.
- 闲逛者,漫步者 hiker, walker, stroller, rover, roamer, wanderer, wayfarer.

rambling adj.
- 蔓生的,芜杂的 spreading, sprawling, straggling, trailing.
- 迂回的,兜圈子的 circuitous, roundabout, digressive, wordy, long-winded, long-drawn-out, disconnected, incoherent.

rampage v.
- 横冲直撞,暴跳 run wild, run amok, run riot, rush, tear, storm, rage, rant, rave.

n.
- 盛怒,狂怒 rage, fury, frenzy, storm, uproar, violence, destruction.

on the rampage
- 横冲直撞 amok, berserk, violent, out of control.

rampant adj.
- 广泛流传的,不可控制的 unrestrained, uncontrolled, unbridled, unchecked, wanton, excessive, fierce, violent, raging, wild, riotous, rank, profuse, rife, widespread, prevalent.

random adj.
- 随便的,任意的,无目的的,无计划的 arbitrary, chance, fortuitous, casual, incidental, haphazard, irregular, unsystematic, unplanned, accidental, aimless, purposeless, indiscriminate.

range n.
- 视觉(听觉)范围 scope, compass, scale, gamut, spectrum, sweep, spread, extent, distance, reach, span, limits, bounds, parameters, area, field, domain, province, sphere, orbit.

v.
- 延伸 extend, stretch, reach, spread, vary, fluctuate.
- 把……排列整齐 align, arrange, order, rank, classify, catalogue.

rank¹ n.
- 等级,程度 grade, degree, class, caste, status, standing, position, station, condition, estate, echelon, level, stratum, tier, classification, sort, type, group, division.
- 行;列;排 row, line, range, clown, file, series, order, formation.

v.
- 把……分等,把……分级 grade, class, rate, place,

position, range, sort, classify, categorize, order, arrange, organize, marshal.

rank² adj.
☞ 十足的,不折不扣的 utter, total, complete, absolute, unmitigated, thorough, sheer, downright, out-and-out, arrant, gross, flagrant, glaring, outrageous.
☞ (气味或味道)恶臭难闻的,令人讨厌的 foul, repulsive, disgusting, revolting, stinking, putrid, rancid, stale.

rap v.
☞ 轻敲,急拍 knock, hit, strike, tap, thump.
☞ 责骂 peprove, reprimand, criticize, censure.
n.
☞ 轻敲声,叩击声 knock, blow, tap, thump.
☞ 责备,惩戒 rubuke, reprimand, censure, blame, punishment.

rapid adj.
☞ 快的,迅速的 swift, speedy, quick, fast, express, lightning, prompt, brisk, hurried, hasty, precipitate, headlong.

rapport n.
☞ 和睦 bond, link, affinity, relationship, empathy, sympathy, understanding, harmony.

rare adj.
☞ 稀有的,罕见的 uncommon, unusual, scarce, sparse, sporadic, infrequent.
☞ 优美的,精心的 exquisite, superb, excellent, superlative, incomparable, exceptional, remarkable, precious.

rarely adv.
☞ 难得,非常地 seldom, hardly ever, infrequently, little.

rarity n.
☞ 稀有,稀薄 curiosity, curio, gem, pearl, treasure, find.
☞ 罕见的东西 uncommonness, unusualness, strangeness, scarcity, shortage, sparseness, infrequency.

rate n.
☞ 速度,速率 speed, velocity, tempo, time, ratio, proportion, relation, degree, grade, rank, rating, standard, basis, measure, scale.
☞ 费用 charge, fee, hire, toll, tariff, price, cost, value, worth, tax, duty, amount, figure, percentage.
v.
☞ 判断,断定 judge, consider, deem, count, reckon, figure, estimate, evaluate, assess, weigh, measure, grade, rank, class, classify.
☞ 赞赏,钦佩 admire, respect, esteem, value, prize.
☞ 应得,应受 deserve, merit.

rather adv.
☞ 适度地,相当地 moderately, relatively, slightly, a bit, somewhat, fairly, quite, pretty, noticeably, significantly, very.

ratify v.
☞ 批准,认可 approve, uphold, endorse, sign, legalize, sanction, authorize, establish, affirm, confirm, certify, validate, authenticate.

rating n.
☞ (广播,电视的)收看(听)率 class, rank, degree, status, standing, position, placing, order, grade, mark, evaluation, assessment, classification, category.

ratio n.
☞ 比率 percentage, fraction, proportion, relation, relationship, correspondence, correlation.

ration n.
☞ (食物的)定量 quota, allowance, allocation, allotment, share, portion, helping, part, measure, amount.
v.
☞ 定量供应 apportion, allot, allocate, share, deal out, distribute, doleout, dispense, supply, issue, control, restrict, limit, conserve, save.

rational adj.
☞ 有推理能力的,合理的 logical, reasonable, sound, well-founded, realistic, sensible, clear-headed, judicious, wise, sane, normal, balanced, lucid, reasoning, thinking, intelligent, enlightened.

rationale n.
☞ 理性 logic, reasoning, philosophy, principle, basis, grounds, explanation, reason, motive, motivation, theory.

rattle v.
☞ 喋喋不休 reel off, list, run through, recite, repeat.

raw adj.
☞ 生的 uncooked, fresh.
☞ 未加工的,处于自然状态的 unprocessd, unrefined, untreated, crude, natural.
☞ 简单的,朴素的 plain, bare, naked, basic, harsh, brutal, realistic.
☞ 疼痛的 sratched, grazed, scraped, open, bloody, sore, tender, sensitive.
☞ (天气)阴冷的,寒冷的 cold, chilly, bitter, biting, piercing, freezing, bleak.
☞ 未受训练的 new, green, immature, callow, inexperienced, untrained, unskilled.

ray n.
☞ 光线,射线 beam, shaft, flash, gleam, flicker, glimmer, glint, spark, trace, hint, indication.

reach v.
☞ 抵达,到达 arrive at, get to, attain, achieve, make, amount to, hit, strike, touch, contact, stretch, extend, grasp.
n.
☞ 伸,伸出 range, scope, compass, distance, spread, extent, stretch, grasp, jurisdiction, power, influence.

react v.
☞ 起作用,有影响,起反应 respond, retaliate, reciprocate, reply, answer, acknowledge, act, behave.

reaction n.
☞ 反应 response, effect, reply, answer, acknowledgement, feedback, counteraction, reflex, recoil, reciprocation, retaliation.

reactionary adj.

☞ 反动的 conservative, right-wing, rightist, die-hard, counter-revolutionary.

n.
☞ 反动分子 conservative, right-winger, rightist, die-hard, counter-revolutionary.

read v.
☞ 理解 study, peruse, pore over, scan, skim, decipher, decode, interpret, construe, understand, comprehend.
☞ 朗读,朗诵 recite, deliver, speak, utter.
☞ 显示 indicate, show, display, register, record.

readable adj.
☞ 易读的 legible, decipherable, intelligible, clear, understandable, comprehensible.
☞ 使人爱读的 interesting, enjoyable, entertaining, gripping, unputdownable

readily adv.
☞ 准备好地,愿意地,快地,有效地,可用地 willingly, unhesitatingly, gladly, eagerly, promptly, quickly, freely. smoothly, easily, effortlessly.

reading n.
☞ 阅读 study, perusal, scrutiny, examination, inspection, interpretation, understanding, rendering, version, rendition, recital.
☞ 见解 passage, lesson.

ready adj.
☞ 准备好的 prepared, waiting, set, fit, arranged, organized, completed, finished.
☞ 愿意的 willing, inclined, disposed, happy, game, eager, keen.
☞ 可用的 available, to hand, present, near, accessible, convenient, handy.
☞ 快的 prompt, immediate, quick, sharp, astute, perceptive, alert.

real adj.
☞ 真实的,实际的 actual, existing, physical, material, substantial, tangible, genuine, authentic, bona fide, official, rightful, legitimate, valid, true, factual, certain, sure, positive, veritable, honest, sincere, heartfelt, unfeigned, unaffected.

realistic adj.
☞ 实际的,现实主义的 practical, down-to-earth, commonsense, sensible, level-headed, clear-sighted, businesslike, hard-headed, pragmatic, matter-of-fact, rational, logical, objective, detached, unsentimental, unromantic.
☞ 逼真的 lifelike, faithful, truthful, true, genuine, authentic, natural, real, real-life, graphic, representational.

reality n.
☞ 真实,实际 truth, fact, certainty, realism, actuality, existence, materiality, tangibility, genuineness, authenticity, validity.

realize v.
☞ 认识到,了解 understand, comprehend, grasp, catch on, cotton on, recognize, accept, appreciate.
☞ 使(计划等)实现 achieve,

accomplish, fulfil, complete, implement, perform.
☞ 把(产业等)变为现钱 sell for, fetch, make, earn, produce, net, clear.

really adj.
☞ 事实上 actually, truly, honestly, sincerely, genuinely, positively, certainly, absolutely, categorically, very, indeed.

realm n.
☞ 世界,王国 kingdom, monarchy, principality, empire, country, state, land, territory, area, region, province, domain, sphere, orbit, field, department.

rear n.
☞ 后部,后面 back, stern, end, tail, rump, buttocks, posterior, behind, bottom, backside.

reason n.
☞ 理由,原因 cause, motive, incentive, rationale, explanation, excuse, justification, defence, warrant, ground, basis, case, argument, aim, intention, purpose, object, end, goal.
☞ 理智,理性 sense, logic, reasoning, rationality, sanity, mind, wit, brain, intellect, understanding, wisdom, judgement, common sense, gumption.
v.
☞ 思考,推理 work out, solve, resolve, conclude, deduce, infer, think.

reason with
☞ 劝说,说服 urge, persuade, move, remonstrate with, argue with, debate with, discuss with.

reasonable adj.
☞ 有普通常识的,明智的 sensible, wise, well-advised, sane, intelligent, rational, logical, practical, sound, reasoned, well-thought-out, plausible, credible, possible, viable.
☞ 公平的,公道的(价格) acceptable, satisfactory, tolerable, moderate, average, fair, just, modest, inexpensive.

reasoning n.
☞ 推理 logic, thinking, thought, analysis, interpretation, deduction, supposition, hypothesis, argument, case, proof.

reassure v.
☞ 使放心,使消除疑虑 comfort, cheer, encourage, hearten, inspirit, brace, bolster.

rebel v.
☞ 反抗,对抗 revolt, mutiny, rise up, run riot, dissent, disobey, defy, resist, recoil, shrink.

rebellion n.
☞ 反抗,对抗 revolt, revolution, rising, uprising, insurrection, insurgence, mutiny, resistance, opposition, defiance, disobedience, insubordination, dissent, heresy.

rebellious adj.
☞ 反叛的,反抗的 revolutionary, insurrectionary, insurgent, seditious, mutinous, resistant, defiant, disobedient, insubordinate, unruly,

disorderly, ungovernable, unmanageable, intractable, obstinate.

rebuke v.
☞ 指责,非难 reprove, castigate, chide, scold, tell of, admonish, tick off scold, tell of, reprimand, upbraid, rate, censure, blame, reproach.

recall v.
☞ 回忆,回想 remember, recollect, cast one's mind back, evoke, bring, back.

recede v.
☞ 后退 go back, return, retire, withdraw, retreat, ebb, wane, sink, decline, shrink. slacken, subside, abate.

receipt n.
☞ 收据 voucher, ticket, slip, counterfoil, stub, acknowledgement.
☞ 收到 receiving, reception, acceptance, delivery.

receipts n.
☞ 收入 takings, income, proceeds, profits, gains, return.

receive v.
☞ 收到,接到 take, accept, get, obtain, derive, acquire, pick up, collect, inherit.
☞ 准予进入 admit, let in, greet, welcome, entertain, accommodate.
☞ 受到,体验,经历,感受 experience, undergo, suffer, sustain, meet with, encounter.
☞ 听取,受理 react to, respond to, hear, perceive, apprehend.

recent adj.
☞ 最近的,近来 late, latest, current, present day, contemporary, modern, up-to-date, new, novel, fresh, young.

recently adv.
☞ 最近地,近来的 lately, newly, freshly.

reception n.
☞ 欢迎,接待 acceptance, admission, greeting, recognition, welcome, treatment, response, reaction, acknowledgement, receipt.
☞ 宴会,招待会 party, function, do, entertainment.

receptive adj.
☞ 善于接受的 open-minded, amenable, accommodating, suggestible, susceptible, sensitive, responsive, open, accessible, approachable, friendly, hospitable, welcoming, sympathetic, favourable, interested.

recession n.
☞ 后退,撤回,衰退,暴跌 slump, depression, downturn, decline.

recipe n.
☞ 烹饪法,食谱 formula, prescription, ingredients, instructions, directions, method, system, procedure, technique.

recite v.
☞ 背诵,列举 repeat, tell, narrate, relate, recount, speak, deliver, articulate, declaim, perform, reel off, itemize, enumerate.

reckon v.

- 计算 calculate, compute, figure out, work out, and up, total, tally, count, number, enumerate.
- 认为 deem, regard, consider, esteem, value, rate, judge, evaluate, asses, estimate, gauge.
- 将……加以考虑 think, believe, imagine, fancy, suppose, surmise, assume, guess, conjecture.

reckon on
- 依赖 rely on, depend on, bank on, count on, trust in, hope for, expect, anticipate, foresee, plan for, bargain for, figure on, take into account, face.

reckoning n.
- 估算 calculation, computation, estimate.
- 账单 bill, account, charge, due, score, settlement.
- 惩罚,报应,判决 judgement, retribution, doom.

reclaim v.
- 回收 recover, regain, recapture, retrieve, salvage, rescue, redeem, restore, reinstate, regenerate.

recognition n.
- 认出,识别 indentification, detection, discovery, recollection, recall, remembrance, awareness, perception, realization, understanding.
- 招供,交代 confession, admission, acceptance, acknowledgement, gratitude, appreciation, honour, respect, greeting, salute.

recognize v.
- 认识,认出 identify, know, remember, recollect, recall, place, see, notice, spot, perceive.
- 承认 confess, own, acknowledge, accept, admit, grant, concede, allow, appreciate, understand, realize.

recollect v.
- 回忆,想起 recall, remember, cast one's mind back, reminisce.

recollection n.
- 回忆,记忆力 recall, remembrance, memory, souvenir, reminiscence, impression.

recommend v.
- 推荐,介绍,劝告,建议 advocate, urge, exhort, advise, counsel, suggest, propose, put forward, advance, praise, commend, plug, endorse, approve, vouch for.

recommendation n.
- 推荐,介绍 advice, counsel, suggestion, proposal, advocacy, endorsement, approval, sanction, blessing, praise, commendation, plug, reference, testimonial.

reconcile v.
- 使和解,调解,使一致 reunite, conciliate, pacify, appease, placate, propitiate, accord, harmonize, accommodate, adjust, resolve, settle, square.

reconciliation n.

☞ 和解 reunion, conciliation, pacification, appeasement, propitiation, rapprochement, détente, settlement, agreement, harmony, accommodation, adjustment, compromise.

reconstruct v.
☞ 重建 remake, rebuild, reassemble, re-establish, refashion, remodel, reform, reorganize, recreate, restore, renovate, regenerate.

record n.
☞ 记录,记载 register, log, report, account, minutes, memorandum, note, entry, document, file, dossier, diary, journal, memoir, history, annals, archives, documentation, evidence, testimony, trace.

☞ 唱片 recording, disc, single, CD, compact disc, album, release, LP.

☞ 最高纪录 rastest time, best performance, personal best world record.

☞ 履历 background, track record, curriculum vitae, career.

v.
☞ 记录,记载 note, enter, inscribe, write down, transcribe, register, log, put down, enrol, report, minute, chronicle, document, keep, preserve.

☞ 录音 tape-record, tape, videotape, video, cut.

recording n.
☞ 录音的节目 release, performance, record, disc, CD, cassette, tape, video.

recover v.
☞ 复原,痊愈 get better, improve, pick up, rally, mend, heal, pull through, get over, recuperate, revive, convalesce, come round.

☞ 恢复原状 regain, get back, recoup, retrieve, retake, recapture, repossess, reclaim, restore.

recovery n.
☞ 复原,恢复健康 recuperation, convalescence, rehabilitation, mending, healing, improvement, upturn, rally, revival, restoration.

☞ 补偿 retrieval, salvage, reclamation, repossession, recapture.

recreation n.
☞ 消遣,娱乐 fun, enjoyment, pleasure, amusement, diversion, distraction, entertainment, hobby, pastime, game, sport, play, leisure, relaxation, refreshment.

recruit v.
☞ 吸收(新成员),征募(新兵) enlist, draft, conscript, enroll, sign up, engage, take on, mobilize, raise, gather, obtain, procure.

n.
☞ 新手 beginner, novice, initiate, learner, trainee, apprentice, conscript, convert.

rectify v.
☞ 纠正,矫正 correct, put right, right, remedy, cure, repair, fix, mend, improve, amend, adjust, reform.

recycle v.
- ☞ (使)再循环 reuse, reprocess, reclaim, recover, save.

red adj.
- ☞ 鲜红色,鲜红的 scarlet, vermilion, cherry, ruby, crimson, maroon, pink, reddish, bloodshot, inflamed.
- ☞ 红润的,有血色的 ruddy, florid, glowing, rosy, flushed, blushing, embarrassed, shamefaced.

redden v.
- ☞ 使红,变红 blush, flush, colour, go red, crimson.

reduce v.
- ☞ 减少,减小 lessen, decrease, contract, shrink, slim, shorten, curtail, trim, cut, slash, discount, rebate, lower, moderate, weaken, diminish, impair.
- ☞ 使处于 drive, force, degrade, downgrade, demote, humble, humiliate, impoverish, subdue, overpower, master, vanquish.

reduction n.
- ☞ 减少,减入 decrease, drop, fall, decline, lessening, moderation, weakening, diminution, contraction, compression, shrinkage, narrowing, shortening, curtailment, restriction, limitation, cutback, cut, discount, rebate, devaluation, depreciation, deduction, subtraction, loss.

reel v.
- ☞ 卷,绕 stagger, totter, wobble, rock, sway, waver, falter, stumble, lurch, pitch, roll, revolve, gyrate, spin, wheel, twirl, whirl, swirl.

refer v.
- ☞ 把……委托 send, direct, point, guide, pass on, transfer, commit, deliver.
- ☞ 参阅 consult, look up, turn to, resort to.
- ☞ 提到,暗指 aallude, mention, touch on, speak of, bring up, recommend, cite, quote.
- ☞ 涉及,有关 apply, concern, relate, belong, pertain.

reference n.
- ☞ 提及,暗指 allusion, remark, mention, citation, quotation, illustration, instance, note.
- ☞ 证明,证明书 testimonial, recommendation, endorsement, character.
- ☞ 关联,关系 relation, regard, respect, connection, bearing.

refine v.
- ☞ 精炼,提纯,使文雅,变得文雅 process, treat, purify, clarify, filter, distil, polish, hone, improve, perfect, elevate, exalt.

refined adj.
- ☞ 文雅的 civilized, cultured, cultivated, polished, sophisticated, urbane, genteel, gentlemanly, ladylike, well-bred, well-mannered, polited, civil, elegant, fine, delicate, subtle, precise, exact, sensitive, discriminating.

refinement n.
- ☞ 改良 modification, alteration, amendment, improvement.
- ☞ 优美,文雅 cultivation,

sophistication, urbanity, gentility, breeding, style, elegance, taste, discrimination, subtlety, finesse.

reflect v.
- 反射,反映 mirror, echo, imitate, reproduce, portray, depict, show, reveal, display, exhibit, manifest, demonstrate, indicate, express, communicate.
- 考虑,想到 think, ponder, consider, mull(over), deliberate, contemplate, meditate, muse.

reflection n.
- 映像,倒影 image, likeness, echo, impression, indication, manifestation, observation, view, opinion.
- 思考,考虑 thinking, thought, study, consideration, deliberation, contemplation, meditation, musing.

reform v.
- 改革,改变 change, amend, improve, ameliorate, better, rectify, correct, mend, repair, rehabilitate, remodel, revamp, renovate, restore, regenerate, reconstitute, reorganize, shake up, revolutionize, purge.

n.
- 改革,改良 change, amendment, improvement, rectification, correction, rehabilitation, renovation, reorganization, shake-up, purge.

refresh v.
- 使……清新 cool, freshen, enliven, invigorate, fortify, revive, restore, renew, rejuvenate, revitalize, reinvigorate.
- 提神 jog, stimulate, prompt, prod.

refreshing adj.
- 清新的 cool, thirst-quenching, bracing, invigorating, energizing, stimulating, inspiring, fresh, new, novel, original.

refreshment n.
- 提神的东西 sustenance, food, drink, snack, revival, restoration, renewal, reanimation, reinvigoration, revitalization.

refuge n.
- 庇护,避难所 sanctuary, asylum, shelter, protection, security, retreat, hideout, hide-away, resort, harbour, haven.

refugee n.
- 难民,避难者 exile, émigré, displaced, person, fugitive, runaway, escapee.

refund v.
- 退还 repay, reimburse, rebate, return, restore.

n.
- 偿还额 repayment, reimbursement, rebate, return.

refusal n.
- 拒绝,回绝 rejection, no, rebuff, repudiation, denial, negation.

refuse^1 v.
- 拒绝 reject, turn down, decline, spurn, repudiate, rebuff, repel, deny, withhold.

refuse^2 n.

☞ 垃圾,废物 rubbish, waste, trash, garbage, junk, litter.

refute v.
☞ 反驳,驳斥 disprove, rebut, confute, give the lie to, discredit, counter, negate.

regain v.
☞ 恢复 recover, get back, recoup, reclaim, repossess, retake, recapture, retrieve, return to.

regard v.
☞ 视为,认作 consider, deem, judge, rate, value, think, believe, suppose, imagine, look upon, view, observe, watch.

n.
☞ 注意,关心 care, concern, consideration, attention, notice, heed, respect, deference, honour, esteem, admiration, affection, love, sympathy.

regarding prep.
☞ 关于,有关 with regard to, as regards, concerning, with reference to, re, about, as to.

regardless adj.
☞ 不管,不考虑的 disregarding, heedless, unmindful, neglectful, inattentive, unconcerned, indifferent.

regime n.
☞ 政体,制度 government, rule, administration, management, leadership, command, control, establishment, system.

region n.
☞ 地区,领域,区域,范围 land, terrain, territory, country, province, area, district, zone, sector, neighbourhood, range, scope, expanse, domain, realm, sphere, field, division, section, part, place.

register n.
☞ 登记,名单 roll, roster, list, index, catalogue, directory, log, record, chronicle, annals, archives, file, ledger, schedule, diary, almanac.

v.
☞ 登记,注册 record, note, log, enter, inscribe, mark, list, catalogue, chronicle, enrol, enlist, sign on, check in.
☞ 指出,显示 show, reveal, betray, display, exhibit, manifest, express, say, read, indicate.

regret v.
☞ 悲痛,惋惜 rue, repent, lament, mourn, grieve, deplore.

n.
☞ 惋惜,懊悔 remorse, contrition, compunction, self-reproach, shame, sorrow, grief, disappointment, bitterness.

regretful adj.
☞ 哀惜的,遗憾的 remorseful, rueful, repentant, contrite, penitent, conscience-stricken, ashamed, sorry, apologetic, sad, sorrowful, disappointed.

regrettable adj.
☞ 可悲的,不幸的 unfortunate, unlucky, unhappy, sad, disappointing, upsetting, distressing, lamentable, deplorable, shameful, wrong, ill-advised.

regular adj.
☞ 有规则的,正规的 routine, habitual, typical, usual,

customary, time-honoured, conventional, orthodox, correct, official, standard, normal, ordinary, common, commonplace, everyday.
☞ 固定的,整齐的 periodic, rhythmic, steady, constant, fixed, set, unvarying, uniform, even, level, smooth, balanced, symmetrical, orderly, systematic, methodical.

regulate v.
☞ 管理,控制 control, direct, guide, govern, rule, administer, manage, handle, conduct, run, organize, order, arrange, settle, square, monitor, set, adjust, tune, moderate, balance.

regulation n.
☞ 规则,规定 rule, statute, law, ordinance, edict, decree, order, commandment, precept, dictate, requirement.
adj.
☞ 正规的,规定的 standard, official, statutory, prescribed, required, orthodox, accepted, customary, usual, normal.

rehearsal n.
☞ 练习,演习 practice, drill, exercise, dry run, run-through, preparation, reading, recital, narration, account, enumeration, list.

rehearse v.
☞ 演练,练习 practise, drill, train, go over, prepare, try out, repeat, recite, recount, relate.

reign n.
☞ 统治,主权 rule, sway, monarchy, empire, sovereignty, supremacy, power, command, dominion, control, influence.
v.
☞ 统治 rule, govern, command, prevail, predominunce, influence.

reject v.
☞ 拒绝,排除 refuse, deny, decline, turn down, veto, disallow, condemn, despise, spurn, rebuff, jilt, exclude, repudiate, repel, renounce, eliminate, scrap, discard, jettison, cast off.

rejection n.
☞ 拒绝,被弃 refusal, denial, veto, dismissal, rebuff, brush-off, exclusion, repudiation, renunciation, elimination.

rejoice v.
☞ 高兴,快乐 celebrate, revel, delight, glory, exult, triumph.

rejoicing n.
☞ 高兴,欣喜 celebration, revelry, merrymaking, festivity, happiness, gladness, joy, delight, elation, jubilation, exultation, triumph.

relapse v.
☞ (疾病)重发 worsen, deteriorate, degenerate, weaken, sink, fail, lapse, revert, regress, backslide.
n.
☞ 复发,重犯 worsening, deterioration, setback, recurrence, weakening, lapse, reversion, regression, backsliding.

relate v.
☞ 与……相联系 link, connect,

join, couple, ally, associate, correlate.
- 关联 refer, apply, concern, pertain, appertain.
- 讲叙,叙述 tell, recount, narrate, report, describe, recite.

related *adj*.
- 相关的,有联系的 kindred, akin, affiliated, allied, associated, connected, linked, interrelated, interconnected, accompanying, concomitant, joint, mutual.

relation *n*.
- 联系,关系 link, connection, bond, relationship, correlation, comparison, similarity, affiliation, interrelation, interconnection, interdependence, regard, reference.
- 亲戚,亲属 relative, family, kin, kindred.

relations *n*.
- 亲属 relatives, family, kin, kindred.
- 关系 relationship, terms, rapport, liaison, intercourse, affairs, dealings, interaction, communications, contact, associations, connections.

relationship *n*.
- 联系 bond, link, connection, association, liaison, rapport, affinity, closeness, similarity, parallel, correlation, ratio, proportion.

relative *adj*.
- 相对的 comparative, proportional, proportionate, commensurate, corresponding, respective; appropriate, relevant, applicable, related, connected, interrelated, reciprocal, dependent.

n.
- 亲属 relation, family, kin.

relax *v*.
- 放松 loosen, lessen, reduce, diminish, weaken, lower, soften, moderate, abate, remit, relieve, ease, rest, unwind, calm, tranquillize, sedate.

relaxation *n*.
- 休闲 rest, repose, refreshment, leisure, recreation, fun, amusement, entertainment, enjoyment, pleasure.
- 放松 slackening, lessoning, reduction, moderation, abatement, let up, détente, easing.

relaxed *adj*.
- 松懈的,放松的 informal, casual, laid-back, easy-going, carefree, happy-go-lucky, cool, calm, composed, collected, unhurried, leisurely.

relay *n*.
- 转播 broadcast, transmission, programme, communication, message, dispatch.
- 接力 shift, turn.

v.
- 转播 broadcast, transmit, communicate, send, spread, carry, supply.

release *v*.
- 释放 loose, unloose, unleash, unfasten, extricate, free, liberate, deliver, emancipate, acquit, absolve, exonerate, excuse, exempt, discharge,

issue, publish, circulate, distribute, present, launch, unveil.

n.

☞解放 freedom, liberty, liberation, deliverance, emancipation, acquittal, absolution, exoneration, exemption, discharge, issue, publication, announcement, proclamation.

relent v.
☞减弱,缓和 give in, give way, yield, capitulate, unbend, relax, slacken, soften, weaken.

relevant adj.
☞相关的 pertinent, material, significant, germane, related, applicable, apposite, apt, appropriate, suitable, fitting, proper, admissible.

reliable adj.
☞可信赖的 unfailing, certain, sure, dependable, responsible, trusty, trustworthy, honest, true, faithful, constant, staunch, solid, safe, sound, stable, predictable, regular.

reliance n.
☞依靠 dependence, trust, faith, belief, credit, confidence, assurance.

relic n.
☞残迹 memento, souvenir, keepsake, token, survival, remains, remnant, scrap, fragment, vestige, trace.

relief n.
☞宽慰 reassurance, consolation, comfort, ease, alleviation, cure, remedy, release, deliverance, help, aid, assistance, support, sustenance, refreshment, diversion, relaxation, rest, respite, break, breather, remission, let-up, abatement.

relieve v.
☞宽慰 reassure, console, comfort, ease, soothe, alleviate, mitigate, cure, release, deliver, free, unburden, lighten, soften, slacken, relax, calm, help, aid, assist, support, sustain.

religious adj.
☞虔诚的 sacred, holy, divine, spiritual, devotional, scriptural, theological, doctrinal.
☞宗教的 devout, godly, pious, God-fearing, church-going, reverent, righteous.

reluctant adj.
☞不情愿的,勉强的 unwilling, disinclined, indisposed, hesitant, slow, backward, loth, averse, unenthusiastic, grudging.

rely v.
☞依靠,依赖 depend, lean, count, bank, reckon, trust, swear by.

remain v.
☞保持,依旧 stay, rest, stand, dwell, abide, last, endure, survive, prevail, persist, continue, linger, wait.

remainder n.
☞剩余物,剩余 rest, balance, surplus, excess, remnant, remains.

remaining adj.
☞剩下的,依旧的 left, unused, unspent, unfinished, residual, outstanding, surviving,

persisting, lingering, lasting, abiding.

remains n.
- 残余,剩余 rest, remainder, residue, dregs, leavings, leftovers, scraps, crumbs, fragments, remnants, oddments, traces, vestiges, relics, body, corpse, carcase, ashes, debris.

remark v.
- 评论,注意,说 comment, observe, note, mention, say, state, declare.

n.
- 评语,意见,评论 comment, observation, opinion, reflection, mention, utterance, statement, assertion, declaration.

remarkable adj.
- 显著的,惊人的 striking, impressive, noteworthy, surprising, amazing, strange, odd, unusual, uncommon, extraordinary, phenomenal, exceptional, outstanding, notable, conspicuous, prominent, distinguished.

remedy n.
- 治疗措施,药品 cure, antidote, countermeasure, corrective, restorative, medicine, treatment, therapy, relief, solution, answer, panacea.

v.
- 修缮,校正,治疗 correct, rectify, put right, redress, counteract, cure, heal, restore, treat, help, relieve, soothe, ease, mitigate, mend, repair, fix, solve.

remember v.
- 记起 recall, recollect, summon up, think back, reminisce, recognize, place.
- 记得 memorize, learn, retain.

remind v.
- 提醒,使……想起 prompt, nudge, hint, jog one's memory, refresh one's memory, bring to mind, call to mind, call up.

reminder n.
- 纪念品 prompt, nudge, hint, suggestion, memorandum, memo, souvenir, memento.

remote adj.
- 遥远的 distant, far, faraway, far-off, outlying, out-of-the-way, inaccessible, god-forsaken, isolated, secluded, lonely.
- 疏远的,冷淡的 detached, aloof, standoffish, uninvolved, reserved, withdrawn.
- 极小的 slight, small, slim, slender, faint, negligible, unlikely, improbable.

remove v.
- 排除,消除,去除 detach, pull of, amputate, cut off, extract, pull out, withdraw, take away, take off, strip, shed, doff, expunge, efface, erase, delete, strike out, get rid of, abolish, purge, eliminate, dismiss, discharge, eject, throw out, oust, depose, displace, dislodge, shift, move, transport, transfer, relocate.

render v.
- 使得 make, cause to be, leave.

☞提供,提出 give, provide, supply, tender, present, submit, hand over, deliver.
☞翻译 translate, transcribe, interpret, explain, clarify, represent, perform, play, sing.

renew v.
☞更新,换新 renovate, modernize, refurbish, refit, recondition, mend, repair, overhaul, remodel, reform, transform, recreate, reconstitute, reestablish, regenerate, revive, resuscitate, refresh, rejuvenate, reinvigorate, revitalize, restore, replace, replenish, restock.
☞补充,使恢复 repeat, restate, reaffirm, extend, prolong, continue, recommence, restart, resume.

renounce v.
☞放弃,弃绝 abandon, forsake, give up, resign, relinquish, surrender, discard, reject, spurn, disown, repudiate, dislaim, deny, recant, abjure.

renovate v.
☞修理,恢复 restore, renew, recondition, repair, overhaul, modernize, refurbish, refit, redecorate, do up, remodel, reform, revamp, improve.

renown n.
☞名望,声誉 fame, celebrity, stardom, acclaim, glory, eminence, illustriousness, distinction, note, mark, esteem, reputation, honour.

renowned adj.
☞著名的,有名的 famous, well-known, celebrated, acclaimed, famed, noted, eminent, distinguished, illustrious, notable.

rent n.
☞租金,地租 rental, lease, hire, payment, fee.
v.
☞租 let, sublet, lease, hire, charter.

repair v.
☞修理,修补 mend, fix, patch up, overhaul, service, rectify, redress, restore, renovate, renew.
n.
☞修补,恢复,修理 mend, patch, darn, overhaul, service, maintenance, restoration, adjustment, improvement.

repay v.
☞偿还,付还 refund, reimburse, compensate, recompense, reward, remunerate, pay, settle, square, get even with, retaliate, reciprocate, revenge, avenge.

repeat v.
☞重复做,重复,背诵 restate, reiterate, recapitulate, echo, quote, recite, relate, retell, reproduce, duplicate, renew, rebroadcast, reshow, replay, rerun, redo.
n.
☞重复,重演 repetition, echo, reproduction, duplicate, rebroadcast, reshowing, replay, rerun.

repeatedly adv.
☞反复地 time after time, time and (time) again, again and again, over and over,

frequently, often.

repel v.
- 🔘 驱开,击退 drive back, repulse, check, hold off, ward off, parry, resist, oppose, fight, refuse, decline, reject, rebuff.
- 🔘 使……厌恶 disgust, revolt, nauseate, sicken, offend.

repetition n.
- 🔘 重复,反复 restatement, reiteration, recapitulation, echo, return, reappearance, recurrence, duplication, tautology.

repetitive adj.
- 🔘 重复的,反复的 recurrent, monotonous, tedious, boring, dull, mechanical, unchanging, unvaried.

replace v.
- 🔘 放回,恢复 put back, return, restore, make good, reinstate, re-establish.
- 🔘 替代,取代 supersede, succeed, follow, supplant, oust, deputize, substitute.

replacement n.
- 🔘 替代物 substitute, stand-in, understudy, fill-in, supply, proxy, surrogate, successor.

replenish v.
- 🔘 补充,再装满 refill, restock, reload, recharge, replace, restore, renew, supply, provide, furnish, stock, fill, top up.

reply v.
- 🔘 回答,答复 answer, respond, retort, rejoin, react, acknowledge, return, echo, reciprocate, counter, retaliate.

n.
- 🔘 回答 answer, response, retort, rejoinder, riposte, repartee, reaction, comeback, acknowledgement, return, echo, retaliation.

report n.
- 🔘 报告,传闻 article, piece, write-up, record, account, relation, narrative, description, story, tale, gossip, hearsay, rumour, talk, statement, communiqué, declaration, announcement, communication, information, news, word, message, note.

v.
- 🔘 报告,汇报 state, announce, declare, proclaim, air, broadcast, relay, publish, circulate, communicate, notify, tell, recount, relate, narrate, describe, detail, cover, document, record, note.

reporter n.
- 🔘 记者,报导者 journalist, correspondent, columnist, newspaperman, newspaperwoman, back, newscaster, commentator, announcer.

represent v.
- 🔘 表示,阐明,象征 stand for, symbolize, designate, denote, mean, express, evoke, depict, portray, describe, picture, draw, sketch, illustrate, exemplify, typify, epitomize, embody, personify, appear as, act as, enact, perform, show, exhibit, be, amount to,

representation n.
☞ 象征, 表示 likeness, image, icon, picture, portrait, illustration, sketch, model, statue, bust, depiction, portrayal, description, account, explanation.
☞ 演出 performance, production, play, show, spectacle.

representative n.
☞ 代表 delegate, deputy, proxy, stand-in, spokesperson, spokesman, spokeswoman, ambassador, commissioner, agent, salesman, saleswoman, rep, traveller.
adj.
☞ 代表的, 象征的 typical, illustrative, exemplary, archetypal, characteristic, usual, normal, symbolic.

repulsive *adj.*
☞ 推斥的, 讨厌的 repellent, repugnant, revolting, disgusting, nauseating, sickening, offensive, distasteful, objectionable, obnoxious, foul, vile, loathsome, abominable, abhorrent, hateful, horrid, unpleasant, disagreeable, ugly, hideous, forbidding.

reputable *adj.*
☞ 受尊敬的, 名誉好的 respectable, reliable, dependable, trustworthy, upright, honourable, creditable, worthy, good, excellent, irreproachable.

reputation n.
☞ 名誉, 名望 honour, character, standing, stature, esteem, opinion, credit, repute, fame, renown, celebrity, distinction, name, good name, bad name, infamy, notoriety.

reputed *adj.*
☞ 驰名的, 号称的 alleged, supposed, said, rumoured, believe, thought, considered, regarded, estimated, reckoned, held, seeming, apparent, ostensible.

request v.
☞ 请求, 要求 ask for, solicit, demand, require, seek, desire, beg, entreat, supplicate, petition, appeal.
n.
☞ 请求, 要求 appeal, call, demand, requisition, desire, application, solicitation, suit, petition, entreaty, supplication, prayer.

require v.
☞ need, want, wish, desire, lack, miss.
☞ 命令, 要求 oblige, force, compel, constrain, make, ask, request, instruct, direct, order, demand, necessitate, take, involve.

requirement n.
☞ 需要, 必须 need, necessity, essential, must, requisite, prerequisite, demand, stipulation, condition, term, specification, proviso, qualification, provision.

requisite *adj.*
☞ 需要的, 必要的 required, needed, necessary, essential, obligatory, compulsory, set,

prescribed.

requisition v.
☞ 需要,要求 request, put in for, demand, commandeer, appropriate, take, confiscate, seize, occupy.

rescue v.
☞ 拯救,救援 save, recover, salvage, deliver, free, liberate, release, redeem, ransom.
n.
☞ 营救 saving, recovery, salvage, deliverance, liberation, release, redemption, salvation.

research n.
☞ 调查,研究 investigation, inquiry, fact-finding, groundwork, examination, analysis, scrutiny, study, search, probe, exploration, experimentation.
v.
☞ 调查,分析 investigate, examine, analyze, scrutinize, study, search, probe, explore, experiment.

resemblance n.
☞ 相似,近似 likeness, similarity, sameness, parity, conformity, closeness, affinity, parallel, comparison, analogy, correspondence, image, facsimile.

resemble v.
☞ 相似 be like, look like, take after, favour, mirror, echo, duplicate, parallel, approach.

resent v.
☞ 愤恨,怨恨 grudge, begrudge, envy, take offence at, take umbrage at, take amiss, object to, grumble at, take exception to, dislike.

resentful adj.
☞ 愤恨的 grudging, envious, jealous, bitter, embittered, hurt, wounded, offended, aggrieved, put out, miffed, peeved, indignant, angry, vindictive.

resentment n.
☞ 愤怒 grudge, envy, jealousy, bitterness, spite, malice, ill-will, ill-feeling, animosity, hurt, umbrage, pique, displeasure, irritation, indignation, vexation, anger, vindictiveness.

reservation n.
☞ 保留 doubt, scepticism, misgiving, qualm, scruple, hesitation, second thought.
☞ 限制 proviso, stipulation, qualification.
☞ 保护区 reserve, preserve, park, sanctuary, homeland, enclave.
☞ 预定 booking, engagement, appointment.

reserve v.
☞ 储备 set apart, earmark, keep, retain, hold back, save, store, stockpile.
☞ 预定 book, engage, order, secure.
n.
☞ 储备 store, stock, supply, fund, stockpile, cache, hoard, saving.
☞ 矜持 shyness, reticence, secretiveness, coolness, aloofness, modesty, restraint.
☞ 保留地 reservation, preserve,

park, sanctuary.
☞ 备用品 replacement, substitute, stand-in.

reserved adj.
☞ 预定的 booked, engaged, taken, spoken, for, set aside, earmarked, meant, intended, designated, destined, saved, held, kept, retained.
☞ 矜持的 shy, retiring, uncommunicative, secretive, silent, taciturn, unsociable, cool, aloof, standoffish, unapproachable, modest, restrained, cautious.

reside v.
☞ 居住 live, inhabit, dwell, lodge, stay, sojourn, settle, remain.

residence n.
☞ 居住地 dwelling, habitation, domicile, abode, seat, place, home, house, lodgings, quarters, hall, manor, mansion, palace, villa, country-house, country-seat.

resident n.
☞ 居民 inhabitant, citizen, local, householder, occupier, tenant, lodger, guest.

residual adj.
☞ 剩下的 remaining, leftover, unused, unconsumed, net.

resign v.
☞ 辞去 stand down, leave, quit, abdicate, vacate, renounce, relinquish, forgo, waive, surrender, yield, abandon, forsake.

resign oneself v.
☞ 听从 reconcile oneself, accept, bow, submit, yield, comply, acquiesce.

resignation n.
☞ 辞职 standing-down, abdication, retirement, departure, notice, renunciation, relinquishment, surrender.
☞ 顺从 acceptance, acquiescence, submission, nonresistance, passivity, patience, stoicism, defeatism.

resigned adj.
☞ 顺从的 reconciled, philosophical, stoical, patient, unprotesting, unresisting, submissive, defeatist.

resist v.
☞ 抵抗 oppose, defy, confront, fight, combat, weather, withstand, repel, counteract, check, avoid, refuse.

resistant adj.
☞ 抵抗的 opposed, antagonistic, defiant, unyielding, intransigent, unwilling.
☞ 坚强的 proof, impervious, immune, invulnerable, tough, strong.

resolute adj.
☞ 决心的 determined, resolved, set, fixed, unwavering, staunch, firm, steadfast, relentless, single-minded, persevering, dogged, tenacious, stubborn, obstinate, strong-willed, undaunted, unflinching, bold.

resolution n.
☞ 决心 determination, resolve, willpower, commitment, dedication, devotion, firmness,

steadfastness, persistence, perseverance, doggedness, tenacity, zeal, courage, boldness.
☞ 决定 decision, judgement, finding, declaration, proposition, motion.

resolve v.
☞ 决心 decide, make up one's mind, determine, fix, settle, conclude, sort out, work out, solve.

resort v.
☞ 常去 go, visit, frequent, patronize, haunt.

resort to
☞ 求助 turn to, use, utilize, employ, exercise.

resource n.
☞ 依靠之物 supply, reserve, stockpile, source, expedient, contrivance, device.
☞ 机智 resourcefulness, initiative, ingenuity, talent, ability, capability.

resourceful adj.
☞ 机智的 ingenious, imaginative, creative, inventive, innovative, original, clever, bright, sharp, quick-witted, able, capable, talented.

resources n.
☞ 资源 materials, supplies, reserves, holdings, funds, money, wealth, riches, capital, assets, property, means.

respect n.
☞ 尊敬,尊重 admiration, esteem, appreciation, recognition, honour, deference, reverence, veneration, politeness, courtesy.
☞ 方面 point, aspect, facet, feature, characteristic, particular, detail, sense, way, regard, reference, relation, connection.

v.
☞ 尊重,重视 admire, esteem, regard, appreciate, value.
☞ 服从,敬意 obey, observe, heed, follow, honour, fulfil.

respectable adj.
☞ 可尊重的 honourable, worthy, respected, dignified, upright, honest, decent, clean-living.
☞ 可接受的 acceptable, tolerable, passable, adequate, fair, reasonable, appreciable, considerable.

respectful adj.
☞ 尊敬人的 deferential, reverential, humble, polite, well-mannered, courteous, civil.

respective adj.
☞ 各自的 corresponding, relevant, various, several, separate, individual, personal, own, particular, special.

respond v.
☞ 回答 answer, reply, retort, acknowledge, react, return, reciprocate.

response n.
☞ 回答 answer, reply, retort, comeback, acknowledgement, reaction, feedback.

responsibility n.
☞ 责任 fault, blame, guilt, culpability, answerability, accountability, duty, obligation,

burden, onus, charge, care, trust, authority, power.

responsible *adj*.
☞ 有责任的 guilty, culpable, at fault, to blame, liable, answerable, accountable.
☞ 可靠的 dependable, reliable, conscientious, trustworthy, honest, sound, steady, sober, mature, sensible, rational.
☞ 责任重大的 important, authoritative, executive, decision-making.

rest[1] *n*.
☞ 休息 leisure, relaxation, repose, lie-down, sleep, snooze, nap, siesta, idleness, inactivity, motionlessness, standstill, stillness, tranquillity, calm.
☞ 停止 break, pause, breathing-space, breather, intermission, interlude, interval, recess, holiday, vacation, halt, cessation, lull, respite.
☞ 支撑 support, prop, stand, base.
v.
☞ 停止 pause, halt, stop, cease.
☞ 休息 relax, repose, sit, recline, lounge, laze, lie down, sleep, snooze, doze.
☞ 取决于 depend, rely, hinge, hang, lie.
☞ 放, 搁 lean, prop, support, stand.

rest[2] *n*.
☞ 剩余部分 remainder, others, balance, surplus, excess, residue, remains, leftovers, remnants.

restaurant *n*.
☞ 饭馆 eating-house, bistro, steakhouse, grill room, dining-room, snack-bar, buffet, cafeteria, café.

restful *adj*.
☞ 恬静的 relaxing, soothing, calm, tranquil, serene, peaceful, quiet, undisturbed, relaxed, comfortable, leisurely, unhurried.

restless *adj*.
☞ 不安定的 fidgety, unsettled, disturbed, troubled, agitated, nervous, anxious, worried, uneasy, fretful, edgy, jumpy, restive, unruly, turbulent, sleepless.

restore *v*.
☞ 放回 replace, return, reinstate, rehabilitate, re-establish, reintroduce, re-enforce.
☞ 修复, 重建 renovate, renew, rebuild, reconstruct, refurbish, retouch, recondition, repair, mend, fix.
☞ 使……恢复 revive, refresh, rejuvenate, revitalize, strengthen.

restrain *v*.
☞ 抑制, 制止 hold back, keep back, suppress, subdue, repress, inhibit, check, curb, bridle, stop, arrest, prevent, bind, tie, chain, fetter, manacle, imprison, jail, confine, restrict, regulate, control, govern.

restrained *adj*.
☞ 受限制的 moderate,

temperate, mild, subdued, muted, quiet, soft, low-key, unobtrusive, discreet, tasteful, calm, controlled, steady, self-controlled.

restraint n.
☞ 控制,抑制,制止 moderation, inhibition, self-control, self-discipline, hold, grip, check, curb, rein, bridle, suppression, bondage, captivity, confinement, imprisonment, bonds, chains, fetters, straitjacket, restriction, control, constraint, limitation, tie, hindrance, prevention.

restrict v.
☞ 限制,制止 limit, bound, demarcate, control, regulate, confine, contain, cramp, constrain, impede, hinder, hamper, handicap, tie, restrain, curtail.

restriction n.
☞ 限制,约束 limit, bound, confine, limitation, constraint, handicap, check, curb, restraint, ban, embargo, control, regulation, rule, stipulation, condition, proviso.

result n.
☞ 结果,成果 effect, consequence, sequel, repercussion, reaction, outcome, upshot, issue, end-product, fruit, score, answer, verdict, judgement, decision, conclusion.

v.
☞ 产生于,来自 follow, ensue, happen, occur, issue, emerge, arise, spring, derive, stem, flow, proceed, develop, end, finish, terminate, culminate.

resume v.
☞ 重新开始,恢复,继续 restart, recommence, reopen, reconvene, continue, carry on, go on, proceed.

resumption n.
☞ 重新开始,恢复,继续 restart, recommencement, reopening, renewal, resurgence, continuation.

retain v.
☞ 保持,保留 keep, hold, reserve, hold back, save, preserve.
☞ 记得,记忆 remember, memorize.
☞ 雇用,聘请 employ, engage, hire, commission.

retaliate v.
☞ 报复,报仇,反击 reciprocate, counter-attack, hit back, strike back, fight back, get one's own back, get even with, take revenge.

retaliation n.
☞ 报复,报仇,反击 reprisal, counter-attack, revenge, vengeance, retribution.

retire v.
☞ 退下,离开 leave, depart, withdraw, retreat, recede.

retirement n.
☞ 退隐,退休,隐居 withdrawal, retreat, solitude, loneliness, seclusion, privacy, obscurity.

retiring adj.
☞ 有隐居倾向的,孤独缄默的 shy, bashful, timid, shrinking, quiet, reticent, reserved, self-effacing, unassertive, modest,

unassuming, humble.

return v.
☞ 回来 come back, reappear, recur, go back, backtrack, regress, revert.

☞ 归还 give back, hand back, send back, deliver, put back, replace, restore.

☞ 报答 reciprocate, requite, repay, refund, reimburse, recompense.

n.

☞ 回来 reappearance, recurrence, comeback, home-coming.

☞ 放回,归还 repayment, recompense, replacement, restoration, reinstatement reciprocation.

☞ 利润,赢利 revenue, income, proceeds, takings, yield, gain, profit, reward, advantage, benefit.

reveal v.
☞ 揭露,显露,显示,显现 expose, uncover, unveil, unmask, show, display, exhibit, manifest, disclose, divulge, betray, leak, tell, impart, communicate, broadcast, publish, announce, proclaim.

revelation n.
☞ 显示,展示 uncovering, unveiling, exposure, unmasking, show, display, exhibition, manifestation, disclosure, confession, admission, betrayed, giveaway, leak, news, information, communication, broadcasting, publication, announcement, proclamation.

revenge n.

☞ 为(自己)报仇,替(某人)报仇 vengeance, satisfaction, reprisal, retaliation, requital, retribution.

v.

☞ 报仇 avenge, repay, retaliate, get one's own back.

revenue n.
☞ 收入总额 income, return, yield, interest, profit, gain, proceeds, receipts, takings.

reverse v.
☞ 推翻,撤消 back, retreat, backtrack, undo, negate, cancel, annul, invalidate, countermand, overrule, revoke, rescind, repeal, retract, quash, overthrow.

☞ 颠倒 transpose, turn round, invert, up-end, overturn, upset, change, alter.

n.

☞ 背面 underside, back, rear, inverse, converse, contrary, opposite, antithesis.

☞ 逆境 misfortune, mishap, misadventure, adversity, affliction, hardship, trial, blow, disappointment, setback, check, delay, problem, difficulty, failure, defeat.

adj.

☞ 颠倒的,相反的 opposite, contrary, converse, inverse, inverted, backward, back, rear.

revert v.
☞ 回复 return, go back, resume, lapse, relapse, regress.

review v.
☞ 回顾,复习 criticize, assess, evaluate, judge, weigh, discuss, examine, inspect, scrutinize, study, survey, recapitulate.

☞ 检查 reassess, re-evaluate, re-examine, reconsider, rethink, revise.

n.
☞ 评论 criticism, critique, assessment, evaluation, judgement, report, commentary, examination, scrutiny, analysis, study, survey, recapitulation, reassessment, re-evaluation, re-examination, revision.

revise *v.*
☞ 修订 change, alter, modify, amend, correct, update, rewrite, reword, recast, revamp, reconsider, re-examine, review.
☞ 复习 study, learn, swot up, cram.

revival *n.*
☞ 复活 resuscitation, revitalization, restoration, renewal, renaissance, rebirth, reawakening, resurgence, upsurge.

revive *v.*
☞ 苏醒 resuscitate, reanimate, revitalize, restore, renew, refresh, animate, invigorate, quicken, rouse, awaken, recover, rally, reawaken, rekindle, reactivate.

revoke *v.*
☞ 撤销 repeal, rescind, quash, abrogate, annul, nullify, invalidate, negate, cancel, countermand, reverse, retract, withdraw.

revolution *n.*
☞ 剧变,革命 revolt, rebellion, mutiny, rising, uprising, insurrection, coup(d'état), reformation, change, transformation, innovation, upheaval, cataclysm.
☞ 旋转 rotation, turn, spin, cycle, circuit, round, circle, orbit, gyration.

revolutionary *n.*
☞ 革命者 rebel, mutineer, insurgent, anarchist, revolutionist.

adj.
☞ 革命的 rebel, rebellious, mutinous, insurgent, subversive, seditious, anarchistic.
☞ 激进的 new, innovative, avant-garde, different, drastic, radical, thoroughgoing.

revolve *v.*
☞ 旋转 rotate, turn, pivot, swivel, spin, wheel, whirl, gyrate, circle, orbit.

revulsion *n.*
☞ 厌恶 repugnance, disgust, distaste, dislike, aversion, hatred, loathing, abhorrence, abomination.

reward *n.*
☞ 报答,报偿 prize, honour, medal, decoration, bounty, pay-off, bonus, premium, payment, remuneration, recompense, repayment, requital, compensation, gain, profit, return, benefit, merit, desert, retribution.

v.
☞ 报答 pay, remunerate, recompense, repay, requite, compensate, honour, decorate.

rewarding *adj.*

☞值得做的 profitable, remunerative, lucrative, productive, fruitful, worthwhile, valuable, advantageous, beneficial, satisfying, gratifying, pleasing, fulfilling, enriching.

rhetoric n.
☞修辞学,修辞 eloquence, oratory, grandiloquence, magniloquence, bombast, pomposity, hyperbole, verbosity, wordiness.

rhetorical adj.
☞修辞学的 oratorical, grandiloquent, magniloquent, bombastic, declamatory, pompous, high-sounding, grand, high-flown, flowery, florid, flamboyant, showy, pretentious, artificial, insincere.

rhyme n.
☞韵,脚韵 poetry, verse, poem, ode, limerick, jingle, song, ditty.

rhythm n.
☞韵律,格律 beat, pulse, time, tempo, metre, measure, movement, flow, lilt, swing, accent, cadence, pattern.

rhythmic adj.
☞韵律的,格律的 rhythmical, metric, metrical, pulsating, throbbing, flowing, lilting, periodic, regular, steady.

rich adj.
☞富的,有钱的 wealthy, affluent, moneyed, prosperous, well-to-do, well-off, loaded.
☞丰富的 plentiful, abundant, copious, profuse, prolific, ample, full.
☞富饶的,丰富的 fertile, fruitful, productive, lush.
☞味浓的 creamy, fatty, full-bodied, heavy, full-flavoured, strong, spicy, savoury, tasty, delicious, luscious, juicy, sweet.
☞生动鲜艳的 deep, intense, vivid, bright, vibrant, warm.
☞昂贵的 expensive, precious, valuable, lavish, sumptuous, opulent, luxurious, splendid, gorgeous, fine, elaborate, ornate.

riddle¹ n.
☞谜 enigma, mystery, conundrum, brain-teaser, puzzle, poser, problem.

riddle² v.
☞打满孔 perforate, pierce, puncture, pepper, fill, permeate, pervade, infest.

ride v.
☞骑 sit, move, progress, travel, journey, gallop, trot, pedal, drive, steer, control, handle, manage.
n.
☞乘车或骑马旅行 journey, trip, outing, jaunt, spin, drive, lift.

ridicule n.
☞讥笑,嘲弄 satire, irony, sarcasm, mockery, jeering, scorn, derision, taunting, teasing, chaff, banter, badinage, laughter.

ridiculous adj.
☞荒谬的,可笑的 ludicrous,

absurd, nonsensical, silly, foolish, stupid, contemptible, derisory, laughable, farcical, comical, funny, hilarious, outrageous, preposterous, incredible, unbelievable.

right adj.
- ☞正确的 correct, accurate, exact, precise, true, factual, actual, real.
- ☞合适的 proper, fitting, seemly, becoming, appropriate, suitable, fit, admissible, satisfactory, reasonable, desirable, favourable, advantageous.
- ☞公正的 fair, just, equitable, lawful, honest, upright, good, virtuous, righteous, moral, ethical, honourable.
- ☞右的 right-wing, conservative, Tory.

right away
- ☞马上 straight away, immediately, at once, now, instantly, directly, forthwith, without delay, promptly.

rightful adj.
- ☞正统的,合法的 legitimate, lawful, legal, just, bona fide, true, real, genuine, valid, authorized, correct, proper, suitable, due.

rigid adj.
- ☞僵硬的 stiff, inflexible, unbending, cast-iron, hard, firm, set, fixed, unalterable, invariable, austere, harsh, severe, unrelenting, strict, rigorous, stringent, stern, uncompromising, unyielding.

rigorous adj.
- ☞严峻的,严厉的 strict, stringent, rigid, firm, exact, precise, accurate, meticulous, painstaking, scrupulous, conscientious, thorough.

rim n.
- ☞边 lip, edge, brim, brink, verge, margin, border, circumference.

ring¹ n.
- ☞环状物 circle, round, loop, hoop, halo, band, girdle, collar, circuit, arena, enclosure.
- ☞一伙 group, cartel, syndicate, association, organization, gang, crew, mob, band, cell, clique, coterie.

v.
- ☞围住 surround, encircle, gird, circumscribe, encompass, enclose.

ring² v.
- ☞铃响 chime, peal, toll, tinkle, clink, jingle, clang, sound, resound, resonate, reverberate, buzz.
- ☞打电话 telephone, phone, call, ring up.

n.
- ☞铃声 chime, peal, toll, tinkle, clink, jingle, clang.
- ☞打电话 phone call, call, buzz, tinkle.

riot n.
- ☞骚乱 insurrection, rising, uprising, revolt, rebellion, anarchy, lawlessness, affray, disturbance, turbulence, disorder, confusion, commotion, tumult, turmoil, uproar, row, quarrel, strife.

rip v.
☞ 撕裂 tear, rend, split, separate, rupture, burst, cut, slit, slash, gash, lacerate, hack.

n.

☞ 撕 tear, rent, split, cleavage, rupture, cut, slit, slash, gash, hole.

rip off
☞ 偷窃,骗钱 overcharge, swindle, defraud, cheat, diddle, do, fleece, sting, con, trick, dupe, exploit.

ripe adj.
☞ 成熟的 ripened, mature, mellow, seasoned, grown, developed, complete, finished, perfect.

☞ 合适的 ready, suitable, right, favourable, auspicious, propitious, timely, opportune.

ripen v.
☞ 使成熟 develop, mature, mellow, season, age.

rise v.
☞ 上升 go up, ascend, climb, mount, slope(up), soar, tower, grow, increase, escalate, intensify.

☞ 站立 stand up, get up, arise, jump up, spring up.

☞ 上涨,增强 advance, progress, improve, prosper.

☞ 出现 originate, spring, flow, issue, emerge, appear.

risk n.
☞ 冒险 danger, peril, jeopardy, hazard, chance, possibility, uncertainty, gamble, speculation, venture, adventure.

risky adj.
☞ 冒险的 dangerous, unsafe, perilous, hazardous, chancy, uncertain, touch-and-go, dicey, tricky, precarious.

ritual n.
☞ 礼仪 custom, tradition, convention, usage, practice, habit, wont, procedure, ordinance, prescription, form, formality, ceremony, ceremonial, solemnity, rite, sacrament, service, liturgy, observance, act.

adj.

☞ 仪式的 customary, traditional, conventional, habitual, routine, procedural, prescribed, set, formal, ceremonial.

rival n.
☞ 竞争者,对手 competitor, contestant, contender, challenger, opponent, adversary, antagonist, match, equal, peer.

rivalry n.
☞ 竞赛 competitiveness, competition, contest, contention, conflict, struggle, strife, opposition, antagonism.

river n.
☞ 河 waterway, watercourse, tributary, stream, brook, beck, creek, estuary.

road n.
☞ 路 roadway, motorway, bypass, highway, thoroughfare, street, avenue, boulevard, crescent, drive, lane, track,

route, course, way, direction.

roar v., n.
- 吼 bellow, yell, shout, cry, bawl, howl, hoot, guffaw, thunder, crash, blare, rumble.

rob v.
- 抢劫 steal from, hold up, raid, burgle, loot, pillage, plunder, sack, rifle, ransack, swindle, rip of, do, cheat, defraud, deprive.

robbery n.
- 抢劫 theft, stealing, larceny, hold-up, stick-up, heist, raid, burglary, pillage, plunder, fraud, embezzlement, swindle, rip-off.

robot n.
- 机器人 automaton, machine, android zmobie.

robust adj.
- 健壮的 strong, sturdy, tough, hardy, vigorous, powerful, muscular, athletic, fit, healthy, well.

rock^1 n.
- 石头 boulder, stone, pebble, crag, outcrop.

rock^2 v.
- 摇滚 sway, swing, tilt, tip, shake, wobble, roll, pitch, toss, lurch, reel, stagger, totter.
- 震惊 shock, stun, daze, dumbfound, astound, astonish, surprise, startle.

rocky^1 adj.
- 多石的 stony, pebbly, craggy, rugged, rough, hard, flinty.

rocky^2 adj.
- 不平衡的 unsteady, shaky, wobbly, staggering, tottering, unstable, unreliable, uncertain, weak.

rod n.
- 杆,竿 bar, shaft, strut, pole, stick, baton, wand, cane, switch, staff, mace, sceptre.

role n.
- 作用,角色 part, character, representation, portrayal, impersonation, function, capacity, task, duty, job, post, position.

roll v.
- 滚动 rotate, revolve, turn, spin, wheel, twirl, whirl, gyrate, move, run, pass.
- 摇摆 wind, coil, furl, twist, curl, wrap, envelop, enfold, bind.
- 翻 rock, sway, swing, pitch, toss, lurch, reel, wallow, undulate.
- 压平 press, flatten, smooth, level.
- 轰鸣 rumble, roar, thunder, boom, resound, reverberate.

n.
- 滚筒 roller, cylinder, drum, reel, spool, bobbin, scroll.
- 记录 register, roster, census, list, inventory, index, catalogue, directory, schedule, record, chronicle, annals.
- 转动 rotation, revolution, cycle, turn, spin, wheel, twirl, whirl, gyration, undulation.
- 轰鸣 rumble, roar, thunder, boom, resonance, reverberation.

roll up
- 集中 arrive, assemble,

romance n.
- 罗曼史 love affair, affair, relationship, liaison, intrigue, passion.
- 爱情小说 love story, novel, story, tale, fairytale, legend, idyll, fiction, fantasy.
- 浪漫 adventure, excitement, melodrama, mystery, charm, fascination, glamour, sentiment.
- 讲虚构的故事 lie, fantasize, exaggerate, overstate.

romantic adj.
- 虚构的 imaginary, fictitious, fanciful, fantastic, legendary, fairy-tale, idyllic, utopian, idealistic, quixotic, visionary, starry-eyed, dreamy, unrealistic, impractical, improbable, wild, extravagant, exciting, fascinating.
- 浪漫的 sentimental, loving, amorous, passionate, tender, fond, lovey-dovey, soppy, mushy, sloppy.

root^1 n.
- 根 tuber, rhizome, stem.
- 根源 origin, source, derivation, cause, starting point, fount, fountainhead, seed, germ, nucleus, heart, core, nub, essence, seat, base, bottom, basis, foundation.

v.
- 扎根 anchor, moor, fasten, fix, set, stick, implant, embed, entrench, establish, ground, base.

root out
- 根除 unearth, dig out, uncover, discover, uproot, eradicate, extirpate, eliminate, exterminate, destroy, abolish, clear away, remove.

root^2 v.
- 寻找 dig, delve, burrow, forage, hunt, rummage, ferret, poke, pry, nose.

roots n.
- 根源 beginning(s), origins, family, heritage, background, birthplace, home.

rope n.
- 绳子 line, cable, cord, string, strand.

v.
- 绑 tie, bind, lash, fasten, hitch, moor, tether.

rope in
- 圈起，包括 enlist, engage, involve, persuade, inveigle.

roster n.
- 花名册 rota, schedule, register, roll, list.

rot v.
- 腐朽 decay, decompose, putrefy, fester, perish, corrode, spoil, go bad, go off, degenerate, deteriorate, crumble, disintegrate, taint, corrupt.

n.
- 腐朽 decay, decomposition, putrefaction, corrosion, rust, mould.
- 胡说 nonsense, rubbish, poppycock, drivel, claptrap.

rotten adj.
- 腐烂的 decayed, decomposed, putrid, addled, bad, off, mouldy, fetid, stinking, rank,

foul, rotting, decaying, disintegrating.
☞ 低贱的 inferior, bad, poor, inadequate, low-grade, lousy, crummy, ropy, mean, nasty, beastly, dirty, despicable, contemptible, dishonourable, wicked.
☞ 糟糕的 ill, sick, unwell, poorly, grotty, rough.

rough *adj.*
☞ 粗糙的 uneven, bumpy, lumpy, rugged, craggy, jagged, irregular, coarse, bristly, scratchy.
☞ 强横的 harsh, severe, tough, hard, cruel, brutal, drastic, extreme, brusque, curt, sharp.
☞ 大概的 approximate, estimated, imprecise, inexact, vague, general, cursory, hasty, incomplete, unfinished, crude, rudimentary.
☞ 汹涌的 choppy, agitated, turbulent, stormy, tempestuous, violent, wild.

round *adj.*
☞ 圆形的 spherical, globular, ball-shaped, circular, ring-shaped, cylindrical, rounded, curved.
☞ 圆胖的 rotund, plump, stout, portly.
n.
☞ 圆型 circle, ring, band, disc, sphere, ball, orb.
☞ 回合 cycle, series, sequence, succession, period, bout, session.
☞ 一圈 beat, circuit, lap, course, routine.
v.
☞ 绕行 circle, skirt, flank, bypass.

round off
☞ 完成 finish (off), complete, end, close, conclude, cap, crown.

round on
☞ 攻击 turn on, attack, lay into, abuse.

round up
☞ 收集 herd, marshal, assemble, gather, rally, collect, group.

roundabout *adj.*
☞ 迂回的 circuitous, tortuous, twisting, winding, indirect, oblique, devious, evasive.

rouse *v.*
☞ 唤醒 wake(up), awaken, arouse, call, stir, move, start, disturb, agitate, anger, provoke, stimulate, instigate, incite, inflame, excite, galvanize, whip up.

rout *n.*
☞ 溃败 defeat, conquest, overthrow, beating, thrashing, flight, stampede.

route *n.*
☞ 路线 course, run, path, road, avenue, way, direction, itinerary, journey, passage, circuit, round, beat.

routine *n.*
☞ 常规 procedure, way, method, system, order, pattern, formula, practice, usage, custom, habit.
adj.
☞ 例行的 customary, habitual, usual, typical, ordinary, run-of-the-mill, normal,

row¹ n.
☞ 排,行 line, tier, bank, rank, range, column, file, queue, string, series, sequence.

row² n.
☞ 吵 argument, quarrel, dispute, controversy, squabble, tiff, slanging match, fight, brawl.
☞ 喧闹 noise, racket, din, uproar, commotion, disturbance, rumpus, fracas.
v.
☞ 争吵 argue, quarrel, wrangle, bicker, squabble, fight, scrap.

royal adj.
☞ 王室的,皇家的 regal, majestic, kingly, queenly, princely, imperial, monarchical, sovereign, august, grand, stately, magnificent, splendid, superb.

rub v.
☞ 搓,擦 apply, spread, smear, stroke, caress, massage, knead, chafe, grate, scrape, abrade, scour, scrub, clean, wipe, smooth, polish, buff, shine.

rubbish n.
☞ 废物,垃圾 refuse, garbage, trash, junk, litter, waste, dross, debris, flotsam and jetsam.
☞ 胡说 nonsense, drivel, claptrap, twaddle, gibberish, gobbledggook, balderdash, poppycock, rot.

rude adj.
☞ 粗鲁的 impolite, discourteous, disrespectful, impertinent, impudent, cheeky, insolent, offensive, insulting, abusive, ill-mannered, ill-bred, uncouth, uncivilized, unrefined, unpolished, uneducated, untutored, uncivil, curt, brusque, abrupt, sharp, short.
☞ 下流的 obscene, vulgar, coarse, dirty, naughty, gross.

rugged adj.
☞ 崎岖的 rough, bumpy, uneven, irregular, jagged, rocky, craggy, stark.
☞ 强壮的,粗鲁的 strong, robust, hardy, tough, muscular, weather-beaten.

ruin n.
☞ 毁灭 destruction, devastation, wreckage, havoc, damage, discrepair, decay, disintegration, breakdown, collapse, fall, downfall, failure, defeat, overthrow, ruination, undoing, insolvency, bankruptcy, crash.

rule n.
☞ 规则 regulation, law, statute, ordinance, decree, order, direction, guide, precept, tenet, canon, principle, formula, guideline, standard, criterion.
☞ 统治 reign, sovereignty, supremacy, dominion, mastery, power, authority, command, control, influence, regime, government, leadership.
☞ 惯例 custom, convention,

practice, routine, habit, wont.
v.
- 统治 reign, govern, command, lead, administer, manage, direct, guide, control, regulate, prevail, dominate.
- 裁决 judge, adjudicate, decide, find, determine, resolve, establish, decree, pronounce.

rule out
- 排除 exclude, eliminate, reject, dismiss, preclude, prevent, ban, prohibit, forbid, disallow.

ruling *n.*
- 裁决 judgement, adjudication, verdict, decision, finding, resolution, decree, pronouncement.

adj.
- 统治的,优势的 reigning, sovereign, supreme, governing, commanding, leading, main, chief, principal, dominant, predominant, controlling.

rumour *n.*
- 谣言 hearsay, gossip, talk, whisper, word, news, report, story, grapevine, bush telegraph

run *v.*
- 跑 sprint, jog, race, career, tear, dash, hurry, rush, speed, bolt, dart, scoot, scuttle.
- 走 go, pass, move, proceed, issue.
- 运作 function, work, operate, perform.
- 经营 head, lead, administer, direct, manage, superintend, supervise, oversee, control, regulate.
- 竞争 compete, contend, stand, challenge.
- 持续 last, continue, extend, reach, stretch, spread, range.
- 流 flow, stream, pour, gush.

n.
- 冲 jog, gallop, race, sprint, spurt, dash, rush.
- 行驶 drive, ride, spin, jaunt, excursion, outing, trip, journey.
- 连续上演 sequence, series, string, chain, course.

run after
- 追随 chase, pursue, follow, tail.

run away
- 逃跑 escape, flee, abscond, bolt, beat it, run off, make off, clear off.

run down
- 诋毁 criticize, belittle, disparage, denigrate, defame.
- 撞倒 run over, knock over, hit, strike.
- 变弱,耗尽 tire, weary, exhaust, weaken.
- 减少,减弱 reduce, decrease, drop, cut, trim, curtail.

run into
- 遇见,碰倒 meet, encounter, run across, bump into, hit, strike, collide with.

run out
- 消退,用尽,到期 expire, terminate, end, cease, close, finish, dry up, fail.

runaway *n.*
- 逃亡者 escaper, escapee, fugitive, absconder, deserter, refugee.

adj.
- 逃跑的,控制不住的 escaped, fugitive, loose, uncontrolled.

rundown *n.*
- 变弱,裁减 reduction, decrease, decline, drop, cut.
- 概要,总结 summary, résumé, synopsis, outline, review, recap, run-through.

runner *n.*
- 赛跑者 jogger, sprinter, athlete, competitor, participant, courier, messenger.

running *adj.*
- 连续的,不间断的 successive, consecutive, unbroken, uninterrupted, continuous, constant, perpetual, incessant, unceasing, moving, flowing.

rural *adj.*
- 农村的,田园的 country, rustic, pastoral, agricultural, agrarian.

rush *v.*
- 冲,奔,急进 hurry, hasten, quicken, accelerate, speed(up), press, push, dispatch, bolt, dart, shoot, fly, tear, career, dash, race, run, sprint, scramble, stampede, charge.

n.
- 冲,奔 hurry, haste, urgency, speed, swiftness, dash, race, scramble, stampede, charge, flow, surge.

rust *n.*
- 锈 corrosion, oxidation.

v.
- 生锈 corrode, decay, rot, oxidize, tarnish, deteriorate, decline.

rustic *adj.*
- 乡村的,粗俗的 pastoral, sylvan, bucolic, countrified, country, rural.
- 纯朴的,粗野的 plain, simple, rough, crude, coarse, rude, clumsy, awkward, artless, unsophisticated, unrefined, uncultured, provincial, uncouth, boorish, oafish.

rusty *adj.*
- 生锈的 corroded, rusted, rust-covered, oxidized, tarnished, discoloured, dull.
- 过时的,破旧的 unpractised, weak, poor, deficient, dated, old-fashioned, outmoded, antiquated, stale, stiff, creaking.

ruthless *adj.*
- 无情的,冷酷的 merciless, pitiless, hard-hearted, hard, heartless, unfeeling, callous, cruel, inhuman, brutal, savage, cur-throat, fierce, ferocious, relentless, unrelenting, inexorable, implacable, harsh, severe.

S

sacred *adj.*
- 神的,神圣的,宗教的 holy, divine, heavenly, blessed,

hallowed, sanctified, consecrated, dedicated, religious, devotional, ecclestical, priestly, saintly, godly, venerable, revered, sacrosanct, inviolable.

sacrifice v.
☞ 供奉,牺牲 surrender, forfeit, relinquish, let go, abandon, renounce, give up, forgo, offer, slaughter.
n.
☞ 献祭,牺牲 offering, immolation, slaughter, destruction, surrender, renunciation, loss.

sad adj.
☞ 悲哀的,忧愁的 unhappy, sorrowful, tearful, grief-stricken, heavy-hearted, upset, distressed, miserable, low-spirited, downcast, glum, long-faced, crestfallen, dejected, down-hearted, despondent, melancholy, depressed, low, gloomy, dismal.
☞ 使人悲哀的,悲惨的,灾难性的 upsetting, distressing, painful, depressing, touching, poignant, heart-rending, tragic, grievous, lamentable, regrettable, , sorry, unfortunate, serious, grave, disastrous.

sadden v.
☞ (使)悲哀,(使)忧愁 upset, distress, grieve, depress, dismay, discourage, dishearten.

saddle v.
☞ 加负担于……,使……负责 burden, encumber, lumber, impose, tax, charge, load.

safe adj.
☞ 安全的,无害的 harmless, innocuous, non-toxic, non-poisonous, uncontaminated.
☞ 未受伤害的,无危险的 unharmed, undamaged, unscathed, uninjured, unhurt, intact, secure, protected, guarded, impregnable, invulnerable, immune.
☞ 谨慎的,小心的 unadventurous, cautious, prudent, conservative, sure, proven, tried, tested, sound, dependable, reliable, trustworthy.

safeguard v.
☞ 保护,防卫 protect, preserve, defend, guard, shied, screen, shelter, secure.
n.
☞ 安全措施,保护 protection, defence, shield, security, surety, guarantee, assurance, insurance, cover, precaution.

safe-keeping n.
☞ 保护,保管 protection, care, custody, keeping, charge, trust, guardianship, surveillance, supervision.

safety n.
☞ 安全,平安 protection, refuge, sanctuary, shelter, cover, security, safeguard, immunity, impregnablity, safeness, harmlessness, reliability, dependability.

sail v.
☞ 驾驶,掌舵 captain, skipper, pilot, navigate, steer.
☞ 掠过,滑过 glide, plane, sweep, float, skim, scud, fly.

☞航向 embark, set sail, weigh anchor, put to sea, cruise, voyage.

sailor n.
☞船员,水手 seafarer, mariner, seaman, marine, rating, yachtsman, yachtswoman.

saintly adj.
☞神圣的,崇高的 godly, pious, devout, god-fearing, holy, religious, blessed, angelic, pure, spotless, innocent, blameless, sinless, virtuous, upright, worthy, righteous.

sake n.
☞利益,缘故 benefit, advantage, good, welfare, wellbeing, gain, profit, behalf, interest, account, regard, respect, cause, reason.

salary n.
☞薪水,工资 pay, remuneration, emolument, stipend, wages, earnings, income.

sale n.
☞出售,出卖 selling, marketing, vending, disposal, trade, traffic, transaction, deal, auction.

salesperson n.
☞售货员,销售员 salesman, saleswoman, sales assistant, shop assistant, shop-boy, shop-girl, shopkeeper, representaive, rep.

salt n.
☞风味,调味品,盐 seasoning, taste, flavour, savour, relish, piquancy.

salty adj.
☞咸的,含盐的 salt, salted, saline, briny, brackish, savoury, spicy, piquant, tangy.

salutary adj.
☞有益的,有好处的 good, beneficial, advantageous, profitable, valuable, helpful, useful, practical, timely.

salute v.
☞欢迎,致敬 greet, acknowledge, recognize, wave, hail, address, nod, bow, honour.
n.
☞问候,敬礼 greeting, acknowledgement, recognition, wave, gesture, hail, address, handshake, nod, bow, tribute, reverence.

salvage v.
☞抢救,增援 save, preserve, conserve, rescue, recover, recuperate, retrieve, reclaim, redeem, repair, restore.

salvation n.
☞拯救,救助 deliverance, liberation, rescue, saving, preservation, redemption, reclamation.

same adj.
☞同样的,相同的 identical, twin, duplicate, indistinguishable, equal, selfsame, very, alike, like, similar, comparable, equivalent, matching, corresponding, mutual, reciprocal, interchangeable, substitutable, synonymous, consistent, uniform, unvarying, changeless, unchanged.

sample n.
☞ 样本,样品 specimen, example, cross-section, model, pattern, swatch, piece, demonstration, illustration, instance, sign, indication, foretaste.
v.
☞ 试用,抽样 try, test, taste, sip, inspect, experience.

sanction n.
☞ 批准,许可 authorization, permission, agreement, ok, approval, to-ahead, ratification, confirmation, support, backing, endorsement, licence, authority.
v.
☞ 批准,认可 authorize, allow, permit, approve, ratify, confirm, support, back, endorse, underwrite, accredit, license, warrant.

sanctions n.
☞ 处罚,制裁 restrictions, boycott, embargo, ban, prohibition, penalty.

sand n.
☞ 沙地,海滩 beach, shore, strand, sands, grit.

sane adj.
☞ 明智的,稳健的 normal, rational, right-minded, all there, balanced, stable, sound, sober, level-headed, sensible, judicious, reasonable, moderate.

sanitary adj.
☞ 卫生的,清洁的 clean, pure, uncontaminated, unpolluted, aseptic, germ-free, disinfected, hygienic, salubrious, healthy, wholesome.

sanity n.
☞ 健全,头脑清醒 normality, rationality, reason, sense, common sense, balance of mind, stability, soundness, level-headedness, judiciousness.

sarcasm n.
☞ 讽刺,讥讽 irony, satire, mockery, sneering, derision, scorn, contempt, cynicism, bitterness.

sarcastic adj.
☞ 讽刺的,嘲弄的 ironical, satirical, mocking, taunting, sneering, derisive, scathing, disparaging, cynical, incisive, cutting, biting, caustic.

satire n.
☞ 讽刺 ridicule, irony, sarcasm, wit, burlesque, skit, send-up, spoof, take-off, parody, caricature, travesty.

satirical adj.
☞ 含有讽刺的,嘲弄的 ironical, sarcastic, mocking, irreverent, taunting, derisive, sardonic, incisive, cutting, biting, caustic, cynical, bitter.

satisfaction n.
☞ 满意,满足 gratification, contentment, happiness, pleasure, enjoyment, comfort, ease, well-being, fulfilment, self-satisfaction, pride.
☞ 报复,补偿 settlement, compensation, reimbursement, indemnification, damages, reparation, amends, redress, recompense, requital, vindication.

satisfactory adj.

satisty v.
☞ 令人满意的,圆满的 acceptable, passable, up to the mark, all right, ok, fair, average, competent, adequate, sufficient, suitable, proper.

satisty v.
☞ 使……满意,使满足 gratify, indulge, content, please, delight, quench, slake, sate, satiate, surfeit.
☞ 足够,达到 meet, fulfil, discharge, settle, answer, fill, suffice, serve, qualify.
☞ 使确信,使消除疑惑 assure, convince, persuade.

savage adj.
☞ 野蛮的,未开化的 wild, untamed, undomesticated, uncivilized, primitive, barbaric, barbarous, fierce, ferocious, vicious, beastly, cruel, inhuman, brutal, sadistic, bloodthirsty, bloody, murderous, pitiless, merciless, ruthless, harsh.

n.
☞ 野蛮人,野人 brute, beast, barbarian.

v.
☞ 袭击,乱咬 attack, bite, claw, tear, maul, mangle.

save v.
☞ 储存,节约 economize, cut back, conserve, preserve, keep, retain, hold, reserve, store, lay up, set aside, put by, hoard, stash, collect, gather.
☞ 拯救,援救 rescue, deliver, liberate, free, salvage, recover, reclaim.
☞ 保全 protect, guard, screen, shield, safeguard, spare, prevent, hinder.

savings n.
☞ 储金,储蓄 capital, investments, nest egg, fund, store, reserves, resources.

savour n.
☞ 味道,风味 taste, flavour, smack, smell, tang, piquancy, salt, spice, relish, zest.

v.
☞ 意味,有……味道 relish, enjoy, delight in, revel in, like, appreciate.

savoury adj.
☞ 香喷喷的,可口的 tasty, appetizing, delicious, mouthwatering, luscious, palatable.
☞ 咸的,辛辣的 salty, spicy, aromatic, piquant, tangy.

say v.
☞ 说,讲 express, phrase, put, render, utter, voice, articulate, enunciate, pronounce, deliver, speak, orate, recite, repeat, read, indicate.
☞ 回答,答复 answer, reply, respond, rejoin, retort, exclaim, ejaculate, comment, remark, observe, mention, add, drawl, mutter, grunt.
☞ 告诉,宣布 tell, instruct, order, communicate, convey, intimate, report, announce, declare, state, assert, affirm, maintain, claim, allege, rumour, suggest, imply, signify, reveal, disclose, divulge.
☞ 假定,估计 guess, estimate, reckon, judge, imagine, suppose, assume, presume,

surmise.

saying n.
- 谚语,格言 adage, proverb, dictum, precept, axiom, aphorism, maxim, motto, slogan, phrase, expression, quotation, statement, remark.

scale¹ n.
- 比例,阶段,规模 ratio, proportion, measure, degree, extent, spread, reach, range, scope, compass, spectrum, gamut, sequence, series, progression, order, hierarchy, ranking, ladder, steps, gradation, graduation, calibration, register.

v.
- 攀登,到达……顶点 climb, ascend, mount, clamber, scramble, shin up, conquer, surmount.

scale² n.
- 鳞状物,鳞 encrustation, deposit, crust, layer, film, lamina, plate, flake, scurf.

scan v.
- 审视,细察 examine, scrutinize, study, search, survey, sweep, investigate, check.
- 扫视,略看 skim, glance at, flick through, thumb through.

scandal n.
- 公愤,可耻的行为 outrage, offence, outcry, uproar, rurore, gossip, rumours, smear, dirt, discredit, dishonour, disgrace, shame, embarrassment, ignominy.

scandalous adj.
- 可耻的,令人震惊的 shocking, appalling, atrocious, abominable, monstrous, unspeakable, outrageous, disgraceful, shameful, disreputable, infamous, improper, unseemly, defamatory, scurrilous, slanderous, libellous, untrue.

scar n.
- 疤,伤痕 mark, lesion, wound, injury, blemish, stigma.

v.
- 留下疤痕 mark, disfigure, spoil, damage, brand, stigmatize.

scarce adj.
- 不定的,缺乏的 few, rare, infrequent, uncommon, unusual, sparse, scanty, insufficient, deficient, lacking.

scarcely adv.
- 刚刚,仅仅 hardly, barely, only just.

scarcity n.
- 不足,缺乏 lack, shortage, dearth, deficiency, insufficiency, paucity, rareness, rarity, infrequency, uncommonness, sparseness, scantiness.

scare v.
- 惊吓,使……惊惧 frighten, startle, alarm, dismay, daunt, intimidate, unnerve, threaten, menace, terrorize, shock, appal, panic, terrify.

n.
- 惊恐,惊吓 fright, start, shock, alarm, panic, hysteria, terror.

scared adj.
☞ 惊恐的, 惊吓的 frightened, fearful, nervous, anxious, worried, startled, shaken, panic-stricken, terrified.

scary adj.
☞ 令人惊慌的, 可怕的 frightening, alarming, daunting, intimidating, disturbing, shocking, horrifying, terrifying, hair-raising, bloodcurdling, spine-chilling, chilling, creepy, eerie, spooky.

scatter v.
☞ 分散, 传播 disperse, dispel, dissipate, disband, disunite, separate, divide, break up, disintegrate, diffuse, broadcast, disseminate, spread, sprinkle, sow, strew, fling, shower.

scattering n.
☞ 少量的, 少数的 sprinkling, few, handful, smattering.

scene n.
☞ 地点, 场景 place, area, spot, locale, site, situation, position, whereabouts, location, locality, environment, milieu, setting, contact, background, backdrop, set, stage.
☞ 风景, 景象 landscape, panorama, view, vista, prospect, sight, spectacle, picture, tableau, pageant.
☞ 实况, 一幕, 一场 episode, incident, part, division, act, clip.
☞ 表演, 情景 fuss, commotion, to-do, performance, drama, exhibition, display, show.

scenery n.
☞ 风致, 风景 landscape, terrain, panorama, view, vista, outlook, scene, background, setting, surroundings, backdrop, set.

scenic adj.
☞ 风景优美的, 天然景色的 panoramic, picturesque, attractive, pretty, beautiful, grand, striking, impressive, spectacular, breathtaking, awe-inspiring.

scent n.
☞ 气味, 香味 perfume, fragrance, aroma, bouquet, smell, odour.
☞ 兽迹, 痕迹 track, trail.
v.
☞ 嗅出, 闻到 smell, sniff (out), nose (out), sense, perceive, detect, discern, recognize.

scented adj.
☞ 好闻的, 有香味的 perfumed, fragrant, sweet-smelling, aromatic.

sceptic n.
☞ 怀疑者, 怀疑论者 doubter, unbeliever, disbeliever, agnostic, atheist, rationalist, questioner, scoffer, cynic.

sceptical adj.
☞ 怀疑的, 不相信的 doubting, doubtful, unconvinced, unbelieving, disbelieving, questioning, distrustful, mistrustful, hesitating, dubious, suspicious, scoffing, cynical, pessimistic.

schedule n.
☞ 时间表, 进度表 timetable, programme, agenda, diary,

calendar, itinerary, plan, scheme, list, inventory, catalogue, table, form.

v.
☞ 列入时间表或进度表,安排 timetable, time, table, programme, plan, organize, arrange, appoint, assign, book, list.

scheme n.
☞ 方案,计划 prorgamme, schedule, plan, project, idea, proposal, proposition, suggestion, draft, outline, blueprint, schema, diagram, chart, layout, pattern, design, shape, configuration, arrangement.
☞ 阴谋,诡计 intrigue, plot, connspiracy, device, stratagem, ruse, ploy, shift, manoeuvre, tactic(s), strategy, procedure, system, method.

v.
☞ 设计,图谋 plot, conspire, connive, collude, intrigue, machinate, manoeuvre, manipulate, pull string, mastermind, plan, project, contrive, devise, frame, work out.

scholar n.
☞ 学者,学生 pupil, student, academic, intellectual, egghead, authority, expert.

scholarly adj.
☞ 博学的,有学问的 learned, erudite, lettered, academic, shcolastic, school, intellectual, highbrow, bookish, studious, knowledgeable, well-read, analytical, scientific.

scholarship n.
☞ 学问,学识 erudition, learnedness, learning, knowledge, wisdom, education, schooling.
☞ 奖学金 grant, award, bursary, endowment, fellowship, exhibition.

school n.
☞ 学校,学生 college, academy, institute, institution, seminary, faculty, department, discipline, class, group, pupils, students.

v.
☞ 教育,训练 educate, teach, instruct, tutor, coach, train, discipline, drill, verse, prime, prepare, indoctrinate.

schooling n.
☞ 教育 education, book-learning, teaching, instruction, tuition, coaching, training, drill, preparation, grounding, guidance, indoctrination.

science n.
☞ 科学,学问 technology, discipline, specialization, knowledge, skill, proficiency, technique, art.

scientific adj.
☞ 科学的 methodical, systematic, controlled, regulated, analytical, mathematical, exact, precise, accurate, scholarly, thorugh.

scold v.
☞ 责骂,责备 chide, tell off, tick off, reprimand, reprove, rebuke, take to task, admonish, upbraid, reproach, blame, censure, lecture, talking-to,

scope n.
- 范围 range, compass, field, area, sphere, ambit, terms of reference, confines, reach, extent, span, breadth, coverage.
- 余地,机会 room, space, capacity, elbow-room, latitude, leeway, freedom, liberty, opportunity.

scorch v.
- 烧焦 burn, signe, char, blacken, scald, roast, sear, parch, shrivel, wither.

scorching adj.
- 灼热的 burning, boiling, baking, roasting, sizzling, blistering, sweltering, torrid, tropical, searing, red-hot.

score n.
- 分数,得分 result, total, sum, tally, points, marks.
- 刻痕,截痕 scratch, line, groove, mark, nick, notch.

v.
- 记录,得分,击败 record, register, chalk up, notch up, count, total, make, earn, gain, achieve, attain, win, have the advantage, have the edge, be one up.
- 刻痕于,截痕于 scratch, scrape, graze, mark, groove, gouge, cut, incise, engrave, indent, nick, slash.

scorn n.
- 蔑视,轻视 contempt, scornfulness, disdain, sneering, derision, mockery, ridicule, sarcasm, disparagement, digust.

v.
- 蔑视,轻视 despise, look down on, disdain, sneer at, scoff at, deride, mock, laugh at, slight, spurn, refuse, reject, dismiss.

scorntful adj.
- 轻蔑的,蔑视的 contemptuous, disdainful, supercilious, haughty, arrogant, sneering, scoffing, derisive, mocking, jeering, sarcastic, scathing, disparaging, insulting, slighting, dismissive.

scramble v.
- 爬,爬行 climb, scale, clamber, crawl, shuffle, scrabble, grope.
- 争夺 rush, hurry, hasten, run, push, jostle, struggle, strive, vie, contend.

n.
- 争取,争夺 rush, hurry, race, dash, hustle, bustle, commotion, confusion, muddle, struggle, free-for-all, melee.

scrap¹ n.
- 小片,碎屑 bit, piece, fragment, part, fraction, crumb, morsel, bite, mouthful, sliver, shred, snippet, atom, iota, grain, particle, mite, trace, vestige, remnant, leftover, waste, junk.

v.
- 废弃 discard, throw away, jettison, shed, abandon, drop, dump, ditch, cancel, axe, demolish, break up, write off.

scrap² n.
- 打架,口角 fight, scuffle, brawl, dust-up, quarrel, row,

argument, squabble, wrangle, dispute, disagreement.
v.
☞ 打架,口角 fight, brawl, quarrel, argue, fall out, squabble, bicker, wrangle, disagree.

scream *v, n*
☞ 尖叫,尖叫声 shriek, screech, cry, shout, yell, bawl, roar, howl, wail, squeal, yelp.

screen *v.*
☞ 放映 show, present, broadcast.
☞ 隐藏,掩护 shield, protect, safeguard, defend, guard, cover, mask, veil, cloak, shroud, hide, conceal, shelter, shade.
☞ 筛选,甄别 sort, grade, sift, sieve, filter, process, evaluate, gauge, examine, scan, vet.
n.
☞ 隔板,遮蔽物 partition, divider, shield, guard, cover, mask, veil, cloak, shroud, concealment, shelter, shade, awning, canopy, net, mesh.

screw *v.*
☞ 旋紧,拧紧,扭紧 fasten, adjust, tighten, contract, compress, squeeze, extract, extort, force, constrain, pressurize, turn, wind, wring, distort, wrinkle.

scribble *v.*
☞ 潦草地书写,乱涂 write, pen, jot, dash off, scrawl, doodle.

scribe *n.*
☞ 书记,抄写者 writer, copyist, amanuensis, secretary, clerk.

script *n.*
☞ 手稿,文稿 text, lines, words, dialogue, screenplay, libretto, book.
☞ 笔迹,手迹 writing, handwriting, hand, longhand, calligraphy, letters, manuscript, copy.

scrupulous *adj.*
☞ 多虑的,谨慎的 painstaking, meticulous, conscientious, careful, rigorous, strict, exact, precise, minute, nice.
☞ 严格认真的,正直的 principled, moral, ethical, honourable, upright.

scrutinize *v.*
☞ 仔细查阅或检查 examine, inspect, study, scan, analyse, sift, investigate, probe, search, explore.

scrutiny *n.*
☞ 细察,调查,详细查验 examination, inspection, study, analysis, investigation, inquiry, search, exploration.

sculpt *v.*
☞ 雕刻,雕塑 sculpture, carve, chisel, hew, cut, model, mould, cast, form, shape, fashion.

sea *n.*
☞ 海,海洋 ocean, main, deep, briny.
☞ 大量 multitude, abundance, profusion, mass.
adj.
☞ 海洋的 marine, maritime, ocean, oceanic, salt, saltwater, aquatic, seafaring.

at sea

☞ 茫然,迷惑 adrift, lost, confused, bewildered, baffled, puzzled, perplexed, mystified.

seal v.
☞ 封,盖章于 close, shut, stop, plug, cork, stopper, waterproof, fasten, secure.
☞ 解决,决定 settle, conclude, finalize, stamp.
n.
☞ 封条 stamp, signet, insignia, imprimatur, authentication, assurance, attestation, confirmation, ratification.

seal off
☞ 封闭 block up, close off, shut off, fence off, cut off, segregate, isolate, quarantine.

seam n.
☞ 接缝,缝 join, joint, weld, closure, line.
☞ 层 layer, stratum, vein, lode.

search v.
☞ 搜寻,探查 seek, look, hunt, rummage, rifle, ransack, scour, comb, sift, probe, explore, frisk, examine, scrutinize, inspect, check, investigate, inquire, pry.
n.
☞ 搜查,搜寻 hunt, quest, pursuit, rummage, probe, exploration, examination, scrutiny, inspection, investigation, inquiry, research, survey.

searching adj.
☞ 锐利的,彻底的 penetrating, piercing, keen, sharp, close, intent, probing, thorough, minute.

seaside n.
☞ 海岸 coast, shore, beach, sands.

season n.
☞ 季,季节 period, spell, phase, term, time, span, interval.
v.
☞ 调味,加味 flavour, spice, salt.

seasonable adj.
☞ 适合季节的,适合时机的 timely, well-timed, welcome, opportune, convenient, suitable, appropriate, fitting.

seasoned adj.
☞ 阅历深的,富有经验的 mature, experienced, practised, well-versed, veteran, old, hardened, toughened, conditioned, acclimatized, weathered.

second¹ adj.
☞ 第二的,额外的,附属的 duplicate, twin, double, repeated, additional, further, extra, supplementary, alternative, other, alternate, next, following, subsequent, succeeding, secondary, subordinate, lower, inferior, lesser, supporting.
n.
☞ 助手,帮手 helper, assistant, backer, supporter.
v.
☞ 赞成,附议 approve, agree with, endorse, back, support, help, assist, aid, further, advance, forward, promote, encourage.

second² n.

☞ 秒,时刻 minute, tick, moment, instant, flash, jiffy.

secondary adj.
☞ 次要的,从属的 subsidiary, subordinate, lower, inferior, lesser, minor, unimportant, ancillary, auxiliary, supporting, relief, back-up, reserve, spare, extra, second, alternative, indirect, derived, resulting.

second-hand adj.
☞ 二手的,用过的 used, old, worn, hand-me-down, borrowed, derivative, secondary, indirect, vicarious.

second-rate adj.
☞ 二等的,平庸的 inferior, substandard, second-class, second-best, poor, low-grade, shoddy, cheap, tawdry, mediocre, undistinguished, uninspired, uninspiring.

secrecy n.
☞ 保密,秘密 privacy, seclusion, confidentiality, confidence, covertness, concealment, disguise, camouflage, furtiveness, surreptitiousness, stealthiness, stealth, mystery.

secret adj.
☞ 秘密的 private, discreet, covert, hidden, concealed, unseen, shrouded, covered, disguised, camouflaged, undercover, furtive, surreptitious, stealthy, sly, underhand, under-the-counter, hole-and-corner, cloak-and-dagger, clandestine, underground, backstairs, back-door.
☞ 机密的,不公开的 classified, restricted, confidential, hush-hush, unpublished, undisclosed, unrevealed, unknown.
☞ 神秘的 cryptic, mysterious, unknown.
☞ 不可思议的,难理解的 cryptic, mysterious, occult, arcane, recondite, deep.
☞ 隐蔽的 secretive, close, retired, secluded, out-of-the-way.

n.
☞ 机密,秘诀 confidence, mystery, enigma, code, key, formula, recipe.

secretary n.
☞ 秘书,书记 personal, assistant, pa, typist, stenographer, clerk.

sect n.
☞ 派别,宗派 denomination, cult, division, subdivision, group, splinter, group, faction, camp, wing, party, school.

section n.
☞ 部门,部分 division, subdivision, chapter, paragraph, passage, instalment, part, component, fraction, fragment, bit, piece, slice, portion, segment, sector, zone, district, area, region, department, branch, wing.

sector n.
☞ 界,部分 zone, district, quarter, area, region, section, division, subdivision, part.

secular adj.
☞ 非宗教性的,世俗的 lay, temporal, worldly, earthly, civil, state, non-religious, profane.

secure adj.
☞ 安全的,牢固的 safe, unharmed, undamaged, protected, sheltered, shielded, immune, impregnable, fortified, fast, tight, fastened, locked, fixed, immovable, stable, steady, solid, sure, conclusive, definite.
☞ 安心的,有把握的 confident, assured, reassured.
v.
☞ 得到 obtain, acquire, gain, get.
☞ 系于 fasten, attach, fix, make fast, tie, moor, lash, chain, lock (up), padlock, bolt, batten down, nail, rivet.

security n.
☞ 保障,安全 safety, immunity, asylum, sanctuary, refuge, cover, protection, defence, surveillance, safe-keeping, preservation, care, custody.
☞ 担保 collateral, surety, pledge, guarantee, warranty, assurance, insurance, precautions, safeguards.
☞ 确定,把握 confidence, conviction, certainty, positiveness.

seduce v.
☞ 诱惑,引诱 entice, lure, allure, attract, tempt, charm, beguile, ensnare, lead, astray, mislead, deceive, corrupt, dishonour, ruin.

seduction n.
☞ 勾引,诱惑 enticement, lure, attraction, temptation, come-on, corruption, ruin.

seductive adj.
☞ 诱惑的,吸引人的 enticing, alluring, attractive, tempting, tantalizing, inviting, come-hither, flirtatious, sexy, provocative, beguiling, captivating, bewitching, iresistible.

see v.
☞ 看到,注意 perceive, glimpse, discern, spot, make out, distinguish, identify, sight, notice, observe, watch, view, look at, mark, note.
☞ 想像 imagine, picture, visualize, envisage, foresee, anticipate.
☞ 理解,明白 understand, comprehend, grasp, fathom, follow, realize, recognize, appreciate, regard, consider, deem.
☞ 发现 discover, find out, learn, ascertain, determine, decide.
☞ 经历,阅历 lead, usher, accompany, escort, court, go out with, date.
☞ 访问,会见 visit, consult, interview, meet.

see to
☞ 负责,照料 attend to, deal with, take care of, look after, arrange, organize, manage, do, fix, repair, sort out.

seed n.
☞ 种子 pip, stone, kernel, nucleus, grain, germ, sperm, ovum, egg, ovule, spawn, embryo, source, start, beginning.

seek v.
☞ 寻找,探索 look for, search for, hunt, pursue, follow,

inquire, ask, invite, request, solicit, petition, entreat, want, desire, aim, aspire, try, attempt, endeavour, strive.

seem v.
☞ 似乎,好像 appear, look, feel, sound, pretend to be.

seeming adj.
☞ 表面上的 apparent, ostensible, outward, superficial, surface, quasi-pseudo, specious.

see-through adj.
☞ 透明的 transparent, translucent, sheer, filmy, gauzy, gossamer(y), flimsy.

segment n.
☞ 部分,片 section, division, compartment, part, bit, piece, slice, portion, wedge.

seize v.
☞ 抓住,捉住 grab, snatch, grasp, clutch, grip, hold, take, confiscate, impound, appropriate, commandeer, hijack, annex, abduct, catch, capture, arrest, apprehend, nab, collar.

seizure n.
☞ 疾病发作 fit, attack, convulsion, paroxysm, spasm.
☞ 强占,没收 taking, confiscation, appropriation, hijack, annexation, abduction, capture, arrest, apprehension.

seldom adv.
☞ 很少,不常 rarely, infrequently, occasionally, hardly ever.

select v.
☞ 选择,挑选 choose, pick, single out, decide on, appoint,
elect, prefer, opt for.
adj.
☞ 有选择的,精选的 selected, choice, top, prime, first-class, first-rate, hand-picked, elite, exclusive, limited, privileged, special, excellent, superior, posh.

selection n.
☞ 选择,挑选 choice, pick, option, preference, assortment, variety, range, line-up, miscellany, medley, potpourri, collection, anthology.

selective adj.
☞ 有选择力的 particular, choosy, careful, discerning, discriminating.

self n.
☞ 自己,自我,私利 ego, personality, identity, person.

self-centred adj.
☞ 自私的 selfish, self-seeking, self-serving, self-interested, egotistic(al), narcissistic, self-absorbed, egocentric.

self-confident adj.
☞ 有自信心的 confident, self-reliant, self-assured, assured, self-possessed, cool, fearless.

self-conscious adj.
☞ 自觉的,害羞的 uncomfortable, ill at ease, awkward, embarrassed, shamefaced, sheepish, shy, bashful, coy, retiring, shrinking, self-effacing, nervous, insecure.

self-control n.
☞ 自制,克己 calmness, composure, cool, patience, self-

restraint, restraint, self-denial, temperance, self-discipline, self-mastery, will-power.

self-evident adj.
☞ 昭然若揭的,不需证明的 obvious, manifest, clear, undeniable, axiomatic, unquestionable, incontrovertible, inescapable.

self-government n.
☞ 自治政府 autonomy, independence, home rule, democracy.

selfish adj.
☞ 自私的 self-interested, self-seeking, self-serving, mean, miserly, mercenary, greedy, covetous, self-centred, egocentric, egotistic.

selfless adj.
☞ 无私的,忘我的 unselfish, altruistic, self-denying, self-sacrificing, generous, philanthropic.

self-respect n.
☞ 自尊,自重 pride, dignity, self-esteem, self-assurance, self-confidence.

self-righteous adj.
☞ 自以为公正善良的 smug, complacent, superior, goody-goody, pious, sanctimonious, holier-than-thou, pietistic, hypocritical, pharisaical.

self-sacrifice n.
☞ 自我牺牲 self-denial, self-renunciation, selflessness, altruism, unselfishness, generosity.

slef-satisfied adj.
☞ 自以为是,自满的 smug, complacent, self-congratulatory, self-righteous.

self-styled adj.
☞ 自谓的 self-appointed, professed, so-called, would-be.

self-supporting adj.
☞ 自足的 self-sufficient, self-financing, independent, self-reliant.

sell v.
☞ 卖,售 barter, exchange, trade, auction, vend, retail, stock, handle, deal in, trade in, traffic in, merchandise, hawk, peddle, push, advertise, promote, market.

seller n.
☞ 出售者,卖方 vendor, merchant, trader, dealer, supplier, stockist, retailer, shopkeeper, salesman, saleswoman, agent, representative, rep, travveller.

semblance n.
☞ 外表,相似 appearance, air, show, pretence, guise, mask, front, facade, venner, apparition, image, resemblance, likeness, similarity.

send v.
☞ 邮寄,送 post, mail, dispatch, consign, remit, forward, convey, deliver.
☞ 派,遣 transmit, broadcast, communicate.
☞ 使……快速移动 propel, drive, move, throw, fling, hurl, launch, fire, shoot, discharge, emit, direct.

send for
☞ 召唤 summon, call for,

request, order, command.
send up
☞ 使滑稽可笑　satirize, mock, ridicule, parody, take off, mimic, imitate.

send-off *n.*
☞ 送行,欢送　farewell, leave-taking, departure, start, goodbye.

senior *adj.*
☞ 年长的,年纪较大的　older, elder, higher, superior, high-ranking, major, chief.

seniority *n.*
☞ 资历深,职位高　priority, precedence, rank, standing, status, age, superiority, importance.

sensation *n.*
☞ 感觉,知觉　feeling, sense, impression, perception, awareness, consciousness, emotion.
☞ 骚动　commotion, stir, agitation, excitement, thrill, furore, outrage, scandal.

sensational *adj.*
☞ 令人激动的,触动的　exciting, thrilling, electrifying, breathtaking, startling, amazing, astounding, staggering, dramatic, spectacular, impressive, exceptional, excellent, wonderful, marvellous, smashing.
☞ 轰动的　scandalous, shocking, horrifying, revealing, melodramatic, lurid.

sense *n.*
☞ 感觉,知觉　feeling, sensation, impression, perception, awareness, consciousness, appreciation, faculty.
☞ 心智健全　reason, logic, mind, brain(s), wit(s), wisdom, intelligence, cleverness, understanding, discernment, judgement, intuition.
☞ 含义,意义　meaning, significance, definition, interpretation, implication, point, purpose, substance.
☞ *v.*
☞ 感觉,了解　feel, suspect, intuit, perseive, detect, notice, observe, realize, appreciate, understand, comprehend, grasp.

senseless *adj.*
☞ 愚蠢的　foolish, stupid, unwise, silly, idiotic, mad, crazy, daft, ridiculous, ludicrous, absurd, meaningless, nonsensical, fatuous, irrational, illogical, unreasonable, pointless, purposeless, futile.
☞ 无感觉的,不醒人事的 unconscious, out, stunned, anaesthetized, deadened, numb, unfeeling.

sensitive *adj.*
☞ 敏感的,容易感受的　susceptible, vulnerable, impressionable, tender, emotional, thin-skinned, temperamental, touchy, irritable, sensitized, responsive, aware, perceptive, discerning, appreciative.
☞ 灵敏的　delicate, fine, exact, precise.

sensual *adj.*

sensuous adj.
☞ 肉欲的,淫荡的 self-indulgent, voluptuous, worldly, physical, animal, carnal, fleshly, bodily, sexual, erotic, sexy, lustful, randy, lecherous, lewd, licentious.

sensuous adj.
☞ 感觉上的,给人美感的 pleasurable, gratifying, voluptuous, rich, lush, luxurious, sumptuous.

sentence n.
☞ 判决,宣判 judgement, decision, verdict, condemnation, pronouncement, ruling, decree, order.
v.
☞ 判决,宣判 judge, pass judgement on, condemn, doom, punish, penalize.

sentiment n.
☞ 意见,观点 thought, idea, feeling, opinion, view, judgement, belief, persuasion, attitude.
☞ 感情,情绪 emotion, sensibility, tenderness, soft-heartedness, remandticism, sentimentality, mawkishness.

sentimental adj.
☞ 感情脆弱的 tender, soft-hearted, emotional, gushing, touching, pathetic, tear-jerking, weepy, maudlin, mawkish, nostalgic, romantic, lovey-dovey, slushy, mushy, sloppy, schmaltzy, soppy, corny.

separable adj.
☞ 可分离的 divisible, detachable, removable, distinguishable, distinct.

separate v.
☞ 分开,隔开 divide, sever, part, split (up), divorce, part company, diverge, disconnect, uncouple, disunite, disaffiliate, disentangle, segregate, isolate, cut off, abstract, remove, detach, withdraw, secede.
adj.
☞ 单独的,分别的 single, individual, particular, independent, alone, solitary, segregated, isolated, apart, divorced, divided, disunited, disconnected, disjointed, detached, unattached, unconnected, unrelated, different, disparate, distinct, discrete, several, sundry.

separation n.
☞ 分离,分开,缺口 division, severance, parting, leave-taking, farewell, split-up, break-up, divorce, split, rift, gap, divergence, disocnnection, disengagement, dissociation, estragement, segregation, isolation, detachment.

suquel n.
☞ 继续,结局 follow-up, continuation, development, result, consequence, outcome, issue, upshot, pay-off, end, conclusion.

sequence n.
☞ 连续,系列 succession, series, run, progression, chain, string, train, line, procession, order, arrangement, course, track, cycle, set.

series n.
☞ 套,系列 set, cycle,

succession, sequence, run, progression, chain, string, line, train, order, arrangement, course.

serious adj.
- 重大的,严重的 important, significant, weighty, momentous, crucial, critical, urgent, pressing, acute, grave, worrying, difficult, dangerous, grim, severe, deep, far-reaching.
- 严肃的,庄重的 unsmiling, long-faced, humourless, solemn, sober, stern, thoughtful, pensive, earnest, sincere.

sermon n.
- 说教,训诫 address, discourse, lecture, harangue, homily, talking-to.

servant n.
- 仆人 domestic, maid, valet, steward, attendant, retainer, hireling, lackey, menial, skivvy, slave, help, helper, assistant, ancillary.

serve v.
- 服务 wait on, attend, minister to, work for, help, aid, assist, benefit, further.
- 适合 fulfil, complete, answer, satisfy, discharge, perform, act, function.
- 提供 distribute, dole out, present, deliver, provide, supply.

service n.
- 服务,工作 employment, work, labour, business, duty, function, performance.
- 利益,好处 use, usefulness, utility, advantage, benefit, help, assistance.
- 维修 servicing, maintenance, overhaul, check.
- 礼拜式 worship, observance, ceremony, rite.

v.
- 维修,检查 maintain, overhaul, check, repair, recondition, tune.

session n.
- 开会,会议 sitting, hearing, meeting, assembly, conference, discussion, period, time, term, semester, year.

set v.
- 放,置 put, place, locate, situate, position, arrange, prepare, lodge, fix, stick, park, deposit.
- 规定,定位 schedule, appoint, designate, specify, name, prescribe, ordain, assign, allocate, impose, fix, establish, determine, decide, conclude, settle, resolve.
- 适应,调整 adjust, regulate, synchronize, co-ordinate.
- 下沉,落 go down, sink, dip, subside, disappear, vanish.
- 凝结 congeal, thicken, gel, gel, stiffen, solidify, harden, crystallize.

n.
- 套,组,系列 batch, series, sequence, kit, outfit, compendium, assortment, collection, class, category, group, band, gang, crowd, circle, clique, faction.

adj.
- 规定的,指定的 scheduled, appointed, arranged, prepared,

prearranged, fixed, established, definite, decided, agreed, settled, firm, strict, rigid, inflexible, prescribed, formal, conventional, traditional, customary, usual, routine, regular, standard, stock, stereotyped, hackneyed.

set about
☞ 着手开始做 begin, start, embark on, undertake, tackle, attack.

set aside
☞ 拨出,留下 put aside, lay aside, keep (back), save, reserve, set apart, separate, select, earmark.
☞ 驳回,宣布……无效 annul, abrogate, cancel, revoke, reverse, overturn, overrule, reject, discard.

set back
☞ 阻碍,耽搁 delay, hold up, slow, retard, hinder, impede.

set off
☞ 出发,开始 leave, depart, set out, start (out), begin.
☞ 引爆 detonate, light, ignite, touch off, trigger off, explode.
☞ 更明显 display, show off, enhance, contrast.

set on
☞ 攻击,唆使 set upon, attack, turn on, go for, fall upon, lay into, beat up.

set out
☞ 出发,开始 leave, depart, set off, start (out), begin.
☞ 展示,陈列 layout, arrange, display, exhibit, present, describe, explain.

set up
☞ 提出,提高 raise, elevate, erect, build, construct, assemble, compose, form, create, establish, institute, found, inaugurate, initiate, begin, start, introduce, organize, arrange, prepare.

setback n.
☞ 顿挫,退步 delay, hold-up, problem, snag, hitch, hiccup, reverse, misfortune, upset, disappointment, defeat.

setting n.
☞ 安装 mounting, frame, surroundings, milieu, environment, background, context, perspective, period, position, location, locale, site, scene, scenery.

settle v.
☞ 了结 arrange, order, adjust, reconcile, resolve, complete, conclude.
☞ 下沉,下降 sink, subside, drop, fall, descend, land, alight.
☞ 决定 choose, appoint, fix, establish, determine, decide, agree, confirm.
☞ 殖民于,殖民 colonize, occupy, populate, people, inhabit, live, reside.
☞ 结清 pay, clear, discharge.

settlement n.
☞ 解决 resolution, agreement, arrangement, decision, conclusion, termination, satisfaction.
☞ 清偿 payment, clearance, clearing, discharge.
☞ 殖民地 colony, outpost, community, kibbutz, camp,

encampment, hamlet, village.

settler n.
☞ 移居者,殖民者 colonist, colonizer, pioneer, frontiersman, frontierswoman, planter, immigrant, incomer, newcomer, squatter.

several adj.
☞ 一些 some, many, various, assorted, sundry, diverse, different, distinct, separate, particular, individual.

severe adj.
☞ 严厉的,剧烈的 stern, disapproving, sober, strait-laced, strict, rigid, unbending, harsh, tough, hard, difficult, demanding, arduous, punishing, rigorous, grim, forbidding, cruel, biting, cutting, scathing, pitiless, merciless, oppressive, relentless, inexorable, acute, bitter, intense, extreme, fierce, violent, distressing, serious, grave, critical, dangerous.
☞ 简朴的 plain, simple, unadorned, unembellished, functional, restrained, austere, ascetic.

sew v.
☞ 缝 stitch, tack, baste, hem, darn, embroider.

sex n.
☞ 性别 gender, sexuality.
☞ 性交 sexual intercourse, intercourse, sexual relations, copulation, coitus, lovemaking, fornication, reproduction, union, intimacy.

sexual adj.
☞ 性的,性别的 sex, reproductive, procreative, genital, coital, venereal, carnal, sensual, erotic.

sexy adj.
☞ 性感的,色情的 sensual, voluptuous, nubile, beddable, seductive, inviting, flirtatious, arousing, provoking, provocative, titillating, pornographic, erotic, salacious, suggestive.

shabby adj.
☞ 衣衫褴褛的 ragged, tattered, frayed, worn, worn-out, mangy, moth-eaten, scruffy, tatty, disreputable, dilapidated, run-down, seedy, dirty, dingy, poky.
☞ 卑鄙的 contemptible, despicable, rotten, mean, low, cheap, shoddy, shameful, dishonourable.

shade n.
☞ 幽暗,阴暗 shadiness, shadow, darkness, obscurity, semi-darkness, dimness, gloom, gloominess, twilight, dusk, gloaming.
☞ 遮光物 awning, canopy, cover, shelter, screen, blind, curtain, shield, visor, umbrella, parasol.
☞ 色度 colour, hue, tint, tone, tinge.
☞ 细微差别 trace, dash, hint, suggestion, suspicion, nuance, gradation, degree, amount, variety.
☞ 灵魂 ghost, spectre, phantom, spirit, apparition, semblance.
v.

☞ 遮蔽,遮 shield, screen, protect, cover, shroud, veil, hide, conceal, obscure, cloud, dim, darken, shadow, overshadow.

shadow n.
☞ 黑暗 shade, darkness, obscurity, semi-darkness, dimness, gloom, twilight, dusk, gloaming, cloud, cover, protection.
☞ 阴影 silhouette, shape, image, representation.
☞ 徵痕 trace, hint, suggestion, suspicion, vestige, remnant.

v.
☞ 遮蔽 overshadow, overhang, shade, shield, screen, obscure, darken.
☞ 跟随 follow, tail, dog, stalk, trail, watch.

shadowy adj.
☞ 暗黑的,朦胧的 dark, gloomy, murky, obscure, dim, faint, indistinct, ill-defined, vague, hazy, nebulous, intangible, unsubstantial, ghostly, spectral, illusory, dreamlike, imaginary, unreal.

shady adj.
☞ 遮荫的 shaded, shadowy, dim, dark, cool, leafy.
☞ 可疑的,有问题的 dubious, questionable, suspect, suspicious, fishy, dishonest, crooked, unreliable, untrustworthy, disreputable, unscrupulous, unethical, underhand.

shake v.
☞ 震动,摇动 wave, flourish, brandish, wag, waggle, agitate, rattle, joggle, jolt, jerk, twitch, convulse, heave, throb, vibrate, oscillate, fluctuate, waver, wobble, totter, sway, rock, tremble, quiver, quake, shiver, shudder.
☞ 惊震 upset, distress, shock, frighten, unnerve, intimidate, disturb, discompose, unsettle, agitate, stir, rouse.

shake off
☞ 摆脱 get rid of, dislodge, lose, elude, give the slip, leave behind, outdistance, outstrip.

shake-up n.
☞ 变动,整顿 reorganization, rearrangement, reshuffle, disturbance, upheaval.

shaky adj.
☞ 颤抖的 trembling, quivering, faltering, tentative, uncertain.
☞ 不稳的 unstable, unsteady, insecure, precarious, wobbly, rocky, tottery, rickety, weak.
☞ 不安的,不可靠的 dubious, questionable, suspect, unreliable, unsound, unsupported.

shallow adj.
☞ 浅的,肤浅的 superficial, surface, skin-deep, slight, flimsy, trivial, frivolous, foolish, idle, empty, meaningless, unscholarly, ignorant, simple.

shame n.
☞ 羞耻,惭愧 disgrace, dishonour, discredit, stain, stigma, disrepute, infamy, scandal, ignominy, humiliation, degradation, shamefacedness, remorse, guilt, embarrassment,

mortification.

v.
☞ 使羞耻,使蒙羞 embarrass, mortify, abash, confound, humiliate, ridicule, humble, put to shame, show up, disgrace, dishonour, discredit, debase, degrade, sully, taint, stain.

shamefaced adj.
☞ 羞耻的 ashamed, conscience-stricken, remorseful, contrite, apologetic, sorry, sheepish, red-faced, blushing, embarrassed, mortified, abashed, humiliated, uncomfortable.

shameful adj.
☞ 可耻的 disgraceful, outrageous, scandalous, indecent, abominable, atrocious, wicked, mean, low, vile, reprehensible, contemptible, unworthy, ignoble.
☞ 丢脸的 embarrassing, mortifying, humiliating, ignominious.

shameless adj.
☞ 无耻的 unashamed, unabashed, unrepentant, impenitent, barefaced, flagrant, blatant, brazen, brash, audacious, insolent, defiant, hardened, incorrigible.
☞ 厚颜的 immodest, indecent, improper, unprincipled, wanton, dissolute, corrupt, depraved.

shape n.
☞ 形状,外形 form, outline, silhouette, profile, model, mould, pattern, cut, lines, contours, figure, physique, build, frame, format, configuration.
☞ 样子,相似 appearance, guise, likeness, semblance.
☞ 情况,状况 condition, state, form, health, trim, fettle.

v.
☞ 塑造,形成 form, fashion, model, mould, cast, forge, sculpt, carve, whittle, make, produce, construct, create, devise, frame, plan, prepare, adapt, adjust, regulate, accommodate, modify, remodel.

share v.
☞ 分给,分摊 divide, split, go halves, partake, participate, share out, distribute, dole out, give out, deal out, apportion, allot, allocate, assign.

n.
☞ 部分,分 portion, ration, quota, allowance, allocation, allotment, lot, part, division, proportion, percentage, cut, dividend, due, contribution, whack.

sharp adj.
☞ 锋利的,尖的 pointed, keen, edged, knife-edged, razor-sharp, cutting, serrated, jagged, barbed, spiky.
☞ 明确的,鲜明的 clear, clear-cut, well-defined, distinct, marked, crisp.
☞ 敏锐的 quick-witted, alert, shrewd, astute, perceptive, observant, discerning, penetrating, clever, crafty, cunning, artful, sly.
☞ 突然的 sudden, abrupt, violent, fierce, intense, extreme, severe, acute,

piercing, stabbing.
- ☞ 辛辣的 pungent, piquant, sour, tart, vinegary, bitter, acerbic, acid.
- ☞ 尖刻的 trenchant, incisive, cutting, biting, caustic, sarcastic, sardonic, scathing, vitriolic, acrimonious.

adv.
- ☞ 准时,正(指时刻) punctually, promptly, on the dot, exactly, precisely, abruptly, suddenly, unexpectedly.

sharpen v.
- ☞ 使尖锐,使敏锐 edge, whet, hone, grind, file.

shatter v.
- ☞ 粉碎,破坏 break, smash, splinter, shiver, crack, split, burst, explode, blast, crush, demolish, destroy, devastate, wreck, ruin, overturn, upset.

shed v.
- ☞ 流出,倾泻 cast, moult, slough, discard, drop, spill, pour, shower, scatter, diffuse, emit, radiate, shine, throw.

sheepish adj.
- ☞ 胆怯的,害羞的 ashamed, shamefaced, embarrassed, mortified, chastened, abashed, uncomfortable, self-conscious, silly, foolish.

sheer adj.
- ☞ 彻底的,绝对的 utter, complete, total, absolute, thorough, mere, pure, unadulterated, downright, out-and-out, rank, thoroughgoing, unqualified, unmitigated.
- ☞ 垂直的 vertical, perpendicular, precipitous, abrupt, steep.
- ☞ 极薄的,透明的 thin, fine, flimsy, gauzy, gossamer, translucent, transparent, see-through.

sheet n.
- ☞ 被单,单子 cover, blanket, covering, coating, coat, film, layer, stratum, skin, membrane, lamina, veneer, overlay, plate, leaf, page, folio, piece, panel, slab, pane, expanse, surface.

shelf n.
- ☞ 搁板,架子 ledge, mantelpiece, sill, step, bench, counter, bar, bank, sandbank, reef, terrace.

shell n.
- ☞ 框架,骨架 covering, hull, husk, pod, rind, crust, case, casing, body, chassis, frame, framework, structure, skeleton.

v.
- ☞ 剥掉,去掉 hull, husk, pod.
- ☞ 轰炸 bomb, bombard, barrage, blitz, attack.

shelter v.
- ☞ 保护,掩护 cover, shroud, screen, shade, shadow, protect, safeguard, defend, guard, shield, harbour, hide, accommodate, put up.

n.
- ☞ 遮蔽,庇护 cover, roof, shade, shadow, protection, defence, guard, security, safety, sanctuary, asylum, haven, refuge, retreat, accommodation, lodging.

sheltered adj.
- ☞ 遮蔽的 covered, shaded,

shielded, protected, cosy, snug, warm, quiet, secluded, isolated, retired, withdrawn, reclusive, cloistered, unworldly.

shield n.
☞ 护板,挡板 buckler, escutcheon, defence, bulwark, rampart, screen, guard, cover, shelter, protection, safeguard.
v.
☞ 保护,防御 defend, guard, protect, safeguard, screen, shade, shadow, cover, shelter.

shift v.
☞ 改变,移动 change, vary, fluctuate, alter, adjust, move, budge, remove, dislodge, displace, relocate, reposition, rearange, transpose, transfer, switch, swerve, veer.
n.
☞ 改换,改变 change, fluctuation, alteration, modification, move, removal, displacement, rearrangement, transposition, transfer, switch.

shifty adj.
☞ 狡猾的,不可靠的 untrustworthy, dishonest, deceitful, scheming, contriving, tricky, wily, crafty, cunning, devious, evasive, slippery, furtive, underhand, dubious, shady.

shine v.
☞ 发光,照耀 beam, radiate, glow, flash, glare, gleam, glint, glitter, sparkle, twinkle, shimmer, glisten, glimmer.
☞ 磨光,擦亮 polish, burnish, buff, brush, rub.
☞ 杰出 excel, stand out.

n.
☞ 光亮,光辉 light, radiance, glow, brightness, glare, gleam, sparkle, skimmer.
☞ 擦亮 gloss, polish, burnish, sheen, lustre, glaze.

shining adj.
☞ 明亮的,光明的 bright, radiant, glowing, beaming, flashing, gleaming, glittering, glistening, shimmering, twinkling, sparkling, brilliant, resplendent, splendid, glorious.
☞ 杰出的,著名的 conspicuous, outstanding, leading, eminent, celebrated, distinguished, illustrious.

shiny adj.
☞ 有光泽的,擦亮的 polished, burnished, sheeny, lustrous, glossy, sleek, bright, gleaming, glistening.

ship n.
☞ 船,舰 vessel, craft, liner, steamer, tanker, trawler, ferry, boat, yacht.

shiver v.
☞ 颤抖 shudder, tremble, quiver, quake, shake, vibrate, palpitate, flutter.
n.
☞ 颤抖 shudder, quiver, shake, tremor, twitch, start, vibration, flutter.

shock v.
☞ 使震惊,惊骇 disgust, revolt, sicken, offend, appal, outrage, scandalize, horrify, astound, stagger, stun, stupefy, numb, paralyse, traumatize, jolt, jar, shake, agitate, unsettle, disquiet, unnerve, confound,

☞ 休克,震惊 fright, start, jolt, impact, collision, surprise, bombshell, thunderbolt, blow, trauma, upset, distress, dismay, consternation, disgust, outrage.

shocking adj.
☞ 令人震惊的,骇人听闻的 appalling, outrageous, scandalous, horrifying, disgraceful, deplorable, intolerable, unbearable, atrocious, abominable, monstrous, unspeakable, detestable, abhorrent, dreadful, awful, terrible, frightful, ghastly, hideous, horrible, disgusting, revolting, repulsive, sickening, nauseating, offensive, distressing.

shoot v.
☞ 开火,发射 fire, discharge, launch, propel, hurl, fling, project.
☞ 飞速通过 dart, bolt, dash, tear, rush, race, sprint, speed, charge, hurtle.
☞ 射杀 hit, kill, blast, bombard, gun down, snipe at, pick off.
n.
☞ 苗,嫩芽 sprout, bud, offshoot, branch, twig, sprig, slip, scion.

short adj.
☞ 短的,短暂的 brief, cursory, fleeting, momentary, transitory, ephemeral, concise, succinct, terse, pithy, compact, compressed, shortened, curtailed, abbreviated, abridged, summarized.
☞ 粗鲁的 brusque, curt, gruff, snappy, sharp, abrupt, blunt, direct, rude, impolite, discourteous, uncivil.
☞ 短少的 small, little, low, petite, diminutive, squat, dumpy.
☞ 不足的,缺少的 inadequate, insufficient, deficient, lacking, wanting, low, poor, meagre, scant, sparse.

shortage n.
☞ 不足,缺少 inadequacy, insufficiency, deficiency, shortfall, deficit, lack, want, need, scarcity, paucity, poverty, dearth, absence.

shortcoming n.
☞ 缺点,短处 defect, imperfection, fault, flaw, drawback, failing, weakness, foible.

shorten v.
☞ 使短,变短 cut, trim, prune, crop, dock, curtail, truncate, abbreviate, abridge, reduce, lessen, decrease, diminish, take up.

shortly adv.
☞ 不久,立刻 soon, before long, presently, by and by.

short-sighted adj.
☞ 近视的 myopic, near-sighted.
☞ 短见的 improvident, imprudent, injudicious, unwise, impolitic, ill-advised, careless, hasty, ill-considered.

shot n.
☞ 弹,炮弹 bullet, missile,

projectile, ball, pellet, slug, discharge, blast.
☞ 试图 attempt, try, effort, endeavour, go, bash, crack, stab, guess, turn.

shoulder v.
☞ 以肩挤 push, shove, jostle, trust, press.
☞ 肩负,承担 accept, assume, take, on, bear, carry, sustain.

shout n, v
☞ 喊叫声,呼喊 call, cry, scream, shriek, yell, roar, bellow, bawl, howl, bay, cheer.

show v.
☞ 出示,展示 reveal, expose, uncover, disclose, divulge, present, offer, exhibit, manifest, display, indicate, register, demonstrate, prove, illustrate, exemplify, explain, instruct, teach, clarify, elucidate.
☞ 引导,送 lead, guide, conduct, usher, escort, accompany, attend.

n.
☞ 显示,外观 ostentation, parade, display, flamboyance, panache, pizzazz, showiness, exhibitionism, affectation, pose, pretence, illusion, semblance, facade, impression, appearance, air.
☞ 展示,表演 demonstration, presentation, exhibition, exposition, fair, display, parade, pageant, extravaganza, spectacle, entertainment, performance, production, staging, showing, representation.

show off
☞ 炫耀,卖弄 parade, strut, swagger, brag, boast, swank, flaunt, brandish, display, exhibit, demonstrate, advertise, set off, enhance.

show up
☞ 露出,显出 arrive, come, turn up, appear, materialize.
☞ 拆穿 humiliate, embarrass, mortify, shame, disgrace, let down.
☞ 揭露 reveal, show, expose, unmask, lay bare, highlight, pinpoint.

shower n.
☞ 阵雨,雹 rain, stream, torrent, deluge, hail, volley, barrage.

v.
☞ 似阵雨般降,大量给予 spray, sprinkle, rain, pour, deluge, inundate, overwhelm, load, heap, lavish.

show-off n.
☞ 喜爱炫耀的人,卖弄的人 swaggerer, braggart, boaster, swanker, exhibitionist, peacock, poser, poseur, egotist.

showy adj.
☞ 显眼的 flashy, flamboyant, ostentatious, gaudy, garish, loud, tawdry, fancy, ornate, pretentious, pompous, swanky, flash.

shrewd adj.
☞ 敏锐的,精明的 astute, judicious, well-advised, calculated, far-siighted, smart, clever, intelligent, sharp, keen, acute, alert, perceptive,

observant, discerning, discriminating, knowing, calculating, cunning, crafty, artful, sly.

shriek v, n
☞ 尖声叫喊,尖叫　scream, screech, squawk, squeal, cry, shout, yell, wail, howl.

shrink v.
☞ 收缩,皱缩　contract, shorten, narrow, decrease, lessen, diminish, dwindle, shrivel, wrinkle, wither.
☞ 退缩,畏缩　recoil, back away, shy away, withdraw, retire, balk, quail, cower, cringe, wince, flinch, shun.

shudder v.
☞ 抽动,发抖　shiver, shake, tremble, quiver, quake, heave, convulse.
n.
☞ 颤抖,发抖　shiver, quiver, tremor, spasm, convulsion.

shuffle v.
☞ 弄混,乱堆　mix (up), intermix, jumble, confuse, disorder, rearrange, reorganize, shift, around, switch.
☞ 曳足而行　shamble, scuffle, scrape, drag, limp, hobbhle.

shut v.
☞ 关,闭　close, slam, seal, fasten, secure, lock, latch, bolt, bar.

shut down
☞ 关闭,停止　close, stop, cease, terminate, halt, discontinue, suspend, switch off, inactivate.

shut in
☞ 囚禁,困住　enclose, box in, hem in, fence in, immure, confine, imprison, cage.

shut off
☞ 停闭(水,煤气等)　seclude, isolate, cut off, separate, segregate.

shut out
☞ 排除　exclude, bar, debar, lock out, ostracize, banish.
☞ 挡住　hide, conceal, cover, mask, screen, veil.

shut up
☞ 闭嘴　silence, gag, quiet, hush up, pipe down, hold one's tongue, clam up.
☞ 关闭　confine, coop up, imprison, incarcerate, jail, intern.

shy adj.
☞ 害羞的,易受惊的,迟疑的　timid, bashful, reticent, reserved, retiring, diffient, coy, self-conscious, inhibited, modest, self-effacing, shrinking, hesitant, cautious, chary, suspicious, nervous.

sick adj.
☞ 不适的,患病的　ill, unwel, indisposed, laid up, poorly, ailing, sickly, under the weather, weak, feeble.
☞ 反胃,作呕　vomiting, queasy, bilious, seasick, airsick.
☞ 厌烦,无趣　bored, fed up, tired, weary, disgusted, nauseated.

sicken v.
☞ 厌恶,厌倦　nauseate, revolt, disgust, repel, put off, turn off.

sickening adj.
☞ 令人厌恶的　nauseating, revolting, disgusting, offensive,

distasteful, foul, vile, loathsome, repulsive.

sickly *adj.*
- 多病的 unhealthy, infirm, delicate, weak, feeble, frail, wan, pallid, ailing, indisposed, sick, bilious, faint, languid.
- 令人作呕的 nauseating, revolting, sweet, syrupy, cloying, mawkish.

sickness *n.*
- 疾病,病 illness, disease, malady, ailment, complaint, affliction, ill-health, indisposition, infirmity.
- 厌恶,厌倦 vomiting, nausea, queasiness, biliousness.

side *n.*
- 边,侧面 edge, margin, fringe, periphery, border, boundary, limit, verge, brink, bank, shore, quarter, region, flank, hank, face, facet, surface.
- 立场,观点 standpoint, viewpoint, view, aspect, angle, slant.
- 队,派系 team, party, faction, camp, cause, interest.

adj.
- 边的,侧的,副的 lateral, flanking, marginal, secondary, subsidiary, subordinate, lesser, minor, incidental, indirect, oblique.

side with
- 支持,袒护 agree with, team up with, support, vote for, favour, prefer.

sidestep *v.*
- 回避 avoid, dodge, duck, evade, elude, skirt, bypass.

sideways *adv.*
- 斜,自一边的 sidewards, edgeways, laterally, obliquely.

adj.
- 向旁边的,横斜的 sideward, side, lateral, slanted, oblique, indirect, sidelong.

sigh *v.*
- 叹气 breathe, exhale, moan, complain, lament, grieve.

sight *n.*
- 视力,视觉 vision, eyesight, seeing, observation, perception.
- 视野,看见 view, look, glance, glimpse, range, field of vision, visibility.
- 景色,景象 appearance, spectacle, show, display, exhibition, scene, eyesore, monstrosity, fright.

v.
- 看见,发现 see, observe, spot, glimpse, perceive, discern, distinguish, make out.

sightseer *n.*
- 观光者,游览者 tourist, visitor, holidaymaker, tripper, excursionist.

sign *n.*
- 记号,象征 symbol, token, character, figure, representation, emblem, badge, insignia, logo.
- 标志,手势 indication, mark, signal, gesture, evidence, manifestation, clue, pointer, hint, suggestion, trace.
- 招牌,告示 notice, poster, board, placard.
- 暗号,征兆 portent, omen, forewarning, foreboding.

v.

☞ 签字,签名 autograph, initial, endorse, write.

sign up
☞ 征募,签约雇用 enlist, enrol, join (up), volunteer, register, sign on, recruit, take on, hire, engage, employ.

signal n.
☞ 信号,暗号 sign, indication, mark, gesture, cue, go-ahead, password, light, indicator, beacon, flare, rocket, alarm, alert, warning, tip-off.
v.
☞ 发信号 wave, gesticulate, gesture, beckon, motion, nod, sign, indicate, communicate.

signature n.
☞ 签名,签字 autograph, initials, mark, endorsement, inscription.

significance n.
☞ 重要,意义 importance, relevance, consequence, matter, interest, consideration, weight, force, meaning, implication, sense, point, message.

significant adj.
☞ 重要的,重大的 important, relevant, consequential, momentous, weighty, serious, noteworthy, critical, vital, marked, considerable, appreciable.
☞ 有含义的,有特殊意义的 meaningful, symbolic, expressive, suggestive, indicative, symptomatic.

signify v.
☞ 表示,象征 mean, denote, symbolize, represent, stand for, indicate, show, express, convey, transmit, communicate, intimate, imply, suggest.
☞ 有关系,有重要性 matter, count.

silence n.
☞ 沉默,寂静 quiet, quietness, hush, peace, stillness, calm, lull, noiselessness, soundlessness, muteness, dumbness, speechlessness, taciturnity, uncommunicativeness, reticence, reserve.
v.
☞ 使安静,使沉默 quiet, quieten, hush, mute, deaden, muffle, stifle, gag, muzzle, suppress, subdue, quell, still, dumbfound.

silent adj.
☞ 静的,沉默的 inaudible, noiseless, soundless, quiet, peaceful, still, hushed, muted, mute, dumb, speechless, tongue-tied, taciturn, mum, reticent, reserved, tacit, unspoken, unexpressed, understood, voiceless, wordless.

silky adj.
☞ 丝般的,柔滑的 silken, fine, sleek, lustrous, glossy, satiny, smooth, soft, velvety.

silly adj.
☞ 愚蠢的,傻的 foolish, stupid, imprudent, senseless, pointless, idiotic, daft, ridiculous, ludicrous, preposterous, absurd, meaningless, irrational, illogical, childish, puerile, immature, irresponsible, scatterbrained.

similar adj.
☞ 相似的,近似的 alike, close,

related, akin, corresponding, equivalent, analogous, comparable, uniform, homogeneous.

similarity n.
☞ 相似,类似 likeness, resemblance, similitude, closeness, relation, correspondence, congruence, equivalence, analogy, comparability, compatibility, agreement, affinity, homogeneity, uniformity.

simple adj.
☞ 坦率的,率直的 easy, elementary, straightforward, uncomplicated, uninvolved, clear, lucid, plain, understandable, comprehensible.
☞ 坦率的,天真的 unsophisticated, natural, innocent, artless, guileless, ingenuous, naive, green, foolish, stupid, silly, idiotic, half-witted, simple-minded, feeble-minded, backward.

simplicity n.
☞ 简朴,质朴 simpleness, ease, straightforwardness, uncomplicatedness, clarity, purity, plainness, restraint, naturalness, innocence, artlessness, candour, openness, sincerity, directness.

simplify v.
☞ 简化,使单纯 disentangle, untangle, decipher, clarify, paraphrase, abridge, reduce, streamline.

simply adv.
☞ 仅仅,绝对地 merely, just, only, solely, purely, utterly, completely, totally, wholly, absolutely, quite, really, undeniably, unquestionably, clearly, plainly, obviously.
☞ 朴实地,朴素地 easily, straightforwardly, directly, intelligibly.

simulate v.
☞ 模拟,模仿 pretend, affect, assume, put on, act, feign, sham, fake, counterfeit, reproduce, duplicate, copy, imitate, mimic, parrot, echo, reflect.

simultaneous adj.
☞ 同时的,同时发生的 synchronous, synchronic, concurrent, contemporaneous, coinciding, parallel.

sin n.
☞ 罪,罪恶 wrong, offence, transgression, trespass, misdeed, lapse, fault, error, crime, wrongdoing, sinfulness, wickedness, unrighteousness, guilt.
v.
☞ 犯罪,违反 offend, transgress, trespass, lapse, err, misbehave, stray, go astray, fall, fall from grace.

sincere adj.
☞ 真实的,诚恳的 honest, thuthful, candid, frank, open, direct, straightforward, plain-spoken, serious, earnest, heartfelt, wholehearted, unmixed, natural, unaffected, artless, guileless, simple.

sincerity n.
☞ 真实,挚诚 honour, integrity, probity, uprightness, honesty,

truthfulness, candour, frankness, openness, directness, straightforwardness, seriousness, earnestness, wholeheartedness, genuineness.

sinful adj.
☞ 罪恶的 wrong, wrongful, criminal, bad, wicked, iniquitous, erring, fallen, immoral, corupt, depraved, impious, ungodly, unholy, irreligious, guilty.

sing v.
☞ 唱,发鸣叫声 chant, intone, vocalize, croon, serenade, yodel, trill, warble, chirp, pipe, whistle, hum.

single adj.
☞ 仅有的,唯一的 one, unique, singular, individual, particular, exclusive, sole, only, lone, solitary, separate, distinct, free, unattached, unmarried, celibate, unshared, undivided, unbroken, simple, one-to-one, man-to-man.

single out
☞ 选择,挑选 choose, select, pick, hand-pick, distinguish, identify, separate, set apart, isolate, highlight, pinpoint.

single-handed adj, adv
☞ 独立的(地),独力的(地) solo, alone, unaccompanied, unaided, unassisted, independent (ly).

single-minded adj.
☞ 赤诚的,一心一意的 determined, resolute, dogged, persevering, tireless, unwavering, fixed, unswerving, undeviating, steadfast, dedicated, devoted.

sinister adj.
☞ 不吉祥的,凶兆的 ominous, menacing, threatening, disturbing, disquieting, unlucky, inauspicious, malevolent, evil.

sink v.
☞ 下沉,沉没 descend, slip, fall, drop, slump, lower, stoop, succumb, lapse, droop, sag, dip, set, disappear, vanish.
☞ 变低,变弱 decrease, lessen, subside, abate, dwindle, diminish, ebb, fade, flag, weaken, fail, decline, worsen, degenerate, degrade, decay, collapse.
☞ 浸入,渗入 founder, dive, plunge, plummet, submerge, immerse, engulf, drown.
☞ 掘,挖 bore, drill, penetrate, dig, excavate, lay, conceal.

sip v.
☞ 啜,呷 taste, sample, drink, sup.
n.
☞ 啜,啜 taste, drop, spoonful, mouthful.

sit v.
☞ 坐落,孵卵 settle, rest, perch, roost, brood, pose.
☞ 坐,使坐 seat, hold, accommodate, contain.
☞ 聚集,开会 meet, assemble, gather, convene, deliberate.

site n.
☞ 位置,地点 location, place, spot, position, situation, station, setting, scene, plot, lot, ground, area.
v.

☞ 位于,设置 locate, place, position, situate, station, set, install.

sitting *n.*
☞ 开会,开庭 session, period, spell, meeting, assembly, hearing, consultation.

situation *n.*
☞ 位置,场所 site, location, position, place, spot, seat, locality, locale, setting, scenario.
☞ 状况,事态 state of affairs, case, circumstances, predicament, state, condition, status, rank, station, post, office, job, employment.

sizable *adj.*
☞ 颇大的,相当大的 large, substantial, considerable, respectable, goodly, largish, biggish, decent, generous.

size *n.*
☞ 大小,尺寸 magnitude, measurement(s), dimensions, proportions, volume, bulk, mass, height, length, extent, range, scale, amount, greatness, largeness, bigness, vastness, immensity.

size up *n.*
☞ 品评,判断 gauge, assess, evaluate, weigh up, measure.

skeleton *n.*
☞ 骨骼,纲要 bones, frame, structure, framework, bare bones, outline, draft, sketch.

sketch *v.*
☞ 起草,略述 draw, depict, portray, represent, pencil, paint, outline, delineate, draft, rough out, block out.
n.
☞ 梗概,素描 drawing, vignette, design, plan, diagram, outline, delineation, skeleton, draft.

skilful *adj.*
☞ 熟练的,灵巧的 able, capable, adept, competent, proficient, deft, adroit, handy, expert, masterly, accomplished, skilled, practised, experienced, professional, clever, tactical, cunning.

skill *n.*
☞ 技能,熟练 skilfulness, ability, aptitude, facility, handiness, talent, knack, art, technique, training, experience, expertise, expertness, mastery, proficiency, competence, accomplishment, cleverness, intelligence.

skilled *adj.*
☞ 有技能的,熟练的 trained, schooled, qualified, proficient, able, skilful.

skin *n.*
☞ 毛皮,牛皮 hide, pelt, membrane, film, coating, surface, outside, peel, rind, husk, casing, crust.
v.
☞ 剥皮 flay, fleece, strip, peel, scrape, graze.

skinny *adj.*
☞ 瘦骨嶙峋的 thin, lean, scrawny, scraggy, skeletal, skin-and-bone, emaciated, underfed, undernourished.

skip *v.*
☞ 跳,跳跃 hop, jump, leap,

dance, gambol, frisk, caper, prance.
- ☞ 略过,遗漏 miss, omit, leave out, cut.

sky n.
- ☞ 天空,天 space, atmosphere, air, heavens, blue.

slack adj.
- ☞ 松驰,不紧的 loose, limp, sagging, baggy.
- ☞ 缓慢的,呆滞的 lazy, sluggish, slow, quiet, idle, inactive.
- ☞ 疏忽的,马虎的 neglectful, negligent, careless, inattentive, remiss, permissive, lax, relaxed, easy-going.

v.
- ☞ 松垮地做,怠惰 idle, shirk, skive, neglect.

slacken v.
- ☞ 放松,减弱 loosen, release, relax, ease, moderate, reduce, lessen, decrease, diminish, abate, slow (down).

slam v.
- ☞ 猛投,猛击 bang, crash, dash, smash, throw, hurl, fling.
- ☞ 抨击,辱骂 criticize, slate, pan.

slander n.
- ☞ 诽谤,诬蔑 defamation, calumny, misrepresentation, libel, scandal, smear, slur, aspersion, backbiting.

v.
- ☞ 诽谤,诬蔑 defame, vilify, malign, denigrate, disparage, libel, smear, slur, backbite.

slanderous adj.
- ☞ 诽谤的,造谣中伤的 defamatory, false, untrue, libellous, damaging, malicious, abusive, insulting.

slant v.
- ☞ 使倾斜,倾向 tilt, slope, incline, lean, list, skew, angle.
- ☞ 歪曲,使……带上色的 distort, twist, warp, bend, weight, bias, colour.

n.
- ☞ 倾斜,倾向 slope, incline, gradient, ramp, camber, pitch, tilt, angle, diagonal.
- ☞ 偏见,歪曲 bias, emphasis, attitude, viewpoint.

slanting adj.
- ☞ 倾斜的,歪斜的 sloping, tilted, oblique, diagonal.

slap n.
- ☞ 拍,掌击 smack, spank, cuff, blow, bang, clap.

v.
- ☞ 拍,猛击 smack, spank, hit, strike, cuff, clout, bang, clap.

slaughter n.
- ☞ 屠杀,杀戮 killing, murder, massacre, extermination, butchery, carnage, blood-bath, bloodshed.

v.
- ☞ 屠杀,杀戮 kill, slay, murder, massacre, exterminate, liquidate, butcher.

slave n.
- ☞ 奴隶,苦工 servant, drudge, vassal, serf, villein, captive.

v.
- ☞ 使苦工,做牛马 toil, labour, drudge, sweat, grind, slog.

slavery n.

☞ 奴役,苦役 servitude, bondage, captivity, enslavement, serfdom, thraldom, subjugation.

sleep v.
☞ 睡,睡眠 doze, snooze, slumber, kip, doss (down), hibernate, drop off, nod off, rest, repose.
n.
☞ 睡眠,冬眠 doze, snooze, nap, forty, winks, shut-eye, kip, slumber, hibernation, rest, repose, siesta.

sleepless adj.
☞ 失眠的,不眠的 unsleeping, awake, wide-awake, alert, vigilant, watchful, wakeful, restless, disturbed, insomniac.

sleepy adj.
☞ 困的,不活动的 drowsy, somnolent, tired, weary, heavy, slow, sluggish, torpid, lethargic, inactive, quiet, dull, soporific, hypnotic.

slender adj.
☞ 纤细的,细长的 slim, thin, lean, slight, svelte, graceful.
☞ 微小的,不足的 faint, remote, slight, inconsiderable, tenuous, flimsy, feeble, inadequate, insufficient, meagre, scanty.

slice n.
☞ 薄片,部分 piece, sliver, wafer, rasher, tranche, slab, wedge, segment, section, share, portion, helping, cut, whack.
v.
☞ 砍,切成薄片 carve, cut, chop, divide, segment.

slide v.
☞ 滑,溜走 slip, slither, skid, skate, ski, toboggan, glide, plane, coast, skim.

slight adj.
☞ 少量的,琐屑的 minor, unimportant, insignificant, negligible, trivial, paltry, modest, small, little, inconsiderable, insubstantial.
☞ 微小的,轻微的 slender, slim, diminutive, petite, delicate.
v.
☞ 轻视,怠慢 scorn, despise, disdain, disparage, insult, affront, offend, snub, cut, cold-shoulder, ignore, disregard, neglect.
n.
☞ 轻蔑,怠慢 insult, affront, slur, snub, rebuff, rudeness, discourtesy, disrespect, contempt, disdain, indifference, disregard, neglect.

slim adj.
☞ 纤细的,苗条的 slender, thin, lean, svelte, trim.
☞ 微小的,渺茫的 slight, remote faint, poor.
v.
☞ 变苗条 lose weight, diet, reduce.

sling v.
☞ 投,掷 throw, hurl, fling, catapult, heave, pitch, lob, toss, chuck.
☞ 悬挂,吊起 hang, suspend, dangle, swing.

slip¹ v.
☞ 溜走,滑行 slide, glide,

skate, skid, stumble, trip, fall, slither, slink, sneak, steal, creep.

n.
☞ 摔跤,失足 mistake, error, slip-up, bloomer, blunder, fault, indiscretion, boob, omission, oversight, failure.

slip² *n.*
☞ 条,片 piece, strip, voucher, chit, coupon, certificate.

slippery *adj.*
☞ 滑的,滑溜的 slippy, icy, greasy, glassy, smooth, dangerous, treacherous, perilous.

☞ 不可靠的,滑头的 dishonest, untrustworthy, false, duplicitous, two-faced, crafty, cunning, devious, evasive, smooth, smarmy.

slit *v.*
☞ 切开,撕裂 cut, gash, slash, slice, split, rip, tear.

n.
☞ 切口,裂口 opening, aperture, vent, cut, incision, gash, slash, split, tear, rent.

slogan *n.*
☞ 口号,标语 jingle, motto, catch-phrase, catchword, watchword, battle-cry, warcry.

slope *v.*
☞ 倾斜,有斜度 slant, lean, tilt, tip, pitch, incline, rise, fall.

n.
☞ 倾斜,斜坡 incline, gradient, ramp, hill, ascent, descent, slant, tilt, pitch, inclination.

slot *n.*
☞ 缝,槽 hole, opening, aperture, slit, vent, groove, channel, gap, space, time, vacancy, place, spot, position, niche.

v.
☞ 安插,开槽于 insert, fit, place, position, assign, pigeonhole.

slow *adj.*
☞ 慢的,缓慢的 leisurely, unhurried, lingering, loitering, dawdling, lazy, sluggish, slow-moving, creeping, gradual, deliberate, measure, plodding, delayed, late, unpunctual.

☞ 迟钝的,笨的 stupid, slow-witted, dim, thick.

☞ 无趣的,无生气的 prolonged, protracted, long-drawn-out, tedious, boring, dull, uninteresting, uneventful.

v.
☞ 减速,缓行 brake, decelerate, delay, hold up, retard, handicap, check, curb, restrict.

sluggish *adj.*
☞ 不活动的,行动缓慢的 lethargic, listless, torpid, heavy, dull, slow, slow-moving, slothful, lazy, idle, inactive, lifeless, unresponsive.

sly *adj.*
☞ 狡猾的,偷偷摸摸的 wily, foxy, crafty, cunning, artful, guileful, clever, canny, shrewd, astute, knowing, subtle, devious, shifty, tricky, furtive, stealthy, surreptitious, underhand, covert, secretive, scheming, conniving, mischievous, roguish.

smack v.
☞ 掌击,拍击 hit, strike, slap, spank, whack, thwack, clap, box, cuff, pat, tap.
n.
☞ 拍击,掌击 blow, slap, spank, whack, thwack, box, cuff, pat, tap.
adv.
☞ 急剧而猛烈地 bang, slap-bang, right, plumb, straight, directly, exactly, precisely.

small adj.
☞ 小的,少的 little, tiny, minute, minuscule, short, slight, puny, petite, diminutive, pint-size(d), miniature, mini, pocket, pocket-sized, young.
☞ 不重要的,琐屑的 petty, trifling, trivial, unimportant, insignificant, minor, inconsiderable, negligible.
☞ 少的,不足的 inadequate, insufficient, scanty, meagre, paltry, mean, limited.

small-minded adj.
☞ 卑鄙的,吝啬的 petty, mean, ungenerous, illiberal, intolerant, bigoted, narrow-minded, parochial, insular, rigid, hidebound.

smart adj.
☞ 时髦的,整洁的 elegant, stylish, chic, fashionable, modish, neat, tidy, spruce, trim, well-groomed.
☞ 聪明的,机灵的 clever, intelligent, bright, sharp, acute, shrewd, astute.
v.
☞ 感到剧痛,引起剧痛 sting, hurt, prick, burn, tingle, twinge, throb.

smash v.
☞ 打碎,打破 break, shatter, shiver, ruin, wreck, demolish, destroy, defeat, crush.
☞ 猛击,重击 crash, collide, strike, bang, bash, thump.
n.
☞ 打碎,捣毁 accident, crash, collision, pile-up.

smear v.
☞ 擦,抹 daub, plaster, spread, cover, coat, rub, smudge, streak.
☞ 中伤,诽谤 defame, malign, vilify, blacken, sully, stain, tarnish.
n.
☞ 污点,污迹 streak, smudge, blot, blotch, splodge, daub.
☞ 中伤,诽谤 defamation, slander, libel, mudslinging, muck-raking.

smell n.
☞ 气味,嗅觉 odour, whiff, scent, perfume, fragrance, bouquet, aroma, stench, stink, pong.
v.
☞ 发出气味,闻 sniff, nose, scent, stink, reek, pong.

smelly adj.
☞ 难闻的,臭的 malodorous, pongy, stinking, reeking, foul, bad, off, fetid, putrid, high, strong.

smile n, v.
☞ 笑,微笑 grin, beam, simper, smirk, leer, laugh.

smoke n.

☞ 烟,烟尘 fumes, exhaust, gas, vapour, mist, fog, smog.
v.
☞ 冒烟,冒气 fume, smoulder, cure, dry.

smoky *adj.*
☞ 发烟多的,充满烟的 sooty, black, grey, grimy, murky, cloudy, hazy, foggy.

smooth *adj.*
☞ 平坦的,不颠簸的 level, plane, even, flat, horizontal, flush.
☞ 流畅的 steady, unbroken, flowing, regular, uniform, rhythmic, easy, effortless.
☞ 平滑的,平静的 shiny, polished, glossy, silky, glassy, calm, undisturbed, serene, tranquil, peaceful.
☞ 温和的,有礼貌的 suave, agreeable, smooth-talking, glib, plausible, persuasive, slick, smarmy, unctuous, ingratiating.
v.
☞ 使光滑,变平滑 iron, press, roll, flatten, level, plane, file, sand, polish.
☞ 变平静,使平静 ease, alleviate, assuage, allay, mitigate, calm, mollify.

smother *v.*
☞ 窒息,闷住 suffocate, asphyxiate, strangle, throttle, ckoke, stifle, extinguish, snuff, muffle, suppress, repress, hide, conceal, cover, shroud, envelop, wrap.

snack *n.*
☞ 快餐,小吃 refreshment(s), bite, nibble, titbit, elevenses.

snap *v.*
☞ 折断,断开 break, crack, split, separate.
☞ 猛咬,咬住 bite, nip, bark, growl, snarl, retort, crackle, pop.
☞ 抓住,攫取 snatch, seize, catch, grasp, grip.
n.
☞ 断开,咬住 break, crack, bite, nip, flick, fillip, crackle, pop.
adj.
☞ 仓促的,突然的 immediate, instant, on-the-spot, abrupt, sudden.

snare *v.*
☞ 捕捉,诱获 trap, ensnare, entrap, catch, net.
n.
☞ 陷阱,圈套 trap, wire, net, noose, catch, pitfall.

snarl[1] *v.*
☞ 咆哮,严厉地说 growl, grumble, complain.

snarl[2] *v.*
☞ 使……挤在一起,挤塞 tangle, knot, ravel, entangle, enmesh, embroil, confuse, muddle, complicate.

snatch *v.*
☞ 抓,攫取 grab, seize, kidnap, take, nab, pluck, pull, wrench, wrest, gain, win, clutch, grasp, grip.

sneak *v.*
☞ 偷偷地溜走,潜行 creep, steal, slip, slink, sidle, skulk, lurk, prowl, smuggle, spirit.
☞ 告密,打小报告 tell tales, split, inform on, grass on.
n.

☞打小报告的人 tell-tale, informer, grass.

sneaking adj.
☞偷偷摸摸的,不适的 private, secret, furtive, surreptitious, hidden, lurking, suppressed, grudging, nagging, niggling, persistent, worrying, uncomfortable, intuitive.

sneer v.
☞嘲笑,讥笑 scorn, disdain, look down on, deride, scoff, jeer, mock, ridicule, gibe, laugh, snigger.
n.
☞嘲笑,讥笑 scorn, disdain, derision, jeer, mockery, ridicule, gibe, snigger.

sniff v.
☞嗅,闻 breathe, inhale, snuff, snuffe, smell, nose, scent.

snigger v, n
☞窃笑,暗笑 laugh, gigle, titter, chuckle, sneer.

snobbery n.
☞势利,谄上欺下 snlbbishness, superciliousness, snootiness, airs, loftiness, arrogance, pride, pretension, condescension.

snobbish adj.
☞谄上的,势利的 supercilious, disdainful, snooty, stuck-up, toffee-nosed, superior, lofty, high-and-mighty, arrogant, pretentious, affected, condescending, patronizing.

soak v.
☞浸,泡 wet, drench, saturate, penetrate, permeate, infuse, bathe, marinate, souse, steep, submerge, immerse.

soaking adj.
☞湿透的,湿的 soaked, drenched, sodden, waterlogged, saturated, sopping, wringing, dripping, streaming.

soar v.
☞翱翔,升高 fly, wing, glide, plane, tower, rise, ascend, climb, mount, escalate, rocket.

sob v.
☞哭泣,呜咽 cry, weep, bawl, howl, blubber, snivel.

sober adj.
☞自制的,适度的 teetotal, temperate, moderate, abstinent, abstemious.
☞清醒的,冷静的 solemn, dignified, serious, staid, steady, sedate, quiet, serene, calm, composed, unruffled, unexcited, cool, dispassionate, level-headed, practical, realistic, reasonable, rational, clear-headed.
☞单调的,朴素的 sombre, drab, dull, plain, subdued, restrained.

so-called adj.
☞所谓的,号称的 alleged, supposed, purported, ostensible, nominal, self-styled, professed, would-be, pretended.

sociable adj.
☞好交际的,好与人交往的 outgoing, gregarious, friendly, affable, companionable, genial, convivial, cordial, warm, hospitable, neighbourly, approachable, accessible, familiar.

social adj.

☞ 社会的,社交的 communal, public, community, common, general, collective, group, organized.

n.
☞ 交谊会,联欢会 party, do, get-together, gathering.

socialize v.
☞ 适应社会生活,参与社交 mix, mingle, fraternize, gettogether, go out, entertain.

society n.
☞ 社会 community, population, culture, civilization, nation, people, mankind, humanity.

☞ 会,协会 club, circle, group, association, organization, company, corporation, league, union, guild, fellowship, fraternity, brotherhood, sisterhood, sorority.

☞ 友谊,交谊 friendship, companionship, camaraderie, fellowship, company.

☞ 名流社会,上层社会 upper classes, aristocracy, gentry, nobility, elite.

soft adj.
☞ 柔和的,柔软的 yielding, pliable, flexible, elastic, plastic, malleable, spongy, squashy, pulpy.

☞ 淡雅的 pale, light, pastel, delicate, subdued, muted, quiet, low, dim, faint, diffuse, mild, bland, gentle, soothing, sweet, mellow, melodious, delcet, pleasant.

☞ 柔滑的,细软的 furry, downy, velvety, silky, smooth.

☞ 温和的,宜人的 lenient, lax, permissive, indulgent, tolerant, easy-going, kind, generous, gentle, merciful, soft-hearted, tender, sensitive, weak, spineless.

soften v.
☞ 变弱,变温和 moderate, temper, mitigate, lessen, diminish, abate, alleviate, lessen, diminish, abate, alleviate, ease, soothe, palliate, quell, assuage, subdue, mollify, appease, calm, still, relax.

☞ 变柔 melt, liquefy, dissolve, reduce.

☞ 使软弱 cushion, pad, muffle, quicken, lower, lighten.

soft-hearted adj.
☞ 软心肠的,仁慈的 sympathetic, compassionate, kind, benevolent, charitable, generous, warm-hearted, tender, sentimental.

soil¹ n.
☞ 土地,泥土 earth, clay, loam, humus, dirt, dust, ground, land, region, country.

soil² v.
☞ 弄污,弄脏 dirty, begrime, stain, spot, smudge, smear, foul, muddy, pollute, defile, besmirch, sully, tarnish.

sole adj.
☞ 唯一的,仅有的 only, unique, exclusive, individual, single, singular, one, lone, solitary, alone.

solemn adj.
☞ 严肃的,崇敬的 serious, grave, sober, sedate, sombre, glum, thoughtful, earnest,

awed, reverential.
☞ 庄重的,令人深思的 grand, stately, majestic, ceremonial, ritual, formal, ceremonious, pompous, dignified, august, venerable, awe-inspiring, impressive, imposing, momentous.

solicit v.
☞ 请求,恳求 ask, request, seek, crave, beg, beseech, entreat, implore, pray, supplicate, sue, petition, canvass, importune.

solicitor n.
☞ 律师 lawyer, advocate, attorney, barrister, QC.

solid adj.
☞ 坚固的,结实的 hard, firm, dense, compact, strong, sturdy, substantial, sound, unshakable.
☞ 连续的,不间断的 unbroken, continuous, uninterrupted.
☞ 可靠的,可依赖的 reliable, dependable, trusty, worthy, decent, upright, sensible, level-headed, stable, serious, sober.
☞ 纯的,实心的 real, genuine, pure, concrete, tangible.

solidify v.
☞ 变坚固,变结实 harden, set, jell, congeal, coagulate, clot, cake, crystallize.

solitary adj.
☞ 独居的,无伴的 sole, single, lone, alone, lonely, lonesome, friendless, unsociable, reclusive, withdrawn, retired, sequestered, cloistered, secluded, separate, isolated, remote, out-of-the-way, inaccessible, unfrequented, unvisited, untrodden.

solitude n.
☞ 孤独,单独 aloneness, loneliness, reclusiveness, retirement, privacy, seclusion, isolation, remoteness.

solution n.
☞ 解答,解决 answer, result, explanation, resolution, key, remedy.
☞ 溶液 mixture, suspension, emulsion, liquid.

solve v.
☞ 解释,解答 work out, figure out, puzzle out, decipher, crack, disentangle, unravel, answer, resolve, settle, clear up, clarify, explain, interpret.

sombre adj.
☞ 昏暗的,阴沉的 dark, funereal, drab, dull, dim, obscure, shady, shadowy, gloomy, dismal, melancholy, mournful, sad, joyless, sober, serious, grave.

sometimes adv.
☞ 不时,有时 occasionally, now and again, now and then, once in a while, from time to time.

song n.
☞ 歌曲,音乐 ballad, madrigal, lullaby, shanty, anthem, hymn, carol, chant, chorus, air, tune, melody, lyric, number, ditty.

soon adv.
☞ 不久,很快 shortly, presently, in a minute, before long, in the near future.

soothe v.
☞ 减轻,缓和 alleviate, relieve, ease, salve, comfort, allay,

calm, compose, tranquillize, settle, still, quiet, hush, lull, pacify, appease, mollify, assuage, mitigate, soften.

sophisticated *adj*.
☞ 老于世故的 urbane, cosmopolitan, worldly, worldly-wise, cultured, cultivated, refined, polished.
☞ 最新式的,复杂的 advanced, highly-developed, complicated, complex, intricate, elaborate, delicate, subtle.

sore *adj*.
☞ 疼痛的 painful, hurting, aching, smarting, stinging, tender, sensitive, inflamed, red, raw.
☞ 恼怒的,伤心的 annoyed, irritated, vexed, angry, upset, hurt, wounded, afflicted, aggrieved, resentful.
n.
☞ 痛处,伤处 wound, lesion, swelling, inflammation, boil, abscess, ucler.

sorrow *n*.
☞ 悲伤,悲哀 sadness, unhappiness, grief, mourning, misery, woe, distress, affliction, anguish, heartache, heatbreak, misfortune, hardship, trouble, worry, trial, tribulation, regret, remorse.

sorry *adj*.
☞ 抱歉的,道歉的 apologetic, regretful, remorseful, contrite, penitent, repentant, conscience-stricken, guilt-ridden, shamefaced.
☞ 可怜的,悲哀的 pathetic, pitiful, poor, wretched, miserable, sad, unhappy, dismal.
☞ 同情的,惋惜的 sympathetic, compassionate, understanding, pitying, concerned, moved.

sort *n*.
☞ 分类,种 kind, type, genre, ilk, family, race, breed, species, genus, variety, order, class, category, group, denomination, style, make, brand, stamp, quality, nature, character, description.
v.
☞ 分类 class, group, categorize, distribute, divide, separate, segregate, sift, screen, grade, rank, order, classify, catalogue, arrange, organize, systematize.

sort out
☞ 整理,拣选 resolve, clear up, clarify, tidy up, neaten, choose, select.

soul *n*.
☞ 精神,灵魂 spirit, psyche, mind, reason, intellect, character, inner, being, essence, life, vital force.
☞ 个人,人类 individual, person, man, creature.

sound¹ *n*.
☞ 声音,噪音 noise, din, report, resonance, reverberation, tone, timbre, tenor, description.
v.
☞ 发声,作声 ring, toll, chime, peal, resound, resonate, reverberate, echo.
☞ 通知,发布 articulate, enunciate, pronounce, voice, express, utter, say, declare,

announce.

sound² adj.
- 完好的,坚固的 fit, well, healthy, vigorous, robust, sturdy, firm, solid, whole, complete, intact, perfect, unbroken, undamaged, unimpaired, unhurt, uninjured.
- 确实的,可靠的 valid, well-founded, reasonable, rational, logical, orthodox, right, true, proven, reliable, trustworthy, secure, substantial, thorough, good.

sound³ v.
- 探测,试探 measure, plumb, fathom, probe, examine, test, inspect, investigate.

sour adj.
- 酸的,有酸味的 tart, sharp, acid, pungent, vinegary, bitter, rancid.
- 坏脾气的 embittered, acrimonious, ill-tempered, peevish, crabbed, crusty, disagreeable.

source n.
- 源头,来源 origin, derivation, beginning, start, commencement, cause, root, rise, spring, fountainhead, wellhead, supply, mine, originator, authority, informant.

souvenir n.
- 纪念物,纪念品 memento, reminder, remembrance, keepsake, relic, token.

sovereign n.
- 最高统治者 uler, monarch, king, queen, emperor, empress, potentate, chief.

adj.
- 最高的,有无限权力的,有主权的 ruling, royal, imperial, absolute, unlimited, supreme, paramount, predominant, principal, chief, dominant, independent, autonomous.

sow v.
- 播种 plant, seed, scatter, strew, spread, disseminate, lodge, implant.

space n.
- 场地,空地 room, place, seat, accommodation, capacity, volume, extent, expansion, scope, range, play, elbow-room, leeway, margin.
- 空白,空间 blank, omission, gap, opening, lacuna, interval, intermission, chasm.

spacious adj.
- 宽广的,宽阔的 roomy, capacious, ample, big, large, sizable, broad, wide, huge, vast, extensive, open, uncrowded.

span n.
- 间距,期间 spread, stretch, reach, range, scope, compass, extent, length, distance, duration, term, period, spell.

v.
- 跨过,架 arch, vault, bridge, link, cross, traverse, extend, cover.

spare adj.
- 多余的,未占用的 reserve, emergency, extra, additional, leftover, remaining, unused, over, surplus, superfluous, supernumerary, unwanted, free, unoccupied.

v.
- 赦免,宽宏 pardon, let off, reprieve, release, free.
- 提供,分出 grant, allow, afford, part with.

sparing adj.
- 节俭的,节约的 economical, thrifty, careful, prudent, frugal, meagre, miserly.

spark n.
- 火光,闪烁 flash, flare, gleam, glint, flicker, hint, trace, vestige, scrap, atom, jot.

v.
- 发出火花,放散火星 kindle, set off, trigger, start, cause, occasion, prompt, provoke, stimulate, stir, excite, inspire.

sparkle v.
- 闪耀,闪烁 twinkle, glitter, scintillate, flash, gleam, glint, glisten, shimmer, coruscate, shine, beam.
- 起泡 effervesce, fizz, bubble.

n.
- 火花,闪烁 twinkle, glitter, flash, gleam, glint, flicker, spark, radiance, brilliance, dazzle, spirit, vitality, life, animation.

sparse adj.
- 稀少的,稀疏的 scarce, scanty, meagre, scattered, infrequent, sporadic.

speak v.
- 说,讲 talk, converse, say, state, declare, express, utter, voice, articulate, enunciate, pronounce, tell, communicate, address, lecture, harangue, hold forth, declaim, argue, discuss.

speaker n.
- 说话者,讲演者 lecturer, orator, spokesperson, spokesman, spokeswoman.

special adj.
- 重大的 important, significant, momentous, major, noteworthy, distinguished, memorable, remarkable, extraordinary, exceptional.
- 特殊的,格外的 different, distinctive, characteristic, peculiar, singular, individual, unique, exclusive, select, choice, particular, specific, unusual, precise, detailed.

specialist n.
- 专家 consultant, authority, expert, master, professional, connoisseur.

speciality n.
- 特征,特质 strength, forte, talent, field, specialty, piece, de resistance.

specific adj.
- 明确的,精确的 precise, exact, fixed, limited, particular, special, definite, unequivocal, clear-cut, explicit, express, unambiguous.

specification n.
- 阐明,记述 requirement, condition, qualification, description, listing, item, particular, detail.

specify v.
- 指定,详细说明 stipulate, spell out, define, particularize, detail, itemize, enumerate, list, mention, cite, name, designate, indicate, describe, delineate.

specimen n.
☞ 样本,标本 sample, example, instance, illustration, model, pattern, paradigm, exembplar, representative, copy, exhibit.

spectacle n.
☞ 展示,场面 show, performance, display, exhibition, parade, pageant, extravaganza, scene, sight, curiosity, wonder, marvel, phenomenon.

spectacular adj.
☞ 富丽的,壮观的 grand, splendid, magnificent, sensational, impressive, striking, stunning, staggering, amazing, remarkable, dramatic, daring, breathtaking, dazzling, eye-catching, colourful.

spectator n.
☞ 观众,旁观者 watcher, viewer, onlooker, looker-on, bystander, passer-by, witness, eye-witness, observer.

spectre n.
☞ 鬼怪,幽灵 ghost, phantom, spirit, wraith, apparition, vision, presence.

speculate v.
☞ 思索,沉思 wonder, contemplate, meditate, muse, reflect, consider, deliberate, theorize, suppose, guess, conjecture, surmise, gamble, risk, hazard, venture.

speech n.
☞ 谈话,讲话 diction, articulation, enunciation, elocution, delivery, utterance, voice, language, tongue, parlance, dialect, jargon.
☞ 演讲 oration, address, discourse, talk, lecture, harangue, spiel, conversation, dialogue, monologue, soliloquy.

speechless adj.
☞ 不会说话的,哑的 dumbfounded, thunderstruck, amazed, aghast, tongue-tied, inarticulate, mute, dumb, silent, mum.

speed n.
☞ 速度 velocity, rate, pace, tempo, quickness, swiftness, rapidity, celerity, alacrity, haste, hurry, dispatch, rush, acceleration.
v.
☞ 迅速前进,快行 race, tear, belt, zoom, career, bowl along, sprint, gallop, hurry, rush, hasten, accelerate, quicken, put one's foot down, step on it.

speedy adj.
☞ 快的,迅速的 fast, quick, swift, rapid, nimble, express, prompt, immediate, hurried, hasty, precipitate, cursory.

spell¹ n.
☞ 一段时间,一段持续时间 period, time, bout, session, term, season, interval, stretch, patch, turn, stint.

spell² n.
☞ 魅力,妩媚 charm, incantation, magic, sorcery, witchery, bewitchment, enchantment, fascination, galmour.

spellbound adj.

spend v.
☞ 入迷的，出神的 transfixed, hypnotized, mesmerized, fascinated, enthralled, gripped, entranced, captivated, bewitched, enchanted, charmed.

spend v.
☞ 花费,开销 disburse, pay out, fork out, shell out, invest, lay out, splash out, waste, squander, fritter, expend, consume, use up, exhaust.
☞ 渡过 pass, fill, occupy, use, employ, apply, devote.

spendthrift n.
☞ 挥霍者,浪费者 squanderer, prodigal, profligate, wastrel.
adj.
☞ 挥霍的,浪费的 improvident, extravagant, prodigal, wasteful.

sphere n.
☞ 球形,球体 ball, globe, orb, round.
☞ 圈子,领域 domain, realm, province, department, territory, field, range, scope, compass, rank, function, capacity.

spherical adj.
☞ 球的,球形的 round, rotund, ball-shaped, globe-shaped.

spicy adj.
☞ 香料的 piquant, hot, pungent, tangy, seasoned, aromatic, fragrant.
☞ 辛辣的,痛快的 racy, risque, ribald, suggestive, indelicate, improper, indecorous, unseemly, scandalous, sensational.

spill v.
☞ 推翻,倾倒 overturn, upset, slop, overflow, disgorge, pout, tip, discharge, shed, scatter.

spin v.
☞ 旋转 turn, revolve, rotate, twist, gyrate, twirl, pirouette, wheel, whirl, swirl, reel.
n.
☞ 旋转 turn, revolution, twist, gyration, twirl, pirouette, whirl, swirl.
☞ 混乱 commotion, agitation, panic, flap, state, tizzy.
☞ 乘车 drive, ride, run.

spin out
☞ 延长 prolong, protract, extend, lengthen, amplify, pad out.

spine n.
☞ 脊椎骨 backbone, spinal column, vertebral column, vertebrae.
☞ 刺,针 thorn, barb, prickle, bristle, quill.

spineless adj.
☞ 柔弱无力的 weak, feeble irresolute, ineffective, cowardly, faint-hearted, lily-livered, yellow, soft, wet, submissive, weak-kneed.

spiral adj.
☞ 螺旋形的,螺线的 winding, coiled, corkscrew, helical, whorled, scrolled, circular.
n.
☞ 螺旋形,螺线 coil, helix, corkscrew, screw, whorl, convolution.

spirit n.
☞ 精神,心灵 soul, psyche, mind, breath, life.
☞ 灵魂 ghost, spectre, phantom, apparition, angel,

demon, fairy, sprite.
☞ 勇气,锐气 liveliness, vivacity, animation, sparkle, vigour, energy, zest, fire, ardour, motivation, enthusiasm, zeal, enterprise, resolution, willpower, courage, backbone, mettle.
☞ 本质,精神 meaning, sense, substance, essence, gist, tenor, character, quality, mood, humour, temper, disposition, temperament, feeling, morale, attitude, outlook.

spirited *adj*.
☞ 精神饱满的,生气勃勃的 lively, vivacious, animated, sparkling, high-spirited, vigorous, energetic, active, ardent, zealous, bold, courageous, mettlesome, plucky.

spiritual *adj*.
☞ 精神的,无实体的 unworldly, incorporeal, immaterial, otherwordly, heavenly, divine, holy, sacred, religious, ecclesiastical.

spit *v*.
☞ 吐痰 expectorate, eject, discharge, splutter, hiss.
n.
☞ 唾液 spittle, saliva, slaver, drool, dribble, sputum, phlegm, expectoration.

spite *n*.
☞ 恶意 spitefulness, malice, venom, gall, bitterness, rancour, animosity, ill feeling, grudge, malevolence, malignity, ill nature, hate, hatred.
v.
☞ 使……恼怒 annoy, irritate, irk, vex, provoke, gall, hurt, injure, offend, put out.

spiteful *adj*.
☞ 恶意的 malicious, venomous, catty, bitchy, snide, barbed, cruel, vindictive, vengeful, malevolent, malignant, ill-natured, ill-disposed, nasty.

splash *v*.
☞ 溅水 bathe, wallow, paddle, wade, dabble, plunge, wet, wash, shower, spray, squirt, sprinkle, spatter, splatter, splodge, spread, daub, plaster, slop, slosh, plop, surge, break, dash, strike, buffet, smack.
☞ 显示,炫耀 publicize, flaunt, blazon, trumpet.
n.
☞ 斑点 spot, patch, splatter, splodge, burst, touch, dash.
☞ 显示,炫耀 publicity, display, ostentation, effect, impact, stir, excitement, sensation.

splendid *adj*.
☞ 壮丽的 brilliant, dazzling, glittering, lustrous, bright, radiant, glowing, glorious, magnificent, gorgeous, resplendent, sumptuous, luxurious, lavish, rich, fine, grand, stately, imposing, impressive, great, outstanding, remarkable, exceptional, sublime, supreme, superb, excellent, first-class, wonderful, marvellous, admirable.

splendour *n*.
☞ 辉煌 brightness, radiance, brilliance, dazzle, lustre, glory,

resplendence, magnificence, richness, grandeur, majesty, solemnity, pomp, ceremony, display, show, spectacle.

split v.

☞ 分开 divide, separate, partition, part, disunite, disband, open, gape, fork, diverge, break, splinter, shiver, snap, crack, burst, rupture, tear, rend, rip, slit, slash, cleave, halve, slice up, share, distribute, parcel out.

n.

☞ 分开 division, separation, partition, break, breach, gap, cleft, crevice, crack, fissure, rupture, tear, rent, rip, rift, slit, slash.

☞ 不合 schism, disunion, dissension, discord, difference, divergence, break-up.

adj.

☞ 分开的 divided, cleft, cloven, bisected, dual, twofold, broken, fractured, cracked, ruptured.

split up

☞ 分开 part, part company, disband, break up, separate, divorce.

spoil v.

☞ 毁坏 mar, upset, wreck, ruin, destroy, damage, impair, harm, hurt, injure, deface, disfigure, blemish.

☞ 溺爱 indulge, pamper, cosset, coddle, mollycoddle, baby, spoon-feed.

sponsor n.

☞ 资助人 patron, backer, angel, promoter, underwriter, guarantor, surety.

v.

☞ 资助 finance, fund, bankroll, subsidize, patronize, back, promote, underwrite, guarantee.

spontaneous adj.

☞ 自觉的 natural, unforced, untaught, instinctive, impulsive, unpremeditated, free, willing, unhesitating, voluntary, unprompted, impromptu, extempore.

sport n.

☞ 运动 game, exercise, activity, pastime, amusement, entertainment, diversion, recreation, play.

☞ 戏谑 fun, mirth, humour, joking, jesting, banter, teasing, mockery, ridicule.

v.

☞ 夸示 wear, display, exhibit, show off.

sporting adj.

☞ 堂堂正正的 sportsmanlike, gentlemanly, decent, considerate, fair.

spot n.

☞ 污点 dot, speckle, fleck, mark, speck, blotch, blot, smudge, daub, splash, stain, discoloration, blemish, flaw, pimple.

☞ 地点 place, point, position, situation, location, site, scene, locality.

☞ 困境 plight, predicament, quandary, difficulty, trouble, mess.

v.

☞ 发现 see, notice, observe,

detect, discern, identify, recognize.

spotless *adj*.
- 无瑕的 immaculate, clean, white, gleaming, spick and span, unmarked, unstained, unblemished, unsullied, pure, chaste, virgin, untouched, innocent, blameless, faultless, irreproachable.

spotted *adj*.
- 有斑点的 dotted, speckled, flecked, mottled, dappled, pied.

spotty *adj*.
- 有斑点的 pimply, pimpled, blotchy, spotted.

spouse *n*.
- 配偶 husband, wife, partner, mate, better, half.

sprawl *v*.
- 伸延 spread, straggle, trail, ramble, flop, slump, slouch, loll, lounge, recline, repose.

spread *v*.
- 伸延 stretch, extend, sprawl, broaden, widen, dilate, expand, swell, mushroom, proliferate, escalate, open, unroll, unfurl, unfold, fan out, cover, lay out, arrange.
- 散布, 传播 scatter, strew, diffuse, radiate, disseminate, broadcast, transmit, communicate, promulgate, propagate, publicize, advertise, publish, circulate, distribute.
- *n*.
- 伸展 stretch, reach, span, extent, expanse, sweep, compass.
- 蔓延 advance, development, expansion, increase, proliferation, escalation, diffusion, dissemination, dispersion.

spring¹ *v*.
- 跳 jump, leap, vault, bound, hop, bounce, rebound, recoil.
- 发生 originate, derive, come, stem, arise, start, proceed, issue, emerge, emanate, appear, sprout, grow, develop.
- *n*.
- 跳 jump, leap, vault, bound, bounce, .
- 弹性 springiness, resilience, give, flexibility, elasticity, buoyancy.

spring² *n*.
- 源头 source, origin, beginning, cause, root, fountainhead, wellhead, wellspring, well, geyser, spa.

springy *adj*.
- 有弹性的 bouncy, resilient, flexible, elastic, stretchy, rubbery, spongy, bouyant.

sprout *v*.
- 发芽 shoot, bud, germinate, grow, develop, come up, spring up.

spy *n*.
- 间谍 secret agent, undercover, agent, double agent, mole, fifth columnist, scout, snooper.
- *v*.
- 发现 spot, glimpse, notice, observe, discover.

squad *n*.
- 班, 分队 crew, team, gang,

squander v.
- 挥霍 waste, misspend, misuse, lavish, blow, fritter away, throw away, dissipate, scatter, spend, expend, consume.

square v.
- 结清，使……一致 settle, reconcile, tally, agree, accord, harmonize, correspond, match, balance, straighten, level, align, adjust, regulate, adapt, tailor, fit, suit.

adj.
- 正方形的 quadrilateral, rectangular, right-angled, perpendicular, straight, true, even, level.
- 公平的 fair, equitable, just, ethical, honourable, honest, genuine, above-board, on the level.

squash v.
- 压碎 crush, flatten, press, squeeze, compress, crowd, trample, stamp, pound, pulp, smash, distort.
- 镇压 suppress, silence, quell, quash, annihilate, put down, snub, humiliate.

squeak v, n
- 发出吱吱声 squeal, whine, creak, peep, cheep.

squeal v, n
- 尖叫 cry, shout, yell, yelp, wail, scream, screech, shriek, squawk.

squeeze v.
- 挤压 press, squash, crush, pinch, nip, compress, grip, clasp, clutch, hug, embrace, enfold, cuddle.
- 绞，扭 wring, wrest, extort, milk, bleed, force, lean on.

n.
- 挤压 press, squash, crush, crowd, congestion, jam.
- 拥抱 hug, embrace, hold, grasp, clasp.

stab v.
- 刺 pierce, puncture, cut, wound, injure, gore, knife, spear, stick, jab, thrust.

n.
- 刺痛 ache, pang, twinge, prick, puncture, cut, incision, gash, wound, jab.
- 尝试 try, attempt, endeavour, bash.

stability n.
- 平稳 steadiness, firmness, soundness, constancy, steadfastness, strength, sturdiness, solidity, durability, permanence.

stable adj.
- 平稳的 steady, firm, secure, fast, sound, sure, constant, steadfast, reliable, established, well-founded, deep-rooted, strong, sturdy, durable, lasting, enduring, abiding, permanent, unchangeable, unalterable, invariable, immutable, fixed, static, balanced.

stack n.
- 堆 heap, pile, mound, mass, load, accumulation, hoard, stockpile.

v.
- 堆积 heap, pile, load, amass,

accumulate, assemble, gather, save, hoard, stockpile.

staff n.
- 全体人员 personnel, workforce, employees, workers, crew, team, teachers, officers.
- 棒,杆 stick, cane, rod, baton, wand, pole, prop.

stage n.
- 阶段 point, juncture, step, phase, period, division, lap, leg, length, level, floor.

v.
- 上演 mount, put on, present, produce, give, do, perform, arrange, organize, stage-manage, orchestrate, engineer.

stagger v.
- 蹒跚 lurch, totter, teeter, wobble, sway, rock, reel, falter, hesitate, waver.
- 吃惊 surprise, amaze, astound, astonish, stun, stupefy, dumbfound, flabbergast, shake, shock, confound, overwhelm.

stagnant adj.
- 停滞的 still, motionless, standing, brackish, stale, sluggish, torpid, lethargic.

stain v.
- 弄脏 mark, spot, blemish, blot, smudge, discolour, dirty, soil, taint, contaminate, sully, tarnish, blacken, disgrace.
- 着色 dye, tint, tinge, colour, paint, varnish.

n.
- 污点 mark, spot, blemish, blot, smudge, discoloration, smear, slur, disgrace, shame, dishonour.

stake¹ n.
- 木桩 post, pole, standard, picket, pale, paling, spike, stick.

stake² n.
- 赌金 bet, wager, pledge, interest, concern, involvement, share, investment, claim.

stale adj.
- 不新鲜的 dry, hard, old, musty, fusty, flat, insipid, tasteless.
- 陈腐的 overused, hackneyed, clicheed, stereotyped, jaded, worn-out, unoriginal, trite, banal, commonplace.

stalemate n.
- 僵局 draw, tie, deadlock, impasse, standstill, halt.

stalk v.
- 偷偷走近 track, trail, hunt, follow, pursue, shadow, tail, haunt.

stammer v.
- 口吃 stutter, stumble, falter, hesitate, splutter.

stamp v.
- 踩 trample, crush, beat, pound.
- 加印盖 imprint, impress, print, inscribe, engrave, emboss, mark, brand, label, categorize, identify, characterize.

n.
- 印章 print, imprint, impression, seal, signature, authorization, mark, hallmark, attestation, brand, cast, mould, cut, form, fashion, sort, kind, type, breed, character,

stance n.
☞ 姿态 posture, deportment, carriage, bearing, position, standpoint, viewpoint, angle, point of view, attitude.

stand v.
☞ 放置 put, place, set, erect, up-end, position, station.
☞ 忍受 bear, tolerate, abide, endure, suffer, experience, undergo, withstand, weather.
☞ 站 rise, get up, stand up.
n.
☞ 基座 base, pedestal, support, frame, rack, table, stage, platform, place, stall, booth.

stand by
☞ 支持 support, back, champion, defend, stick up for, uphold, adhere to, hold to, stick by.

stand down
☞ 退出 step down, resign, abdicate, quit, give up, retire, withdraw.

stand for
☞ 代表 represent, symbolize, mean, signify, denote, indicate.

stand in for
☞ 代替 deputize for, cover for, understudy, replace, substitute for.

stand out
☞ 突出 show, catch the eye, stick out, jut out, project.

stand up for
☞ 捍卫 defend, stick up for, side with, fight for, support, protect, champion, uphold.

stand up to
☞ 抵制 defy, oppose, resist, withstand, endure, face, confront, brave.

standard n.
☞ 标准 norm, average, type, model, pattern, example, sample, guideline, benchmark, touchstone, yardstick, rule, measure, gauge, level, criterion, requirement, specification, grade, quality.
adj.
☞ 标准的 normal, average, typical, stock, classic, basic, staple, usual, customary, popular, prevailing, regular, approved, accepted, recognized, official, orthodox, set, established, definitive.

standardize v.
☞ 标准化 normalize, equalize, homogenize, stereotype, mass-produce.

standpoint n.
☞ 观点 position, station, vantagepoint, stance, viewpoint, angle, point of view.

standsstill n.
☞ 静止 stop, halt, pause, lull, rest, stoppage, jam, jog-jam, hold-up, impasse, deadlock, stalemate.

star n.
☞ 名人 celebrity, personage, luminary, idol, lead, leading man, leading lady, superstar.

stare v.
☞ 注视 gaze, look, watch, gape, gawp, gawk, goggle, glare.
n.
☞ 注视 gaze, look, glare.

start v.
☞ 开始 begin, commence, originate, initiate, introduce, pioneer, create, found, establish, set up, institute, inaugurate, launch, open, kick off, instigate, activate, trigger, set off, set out, leave, depart, appear, arise, issue.
n.
☞ 开始 beginning, commencement, outset, inception, dawn, birth, break, outburst, onset, origin, initiation, introduction, foundation, inauguration, launch, opening, kick-off.

startle v.
☞ 震惊 surprise, amaze, astonish, astound, shock, scare, frighten, alarm, agitate, upset, disturb.

starvation n.
☞ 饥饿, 饿死 hunger, undernourishment, malnutrition, famine.

starve v.
☞ 挨饿, 饿死 hunger, fast, diet, deprive, refuse, deny, die, perish.

starving adj.
☞ 挨饿的 hungry, underfed, undernourished, ravenous, famished.

state v.
☞ 说, 陈述 say, declare, announce, report, communicate, assert, aver, affirm, specify, present, express, put, formulate, articulate, voice.
n.
☞ 情况, 状态 condition, shape, situation, position, circumstances, case.
☞ 国家, 政府 nation, country, land, territory, kingdom, republic, government.
☞ 盛观, 仪礼, 豪华 pomp, ceremony, dignity, majesty, grandeur, glory, splendour.
adj.
☞ 国家的, 礼仪的 national, governmental, public, official, formal, ceremonial, pompous, stately.

stately adj.
☞ 威严的, 堂皇的 grand, imposing, impressive, elegant, majestic, regal, reval, imperial, noble, august, lofty, pompous, dignified, measured, deliberate, solemn, ceremonious.

statement n.
☞ 陈述, 声明 account, report, bulletin, communique, announcement, declaration, proclamation, communication, utterance, testimony.

static adj.
☞ 静止的, 不动的 stationary, motionless, immobile, unmoving, still, inert, resting, fixed, constant, changeless, unvarying, stable.

station n.
☞ 站, 位置 place, location, position, post, headquarters, base, depot.
v.
☞ 置于…… locate, set, establish, install, garrison, post, send, appoint, assign.

stationary adj.

statue n.
☞ 雕像, 塑像 figure, head, bust, effigy, idol, statuette, carving, bronze.

status n.
☞ 重要地位, 要人身分 rank, grade, degree, level, class, station, standing, position, state, condition, prestige, eminence, distinction, importance, consequence, weight.

stay v.
☞ 继续, 保持, 忍耐 last, continue, endure, abide, remain, linger, persist.
☞ 暂住, 停留 reside, dwell, live, settle, sojourn, stop, halt, pause, wait.
n.
☞ 停留, 逗留 visit, holiday, stopover, sojourn.

steady adj.
☞ 坚固的, 稳定的 stable, balanced, poised, fixed, immovable, firm, poised, settled, still, calm, imperturbable, equable, even, uniform, consistent, unvarying, unchanging, constant, persistent, unremitting, incessant, uninterrupted, unbroken, regular, rhythmic, steadfast, unwavering.
v.
☞ 变得牢固, 稳定 balance, stabilize, fix, secure, brace, support.

☞ 不动的, 固定的 motionless, immobile, unmoving, still, static, inert, standing, resting, parked, moored, fixed.

steal v.
☞ 偷, 窃取 thieve, pilfer, filch, pinch, nick, take, appropriate, snatch, swipe, shoplift, poach, embezzle, lift, plagiarize.
☞ 偷偷地移动, 潜行 creep, tiptoe, slip, slink, sneak.

stealthy adj.
☞ 偷偷进行的, 秘密的 surreptitious, clandestine, covert, secret, unobtrusive, secretive, quiet, furtive, sly, cunning, sneaky, underhand.

steam n.
☞ 蒸气 vapour, mist, haze, condensation, moisture, dampness.

steep adj.
☞ 垂直的, 陡峭的 sheer, precipitous, headlong, abrupt, sudden, sharp.
☞ 不合理的, 过分的 excessive, extreme, stiff, unreasonable, high, exorbitant, exrottionate, overpriced.

steer v.
☞ 驾驶, 引导 pilot, guide, direct, control, govern, conduct.

stem¹ n.
☞ 茎 stalk, shoot, stock, branch, trunk.

stem² v.
☞ 阻止, 堵住 stop, halt, arrest, stanch, staunch, block, dam, check, curb, restrain, contain, resist, oppose.

step n.
☞ 步, 举步 pace, stride, footstep, tread, footprint,

print, trace, track.
- 步骤,阶段 move, act, action, deed, measure, procedure, process, proceeding, progression, movement, stage, phase, degree.
- 台阶,梯阶 rung, stair, level, rank, point.

v.
- 走,踏过 pace, stride, tread, stamp, walk, move.

step down
- 辞职,下台 stand down, resign, abdicate, quit, leave, retire, withdraw.

step up
- 增加 increase, raise, augment, boost, build up, intensify, escalate, accelerate, speed up.

stereotype n.
- 模型,模子 formula, convention, mould, pattern, model.

v.
- 用铅板印刷,使固定 categorize, pigeonhole, typecast, standardize, formalize, conventionalize, mass-produce.

stern adj.
- 严厉的,严格的 strict, severe, authoritarian, rigid, inflexible, unyielding, hard, tough, rigorous, stringent, harsh, cruel, unsparing, relentless, unrelenting, grim, forbidding, stark, austere.

stew v.
- 炖,煮 boil, simmer, braise, casserole.

stick¹ v.
- 刺,插 thrust, poke, stab, jab, pierce, penetrate, puncture, spear, transfix.
- 粘,粘接 glue, gum, paste, cement, bond, fuse, weld, solder, adhere, cling, hold.
- 固定,连接 attach, affix, fasten, secure, fix, pin, join, bind.
- 置,装 put, place, position, set, install, deposit, drop.

stick at
- 坚持做 persevere, plug away, persist, continue.

stick out
- 伸出,凸出 protrude, jut out, project, extend.

stick up for
- 坚持,维护 stand up for, speak up for, defend, champion, support, uphold.

stick² n.
- 枯枝,小木棍 branch, twig, wand, baton, staff, sceptre, cane, birch, rod, pole, stake.

sticky adj.
- 粘的 adhesive, gummed, tacky, gluey, gummy, viscous, glutinous, gooey.
- 困难的,不愉快的 difficult, tricky, thorny, awkward, unpleasant, delicate.
- 粘性的,潮湿的 humid, clammy, muggy, close, oppressive, sultry.

stiff adj.
- 坚硬的,不易弯曲的 rigid, inflexible, unbending, unyielding, hard, solid, hardened, solidified, firm, tight, taut, tense.
- 冷淡的,拘谨的 formal,

ceremonious, pompous, stand-offish, cold, prim, priggish, austere, strict, severe, harsh.
☞ 不灵活的,困难的 difficult, hard, tough, arduous, laborious, awkward, exacting, rigorous.

stiffen v.
☞ 使坚硬 harden, solidify, tighten, tense, brace, reinforce, starch, thicken, congeal, coagulate, jell, set.

stifle v.
☞ 使感到窒息 smother, suffocate, asphyxiate, strangle, choke, extinguish, muffle, dampen, deaden, silence, hush, suppress, quell, check, curb, restrain, repress.

still adj.
☞ 寂静的,静止的 stationary, motionless, lifeless, stagnant, smooth, undisturbed, unruffled, calm, tranquil, serene, restful, peaceful, hushed, quiet, silent, noiseless.
v.
☞ 平静,寂静 calm, soothe, allay, tranquillize, subdue, restrain, hush, quieten, silence, pacify, settle, smooth.
adv.
☞ 仍,尚 yet, even so, nevertheless, nonetheless, notwithstanding, however.

stimulate v.
☞ 激励,鼓舞 rouse, arouse, animate, quicken, fire, inflame, inspire, motivate, encourage, induce, urge, impel, spur, prompt, goad, provoke, incite, instigate, trigger off.

stimulus n.
☞ 刺激物,激励物 incentive, encouragement, inducement, spur, goad, provocation, incitement.

sting v.
☞ 螫,刺痛 bite, prick, hurt, injure, wound.
☞ 感到刺痛,刺伤 smart, tingle, burn, pain.
n.
☞ 刺痛,刺伤 bite, nip, prick, smart, tingle.

stingy adj.
☞ 吝啬的,小气的 mean, miserly, niggardly, tight-fisted, parsimonious, penny-pinching.

stipulate v.
☞ 规定,约定 specify, lay down, require, demand, insist on.

stipulation n.
☞ 规定,条件 specification, requirement, demand, condition, proviso.

stir v.
☞ 移动,惹起,激发 move, budge, touch, affect, inspire, excite, thrill, disturb, agitate, shake, tremble, quiver, flutter, rustle.
☞ 搅和,拌匀 mix, blend, beat.
n.
☞ 移动,骚动,激动 activity, movement, bustle, flurry, commotion, ado, fuss, to-do, uproar, tumult, disturbance, disorder, agitation, excitement, ferment.

stir up
☞ 使激动 rouse, arouse,

awaken, animate, quicken, kindle, fire, inflame, stimulate, spur, prompt, provoke, incite, instigate, agitate.

stock n.
☞ 现货,存货 goods, merchandise, wares, commodities, capital, assets, inventory, repertoire, range, variety, assortment, source, supply, fund, reservoir, store, reserve, stockpile, hoard.
☞ 祖先,血统 parentage, ancestry, descent, extraction, family, line, lineage, pedigree, race, breed, species, blood.
☞ 家畜 livestock, animals, cattle, horse, sheep, herds, flocks.
adj.
☞ 普通的,常备的 standard, basic, regular, routine, ordinary, run-of-the-mill, usual, customary, traditional, conventional, set, stereotyped, hackneyed, overused, banal, trite.
v.
☞ 贮存,进货 keep, carry, sell, trade in, deal in, handle, supply, provide.

stock up
☞ 供应,贮存 gather, accumulate, amass, lay in, provision, fill, replenish, store (up), save, hoard, pile up.

stomach n.
☞ 胃 tummy, gut, inside(s), belly, abdomen, paunch, pot.
v.
☞ 忍受,容忍 tolerate, bear, stand, abide, endure, suffer, submit to, take.

stony adj.
☞ 冷酷无情的,铁石心肠的 blank, expressionless, hard, cold, frigid, icy, indifferent, unfeeling, heartless, callous, merciless, pitiless, inexorable, hostile.
☞ 多石的 pebbly, shingly, rocky.

stoop v.
☞ 弯腰,低头 hunch, bow, bend, incline, lean, duck, squat, crouch, kneel.
☞ 卑屈,堕落 descend, sink, lower, oneself, resort, go so far as, condescend, deign.

stop v.
☞ 停止,中止 halt, cease, end, finish, conclude, terminate, discontinue, suspend, interrupt, pause, quit, refrain, desist, pack in.
☞ 防止,阻碍 prevent, bar, frustrate, thwart, intercept, hinder, impede, check, restrain.
☞ 堵塞,填塞 seal, close, plug, block, obstruct, arrest, stem, stanch.
n.
☞ 车站 station, terminus, destination.
☞ 休息 rest, break, pause, stage.
☞ 停止 halt, standstill, stoppage, cessation, end, finish, conclusion, termination, discontinuation.

store v.
☞ 贮存,储藏 save, keep, put aside, lay by, reserve, stock,

lay in, deposit, lay down, lay up, accumulate, hoard, salt away, stockpile, stash .
n.
☞ 供给,贮存 stock, supply, provision, fund, reserve, mine, reservoir, hoard, cache, stockpile, accumulation, quantity, abundance, plenty, lot.
☞ 仓库 storeroom, storehouse, warehouse, repository, depository.

storey *n.*
☞ 一层 floor, level, stage, tier, flight, deck.

storm *n.*
☞ 暴风雪,大风 tempest, thunderstorm, squall, blizzard, gale, hurricane, whirlwind, tornado, cyclone.
☞ 爆发,激动 outburst, uproar, furore, outcry, row, rumpus, commotion, disturbance, tumult, turmoil, stir, agitation, rage, outbreak, attack, assault.
v.
☞ 突击,狂怒 charge, rush, attack, assault, assail, roar, thunder, rage, rant, rave, fume.

stormy *adj.*
☞ 有暴风雨的,有暴风雪的 tempestuous, squally, rough, choppy, turbulent, wild, raging, windy, gusty, blustery, foul.

story *n.*
☞ 故事,传说 tale, fairy-tale, fable, myth, legend, novel, romance, fiction, yarn, anecdote, episode, plot, narrative, history, chronicle, record, account, relation, recital, report, article, feature.
☞ 谎言,假话 lie, falsehood, untruth.

stout *adj.*
☞ 粗壮的,肥大的 fat, plump, fleshy, portly, corpulent, overweight, heavy, bulky, big, brawny, beefy, hulking, burly, muscular, athletic.
☞ 坚固的,结实的 strong, tough, durable, thick, sturdy, robust, hardy, vigorous.
☞ 勇敢的,刚毅的 brave, courageous, valiant, plucky, fearless, bold, intrepid, dauntless, resolute, stalwart.

straight *adj.*
☞ 笔直的,一直的 level, even, flat, horizontal, upright, vertical, aligned, direct, undeviating, unswerving, true, right.
☞ 景然有序的,整齐的 tidy, neat, orderly, shipshape, organized.
☞ 坦诚的,正直的 honourable, honest, law-abiding, respectable, upright, trustworthy, reliable, straightforward, fair, just.
☞ 直率的 frank, candid, blunt, forthright, direct.
☞ 纯的 undiluted, neat, unadulterated, unmixed.
adv.
☞ 正直的,坦然的 directly, point-blank, honestly, frankly, candidly.

straight away
☞ 立刻,马上 at once,

immediately, instantly, right away, directly, now, there, and then.

straighten v.
- 变直,变整洁 unbend, align, tidy, neaten, order, arrange.

straighten out
- 变整洁 clear up, sort out, settle, resolve, correct, rectify, disentangle, regularize.

straightforward adj.
- 直白的 easy, simple, uncomplicated, clear, elementary.
- 直率的,真诚的 honest, truthful, sincere, genuine, open, frank, candid, direct, forthright.

strain¹ v.
- 拉紧 pull, wrench, twist, sprain, tear, stretch, extend, tighten, tauten.
- 紧压,净化 sieve, sift, screen, separate, filter, purify, drain, wring, squeeze, compress, express.
- 奋斗,努力 weaken, tire, tax, overtax, overwork, labour, try, endeavour, struggle, strive, exert, force, drive.

n.
- 负担,努力 stress, anxiety, burden, pressure, tension, tautness, pull, sprain, wrench, injury, exertion, effort, struggle, force.

strain² n.
- 种,血统 stock, ancestry, descent, extraction, family, lineage, pedigree, blood, variety, type.
- 特质,潮流 trait, streak, vein, tendency, trace, suggestion, suspicion.

strained adj.
- 勉强的,被迫的 forced, constrained, laboured, false, artificial, unatural, stiff, tense, unrelaxed, uneasy, uncomfortable, awkward, embarrassed, self-conscious.

strange adj.
- 特别的,奇怪的 odd, peculiar, funny, curious, queer, weird, bizarre, eccentric, abnormal, irregular, uncommon, unusual, exceptional, remarkable, extraordinary, mystifying, perplexing, unexplained.
- 未见的 new, novel, untried, unknown, unheard-of, unfamiliar, unacquainted, foreign, alien, exotic.

stranger n.
- 陌生人,异乡人 newcomer, visitor, guest, non-member, outsider, foreigner, alien.

strategic adj.
- 战略性的,重要的 important, key, critical, decisive, crucial, vital, tactical, planned, calculated, deliberate, politic, diplomatic.

strategy n.
- 政策,策略 tactics, planning, policy, approach, procedure, plan, programme, design, scheme.

stray v.
- 走失,迷失 wander, (off) get lost, err, ramble, roam,

rove, range, meander, straggle, drift, diverge, deviate, digress.
adj.
☞ 走失的,迷路的 lost, abandoned, homeless, wandering, roaming.
☞ 偶然的,怪异的 random, chance, accidental, freak, odd, erratic.

stream n.
☞ 河流 river, creek, brook, beck, burn, rivulet, tributary.
☞ 水流,不断流出 current, drift, flow, run, gush, flood, deluge, cascade, torrent.
v.
☞ 流出 issue, well, surge, run, flow, course, pour, spout, gush, flood, cascade.

streamlined adj.
☞ 流线型的 aerodynamic, smooth, sleek, graceful, efficient, well-run, smooth-running, rationalized, time-saving, organized, slick.

strength n.
☞ 力量,力气,强度 toughness, robustness, sturdiness, lustiness, brawn, muscle, sinew, power, might, force, vigour, energy, stamina, health, fitness, courage, fortitude, spirit, resolution, firmness, effectiveness, potency, concentration, intensity, vehemence.

strengthen v.
☞ 使……更强壮,坚强 reinforce, brace, steel, fortify, buttress, bolster, support, toughen, harden, stiffen, consolidate, substantiate, corroborate, confirm, encourage, hearten, refresh, restore, invigorate, nourish, increase, heighten, intensify.

stress n.
☞ 重要,忧虑 pressure, strain, tension, worry, anxiety, weight, burden, trauma, hassle.
☞ 重点,压力 emphasis, accent, accentuation, beat, force, weight, importance, significance.
v.
☞ 强调,重读 emphasize, accentuate, highlight, underline, underscore, repeat.

stretch n.
☞ 伸展,延伸 expanse, spread, sweep, reach, extent, distance, space, area, tract.
☞ 连续的时间,空间 period, time, term, spell, stint, run.
v.
☞ 拉长,伸展 pull, tighten, tauten, strain, tax, extend, lengthen, elongate, expand, spread, unfold, unroll, inflate, swell, reach.

stretch out
☞ 直躺 extend, relax, hold out, put out, lie down, reach.

strict adj.
☞ 严格的,严厉的 stern, authoritarian, no-nonsense, firm, rigid, inflexible, stringent, rigorous, harsh, severe, austere.
☞ 准确的 exact, precise, accurate, literal, faithful, true, absolute, utter, total, complete, thoroughgoing, meticulous,

scrupulous, particular, religious.

strife n.
- 争吵,冲突 conflict, discord, dissension, controversy, animosity, friction, rivalry, contention, quarrel, row, wrangling, struggle, fighting, combat, battle, warfare.

strike n.
- 罢工 industrial action, work-to-rule, go-slow, stoppage, sit-in, walk-out, mutiny, revolt.
- 击,打 hit, blow, stroke, raid, attack.

v.
- 罢工 stop work, down tools, work to rule, walk out, protest, mutiny, revolt.
- 击,打 hit, knock, collide with, slap, smack, cuff, clout, thump, wallop, beat, pound, hammer, buffet, raid, attack, afflict.
- 给……深刻印象 impress, affect, touch, register.
- 发现,找到 find, discover, unearth, uncover, encounter, reach.

strike out
- 删除,除去 cross out, delete, strike through, cancel, strike off, remove.

striking adj.
- 引人注目的 noticeable, conspicuous, salient, outstanding, remarkable, extraordinary, memorable, impressive, dazzling, arresting, astonishing, stunning.

string n.
- 线,细绳 twine, cord, rope, cable, line, strand, fibre.
- 串 series, succession, sequence, chain, line, row, file, queue, procession, train.

v.
- 连结,上弦 thread, link, connect, tie up, hang, suspend, festoon, loop.

strip¹ v.
- 脱去,剥去 peel, skin, flay, denude, divest, deprive, undress, disrobe, unclothe, uncover, expose, lay bare, bare, empty, clear, gut, ransack, pillage, plunder, loot.

strip² n.
- 带,条 ribbon, thong, strap, belt, sash, band, stripe, lath, slat, piece, bit, slip, shred.

stripe n.
- 带状,条状 band, line, bar, chevron, flash, streak, fleck, strip, belt.

strive v.
- 奋斗,奋勉 try, attempt, endeavour, struggle, strain, work, toil, labour, fight, contend, compete.

stroke n.
- 拍 caress, pat, rub.
- 打击,一击 blow, hit, knock, swipe.
- 一次动作 sweep, flourish, movement, action, move, line.

v.
- 抚摸 caress, fondle, pet, touch, pat, rub, massage.

stroll v.
- 漫步,闲逛 saunter, amble, dawdle, ramble, wander.

n.
- 散步,漫步 saunter, amble,

strong adj.
☞ 强壮的,坚固的 tough, resilient, durable, hard-wearing, heavy-duty, robust, sturdy, firm, sound, lusty, strapping, stout, burly, well-built, beefy, brawny, muscular, sinewy, athletic, fit, healthy, hardy, powerful, mighty, potent.

☞ 强烈的,坚强的 intense, deep, vivid, fierce, violent, vehement, keen, eager, zealous, fervent, ardent, dedicated, staunch, stalwart, determined, resolute, tenacious, strong-minded, strong-willed, self-assertive.

☞ 辛辣 highly-flavoured, piquant, hot, spicy, highly-seasoned, sharp, pungent, undiluted, concentrated.

☞ 有力度的 convincing, persuasive, cogent, effective, telling, forceful, weighty, compelling, urgent.

stronghold n.
☞ 要塞,保垒 citadel, bastion, fort, fortress, castle, keep, refuge.

structure n.
☞ 结构,组成 construction, erection, building, edifice, fabric, framework, form, shape, design, configuration, conformation, make-up, formation, arrangement, organization, set-up.

v.
☞ 构造,组织 construct, assemble, build, form, shape, design, arrange, organize.

struggle v.
☞ 奋斗,努力 strive, work, toil labour, strain, agonize, fight, battle, wrestle, grapple, contend, compete, vie.

n.
☞ 抗争,努力 difficulty, problem, effort, exertion, pains, agony, work, labour, toil, clash, conflict, strife, fight, battle, skirmish, encounter, combat, hostilities, contest.

stubborn adj.
☞ 顽固的,固执的 obstinate, stiff-necked, mulish, pig-headed, obdurate, intransigent, rigid, inflexible, unbending, unyielding, dogged, persistent, tenacious, headstrong, self-willed, wilful, refractory, difficult, unmanageable.

stuck adj.
☞ 粘的 fast, jammed, firm, fixed, fastened, joined, glued, cemented.

☞ 受到打击的 beaten, stumped, baffled.

stuck-up adj.
☞ 自大的,骄傲的 snobbish, toffee-nosed, supercilious, snooty, haughty, high and mighty, condescending, proud, arrogant, conceited, bigheaded.

student n.
☞ 学生 undergraduate, postgraduate, scholar, schoolboy, schoolgirl, pupil, disciple, learner, trainee, apprentice.

studied adj.
☞ 故意的,有意的 deliberate, conscious, wilful, intentional, premeditated, planned, calculated, contrived, forced, unnatural, over-elaborate.

studio n.
☞ 工作室,工作间 workshop, workroom.

study v.
☞ 学习,研究 read, learn, revise, cram, swot, mug up, read up, research, investigate, analyse, survey, scan, examine, scrutinize, peruse, pore over, contemplate, meditate, ponder, consider, deliberate.

n.
☞ 学识 reading, homework, preparation, learning, revision, cramming, swotting, research, investigation, inquiry, analysis, examination, scrutiny, inspection, contemplation, consideration, attention.
☞ 论文 perort, essay, thesis, paper, monograph, survey, review, critique.
☞ 书房 office, den.

stuff v.
☞ 挤塞 pack, stow, load, fill, cram, crowd, force, push, shove, ram, wedge, jam, squeeze, compress.
☞ 暴食,过食 gorge, gormandise, overindulge, guzzle, gobble, sate, satiate.

n.
☞ 材料,质料 material, fabric, matter, substance, essence.
☞ 所有物,财产 belonging, possessions, things, objects, articles, goods, luggage, paraphernalia, gear, clobber, kit, tackle, equipment, materials.

stuffy adj.
☞ 通风不良的,闷热的 musty, stale, airless, unventilated, suffocating, stifling, oppressive, heavy, close, muggy, sultry.
☞ 呆板的 staid, strait-laced, prim, conventional, old-fashioned, pompous, dull, dreary, uninteresting, stodgy.

stumble v.
☞ 绊倒,跌 trip, slip, fall, lurch, reel, stagger, flounder, blunder.
☞ 结巴 stammer, stutter, hesitate, falter.

stumble on
☞ 偶然发现 come across, chance upon, happen upon, find, discover, encounter.

stun v.
☞ 把……打晕,使震惊 amaze, astonish, astound, stagger, shock, daze, stupefy, dumbfound, flabbergast, overcome, confound, confuse, bewilder.

stunning adj.
☞ 漂亮的,极好的 beautiful, lovely, gorgeous, ravishing, dazzling, brilliant, striking, impressive, spectacular, remarkable, wonderful, marvellous, great, sensational.

stupid adj.
☞ 愚蠢的 silly, foolish, irresponsible, ill-advised, indiscreet, foolhardy, rash, senseless, mad, lunatic,

brainless, half-witted, idiotic, imbecilic, moronic, feeble-witted, idiotic, imbecilic, moronic, feeble-minded, simple-minded, slow, dim, dull, dense, thick, dumb, dopey, crass, inane, puerile, mindless, futile, pointless, meaningless, nonsensical, absurd, ludicrous, ridiculous, laughable.

☞ 迟钝的 dazed, groggy, stupefied, stunned, sluggish, semiconscious.

sturdy adj.

☞ 坚实的,强健的 strong, robust, durable, well-made, stout, substantial, solid, well-built, powerful, muscular, athletic, hardy, vigorous, flourishing, hearty, staunch, stalwart, steadfast, firm, resolute, determined.

stutter v.

☞ 结结巴巴的说 stammer, hesitate, falter, stumble, mumble.

style n.

☞ 样式,款式 appearance, cut, design, pattern, shape, form, sort, type, kind, genre, variety, category.

☞ 时髦,气派 elegance, smartness, chic, flair, panache, stylishness, taste, polish, refinement, sophistication, urbanity, fashion, vogue, trend, mode, dressiness, flamboyance, affluence, luxury, grandeur.

☞ 方法,手段 technique, approach, method, manner, mode, fashion, way, custom.

☞ 文体 wording, phrasing, expression, tone, tenor.

v.

☞ 设计 design, cut, tailor, fashion, shape, adapt.

☞ 称呼 designate, term, name, call, address, title, dub, label.

stylish adj.

☞ 流行的 chic, fashionable, a la mode, modish, in vogue, voguish, trendy, snappy, natty, snazzy, dressy, smart, elegant, classy, polished, refined, sophisticated, urbane.

subconscious adj.

☞ 下意识的 subliminal, unconscious, intuitive, inner, innermost, hidden, latent, repressed, suppressed.

subdue v.

☞ 克服 overcome, quell, suppress, repress, overpower, crush, defeat, conquer, vanquish, overrun, subject, subjugate, humble, break, tame, master, discipline, control, check, moderate, reduce, soften, quienten, damp, mellow.

subject n.

☞ 主题 topic, theme, matter, issue, question, point, case, affair, business, discipline, field.

☞ 臣民 national, citizen, participant, client, patient, victim.

adj.

☞ 容易受 liable, disposed, prone, susceptible, vulnerable, open, exposed.

☞ 从属的 subjugated, captive,

bound, obedient, answerable, subordinate, inferior, subservient, submissive.
☞ 以……为条件 dependent, contingent, conditional.
v.
☞ 使……遭受 expose, lay open, submit, subjugate, subdue.

sublime *adj.*
☞ 崇高的 exalted, elevated, high, lofty, noble, majestic, great, grand, imposing, magnificent, glorious, transcendent, spirtual.

submerge *v.*
☞ 潜入 submerse, immerse, plunge, duck, dip, sink, drown, engulf, overwhelm, swamp, flood, inundate, deluge.

submerged *adj.*
☞ 潜水的 submersed, immersed, underwater, sunk, sunken, drowned, swamped, inundated, hidden, concealed, unseen.

submission *n.*
☞ 屈服 surrender, capitulation, resignation, acquiescence, assent, compliance, obedience, deference, submissiveness, meekness, passivity.
☞ 提交 presentation, offering, contribution, entry, suggestion, proposal.

submissive *adj.*
☞ 屈认的 yielding, unresisting, resigned, patient, uncomplaining, accommodating, biddable, obedient, deferential, ingratiating, subservient, humble, meek, docile, subdued, passive.

submit *v.*
☞ 屈从 yield, give in, surrender, capitulate, knuckle under, bow, bend, stoop, succemb, agree, comply.
☞ 呈送 present, tender, offer, put forward, suggest, propose, table, state, claim, argue.

subordinate *adj.*
☞ 下级的 secondary, auxiliary, ancillary, subsidiary, dependent, inferior, lower, junior, minor, lesser.
n.
☞ 属下 inferior, junior, assistant, attendant, second, aide, dependant, underling.

subscribe *v.*
☞ 赞同 support, endorse, back, advocate, approve, agree.
☞ 认捐 give, donate, contribute.

subscription *n.*
☞ 订阅 membership fee, dues, payment, donation, contribution, offering, gift.

subsequent *adj.*
☞ 随后的 following, later, future, next, succeeding, consequent, resulting, ensuing.

subsidiary *adj.*
☞ 辅助的 auxiliary, supplementary, additional, ancillary, assistant, supporting, contributory, secondary, subordinate, lesser, minor.
n.
☞ 附属公司 branch, offshoot, division, section, part.

subsidize v.
☞ 补助 support, back, underwrite, sponsor, finance, fund, aid, promote.

subsidy n.
☞ 津贴 grant, allowance, assistance, help, aid, contribution, sponsorship, finance, support, backing.

substance n.
☞ 物质 matter, material, stuff, fabric, essence, pith, entity, body, solidity, concreteness, reality, actuality, ground, foundation.
☞ 实质 subject, subject-matter, theme, gist, meaning, significance, force.

substandard adj.
☞ 不合标准的 second-rate, inferior, imperfect, damaged, shoddy, poor, inadequate, unacceptable.

substantial adj.
☞ 相当的, 重要的 large, big, sizable, ample, generous, great, considerable, significant, important, worthwhile, massive, bulky, hefty, well-built, stout, sturdy, strong, sound, durable.

substantiate v.
☞ 证实 prove, verify, confirm, support, corroborate, authenticate, validate.

substitute v.
☞ 代替 change, exchange, swap, switch, interchange, replace.
☞ 代理 stand in, fill in, cover, deputize, understudy, relieve.
n.
☞ 代替, 代理 reserve, stand-by, temp, supply, locum, understudy, stand-in, replacement, relief, surrogate, proxy, agent, deputy, makeshift, stopgap.
adj.
☞ 代替的 reserve, temporary, acting, surrogate, proxy, replacement, alternative.

subtle adj.
☞ 精巧的 delicate, understated, implied, indirect, slight, tenuous, faint, mild, fine, nice, refined, sophisticated, deep, profound.
☞ 狡猾的 artful, cunning, crafty, sly, devious, shrewd, astute.

subtract v.
☞ 减去 deduct, take away, remove, withdraw, debit, detract, diminish.

suburbs n.
☞ 郊区 subuibia, commuter belt, residential area, outskirts.

succeed v.
☞ 成功 triumph, make it, get on, thrive, flourish, prosper, make good, manage, work.
☞ 随…而至 follow, replace, result, ensue.

succeeding adj.
☞ 随之而来的 following, next, subsequent, ensuing, coming, to come, later, successive.

success n.
☞ 成功 triumph, victory, luck, fortune, prosperity, fame, eminence, happiness.

☞ 成功的人或物　celebrity, star, somebody, winner, bestseller, hit, sensation.

successful adj.
☞ 成功的　victorious, winning, lucky, fortunate, prosperous, wealthy, thriving, flourishing, booming, moneymaking, lucrative, profitable, rewarding, satisfying, fruitful, productive.

succession n.
☞ 连续　sequence, series, order, progression, run, chain, string, cycle, continuation, flow, course, line, train, procession.

successive adj.
☞ 连续的　connsecutive, sequential, following, succeeding.

succinct adj.
☞ 简洁的　short, brief, terse, pithy, concise, compact, condensed, summary.

succumb v.
☞ 屈从　give way, yield, give in, submit, knuckle under, surrender, capitulate, collapse, fall.

suck v.
☞ 吸吮　draw in, imbibe, absorb, soak up, extract, drain.

sudden adj.
☞ 突然　unexpected, unforeseen, surprising, startling, abrupt, sharp, quick, swift, rapid, prompt, hurried, hasty, rash, impetuous, impulsive, snap.

sue v.
☞ 起诉　prosecute, charge, indict, summon, solicit, appeal.

suffer v.
☞ 伤害　hurt, ache, agonize, grieve, sorrow.
☞ 忍受　bear, support, tolerate, endure, sustain, experience, undergo, go through, feel.

suffering n.
☞ 苦难　pain, discomfort, agony, anguish, affliction, distress, misery, hardship, ordeal, torment, torture.

sufficient adj.
☞ 充足的　enough, adequate, satisfactory, effective.

suffocate v.
☞ 窒息　asphyxiate, smother, stifle, choke, strangle, throttle.

suggestion n.
☞ 建议　proposal, proposition, motion, recommendation, idea, plan.
☞ 暗示　implication, insinuation, innuendo, hint, intimation, suspicion, trace, indication.

suggestive adj.
☞ 暗示的　evocative, reminiscent, expressive, meaning, indicative.

suit v.
☞ 令……满意　satisfy, gratify, please, answer, match, tally, agree, correspond, harmonize.
☞ 适合　fit, befit, become, tailor, adapt, adjust, accommodate, modify.
n.
☞ 服装　outfit, costume, dress, clothing.

suitable adj.
☞ 合适的　appropriate, fitting, convenient, opportune, suited,

sum n.
☞ 合计 total, sum total, aggregate, whole, entirety, number, quantity, amount, tally, reckoning, score, result.

sum up
☞ 概括 summarize, review, recapitulate, conclude, close.

summarize v.
☞ 概括 outline, precis, condense, abridge, abbreviate, shorten, sum up, encapsulate, revies.

summmary n.
☞ 摘要 svnopsis, resume, outline, abstract, precis, condensation, digest, compendium, abridgement, summing-up, review, recapitulation.
adj.
☞ 概要的 short, succinct, brief, cursory, hasty, prompt, direct, unceremonious, arbitrary.

summit n.
☞ 顶点 top, peak, pinnacle, apex, point, crown, head, zenith, acme, culmination, height.

summon v.
☞ 召唤 call, send for, invite, bid, beckon, gather, assemble, convene, rally, muster, mobilize, rouse, arouse.

sumptuous adj.
☞ 奢侈的 luxurious, plush, lavish, extravagant, opulent, rich, costly, expensive, dear, splendid, magnificent, gorgeous superb, grand.

sunbathe v.
☞ 日光浴 sun, bask, tan, brown, bake.

sunburnt adj.
☞ 晒黑的 brown, tanned, bronzed, weather-beaten, burnt, red, blistered, peeling.

sunny adj.
☞ 晴朗的 fine, cloudless, clear, summery, sunshiny, sunlit, bright, brilliant.
☞ 开朗的 cheerful, happy, joyful, smiling, beaming, radiant, light-hearted, buoyant, optimistic, pleasant.

sunrise n.
☞ 日出 dawn, crack of dawn, daybreak, daylight.

sunset n.
☞ 日落 sundown, dusk, twilight, gloaming, evening, nightfall.

superb adj.
☞ 极佳的 excellent, first-rate, first-class, superior, choice, fine, exquisite, gorgeous, magnificent, splendid, grand, wonderful, marvellous, admirable, impressive, breathtaking.

superficial adj.
☞ 表面的 surface, external, exterior, outward, apparent, seeming, cosmetic, skin-deep, shallow, slight, trivial, lightweight, frivolous, casual, cursory, sketchy, hasty,

superfluous adj.
- 多余的 extra, spare, excess, surplus, remaining, redundant, supernumerary, unnecessary, needless, unwanted, uncalled-for, excessive.

superintend v.
- 监督 supervise, oversee, overlook, inspect, run, manage, administer, direct, control, handle.

superior adj.
- 上等的 excellent, first-class, first-rate, top-notch, top-flight, high-class, exclusive, choice, select, fine, de luxe, admirable, distinguished, exceptional, unrivalled, par excellence.
- 较……好,高于 better, preferred, greater, higher, senior.
- 傲慢的 haughty, lordly, pretentious, snobbish, snooty, supercilious, disdainful, condescending, patronizing.
- n.
- 上司 senior, elder, better, boss, chief, principal, director, manager, foreman, supervisor.

superiority n.
- 优越 advantage, lead, edge, supremacy, ascendancy, pre-eminence, predominance.

superstition n.
- 迷信 myth, old wives' tale, fallacy, delusion, illusion.

superstitious adj.
- 迷信的 mythical, false, fallacious, irrational, groundless, delusive, illusory.

supervise v.
- 监督 oversee, watch over, look after, superintend, run, manage, administer, direct, conduct, preside over, control, handle.

supervision n.
- 监督 surveillance, care, charge, superintendence, oversight, running, management, administration, direction, control, guidance, instruction.

supervisor n.
- 主管,上司 overseer, inspector, superintendent, boss, chief, director, administrator, manager, foreman, forewoman.

supplant v.
- 取代 replace, supersede, usurp, oust, displace, remove, overthrow, topple, unseat.

supplement n.
- 补充 addition, extra, insert, pull-out, addendum, appendix, codicil, postscript, sequel.
- v.
- 补充 add to, augment, boost, reinforce, fill up, top up, complement, extend, eke out.

supplementary adj.
- 补充的 additional, extra, auxliary, secondary, complementary, accompanying.

supplier n.
- 供应商 dealer, seller, vendor, wholesaler, retailer.

supplies n.
- 供应物 stores, provisions, food, equipment, materials, necessities.

supply v.
☞ 供应 provide, furnish, equip, outfit, stock, fill, replenish, give, donate, grant, endow, contribute, yield, produce, sell.

n.
☞ 给养 source, amount, quantity, stock, fund, reservoir, store, reserve, stockpile, hoard, cache.

supprt v.
☞ 支持 back, second, defend, champion, advocate, promote, foster, help, aid, assist, rally round, finance, fund, subsidize, underwrite.
☞ 支撑 hold up, bear, carry, sustain, brace, reinforce, strengthen, prop, buttress, bolster.
☞ 维持 maintain, keep, provide for, feed, nuurish.
☞ 拥护 endorse, confirm, verify, authenticate, corroborate, substantiate, document.

n.
☞ 支持 backing, allegiance, loyalty, defence, protection, patronage, sponsorship, approval, encouragement, comfort, relief, help, aid, assistance.
☞ 支撑物 prop, stay, post, pillar, brace, crutch, roundation, underpinning.

supporter n.
☞ 支持者 fan, follower, adherent, advocate, champion, defender, seconder, patron, sponsor, helper, ally, friend.

suppose v.
☞ 假设 assume, presume, expect, infer, conclude, guess, conjecture, surmise, believe, think, consider, judge, imagine, conceive, fancy, pretend, postulate, hypothesize.

supposed adj.
☞ 传闻的 alleged, reported, rumoured, assumed, presumed, reputed, putative, imagined, hypothetical.

supposed to
☞ 预定的 meant to, intended to, expected to, required to, obliged to.

supreme adj.
☞ 最好的 best, greatest, highest, top, crowning, culminating, first, leading, foremost, chief, principal, head, sovereign, pre-eminent, predominant, prevailing, world-beating, unsurpassed, second-to-none, incomparaable, matchless, consummate, transcendent, superlative, prime, ultimate, extreme, final.

sure adj.
☞ 肯定的 certain, convinced, assured, confident, decided, positive, definite, unmistakable, clear, accurate, precise, unquestionable, indisputable, undoubted, undeniable, irrvocable, inevitable, bound.
☞ 安全的 safe, secure, fast, solid, firm, steady, stable, guananteed, reliable, dependable, trustworthy, steadfast, unwavering, unerring, unfailing, infallible, effective.

surface n.
- 表面 outside, exterior, facade, veneer, covering, skin, top, side, face, plane.

v.
- 浮在表面 rise, arise, come up, emerge, appear, materialise, come to light.

surpass v.
- 超越 beat, outdo, exceed, outstrip, better, excel, transcend, outshine, eclipse.

surplus n.
- 多余 excess, residue, remainder, balance, superfluity, glut, surfeit.

adj.
- 多余的 excess, superfluous, redundant, extra, spare, remaining, unused.

surprise v.
- 吃惊 startle, amaze, astonish, astound, stagger, flabbergast, bewilder, confuse, nonplus, disconcert, dismay.

n.
- 吃惊 amazement, astonishment, incredulity, wonder, bewilderment, dismay, shock, start, bombshell, revelation.

surprised adj.
- 吃惊的 startled, amazed, astonished, astounded, staggered, flabbergasted, thunderstruck, dumbfounded, speechless, shocked, nonplussed.

surprising adj.
- 使人吃惊的 amazing, astonishing, astounding, staggering, stunning, incredible, extraordinary, remarkable, startling, unexpected, unforeseen.

surrender v.
- 投降 capitulate, submit, resign, concede, yield, give in, cede, give up, quit, relinquish, abandon, renounce, forgo, waive.

n.
- 投降 capitulation, resignation, submission, yielding, relinquishment, renunciation.

surround v.
- 环绕 encircle, ring, girdle, encompass, envelop, encase, enclose, hem in, besiege.

surrounding adj.
- 周围的 encircling, bordering, adjacent, adjoining, nerghbouring, nearby.

surroundings n.
- 周围 neighbourhood, vicinity, locality, setting, environment, background, milieu, ambience.

survey v.
- 调查,测量 view, contemplate, observe, supervise, scan, scrutinize, examine, inspect, study, research, review, consider, estimate, evaluate, assess, measure, plot, plan, map, chart, reconnoitre.

n.
- 调查 review, overview, scrutiny, examination, inspection, study, pull, appraisal, assessment, measurement.

survive v.

☞ 比……活得久 outlive, outlast, endure, last, stay, remain, live, exist, withstand, weather.

suspect v.
☞ 怀疑 doubt, distrust, mistrust, call into question.
☞ 猜想 believe, fancy, feel, guess, conjecture, speculate, surmise, suppose, consider, conclude, infer.

adj.
☞ 怀疑的 suspicious, doubtful, dubious, questionable, debatable, unreliable, iffy, dodgy, fishy.

suspend v.
☞ 悬挂 hang, dangle, swing.
☞ 中止 adjourn, interrupt, discontinue, cease, delay, defer, postpone, put off, shelve.

suspense n.
☞ 悬念 uncertainty, insecurity, anxiety, tension, apprehension, anticipation, expectation, expectancy, excitement.

suspension n.
☞ 中止 adjournment, interruption, break, intermission, respite, remission, stay, moratorium, delay, deferral, postponement, abeyance.

suspicion n.
☞ 怀疑 doubt, scepticism, distrust, mistrust, wariness, caution, misgiving, apprehension.
☞ 有点儿 trace, hint, suggestion, soupcon, touch, tinge, shade, glimmer, shadow.
☞ 疑心 idea, notion, hunch.

suspicious *adj.*
☞ 怀疑的 doubtful, sceptical, unbelieving, suspecting, distrustful, mistrustful, wary, chary, apprehensive, uneasy.
☞ 可疑的 dubious, questionable, suspect, irregular, shifty, shady, dodgy, fishy.

sustain v.
☞ 维持 nourish, provide for, nurture, foster, help, aid, assist, comfort, relieve, support, uphold, endorse, bear, carry.
☞ 保持 maintain, keep going, keep up, continue, prolong, hold.

swallow v.
☞ 吞吃 consume, devour, eat, gobble, up, guzzle, drink, quaff, knock back, gulp down.

swarm n.
☞ 群 crowd, throng, mob, mass, multitude, myriad, host, army, horde, herd, flock, drove, shoal.
v.
☞ 群集 1 flock, flood, stream, mass, congregate, crowd, throng.
☞ 充满 teem, crawl, bristle, abound.

sway v.
☞ 摇摆 rock, roll, lurch, swing, wave, oscillate, fluctuate, bend, incline, lean, divert, veer, swerve.
☞ 影响 influence, affect, persuade, induce, convince, convert, overrule, dominate, govern.

swear v.
- 发誓 vow, promise, pledge, avow, attest, asseverate, testify, affirm, assert, declare, insist.
- 诅咒 curse, blaspheme.

swear-word n.
- 咒骂 expletive, four-letter word, curse, oath, imprecation, obscenity, profanity, blasphemy, swearing, bad language.

sweat n.
- 汗 perspiration, moisture, stickiness.
- 焦虑 anxiety, worry, agitation, panic.
- 吃力,辛苦 toil, labour, drudgery, chore.

v.
- 流汗 perspire, swelter, exude.

sweaty adj.
- 出汗的 damp, moist, clammy, sticky, sweating, perspiring.

sweep v.
- 扫除 brush, dust, clean, clear, remove.
- 掠过,环视 pass, sail, fly, glide, scud, skim, glance, whisk, tear, hurtle.

sweeping adj.
- 全面的 general, global, all-inclusive, all-embracing, blanket, across-the-board, broad, wide-ranging, extensive, far-reaching, comprehensive, thoroughgoing, radical, wholesale, indiscriminate, oversimplified, simplistic.

sweet adj.
- 甜的 sugary, syrupy, sweetened, honeyed, saccarine, luscious, delicious.
- 可爱的 pleasant, delightful, lovely, arractive, beautiful, pretty, winsome, cute, appealing, lovable, charming, agreeable, amiable, affectionate, tender, kind, treasured, precious, dear, darling.
- 清爽的 freash, clean, wholesome, pure, clear, perfumed, fragrant, aromatic, balmy.
- 悠扬的 melodious, tuneful, harmonious, euphonious, musical, dulcet, soft, mellow.

n.
- 甜点 dessert, pudding, afters.

sweeten v.
- 使变甜 sugar, honey, mellow, soften, soothe, appease, temper, cushion.

swell v.
- 膨胀 expand, dilate, inflate, blow up, puff up, bloat, distend, fatten, bulge, balloon, billow, surge, rise, mount, increase, enlarge, extend, grow, augment, heighten, intensify.

n.
- 增加 billow, wave, undulation, surge, rise, increase, enlargement.

swelling n.
- 红肿 lump, tumour, bump, bruise, blister, boil, inflammation, bulge, protuberance, puffiness, distension, enlargement.

swift adj.
☞ 快捷的 fast, quick, rapid, speedy, express, flying, hurried, hasty, short, brief, sudden, prompt, ready, agile, nimble, nippy.

swimsuit n.
☞ 泳衣 swimming costume, bathing-costume, bathing-suit, bikini, trunks.

swindle v.
☞ 欺骗 cheat, defraud, diddle, do, overcharge, fleece, rip off, trick, deceive, dupe, con, bamboozle..
n.
☞ 欺骗 fraud, fiddle, racket, sharp practice, double-dealing, trickery, deception, con, rip-off.

swindler n.
☞ 骗子 cheat, fraud, impostor, con man, trickster, shark, rogue, rascal.

swing v.
☞ 悬挂,摆动 hang, suspend, dangle, wave, brandish, sway, rock, oscillate, vibrate, fluctuate, vary, veer, swerve, turn, whirl, twirl, spin, rotate.
n.
☞ 摆动 sway, rock, oscillation, vibration, fluctuation, variation, change, shift, movement, motion, rhythm.

swirl v.
☞ 漩涡 churn, agitate, spin, twirl, whirl, wheel, eddy, twist, curl.

switch v.
☞ 切换 change, exchange, swap, trade, interchange, transpose, substitute, replace, shift, rearrange, turn, veer, deviate, divert, deflect.
n.
☞ 切换 change, alteration, shift, exchange, swap, interchange, substitution, replacement.

swollen adj.
☞ 肿胀的 bloated, distended, inflated, tumid, puffed up, puffy, inflamed, enlarged, bulbous, bulging.

sword n.
☞ 剑 blade, foil, rapier, sabre, scimitar.

symbol n.
☞ 象征 sign, token, representation, mark, emblem, badge, logo, character, ideograph, figure, image.

symbolic adj.
☞ 象征的 symbolical, representative, emblematic, token, figurative, metaphorical, allegorical, meaningful, significant.

symbolize v.
☞ 象征 represent, stand for, denote, mean, signify, typify, exemplify, epitomize, personify.

symmetry n.
☞ 对称 balance, evenness, regularity, parallelism, correspondence, proportion, harmony, agreement.

sympathetic adj.
☞ 同情的 understanding, appreciative, supportive, comforting, consoling, commiserating, pitying,

interested, concerned, solicitous, caring, compassionate, tender, kind, warm-hearted, well-disposed, affectionate, agreeable, friendly, congenial, like-minded, compatible.

sympathize v.
☞同情 understand, comfort, commiserate, pity, feel for, empathize, identify with, respond to.

sympathy n.
☞同情 1 understanding, comfort, consolation, condolences, commiseration, pity, compassion, tenderness, kindness, warmth, thoughtfulness, empathy, fellow-feeling, affinity, rapport.
☞赞同 agreement, accord, correspondence, harmony.

symptom n.
☞症状 sign, indication, evidence, manifestation, expression, feature, characteristic, mark, token, warning.

synonymous adj.
☞同义的 interchangeable, substitutable, the same, identical, similar, comparable, tantamount, equivalent, corresponding.

synopsis n.
☞大纲 outline, abstract, summary, resume, precis, condensation, digest, abridgement, review, recapitulation.

system n.
☞方式 method, mode, technique, procedure, process, routine, practice, usage, rule.
☞制度 organization, structure, set-up, systematization, coordination, orderliness, methodology, logic, classification, arrangement, order, plan, scheme.

systematic adj.
☞系统的 methodical, logical, ordered, well-ordered, planned, well-planned, organized, well-organized, structured, systematized, standardized, orderly, businesslike, efficient.

T

table n.
☞桌子 board, slab, counter, worktop, desk, bench, stand.
☞图表 digaram, chart, graph, timetable, schedule, programme, list, inventory, catalogue, index, register, record.

v.
☞提议 propose, suggest, submit, put forward.

tackle n.
☞擒抱 attack, challenge, interception, intervention, block.
☞工具 equipment, tools,

implements, apparatus, rig, outfit, gear, trappings, paraphernalia.

v.

☞ 处理,抓住 begin, embark on, set about, try, attempt, undertake, take on, challenge, confront, encounter, face up to, grapple with, deal with, attend to, handle, grab, seize, grasp.

tact *n*.

☞ 圆滑,机智 tactfulness, diplomacy, discretion, prudence, delicacy, sensitivity, perception, discernment, judgement, understanding, thoughtfulness, consideration, skill, adroitness, finesse.

tactful *adj*.

☞ 机智的 diplomatic, discreet, politic, judicious, prudent, careful, delicate, subtle, sensitive, perceptive, discerning, understanding, thoughtful, considerate, polite, skilful, adroit.

tactical *adj*.

☞ 战术的 strategic, planned, calculated, artful, cunning, shrewd, skilful, clever, smart, prudent, politic, judicious.

tactics *n*.

☞ 战术 strategy, campaign, plan, policy, aproach, line of attack, moves, manoeuvres.

tactless *adj*.

☞ 不圆滑 undiplomatic, indiscreet, indelicate, inappropriate, impolitic, imprudent, careless, clumsy, blundering, insensitive, unfeeling, hurtful, unkind, thoughtless, inconsiderate, rude, impolite, discourteous.

tag *n*.

☞ 标签 label, sticker, tab, ticket, mark, identification, note, slip, docket.

v.

☞ 加标签 label, mark, identify, designate, term, call, name, christen, nkickname, style, dub.

☞ 附加 add, append, annex, adjoin, affix, fasten.

tail *n*.

☞ 尾部 end, extremity, rear, rear end, rump, behind (infml), *posterior*, *appendage*.

v.

☞ 尾随 follow, pursue, shadow, dog, stalk, track, trail.

tail off

☞ 降弱 decrease, decline, drop, fall away, fade, wane, dwindle, taper off, peter out, die (out).

tailor *n*.

☞ 裁缝 outfitter, dressmaker.

v.

☞ 缝制 fit, suit, cut, trim, style, fashion, shape, mould, alter, modify, adapt, adjust, accommodate.

tailor-made *adj*.

☞ 合身的 made-to-measure, custom-built, ideal, perfect, right, suited, fitted.

take *v*.

☞ 抓 seize, grab, snatch, grasp, hold, catch, capture, get, obtain, acquire, secure, gain, win, derive, adopt, assume, pick, choose, select, accept,

receive.
- ☞ 拿走 remove, eliminate, take away, subtract, deduct, steal, filch, purloin, nick, pinch, appropriate, abduct, carry off.
- ☞ 需要 need, necessitate, require, demand, call for.
- ☞ 带走 convey, carry, bring, transport, ferry, accompany, escort, lead, guide, conduct, unsher.
- ☞ 忍受 bear, tolerate, stand, stomach, abide, endure, suffer, undergo, withstand.

take aback
- ☞ 使吃惊 surprise, astonish, astound, stagger, stun, startle, disconcert, bewilder, dismay, upset.

take apart
- ☞ 分解 take to pieces, dismantle, disassemble, analyse.

take back
- ☞ 取回,取消 reclaim, repossess, withdraw, retract, recant, repudiate, deny, eat one's words.

take down
- ☞ 拆掉 dismantle, disassemble, demolish, raze, level, lower.
- ☞ 记下 note, record, write down, put down, set down, transcribe.

take in
- ☞ 理解 absorb, assimilate, digest, realize, appreciate, understand, comprehend, grasp, admit, receive, shelter, accommodate, contain, include, comprise, incorporate, embrace, encompass, cover.
- ☞ 欺骗 deceive, fool, dupe, con, mislead, trick, hoodwink, bamboozle, cheat, swindle.

take off
- ☞ 拿开 remove, doff, divest, shed, discard, drop.

take on
- ☞ 接受 accept, assume, acquire, undertake, tackle, face, contend with, fight, oppose.
- ☞ 雇用 employ, hire, enlist, recruit, engage, retain.

take up
- ☞ 占领 occupy, fill, engage, engross, absorb, monopolize, use up.
- ☞ 开始 start, begin, embark on, pursue, carry on, continue.
- ☞ 拿起 raise, lift.

takeover *n*.
- ☞ 接管,接收 merger, amalgamation, combination, incorporation, coup.

tale *n*.
- ☞ 故事 story, yarn, anecdote, spiel, narrative, account, report, rumour, tall story, old wives'tale, superstition, fable, myth, legend, saga, lie, fib, falsehood, untruth, fabrication.

talent *n*.
- ☞ 才能 gift, endowment, genius, flair, feel, knack, bent, aptitude, faculty, skill, ability, capacity, power, strength, forte.

talented *adj*.
- ☞ 有才能的 gifted, brilliant, well-endowed, versatile, accomplished, able, capable, proficient, adept, adroit, deft, clever, skilful.

talk *v*.

☞ 讲话 speak, utter, articulate, say, communicate, converse, chat, gossip, natter, chatter, discuss, confer, negotiate.

n.
☞ 谈话 conversation, dialogue, discussion, conference, meeting, consultation, negotiation, chat, chatter, natter, gossip, hearsay, rumour, tittle-tattle.

☞ 讲演 lecture, seminar, symposium, speech, address, discourse, sermon, spiel.

☞ 言谈 language, dialect, slang, jargon, speech, utterance, words.

talk into
☞ 说服 encourage, coax, sway, persuade, convince, bring round, win over.

talk out of
☞ 打消某人念头 discourage, deter, put off, dissuade.

talkative *adj.*
☞ 啰嗦的，唠叨的 garrulous, voluble, vocal, communicative, forthcoming, unreserved, expansive, chatty, gossipy, verbose, wordy.

tall *adj.*
☞ 高的 high, lofty, elevated, soaring, towering, big, great, giant, gigantic.

tame *adj.*
☞ 家养的 domesticated, broken in, trained, disciplined, manageable, tractable, amenable, gentle, docile, meek, submissive, unresisting, obedient, biddable.

☞ 无生气的 dull, boring, tedious, uninteresting, humdrum, flat, bland, insipid, weak, feeble, uninspired, unadventurous, unenterprising, lifeless, spiritlesss.

v.
☞ 驯养 domesticate, house-train, break in, train, discipline, master, subjugate, conquer, brdle, curb, repress, suppress, quell, subdue, temper, soften, mellow, calm, pacify, humble.

tangible *adj.*
☞ 具体的 touchable, tactile, palpable, solid, concrete, material, substantial, physical, real, actual, perceptible, discernible, evident, manifest, definite, positive.

tangle *n.*
☞ 纠缠 knot, snarl-up, twist, coil, convolution, mesh, web, maze, labyrinth, mess, muddle, jumble, mix-up, confusion, entanglement, embroilment, complication.

v.
☞ 纠缠 entangle, knot, snarl, ravel, twist, coil, interweave, interlace, intertwine, catch, ensnare, entrap, enmesh, embroil, implicate, involve, muddle, confuse.

tangled *adj.*
☞ 纠缠的 knotty, snarled, matted, tousled, dishevelled, messy, muddled, jumbled, confused, twisted, convoluted, tortuous, involved, complicated, complex, intricate.

tap[1] *v.*
☞ 轻拍 hit, strike, knock, rap,

beat, drum, pat, touch.
n.
☞ 轻拍 knock, rap, beat, pat, touch.

tap² n.
☞ 水龙头 stopcock, valve, faucet, spigot, spout.
☞ 栓,塞 stopper, plug, bung.
v.
☞ 开发 use, utilize, exploit, mine, quarry, siphon, bleed, milk, drain.

tape n.
☞ 带,条 band, strip, binding, ribbon, video, cassette.
v.
☞ 录 record, video, bind, secure, stick, seal.

target n.
☞ 目标 aim, object, end, purpose, intention, ambition, goal, destination, objective, butt, mark, victim, prey, quarry.

tarnish v.
☞ 使变色,沾污 discolour, corrode, rust, dull, dim, darken, blacken, sully, taint, stain, blemish, spot, blot, mar, spoil.

task n.
☞ 任务 job, chore, duty, charge, imposition, assignment, exercise, mission, errand, undertaking, enterprise, business, occupation, activity, employment, work, labour, toil, burden.

taste n.
☞ 味道 flavour, savour, relish, smack, tang.
☞ 一口,少量 sample, bit, piece, morsel, titbit, bite, nibble, mouthful, sip, drop, dash, soupcon.
☞ 喜好 liking, fondness, partiality, preference, inclination, leaning, desire, appetite.
☞ 品味,眼光 discrimination, discernment, judgement, perception, appreciation, sensitivity, refinement, polish, culture, cultivation, breeding, decorum, finesse, style, elegance, tastefulness.
v.
☞ 品尝 savour, relish, sample, nibble, sip, try, test, differentiate, distinguish, discern, perceive, experience, undergo, feel, encounter, meet, know.

tasteful adj.
☞ 有品味的 refined, polished, cultured, cultivated, elegant, smart, stylish, aesthetic, artistic, harmonious, beautiful, exquisite, delicate, graceful, restrained, well-judged, judicious, correct, fastidious, discriminating.

tasteless adj.
☞ 无味的 flavourless, insipid, bland, mild, weak, watery, flat, stale, dull, boring, uninteresting, vapid.
☞ 无品味的 inelegant, graceless, unseemly, improper, indiscreet, crass, rude, crude, vulgar, kitsch, naff, cheap, tawdry, flashy, gaudy, garish, loud.

tasty *adj.*
☞ 美味的　luscious, palatable, appetizing, mouthwatering, delicious, flavoursome, succulent, scrumptious, yummy, tangy, piquant, savoury, sweet.

taunt *v.*
☞ 嘲笑　tease, torment, provoke, bait, goad, jeer, mock, ridicule, gibe, rib, deride, sneer, insult, revile, reproach.
n.
☞ 嘲笑　jeer, catcall, gibe, dig, sneer, insult, reproach, taunting, teasing, provocation, ridicule, sarcasm, derision, censure.

tax *n.*
☞ 收税　levy, charge, rate, tariff, customs, contribution, imposition, burden, load.
v.
☞ 收税　levy, charge, demand, exact, assess, impose, burden, load, strain, stretch, try, tire, weary, exhaust, drain, sap, weaken.

teach *v.*
☞ 教授　instruct, train, coach, tutor, lecture, drill, ground, verse, discipline, school, educate, enlighten, edify, inform, impart, inculcate, advise, counsel, guide, direct, show, demonstrate.

teacher *n.*
☞ 教师　schoolteacher, schoolmaster, master, schoolmistress, mistress, educator, pedagogue, tutor, lecturer, professor, don, instructor, trainer, coach, adviser, counsellor, mentor, guide, guru.

teaching *n.*
☞ 教授　instruction, tuition, training, grounding, schooling, education, pedagogy, indoctrination.
☞ 教条　dogma, doctrine, tenet, precept, principle.

team *n.*
☞ 队　side, line-up, squad, shift, crew, gang, band, group, company, stable.

team up
☞ 团结　join, unite, couple, combine, band together, co-operate, collaborate, work together.

tear *v.*
☞ 撕　rip, rend, divide, rupture, sever, shred, scratch, claw, gash, lacerate, mutilate, mangle.
☞ 抓　pull, snatch, grab, seize, wrest.
☞ 冲　dash, rush, hurry, speed, race, run, sprint, fly, shoot, dart, bolt, belt, career, charge.
n.
☞ 撕　rip, rent, slit, hole, split, rupture, scratch, gash, laceration.

tearful *adj.*
☞ 眼泪汪汪的　crying, weeping, sobbing, whimpering, blubbering, sad, sorrowful, upset, distressed, emotional, weepy.

tears *n.*

☞ 哭泣 crying, weeping, sobbing, wailing, whimpering, blubbering, sorrow, distress.

tease v.
☞ 嘲弄 taunt, provoke, bait, annoy, irritate, aggravate, needle, badger, worry, pester, plague, torment, tantalize, mock, ridicule, gibe, banter, rag, rib.

technical adj.
☞ 技术的 mechanical, scientific, technological, electronic, computerized, specialized, expert, professional.

technique n.
☞ 技术 method, system, procedure, manner, fashion, style, mode, way, means, approach, course, performance, execution, delivery, artistry, craftsmanship, skill, facility, proficiency, expertise, know-how, art, craft, knack, touch.

tedious adj.
☞ 无聊的 boring, monotonous, uninteresting, unexciting, dull, dreary, drab, banal, humdrum, tiresome, wearisome, tiring, laborious, long-winded, long-drawn-out.

teenage adj.
☞ 十几岁的 teenaged, adolescent, young, youthful, juvenile, immature.

teenager n.
☞ 十几岁孩子 adolescent, youth, boy, girl, minor, juvenile.

telephone n.
☞ 电话 phone, handset, receiver, blower.
v.
☞ 打电话 phone, ring (up), call (up), dial, buzz, contact, get in touch.

telescope v.
☞ 缩短 contract, shrink, compress, condense, abridge, squash, crush, shorten, curtail, truncate, abbreviate, reduce, cut, trim.

television n.
☞ 电视 tv, receiver, set, telly, the box, goggle-box, idiot box, small screen.

tell v.
☞ 告诉 inform, notify, let know, acquaint, impart, communicate, speak, utter, say, state, confess, divulge, disclose, reveal.
☞ 讲述 narrate, recount, relate, report, announce, describe, protray, mention.
☞ 命令 order, command, direct, instruct, authorize.
☞ 分辨 differentiate, distinguish, discriminate, discern, recognize, identify, discover, see, understand, comprehend.

tell off
☞ 责怪 scold, chide, tick off, upbraid, reprimand, rebuke, reprove, lecture, berate, dress down, reproach, censure.

temper n.
☞ 性情 mood, humour, nature, temperament, character, disposition, constitution.
☞ 愤怒 anger, rage, fury, passion, tantrum, annoyance,

irritability, ill-humour.
☞冷静 calm, composure, self-control.

v.

☞抑制,减轻 moderate, lessen, reduce, calm, soothe, allay, assuage, palliate, mitigate, modify, soften.

☞锻炼,回火 harden, toughen, strengthen.

temperament n.

☞气质 nature, character, personality, disposition, tendency, bent, constitution, make-up, soul, spirit, mood, humour, temper, state of mind, attitude, outlook.

temperamental adj.

☞情绪的 moody, emotional, neurotic, highly-strung, sensitive, touchy, irritable, impatient, passionate, fiery, excitable, explosive, volatile, mercurial, capricious, unpredictable, unreliable.

☞天生的 natural, inborn, innate, inherent, constitutional, ingrained.

temperance n.

☞克制 teetotalism, prohibition, abstinence, abstemiousness, sobriety, continence, moderation, restraint, self-restraint, self-control, self-discipline, self-denial.

temperate adj.

☞温和的 mild, clement, balmy, fair, equable, balanced, stable, gentle, pleasant, agreeable.

☞克制的 teetotal, abstinent, abstemious, sober, continent, moderate, restrained, controlled, even-tempered, calm, composed, reasonable, sensible.

tempestuous adj.

☞剧烈的 stormy, windy, gusty, blustery, squally, turbulent, tumultuous, rough, wild, violent, furious, raging, heated, passionate, intense.

temple n.

☞庙 shrine, sanctuary, church, tabernacle, mosque, pagoda.

tempo n.

☞节奏 time, rhythm, metre, beat, pulse, speed, velocity, rate, pace.

temporary adj.

☞临时的 impermanent, provisional, interim, makeshift, stopgap, temporal, transient, transitory, passing, ephemeral, evanescent, fleeting, brief, short-lived, momentary.

tempt v.

☞引诱 entice, coax, persuade, woo, bait, lure, allure, attract, draw, seduce, invite, tantalize, provoke, incite.

temptation n.

☞诱惑 enticement, inducement, goal, target, depot, station, garage, terminal.

terms n.

☞关系 relations, relationship, footing, standing, position.
☞条件 conditions, specifications, stipulations, provisos, provisions, qualifications, particulars.
☞费用 rates, charges, fees,

prices, tariff.

terrain n.
☞ 领域 land, ground, territory, country, countryside, landscape, topography.

terrestrial adj.
☞ 领土的 earthly, worldly, global, mundane.

terrible adj.
☞ 可怕的 bad, awful, frightful, dreadful, shocking, appalling, outrageous, disgusting, revolting, repulsive, offensive, abhorrent, hateful, horrid, horrible, unpleasant, obnoxious, foul, vile, hideous, gruesome, horrific, harrowing, distressing, grave, serious, severe, extreme, desperate.

terribly adv.
☞ 非常 very, much, greatly, extremely, exceedingly, awfully, frightfully, decidedly, seriously.

terrific adj.
☞ 极佳的 excellent, wonderful, marvellous, super, smashing, outstanding, brilliant, magnificent, superb, fabulous, fantastic, sensational, amazing, stupendous, breathtaking.
☞ 巨大的 huge, enormous, gigantic, tremendous, great, intense, extreme, excessive.

terrify v.
☞ 恐怖 petrify, horrify, appal, shock, terrorize, intimidate, frighten, scare, alarm, dismay.

territory n.
☞ 领土 country, land, state, dependency, province, domain, preserve, jurisdiction, sector, region, area, district, zone, tract, terrain.

terror n.
☞ 恐惧 fear, panic, dread, trepidation, horror, shock, fright, alarm, dismay, consternation, terrorism, intimidation.

terrorize v.
☞ 使恐惧 threaten, menace, intimidate, oppress, coerce, bully, browbeat, frighten, scare, alarm, terrify, petrify, horrify, shock.

terse adj.
☞ 简洁的 short, brief, succinct, concise, compact, condensed, epigrammatic, pithy, incisive, snappy, curt, brusque, abrupt, laconic.

test v.
☞ 测试 try, experiment, examine, assess, evaluate, check, investigate, analyse, screen, prove, verify.
n.
☞ 试验 trial, try-out, experiment, examination, assessment, evaluation, check, investigation, analysis, proof, probation, ordeal.

testify v.
☞ 验证 give evidence, depose, state, declare, assert, swear, avow, attest, vouch, certify, corroborate, affirm, show, bear, witness.

testimony n.
☞ 证据 evidence, statement, affidavit, submission,

deposition, declaration, profession, attestation, affirmation, support, proof, verification, confirmation, witness, demonstration, manifestation, indication.

text n.
☞ 内容，文本　words, wording, content, matter, body, subject, topic, theme, reading, passage, paragraph, sentence, book, textbook, source.

texture n.
☞ 质地　consistency, feel, surface, grain, weave, tissue, fabric, structure, composition, constitution, character, quality.

thank v.
☞ 感谢　say thank you, be grateful, appreciate, acknowledge, recognize, credit.

thankful adj.
☞ 充满感激的　grateful, appreciative, obliged, indebted, pleased, contented, relieved.

thankless adj.
☞ 徒劳的　unrecognized, unappreciated, unrequited, unrewarding, unprofitable, fruitless.

thanks n.
☞ 谢谢　gratitude, gratefulness, appreciation, acknowledgement, recognition, credit, thanksgiving, thank-offering.

thanks to
☞ 多亏　beacause of, owing to, due to, on account of, as a result of, through.

theatrical adj.
☞ 戏剧性的　dramatic, thespian.
☞ 夸张的　melodramatic, histrionic, mannered, affected, artificial, pompous, ostentatious, showy, extravagant, exaggerated, overdone.

theft n.
☞ 偷窃　robbery, thieving, stealing, pilfering, larceny, shop-lifting, kleptomania, fraud, embezzlement.

theme n.
☞ 主题　subject, topic, thread, motif, keynote, idea, gist, essence, burden, argument, thesis, dissertation, composition, essay, text, matter.

theoretical adj.
☞ 理论的　hypothetical, conjectural, speculative, abstract, academic, doctrinaire, pure, ideal.

theorize v.
☞ 理论化　hypothesize, suppose, guess, conjecture, speculate, postulate, propound, formulate.

theory n.
☞ 理论　hypothesis, supposition, assumption, presumption, surmise, guess, conjecture, speculation, idea, notion, abstraction, philosophy, thesis, plan, proposal, scheme, system.

therapy n.
☞ 疗法　treatment, remedy, cure, healing, tonic.

therefore adv.
☞ 因此　so, then, consequently,

thesis n.
- 论文 dissertation, essay, composition, treatise, paper, monograph.
- 主题 subject, topic, theme, idea, opinion, view, theory, hypothesis, proposal, proposition, premise, statement, argument, contention.

thick adj.
- 宽厚的 wide, broad, fat, heavy, solid, dense, impenetrable, close, compact, concentrated, condensed, viscous, coagulated, clotted.
- 浓的 full, packed, crowded, chock-a-block, swarming, teeming, bristling, brimming, bursting, numerous, abundant.
- 蠢的 stupid, foolish, slow, dull, dim-witted, brainless, simple.

thicken v.
- 使密 condense, stiffen, congeal, coagulate, clot, cake, gel, jell, set.

thickness n.
- 宽,密 width, breadth, diameter, density, viscosity, bulk, body.
- 层 layer, stratum, ply, sheet, coat.

thick-skinned adj.
- 皮厚的 insensitive, unfeeling, callous, tough, hardened, hard-boiled.

thief n.
- 贼 robber, bandit, mugger, pickpocket, shop-lifter, burglar, house-breaker, plunderer, poacher, stealer, pilferer, filcher, kleptomaniac, swindler, embezzler.

thin adj.
- 单薄的 lean, slim, slender, narrow, attenuated, slight, skinny, bony, skeletal, scraggy, scrawny, lanky, gaunt, spare, underweight, undernourished, emaciated.
- 纤细的 fine, delicate, light, flimsy, filmy, gossamer, sheer, see-through, transparent, translucent.
- 稀松的 sparse, scarce, scattered, scant, meagre, poor, inadequate, deficient, scanty, skimpy.
- 稀的 weak, feeble, runny, watery, diluted.

v.
- 使变瘦薄 narrow, attenuate, diminish, reduce, trim, weed out.
- 使变稀 weaken, dilute, water down, rarefy, refine.

thing n.
- 事物 article, object, entity, creature, body, substance, item, detail, particular, feature, factor, element, point, fact, concept, thought.
- 装置 device, contrivance, gadget, tool, implement, instrument, apparatus, machine, mechanism.
- 行为 act, deed, feat, action, task, responsibility, problem.
- 情况 circumstance, eventuality, happening, occurrence, event, incident, phenomenon, occurrence, event,

things *n.*
- 东西 belongings, possessions, effects, paraphernalia, stuff, goods, luggage, gear, clobber, odds and ends, bits and pieces.

think *v.*
- 认为 believe, hold, consider, regard, esteem, deem, judge, estimate, reckon, calculate, determine, conclude, reason.
- 想象 conceive, imagine, suppose, presume, surmise, expect, foresee, envisage, anticipate.
- 考虑 ponder, mull over, chew over, ruminate, meditate, contemplate, muse, cogitate, reflect, deliberate, weigh up, recall, recollect, remember.

think up
- 想出 devise, contrive, dream up, imagine, conceive, visualize, invent, design, create, concoct.

thinker *n.*
- 思想者 philosopher, theorist, ideologist, brain, intellect, mastermind.

thinking *n.*
- 想法 reasoning, philosophy, thoughts, conclusions, theory, idea, opinion, view, outlook, position, judgement, assessment.

third-rate *adj.*
- 三流的 low-grade, poor, bad, inferior, mediocre, indifferent, shoddy, cheap and nasty.

incident, phenomenon, affair, proceeding.

thirst *n.*
- 干渴 thirstiness, dryness, drought.
- 渴望 desire, longing, yearning, hankering, craving, hunger, appetite, lust, passion, eagerness, keeness.

thirsty *adj.*
- 干的 dry, parched, gasping, dehydrated, arid.
- 渴望的 desirous, longing, yearning, hankering, craving, hungry, burning, itching, dying, eager, avid, greedy.

thorn *n.*
- 刺 spike, point, barb, prickle, spine, bristle, needle.

thorough *adj.*
- 全部的,彻底的 full, complete, total, entire, utter, absolute, perfect, pure, sheer, unqualified, unmitigated, out-and-out, downright, sweeping, all-embracing, comprehensive, all-inclusive, exhaustive, thoroughgoning, intensive, in-depth, conscientious, efficient, painstaking, scrupulous, meticulous, careful.

though *conj.*
- 虽然 although, even if, notwithstanding, while, allowing, granted.

adv.
- 然而 however, nevertheless, nonetheless, yet, still, even so, all the same, for all that.

thought *n.*
- 考虑 thinking, attention, heed, regard, consideration, study, scrutiny, introspection,

meditation, contemplation, cogitation, reflection, deliberation.
- 想法 idea, notion, concept, conception, belief, conviction, opinion, view, judgement, assessment, conclusion, plan, design, intention, purpose, aim, hope, dream, expectation, anticipation.
- 关心 thoughtfulness, consideration, kindness, care, concern, compassion, sympathy, gesture, touch.

thoughtful adj.
- 有想法的 pensive, wistful, dreamy, abstracted, reflective, contemplative, introspective, thinking, absorbed, studious, serious, solemn.
- 体贴的 considerate, kind, unselfish, helpful, caring, attentive, heedful, mindful, careful, prudent, cautious, wary.

thoughtless adj.
- 自私的 inconsiderate, unthinking, insensitive, unfeeling, tactless, undiplomatic, unkind, selfish, uncaring.
- 不注意的,粗心的 absent-minded, inattentive, heedless, mindless, foolish, stupid, silly, rash, reckless, ill-considered, imprudent, careless, negligent, remiss.

thread n.
- 线 cotton, yarn, strand, fibre, filament, string, line.
- 主线 course, direction, drift, tenor, theme, motif, plot, storyline.

threat n.
- 威胁 menace, warning, omen, portent, presage, foreboding, danger, risk, hazard, peril.

threaten v.
- 威胁 menace, intimidate, browbeat, pressurize, bully, terrorize, warn, portend, presage, forebode, foreshadow, endanger, jeopardize, imperil.

threatening adj.
- 威慑的 menacing, intimidatory, warning, cautionary, ominous, inauspicious, sinister, grim, looming, impending.

thrift n.
- 节俭 economy, husbandry, saving, conservation, frugality, prudence, carefulness.

thrifty adj.
- 节俭的 economical, saving, frugal, sparing, prudent, careful.

thrill n.
- 刺激 excitement, adventure, pleasure, stimulation, charge, kick, sensation, glow, tingle, throb, shudder, quiver, tremor.

v.
- 刺激 excite, electrify, galvanize, exhilarate, rouse, arouse, move, stir, stimulate, flush, glow, tingle, throb, shudder, tremble, quiver, shake.

thrive v.
- 繁荣 flourish, prosper, boom, grow, increase, advance,

develop, bloom, blossom, gain, profit, succeed.

through *prep.*
- 通过 between, by, via, by way of, by means of, using.
- 自始至终 throughout, during, in.
- 经由 because of, as a result of, thanks to.

throw *v.*
- 抛投,掷掷 hurl, heave, lob, pitch, chuck, sling, cast, fling, toss, launch, propel, send.
- 发射 shed, cast, project, direct.
- 推翻 bring down, floor, upset, overturn, dislodge, unseat, unsaddle, unhorse.
- perplex, baffle, confound, confuse, disconcert, astonish, dumbfound.

n.
- 扔,投,掷 heave, lob, pitch, sling, fling, toss, cast.

throw away
- 舍弃 discard, jettison, dump, scrap, dispose of, throw out.
- 浪费 waste, squander, fritter away.

thrust *v.*
- 刺,戳,插入 push, shove, butt, ram, jam, wedge, stick, poke, prod, jab, lunge, pierce, stab, plunge, press, force, impel, drive, propel.

n.
- 推插,冲刺,攻击 push, shove, poke, prod, lunge, stab, drive, impetus, momentum.

thump *n.*
- 击打 knock, blow, punch, clout, box, cuff, smack, whack, wallop, crash, bang, thud, beat, throb.

v.
- 击打 hit, strike, knock, punch, clout, box, cuff, smack, thrash, whack, wallop, crash, bang, thud, batter, pound, hammer, beat, throb.

thunder *n.*
- 打雷 boom, reverberation, crash, bang, crack, clap, peal, rumble, roll, roar, blast, explosion.

v.
- 打雷 boom, resound, reverberate, crash, bang, crack, clap, peal, rumble, roll, roar, blast.

thunderous *adj.*
- 雷鸣般的 booming, resounding, reverberating, roaring, loud, noisy, deafening, ear-splitting.

thus *adv.*
- 这样 so, hence, therefore, consequently, then, accordingly, like this, in this way, as follows.

thwart *v.*
- 阻挠 frustrate, foil, stymie, defeat, hinder, impede, obstruct, block, check, baffle, stop, prevent, oppose.

ticket *n.*
- 票,入场券 pass, card, certificate, token, voucher, coupon, docket, slip, label, tag, sticker.

tide *n.*
- 潮流 current, ebb, flow,

stream, flux, movement, course, direction, drift, trend, tendency.

tidy adj.
- ☞整洁的 neat, orderly, methodical, systematic, organized, clean, spick-and-span, shipshape, smart, spruce, trim, well-kept, ordered, uncluttered.
- ☞相当大的 large, substantial, sizable, considerable, good, generous, ample.

v.
- ☞使整洁 neaten, straighten, order, arrange, clean, smarten, spruce up, groom.

tie v.
- ☞系于 knot, fasten, secure, moor, tether, attach, join, connect, link, unite, rope, lash, strap, bind, restrain, restrict, confine, limit, hamper, hinder.

n.
- ☞系紧 knot, fastening, joint, connection, link, liaison, relationship, bond, affiliation, obligation, commitment, duty, restraint, restriction, limitation, hindrance.
- ☞平手 draw, dead heat, stalemate, deadlock.

tie up
- ☞束紧,绑系 moor, tether, attach, secure, rope, lash, bind, truss, wrap up, restrain.
- ☞阻断 conclude, terminate, wind up, settle.
- ☞忙碌 occupy, engage, engross.

tight adj.
- ☞紧的 taut, stretched, tense, rigid, stiff, firm, fixed, fast, secure, close, cramped, constricted, compact, snug, close-fitting.
- ☞不漏的 sealed, hermetic, proof, impervious, airtight, watertight.
- ☞吝啬的 mean, stingy, miserly, niggardly, parsimonious, tight-fisted.
- ☞严格的 strict, severe, stringent, rigorous.

tighten v.
- ☞使紧 tauten, stretch, tense, stiffen, fix, fasten, secure, narrow, close, cramp, constrict, crush, squeeze.

tight-fisted adj.
- ☞吝啬的 mean, stingy, miserly, mingy, niggardly, penny-pinching, sparing, parsimonious, tight, grasping.

tilt v.
- ☞倾斜 slope, incline, slant, pitch, list, tip, lean.

n.
- ☞倾斜 slope, incline, angle, inclination, slant, pitch, list.

timber n.
- ☞木料 wood, trees forest, beam, lath, plank, board, log.

time n.
- ☞时期 spell, stretch, period, term, season, session, span, duration, interval, space, while.
- ☞拍子 tempo, beat, rhythm, metre, measure.
- ☞时刻 moment, point, juncture, stage, instance, occasion, date, day, hour.
- ☞时代 age, era, epoch, life,

lifetime, generation, heyday, peak.

v.

☞计时 clock, measure, meter, regulate, control, set, schedule, timetable.

timeless adj.

☞永恒的 ageless, immortal, everlasting, eternal, endless, permanent, changeless, unchanging.

timely adj.

☞适时的 well-timed, seasonable, suitable, appropriate, convenient, opportune, propitious, prompt, punctual.

timetable n.

☞时刻表 schedule, programme, agenda, calendar, diary, rota, roster, list, listing, curriculum.

timid adj.

☞害羞的 shy, bashful, modest, shrinking, retiring, nervous, apprehensive, afraid, timorous, fearful, cowardly, faint-hearted, spineless, irresolute.

tinge n.

☞色调 tint, dye, colour, shade, touch, trace, suggestion, hint, smack, flavour, pinch, drop, dash, bit, sprinkling, smattering.

v.

☞使……带色 tint, dye, stain, colour, shade, suffuse, imbue.

tint n.

☞色泽 dye, stain, rinse, wash, colour, hue, shade, tincture, tinge, tone, cast, streak, trace, touch.

v.

☞微染 dye, colour, tinge, streak, stain, taint, affect.

tiny adj.

☞微小的 minute, microscopic, infinitesimal, teeny, small, little, slight, negligible, insignificant, diminutive, petite, dwarfish, pint-sized, pocket, miniature, mini.

tip^1 n.

☞尖端 end, extremity, point, nib, apex, peak, pinnacle, summit, acme, top, cap, crown, head.

v.

☞顶端装上 cap, crown, top, surmount.

tip^2 v.

☞倾斜,翻倒 lean, incline, slant, list, tilt, topple over, capsize, upset, overturn, spill, pout out, empty, unload, dump.

tip^3 n.

☞告诫 clue, pointer, hint, suggestion, advice, warning, tip-off, information, inside, information, forecast.

☞小费 gratuity, gift, perquisite.

v.

☞劝告 advise, suggest, warn, caution, forewarn, tip off, inform, tell.

☞给小费 reward, remunerate.

tire v.

☞使疲惫 weary, fatigue, wear out, exhaust, drain, enervate.

tired adj.

☞疲惫的 weary, drowsy,

sleepy, flagging, fatigued, worn out, exhausted, dog-tired, drained, jaded, bushed, whacked, shattered, beat, dead-beat, all in, knackered.
☞ 不耐烦的 fed up, bored, sick.

tireless adj.
☞ 不会疲倦的 untiring, unwearied, unflagging, indefatigable, energetic, vigorous, diligent, industrious, resolute, determined.

tiresome adj.
☞ 烦人的 troublesome, tring, annoying, irritating, exasperating, wearisome, dull, boring, tedious, monotonous, uninteresting, tiring, fatiguing, laborious.

tiring adj.
☞ 烦人的 wearying, fatiguing, exhausting, draining, demanding, exacting, taxing, arduous, strenuous, laborious.

tissue n.
☞ 组织 substance, matter, material, fabric, stuff, gauze, web, mesh, network, structure, texture.

titillate v.
☞ 刺激,搔痒 stimulate, arouse, excite, thrill, tickle, provoke, tease, tantalize, intrigue, interest.

title n.
☞ 名义 name, appellation, denomination, term, designation, label, epithet, nickname, pseudonvm, rank, status, office, position.
☞ 标题 heading, headline, caption, legend, inscription.
☞ 权力 right, prerogative, privilege, claim, entitlement, ownership, deeds.
v.
☞ 命名 entitle, name, call, dub, style, term, designate, label.

titter v.
☞ 窃笑 laugh, chortle, chuckle, giggle, snigger, mock.

toast v.
☞ 烤 grill, brown, roast, heat, warm.
n.
☞ 干杯 drink, pledge, tribute, salute, compliment, health.

together adv.
☞ 一起 jointly, in concert, side bi side, shoulder to shoulder, in unison, as one, simultaneously, at the same time, all at once, collectively, enmasse, closely, continuously, consecutively, successively, in succession, in a row, hand in hand.

toil n.
☞ 劳作 labour, hard work, donkey-work, drudgery, sweat, graft, industry, application, effort, exertion, elbow, grease.
v.
☞ 劳作 labour, work, slave, drudge, sweat, grind, slog, graft, plug away, persevere, strive, struggle.

toilet n.
☞ 洗手间 lavatory, wc, loo, bathroom, cloakroom, washroom, rest room, public convenience, ladies, gents,

urinal, convenience, powder room.

token n.
☞ 标志 symbol, emblem, representation, mark, sign, indication, manifestation, demonstration, expression, evidence, proof, clue, warning, reminder, memorial, memento, souvenir, keepsake.
☞ 代用品 voucher, coupon, counter, disc.
adj.
☞ 象征的 symbolic, emblematic, nominal, minimal, perfunctory, superficial, cosmetic, hollow, insincere.

tolerable *adj.*
☞ 忍耐的 bearable, endurable, sufferable, acceptable, passable, adequate, reasonable, fair, average, all right. ok, not bad, mediocre, indifferent, so-so, unexceptional, ordinary, run-of-the-mill.

tolerance n.
☞ 忍耐力 toleration, patience, forbearance, open-mindedness, broad-mindedness, magnanimity, sympathy, understanding, lenity, indulgence, permissiveness.

tolerant *adj.*
☞ 有忍耐力的 patient, forbearing, long-suffering, open-minded, fair, unprejudiced, broad-minded, liberal, charitable, kind-hearted, sympathetic, understanding, forgiving, lenient, indulgent, easy-going, permissive, lax, soft.

tolerate v.
☞ 忍受 endure, suffer, put up with, bear, stand, abide, stomach, swallow, take, receive, accept, admit, allow, permit, condone, countenance, indulge.

toll¹ v.
☞ 鸣响 ring, peal, chime, knell, sound, strike announce, call.

toll² n.
☞ 使用费 charge, fee, payment, levy, tax, duty, tariff, rate, cost, penalty, demand, loss.

tomb n.
☞ 墓 grave, burial-place, vault, crypt, sepulchre, catacomb, mausoleum, cenotaph.

tone n.
☞ 语气 note, timbre, pitch, volume, intonation, modulation, inflection, accent, stres, emphasis, force, strength.
☞ 色调 tint, tinge, colour, hue, shade, cast, tonality.
☞ 状况 air, manner, attitude, mood, spirit, humour, temper, character, quality, feel, style, effect, vein, tenor, drift.
v.
☞ 使协调 match, co-ordinate, blend, harmonize.

tongue n.
☞ 语气 language, speech, discourse, talk, utterance, articulation, parlance, vernacular, idiom, dialect, patois.

tongue-tied *adj.*
☞ 木讷的 speechless,

dumbstruck, inarticulate, silent, mute, dumb, voiceless.

too *adv*.
- 也 also, as well, in addition, besides, moreover, likewise.
- 太 excessively, inordinately, unduly, over, overly, unreasonably, ridiculously, extremely, evry.

tool *n*.
- 工具 implement, instrument, utensil, gadget, device, contrivance, contraption, apparatus, appliance, machine, means, vehicle, medium, agency, agent, intermediary.
- 走狗 puppet, pawn, dupe, stooge, minion, hireling.

top *n*.
- 顶 head, tip, vertex, apex, crest, crown, peak, pinnacle, summit, acme, zenith, culmination, height.
- 盖 lid, cap, cover, cork, stopper.

adj.
- 最高的 highest, topmost, upmost, uppermost, upper, superior, head, chief, leading, first, foremost, principal, sovereign, ruling, pre-eminent, dominant, prime, paramount, greatest, maximum, best, finest, supreme, crowning, culminating.

v.
- 加盖子 tip, cap, crown, cover, finish (off), decorate, garnish.
- 超过 beat, exceed, outstrip, better, excel, best, surpass, eclipse, outshine, outdo, surmount, transcend.
- 领导 head, lead, rule, command.

topic *n*.
- 主题 subject, theme, issue, question, matter, point, thesis, text.

torment *v*.
- 折磨 tease, provoke, annoy, vex, trouble, worry, harass, hound, pester, bother, bedevil, plague, afflict, distress, harrow, pain, torture, persecute.

n.
- 折磨 provocation, annoyance, vexation, bane, scourge, trouble, bother, nuisance, harassment, worry, anguish, distress, misery, affliction, suffering, pain, agony, ordeal, torture, persecution.

torrent *n*.
- 急流 stream, volley, outburst, gush, rush, flood, spate, deluge, cascade, downpour.

torture *v*.
- 折磨 pain, agonize, excruciate, crucify, rack, martyr, persecute, torment, afflict, distress.

n.
- 折磨 pain, agony, suffering, affliction, distress, misery, anguish, torment, martyrdom, persecution.

toss *v*.
- 扔 flip, cast, fling, throw, chuck, sling, hurl, lob.
- 摇 roll, heave, pitch, lurch, jolt, shake, agitate, rock,

thrash, squirm, wriggle.
n.
☞ 扔 flip, cast, fling, throw, pitch.

total *n.*
☞ 总量 sum, whole, entirety, totality, all, lot, mass, aggregate, amount.
adj.
☞ 全部的 full, complete, entire, whole, integral, all-out, utter, absolute, unconditional, unqualified, outright, undisputed, perfect, consummate, thoroughgoing, sheer, downright, thorough.
v.
☞ 总计 add (up), sum (up), tot (up), count (up), reckon, amount to, come to, reach.

totter *v.*
☞ 蹒跚 stagger, reel, lurch, stumble, falter, waver, teeter, sway, rock, shake, quiver, tremble.

touch *n.*
☞ 摸 feel, texture, brush, stroke, caress, pat, tap, contact.
☞ 一些 trace, spot, dash, pinch, soupcon, suspicion, hint, suggestion, speck, jot, tinge, smack.
☞ 手法 skill, art, knack, flair, style, method, manner, technique, approach.
v.
☞ 摸 feel, handle, finger, brush, graze, stroke, caress, fondle, pat, tap, hit, strike, contact, meet, abut, adjoin, border.

☞ 感动 move, stir, upset, disturb, impress, inspire, influence, affect, concern, regard.
☞ 到达 reach, attain, equal, match, rival, better.

touch on
☞ 提到 mention, broach, speak of, remark on, refer to, allude to, cover, deal with.

touched *adj.*
☞ 感动的 moved, stirred, affected, disturbed, impressed.
☞ 微疯的 mad, crazy, deranged, disturbed, eccentric, dotty, daft, barmy.

touching *adj.*
☞ 令人感动的 moving, stirring, affecting, poignant, pitiable, pitiful, pathetic, sad, emotional, tender.

touchy *adj.*
☞ 易怒的 irritable, irascible, quick-tempered, bad-tempered, grumpy, grouchy, crabbed, cross, peevish, captious, edgy, over-sensitive.

tough *adj.*
☞ 结实的 strong, durable, resilient, resistant, hardy, sturdy, solid, rigid, stiff, inflexible, hard, leathery.
☞ 凶恶的 rough, violent, vicious, callous, hardened, obstinate.
☞ 严厉的 harsh, severe, strict, stern, firm, resolute, determined, tenacious.
☞ 艰难的 arduous, laborious, exacting, hard, difficult, puzzling, perplexing, baffling, knotty, thorny, troublesome.

n.
☞ 恶棍 brute, thug, bully, ruffian, hooligan, lout, yob.

tour
n.
☞ 旅游 circuit, round, visit, expedition, journey, trip, outing, excursion, drive, ride, course.
v.
☞ 旅游 visit, go round, sightsee, explore, travel, journey, drive, ride.

tourist n.
☞ 游客 holidaymaker, visitor, sightseer, tripper, excursionist, traveller, voyager, globetrotter.

tournament n.
☞ 锦标赛 championship, series, competition, contest, match, event, meeting.

tow v.
☞ 拖 pull, tug, draw, trail, drag, lug, haul, transport.

towards prep.
☞ 向 to, approaching, nearing, close to, nearly, almost.

tower n.
☞ 塔 steeple, spire, belfry, turret, fortification, bastion, citadel, fort, fortress, castle, keep.
v.
☞ 高耸 rise, rear, ascend, mount, soar, loom, overlook, dominate, surpass, transcend, exceed, top.

towering adj.
☞ 高耸的 soaring, tall, high, lofty, elevated, monumental, colossal, gigantic, great, magnificent, imposing, impressive, sublime, supreme, surpassing, overpowering, extreme, inordinate.

toxic adj.
☞ 有毒的 poisonous, harmful, noxious, unhealthy, dangerous, deadly, lethal.

toy n.
☞ 玩具 plaything, game, doll, knick-knack.
v.
☞ 玩耍 play, tinker, fiddle, sport, trifle, dally.

trace n.
☞ 痕迹 trail, track, spoor, footprint, footmark, mark, token, sign, indication, evidence, record, relic, remains, remnant, vestige, shadow, hint, suggestion, suspicion, soupcon, dash, drop, spot, bit, jot, touch, tinge, smack.
☞ 追踪,查出 find, discover, detect, unearth, track (down), trail, stalk, hunt, seek, follow, pursue, shadow.

track n.
☞ 足迹,痕迹 footstep, footprint, footmark, scent, spoor, trail, wake, mark, trace, slot, groove, rail, path, way, route, orbit, line, course, drift, sequence.
v.
☞ 追踪,尾随 stalk, trail, hunt, trace, follow, pursue, chase, dog, tail, shadow.

track down
☞ 追踪,搜查而发现 find, discover, trace, hunt down, run to earth, sniff out, ferret out,

dig up, unearth, expose, catch, capture.

trade n.
☞ 贸易，交易　commerce, traffic, business, dealing, buying, selling, shopkeeping, barter, exchange, transactions, custom.
☞ 职业，手艺　occupation, job, business, profession, calling, craft, skill.
v.
☞ 交易，买卖　traffic, peddle, do business, deal, transact, buy, sell, barter, exchange, swap, switch, bargain.

trademark n.
☞ 商标　brand, label, name, sign, symbol, logo, insignia, crest, emblem, badge, hallmark.

trader n.
☞ 商人，贸易者　merchant, tradesman, broker, dealer, buyer, seller, vendor, supplier, wholesaler, retailer, shopkeeper, trafficker, peddler.

tradition n.
☞ 传统，习惯　convention, custom, usage, way, habit, routine, ritual, institution, folklore.

traditional adj.
☞ 传统的　conventional, customary, habitual, usual, accustomed, established, fixed, long-established, time-honoured, old, historic, folk, oral, unwritten.

traffic n.
☞ 交通，通行　vehicles, shipping, transport, transportation, freight, passengers.
☞ 走私　trade, commerce, business, dealing, trafficking, barter, exchange.
v.
☞ 做生意，从事贸易　peddle, buy, sell, trade, do business, deal, bargain, barter, exchange.

tragedy n.
☞ 悲剧　adversity, misfortune, unhappiness, affliction, blow, calamity, disaster, catastrophe.

tragic adj.
☞ 悲惨的，悲剧的　sad, sorrowful, miserable, unhappy, unfortunate, unlucky, ill-fated, pitiable, pathetic, heartbreaking, shocking, appalling, dreadful, awful, dire, calamitous, disastrous, catastrophic, deadly, fatal.

trail v.
☞ 拉，拖　drag, pull, tow, droop, dangle, extend, stream, straggle, dawdle, lag, loiter, linger.
☞ 追踪，尾随　track, stalk, hunt, follow, pursue, chase, shadow, tail.
n.
☞ 痕迹，踪迹　track, footprints, footmarks, scent, trace, path, footpath, road, route, way.

train v.
☞ 训练，教育　teach, instruct, coach, tutor, educate, improve, school, discipline, prepare, drill, exercise, work out, practise, rehearse.
☞ 指向，瞄准　point, direct,

aim, level.
n.
- 随从 retinue, entourage, attendants, court, household, staff, followers, following.
- 系列,连续 sequence, succession, series, progression, order, string, chain, line, file, procession, convoy, cortege, caravan.

trainer *n.*
- 训练者 teacher, instructor, coach, tutor, handler.

training *n.*
- 教育,训练 teaching, instruction, coaching, tuition, education, schooling, discipline, preparation, grounding, drill, exercise, working-out, practice, learning, apprenticeship.

trait *n.*
- 特点,特性 feature, attribute, quality, characteristic, idiosyncrasy, peculiarity, quirk.

traitor *n.*
- 叛徒,叛逆 betrayer, informer, deceiver, double-crosser, turncoat, renegade, deserter, defector, quisling, collaborator.

tramp *v.*
- 踩,步行 walk, march, tread, stamp, stomp, stump, plod, trudge, traipse, trail, trek, hike, ramble, roam, rove.
n.
- 流浪汉,游民 vagrant, vagabond, hobo, down-and-out, dosser.

trample *v.*
- 踏碎,踩躏 tread, stamp, crush, squash, flatten.

tranquil *adj.*
- 安静的,平静的 calm, composed, cool, imperturbable, unexcited, placid, sedate, relaxed, laid-back, seren, peaceful, restful, still, undisturbed, untroubled, quiet, hushed, silent.

tranquillizer *n.*
- 镇静剂 sedative, opiate, narcotic, barbiturate.

transaction *n.*
- 交易,事项 deal, bargain, agreement, arrangement, negotiation, business, affair, matter, proceeding, enterprise, undertaking, deed, action, execution, discharge.

transcend *v.*
- 超出,超越 surpass, excel, outshine, eclipse, outdo, outstrip, beat, surmount, exceed, overstep.

transcribe *v.*
- 抄写,转录 write out, copy, reproduce, rewrite, transliterate, translate, render, take down, note, record.

transcript *n.*
- 抄本,副本 transcription, copy, reproduction, duplicate, transliteration, translation, version, note, record, manuscript.

transfer *v.*
- 迁移,移交 change, transpose, move, shift, remove, relocate, transplant, transport, carry, convey, transmit, consign, grant, hand over.

n.
☞ 转移，换车 change, changeover, transposition, move, shift, removal, relocation, displacement, transmission, handover, transference.

transform *v.*
☞ 改变 change, alter, adapt, convert, remodel, reconstruct, transfigure, revolutionize.

transformation *n.*
☞ 变化，变质 change, alteration, mutation, conversion, metamorphosis, transfiguration, revolution.

transient *adj.*
☞ 短暂，暂时的 transitory, passing, flying, fleeting, brief, short, momentary, ephemeral, short-lived, temporary, short-term.

transit *n.*
☞ 通过，运送 passage, journey, travel, movement, transfer, transportation, conveyance, carriage, haulage, shipment.

transition *n.*
☞ 过渡，变化 passage, passing, progress, progression, development, evolution, flux, change, alteration, conversion, transformation, shift.

transitional *adj.*
☞ 过渡 provisional, temporary, passing, intermediate, developmental, changing, fluid, unsettled.

translate *v.*
☞ 翻译 interpret, render, paraphrase, simplify, decode, decipher, transliterate, transcribe, change, alter, convert, transform, improve.

translation *n.*
☞ 翻译 rendering, version, interpretation, gloss, crib, rewording, rephrasing, paraphrase, simplification, transliteration, transcription, change, alteration, conversion, transformation.

transmission *n.*
☞ 传送，传播 broadcasting, diffusion, spread, communication, conveyance, carriage, transport, shipment, sending, dispatch, relaying, transfer.
☞ 播送 broadcast, programme, show, signal.

transmit *v.*
☞ 传送，传播 communicate, impart, convey, carry, bear, transport, send, dispatch, forward, relay, transfer, broadcast, radio, disseminate, network, diffuse, spread.

transparency *n.*
☞ 幻灯片 slide, photograph, picture.

transparent *adj.*
☞ 透明的 clear, see-through, translucent, sheer.
☞ 明显的，显然的 plain, distinct, clear, lucid, explicit, unambiguous, unequivocal, apparent, visible, obvious, evident, manifest, patent, undisguised, open, candid, straightforward.

transplant *v.*

☞移植 move, shift, displace, remove, uproot, transfer, relocate, resettle, repot.

transport v.
☞运送,运输 convey, carry, bear, take, fetch, bring, move, shift, transfer, ship, haul, remove, deport.

n.
☞运输,运输工具 conveyance, carriage, transfer, transportation, shipment, shipping, haulage, removal.

trap n.
☞陷阱 snare, net, noose, springe, gin, booby-trap, pitfall, danger, hazard, ambush, trick, wile, ruse, stratagem, device, trickery, artifice, deception.

☞诱捕,使落入圈套 snare, net, entrap, ensnare, enmesh, catch, take, ambush, corner, trick, deceive, dupe.

trash n.
☞垃圾 rubbish, garbage, refuse, junk, waste, litter, sweepings, offscourings, scum, dregs.

trauma n.
☞痛苦,损伤 injury, wound, hurt, damage, pain, suffering, anguish, agony, torture, ordeal, shock, jolt, upset, disturbance, upheaval, strain, stress.

traumatic adj.
☞痛苦的 painful, hurtful, injurious, wounding, shocking, upsetting, distressing, disturbing, unpleasant, frightening, stressful.

travel v.
☞旅行,行进 journey, voyage, go, wend, move, proceed, progress, wander, ramble, roam, rove, tour, cross, traverse.

n.
☞旅行,游历 travelling, touring, tourism, globetrotting.

traveller n.
☞游客,旅行者 tourist, explorer, voyager, globetrotter, holidaymaker, tripper, excursionist, passenger, commuter, wanderer, rambler, hiker, wayfarer, migrant, nomad, gypsy, itinerant, tinker, vagrant.

☞推销员 salesman, saleswoman, representative, rep, agent.

travelling adj.
☞旅行,游历 touring, wandering, roaming, roving, wayfaring, migrant, migratory, nomadic, itinerant, peripatetic, mobile, moving, vagrant, homeless.

travels n.
☞游历,行程 voyage, expedition, passage, journey, trip, excursion, tour, wanderings.

treacherous adj.
☞不忠的,靠不住的 traitorous, disloyal, unfaithful, faithless, unreliable, untrustworthy, false, untrue, deceitful, double, crossing.
☞危险的 dangerous, hazardous, risky, perilous, precarious, icy, slippery.

treachery n.
☞ 不忠,叛逆 treason, betrayal, disloyalty, infidelity, falseness, duplicity, double-dealing.

tread v.
☞ 践踏,踩 walk, step, pace, stride, march, tramp, trudge, plod, stamp, trample, walk on, press, crush, squash.
n.
☞ 步法,踏 walk, footfall, footstep, pace, stride.

treason n.
☞ 叛国,不忠 treachery, perfidy, disloyalty, duplicity, subversion, sedition, mutiny, rebellion.

treasure n.
☞ 珍宝,财宝 fortune, wealth, riches, money, cash, gold, jewels, hoard, cache.
v.
☞ 珍爱 prize, value, esteem, revere, worship, love, adore, idolize, cherish preserve, guard.

treat n.
☞ 乐事,款待 indulgence, gratification, pleasure, delight, enjoyment, fun, entertainment, excursion, outing, party, celebration, feast, banquet, gift, surprise, thrill.
v.
☞ 处理,看待 deal with, manage, handle, use, regard, consider, discuss, cover.
☞ 治疗,照顾 tend, nurse, minister to, attend to, care for, heal, cure.
☞ 招待,宴请 pay for, buy, stand, give, provide, entertain, regale, feast.

treatment n.
☞ 治疗,照顾 healing, cure, remedy, medication, therapy, surgery, care, nursing.
☞ 处理,对待 management, handling, use, usage, conduct, discussion, coverage.

treaty n.
☞ 协议,合同 pact, convention, agreement, covenant, compact, negotiation, contract, bond, alliance.

tree n.
☞ 树,树木 bush, shrub, evergreen, conifer.

tremble v.
☞ 颤抖,震颤 shake, vibrate, quake, shiver, shudder, quiver, wobble, rock.
n.
☞ 发抖,震颤 shake, vibration, quake, shiver, shudder, quiver, tremor, wobble.

tremendous adj.
☞ 巨大的 wonderful, marvellous, stupendous, sensational, spectacular, extraordinary, amazing, incredible, terrific, impressive, huge, immense, vast, colossal, gigantic, towering, formidable.

tremor n.
☞ 震动,震颤 shake, quiver, tremble, shiver, quake, quaver, wobble, vibration, agitation, thrill, shock, earthquake.

trend n.
☞ 潮流,趋势 course, flow, drift, tendency, inclination, leaning, craze, rage, fashion, vogue, mode, style, look.

trial n.
- 审讯,审判 litigation, lawsuit, hearing, inquiry, tribunal.
- 考验,实验 experiment, test, examination, check, dry run, dummy run, practice, rehearsal, audition, contest.
- 烦恼,磨炼 affliction, suffering, grief, misery, distress, adversity, hardship, ordeal, trouble, nuisance, vexation, tribulation.

adj.
- 实验的,试用的 experimental, test, pilot, exploratory, provisional, probationary.

tribe n.
- 部落 race, nation, people, clan, family, house, dynasty, blood, stock, group, caste, class, division, branch.

tribute n.
- 献礼,颂辞 praise, credit, commendation, compliment, accolade, homage, respect, honour, acknowledgement, recognition, tratitude.
- 贡金 payment, levy, charge, tax, duty, gift, offering, contribution.

trick n.
- 诡计,计谋 fraud, swindle, deception, deceit, artifice, illusion, hoax, practical joke, joke, leg-pull, prank, antic, caper, frolic, feat, stunt, ruse, wile, dodge, subterfuge, trap, device, knack, technique, secret.

adj.
- 欺诈的 false, mock, artificial, imitation, ersatz, fake, forged, counterfeit, feigned, sham, bogus.

v.
- 欺骗,欺诈 deceive, delude, dupe, fool, hoodwink, beguile, mislead, bluff, hoax, pull, someone's leg, cheat, swindle, diddle, defraud, con, trap, outwit.

trickery n.
- 欺骗,欺诈 deception, illusion, sleight-of-hand, pretence, artifice, guile, deceit, dishonesty, cheating, swindling, fraud, imposture, double-dealing, monkey business, funny business, chicanery, skulduggery, hocus-pocus.

trickle v.
- 细流,滴流 dribble, run, leak, seep, ooze, exude, drip, drop, filter, percolate.

n.
- 滴流,细流 dribble, drip, drop, leak, seepage.

tricky adj.
- 不易处理的 difficult, awkward, problematic, complicated, knotty, thorny, delicate, ticklish.
- 狡猾的,奸诈的 crafty, artful, cunning, sly, wily, foxy, subtle, devious, slippery, scheming, deceitful.

trifle n.
- 琐事,小事 little, bit, spot, drop, dash, touch, trace.
- 廉价货,小玩意 toy, plaything, trinket, bauble, knick-knack, triviality, nothing.

trifling adj.

☞ 不重要的,微小的 small, paltry, slight, negligible, inconsiderable, unimportant, insignificant, minor, trivial, petty, silly, frivolous, idle, empty, worthless.

trigger v.
☞ 引发,引起 cause, start, initiate, activate, set off, spark off, provoke, prompt, elicit, generate, produce.
n.
☞ 扳柄,触发器 lever, catch, switch, spur, stimulus.

trim adj.
☞ 整齐的,整洁的 neat, tidy, orderly, shipshape, spick-and-span, spruce, smart, dapper.
☞ 纤细的 slim, slender, streamlined, compact.
v.
☞ 使整齐 cut, clip, crop, dock, prune, pare, shave.
☞ 修饰,整饰 decorate, ornament, embellish, garnish, dress, array, adjust, arrange, order, neaten, tidy.
n.
☞ 齐备,整齐 condition, state, order, form, shape, fitness, health.

trimmings n.
☞ 装饰物 garnish, decorations, ornaments, frills, extras, accessories.
☞ 边角料 cuttings, clippings, parings, ends.

trip n.
☞ 旅行 outing, excursion, tour, jaunt, ride, drive, spin, journey, voyage, expedition, foray.

v.
☞ 颠簸,跌倒 stumble, slip, fall, tumble, stagger, totter, blunder.

triumph n.
☞ 成功,胜利 win, victory, conquest, walk-over, success, achievement, accomplishment, feat, coup, masterstroke, hit, sensation.
☞ 欢喜,得意 exultation, jubilation, rejoicing, celebration, elation, joy, happiness.
v.
☞ 获胜,成功 win, succeed, prosper, conquer, vanquish, overcome, overwhelm, prevail, dominate, celebrate, rejoice, glory, gloat.

triumphant adj.
☞ 成功的,喜悦的 winning, victorious, conquering, successful, exultant, jubilant, rejoicing, celebratory, glorious, elated, joyful, proud, boastful, bloating, swaggering.

trivial adj.
☞ 琐碎的,不重要的 unimportant, insignificant, inconsequential, incidental, minor, petty, paltry, trifling, small, little, inconsiderable, negligible, worthless, meaningless, frivolous, banal, trite, commonplace, everyday.

triviality n.
☞ 琐屑,平凡 unimportance, insignificance, pettiness, smallness, worthlessness, meaninglessness, frivolity, trifle, detail, technicality.

troop n.

☞ 群 contingent, squadron, unit, division, company, squad, team, crew, gang, band, bunch, group, body, pack, herd, flock, horde, crowd, throng, multitude.
v.
☞ 集结，成群而行 go, march, parade, stream, flock, swarm, throng.

troops n.
☞ 军队，部队 army, military, soldiers, servicemen, servicewomen.

tropical adj.
☞ 热带的 hot, torrid, sultry, sweltering, stifling, steamy, humid.

trot v.
☞ 小跑，快步跑 jog, run, scamper, scuttle, scurry.

trouble n.
☞ 困境，困难 problem, difficulty, struggle, annoyance, irritation, bother, nuisance, inconvenience, misfortune, adversity, trial, tribulation, pain, suffering, affliction, distress, grief, woe, heartache, concern, uneasiness, worry, anxiety, agitation.
☞ 不安，扰乱 unrest, strife, tumult, commotion, disturbance, disorder, upheaval.
☞ 苦恼，烦恼 disorder, complaint, ailment, illness, disease, disability, defect.
☞ 辛劳，烦劳 effort, exertion, pains, care, attention, thought.
v.
☞ 恼人 annoy, vex, harass, torment, bother, inconvenience, disturb, upset, distress, sadden, pain, afflict, burden, worry, agitate, disconcert, perplex.

troublemaker n.
☞ 惹是生非者 agitator, rabble-rouser, incendiary, instigator, ringleader, stirrer, mischief-maker.

troublesome adj.
☞ 令人讨厌的 annoying, irritating, vexatious, irksome, bothersome, inconvenient, difficult, hard, tricky, thorny, taxing, demanding, laborious, tiresome, wearisome.
☞ 麻烦的 unruly, rowdy, turbulent, trying, unco-operative, insubordinate, rebellious.

trousers n.
☞ 裤子 pants, slacks, jeans, denims, levis, flannels, bags, dungarees, breeches, shorts.

truce n.
☞ 休战，停火 cease-fire, peace, armistice, cessation, moratorium, suspension, stay, respite, let-up, lull, rest, break, interval, intermission.

truck n.
☞ 卡车 lorry, van, wagon, trailer, float, cart, barrow.

true adj.
☞ 真实的，确实的 real, genuine, authentic, actual, veritable, exact, precise, accurate, correct, right, factual, truthful, veracious, sincere, honest, legitimate, valid, rightful, proper.

忠诚的,忠心的
faithful, loyal, constant, steadfast, staunch, firm, trustworthy, trusty, honourable, dedicated, devoted.

truly *adv.*
真实地,正确地
very, greatly, extremely, really, genuinely, sincerely, honestly, truthfully, undeniably, indubitably, indeed, in fact, in reality, exactly, precisely, correctly, rightly, properly.

trunk *n.*
箱子
case, suitcase, chest, coffer, box, crate.
树干
torso, body, frame, shaft, stock, stem, stalk.

trust *n.*
信任,相信
faith, belief, credence, credit, hope, expectation, reliance, confidence, assurance, conviction, certainty.
信托物,信托
care, charge, custody, safekeeping, guardianship, protection, responsibility, duty.
v.
相信,信任
believe, imagine, assume, presume, suppose, surmise, hope, expect, rely on, depend on, count on, bank on, swear by.
委托,托付
entrust, commit, consign, confide, give, assign, delegate.

trusting *adj.*
信任的,不疑的
trustful, credulous, gullible, naive, innocent, unquestioning, unsuspecting, unguarded, unwary.

trustworthy *adj.*
值得信任的
honest, upright, honourable, principled, dependable, reliable, steadfast, true, responsible, sensible.

truth *n.*
真理,事实,真实
truthfulness, veracity, candour, frankness, hnoesty, sincerity, genuineness, authenticity, realism, exactness, precision, accuracy, validity, legitimacy, honour, integrity, uprightness, faithfulness, fidelity, loyalty, constancy.
真相
facts, reality, actuality, fact, axiom, maxim, principle, truism.

truthful *adj.*
真实的
veracious, frank, candid, straight, honest, sincere, true, veritable, exact, precise, accurate, correct, realistic, faithful, trustworthy, reliable.

try *v.*
试图,企图
attempt, endeavour, venture, undertake, seek, strive.
审判
hear, judge.
试验
experiment, test, sample, taste, inspect, examine, investigate, evaluate, appraise.
n.
尝试,努力
attempt, endeavour, effort, go, bash, crack, crack, shot, stab.
试验
experiment, test, trial, ample, taste.

trying *adj.*

☞难堪的,考验的 annoying, irritating, aggravating, vexatious, exasperating, troublesome, tiresome, wearisome, difficult, hard, tough, arduous, taxing, demanding, testing.

tub n.
☞桶,浴盆 bath, basin, vat, tun, butt, cask, barrel, keg.

tube n.
☞管,筒 hose, pipe, cylinder, duct, conduit, spout, channel.

tug v.
☞拉,曳 pull, draw, tow, haul, drag, lug, heave, wrench, jerk, pluck.
n.
☞拉扯,拖曳 pull, tow, haul, heave, wrench, jerk, pluck.

tuition n.
☞教学,教授 teaching, instruction, coaching, training, lessons, schooling, education.

tumble v.
☞跌倒,跌落 fall, stumble, trip, topple, overthrow, drop, flop, collapse, plummet, pitch, roll, toss.
n.
☞跌落,摔落 fall, stumble, trip, drop, plunge, roll, toss.

tumult n.
☞烦乱,纷扰 commotion, turmoil, disturbance, upheaval, stir, agitation, unrest, disorder, chaos, pandemonium, noise, clamour, din, racket, hubbub, hullabaloo, row, rumpus, uproar, riot, fracas, brawl, affray, strife.

tumultuous adj.
☞骚乱的,喧闹的 turbulent, stormy, raging, fierce, violent, wild, hectic, boisterous, rowdy, noisy, disorderly, unruly, riotous, restless, agitated, troubled, disturbed, excited.

tune n.
☞调子,曲 melody, theme, motif, song, air, strain.
v.
☞调整 pitch, harmonize, set, regulate, adjust, adapt, temper, attune, synchronize.

tuneful adj.
☞谐美的 melodious, melodic, catchy, musical, euphonious, harmonious, pleasant, mellow, sonorous.

tunnel n.
☞隧道,地下通道 passage, passageway, gallery, subway, underpass, burrow, hole, mine, shaft, chimney.
v.
☞在……挖地道 burrow, dig, excavate, mine, bore, penetrate, undermine, sap.

turbulent adj.
☞狂烈的,混乱的 rough, choppy, stormy, blustery, tempestuous, raging, furious, violent, wild, tumultuous, unbridled, boisterous, rowdy, disorderly, unruly, undisciplined, obstreperous, rebellious, mutinous, riotous, agitated, unsettled, unstable, confused, disordered.

turmoil n.

☞ 骚动,混乱 confusion, disorder, tumult, commotion, disturbance, trouble, disquiet, agitation, turbulence, stir, ferment, flurry, bustle, chaos, pandemonium, bedlam, noise, din, hubbub, row, uproar.

turn v.
☞ 转动,翻转 revolve, circle, spin, twirl, whirl, twist, gyrate, pivot, hinge, swivel, rotate, roll, move, shift, invert, reverse, bend, veer, swerve, divert.
☞ 改变 make, transform, change, alter, modify, convert, adapt, adjust, fit, mould, shape, form, fashion, remodel.
☞ 变得 go, become, grow.
☞ 求助 resort, have recourse, apply, appeal.
☞ 变坏,变差 sour, curdle, spoil, go off, go bad.

n.
☞ 旋转,翻动 revolution, cycle, round, circle, rotation, spin, twirl, twist, gyration, bend, curve, loop, reversal.
☞ 改变,变化 change, alteration, shift, deviation.
☞ 行为,动作 act, performance, performer.
☞ 轮到 go, chance, opportunity, occasion, stint, period, speel.

turn away
☞ 拒绝 reject, avert, deflect, deviate, depart.

turn down
☞ 拒绝 reject, decline, refuse, spurn, rubuff, repudiate.
☞ 扭小,转小 lower, lessen, quieten, soften, mute, muffle.

turn in
☞ 就寝 go to bed, retire.
☞ 上交,交出 hand over, give up, surrender, deliver, hand in, tender, submit, return, give back.

turn off
☞ 放弃,失去 branch off, leave, quit, depart from, deviate, divert.
☞ 关上,扭上 switch off, turn out, stop, shut down, unplug, disconnect.

turn on
☞ 打开,开启 switch on, start (up), activate, connect.
☞ 激起,使……兴奋 arouse, stimulate, excite, thrill, please, attract.
☞ 依赖,视……而定 hinge on, depend on, rest on.
☞ 敌对,攻击 attack, round on, fall on.

turn out
☞ 结果,证明为 happen, come about, transpire, ensue, result, end up, become, develop, emerge.
☞ 关掉 switch off, turn off, unplug, disconnect.
☞ 穿着……的 appear, present, dress, clothe.
☞ 生产,产出 produce, make, manufacture, fabricate, assemble.
☞ 驱逐,迫使……放弃 evict, throw out, expel, deport, banish, dismiss, discharge, drum out, kick out, sack.
☞ 清空 empty, clear, clean out.

turn over
- 仔细考虑 think over, think about, mull over, ponder, deliberate, reflect on, contemplate, consider, examine.
- 上交,提交 hand over, surrender, deliver, transfer.
- 颠覆,翻转 overturn, upset, upend, invert, capsize, keel over.

turn up
- 出现,出席 attend, come, arrive, appear, show up.
- 增加,扩大 amplify, intensify, raise, increase.
- 偶然被发现 discover, find, unearth, dig up, expose, disclose, reveal, show.

turning n.
- 转变处,岔路口 turn-off, junction, crossroads, fork, bend, curve, turn.

turning-point n.
- 转折点,转机 crossroads, watershed, crux, crisis.

turnout n.
- 一批到会者 attendance, audience, gate, crowd, assembly, congregation.
- 装束,装备 appearance, outfit, dress, clothes.

tutor n.
- 导师 teacher, instructor, coach, educator, lecturer, supervisor, guide, mentor, guru, guardian.

v.
- 教授,指导 teach, instruct, train, drill, coach, educate, school, lecture, supervise, direct, guide.

twilight n.
- 曙光,微明 dusk, half-light, gloaming, gloom, dimness, sunset, evening.

twin n.
- 双胞胎之一 double, look-alike, likeness, duplicate, clone, match, counterpart, corollary, fellow, mate.

adj.
- 完全相似的 identical, matching, corresponding, symmetrical, parallel, matched, paired, double, dual, duplicate, twofold.

v.
- 匹配,成对 match, pair, couple, link, join.

twinkle v.
- 闪烁,闪耀 sparkle, glitter, shimmer, glisten, glimmer, flicker, wink, flash, glint, gleam, shine.

n.
- 闪烁,闪光 sparkle, scintillation, glitter, shimmer, glisten, glimmer, flicker, wink, flash, glint, gleam, light.

twirl v.
- 转动,扭动 spin, whirl, pirouette, wheel, rotate, revolve, swivel, pivot, turn, twist, gyrate, wind, coil.

n.
- 旋转,扭曲 spin, whirl, pirouette, rotation, revolution, turn, twist, gyration, convlution, spiral, coil.

twist v.
- 转动,绞 turn, screw, wring, spin, swivel, wind, zigzag, bend, coil, spiral, curl, wreathe, twine, entwine,

intertwine, weave, entangle, wriggle, squirm, writhe.
- 曲解 change, alter, garble, misquote, misrepresent, distort, contort, warp, pervert.

n.
- 扭,拧 turn, screw, spin, roll, bend, curve, arc, curl, loop, zigzag, coil, spiral, convolution, squiggle, tangle.
- 弯曲 change, variation, break.
- 曲解 perversion, distortion, contortion.
- 失常,癖 surprise, quirk, oddity, peculiarity.

twisted adj.
- 扭曲的,不自然的 warped, perverted, deviant, unnatural.

two-faced adj.
- 两面的,伪虚的 hypocritical, insincere, false, lying, deceitful, treacherous, double-dealing, devious, untrustworthy.

tycoon n.
- 大亨,大实业家 industrialist, entrepreneur, captain of industry, magnate, mogul, baron, supremo, capitalist, financier.

type n.
- 类型,样式 sort, kind, form, genre, variety, strain, species, breed, group, class, category, subdivision, classification, description, designation, stamp, mark, order, standard.
- 典型,模范 archetype, embodiment, prototype, original, model, pattern, specimen, example.
- 字体,铅字 print, printing, characters, letters, lettering, face, fount, font.

typhoon n.
- 飓风 whirlwind, cyclone, tornado, twister, hurricane, tempest, storm, squall.

typical adj.
- 典型的 standard, normal, usual, average, conventional, orthodox, stock, model, representative, illustrative, indicative, characteristic, distinctive.

typify v.
- 代表,作为……的象征 embody, epitomize, encapsulate, personnify, characterize, exemplify, symbolize, represent, illustrate.

U

ugly adj.
- 难看的,丑的 unattractive, unsightly, plain, unprepossessing, ill-favoured, hideous, monstrous, misshapen, deformed.
- 讨厌的 unpleasant, disagreeable, nasty, horrid, objectionable, offensive, disgusting, revolting, repulsive, vile, frightful, terrible.

ultimate adj.

☞ 最终的,基本的 final, last, closing, concluding, eventual, terminal, furthest, remotest, extreme, utmost, greatest, highest, supreme, superlative, perfect, radical, fundamental, primary.

ultimately *adv*.
☞ 最终 finally, eventually, at last, in the end, after all.

unabashed *adj*.
☞ 不脸红的,满不在乎的 unashamed, unembarrassed, brazen, blatant, bold, confident, undaunted, unconcerned, undismayed.

unable *adj*.
☞ 不能的 incapable, powerless, impotent, unequipped, unqualified, unfit, incompetent, inadequate.

unacceptable *adj*.
☞ 不能接受的,不受欢迎的 intolerable, inadmissible, unsatisfactory, undesirable, unwelcome, objectionable, offensive, unpleasant.

unaccompanied *adj*.
☞ 无伴的,无伴奏的 alone, unescorted, unattended, lone, solo, single-handed.

unaccountable *adj*.
☞ 无法解释的,不能说明的 unexplainable, unfathomable, impenetrable, incomprehensible, baffling, puzzling, mysterious, astonishing, extraordinary, strange, odd, peculiar, singular, unusual, uncommon, unheard-of.

unaccustomed *adj*.

不习惯的,不适应的
unused, unacquainted, unfamiliar, unpractised, inexperienced.

☞ 不寻常的,奇异的 strange, unusual, uncommon, different, new, unexpected, surprising, uncharacteristic, unprecedented.

unalterable *adj*.
☞ 不可改变的,固定的 unchangeable, invariable, unchanging, immutable, final, inflexible, unyielding, rigid, fixed, permanent.

unanimous *adj*.
☞ 无异议的,全体一致的 united, concerted, joint, common, as one, in agreement, in accord, harmonious.

unarmed *adj*.
☞ 未武装的,徒手的 defenceless, unprotected, exposed, open, vulnerable, weak, helpless.

unashamed *adj*.
☞ 无耻的,公然的 shameless, unabashed, impenitent, unrepentant, unconcealed, undisguised, open, blatant.

unassuming *adj*.
☞ 不爱表现的,不出风头的 unassertive, self-effacing, retiring, modest, humble, meek, unobtrusive, unpretentious, simple, restrained.

unattached *adj*.
☞ 独立的,单身的 unmarried, single, free, available, footloose, fancy-free, independent, unaffiliated.

unavoidable adj.
☞ 无可避免的,不得已的 inevitable, inescapable, inexorable, certain, sure, fated, destined, obligatory, compulsory, mandatory, necessary.

unaware adj.
☞ 未察觉的,无意的 oblivious, unconscious, ignorant, uninformed, unknowing, unsuspecting, unmindful, heedless, blind, deaf.

unbalanced adj.
☞ 不正常的,错乱的 insane, mad, crazy, lunatic, deranged, disturbed, demented, irrational, unsound.
☞ 不全面的 biased, prejudiced, one-sided, partisan, unfair, unjust, unequal, uneven, asymmetrical, lopsided, unsteady, unstable.

unbearable adj.
☞ 不能忍受的,难堪的 intolerable, unacceptable, insupportable, insufferable, unendurable, excruciating.

unbelief n.
☞ 不信上帝,不信宗教 atheism, agnosticism, scepticism, doubt, incredulity, disbelief.

unbelievable adj.
☞ 不信的,怀疑的 incredible, inconceivable, unthinkable, unimaginable, astonishing, staggering, extraordinary, impossible, improbable, unlikely, implausible, unconvincing, far-fetched, preposterous.

unbridled adj.
☞ 放纵的,无约束的 immoderate, excessive, uncontrolled, unrestrained, unchecked.

unbroken adj.
☞ 完整的 intact, whole, entire, complete, solid, undivided.
☞ 不间断的,未受阻碍的 uninterrupted, continuous, endless, ceaseless, incessant, unceasing, constant, perpetual, progressive, successive.
☞ 未被打破的,未被超过的 unbeaten, unsurpassed, unequalled, unmatched.

uncanny adj.
☞ 怪异的,神秘的 weird, strange, queer, bizarre, mysterious, unaccountable, incredible, remarkable, extraordinary, fantastic, unnatural, unearthly, supernatural, eerie, creepy, spooky.

uncivilized adj.
☞ 未开化的 primitive, barbaric, savage, wild, untamed, uncultured, unsophisticated, unenlightened, uneducated, illiterate, uncouth, antisocial.

unclean adj.
☞ 不洁净的 dirty, soiled, filthy, foul, polluted, contaminated, tainted, impure, unhygienic, unwholesome, corrupt, defiled, sullied.

unclear adj.
☞ 朦胧的,不清楚的 indistinct, hazy, dim, obscure, vague,

indefinite, ambiguous, equivocal, uncertain, unsure, doubtful, dubious.

uncomfortable adj.
☞ 不适应的,难弄的 cramped, hard, cold, ill-fitting, irritating, painful, disagreeable.
☞ 不安的,忧虑的 awkward, self-conscious, uneasy, troubled, worried, disturbed, distressed, disquieted, conscience-stricken.

uncommon adj.
☞ 不普通的,不凡的,显著的 rare, scarce, infrequent, unusual, abnormal, atypical, unfamiliar, strange, odd, curious, bizarre, extraordinary, remarkable, notable, outstanding, exceptional, distinctive, special.

unconscious adj.
☞ 失去知觉的 stunned, knocked out, out, out cold, out for the count, senseless, insensible.
☞ 不能察觉的,不知道的 unaware, oblivious, blind, deaf, heedless, unmindful, ignorant.
☞ 无意识的 involuntary, automatic, reflex, instinctive, impulsive, innate, subconscious, subliminal, repressed, suppressed, latent, unwitting, inadvertent, accidental, unintentional.

unconventional adj.
☞ 不寻常的,不依惯例的 unorthodox, alternative, different, offbeat, eccentric, idiosyncratic, individual, original, odd, unusual, irregular, abnormal, bizarre, way-out.

under prep.
☞ 在……下面 below, underneath, beneath, lower than, less than, inferior to, subordinate to.

under way
☞ 正在进行 moving, in motion, going, in operation, started, begun, in progress, afoot.

undercover adj.
☞ 秘密的,暗中从事的 secret, hush-hush, private, confidential, spy, intelligence, underground, clandestine, surreptitious, furtive, covert, hidden, concealed.

underestimate v.
☞ 低估 underrate, undervalue, misjudge, miscalculate, minimize, belittle, disparage, dismiss.

undergo v.
☞ 经受,经历 experience, suffer, sustain, submit to, bear, stand, endure, weather, withstand.

underground adj.
☞ 在地下的,地下的 subterranean, buried, sunken, covered, hidden, concealed.
☞ 秘密的 secret, covert, undercover, revolutionary, subversive, radical, experimental, avant-garde, alternative, unorthodox, unofficial.

underhand adj.
☞ 秘密的,欺骗的,狡诈的 unscrupulous, unethical, immoral, improper, sly, crafty, sneaky, stealthy, surreptitious,

furtive, devious, dishoest, deceitful, deceptive, fraudulent, crooked, shady.

underline v.
☞ 画线于……下面,强调
mark, underscore, stress, emphasize, accentuate, italicize, highlight, point up.

underlying adj.
☞ 基本的,地下的 basic, fundamental, essential, primary, elementary root, intrinsic, latent, hidden, lurking, veiled.

undermine v.
☞ 挖地道,从基础损坏 mine, tunnel, excavate, erode, wear away, weaken, sap, sabotage, subvert, vitiate, mar, impair.

underprivileged adj.
☞ 没有地位的,贫困的 disadvantaged, deprived, poor, needy, impoverished, destitute, oppressed.

understand v.
☞ 理解,清楚 grasp, comprehend, take in, follow, get, cotton on, fathom, penetrate, make out, discern, see, realize, recognize, appreciate, accept.
☞ 同情 sympathize, empathize.
☞ 认为,相信 believe, think, know, hear, learn, gather, assume, presume, suppose, conclude.

understanding n.
☞ 理解力,了解 grasp, comprehension, knowledge, wisdom, intelligence, intellect, sense, judgement, discernment, insight, appreciation, awareness, impression, perception, belief, idea, notion, opinion, interpretation.
☞ 协定,协议 agreement, arrangement, pact, accord, harmony.
☞ 同情心,体谅 sympathy, empathy.

adj.
☞ 同情的,体谅的 sympathetic, compassionate, kind, considerate, sensitive, tender, loving, patient, tolerant, forbearing, forgiving.

undertake v.
☞ 确定,许诺 pledge, agree, promise, guarantee, agree, contract, covenant.
☞ 着手,担承,开始 begin, commence, embark on, tackle, try, attempt, endeavour, take on, accept, assume.

undertaking n.
☞ 事业,企业 enterprise, venture, business, affair, task, project, operation, attempt, endeavour, effort.
☞ 承诺,保证 pledge, vow, commitment, promise, word, assurance.

undertone n.
☞ 暗示,潜伏的感情或意思 hint, suggestion, whisper, murmur, trace, tinge, touch, flavour, feeling, atmosphere, undercurrent.

undervalue v.
☞ 低估……的价值 underrate, underestimate, misjudge, minimize, depreciate, disparage, dismiss.

underwater adj.

☞水面下的,水中的 subaquatic, undersea, submarine, submerged, sunken.

underwear n.
☞内衣 underclothes, undergarments, lingerie, undies, smalls.

underweight adj.
☞重量不足的 thin, undersized, underfed, undernourished, half-starved.

underwrite v.
☞负责保险,认购 endorse, authorize, sanction, approve, back, guarantee, insure, sponsor, fund, finance, subsidize, subscribe, sign, initial, countersign.

undesirable adj.
☞不受欢迎的,讨厌的 unwanted, unwelcome, unacceptable, unsuitable, unpleasant, disagreeable, distasteful, repugnant, offensive, objectionable, obnoxious.

undo v.
☞解开,松开 unfasten, untie, unbuckle, unbutton, unzip, unlock, unwrap, unwind, open, loose, loosen, separate.
☞破坏 annul, nullify, invalidate, cancel, offset, neutralize, reverse, overturn, upset, quash, defeat, undermine, subvert, mar, spoil, ruin, wreck, shatter, destroy.

undone adj.
☞未完成的,未做的 left, unaccomplished, unfulfilled, unfinished, uncompleted, incomplete, outstanding, omitted, neglected, forgotten.
☞松开的 unfastened, untied, unlaced, unbuttoned, unlocked, open, loose.

undoubted adj.
☞确定的,无疑的 unchallenged, undisputed, acknowledged, unquestionable, indisputable, incontrovertible, undesirable, indubitable, sure, certain, definite, obvious, patent.

unearth v.
☞发掘,发现 dig up, exhume, disinter, excavate, uncover, expose, reveal, find, discover, detect.

unearthly adj.
☞超自然的,神秘的 supernatural, ghostly, eerie, uncanny, weird, strange, spine-chilling.
☞不合理的 unreasonable, outrageous, ungodly.

uneven adj.
☞不平坦的 rough, bumpy.
☞不平衡的 odd, unequal, inequitable, unfair, unbalanced, one-sided, asymmetrical, lopsided, crooked.
☞不规则的 irregular, intermittent, spasmodic, fitful, jerky, unsteady, variable, changeable, fluctuating, erratic, inconsistent, patchy.

uneventful adj.
☞平静无事的 uninteresting, unexciting, quiet, unvaried, boring, monotonous, tedious, dull, routine, ordinary, commonplace, unremarkable, unexceptional, unmemorable.

unexceptional adj.
☞ 平常的 unremarkable, unmemorable, typical, average, normal, usual, ordinary, indifferent, mediocre, unimpressive.

unexpected adj.
☞ 意外的,未料到的 unforeseen, unanticipated, unpredictable, chance, accidental, fortuitous, sudden, abrupt, surprising, startling, amazing, astonishing, unusual.

unfair adj.
☞ 不公平的,不公正的 unjust, inequitable, partial, biased, prejudiced, bigoted, discriminatory, unbalance, one-sided, partisan, arbitrary, undeserved, unmerited, unwarranted, uncalled-for, unethical, unscrupulous, unprincipled, wrongful, dishonest.

unfaithful adj.
☞ 不忠实的,不信实的 disloyal, treacherous, false, untrue, deceitful, dishonest, untrustworthy, unreliable, fickle, inconstant, adulterous, two-timing, duplicitous, double-dealing, faithless, unbelieving, godless.

unfamiliar adj.
☞ 不熟的,生疏的 strange, unusual, uncommon, curious, alien, foreign, uncharted, unexplored, unknown, different, new, novel, unaccustomed, unacquainted, inexperienced, unpractised, unskilled, unversed.

unfashionable adj.
☞ 过时的,不合潮流的 outmoded, dated, out of date, out, passe, old-fashioned, antiquated, obsolete.

unfasten v.
☞ 打开,松开 undo, untie, loosen, unlock, open, uncouple, disconnect, separate, detach.

unfinished adj.
☞ 未完成的,未成功的 incomplete, uncompleted, half-done, sketchy, rough, crude, imperfect, lacking, wanting, deficient, undone, unaccomplished, unfulfilled.

unfit adj.
☞ 不合适的,不胜任的 unsuitable, inappropriate, unsuited, ill-equipped, unqualified, ineligible, untrained, unprepared, unequal, incapable, incompetent, inadequate, ineffective, useless.
☞ 不健康的 unhealthy, out of condition, flabby, feeble, decrepit.

unfold v.
☞ 开展,开发 develop, evolve.
☞ 显现,表露 reveal, disclose, show, present, describe, explain, clarify, elaborate.
☞ 展开,打开 open, spread, flatten, straighten, stretch out, undo, unfurl, unroll, uncoil, unwrap, uncover.

unforeseen adj.
☞ 未预见到的 unpredicted, unexpected, unanticipated, surprising, startling, sudden, unavoidable.

unforgettable adj.
- 永远记得的,不能忘记的 memorable, momentous, historic, noteworthy, notable, impressive, remarkable, exceptional, extraordinary.

unforgivable adj.
- 不能原谅的 unpardonable, inexcusable, unjustifiable, indefensible, reprehensible, shameful, disgraceful, deplorable.

unfortunate adj.
- 不幸运的,倒霉的 unlucky, luckless, hapless, unsuccessful, poor, wretched, unhappy, doomed, ill-fated, hopeless, disastrous, ruinous.
- 令人遗憾的 regrettable, lamentable, deplorable, adverse, unfavourable, unsuitable, inappropriate, inopportune, untimely, ill-timed.

unfounded adj.
- 无根据的,无稽的 baseless, groundless, unsupported, unsubstantiated, unproven, unjustified, idle, false, spurious, trumped-up, fabricated.

unfriendly adj.
- 不友好的,有敌意的 unsociable, standoffish, aloof, distant, unapproachable, inhospitable, uncongenial, unneighbourly, unwelcoming, cold, chilly, hostile, aggressive, quarrelsome, inimical, antagonistic, ill-disposed, disagreeable, surly, sour.

unguarded adj.
- 不小心的 unwary, careless, incautious, imprudent, impolitic, indiscreet, undiplomatic, thoughtless, unthinking, heedless, foolish, foolhardy, rash, ill-considered.
- 不设防的 undefended, unprotected, exposed, vulnerable, defenceless.

unhappy adj.
- 不高兴的,悲哀的 sad, sorrowful, miserable, melancholy, depressed, dispirited, despondent, dejected, downcast, crestfallen, long-faced, gloomy.
- 不幸的,不适当的 unfortunate, unlucky, ill-fated, unsuitable, inappropriate, inapt, ill-chosen, tactless, awkward, clumsy.

uniform n.
- 制服,服装 outfit, costume, livery, insignia, regalia, robes, dress, suit.

  adj.
- 相同的,一致的 same, identical, like, alike, similar, homogeneous, consistent, regular, equal, smooth, even, flat, monotonous, unvarying, unchanging, constant, unbroken.

unify v.
- 统一,结合 unite, join, bind, combine, integrate, merge, amalgamate, consolidate, fuse, weld.

union n.
- 联盟,联合 alliance, coalition, league, association, federation, confederation, confederacy,

merger, combination, amalgamation, blend, mixture, synthesis, fusion, unification, unity.

unique adj.
☞ 独一无二的 single, one-off, sole, only, lone, solitary, unmatched, matchless, peerless, unequalled, unparalleled, unrivalled, incomparable, inimitable.

unit n.
☞ 部分,单位组织 item, part, element, constituent, piece, component, module, section, segment, portion, entity, whole, one, system, assembly.

unite v.
☞ 联合,合并 join, link, couple, marry, ally, co-operate, band, associate, federate, confederate, combine, pool, amalgamate, merge, blend, unify, consolidate, coalesce, fuse.

united adj.
☞ 联合的,一致的 allied, affiliated, corporate, unified, combined, pooled, collective, concerted, one, unanimous, agreed, in agreement, in accord, like-minded.

unity n.
☞ 团结,一致 agreement, accord, concord, harmony, peace, consensus, unanimity, solidarity, integrity, oneness, wholeness, union, unification.

universal adj.
☞ 宇宙的,整体的 worldwide, global, all-embracing, all-inclusive, general, common, across-the-board, total, whole, entire, all-round, unlimited.

unload v.
☞ 卸下,除去 unpack, empty, discharge, dump, offload, unburden, relieve.

unmarried adj.
☞ 独身的 single, unwed, celibate, unattached, available.

unnecessary adj.
☞ 不必要的,多余的 unneeded, needless, uncalled-for, unwanted, non-essential, dispensable, expendable, superfluous, redundant, tautological.

unparalleled adj.
☞ 无比的,空前的 unequalled, unmatched, matchless, peerless, incomparable, unrivalled, unsurpasssed, supreme, superlative, rare, exceptional, unprecedented.

unpleasant adj.
☞ 不愉快的,不中意的 disagreeable, ill-natured, nasty, objectionable, offensive, distasteful, unpalatable, unattractive, repulsive, bad, troublesome.

unpopular adj.
☞ 不受欢迎的,不受喜爱的 disliked, hated, detested, unloved, unsought-after, unfashionable, undesirable, unwelcome, unwanted, rejected, shunned, avoided, neglected.

unreal adj.
☞ 不真实的,空想的 false, artificial, synthetic, mock, fake, sham, imaginary, visionary, fanciful, make-believe, pretend,

fictitious, made-up, fairy-tale, legendary, mythical, fantastic, illusory, immaterial, insubstantial, hypothetical.

unreliable adj.
☞ 靠不住的，不能相信的
unsound, fallible, deceptive, false, mistaken, erroneous, inaccurate, unconvincing, implausible, uncertain, undependable, untrustworthy, unstable, fickle, irresponsible.

unsatisfactory adj.
☞ 不令人满意的，不适合的
unacceptable, imperfect, defective, faulty, inferior, poor, weak, inadequate, insufficient, deficient, unsuitable, displeasing, dissatisfying, unsatisfying, frustrating, disappointing.

unusual adj.
☞ 不寻常的，奇异的
uncommon, rare, unfamiliar, strange, odd, curious, queer, bizarre, unconventional, irregular, abnormal, extraordinary, remarkable, exceptional, different, surprising, unexpected.

unwilling adj.
☞ 不情愿的 reluctant, disinclined, indisposed, resistant, opposed, averse, loath, slow, unenthusiastic, grudging.

upbringing n.
☞ 教育，养育 bringing-up, raising, rearing, breeding, parenting, care, nurture, cultivation, education, training, instruction, teaching.

update v.
☞ 使……现代化，使……合时代
modernize, revise, amend, correct, renew, renovate, revamp.

upgrade v.
☞ 提高 promote, advance, elevate, raise, improve, enhance.

upheaval n.
☞ 剧变，骤变 disruption, disturbance, upset, chaos, confusion, disorder, turmoil, shake-up, revolution, overthrow.

uphold v.
☞ 支持，赞成 support, maintain, hold to, stand by, defend, champion, advocate, promote, back, endorse, sustain, fortify, strengthen, justify, vindicate.

upper adj.
☞ 在上的，较高的 higher, loftier, superior, senior, top, topmost, uppermost, high, elevated, exalted, eminent, important.

uppermost adj.
☞ 最高的，最主要的 highest, loftiest, top, topmost, greatest, supreme, first, primmary, foremost, leading, principal, main, chief, dominant, predominant, parmount, pre-eminent.

uprising n.
☞ 起义，反抗 rebellion, revolt, mutiny, rising, insurgence, insurrection, revolution.

uproar n.
☞ 喧嚣，骚动 noise, din, racket, hubbub, hullabaloo, pandemonium, tumult, trumoil, turbulence, commotion, confusion, disorder, clamour, outcry, furore, riot, rumpus.

upset v.

- 使……悲哀,扰乱 distress, grieve, dismay, trouble, worry, agitate, disturb, bother, fluster, ruffle, discompose, shake, unnerve, disconcert, confuse, disorganize.
- 打翻,倾覆 tip, spill, overturn, capsize, topple, overthrow, destabilize, unsteady.

n.
- 扰乱,倾覆 trouble, worry, agitation, disturbance, bother, disruption, upheaval, shake-up, reverse, surprise, shock.
- 不适 disorder, complaint, bug, illness, sickness.

upside down adv.
- 翻转,倾覆 inverted, upturned, wrong way up, upset, overturned, disordered, muddled, jumbled, confused, topsy-turvy, chaotic.

up-to-date adj.
- 现代化的,最新式的 current, contemporary, modern, fashionable, trendy, latest, recent, new.

upturn n.
- 向上转,情况转好 revival, recovery, upsurge, upswing, rise, increase, boost, improvement.

urban adj.
- 城市的,都市的 town, city, inner-city, metropolitan, municipal, civic, built-up.

urge v.
- 力劝,推进,敦促 advise, counsel, recommend, advocate, encourage, exhort, implore, beg, beseech, entreat, plead, press, constrain, compel, force, push, drive, imple, goad, spur, hasten, induce, incite, instigate.

n.
- 强烈的欲望 desire, wish, inclination, fancy, longing, yearning, itch, impulse, compulsion, impetus, drive, eagerness.

urgency n.
- 紧急,急迫 hurry, haste, pressure, stress, importance, seriousness, gravity, imperativeness, need, necessity.

urgent adj.
- 紧急的,急迫的 immediate, instant, top-priority, important, critical, crucial, imperative, exigent, pressing, compelling, persuasive, earnest, eager, insitent, persistent.

usable adj.
- 可用的,能用的 working, operational, serviceable, functional, practical, exploitable, available, current, valid.

usage n.
- 用法,对待 treatment, handling, management, control, running, operation, employment, application, use.
- 风俗,习惯 tradition, custom, practice, habit, convention, etiquette, rule, regulation, form, routine, procedure, method.

use v.
- 利用,使用 utilize, employ, exercise, practise, operate, work, apply, wield, handle, treat, manipulate, exploit, enjoy, consume, exhaust, expend, spend.

n.
- 利用,用途 utility, usefulness, value, worth, profit, advantage,

benefit, good, avail, help, service, point, object, end, purpose, reason, cause, occasion, need, necessity, usage, application, employment, operation, exercise.

use up
☞ 耗尽,用光　finish, exhaust, drain, sap, deplete, consume, devour, absorb, waste, squander, fritter.

usued adj.
☞ 用旧了的　second-hand, cast-off, hand-me-down, nearly new, worn, dog-eared soiled.

useful adj.
☞ 有用的,有帮助的　handy, convenient, all-purpose, practical, effcetive, productive, fruitful, profitable, valuable, worthwhile, advantageous, beneficial, helpful.

useless adj.
☞ 无用的,无效的　futile, fruitless, unproductive, vain, idle, unavailing, hopeless, pointless, worthless, unusable, broken-down, clapped-out, unworkable, impractical, ineffective, inefficient, incompetent, weak.

usher n.
☞ 招待员　usherette, doorkeeper, attendant, escort, guide.
v.
☞ 引导,招待　escort, accompany, conduct, lead, direct, guide, show, pilot, steer.

usual adj.
☞ 正常的,平常的　normal, typical, stock, standard, regular, routine, habitual, customary, conventional, accepted, recognized, accustomed, familiar, common, everyday, general, ordinary, unexceptional, expected, predictable.

usually adv.
☞ 通常地,惯例地　normally, generally, as a rule, ordinarily, typically, traditionally, regularly, commonly, by and large, on the whole, mainly, chiefly, mostly.

utensil n.
☞ 器具,器皿　tool, implement, instrument, device, contrivance, gadget, apparatus, appliance.

utility n.
☞ 有用,实用　usefulness, use, value, profit, advantage, benefit, avail, service, convenience, practicality, efficacy, efficiency, fitness, serviceableness.

utmost adj.
☞ 极度的,最大的　extreme, maximum, greatest, highest, supreme, paramount.
☞ 最终的　farthest, furthermost, remotest, outermost, ultimate, final, last.
n.
☞ 极限,最大可能　best, hardest, most, maximum.

utter adj.
☞ 完全的,全然的　absolute, complete, total, entire, thoroughgoing, out-and-out, downright, sheer, stark, arrant, unmitigated, unqualified, perfect, consummate.
v.
☞ 说,讲　speak, say, voice, vocalize, verbalize, express, articulate, enunciate, sound, pronounce, deliver, state, declare, announce, proclaim, tell, reveal, divulge.

utterly adv.
☞ 完全地 absolutely, completely, totally, fully, entirely, wholly, thoroughly, downright, perfectly.

u-turn n.
☞ 逆转, 回转 about-turn, volte-face, reversal, backtrack.

V

vacancy n.
☞ 空缺 opportunity, opening, position, post, job, place, room, situation.

vacant adj.
☞ 空的, 未被占用的 empty, unoccupied, unfilled, free, available, void, not in use, unused, uninhabited.
☞ 空间的, 空白的 blank, expressionless, vacuous, inane, inattentive, absent, absent-minded, unthinking, dreamy.

vacuum n.
☞ 真空 emptiness, void, nothingness, vacuity, space, chasm, gap.

vague adj.
☞ 不清楚的, 含混的 ill-defined, blurred, indistinct, hazy, dim, shadowy, misty, fuzzy, nebulous, obscure.
☞ 突然的, 含糊的 indefinite, imprecise, unclear, uncertain, undefined, undetermined, unspecific, generalized, inexact, ambiguous, evasive, loose, woolly.

vain adj.
☞ 无效的, 徒然的 useless, worthless, futile, abortive, fruitless, pointless, unproductive, unprofitable, unavailing, hollow, groundless, empty, trivial, unimportant.
☞ 自负的, 自视过高的 pround, conceited, self-satisfied, arrogant, self-important, geotistical, bigheaded, swollen-headed, stuck-up, affected, pretentious, ostentatious, swaggering.

valid adj.
☞ 正常的, 健全的 logical, well-founded, well-grounded, sound, good, cogent, convincing, telling, conclusive, reliable, substantial, weighty, powerful, just.
☞ 有效的, 有法律效力的 official, legal, lawful, legitimate, authentic, bona fide, genuine, binding, proper.

valley n.
☞ 谷, 山谷 dale, vale, dell, glen, hollow, depression, gulch.

valuable adj.
☞ 贵重的, 有很大价值的 precious, prized, valued, costly, expensive, dear, high-priced, treasured, cherished, estimable.
☞ 很有用的 helpful, worthwhile, useful, beneficial, invaluable, constructive, fruitful, profitable, important,

serviceable, worthy, handy.

value n.
- 价值 cost, price, rate, worth.
- 有效性,重要性 use, usefulness, utility, merit, importance, desirability, benefit, advantage, significance, good, profit.

v.
- 珍惜,重视 prize, appreciate, treasure, esteem, hold dear, respect, cherish.
- 估……的价格 evaluate, assess, estimate, price, appraise, survey, rate.

vanish v.
- 消失,消减 disappear, fade, dissolve, evaporate, disperse, melt, die out, depart, , exit, fizzle out, peter out.

vanity n.
- 自负,自大 conceit, conceitedness, pride, arrogance, self-conceit, self-love, self-satisfaction, narcissism, egotism, pretension, ostentation, affectation, airs, bigheadedness, swollen-headedness.
- 空虚,无价值 worthlessness, uselessness, emptiness, futility, pointlessness, unreality, hollowness, fruitlessness, triviality.

vapour n.
- 雾,烟,水分 steam, mist, fog, smoke, breath, fumes, haze, damp, dampness, exhalation.

variable adj.
- 变化的,易变的 changeable, inconstant, varying, shifting, mutable, unpredictable, fluctuating, fitful, unstable, unsteady, wavering, vacillating, temperamental, fickle, flexible.

variance n.
- 不同 variation, difference, discrepancy, divergence, inconsistency, disagreement.
- 意见不同 disagreement, disharmony, conflict, discord, division, dissent, dissension, quarrelling, strife.

variation n.
- 变异,变化 diversity, variety, deviation, discrepancy, diversification, alteration, change, difference, departure, modification, modulation, inflection, novelty, innovation.

varied adj.
- 各式各样的,多变化的 assorted, diverse, miscellaneous, mixed, various, sundry, heterogeneous, different, wide-ranging.

variety n.
- 种种 assortment, miscellany, mixture, collection, medley, pot-pourri, range.
- 异种,异类 difference, diversity, dissimilarity, discrepancy, variation, multiplicity.
- 品种,种类 sort, kind, class, category, species, type, breed, brand, make, strain.

various adj.
- 不同的,种种的 different, differing, diverse, varied, varying, assorted, miscellaneous, heterogeneous,

vary v.
☞ 改变,使不同 change, alter, modify, modulate, diversify, reorder, transform, alternate, inflect, permutate.
☞ 使有变化 diverge, differ, disagree, depart, fluctuate.

vast adj.
☞ 巨大的,广大的 huge, immense, massive, gigantic, enormous, great, colossal, extensive, tremendous, sweeping, unlimited, fathomless, immeasurable, never-ending, monumental, monstrous, far-flung.

distinct, diversified, mixed, many, several.

vehicle n.
☞ 运输,运送 conveyance, transport.
☞ 媒介物 means, agency, channel, medium, mechanism, organ.

veil v.
☞ 蒙面纱,遮掩 screen, cloak, cover, mask, shadow, shield, obscure, conceal, hide, disguise, shade.
n.
☞ 面纱,面罩 cover, cloak, curtain, mask, screen, disguise, film, blind, shade, shroud.

vein n.
☞ 静脉 streak, stripe, stratum, seam, lode, blood vessel.
☞ 心情,心思 mood, tendency, bent, strain, temper, tenor, tone, frame of mind, mode, style.

venerable adj.
☞ 令人肃然起敬的 respected, esteemed, honoured, venerated, dignified, grave, wise, august, aged, worshipped.

venerate v.
☞ 崇敬,对……深怀敬意 revere, respect, honour, esteem, worship, hallow, adore.

venture v.
☞ 敢,敢于 dare, advance, make bold, put forward, presume, suggest, volunteer.
☞ 冒险 risk, hazard, endanger, imperil, jeopardize, speculate, wager, stake.
n.
☞ 冒险 risk, chance, hazard, speculation, gamble, undertaking, project, adventure, endeavour, enterprise, operation, fling.

verbal adj.
☞ 口头的,逐字的 spoken, oral, verbatim, unwritten, word-of-mouth.

verge n.
☞ 边,缘 border, edge, margin, limit, rim, brim, brink, boundary, threshold, extreme, edging.

verge on
☞ 接近,濒临 approach, border on, come close to, near.

verify v.
☞ 证实,证明 confirm, corroborate, substantiate, bear out, prove, support, validate, testify, attest.

versatile adj.
☞ 多才多艺的,多方面的

verse n.
- 诗,韵文 poetry, rhyme, stanza, metre, doggerel, jingle.

version n.
- 看法,翻译 rendering, reading, interpretation, account, translation, paraphrase, adaptation, portrayal.
- 版本,译本 type, kind, variant, form, model, style, design.

vertical adj.
- 垂直的,竖的 upright, perpendicular, upstanding, erect, on end.

very adv.
- 很,非常 extremely, greatly, highly, deeply, truly, terribly, remarkably, excessively, exceeding(ly), acutely, particularly, really, absolutely, noticeably, unusually.

  adj.
- 真的,真正的,确切的 actual, real, same, selfsame, identical, true, genuine, simple, utter, sheer, pure, perfect, plain, mere, bare, exact, appropriate.

vet v.
- 检查,诊察,核对 investigate, examine, check, scan, inspect, survey, review, appraise, audit.

veteran n.
- 老兵,老手,富有经验的人 master, pastmaster, old hand, old stager, old-timer, pro, warhorse.

  adj.
- 老练的,有经验的 experienced, practised, seasoned, long-serving, expert, adept, proficient, old.

vibrate v.
- (使)摆动,摇动,振动 quiver, pulsate, shudder, shiver, resonate, reverberate, throb, oscillate, tremble, sway, swing, shake.

vice n.
- 坏毛病,坏习惯,罪恶 evil, evil-doing, depravity, immorality, wickedness, sin, corruption, blemish, bad habit, besetting sin.

vicious adj.
- 中伤的,恶意的 wicked, bad, wrong, immoral, depraved, unprincipled, diabolical, corrupt, debased, perverted, profligate, vile, heinous.
- 残酷的,凶恶的 malicious, spiteful, vindictive, virulent, cruel, mean, nasty, slanderous, venomous, defamatory.
- 暴力的 savage, wild, violent, barbarous, brutal, dangerous.

victim n.
- 受骗者,牺牲品 sufferer, casualty, prey, scapegoat, martyr, sacrifice, fatality.

victorious adj.
- 胜利的,得胜的 conquering, champion, triumphant, winning, unbeaten, successful, prize-winning, top, first.

victory n.
☞ 胜利 conquest, win, triumph, success, superiority, mastery, vanquishment, subjugation, overcoming.

view n.
☞ 观点,见解 opinion, attitude, belief, judgement, estimation, feeling, sentiment, impression, notion.

☞ 景色,看得见的东西,风景 sight, scene, vision, vista, outlook, prospect, perspective, panorama, landscape.

☞ 考察,观察 survey, inspection, examination, observation, scrutiny, scan.

☞ 看 glimpse, look, sight, perception.

v.
☞ 考虑 consider, regard, contemplate, judge, think about, speculate.

☞ 观察 observe, watch, see, examine, inspect, look at, scan, survey, witness, perceive.

viewer n.
☞ 观察者 spectator, watcher, observer, onlooker.

viewpoint n.
☞ 观点,看法 attitude, position, perspective, slant, standpoint, stance, opinion, angle, feeling.

vigilant adj.
☞ 机警的 watchful, alert, attentive, observant, on on's guard, on the lookout, cautious, wide-awake, sleepless, unsleeping.

vigorous adj.
☞ 精力充沛的,强有力的 energetic, active, lively, healthy, strong, strenuous, robust, lusty, sound, vital, brisk, dynamic, forceful, forcible, powerful, stout, spirited, full-blooded, effcetive, effcient, enterprising, flourishing, intense.

vigour n.
☞ 精力,活力 energy, vitality, liveliness, health, robustness, stamina, strength, resilience, soundness, spirit, verve, gusto, activity, animation, power, potency, force, forcefulness, might, dash, dynamism.

vile adj.
☞ 讨厌的,卑鄙的 base, contemptible, debased, depraved, degenerate, bad, wicked, wretched, worthless, sinful, miserable, mean, evil, impure, corrupt, despicable, disgraceful, degrading, vicious, appalling.

☞ 极坏的 disgusting, foul, nauseating, sickening, repulsive, repugnant, revolting, noxious, offensive, nasty, loathsome, horrid.

villain n.
☞ 坏人,恶棍 evil-doer, miscreant, scoundrel, rogue, malefactor, criminal, reprobate, rascal.

villainous adj.
☞ 恶棍的,讨厌的,极坏的 wicked, bad, criminal, evil, sinful, vicious, notorious, , cruel, inhuman, vile, depraved, disgraceful, terrible.

vindicate v.

- 辩护,表现 clear, acquit, excuse, exonerate, absolve, rehabilitate.
- 证明,证实 justify, uphold, support, maintain, defend, establish, advocate, assert, verify.

vindictive adj.
- 存心报复的,惩罚性的 spiteful, unforgiving, implacable, vengeful, relentless, unrelenting, revengeful, resentful, punitive, venomous, malevolent, malicious.

violate v.
- 违反,违背 contravene, disobey, disregard, transgress, break, flout, infringe.
- 亵渎,玷污 outrage, debauch, defile, rape, ravish, dishonour, profane, invade.

violence n.
- 暴力,伤害 force, strength, power, vehemence, might, intensity, ferocity, fierceness, severity, tumult, turbulence, wildness.
- 猛烈,激烈 brutality, destructiveness, cruelty, bloodshed, murderousness, savagery, passion, fighting, frenzy, fury, hostilities.

violent adj.
- 猛烈的,激烈的,剧烈的 intense, strong, severe, sharp, acute, extreme, harmful, destructive, devastating, injurious, powerful, painful, agonizing, forceful, forcible, harsh, ruinous, rough, vehement, tumultuous, turbulent.
- 暴力的,由暴力所致的 cruel, brutal, aggressive, bloodthirsty, impetuous, hot-headed, murderous, savage, wild, vicious, unrestrained, uncontrollable, ungovernable, passionate, furious, intemperate, maddened, outrageous, riotous, fiery.

virgin n.
- 处女 girl, maiden, celibate, vestal.

adj.
- 未开发的,未使用的 virginal, chaste, intact, immaculate, maidenly, pure, modest, new, fresh, spotless, stainless, undefiled, untouched, unsullied.

virtual adj.
- 实际上的,事实上的 effective, essential, practical, implied, implicit, potential.

virtually adv.
- 实际上地 practically, in effect, almost, nearly, as good as, in essence.

virtue n.
- 美德,优良品质 goodness, morality, rectitude, uprightness, worthiness, righteousness, probity, integrity, honour, incorruptibility, justice, high-mindedness, excellence.
- 优点,长处 quality, worth, merit, advantage, asset, credit, strength.

virtuous adj.
- 有道德的 good, moral, righteous, upright, worthy, honourable, irreproachable, incorruptible, exemplary, unimpeachable, high-principled,

visible *adj.*
☞ **看得见的** perceptible, discernible, detectable, apparent, noticeable, observable, distinguishable, discoverable, evident, unconcealed, undisguised, unmistakable, conspicuous, clear, obvious, manifest, open, palpable, plain, patent.

vision *n.*
☞ **幻象,幻影** apparition, hallucination, illusion, delusion, mirage, phantom, ghost, chimera, spectre, wraith.
☞ **想法,想象力** idea, ideal, conception, insight, view, picture, image, fantasy, dream, daydream.
☞ **洞察力,远见** sight, seeing, eyesight, perception, discernment, far-sightedness, foresight, penetration.

visit *v.*
☞ **拜访,访问** call on, call in, stay with, stay at, drop in on, stop by, look in, look up, pop in, see.
n.
☞ **访问,参观** call, stay, stop, excursion, sojourn.

visitor *n.*
☞ **访问者,造访者** caller, guest, company, tourist, holidaymaker.

vital *adj.*
☞ **重要的,致命的** critical, crucial, important, imperative, key, significant, basic, fundamental, essential, necessary, requisite, indispensable, urgent, life-or-death, decisive, forceful.
☞ **充满活力的** living, alive, lively, life-giving, invigorating, spirited, vivacious, vibrant, vigorous, dynamic, animated, energetic, quickening.

vitality *v.*
☞ **生命力,活力** life, liveliness, animation, vigour, energy, vivacity, spirit, sparkle, exuberance, go, strength, stamina.

vivid *adj.*
☞ **鲜明的,栩栩如生的** bright, colourful, intense, strong, rich, vibrant, brilliant, glowing, dazzling, vigorous, expressive, dramatic, flamboyant, animated, lively, lifelike, spirited.
☞ **强烈的,生动的** memorable, powerful, graphic, clear, distinct, striking, sharp, realistic.

vocabulary *n.*
☞ **词汇,词汇量** language, words, glossary, lexicon, dictionary, word-book, thesaurus, idiom.

vocation *n.*
☞ **职业,工作** calling, pursuit, career, metier, mission, profession, trade, employment, work, role, post, job, business, office.

voice *n.*
☞ **声音,嗓子** speech, utterance, articulation, language, words, sound, tone, intonation, inflection,

expression, mouthpiece, medium, instrument, organ.
☞ 意见,发言权 say, vote, opinion, view, decision, option, will.
v.
☞ 道出,宣述 express, say, utter, air, articulate, speak of, verbalize, assert, convey, disclose, divulge, declare, enunciate.

void adj.
☞ 空闲的 empty, emptied, free, unfilled, unoccupied, vacant, clear, bare, blank, drained.
☞ 无用的 annulled, inoperative, invalid, cancelled, ineffective, futile, useless, vain, worthless.
n.
☞ 空虚 emptiness, vacuity, vacuum, chasm, blank, blankness, space, lack, want, cavity, gap, hollow, opening.

volume n.
☞ 体积 bulk, size, capacity, dimensions, amount, mass, quantity, aggregate, amplitude, body.
☞ 册 book, tome, publication.

voluntary adj.
☞ 自愿的,自发的 free, gratuitous, optional, spontaneous, unforced, willing, unpaid, honorary.
☞ 有目的的 conscious, deliberate, purposeful, intended, intentional, wilful.

volunteer v.
☞ 自愿提供,自愿贡献 offer, propose, put forward, present, suggest, step forward, advance.

vote n.
☞ 投票,选票 ballot, poll, election, franchise, referendum.
v.
☞ 投票,表决 elect, ballot, choose, opt, plump for, declare, return.

vow v.
☞ 发誓,许愿 promise, pledge, swear, dedicate, devote, profess, consecrate, affirm.
n.
☞ 誓言,许愿 promise, oath, pledge.

voyage n.
☞ 旅行 journey, trip, passage, expedition, crossing.

vulnerable adj.
☞ 脆弱的,易受伤害的 unprotected, exposed, defenceless, susceptible, weak, sensitive, wide open.

W

waddle v.
☞ 摇摇摆摆地走 toddle, totter, wobble, sway, rock, shuffle.

wage n.
☞ 工资,报酬 pay, fee, earnings, salary, wage-packet, payment, stipend, remuneration, allowance, reward, hire, compensation, recompense.

v.
- 开展 carry on, conduct, engage in, undertake, practise, pursue.

wail *v.*
- 哭泣,哀泣 moan, cry, howl, lament, weep, complain, yowl.

n.
- 哭泣,哀悼 moan, cry, howl, lament, complaint, weeping.

wait *v.*
- 延缓,耽搁 delay, linger, hold back, hesitate, pause, hang around, hang fire, remain, rest, stay.

n.
- 延缓 hold-up, hesitation, delay, interval, pause, halt.

waive *v.*
- 放弃,不坚持 renounce, forgo, resign, surrender, yield.

wake[1] *v.*
- 醒,唤醒 rise, get up, arise, rouse, came to, bring round.
- 激起,唤起 stimulate, stir, activate, arouse, animate, excite, fire.

n.
- 守丧,守尸 funeral, death-watch, vigil, watch.

wake[2] *n.*
- 航迹 trail, track, path, aftermath, backwash, wash, rear, train, waves.

walk *v.*
- 行走,步行 step, stride, pace, proceed, advance, march, plod, tramp, traipse, trek, trudge, saunter, amble, stroll, tread, hike, promenade, move, hoof it, accompany, escort.

n.
- 步态,步法 carriage, gait, step, pace, stride.
- 散步,步行 stroll, amble, ramble, saunter, march, hike, tramp, trek, traipse, trudge, trail.
- 人行道,步道 footpath, path, walkway, avenue, pathway, promenade, alley, esplanade, lane, pavement, sidewalk.

walk of life
- 职业,身份,生活方式 field, area, sphere, line, activity, arena, course, pursuit, calling, metier, career, vocation, profession, trade.

walker *n.*
- 步行者 pedestrian, rambler, hiker.

walk-out *n.*
- 罢工 strike, stoppage, industrial action, protest, rebellion, revolt.

walk-over *n.*
- 轻易获得的胜利 pushover, doddle, child's play, piece of cake, cinch.

wall *n.*
- 墙,壁 partition, screen, panel, divider, fence, hedge, enclosure, membrane, bulkhead.
- 栏杆,短墙 fortification, barricade, rampart, parapet, stockade, embankment, bulwark, palisade.
- 似墙之物 obstacle, obstruction, barrier, block, impediment.

wander *v.*
- 漫步,漫游 roam, rove,

ramble, meander, saunter, stroll, prowl, drift, range, stray, straggle.
☞迷失,走岔 digress, diverge, deviate, depart, go astray, swerve, veer, err.
☞乱聊,离题 ramble, rave, babble, gibber.

wanderer *n.*
☞行者 itinerant, traveller, voyager, drifter, rover, rambler, stroller, stray, straggler, ranger, nomad, gypsy, vagrant, vagabond, rolling stone.

wane *v.*
☞减少,变小 diminish, decrease, decline, weaken, subside, fade, dwindle, ebb, lessen, abate, sink, drop, taper off, dim, droop, contract, shrink, fail, wither.

want *v.*
☞希望,欲望 desire, wish, crave, covet, fancy, long for, pine for, yearn for, hunger for, thirst.
☞需要,要 need, require, demand, lack, miss, call for.
n.
☞欲望 desire, demand, longing, requirement, wish, need, appetite.
☞缺少,稀少 lack, dearth, insufficiency, deficiency, shortage, inadequacy.
☞欲得之物 poverty, privation, destitution.

wanting *adj.*
☞缺少的,不够的 absent, missing, lacking, short, insufficient.
☞不够格的 inadequate, imperfect, faulty, defective, substandard, poor, deficient, unsatisfactory.

war *n.*
☞战争 warfare, hostilities, fighting, battle, combat, conflict, strife, struggle, bloodshed, contest, contention, enmity.
v.
☞作战 wage war, fight, take up arms, battle, clash, combat, strive, struggle, contest, contend.

warden *n.*
☞看守人,监护人 keeper, custodian, guardian, warder, caretaker, curator, ranger, steward, watchman, superintendent, administrator, janitor.

wardrobe *n.*
☞衣橱 cupboard, closet.
☞衣服 clothes, outfit, attire.

warehouse *n.*
☞仓库 store, storehouse, depot, depository, repository, stockroom, entrepot.

wares *n.*
☞商品,货物 goods, merchandise, commodities, stock, products, produce, stuff.

warfare *n.*
☞战争 war, fighting, hostilities, battle, arms, combat, struggle, passage of arms, contest, conflict, contention, discord, blows.

warm *adj.*
☞热的 heated, tepid,

lukewarm.
- ☞ 热情的,热心的 ardent, passionate, fervent, vehement, earnest, zealous.
- ☞ 柔和的,同情的 friendly, amiable, cordial, affable, kindly, genial, hearty, hospitable, sympathetic, affectionate, tender.
- ☞ 温和的,温暖的 fine, sunny, balmy, temperate, close.

warm colours:
- ☞ 暖色调的 rich, intense, mellow, cheerful.

v.
- ☞ 加热,变暖 heat (up), reheat, melt, thaw.
- ☞ 使……感到激动,亲切 animate, interest, please, delight, stimulate, stir, rouse, excite.

warmth n.
- ☞ 温暖 warmness, heat.
- ☞ 亲切 friendliness, affection, cordiality, tenderness.
- ☞ 热切 ardour, enthusiasm, passion, fervour, zeal, eagerness.

warn v.
- ☞ 警告,预告 caution, alert, admonish, advise, notify, counsel, put on one's guard, inform, tip off.

warning n.
- ☞ 注意,警告 caution, alert, admonition, advice, notification, notice, advance notice, counsel, hint, lesson, alarm, threat, tip-off.
- ☞ 预兆,警号 omen, augury, premonition, presage, sign, signal, portent.

warrant n.
- ☞ 受权,批准,权威 authorization, authority, sanction, permit, permission, licence, guarantee, warranty, security, pledge, commission, voucher.

v.
- ☞ 保证,担保 guarantee, pledge, certify, assure, declare, affirm, vouch for, answer for, underwrite, uphold, endorse.
- ☞ 有权力,有理由授权 authorize, entitle, empower, sanction, permit, allow, license, justify, excuse, approve, call for, commission, necessitate, require.

wary *adj*.
- ☞ 小心的 cautious, guarded, careful, chary, on one's guard, on the lookout, prudent, distrustful, suspicious, heedful, attentive, alert, watchful, vitilant, wide-awake.

wash v.
- ☞ 洗、擦 clean, cleanse, launder, scrub, swab down, rinse, swill.
- ☞ 洗澡 bathe, bath, shower, douche, shampoo.

n.
- ☞ 冲洗,洗的衣服 cleanintg, cleansing, bath, bathe, laundry, laundering, scrub, shower, shampoo, washing, rinse.
- ☞ 冲击,流水声 flow, sweep, wave, swell.

wash-out n.
- ☞ 失败,塌方 failure, disaster, disappointment, fiasco, flop, debacle.

waste v.
- 浪费,徒耗 squander, misspend, misuse, fritter away, dissipate, lavish, spend, throw away, blow.
- 耗损,损毁 consume, erode, exhaust, drain, destroy, spoil.

n.
- 浪费,损失 squandering, dissipation, prodigality, wastefulness, extravagance, loss.
- 误用,滥用 misapplication, misuse, abuse, neglect.
- 废物 rubbish, refuse, trash, garbage, dregs, leftovers, debris, dregs, effluent, litter, scrap, slops, offscouring(s), dross.

adj.
- 无用的,废弃的 useless, worthless, unwanted, unused, left-over, superfluous, supernumerary, extra.
- 荒芜的,无用的 barren, desolate, empty, uninhabited, bare, devastated, uncultivated, unprofitable, wild, dismal, dreary.

wasted adj.
- 无用的,无益的 unnecessary, needless, useless.
- 瘦弱的,衰弱的 emaciated, withered, shrivelled, gaunt, washed-out, spent.

wasteful adj.
- 浪费的 extravagant, spendthrift, prodigal, profligate, uneconomical, thriftless, unthrifty, ruinous, lavish, improvident.

wasteland n.
- 荒地 wilderness, desert, barrenness, waste, wild(s), void.

watch v.
- 看 observe, see, look at, regard, note, notice, mark, stare at, peer at, gaze at, view.
- 照顾 guard, look after, keep an eye on, mind, protect, superintend, take care of, keep.
- 注意,当心 pay attention, be careful, take heed, look out.

n.
- 手表 timepiece, wristwatch, clock, chronometer.
- 监视,观察 vigilance, watchfulness, vigil, observation, surveillance, notice, lookout, attention, heed, alertness, inspection, supervision.

watch out
- 警惕,提防 notice, be vigilant, look out, keep one's eyes open.

watch over
- 照顾,照看,保护 guard, protect, stand guard over, keep an eye on, look after, mind, shield, defend, shelter, preserve.

watchdog n.
- 看门狗 guard dog, house-dog.
- 忠实的看守人 monitor, inspector, scrutineer, vigilante, ombudsman, guardian, custodian, protector.

watcher n.
- 看守人,监视者 spectator, observer, onlooker, looker-on, viewer, lookout, spy, withess.

watchful adj.

☞ 注意的,警惕的 vigilant, attentive, heedful, observant, alert, guarded, on one's guard, wide awake, suspicious, wary, chary, cautious.

watchman n.
☞ 巡夜者,看守人 guard, security guard, carteaker, custodian.

water n.
☞ 水 rain, sea, ocean, lake, river, stream.

v.
☞ 给……浇水,灌溉 wet, moisten, dampen, soak, spray, sprinkle, irrigate, drench, flood, hose.

water down
☞ 加水于,冲淡 dilute, thin, water, weaken, adulterate, mix, tone down, soften, qualify.

waterfall n.
☞ 瀑布 fall, cascade, chute, cataract, torrent.

watertight adj.
☞ 不透水的,防水的 waterproof, sound, hermetic.
☞ 严谨的,无漏洞的 impregnable, unassailable, airtight, flawless, foolproof, firm, incontrovertible.

watery adj.
☞ 水的,含水的 liquid, fluid, moist, wet, damp.
☞ 淡的 weak, watered-down, diluted, insipid, tasteless, thin, runny, soggy, flavourless, washy, wishy-washy.

wave v.
☞ 使……向某方向移动,做手势 beckon, gesture, gesticulate, indicate, sign, signal, direct.
☞ 挥舞,挥动 brandish, flourish, flap, flutter, shake, sway, swing, waft, quiver, ripple.

n.
☞ 波浪,破浪 breakr, roller, billow, ripple, tidal wave, wavelet, undulation, white horse.
☞ 潮涌 surge, sweep, swell, upsurge, ground swell, current, drift, movement, rush, tendency, trend, stream, flood, outbreak, rash.

way n.
☞ 手段,方法 method, approach, manner, technique, procedure, means, mode, system, fashion.
☞ 方式,习惯 custom, practice, habit, usage, characteristic, idiosyncrasy, trait, style, conduct, natur.
☞ 方向,路线 direction, course, route, path, road, channel, access, avenue, track, passage, highway, street, thoroughfare, lane.

by the way
☞ 顺便提及,顺便提一下 incidentally, in passing.

weak adj.
☞ 衰弱的,脆的 feeble, frail, infirm, unhealthy, sickly, delicate, debilitated, exhausted, fragile, flimsy.
☞ 易破的,不能抵抗攻击的 vulnerable, unprotected, unguarded, defenceless, exposed.

- 不耐用的 powerless, impotent, spineless, cowardly, indecisive, ineffectual, irresolute, poor, lacking, lame, inadequate, defective, deficient, inconclusive, unconvincing, untenable.
- 弱的,易坏的 faint, slight, low, soft, muffled, dull, imperceptible.
- 淡的,多水的 insipid, tasteless, watery, thin, diluted, runny.

weaken v.
- 变弱,减少 enfeeble, exhaust, debilitate, sap, undermine, dilute, diminish, lower, lessen, reduce, moderate, mitigate, temper, soften (up), thin, water down.
- 变小,减弱 tire, flag, fail, give way, droop, fade, abate, ease up, dwindle.

weakness n.
- 薄弱,无力 feebleness, debility, infirmity, impotence, frailty, powerlessness, vulnerability.
- 缺点,弱点 fault, failing, flaw, shortcoming, blemish, defect, deficiency, flible.
- 喜好 liking, inclination, fondness, penchant, passion, soft spot.

wealth n.
- 财富,财产 money, cash, riches, assets, affluence, prosperity, funds, mammon, fortune, capital, opulence, means, substance, resources, goods, possessions, property, estate.
- 大量,丰富 abundance, plenty, bounty, fullness, profusion, store.

wealthy adj.
- 富有的,丰裕的 rich, prosperous, affluent, well-off, moneyed, opulent, comfortable, well-heeled, well-to-do, flush, loaded, rolling in it.

wear v.
- 穿上 dress in, have on, put on, don, sport, carry, bear, display, show.
- 消耗,耗损 deteriorate, erode, corrode, consume, rub, abrade, waste, grind.

n.
- 服装 clothes, clothing, dress, garments, outfit, costume, attire.
- 耗损 deterioration, erosion, corrosion, wear and tear, friction, abrasion.

wear off
- 磨掉,逐渐减弱,消失 decrease, abate, dwindle, diminish, subside, wane, weaken, fade, lessen, ebb, peter out, disappear.

wear out
- 用尽 exhaust, fatigue, tire (out), enervate, sap.
- 损坏,穿烂 deteriorate, wear through, erode, impair, consume, fray.

wearing adj.
- 令人厌烦的,令人疲惫的 exhausting, fatiguing, tiresome, tiring, wearisome, trying, taxing, oppressive, irksome, exasperating.

weary adj.

wearisome adj.
☞ 令人疲倦的,令人厌烦的 tiring, fatiguing, exhausting, taxing, trying.

weather n.
☞ 天气 climate, conditions, temperature.

v.
☞ 平安渡过,捱过 endure, survive, live through, come through, ride out, rise above, stick out, withstand, surmount, stand, brave, overcome, resist, pull through, suffer.
☞ 暴露,风干 expose, toughen, season, harden.

weave v.
☞ 编织 interlace, lace, plait, braid, intertwine, spin, knit, entwine, intercross, fuse, merge, unite.
☞ 编排,编作 create, compose, construct, contrive, put together, fabricate.
☞ 编织,曲折 wind, twist, zigzag, criss-cross.

web n.
☞ 网 network, net, netting, lattice, mesh, webbing, interlacing, weft, snare, tangle, trap.

wedding n.
☞ 结婚,婚礼 marriage, matrimony, nuptials, wedlock, bridal.

weep v.

☞ 疲倦的 tired, exhausted, fatigued, sleepy, worn out, drained, drowsy, jaded, all in, done in, fagged out, knackered, dead beat, dog-tired, whacked.

☞ 哭,哭泣 cry, sob, moan, lament, wail, mourn, grieve, bawl, blubber, snivel, whimper, blub.

weigh v.
☞ 重压,压低 bear down, oppress.
☞ 比较,权衡 consider, contemplate, evaluate, meditate on, mull over, ponder, think over, examine, reflect on, deliberate.

weigh down
☞ 沉重的压在心头,使担心,使忧虑 oppress, overload, load, burden, bear down, weigh upon, press down, get down, depress, afflct, trouble, worry.

weigh up
☞ 仔细估量,慎重考虑 assess, examine, size up, balance, consider, contemplate, deliberate, mull over, ponder, think over, discuss, chew over

weight n.
☞ 重量,重力 heaviness, gravity, burden, load, pressure, mass, force, ballast, tonnage, poundage.
☞ 重要,重大 importance, significance, substance, consequence, impact, moment, influence, value, authority, clout, power, preponderance, consideration.

v.
☞ 加负,重担 load, weigh down, oppress, handicap.
☞ 偏重 bias, unbalance, slant, prejudice.

weighty adj.

- ☞ 重的 heavy, burdensome, substantial, bulky.
- ☞ 重要的 important, significant, consequential, crucial, critical, momentous, serious, grave, solemn.
- ☞ 困难的,繁重的 demanding, difficult, exacting, taxing.

weird adj.
- ☞ 怪异的 strange, uncanny, bizarre, eerie, creepy, supernatured, unnatural, ghostly, freakish, mysterious, queer, grotesque, spooky, far-out, way-out.

welcome adj.
- ☞ 受欢迎的 acceptable, desirable, pleasing, pleasant, agreeable, gratifying, appreciated, delightful, refreshing.

n.
- ☞ 欢迎,接待 reception, greeting, salutation, acceptance, hospitality, red carpet.

v.
- ☞ 欢迎,接待 greet, hail, receive, salute, meet, accept, approve of, embrace.

welfare n.
- ☞ 福利,幸福 well-being, health, prosperity, happiness, benefit, good, advantage, interest, profit, success.

well¹ n.
- ☞ 井 spring, well-spring, fountain, fount, source, reservoir, well-head, waterhole.

v.
- ☞ 涌出,流出 flow, spring, surge, gush, stream, brim over, jet, spout, spurt, swell, pour, flood, ooze, run, trickle, rise, seep.

well² adv.
- ☞ 很好地 rightly, correctly, properly, skilfully, ably, expertly, successfully, adequately, sufficiently, suitably, easily, satisfactorily, thoroughly, greatly, fully, considerably, completely, agreeably, pleasantly, happily, kindly, favourably, splendidly, substantially, comfortably, readily, carefully, clearly, highly, deeply, justly.

adj.
- ☞ 健康的 healthy, in good health, fit, able-bodied, sound, robust, strong, thriving, flourishing.
- ☞ 适宜的,合适的 satisfactory, right, all right, good, pleasing, proper, agreeable, fine, lucky, fortunate.

well-being n.
- ☞ 安逸,自在 welfare, happiness, comfort, good.

well-bred adj.
- ☞ 教育良好的 well-mannered, polite, well-brought-up, mannerly, courteous, civil, refined, cultivated, cultured, genteel.

well-dressed adj.
- ☞ 时髦的,整齐的 smart, well-groomed, elegant, fashionable, neat, trim, spruce, tidy.

well-known adj.
- ☞ 著名的,出名的 famous, renowned, celebrated, famed,

eminent, notable, noted, illustrious, familiar.

well-off adj.
☞ 富有的,充分的 rich, wealthy, affluent, prosperous, well-to-do, moneyed, thriving, successful, comfortable, fortunate.

wet adj.
☞ 潮湿的,湿的 damp, moist, soaked, soaking, sodden, saturated, soggy, sopping, watery, waterlogged, drenched, dripping, spongy, dank, clammy.

☞ 下雨的 raining, rainy, showery, teeming, pouring, drizzling, humid.

☞ 弱的,胆怯的 weak, feeble, weedy, spineless, soft, ineffectual, nammby-pamby, irresolute, timorous.

n.
☞ 潮湿 wetness, moisture, damp, dampness, liquid, water, clamminess, condensation, humidity, rain, drizzle.

v.
☞ 使湿 moisten, damp, dampen, soak, saturate, drench, steep, water, irrigate, spray, splash, sprinkle, imbue, dip.

wheel n.
☞ 滚动,旋转 turn, revolution, circle, rotation, gyration, pivot, roll, spin, twirl, whirl.

v.
☞ 旋转 turn, rotate, circle, gyrate, orbit, spin, twirl, whirl, swing, roll, revolve, swivel.

whereabouts n.
☞ 下落,所在 location, position, place, situation, site, vicinity.

whip v.
☞ 鞭打 beat, flog, lash, flagellate, scourge, birch, cane, strap, thrash, punish, chastise, discipline, castigate.

☞ 突然,攫取 pull, jerk, snatch, whisk, dash, dart, rush, tear, flit, flash, fly.

☞ 煽动 goad, drive, spur, push, urge, stir, rouse, agitate, incite, provoke, instigate.

n.
☞ 鞭 lash, scourge, switch, birch, cane, horsewhip, riding-crop, cat-o'-nine-tails.

whirl v.
☞ 旋转,打转 swirl, spin, turn, twist, twirl, pivot, pirouette, swivel, wheel, rotate, revolve, reel, roll, gyrate, circle.

n.
☞ 旋转,曲折 spin, twirl, twist, gyration, revolution, pirouette, swirl, turn, wheel, rotation, circle, reel, roll.

☞ 嘈杂,混乱 confusion, daze, flurry, commotion, agitation, bustle, hubbub, hurly-burly, giddiness, tumult, uproar.

whirlwind n.
☞ 旋风 tornado, cyclone, vortex.

adj.
☞ 急促的 hasty, impulsive, quick, rapid, speedy, swift, lightning, headlong, impetuous, rash.

whisper v.
☞ 低语,私语 murmur, mutter,

mumble, breathe, hiss, rustle, sigh.
☞ 私下诉说　hint, intimate, insinuate, gossip, divulge.

n.
☞ 沙沙地响，低语　murmur, undertone, sigh, hiss, rustle.
☞ 暗示，传闻　hint, suggestion, suspicion, breath, whiff, rumour, report, innuendo, insinuation, trace, tinge, soupcon, buzz.

white *adj.*
☞ 苍白的　pale, pallid, wan, ashen, colourless, anaemic, pasty.
☞ 白色的　light, snowy, milky, creamy, ivory, hoary, silver, grey.
☞ 纯净的　pure, immaculate, spotless, stainless, undefiled.

whiten *v.*
☞ 变白，漂白　bleach, blanch, whitewash, pale, fade.

whole *adj.*
☞ 完全的　complete, entire, integral, full, total, unabridged, uncut, undivided, unedited.
☞ 完整的　intact, unharmed, undamaged, unbroken, inviolate, perfect, in one piece, mint, unhurt.
☞ 完好的　well, healthy, fit, sound, strong.

n.
☞ 整体　total, aggregate, sum total, entirety, all, fullness, totality, ensemble, entity, unit, lot, piece, everything.

on the whole
☞ 总体而言　generally, mostly, in general, generally speaking, as a rule, for the most part, all in all, all things considered, by and large.

whole-hearted *adj.*
☞ 全心全意的　unreserved, unqualified, passionate, enthusiastic, earnest, committed, dedicated, devoted, heartfelt, emphatic, warm, sincere, unfeigned, genuine, complete, true, real, zealous.

wholesale *adj.*
☞ 大量的，批发的　comprehensive, far-reaching, extensive, sweeping, wide-ranging, mass, broad, outright, total, massive, indiscriminate.

wholesome *adj.*
☞ 有营养的　healthy, hygienic, salubrious, sanitary, nutritious, nourishing, beneficial, salutary, invigorating, bracing.
☞ 高尚的　moral, decent, clean, proper, improving, edifying, uplifting, pure, virtuous, rigteous, honourable, respectable.

wholly *adv.*
☞ 充满地，全部地　completely, entirely, fully, purely, absolutely, totally, utterly, , comprehensively, altogether, perfectly, thoroughly, all, exclusively, only.

wicked *adj.*
☞ 不讲道德的　evil, sinful, immoral, depraved, corrupt, vicious, unprincipled, iniquitous, heinous, debased, abominable, ungodly, unrighteous, shameful.
☞ 可怕的，令人厌恶的　bad, unpleasant, difficult, dreadful,

distressing, awful, atrocious, severe, intense, nasty, injurious, troublesome, terrible, foul, fierce.
☞ 淘气的 naughty, mischievous, roguish.

wide adj.
☞ 宽广的 broad, roomy, spacious, vast, immense.
☞ 普遍的 dilated, expanded, full.
☞ 广泛的 extensive, wide-ranging, comprehensive, far-reaching, general.
☞ 宽松的 loose, baggy.
☞ 遥远的 off-target, distant, remote.

adv.
☞ 迷途地 astray, off course, off target, off the mark.
☞ 全部 fully, completely, all the way.

widen v.
☞ 加宽 distend, dilate, expand, extend, spread, stretch, enlarge, broaden.

widespread adj.
☞ 普及的，广布的 extensive, prevalent, rife, general, sweeping, universal, wholesale, far-reaching, unlimited, broad, common, pervasive, far-flung.

width n.
☞ 宽广，广博 breadth, diameter, wideness, compass, thickness, span, scope, range, measure, girth, beam, amplitude, extent, reach.

wield v.
☞ 使用，挥舞 brandish, flourish, swing, wave, handle, ply, manage, manipulate.

☞ 运用 have, hold, possess, employ, exert, exercise, use, utilize, maintain, commmand.

wife n.
☞ 妻子 partner, spouse, mate, better half, bride.

wild adj.
☞ 野生的 untamed, feral, savage, barbarous, primitive, uncivilized, natural, ferocious, fierce.
☞ 荒野的，荒凉的 uncultivated, desolate, waste, uninhabited.
☞ 失控的 unrestrained, unruly, unmanageable, violent, turbulent, rowdy, lawless, disorderly, riotous, boisterous.
☞ 剧烈的，暴风骤雨的 stormy, tempestuous, rough, blustery, choppy.
☞ 凌乱的 untidy, unkenpt, messy, dishevelled, tousled.
☞ 轻率的，鲁莽的 reckless, rash, imprudent, foolish, foolhardy, impracticable, irrational, outrageous, preposterous, wayward, extravagant.
☞ 混乱的，狂乱的 mad, crazy, frenzied, distraught, demented.

wilful adj.
☞ 有意的 deliberate, conscious, intentional, voluntary, premeditated.
☞ 固执的 self-willed, obstinate, stubborn, pig-headed, obdurate, intransigent, inflexible, perverse, wayward, contrary.

will n.
☞ 心愿 volition, choice, option, preference, decision, discretion.
☞ 愿望 wish, desire,

inclination, feeling, fancy, disposition, mind.
- 目的,决心 purpose, resolve, resolution, determination, will-power, aim, intention, command.

v.
- 需要,要 want, desire, choose, compel, command, decree, order, ordain.
- 遗留 bequeath, leave, hand down, pass on, transfer, confer, dispose of.

willing adj.
- 情愿的 disposed, inclined, agreeable, compliant, ready, prepared, consenting, content, amenable, biddable, happy, eager, enthusiastic.

win v.
- 获胜 triumph, succeed, prevail, overcome, conquer, come first, carry off, finish first.
- 赢得 gain, acquire, achieve, attain, accomplish, receive, procure, secure, obtain, get, earn, catch, net.

n.
- 胜利,收益 victory, triumph, conquest, success, mastery.

win over
- 赢得……的同意或支持 persuade, prevail upon, convince, influence, convert, sway, talk round, charm, allure, attract.

wind¹ n.
- 风 air, breeze, draught, gust, puff, breath, air-current, current, bluster, gale, hurricane, tornado, cyclone.

wind² v.
- 缠绕,蜿蜒 coil, twist, turn, curl, curve, bend, loop, spiral, zigzag, twine, encircle, furl, deviate, meander, ramble, wreath, roll, reel.

wind down
- 降低 slow (down), slacken off, lessen, reduce, subside, diminish, dwindle, decline.
- 干劲减小 relax, unwind, quieten, down, ease up, calm down.

wind up
- 结束 close (down), end, conclude, terminate, finalize, finish, liquidate.
- 终结 end up, finish up, find oneself, settle.
- 使……振奋 annoy, irritate, disconcert, fool, trick, kid.

window n.
- 窗口 pane, light, opening, skylight, rose-window, casement, oriel, dormer.

windy adj.
- 有风的,多风的 breezy, blowy, blustery, squally, windswept, stormy, tempestuous, gusty.

wing n.
- 翼,部分,侧面 branch, arm, section, faction, group, grouping, flank, circle, coterie, set, segment, side, annexe, adjunct, extension.

wink v.
- 眨眼,闪耀 blink, flutter, glimmer, glint, twinkle, gleam, sparkle, flicker, flash.

n.

☞ 眨眼,闪耀 blink, flutter, sparkle, twinkle, glimmering, gleam, glint.
☞ 瞬间 instant, second, split second, flash.

winner n.
☞ 胜利者 champion, victor, prizewinner, medallist, title-holder, world-beater, conqueror.

winning adj.
☞ 得胜的 conquering, triumphant, unbeaten, undefeated, victorious, successful.
☞ 迷人的 winsome, charming, attractive, captivating, engaging, fetching, enchanting, endearing, delightful, amiable, alluring, lovely, pleasing, sweet.

wintry adj.
☞ 寒冷的 cold, chilly, bleak, cheerless, desolate, dismal, harsh, snowy, frosty, freezing, frozen, icy.

wipe v.
☞ 擦去 rub, clean, dry, dust, brush, mop, swab, sponge, clear.
☞ 除去 remove, erase, take away, take off.

wipe out
☞ 消灭,擦去 eradicate, obliterate, destroy, massacre, exterminate, annihilate, erase, expunge, raze, abolish, blot out, efface.

wisdom n.
☞ 智慧,学识 discernment, penetration, sagacity, reason, sense, astuteness, comprehension, enlightenment, judgement, judiciousness, understanding, knowledge, learning, intelligence, erudition, foresight, prudence.

wise adj.
☞ 聪明的,明智的 discerning, sagacious, perceptive, rational, informed, well-informed, understanding, erudite, enlightened, knowing, intelligent, clever, aware, experienced.
☞ 贤明的,精明的 well-advised, judicious, prudent, reasonable, sensible, sound, long-sighted, shrewd.

wish v.
☞ 意欲 desire, want, yearn, long, hanker, covet, crave, aspire, hope, hunger, thirst, prefer, need.
☞ 想要 ask, bid, require, order, instruct, direct, command.

n.
☞ 愿望 desire, want, hankering, aspiration, inclination, hunger, thirst, liking, preference, yearning, urge, whim, hope.
☞ 请求 request, bidding, order, command, will.

wistful adj.
☞ 向往的 thoughtful, pensive, musing, reflective, wishful, contemplative, dreamy, dreaming, meditative.
☞ 忧愁而渴望的 melancholy, sad, forlorn, disconsolate, longing, mournful.

wit n.
- 机智,理解力 humour, repartee, facetiousness, drollery, banter, jocularity, levity.
- 理智,才智 intelligence, cleverness, brains, sense, reason, common, sense, wisdom, understanding, judgement, insight, intellect.
- 有才智的人,才子 humorist, comedian, comic, satirist, joker, wag.

witch n.
- 女巫 sorceress, enchantress, occultist, magician, hag.

witchcraff n.
- 巫术,魔力 sorcery, magic, wizardry, occultism, the occult, the black art, black magic, enchantment, necromancy, voodoo, spell, incantation, divination, conjuration.

withdraw v.
- 离开 recoil, shrink back, draw back, pull back.
- 撤消 recant, disclaim, take back, revoke, rescind, retract, cancel, abjure, recall, take away.
- 退出,撤出 depart, go (away), absent oneself, retire, remove, leave, back out, fall back, drop out, retreat, secede.
- 拉开 draw out, extract, pull out.

withdrawal n.
- 撤回 repudiation, recantation, disclaimer, disavowal, revocation, recall, secession, abjuration.
- 退出 departure, exit, exodus, retirement, retreat.

withdrawn adj.
- 沉默寡言的,不爱交际的 reserved, unsociable, shy, introvert, quiet, retiring, aloof, detached, shrinking, uncommunicative, taciturn, silent.
- 孤独的,孤僻的 remote, isolated, distant, secluded, out-of-the-way, private, hidden, solitary.

withhold v.
- 保留,抑制 keep back, retain, hold back, suppress, restrain, repress, control, check, reserve, deduct, refuse, hide, conceal.

withstand v.
- 抵抗,经得起 resist, oppose, stand fast, stand one's ground, stand, stand up to, confront, brave, face, copy with, take on, thwart, defy, hold one's ground, hold out, last, out, hold off, endure, bear, tolerate, put up with, survive, weather.

witness n.
- 证明 testifier.
- 证人 onlooker, eye-witness, looker-on, observer, spectator, viewer, watcher, bystander.

v.
- 目击 see, observe, notice, note, view, watch, look on, mark, perceive.
- 证明,作证 testify, attest, bear witness, depose, confirm, bear out, corroborate.

witty adj.
- 诙谐的,风趣的 humorous, amusing, comic, sharp-witted, droll, whimsical, original,

brilliant, clever, ingenious, lively, sparkling, funny, facetious, fanciful, jocular.

woman n.
☞ 女性 female, lady, girl, matriarch, maiden, maid.

womanly adj.
☞ 女性的 feminine, female, ladylike, womanish.

wonder n.
☞ 奇迹,奇事 marvel, phenomenon, miracle, prodigy, sight, spectacle, rarity, curiosity.
☞ 惊奇,惊愕 awe, amazement, astonishment, admiration, wonderment, fascination, surprise, bewilderment.
v.
☞ 觉得好奇,想知道 meditate, speculate, ponder, ask oneself, question, conjecture, puzzle, enquire, query, doubt, think.
☞ 吃惊,惊奇 marvel, gape, be amazed, be surprised.

wonderful adj.
☞ 了不起的,令人羡慕的 marvellous, magnificent, outtanding, excellent, superb, admirable, delightful, phenomenal, sensational, stupendous, tremendous, super, terrific, brilliant, great, fabulous, fantastic.
☞ 令人惊奇的,令人吃惊的 amazing, astonishing, astounding, startling, surprising, extraordinary, incredible, remarkable, staggering, strange.

wood n.
☞ 木材 timber, lumber, planks.
☞ 森林 forest, woods, woodland, trees, plantation, thicket, grove, coppice, copse, spinney.

wooden adj.
☞ 木质的 timber, woody.
☞ 呆滞的 emotionless, expressionless, awkward, clumsy, stilted, lifeless, spiritless, unemotional, stiff, rigid, leaden, deadpan, blank, empty, slow.

word n.
☞ 词,语 name, term, expression, designation, utterance, vocable.
☞ 谈话,言辞 conversation, chat, talk, discussion, consultation.
☞ 消息,音讯 information, news, report, communication, notice, message, bulletin, communique, statement, dispatch, declaration, comment, assertion, account, remark, advice, warning.
☞ 保证,诺言 promise, pledge, oath, assurance, vow, guarantee.
☞ 口令,命令 command, order, decree, commandment, go-ahead, green light.
v.
☞ 用言语,表达,说出 phrase, express, couch, put, say, explain, write.

words n.
☞ 争吵 argument, dispute, quarrel, disagreement, altercation, bickering, row, squabble.

☞ 作品, 文字　lyrics, libretto, text, book.

wordy adj.
☞ 啰嗦的　verbose, long-winded, loquacious, garrulous, prolix, rambling, diffuse, discursive.

work n.
☞ 事业, 工作　occupation, job, employment, profession, trade, business, career, calling, vacation, line, metier, livelihood, craft, skill.
☞ 责任, 任务　task, assignment, undertaking, job, chore, responsibility, duty, commission.
☞ 努力, 勤勉　toil, labour, drudgery, effort, exertion, industry, slog, graft, elbow grease.
☞ 产品, 作品　creation, production, achievement, composition, opus.

v.
☞ 工作　be employed, have a job, earn one's living.
☞ 劳动　labour, toil, drudge, slave.
☞ 起作用, 使用　function, go, operate, perform, run, handle, manage, use, control.
☞ 完成, 造成　bring about, accomplish, achieve, create, cause, pull off.
☞ 耕种, 劳动　cultivate, farm, dig, till.
☞ 压成, 形成　manipulate, knead, mould, shape, form, fashion, make, process.

work out
☞ 解决　solve, resolve, calculate, figure out, puzzle out, sort out, understand, clear up.
☞ 结果为　develop, evolve, go well, succeed, prosper, turn out, pan out.
☞ 设计, 发明　plan, devise, arrange, contrive, invent, construct, put together.
☞ 算出　add up to, amount to, total, come out.

work up
☞ 激发, 激起　incite, stir up, rouse, arouse, animate, excite, move, stimulate, inflame, spur, instigate, agitate, generate.

worker n.
☞ 工作者　employee, labourer, working man, working woman, artisan, craftsman, tradesman, hand, operative, wage-earner, breadwinner, proletarian.

workforce n.
☞ 劳动力　workers, employees, personnel, labour, force, staff, labour, work-people, shop-floor.

working n.
☞ 运作情况, 作用结果　functioning, operation, running, routine, manner, method, action.

adj.
☞ 起作用的　functioning, operational, running, operative, going.
☞ 活动的, 雇佣的　employed, active.

workmanship n.
☞ 手艺, 工艺　skill, craft, craftsmanship, expertise, art, handicraft, handiwork, technique, execution, manufacture, work, finish.

works n.
- 🈂 工厂　factory, plant, workshop, mill, foundry, shop.
- 🈂 工作　actions, acts, doings.
- 🈂 产品，作品　productions, output, oeuvre, writings, books.
- 🈂 机体　machinery, mechanism, workings, action, movement, parts, installations.

workshop n.
- 🈂 车间　works, workroom, atelier, studio, factory, plant, mill, shop.
- 🈂 研讨会　study group, seminar, symposium, discussion group, class.

world n.
- 🈂 世界　earth, globe, planet, star, universe, cosmos, creation, nature.
- 🈂 人类　everybody, everyone, people, humanity.
- 🈂 领域　sphere, realm, field, area, domain, division, system, society, province, kingdom.
- 🈂 时代　times, epoch, era, period, age, days, life.

worldly adj.
- 🈂 世俗的　temporal, earthly, mundane, terrestrial, physical, secular, unspiritual, profane.
- 🈂 世间的　worldly-wise, sophisticated, urbane, cosmopolitan, experienced, knowing.
- 🈂 物质的　materialistic, selfish, ambitious, grasping, greedy, covetous, avaricious.

worn adj.
- 🈂 破旧的　shabby, threadbare, worn-out, tatty, tattered, frayed, ragged.
- 🈂 疲倦的　exhausted, tired, weary, spent, fatigued, careworn, drawn, haggard, jaded.

worn out
- 🈂 穿烂的　shabby, threadbare, useless, used, tatty, tattered, on its last legs, ragged, moth-eaten, frayed, decrepit.
- 🈂 磨破的　tired out, exhausted, weary, done in, all in, dog-tired, knackered.

worried adj.
- 🈂 忧愁的　anxious, troubled, uneasy, ill at ease, apprehensive, concerned, bothered, upset, fearful, afraid, frightened, on edge, overwrought, tense, strained, nervous, disturbed, distraught, distracted, fretful, distressed, agonized.

worry v.
- 🈂 使困扰　be anxious, be troubled, be distressed, agonize, fret.
- 🈂 使烦恼　irritate, plague, pester, torment, upset, unsettle, annoy, bother, disturb, vex, tease, nag, harass, harry, perturb, hassle.
- 🈂 折磨　attack, go for, savage.

n.
- 🈂 忧虑，关切　problem, trouble, responsibility, burden, concern, care, trial, annoyance, irritation, vexation.
- 🈂 苦恼，焦虑　anxiety, apprehension, unease, misgiving, fear, disturbance, torment, misery, perplexity.

vorsen v.
- 使恶化 eeacerbate, aggravate, intensify.
- 使更坏 get worse, weaken, deterurate, degenerate, decline, sink go downhill.

worship v.
- 崇拜 venerate, revere, reverence, adore, exalt, gorify, honour, praise, idolize, love, respect, pray to, deify.

n.
- 崇拜 veneration, adoration, devotion(s), honour, glory, glorification, exaltation, praise, prayer(s), respect, regard, love, adulation, deifcation, idolatory.

worth n.
- 价值 worthness, merit, value, benefit, advantage, importance, significance, use, usefulness, utility, quality, good, virtue, excellence, credit, desert(s), price, help, assistance.

worthless adj.
- 无价值的,无用的 valueless, useless, pointless, meaningless, futile, unavailing, unimportant, nsignificat, trivial, unusable, poor, trashy, trifling, paltry.
- 卑微的 contemptible, despicable, good-for-nothing, vile.

worthwhile adj.
- 值得的,有用的 profitable, useful, valuable, good, helpful, beneficial, gainful, justifiable, productive.

worthy adj.
- 值得……的 laudable, creditable, commendable, valuable, worthwhile, afinirable, fit, deserving, appropriate, respectable, reputable, good, honest, honourable, excellent, decent, upright, righteous.

wound n.
- 伤口 inury, trauma, hurt, cut, gash, lesion, scar.
- 创伤,痛苦 hurt, distress, trauma, torment, heartbreak, harm, damage, anguish, grief, shock.

v.
- 伤 damage, harm, hurt, injure, hit, cut, gash, lacerate, slash, pierce.
- 伤害 distress, offend, insult, pain, mortify, upset, slight, grieve.

wrap v.
- 包,裹,缠 envelop, fold, enclose, cover, pack, shroud, wind, surround, package, muffle, cocoon, cloak, roll up, bind, bundle, up, immerse.

wrap up
- 包,裹 wrap, pack up, package, parcel.
- 完成 conclude, finish off, end, bring to a close, terminate, wind up, complete, round off.

wrapper n.
- 包装纸,用于包装或包裹之物 wrapping, packaging, envelope, cover, jacket, dust jacket, sheath, sleeve, paper.

wreck v.
- 使破坏,使毁灭,使失事 destroy, ruin, demolish,

devastate, shatter, smash, break, spoil, play havoc, with, ravage, write off.

n.

☞ 破坏,毁灭 ruin, destruction, devastation, mess, demolition, ruination, write-off, disaster, loss, disruption.

wreckage n.

☞ 残骸,残余物 debris, remains, rubble, ruin, fragments, flotsam, pieces.

write v.

☞ 书写,写下 pen, inscribe, record, jot down, set down, take down, transcribe, scribble, scrawl, correspond, communicate, draft, draw up, copy, compose, create.

writer n.

☞ 作者,著者 author, scribe, wordsmith, novelist, dramatist, essayist, playwright, columnist, diarist, hack, penpusher, scribbler, secretary, copyist, clerk.

writing n.

☞ 笔迹,书法 handwriting, calligraphy, script, penmanship, scrawl, scribble, hand, print.

☞ 作品,著作 document, letter, book, composition, letters, literature, work, publication.

wrong adj.

☞ 错误的,不正确的 inaccurate, incorrect, mistaken, erroneous, false, fallacious, in error, imprecise.

☞ 不适合的,不恰当的 inappropriate, unsuitable, unseemly, improper, indecorous, unconventional, unfitting, incongruous, inapt.

☞ 不公平的,不道德的 unjust, unethical, unfair, unlawful, immoral, illegal, illicit, dishonest, criminal, crooked, reprehensible, blameworthy, guilty, to blame, bad, wicked, sinful, iniquitous, evil.

☞ 犯罪的,不正常的 defective, faulty, out of order, amiss, awry.

adv.

☞ 错误地,不正当地 amiss, astray, awry, inaccurately, incorrectly, wrongly, mistakenly, faultily, badly, erroneously, improperly.

n.

☞ 错误,罪恶,过失 sin, misdeed, offence, crime, immorality, sinfulness, transgression, wickedness, wrong-doing, trespass, injury, grievance, abuse, injustice, iniquity, inequity, infringement, unfairness, error.

v.

☞ 冤枉,无礼地对待 abuse, ill-treat, mistreat, maltreat, injure, ill-use, hurt, harm, discredit, dishonour, misrepresent, malign, oppress, cheat.

wrongful adj.

☞ 不公正的,非法的 immoral, improper, unfair, unethical, unjust, unlawful, illegal, illegitimate, illicit, dishonest, criminal, blameworthy, dishonourable, wrong, reprehensible, wicked, evil.

Y

yardstick n.
- 标准,码尺 measure, gauge, criterion, standard, benchmark, touchstone, comparison.

yarn n.
- 纱,纱线 thread, fibre, strand.
- 故事,传奇 story, tale, anecdote, fable, fabrication, tall story, cock-and-bull story (infml).

yearly adj.
- 每年的,周年的 annual, per year, perennial.

adv.
- 每年地,一年一度地, annually, every year, once a year, perennially.

yearn for
- 渴望,希望 long for, pine for, desire, want, wish for, ache for, languish for, itch for.

yell v.
- 大喊,叫 shout, scream, bellow, roar, bawl, shriek, squeal, howl, holler, screech, squall, yelp, yowl, whoop.

n.
- 大喊,叫 shout, scream, cry, roar, bellow, shriek, howl, screech, squall, whoop.

yield v.
- 屈服,放弃 surrender, relinquish, abandon, abdicate, cede, part with, relinquish.
- 服从,让步 give way, capitulate, concede, submit, succumb, give(in), admit defeat, bow, cave in, knuckle under, resign oneself, go along with, permit, allow, acquiesce, accede, agree, comply, consent.
- 出产 produce, bear, supply, provide, generate, bring in, bring forth, furnish, return, earn, pay.

n.
- 产量,收成 return, product, earnings, harvest, crop, produce, output, profit, revenue, takings, proceeds, income.

young adj.
- 年轻的,年幼的 youthful, juvenile, bay, infant, junior, adolescent.
- 未成熟的,没有经验的 immature, early, new, recent, green, growing, fledgling, unfledged, inexperienced.

n.
- 青年,年轻人 offspring, babies, issue, litter, progeny, brook, children, family.

youngster n.
- 小孩,年轻人 child, boy, girl, toddler, youth, teenager, kid.

youth n.
- 青年,小伙子 adikescent, youngster, juvenile, teenager, kid, boy, young man.
- 青年们 young people, the young, younger generation.

☞青少年时期,青春 adolescence, childhood, immaturity, boyhood, girlhood.

youthful *adj.*
☞年轻的,青年的 young, boyish, girlish, childish, immature, juvenile, inexperienced, fresh, active, lively, wellpreserved.

Z

zeal *n.*
☞热心 ardour, fervour, passion, warmth, fire, enthusiasm, devotion, spirit, keeness, zest, eagerness, earnestness, dedication, fanaticism, gusto, verve.

zealous *adj.*
☞热情的 ardent, fervent, impassioned, passionate, devoted, burning, enthusiastic, intense, fanatical, militant, keen, eager, earnest, spirited.

zenith *n.*
☞顶点 summit, peak, height, pinnacle, apex, high point, top, optimum, climax, culmination, acme, meridian, vertex.

zero *n.*
☞零 nothing, nought, nil, nadir, bottom, cipher, zilch, duck, love.

zest *n.*
☞热情 gusto, appetite, enthusiasm, enjoyment, keenness, zeal, exuberance, interest.
☞味道 flavour, taste, relish, savour, spice, tang, piquancy.

zigzag *v.*
☞使成之字形,蜿蜒 meander, snake, wind, twist, curve.
adj.
☞曲折的 meandering, crooked, serpentine, sinuous, twisting, winding.

zone *n.*
☞区域 region, area, district, territory, section, sector, belt, sphere, tract, stratum.

推 荐 书 目

英汉小词典	5.80 元
汉英小词典	6.80 元
学生英汉小词典	9.80 元
实用英汉词典	12.80 元
实用汉英词典	16.80 元
英汉汉英词典	12.80 元
同义词反义词词典	8.80 元
成语词典	9.80 元
组词造句词典	8.80 元
大学英语四级词汇应试手册	4.80 元
大学英语六级词汇应试手册	5.80 元
MBA 应试英语词汇手册	4.80 元
新时代实用英汉大辞典	38.80 元

图书在版编目(CIP)数据

英汉双解同义词词典 / 蔺红英,张杰编.
北京：外文出版社,1999.8
ISBN 7—119—02438—8

Ⅰ.英… Ⅱ.①蔺… ②张… Ⅲ.英汉—同义词—双解词典—英、汉
Ⅳ.H313.2

中国版本图书馆 CIP 数据核字（1999）第 29306 号

外文出版社网址：
http://www.flp.com.cn
外文出版社电子信箱：
info@flp.com.cn
sales@flp.com.cn

英汉双解同义词词典

编　者　蔺红英　张　杰

责任编辑　刘承忠
封面设计　王　博
出版发行　外文出版社
社　　址　北京市百万庄大街 24 号　　邮政编码　100037
电　　话　（010）68320579（总编室）
　　　　　（010）68329514 / 68327211（推广发行部）
印　　刷　新华出版社印刷厂
经　　销　新华书店 / 外文书店
开　　本　大 64 开　　　　　　　　　字　　数　650 千字
印　　数　30001—38000 册　　　　　印　　张　10
版　　次　2003 年第 1 版第 4 次印刷
装　别　平
书　　号　ISBN 7—119—02438—8 / H·814（外）
定　　价　12.80 元

版权所有　侵权必究